WEYERHAEUSER ENVIRONMENTAL BOOKS

William Cronon, Editor

Weyerhaeuser Environmental Books explore human relationships with natural environments in all their variety and complexity. They seek to cast new light on the ways that natural systems affect human communities, the ways that people affect the environments of which they are a part, and the ways that different cultural conceptions of nature profoundly shape our sense of the world around us. A complete list of the books in the series appears at the end of this book.

Vacationland

Tourism and Environment in the
Colorado High Country

WILLIAM PHILPOTT

Foreword by

William Cronon

W

UNIVERSITY OF WASHINGTON PRESS

Seattle and London

VACATIONLAND is published with the assistance of a grant from the Weyerhaeuser Environmental Books Endowment, established by the Weyerhaeuser Company Foundation, members of the Weyerhaeuser family, and Janet and Jack Creighton.

FRONTISPIECE: Cover of the Colorado state "lure book," published by the state's Division of Commerce and Development, ca. 1964. Courtesy Colorado Tourism Office.

© 2013 by the University of Washington Press
Printed and bound in the United States of America
Composed in Sorts Mill Goudy, courtesy of the League of Moveable Type
Display types set in League Gothic, courtesy of the League of Moveable Type,
and Mission Script, courtesy of the Lost Type Co-op
17 16 15 14 13 13   5 4 3 2 1

University of Washington Press
PO BOX 50096, SEATTLE, WA 98145, USA
www.washington.edu/uwpress

Library of Congress Cataloging-in-Publication Data
Philpott, William, 1970–
Vacationland : tourism and environment in the Colorado high country /
William Philpott; foreword by William Cronon.
pages   cm
Includes bibliographical references and index.
ISBN 978-0-295-99273-0 (cloth : alk. paper)
1. Tourism—Colorado—History. 2. Mountain life—Colorado—History.
3. Colorado—Economic conditions. 4. Colorado—Environmental conditions.
5. Colorado—Description and Travel.
1. Title.
G155.U6P47 2013   338.4'79788—dc23   2012050749

For

Mom, Dad, and Kath
Shelby, Carly, and Peter

and in memory of

Sylvia and Lloyd Hegeman
Lois and Ivan Philpott

CONTENTS

ILLUSTRATIONS

Maps

Figures

FOREWORD

At Home and at Play in the High Country

William Cronon

AMERICANS HAVE LONG HAD A LOVE-HATE RELATIONSHIP WITH TOUR-
ism. The impulse to leave home to experience for oneself the length and
breadth of this vast land has been a quintessential part of our national heritage since the earliest days of the Republic. From the nineteenth century
forward, the wonders of wild places and natural landscapes have exercised
an especially powerful attraction, encouraging journeys for growing numbers of travelers first by coach or horseback, then by railroad, and eventually
by automobile and jet plane. Given how important such experiences have
been to American national identity, especially as increasing numbers of citizens have had the time and money to make such trips, one might almost say
that we have become a nation of tourists.

But there also has been a long-standing tendency for Americans to resist
counting themselves among the tourist hordes. In the nineteenth century,
a visit to Niagara Falls became de rigueur for well-to-do travelers on both
sides of the Atlantic, so much so that in the decades following the Civil
War, there were more and more laments that crowds on the banks of the
Niagara River were detracting from the very sublimity they had come to
see. Such concerns were so great that when the Washburn-Langford-Doane
Expedition visited Yellowstone in 1870, followed by the Hayden Expedition
a year later, the tourist excesses of Niagara were invoked as the reason why
that wondrous landscape of geysers and hot springs should be set aside as
the first national park in 1872. And yet not much time had to pass before
successful marketing efforts, first by the Northern Pacific Railroad and then

by the National Park Service, yielded the same complaints about tourist crowds at Old Faithful that had bedeviled Niagara.

Here, then, is one of the chief paradoxes of tourism: by identifying must-see destinations and encouraging travelers to construct itineraries to visit them, promoters attract (and profit from) the very crowds those travelers hope to flee. There are other paradoxes as well. Although the industry often marketed natural wonders and wild landscapes, ranging from the Adirondacks to Niagara to the Great Smokies to Yellowstone to Grand Canyon to Yosemite, it also required the creation of what amounted to urban infrastructures in these places to service all the people who came to see them. Great resort hotels like Grand Canyon's El Tovar and Yosemite's Ahwahnee were constructed, along with highly engineered roads and campgrounds; elaborate water supplies, electrical distribution networks, and sewage systems; and all the other amenities that marked tourist landscapes as being not so different from the semi-urban, semi-natural suburbs that growing numbers of tourists called home. To maintain all this infrastructure and to provide the services travelers expected to find, large numbers of workers had to be hired, who themselves required housing and amenities, thereby becoming residents in places most people only visited. Many tolerated low wages and difficult living conditions because they loved the beauty and the recreational opportunities as much as the tourists did. What emerged were hybrid landscapes and communities influenced and defined by the tourist experiences they fostered.

Few areas of the country better illustrate these paradoxical tendencies than Colorado, especially in the decades following World War II. Tourists had begun discovering the Rocky Mountains in the late nineteenth and early twentieth centuries with the help of the Denver & Rio Grande Railroad, the emergence of resort communities like Estes Park and Colorado Springs, and the opening of Rocky Mountain National Park in 1915. But the transformation of Colorado into one of the nation's most iconic tourist landscapes really accelerated during the middle decades of the twentieth century, when the state's mountainous terrain became more accessible than ever before. Diesel engines, electric motors, and cables on pulleys made it possible to transport people with wooden, metal, or fiberglass planks on their feet to the tops of mountains, saving them the trouble of the upward climb so they could concentrate instead on the downward schuss. The first mechanized rope tow for Colorado skiers, constructed west of Denver on Berthoud Pass in 1937, was followed after the war by much larger and more ambitious ventures. To bring tourists en masse to these new ski areas, two other innovations proved indispensible. Air transport, first with propeller planes and then with jets, made it possible for travelers from faraway places to reach the mountains for relatively short visits, even during the winter. Automobiles proved just as essential, aided and abetted by the construction of high-speed four-lane highways made possible by the National Interstate and Defense Highways Act of 1956.

Without skis, jets, cars, and highways, Colorado would never have become the tourist playground that it is today. This remarkable transformation is the subject of William Philpott's fine new environmental history, *Vacationland: Tourism and Environment in the Colorado High Country*. It combines meticulous scholarship with deep interpretive insight and genuine literary grace to tell fascinating stories about places many Americans visit without ever really knowing them very well. Wearing his erudition lightly, Philpott helps us understand how veterans associated with the U.S. Army's Tenth Mountain Division, trained to fight in craggy terrain under arctic conditions, played key roles in applying their alpine know-how from the Italian theater of the war to tourist destinations in the Rockies. Thus, the down-on-its-heels silver-mining town of Aspen, which had barely seven hundred inhabitants in 1930, was remade when Friedl Pfeifer of the Tenth Mountain Division partnered with the Chicago industrialist Walter Paepcke to redevelop the community into an upscale ski resort and cultural center. Likewise, it was the Tenth Mountain Division's Pete Seibert who teamed up with a Colorado local, Earl Eaton, to recruit a group of investors to finance and build the equally successful ski resort of Vail.

The role of these army veterans in promoting winter sports in postwar America is well known to those familiar with the history of skiing in the United States. What Philpott adds to the story is a far more systematic overview of the many other elements that had to join together before the Colorado high country could become one of America's most popular playgrounds. In particular, he demonstrates and explores in fascinating detail the crucial role of new forms of transportation, especially Interstate 70, in opening up remote mountain valleys that had been all but inaccessible during the winter. Aspen's growth, for instance, initially benefited from the private airstrip that Walter Paepcke constructed there in 1946, which was later supplemented by the Glenwood Springs exit of I-70. The founders of Vail chose its site in full anticipation of the interstate's construction, developing their ski resort on the slopes immediately above and adjacent to the highway. This all-important road—90 percent funded by the federal government—became the object of heated political contestation as communities sought to influence its route through some of the nation's most challenging terrain. Those lucky enough to be nearby—and also skilled enough to attract large-scale capital investment—flourished as never before, while those far away languished.

Philpott does a superb job of weaving together the histories of recreation, highway engineering, real estate development, and changing cultural attitudes toward nature and recreation. In so doing, he quietly challenges the interpretation of tourism that Hal Rothman developed in his provocative 1999 book, *Devil's Bargains*. For Rothman, tourism was generally a net loss for western communities that found themselves colonized by hordes of outsiders. Philpott pulls no punches in assessing the negative consequences of tourist development in Colorado, but for him, the overall impact of tourism is far more ambiguous—a more complex and intriguing mixture of gains and losses.

Perhaps the most striking finding that Philpott offers in this fine book is one with implications far beyond the Rocky Mountains—indeed, beyond the boundaries of the United States. If one paradox of tourism is that people love to tour but resist seeing themselves as tourists, then their relationship to recreational landscapes becomes all the more perplexing as tourists and residents become more difficult to distinguish. As the Colorado high country emerged in the second half of the twentieth century as one of the nation's premier recreational landscapes, more and more Americans chose to move there permanently—to be near the mountains, near the ski resorts, near the wilderness areas. Some came as wageworkers for the tourist industry; some ran businesses that served the tourists; some chose the mountains as their retirement homes; and a great many found the kinds of jobs that employ Americans everywhere. In so doing, they put down roots and chose to become Coloradans. The longer they stayed, the harder it was to know whether they should be counted—in the language of Rothman's *Devil's Bargains*—as the colonizers or the colonized.

Whether they worked nine-to-five jobs in Denver or long hours during the dark winter months in ski towns, these permanent Colorado residents recreated like tourists on the weekends and whenever they could pry loose longer blocks of time. Were they still tourists when they did so? That there is no clear answer to this question is the riddle at the heart of *Vacationland*. When people choose to live and work in a place that they, like everyone else, regard as a playground, then perhaps the categories of tourist and resident have merged into something far more hybrid and intriguing. And because such landscapes loom large in the dreams of so many people, as places not just to visit but to call home, they raise vital questions not just about tourism, not just about the Colorado high country, but about the role of leisure and recreation in modern life itself.

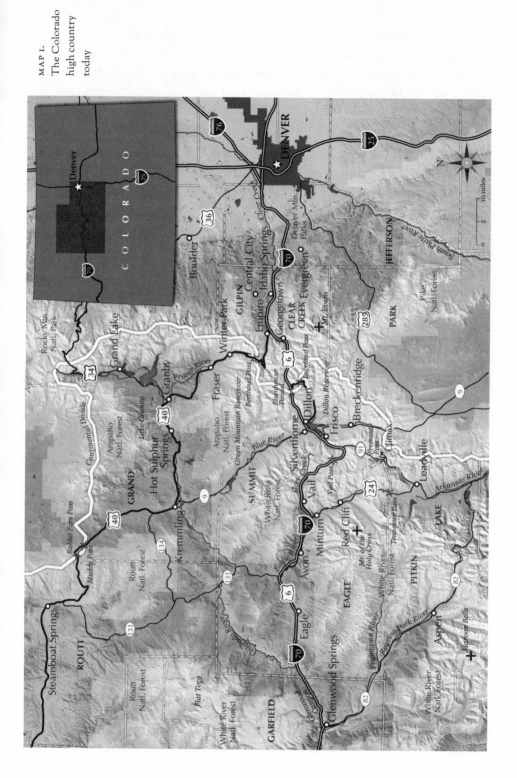

MAP 1.
The Colorado
high country
today

Vacationland

1.1 To see the land like tourists. In ads like this in the 1950s, Colorado's state publicity committee tried to sell local residents on the economic value of tourism. But even more, the ads encouraged locals to see the high country from a tourist's point of view—and to learn to sell it accordingly. Courtesy Colorado Tourism Office.

INTRODUCTION

Seeing Like a Tourist

ON THE THURSDAY BEFORE MEMORIAL DAY 1956, AS THE MUD IN ASPEN'S
streets hardened and the meltwater rivulets up on the mountainside spar-
kled in the late spring sun, locals picked up the *Aspen Times* and found
something unusual on page 2. The state publicity committee had taken out
a full-page advertisement hailing the imminent tourist season.[1] Only the
ad was not directed at tourists. It was aimed at their *hosts*—Aspen residents
themselves. The publicity committee wanted Aspenites to get excited about
the fast-growing vacation trade. "Colorado's Tourist Business Is Big Business," proclaimed the ad. And it offered statistics to back it up: more than
3.3 million out-of-state visitors to Colorado in 1952, spending close to $254
million, or almost $200 in "new money" for every man, woman, and child in
the state. Presumably that should please people in a place like Aspen, a classic western resource town that had been hard hit by the protracted slumps
in ranching and mining.

But if locals stood to profit off tourism, they were not quite ready for the
onslaught yet—at least not by the publicity committee's reckoning. They
needed a little sales training first. At some point during the season, some
flatlander would surely ask where the nearest ghost town was, or whether
there was a decent restaurant around, or what time of year the deer turned
into elk. So locals had to be ready to turn on the Old West hospitality and
talk about Colorado in a visitor-friendly way. That meant people used to
valuing the land more for mining or ranching than for hiking or sightseeing—more for livelihood than for leisure—had to learn how to see their

3

home environment through the eyes of tourists. As the committee gently chided, "Most of us folks living in Colorado don't fully realize what we have to offer vacationists."

So the ad offered six selling points for locals to keep in mind when talking to tourists. There was scenery ("white-robed peaks . . . pine-scented forests . . . glacier-gouged canyons and peaceful green valleys") and lovely summer weather (the "magic ingredient" that "none of us really appreciates . . . until we come back to it after a trip"). There were modern paved highways for easy exploring. There were festivals and rodeos, and there were outdoor sports. And not least, there was Wild West mystique. Coloradans themselves might "never think of it," the ad noted, but visitors imagined the state "as the last American frontier, the real Old West of gold mines, prospectors, ghost towns, cowboys and Indians. The romance of Colorado has a powerful appeal."

Six selling points, six qualities of the Colorado high country as tourists saw it. Or, at least, as state publicists *wanted* them to see it, and wanted locals to learn to talk it up. Historically, others had envisioned Colorado's mountain settings in starkly different ways: as storehouses of raw materials, sources of sustenance, obstacles to progress, spiritual places, homes. But now the state's top advertising agency was prescribing a new way of seeing. "THIS is Colorado," the ad declared, as if its vision now supplanted all others: "America's No. 1 Vacationland."

To see the high country like tourists: this was something a lot of people were learning to do in the decades after World War II. The state publicity committee was not the only one teaching this view, nor were the residents of mountain towns the only students. On license plates, there was a tourist-marketing slogan: "Colorful Colorado." In schools, Colorado history and geography textbooks similarly lifted language and imagery from tourist advertising, especially when discussing the mountains. (One textbook prompted schoolchildren to "imagine that you are a guide for group of tourists visiting our state. What points of interest would you suggest they visit?") Grade-school teachers brought glossy tourist magazines like *Colorado Wonderland* into the curriculum and had pupils decorate the classroom with the vivid, postcardlike pictures. Even Colorado histories written for adults cited tourist advertising clichés as fact, filling Coloradans' heads with the notion that theirs was indeed a natural vacation state.[2] And if you looked up "Colorado" in the venerable Encyclopædia Britannica's *Book of the Year*, the entry you read was written by a staffer in the state advertising office.[3] With so many—and such authoritative—sources of information conflating tourism with Colorado, it makes sense that when the Gallup Poll asked postwar Americans to name the state they considered most scenic, or the state where they would most like to vacation, Colorado almost always ranked in the top five.[4]

So it is in our own time. Mention the Colorado high country today and vacation imagery springs to most people's minds: scenery, camping, hiking, skiing, posh resorts like Aspen and Vail. Tourism has become so deeply rooted in the landscape, economy, and popular sense of place that neither locals nor outsiders need reminding anymore. This has not always been true. As recently as the 1940s, the high country, far from a renowned vacation destination, was little visited and little known. Once tourism took root, though, the region's transformation was rapid and complete.

On one level, this book tells how this happened—how a remote, obscure region became such a celebrated vacationland in just a few decades after World War II. But the story speaks to much bigger questions, ones that sweep far beyond this one pocket of the Rocky Mountain West. The story of the Colorado high country is really the story of postwar consumerism and the ways it reshaped the American landscape, American environmental attitudes, and the American economy and culture of place. This book tries to get at the question, If we have become a republic of consumers, how has that, quite literally, played out on the ground?[5] Seeing what happened up in the high country, a setting that became an object of intense consumer desire, can shed a lot of light.

And so, even as *Vacationland* is the story of tourist development in one place, it is also the story of how places themselves became products: manufactured, packaged, branded, and marketed like so many consumer goods. It is the story of the profitable and prolific place-making industry that emerged, the new kinds of planning that accompanied it, and the new kinds of landscapes that resulted. And it is the story of the new ways that Americans themselves learned to relate to place—and to nature and environment along with it. These changes, it turns out, go a long way toward explaining some of the signature trends in postwar American history, including mass suburbanization, economic and geographic decentralization, and Sunbelt migration, as well as the deepening American dependence on automobiles and, by the 1960s and 1970s, the rise of widespread popular concern for the environment. As more and more Americans learned to do as Aspenites were asked—see the land through the eyes of tourists—the reverberations traveled throughout Colorado, throughout the West, and throughout the nation as a whole.

TRACING TOURISM'S HISTORY AND TRACKING ITS CONSEQUENCES CAN BE knotty. For one thing, there is no clear consensus on what exactly "tourism" is. Everyone can agree that tourists travel for pleasure. But some insist on more rigid definitions, usually having to do with how far from home people go and how long they stay.[6] Such definitions serve a purpose, but by divorcing tourism from all other kinds of leisure and recreation—and for that matter, everyday life—they lose sight of the ways tourism blurred together with the wider world.[7]

Consider, for example, the themes tourist boosters used to sell the Colorado mountains. They promised vacations that were wholesome, family-friendly, luxurious, safe, casually paced, comfortable, and car-convenient. And they promised an escape from city stresses and the workaday world, a retreat to a landscape of scenic beauty, fresh air, green open space, and easily accessible outdoor leisure all around. These were not just ideals for a good vacation. They were also at the heart of the postwar suburban dream. By highlighting them, tourist boosters played to an essentially suburban way of relating to nature and place—one that would have been familiar and appealing to the great many postwar vacationers who themselves hailed from suburbia, or aspired to. Suburban living, then, was not just something tourists escaped temporarily *from*; it profoundly colored what kinds of places they yearned to escape *to*. We miss this connection if we insist on seeing tourism separately from the values and practices of everyday life.[8]

Rigid definitions also lose sight of influences that ran in the other direction, as tourism affected the day-to-day leisure habits and lifestyles of people who were not, by the usual understanding, tourists. In Colorado's case, the environmental imagery crafted by tourist promoters, and the precedents tourists themselves set in claiming certain places for play, tempted many other people to make their new homes in or near the recreation-rich Rockies. Since these people became full- or part-time residents and engaged in recreation near where they lived and worked, they were not tourists in any traditional sense. But they viewed and valued landscapes much as tourists did—and much as the marketers of tourism would have them do. And they moved and migrated along tourist-blazed trails. As Colorado—and other vacation-destination states like California and Florida—attracted flocks of postwar visitors, they attracted flocks of recreation-minded resettlers too.

The allure of living where tourists played was far from the only factor fueling these states' population boom, but it was a significant one.

So instead of defining tourism narrowly, I use the word loosely. I apply it to short-term visiting and sightseeing, of course, but also to seasonal residency, second-home-owning, and other phenomena that saw people staying in place longer than conventional tourists do. I apply it to vacationers who returned to the same resort or dude ranch every year, even though tourists are not usually seen as bonding closely to any one place. And I apply it to sports like skiing and fly-fishing, whose serious devotees are surely loath to see themselves as tourists. I do this in part because I want to get beyond the cartoonish stigmas so often attached to tourism. But even more, I want to underscore just how pervasively tourism has shaded into other realms, including the ways we spend our leisure time when not on vacation and the ways we interact on an everyday basis with the outdoors.

Another problem: what do we mean when we talk of a "tourist industry"? This is another term I use often, for simplicity's sake. But in fact the tourist industry is not a single industry at all. It is a crazy quilt of airlines, car-rental firms, hotels, motels, resorts, restaurants, travel agents, tour operators, theme parks, makers and sellers of recreational equipment and souvenirs, and many other private enterprises that serve tourists. (And few of these businesses cater exclusively to leisure travelers, making it even harder to assess the scope and impact of the "industry.") Then there are countless public or quasi-public entities that variously deal with tourists: chambers of commerce, publicity bureaus, recreation districts, land-management agencies, planning commissions, highway departments, and many more, all of whose roles we must weigh as we trace the rise of large-scale tourism as a historical phenomenon.[9]

And the economic effects of tourism are by no means limited to its industry. In fact, it is arguable that tourist dynamics unleashed an entirely new model of economic growth. One thing that struck—and sometimes exhilarated, sometimes alarmed—people in Colorado was the way their vacationland kept growing and growing, in both prosperity and population. It was not clear how this happened. Conventional economic-development wisdom said that people followed jobs, so you needed some sort of job generator—a mine or factory, for example—to spur growth. But the vacationland did not seem to live by the same rules. Certainly some of its population explosion could be credited to jobs in the thriving tourist industry itself or to the research- and defense-related industries in the Denver metro area.

But more and more people moving into the region seemed not to be following jobs at all. Instead, they came for the environmental and recreational amenities, the quality of life. And they brought their businesses with them, or started new ones, or freelanced, or telecommuted (once that technology came about), or simply lived off their pensions or trusts. In other words, in defiance of all existing economic models, the high country's environmental qualities seemed to be generating growth *on their own*.[10] While this remains a somewhat controversial concept, it is a growth scenario much more familiar to us now, and once again it shows how tourism's economic influence reached far beyond the industry itself.

Beyond its economic impacts, tourism brings people into contact who might otherwise never meet, which means its history is also profoundly *social*. In places where it takes root, it brings not just tourists themselves but also investors, promoters, entrepreneurs, and workers, who end up altering their destination's demographics, social dynamics, and relations of property and power. Not to mention relations of employment and labor, for the production of tourist experiences takes a lot of work, often by immigrant or indigenous workers of low incomes, who may find themselves serving or performing for people of very different value systems, histories, cultural identities, class statuses, and races. Tourism may draw such people together, furthering friendship and understanding. But it may just as easily trade on stereotypes or exotic or derogatory notions of the "other," driving people apart. In the process, it can bring shattering change. Many observers have pointed to tourism's colonial or imperial tendencies—not just in the economic and social senses, but in the cultural sense too. And the changes do not just affect the people being visited or "toured."[11] Cultural impacts rebound the other direction too, as tourists gain exposure to new outlooks and lifeways and may be moved to rethink their own as a result.[12] In Colorado, the vacation mystique that came to surround the high country inspired many people to reshape their lives, identities, and politics around the state's leisure amenities.

But if the history of tourism is about human contact and conflict, at its very heart it is also about the interaction between people and place. After all, tourism is an utterly landscape-specific phenomenon. At its most basic level, it involves people laying claim to certain kinds of physical settings for their own or their customers' pleasure. Many of the social and cultural conflicts mentioned in the previous paragraph boil down to this: Who gets to live, work, or play in this landscape? Profit off it? Claim belonging to it?

Define its beauty, its value, or the ways it will be owned, altered, or used? So tourism raises issues that are not just social and cultural but deeply *environmental*. They are the issues at the heart of this book.

Crucial to this inquiry is the history of how landscapes were framed, explained, and made meaningful for tourists—for example, through advertising, guidebooks, literary and pictorial representations, or prior visitors' travel accounts. Of course, tourists did not necessarily see places exactly as they were "taught" to, nor did they attach exactly the same meanings to them that, say, ad writers or poets did. But ad writers and poets are children of cultural context, and they write for others who are too—which suggests that, by looking for patterns in how tourist scenes in a given era were interpreted and framed, we can learn a great deal about the environmental ideals of that time.[13] And while it is treacherous to generalize about such things, it is possible to discern a broad shift from the nineteenth century, when tourist landscapes were purveyed and portrayed primarily in terms of their collective value; to the mid-twentieth century, by which time the emphasis had moved noticeably toward the emotional benefits that tourist landscapes could bring to the individual.

There is a rich literature on travel in the nineteenth-century United States, and most of it underscores the collective nature of tourism—that is, that tourists in those times were pointed toward natural settings that supposedly bore significance for the wider culture. Wealthy antebellum tourists were encouraged to treat sightseeing as a means to cultural literacy: there emerged a canon of picturesque sights, and visiting and learning to "read" them helped tourists gain membership in a shared elite culture. Even more, collecting these sights was a means to assemble and assert a shared national culture. The most renowned and revered scenic monuments were those that supposedly demonstrated the young nation's distinctiveness from Europe and its superiority, particularly its favored position in the eyes of God.[14] The notion that tourists could collectively affirm an American national identity did not stop with elite eastern sightseers of the early republic. It was an important reason for tourism spreading west to iconic landscapes like Yellowstone, Yosemite, and the Rockies after the Civil War; it carried over to the middle-class tourists who began taking to the rails later in the Gilded Age; and it persisted for decades into the twentieth century. For middle-class tourists, seeing America's great natural places became a "ritual of citizenship," as historian Marguerite Shaffer puts it, in a time when disconcerting changes seemed to challenge national unity and order. In other words, the tradition continued of Americans looking to tourist places for primarily collective benefits.[15]

But tourism changed over the course of the twentieth century, and with it the ways in which destination landscapes were presented to tourists. The shift reflected in part the growing participation in tourism, especially with the dawn of the automobile age. But it also reflected a shift in the wider consumer culture of which tourism is a part. The shift was toward consumerism—that is, the emerging ideal that people could and should seek personal fulfillment, and define themselves and their places in society, through the things they consumed. It was no less than a new consciousness, a new "logic of living," to quote historian Roland Marchand—and as that apt phrase suggests, its implications were sweeping.[16] Arguably, it would influence Americans' ways of seeing and understanding everything, certainly including place and nature. With the triumph of consumerism, natural things took on new meanings for how they could help consumers define, excite, aggrandize, soothe, please, or reassure themselves.[17] That was no less true of the landscapes tourists visited. As Americans settled into a consumerist mind-set, tourist settings became less valuable for their presumed ability to evoke a shared cultural or national identity and more valuable for the personal pleasure or fulfillment a tourist could supposedly derive from visiting there.[18]

Powerful implications flowed from presenting places in this way—implications not just for tourist settings and tourists but, more broadly, for American consumer culture and shifting American living patterns. You might say that tourist promoters added a new twist to the consumerist "logic of living": they made it location-specific. They held out the idea that pleasure and personal fulfillment could come through the consumption of *particular places*. And that, in turn, had major ramifications for popular notions of the American dream, for twentieth-century visions of the good life. It focused such visions more than ever on certain states or sections of the country whose climate, scenery, and other environmental qualities had been successfully marketed to seem naturally suited to leisure. California was the first and best example, its dazzling population growth throughout the twentieth century a testament to its mighty allure. But in the decades after 1945, other states closely associated with tourism, especially in the West and South, also became magnets—not just for tourists but for hordes of permanent new residents seeking to live a vacation-like lifestyle full-time. Yes, the twentieth-century good life had a lot to do with consuming goods, but it also had a lot to do with consuming places: places like these. Without grasping these spatial, geographical, and environmental dimensions, we cannot fully understand popular notions of the postwar good life. This is true even for the great majority of people who did *not* move to California or other vacation states, because those states' mystique ended up influencing residential landscapes and living patterns all across the country. In suburbia, especially, many Americans tried to re-create—through house architecture, interior design, leisure activities, and the design of suburban enclaves themselves—something of these states' casual, outdoor- and recreation-oriented way of life.[19]

SO TOURISM HELPED RESHAPE AMERICANS' RELATIONSHIP TO REGION, environment, and place. Exploring the effects—on people's lifestyles and living patterns, on their environmental attitudes and agendas, and on the ways they arranged themselves on the land—is a major concern of this book. But so are questions we began with: What caused tourism to take root in the settings it did in the first place? By what means did a particular region enter popular culture as a "vacationland"? How did its perceived qualities get linked up to prevailing notions of leisure, pleasure, and the good life? A good way to explore such questions is to ground them in a specific place, to look closely at how tourism has transformed that one place and how people have reacted to the transformation.

The place where I do this is the so-called Colorado high country. The toponym deserves some explanation, as it has wide currency but no firm definition. Today, you will hear "high country" used all over the West to refer to the higher or more mountainous part of this or that state.[20] Sometimes, when you are already in the mountains, it refers more specifically to their uppermost reaches, and to the higher meadows and plateaus, as distinguished from the lower slopes and valley bottoms: *the elk migrate up to the high country for the summer.* And like so many words in this book, it is a very common marketing phrase. Search for it on the Internet, for example, and you will find countless real estate companies, property rental firms, outfitters, and motels carrying the name.

The term is especially common in Colorado. There, in advertising, weather forecasts, and other everyday parlance, "high country" most often refers generally to the state's mountainous middle section, between the Front Range foothills and the Colorado Plateau. But for the purposes of this book, I am most interested in a subset of this area: the rugged swath stretching directly west of Denver through the central and west-central part of the state. Politically, my high country includes all or part of the counties of Clear Creek, Grand, Summit, Lake, Eagle, Garfield, and Pitkin. Unusually for American political jurisdictions, these counties' boundaries generally correspond to watershed boundaries, so that hydrologically my high country takes in the basins of Clear Creek and the Fraser, Blue, extreme upper Arkansas, Eagle, Roaring Fork, and Fryingpan Rivers. Topographically, it includes these river valleys along with the intervening mountains—the Gore, Sawatch, Williams Fork, and Tenmile ranges and some of the many ridges and peaks that are usually lumped together as the Front Range.

Today these counties, watersheds, valleys, and mountains have at least one key thing in common: if you drive to any of them from Denver, you will likely find yourself taking Interstate 70 at least part of the way. In fact, much of the region I write about may properly be called the I-70 corridor. But that name is anachronistic for much of the history this book covers. It was not even clear that there *would* be an I-70 west of Denver until 1957; even then, it took another three years to decide what exact route it would take. Actual construction took over thirty years more. Still, Interstate 70 is a decisive part of the story I tell. All of the counties I cover either ended up on the interstate or *could* have, had the planning and politicking gone another way. That planning and politicking plays a key part in this story. It is no exaggeration to say that the moment the planning and politicking gave way to actual construction, I-70 began to reshape this region's geography. The superhighway slashed directly across the supposedly impenetrable north-south ranges, ending the relative isolation of the valleys and towns in between, tying them to each other and to Denver in a single corridor: a cohesive geographical unit where none had existed before. I-70's ability to handle—and channel—large numbers of leisure seekers along this corridor would have historic consequences.

And that is why I pick this region to explore the making of a vacationland. Before 1945 this region was obscure, hard to reach, little visited. But in the ensuing decades, it underwent rapid, extensive tourist development and gained international repute as a vacationland. By the 1970s people were pouring into the high country for its scenery and for skiing, fishing, hiking, camping, boating, and other outdoor recreation. They were flocking to Aspen, Vail, and the other resorts that had appeared across the area, like Breckenridge, Keystone, Copper Mountain, Dillon, and Winter Park. They were descending on the region's two national forests, placing them both among the nation's top ten for recreational use. And they were speeding along the region's highways, especially Interstate 70, the high-volume, high-speed artery that fed vacationers into the high country and tied it all together. The scale and speed of the high country's tourist transformation makes it an ideal place to study the origins and effects of such a change.

Colorado was actually already on the tourist map long before World War II. But not the high country itself—and certainly not on such a popular scale. Earlier tourism was restricted socially to a more elite clientele. And it was restricted spatially, rarely ever venturing into the heart of the high country.

Already in the 1860s, American and European visitors were exalting Colorado's scenery. The scenery was "natural," in a sense, but it also required some cultural construction—and a good dose of boosterism. The cultural part was the abiding nineteenth-century popularity of the picturesque. The booster part involved people like William Byers, the founding editor of Denver's first newspaper, the Rocky Mountain News. In the 1860s Byers led dignitaries on jaunts around the mountains, showing them the spots that most lived up to picturesque standards, knowing his guests would then convey the charms of the scenery back East. It worked. When the influential Massachusetts newspaperman Samuel Bowles, for example, published an evocative account of his tour with Byers, or when celebrated landscape painter Albert Bierstadt exhibited his theatrical canvases based on the alpine vistas Byers had taken him to see, they helped build Colorado's image as America's new scenic wonderland—the "Switzerland of America," as Bowles christened it.[21]

In 1870 Colorado got its first rail link to the rest of the country; soon after, it got the first of its many pleasure resorts. They were only for the very rich, though. Only the rich could afford the long, costly rail journey to Colorado; and in any case, Colorado's promoters, like most in the West, preferred to cater to the "investor class," because they were the ones who might come back to help capitalize the territory's growth.[22] It is also significant for our story that those early resorts were not up in the high country. Instead, they clung to the easternmost edge of the Rockies—as in the case of Manitou and Colorado Springs, the fashionable spas the Denver & Rio Grande Railway (D&RG) built at the base of Pikes Peak.[23]

There was a legend of a creature that lived deeper in the mountains, where few flatlanders dared to go. Mountainfolk liked to tell tourists of the "slide-rock bolter," a monstrous whalelike beast with a hooked tail and a cavernous, scooplike mouth. The beast would hook its tail over the crest of a ridge—so went the story—and wait quietly for tourists, with their telltale clothing and guidebooks, to wander into the valley below. Then the bolter would suddenly release its tail, swoop down the mountainside on its belly like a toboggan, and scoop the hapless tourists into its gaping maw.[24] It was a classic "stupid tourist" story, purportedly explaining those scars up on steep slopes that were actually left by avalanches or rockslides. But it was also a tale that played on perceptions of the high country as primeval and wild, a bit too rough for visitors to risk.

Probably few were gullible enough to believe in the slide-rock bolter. Still, the high country kept its reputation for remoteness and inhospitableness: few Victorian tourists ventured into the region, and those who did went few places therein. Access was severely limited by the reach of the railroads. Many visitors did take day trips up Clear Creek to marvel at the pitted minescape around Central City, dip into the mineral waters at Idaho Springs, or ride the famous Georgetown Loop, a spectacular spiral of track about forty miles west of Denver.[25] But that was as far into the mountains as rails reached in the 1870s. The early 1880s finally brought railroad access to the heart of the high country, as two lines beat their way to Leadville, the latest boomtown. But even as the "Cloud City" mines and great belching smelters became another popular sightseeing excursion, Leadville could hardly be called a tourist town. The sightseers rarely tarried for long, retreating quickly to their accommodations in Denver, Manitou, or Colorado Springs. And popular perceptions still held the high country to be impenetrable. Even with rail service to Leadville (and by the late 1880s to the newest silver boomtown of Aspen), there was still no route straight west from Denver. Instead, the tracks to Aspen and Leadville took circuitous paths, swinging far to the south to avoid the daunting ranges directly to Denver's west. Grand County, though a short distance from Denver, just on the other side of the Front Range, had no rail access at all. William Byers spent years trying to establish a luxury spa there—Hot Sulphur Springs, his would-be "Saratoga West"—but without a railroad to reach it, the resort languished in obscurity.

To say the railroads limited tourist access, though, is too deterministic. Again, what ultimately dictated the travel patterns of the day was culture. Victorian visitors could have chosen to leave the rail corridors behind and plunge into the rugged middle of Colorado—but few did, because it was not the Victorian taste to do so. Wealthy Victorian travelers preferred to spend their days on the verandas and carriage paths or in the pavilions, casinos, and ballrooms of Manitou and Colorado Springs—resorts that, like Saratoga, Carlsbad, and other eastern and European forebears, styled themselves as enclaves of comfort and sophistication, sheltered from the harshness of the elements.[26] It is revealing that when western Colorado finally got its first major leisure destination—Glenwood Springs, a railroad spa developed in the 1880s and 1890s with capital from Aspen, Colorado Springs, and England—it adhered to this same formula, an island of luxury amid the rugged Rockies, with its bathhouse-casino echoing Viennese architecture, its resort hotel modeled after Rome's Villa Medici, and its golf course and polo grounds evoking an English estate.[27]

Vacationers who "took the waters" at Manitou or Glenwood were exhilarated by the proximity of the Rocky Mountains and often took short, easy walks, rides, or excursions to scenic spots close by. But before the 1890s, at least, they showed little interest in foraying any farther, in leaving behind the comfort of their little resort islands to truly immerse themselves in the outdoors. This cautious keeping of distance echoed another elite travel convention of the day: scenic sightseeing. Here again, the pattern had been set in Europe and the East, with generations of genteel travelers visiting places like the Swiss Alps, the English Lake District, the Hudson River valley, and Niagara Falls. Such travels were supposed to demonstrate tourists' cultural refinement, their ability to understand and appreciate scenery. Interest focused especially on landscapes that met the aesthetic standards of the "sublime" or the "picturesque," mentioned earlier.[28] Importantly, these aesthetic ideals served to minimize sightseers' physical contact with the landscapes they visited, privileging instead the act of gazing from a distance.[29] Instead of actually venturing into the Rockies, then, Victorian tourists usually stopped at prescribed viewpoints that properly framed distant vistas for them. Or if they did venture deeper into the mountains, they did so by train, confining themselves to the safety of the coach and letting the window frame the views.[30] Either way, they contemplated the peaks passively, from afar, much as they might regard a Bierstadt canvas on a gallery wall.

If tourists did not spread much into the high country in the nineteenth century, there were hints of change by the early twentieth. Fears of excessive urbanization and "overcivilization" began to push elite leisure tastes toward more rustic settings and active pursuits. Passive landscape contemplation lost ground to vigorous outdoor activities that were supposed to build body and character, like camping, hunting, and fishing. Remote, rough landscapes that elites had shunned came into favor. And growing numbers of the elites, especially male outdoor enthusiasts, began venturing deep into the high country. Theodore Roosevelt, champion of the "strenuous life," drew publicity to the area when he went on a 1905 bear hunt in the "primitive areas" near Glenwood Springs.[31]

But the foothills and mountains closest to Denver drew the most new interest, as affluent Denverites seeking the strenuous life began heading to the hills. Three pastimes in particular—scenic motoring, mountain climbing, and the newly introduced Norwegian "skisport"—caught on with Denver's wealthy.[32] All three spawned organizations that doubled as both social clubs and promotional groups for their pet pastimes. The Colorado Automobile Club pushed for scenic roads in the foothills and mountains near Denver, laying the groundwork for future automobile tourism.[33] The Colorado Mountain Club sponsored hiking and climbing trips and worked to spread appreciation and enjoyment of the Rockies.[34] And by the mid-1910s, Denver's first ski clubs, together with members of the Mountain Club who also had taken up skiing, were organizing ski outings and carnivals. By the late 1910s, they were building ski jumps at spots like Genesee Mountain, twenty miles from Denver. By the early 1930s, Denver's Arlberg Club would lead a shift away from Nordic to Alpine skiing and help develop some of Colorado's first primitive downhill ski areas.[35]

With leisure travel becoming a larger and more middle-class phenomenon from 1900 through the 1910s, the push for recreational facilities won new allies: Denver officials and business boosters, who were realizing that the city could make a mint off automobile tourists if it could position itself as a gateway to the emerging mountain playground. An important result was the decision, in 1912, to start developing a system of city-owned mountain parks, mostly in the foothills, linked to each other and to Denver by scenic drives.[36] Boosters also joined recreational enthusiasts in lobbying for two new national parks near Denver: Denver National Park, which would have enshrined the spectacular lake-and-peak landscape around Mount Evans— scenery that Bierstadt had made famous—and Rocky Mountain National Park, which would encompass the Front Range around Longs Peak, northwest of the city. The first park never became reality, but the second did in 1915.[37] The growth of the national park system, in turn, compelled the U.S. Forest Service to begin serving recreational interests too. In 1919 the Forest Service hired its first "recreation engineer," Arthur Carhart, whose initial charge was to devise a plan to handle the burgeoning demand for recreation around Mount Evans.[38] Remember Carhart's name, for while his time with the Forest Service was brief, he would reemerge after World War II as one of the nation's leading advocates for recreation planning and so would help usher in a new era of environmental politics in Colorado.

In the late 1930s came another major precedent for postwar tourism: the high country's first mechanized ski mountains. In 1937 the Colorado Winter Sports Council, a group made up of Denver ski club members and businessmen, built the state's first public rope tow about fifty-three miles west of Denver, atop Berthoud Pass. The next year, Denver parks and improvements manager George Cranmer began planning a city-owned ski area fourteen miles farther down the road, at the west portal of the Moffat railroad tunnel in Grand County. Already at this location, the Arlberg Club, Forest Service, and Civilian Conservation Corps had cleared some ski trails and built a shelter. Now Cranmer, using city workers, Arlberg and Colorado Mountain Club volunteers, and funding from private donations, city coffers, and the federal Public Works Administration, got more trails cleared, a J-bar (ski tow) installed, and a warming house built at the base. Winter Park opened in January 1940 and quickly became a favorite weekend retreat for Denverites, particularly Denver children learning to ski.[39] Winter Park and Berthoud Pass owed their popularity in large measure to their mechanical lifts, which made the uphill part of downhill skiing much less taxing. But convenience to Denver figured heavily too. Both ski areas sat right on U.S. Highway 40 (and by fortuitous timing, paving of Highway 40 over Berthoud Pass was completed in 1938, further easing the drive from Denver). Even better, Winter Park's location at the west portal of the Moffat Tunnel meant high-country skiing was now just a quick train trip from Denver. Over the next several decades, thousands upon thousands of Denverites, especially youngsters, would make that train trip for a Saturday or Sunday on the slopes.

Despite such developments, recreation's impact on the high country remained rather limited. Given the growing demand from Denverites, the greatest impact came in the foothills and mountains nearest the city. The rest of the high country remained little visited, especially by leisure seekers from out of state. This was especially true of the high country's old mining towns. These, for the most part, languished in a state of long-term depression and decay, as they had ever since the catastrophic silver market crash of 1893. As yet, tourists showed scant interest in visiting these old towns, nor boosters in getting them to. The one exception proved the rule: Central City, the old gold-mining town, was "discovered" by Denver socialites in the 1930s and partially rehabilitated as a summer opera and theater venue. But

1.2 Denver's mountain playground. At the city-owned Winter Park ski area, seen here in the late 1940s, skiers navigate the practice slope, while others line up in front of the warming shelters at the base to ride the J-bar tow back up. Behind the shelters, the "ski train," which many Denverites rode to and from Winter Park, emerges from the Moffat Tunnel, belching smoke. The pipeline running down the mountain (in shadow, at right) carries water destined for Denver, suggesting another claim that the city's residents placed on the high country environment. Courtesy Sanborn Ltd.

Central sat just forty miles from downtown Denver, and it was promoted as an extension of the city's cultural and high-society scene.[40] So, like Berthoud Pass and Winter Park, it fit the pattern of Denver-driven recreational development near the city rather than signaling a trend toward more extensive tourist development throughout the entire high country.

Still, there were rumblings of what would happen after the war. Ongoing efforts to improve the U.S. and state highways, like U.S. 40, were beginning to make long-isolated pockets of the high country more accessible. The 1930s fascination with local and "folk" heritage was beginning to spark interest in historic buildings and townscapes that mining's collapse had left neglected.[41] And residents in some high-country towns were, like their Denver counterparts, beginning to show heightened interest in outdoor recreation. In the 1910s and 1920s, ski jumps appeared in Dillon, Steamboat Springs, and Hot Sulphur Springs, and ski clubs popped up in many mountain communities, including Steamboat Springs, Leadville, Frisco, and

Grand Lake. Aspen's ski club launched in 1937, and one of its first initiatives was to clear Aspen Mountain's first ski run and build a primitive ski tow. Tows also appeared on town ski hills in Climax, Glenwood Springs, and Steamboat Springs, and at Hoosier Pass near Breckenridge, in the years and months before the war.[42]

Perhaps most significantly, World War II brought a big new crowd of ski enthusiasts to Colorado—based not in Denver this time but in the heart of the high country itself. It happened when the army stationed its new Tenth Mountain Division, a select unit training in skiing and other mountain military skills, at Camp Hale near Leadville. Many soldiers of the Tenth fell in love with the high country; many resolved to return after the war—and as we will soon see, many of them did return, helping to build the postwar ski industry.[43]

Before war's end, then, there were already hints of what the high country would become. But while ski enthusiasts in some towns began to see the potential economic benefits of skiing, local boosters did not yet see tourism or outdoor recreation as anything to base an entire local or regional economy on, nor were many tourists themselves yet sold on the high country as a destination. Only in the aftermath of World War II did that begin to change in a serious way, as boosters figured out how to package and promote the high country to a new generation of leisure seekers, and as tourism in the region began to burgeon on a scale that virtually no one, before the war, would have ever thought possible.

NO REGION, HOWEVER REMOTE, EXISTS IN A HISTORICAL VACUUM. TO understand the path the high country followed after 1945, we must look beyond the region, beyond Colorado, to national trends that helped bring change. There was greater affluence in the wake of the war and increased ease of highway and air travel. There was the desire of many Americans, especially white and middle-class, to escape "urban problems." There was the resulting boom in demand for commercial travel and outdoor recreation. But national factors alone cannot answer the questions posed earlier: How does a certain setting become a vacationland? Why did so many postwar leisure seekers seek out this particular place?

To grasp that part of the story, we must look to the state and local level. Among other factors, we must ponder the roles of what I call, for lack of better terms, tourist "boosters" or "promoters." Like the tourist industry itself, they were far from monolithic. Included among them were the expected local chambers of commerce, local civic leaders, owners of tourist businesses like motels and dude ranches, and their respective state organizations. There were also booster groups that have largely been forgotten, like highway associations, as well as entities that are not usually counted as boosters but did a great deal to publicize tourism and build tourist infrastructure, like the state highway department and the U.S. Forest Service. And it turns out that some of the most energetic boosters were recreational enthusiasts themselves, including ski clubs, outing clubs, and even conservation-recreation groups like the local and state chapters of the Izaak Walton League. It might sound strange, but recreational enthusiasts' role in this story suggests that tourist boosting had a noncommercial, idealistic side to it—an idealism that would resurface in unexpected ways with the rise of popular environmentalism in the late 1950s and 1960s. In any case, tourist boosters were a diverse lot, coordinated loosely if at all—and yet they pursued surprisingly consistent, mutually reinforcing strategies for fostering high-country tourism, which meant that their collective impact was significant.

The claim here is not that the tourist boosters' strategies were in any way unusual or innovative. On the contrary, they were highly derivative. They were pretty much the same strategies boosters all over the country were using—and for that matter, the same strategies that typified twentieth-century advertising in general. To create demand for their product, Colorado boosters used tricks that had been advertisers' stock-in-trade at least since the 1920s: vivid visual imagery; snappy, simple, and repetitive language; and unsubtle personal, emotional appeals, all aimed at establishing and cementing a brand. In this case, it was the land itself that got branded.[44] Boosters translated the high country's complex topography and climate into simplified, stereotyped images and clichés, endlessly reproduced in brochures, advertisements, guidebooks, postcards, magazine articles, and other materials.

Key to tourist promotion—and again, key to all modern advertising—was getting consumers to forge a personal bond with the branded product, to invest emotionally in it, to see it as an expression or extension of themselves.[45] Colorado tourist boosters tried this strategy too. In their portrayals, the high country became a land not just of scenic peaks and perfect climate but of thrills and tranquility and other mighty emotions. And it became a land where you could realize yourself in your own eyes and the eyes of others: by indulging your adventurous side, achieving inner peace, discovering your inner pioneer, showing yourself to be sophisticated, strengthening family bonds. The overarching message—that you could achieve self-fulfill-ment and social definition by consuming *this product*—was the message that, more than any other, characterized twentieth-century advertising (and still drives advertising today). It was the same way that consumers were being "taught" to think about almost everything they bought, from cars to clothes to detergents to deodorants. So to say that high-country boosters used this approach is not to argue they were onto anything original. It is, instead, to suggest that they made an unfamiliar place accessible and desirable by translating it into familiar, mainstream terms—terms that any American consumer could understand.

Paralleling efforts to craft a tourist-friendly image were efforts to build tourist-friendly infrastructure. In a very real sense, infrastructure packaged new places for tourists. Whenever motels appeared in an old mining town, campground facilities in a forest, or an entire resort village in a former sheep pasture, a setting that had been unremarkable or unwelcoming to vacation-ers gained the ability to attract and accommodate them. Suddenly the set-ting became an entry in travel guides, a spot on the tourist map. True, place making involved much more than just infrastructure. A "place" takes shape also from the ways in which people perceive, portray, and promote it; con-nect personally to it; and play out their cultural values, social dynamics, and relations of power within it.[46] Still, places are, by definition, physical, geo-graphical entities, so when it came to packaging new places for recreational visitors, creating the necessary physical infrastructure was an indispensable step.

Again, a whole host of independent actors did this work. And again, instead of being especially innovative, they mostly drew on tried-and-true marketing themes. This time, the favored theme was convenience. Whether elaborate (like mechanical ski lifts) or simple (like marked hiking trails), recreational infrastructure was almost always designed to facilitate people's access to outdoor leisure while minimizing discomfort, difficulty, and risk. Defined this way, the most essential infrastructure was a good road, and the surest way to package a place for postwar tourists was to build a modern paved highway to it. In the high country, the ultimate highway was Inter-state 70 itself. Planning for the interstate, which began in the 1950s, called for tunnels, shelves, cuts and fills, rock blasting, relocated streams, and other heavy-handed interventions, so visitors would be able to speed into the high country without worrying too much about snow, steep inclines, sharp curves, or other hazards. They could even feel safe enough to enjoy the scenery along the way. I–70 packaged a place, all right: it created an entirely new corridor, tying together a motley collection of rural settings that tourists had once shunned, tugging them directly into the mass-market mainstream. Of all the image and infrastructure building going on in the high country, it was the planning and construction of I–70 that most decisively rearranged the region's geography and readied its nature for tourists to consume. It, more than any other factor, made tourism big business and thrust the high country into the popular consciousness as a place where people went on vacation.

Thus my title: "vacationland." It is an almost throwaway cliché, the kind of word you'd see in a postcard caption or magazine ad and never give a second thought to. But like all the advertising catchwords in this book, "vacationland" turns out to be a multivalent term, containing much more than it first appears to. When we call someplace a vacationland, we buy into efforts to brand that land and link it to escapist and other exciting consumer fantasies. We let the marketing of land shape our sense of region and place. At the same time, when we talk of a vacationland, we are expressing a set of environmental values. We are asserting that this landscape finds its highest worth in being pretty to look at or nice to play in—that it is more valuable to us for aesthetic, atmospheric, or recreational qualities than for any resources it may yield. Finally, "vacationland" evokes a certain kind of spatial arrangement, a certain regional geography, a way of ordering the land. No one would use the word to refer to a city. Instead, it suggests an expanse of territory outside any metropolitan area, where there are resorts and other recreational clusters, but in between, lots of pretty scenery and open, lightly developed or natural space. By making "vacationland" my title, then, I mean to suggest that the true significance of tourist development—and of the wider phenomenon of packaging and marketing places—lies in the new kinds of landscapes it has created and the new environmental values and outdoor-oriented living patterns it has instilled.

We *have* learned to see the land like tourists. But does that mean we relate to our surroundings more superficially than before, as tourists are so often assumed to do? In Colorado's case, many people who bought into the marketing of recreation forged surprisingly strong bonds with the places that were marketed to them. Many ended up making the vacationland their home, reorienting their living patterns, their family lives, their personal identities, and even their politics around it.[47] This, in turn, brought about broader shifts, as recreational profits created an incentive to care for the beauty and integrity of the mountains and as popular support surged for certain kinds of environmental protection.[48] But the result was no environmental utopia. The new development patterns proved ecologically troubling in their own ways, and the new environmental politics inherited blind spots and weaknesses from the leisure mind-set that had given it rise.

All of that is part of our story. To tour the postwar history of the high country is to see the sometimes perplexing new landscape of American consumerism take shape, not just in physical form but in our eyes and minds.

CHAPTER 1

Selling the Scene

AFTER MONTHS OF PLANNING AND PREPARATION, THE TENTH MOUN-
tain Division invaded Aspen in early June 1943. The Third Platoon of the
Tenth Recon spearheaded the attack. Striking out from Camp Hale, some
twenty miles away, the elite unit traversed the steep-sided Williams Range,
crested Red Mountain, and descended its southern face to Hunter Creek.
Just beyond huddled vulnerable little Aspen, with its few hundred unarmed
residents. The troops met no resistance as they forded the creek and
advanced on the town. In fact, scores of townspeople turned out to cheer
the invaders as they marched down the main street.

The "invasion," of course, was a training exercise, and the people of
Aspen had met and befriended many of these Tenth Mountain men before.
When the whole maneuver was over, trainees and townspeople went
together for beers at the Hotel Jerome. That evening, after the soldiers had
pitched camp, the socializing resumed, beers giving way to stiffer drinks.
Hotel owner Laurence Elisha mixed glass after glass of the house specialty—a thick milkshake generously spiked with whiskey, lovingly dubbed
the "Aspen crud."[1]

For most of the men, memories of the experience probably dissolved
quickly into a crud-induced haze. But at least one soldier—Corporal Fried-
rich "Friedl" Pfeifer—remembered that sunny June day for the rest of his life.
Even fifty years later, he vividly recalled how he felt as his platoon marched
down Hunter Creek and came upon Aspen. He felt like he had stumbled
upon his hometown, the Austrian ski hamlet of St. Anton am Arlberg,

re-created in the Colorado Rockies. Here, halfway around the globe, he saw the same alpine meadows, the same hardy little mountain-bound town, the same steep slopes running right down to the streets, that he had known as a child. It was a revelatory moment for Pfeifer, one that "would change my life," he later said.[2] Because it was then that he first dreamt of making Aspen a "skiing community": an American St. Anton, where locals and visitors alike would take to the slopes, children would grow up on skis, and the sport would shape people's identities and everyday lives. The whole thing seemed almost predestined, as Pfeifer looked upon Aspen that day in June 1943. "It's made for skiing, it's just a creation for skiing," he later said of Aspen's alpine setting. "God must have created it just for this."[3]

Pfeifer's revelatory first sight marked a critical moment in Aspen's history, for it set in motion the town's reinvention as one of the world's leading ski resorts. But it also carried historical importance far beyond this one community. The Austrian's vision of Aspen and its mountain-meadow surroundings presaged the new ways of seeing the Colorado high country that would assume increasing power after World War II. Most earlier comers had thought this mountainous middle section of Colorado was "created" or "made for" mining, ranching, and other forms of production and extraction. But more and more in the prosperous decades after the war, people would look at the high country through different eyes. They would reassess the environment in light of the booming demand for commercial leisure, and they would decide that the region's most valuable resources were no longer its minerals, timber, or grazing range, but its scenery, climate, recreational amenities, and rustic atmosphere. And they would work to recast the high country in the public imagination, drawing new attention to settings that had gone little noticed or little visited, reimagining them as vacationlands naturally suited for play. Aspen would go first. With the arrival of Pfeifer and like-minded thinkers in the 1940s, it would become the first former mining town to undergo a near-complete conversion to a tourist economy, tourist landscape, and tourist-oriented way of life, setting a precedent for other places to follow.

To be sure, not everyone shared in the grand visions of tourist development. There were still plenty of investors, policy makers, boosters, "expert" observers, and ordinary citizens who scoffed at the idea that mere play would ever bring much wealth to the stagnant high country. They felt sure, based on historical precedent, that only mines and ranches could make a thriving countryside, only factories and processing plants could make prosperous towns. Extraction and production had triggered the booms of the past as surely they would in the future—so went that view. But the recreational re-visioning of the high country gained undeniable strength over the course of the 1940s and 1950s. Behind it coalesced a loose but growing coalition of boosters, working at the state and local levels to promote high-country tour-ism. With varying degrees of sophistication, but with a surprising degree of consistency, they advertised the recreational qualities of the high country, constructing for it a highly marketable new image as a land nature-made for leisure.

IF ASPEN'S PACESETTING CONVERSION TO TOURISM BEGAN IN EARNEST with Pfeifer's "invasion" in 1943, it accelerated two years later when Chi-cago industrialist Walter Paepcke brought his own resort-building vision to town. Like the wealthy Denverites who had pushed for scenic drives, ski hills, and mountain parks in the early twentieth century, both Paepcke and Pfeifer combined profit- and pleasure-seeking motives. But unlike those earlier Denver promoters, Pfeifer and Paepcke fixed their tourist visions on a living, functioning community. They envisioned this community as a perfect place for pleasure, though it was not actually "made for" that any more than it was made for mining or ranching. Pfeifer and Paepcke would need to change many things about Aspen and its environs to create the lei-sure atmosphere they desired. Paepcke in particular would see fit to modify land and buildings; local culture, law, and livelihood; property ownership and even the makeup of the populace—all to turn Aspen into the pleasure resort he envisioned. As Aspen in the 1940s showed, when tourism took root in a place, it had a way of changing almost everything.

As for Friedl Pfeifer, while growing up in the Austrian Tyrol in the 1920s and 1930s, he never guessed he would end up in the American West. But he did, just like so many other people, military and civilian, who either found themselves stationed in the West during World War II or flocked to the region to take wartime jobs. After V-J Day many of these newcomers stayed or returned, drawn by the lifestyle, scenery, or climate—or most often the jobs, as western metropolises like Los Angeles remained flush despite demobilization, and jobs were abundant.[4]

So Pfeifer was one of many who found his future western home during the war and returned after the peace. His route had been more circuitous than most, though. Born into a St. Anton farm family, he had grown into a champion ski racer, fled Austria after the Anschluss, taught skiing in

Australia, and then directed the ski school at Sun Valley, the Union Pacific Railroad's ritzy new resort in Idaho—all this before the United States entered the war, the navy converted Sun Valley into a convalescent center, and Pfeifer volunteered for the army's new Tenth Mountain Division as a "soldier on skis." That was the decision that brought him to Camp Hale, Colorado, and thence to Aspen. But before he could settle there, he still had to fight with the Tenth in Italy, suffer near-fatal wounds in the battle of Riva Ridge, and recuperate in military hospitals in Florida, California, and Colorado Springs. Only then was he finally able to return to the town that had so bewitched him in 1943. Discharged from the army, he raced back to Aspen and rented a house for himself and his wife and toddler daughter. "I felt," he marveled years later, "like I had come home."[5]

It is safe to say it was not a bustling, Los Angeles–like economy that drew him. Aspen had been built on silver mining, and the silver market had crashed in 1893—which meant the town, when Pfeifer first saw it, was slumbering through its fiftieth consecutive "quiet year," as locals called them. What excited Pfeifer was not the economic but the physical environment. Mountains for him were objects of reverence; he was taken with the way Aspen nestled, St. Anton–like, amid them, and the steep mountain that rose directly above town seemed to him divinely created for skiing. Actually, it was artificially created too: by the time Pfeifer arrived, the telltale signs of ski development were already visible up on Aspen Mountain, called Ajax by the locals. In 1936 three men—an Olympic bobsledder, an eastern investor, and a mining man who had spent his boyhood in Aspen—had announced plans for a ski resort several miles south of town, and they had brought in Swiss mountaineer André Roch to design the ski runs.[6] Roch also mapped out a run on Ajax, which the newly organized town ski club, together with crews from the Works Progress Administration, cleared in summer 1937. Called the Roch Run, it streaked down the steepest part of the mountain and for part of its length zigzagged back and forth in a harrowing "corkscrew." Soon the ski club added a crude "boat tow" to haul skiers up the mountainside, cut more trails, built a jump, and began hosting races, culminating in the 1941 National Alpine Championships. So when Pfeifer first saw Aspen, it was already on the map for those in the skiing know.[7]

But it was really just an old mining town with a few ski runs. Pfeifer imagined it becoming something more: what he called a "skiing community," a town defined by the sport. He imagined teaching locals, especially children, to ski, strengthening them in body, character, and spirit, instilling

Mill St. - Aspen, Colo. · Showing Ski Run

1.1 Signs of skiing to come. Aspen languished in the late Depression years, with uncrowded streets, vacant weed lots where the houses of miners and merchants had once stood, and grand but run-down buildings like the Wheeler Opera House (*at right*) standing as silent reminders of the town's onetime silver wealth. But up on the slopes of Ajax, there were already signs of the massive postwar transformation to come: the straight-line cut through the trees where townspeople had built the town's first ski tow and, next to it, the unmistakable "corkscrew" of the Roch ski run. Courtesy Denver Public Library.

in them the same reverence for mountains that he felt. He would mentor them into champions whose racing trophies would restore pride to the town. And people from around the world would come to Aspen for its ski school, rescuing the local economy from dependence on a dead old industry. Pfeifer believed all of this really could happen—because it already had in his hometown of St. Anton. There, he had seen how local farmers made money by hiring out their sleighs as taxis, local tailors by sewing and selling ski clothes, local homeowners by renting rooms to tourists, local skiers by teaching the tourists how to ski. He had seen how St. Anton's young skiers (like himself) had brought repute to the town by winning races all over Europe. And he had seen how wealthy visitors from Britain, the Continent, and even America flocked to St. Anton's ski school to learn its renowned "Arlberg" technique (invented by Pfeifer's own mentor, Hannes Schneider).

St. Antonites, in short, had revived and reoriented everything about their town to center around skiing—from its economy to its communal identity, from the way its land was used to the way its kids were raised. Pfeifer thought he could help Aspenites do the same.[8]

Before being shipped off to Italy, Pfeifer and other soldiers of the Tenth Mountain Division befriended a number of people in town, especially Aspen Ski Club members like Hotel Jerome owner Laurence Elisha, shoemaker and ski shop proprietor Mike Magnifico, and Midnight Mine owners Fred and Frank Willoughby. Townspeople and Tenth Mountain men spent winter Saturdays slogging or boat-towing up the mountain together and racing down as fast as they dared; then, as the sun slipped behind the Elk Range, they might crowd into Magnifico's ski shop, where tales of the day's thrills mingled with the rich and oily fragrance of varnished wood, leather, and ski wax. Many evenings ended with cruds at the Jerome. In his friendships with these local ski fanatics, Pfeifer sensed support for his dream of making Aspen a skiing community.[9] It is hard to gauge what other Aspenites thought, though. When Pfeifer, at Elisha's urging, went before the city council to outline his ideas, the town clerk made only brief note of his presentation and none at all of how the council reacted. "Mr phiffer spoke on future of aspen skiing and his plans," she scrawled, not quite sure what to make of the Austrian's last name, much less his grand vision.[10]

Converting local residents to the idea of a skiing community was one thing. Converting the local landscape was another. When Pfeifer stood atop Aspen Mountain, he wrote years later, "I envisioned the [ski] runs cut naturally with the contours of the mountain, blending with the meadows, gorges, and glades." So naturally did the terrain seem to lend itself to the sport that Pfeifer invoked Providence to explain it. But people before him had already claimed the terrain for another use: mining. Unseen to Pfeifer, as he admired the mountain's physical contours, were contours of another kind: invisible property lines crisscrossing the slopes, a crazy mosaic of mining claims dating back to 1879. Before leaving for Italy, Pfeifer spent weekends traipsing over the mountain face, sizing up possible locations for runs and lifts.[11] But before he could build anything, he would have to negotiate the legal landscape that overlaid the physical one. Everywhere he wanted a trail or tow, he would have to track down the claim holders or their heirs and secure a deed, lease, or easement for that piece of land.

He got help from his ski club friends. The Willoughby brothers offered rights-of-way for tows and trails to pass over their Midnight Mine property, and Magnifico sold Pfeifer some scraps of mountainside he had bought for back taxes.[12] Much trickier was getting access to the Smuggler-Durant property, one of Aspen's richest claims back in the 1880s. The route Pfeifer had picked for his main tow ran right over this property, necessitating an easement, purchase, or lease. But owner D. R. C. "Darcy" Brown Jr., whose father had made millions off the Smuggler mine, was skeptical at first that Pfeifer's plans were serious and not just cover for a shady speculative scheme. Only after a year of negotiating, largely involving surrogates because Pfeifer was hospitalized and Brown was stationed in the Pacific, did Brown finally agree in late 1945 to lease his land. Pfeifer secured a third lease, covering the Spar Consolidated claims, soon after, so that by March 1946 he had surface rights for all his planned ski tows and trails.[13]

Leasing claims was long-standing practice in mining districts like Aspen. It was a new twist, though, for the lessee to be utterly uninterested in mining. Indeed, Pfeifer did not even bother to lease underground mineral rights; his leases applied only to the surface. And remaking the surface for skiing would involve removing evidence of mining—like pits, headframes, ore bins, and waste rock dumps—to make way for lift towers and ski runs. In other words, for the first time in Aspen, someone was using land for purposes that were not just different from but incompatible with mining. Seen in this light, Pfeifer's three leases on Aspen Mountain marked a historic first step toward the overhauling of the local landscape into a landscape of leisure.

The human landscape began to change likewise. Aspen's population swelled immediately after the war, and many of the newcomers looked a lot like Pfeifer: newly discharged Tenth Mountain veterans who gravitated back to Aspen primarily for recreational reasons—primarily, that is, for skiing. Some, like Percy Rideout and Johnny Litchfield, worked for Pfeifer's ski school; others started shops or other businesses; each had his own story. But for all of them, Aspen's allure lay chiefly in skiing. And they, like Pfeifer, began to change the landscape to cater to skiers. Litchfield, for one, bought an old saloon where miners had once gathered, cleaned up its vintage 1892 woodwork (finding, to his delight, colorful inlay designs under the half century of grime), and reopened it as a funky, fashionable new tavern called the Red Onion. Fritz Benedict, newly trained as an architect, paid twelve thousand dollars for six hundred acres of ranchland on Red Mountain, overlooking Aspen on the north, and began surveying streets and lot lines amid the grass, scrub oak, and sage. Red Mountain, Aspen's first luxury-home subdivision, opened to buyers in 1947. Ranchland, like mining land, was giving way to the emerging landscape of leisure.[14]

Meanwhile, Pfeifer went about creating the infrastructure for his skiing community. He partnered with Mike Magnifico to expand the ski shop to handle many more customers, and he struck an agreement with the Aspen Ski Club to build a new rope tow. Ski club volunteers also spent the summer and fall of 1945 digging out boulders and chopping down aspens and pines on the mountain to make way for more ski trails. The clearances they left on the slopes, visible from anywhere in town, were the clearest signs yet of Aspen's nascent recreational makeover. Pfeifer's ski school opened in December and started slow, but by February 1946 scores of skiers dotted the steep face of Aspen Mountain, skidding and tumbling their way down the runs.[15]

Neither Pfeifer nor his fellow Tenth Mountain veterans had the means to make wholesale changes in Aspen. But the small shifts they set in motion set the stage for bigger ones to come. The men represented a new kind of local who would soon become much more numerous: the kind whose lifestyle choices—including the choice of where to live—revolved around outdoor leisure. They brought new ways of seeing the land: Pfeifer looking at Aspen Mountain and seeing ski terrain, Benedict casting his eye on the mountain opposite and imagining vacation houses with scenic valley views. And Pfeifer worked especially hard to win others to his way of seeing. Aspen as a skiing community, Aspen as a natural place for skiing—he painted these pictures over and over for local officials, ski club members, and ski journalists. In turn, the ski magazines spread his vision across the nation. "He has visions of lodges and ski huts dotting the Colorado snow basins," one magazine said of Pfeifer, "so ski trips can be made throughout the entire area."[16] Colorado's high country, remade as a paradise for skiers—images like this one focused armchair skiers' sights on Aspen and the surrounding area, often for the first time, and encouraged them to view this place with an eye toward leisure, just as Friedl Pfeifer had when he first saw it.

A shift in perceptions of a place is admittedly abstract. But in Aspen it took on concrete form every time someone like Pfeifer and Benedict bought or leased property. By bits and pieces, the local landscape was coming under the control of leisure-minded people, people who aimed to modify the land to fit their recreational ideals. That said, nothing Pfeifer was doing could have prepared Aspenites for the sweeping changes that were about to come at the hands of another leisure-minded newcomer, this one with far deeper pockets and far more propensity to seek total control over the local landscape. Nothing could have prepared Aspenites for Walter Paepcke.

If Friedl Pfeifer stood for one postwar western "type," the veteran who returned after the war to settle into civilian life, then Walter Paepcke stood for two others.[17] He was the tourist who went west on vacation, and he was the entrepreneur who sensed a new dynamism in the region and seized the opportunity to invest there. What makes Paepcke significant is that he melded these two types into one. He invested in the West all right, but instead of sectors like mining or manufacturing, he poured his capital into leisure. He built a business selling the same vacation experiences he had originally come west to enjoy.

Paepcke, founder and owner of a Chicago box-making firm called Container Corporation of America, was not your typical businessman. Long before investing in Aspen, he was known for his unusual devotion to matters artistic and intellectual. In the late 1930s he had staked his entrepreneurial identity on an idealistic crusade to enlighten business and society by infusing them with the values of the humanities and arts. His co-crusaders included faculty and administrators at the University of Chicago and a cadre of modernist artists and designers, formerly at Germany's renowned Bauhaus, who had fled fascism to settle in Chicago and other U.S. cities. All of them, in one way or another, were working to harness the arts and humanities to practical ends, and so uplift society. Their crusade took on new urgency in the 1940s, when the world, having emerged from a catastrophic global conflict, blundered into the chill of the Cold War—and into an apparent date with nuclear holocaust. Only the teachings of the arts and humanities could cure humankind of its addiction to technology, science, and power, these cultural reformers believed. Paepcke was their chief corporate sponsor, lending vocal support, money, marketing, and logistical help. Understanding this, his sincere belief in the social benefits of the arts and humanities, is one key to understanding the ambitious project he undertook in Aspen.[18]

Equally important, though, is to understand that Paepcke saw no contradiction between his idealism and his entrepreneurialism. As president of the Container Corporation, he often used advertising and other business tactics to advance the cause of high culture, while using the cachet of culture to improve his own business's bottom line.[19] He employed that same dual strategy in Aspen. By turning Aspen into a cultural retreat, where visitors would mingle with artists, philosophers, and musicians in the rarefied Rocky Mountain air, Paepcke sincerely hoped to renew guests' minds and spirits and equip them to cope with, even solve, the grim dilemmas of the Cold War. At the same time, he sincerely hoped to turn a profit. And in this sense—this unabashed straddling of idealism and commercialism—Paepcke's Aspen set the tone for the marketing of the good life in postwar Colorado.

Walter Paepcke might never even have gone to Aspen had his wife Elizabeth not "discovered" it on a spur-of-the-moment ski trip in 1939. A fairy-tale hamlet of faded but still charming gingerbread houses, set in a pristine wilderness of sunlight and snow—these were Elizabeth Paepcke's enchanted first impressions of Aspen. She urged Walter to see it for himself. Not being a skier, he declined. But in the spring of 1945, Aspen came up in conversation again—and this time Walter began pondering the real estate potential of the place. Over the next few weeks, he secretly had his secretary and several other proxies ask about the availability of property in Aspen. To avoid sparking a speculative frenzy, he had them divide their inquiries among several sources, and he allowed no one to reveal who was behind the questions. He learned that vacant lots and derelict old buildings could be easily had. So on Memorial Day 1945, he, Elizabeth, and another couple paid a visit to Aspen. And in just his first two days there, Walter bought a pretty Queen Anne residence; settled on prices for several other houses, a downtown commercial block, and hundreds of area lots; and hired town judge William Shaw to negotiate more deals on his behalf. On his next visit, in July, he snapped up more lots and three more houses, including the jewel of the town's West End, an elegant mansard-roofed mansion with matching carriage house, set on a full-block lot, shielded by willows from the street. In Aspen's silvery heyday, this mansion, "Pioneer Park," had been home to the mayor—which was fitting, because Paepcke was about to become the new most powerful person in town.[20]

Despite his aggressive property acquisition, Paepcke's ideas for what to do with Aspen were not so well developed at first. Over the course of 1945, he put forth a series of seemingly ad hoc suggestions for what he figured might happen there. Noteworthy, though, is that all of them reflected his own viewpoint as a vacationer, someone used to seeing the mountains mainly as a playground. Before he actually saw Aspen, he was saying it would be a ski resort. The snow was "the most reliable and perfect" in America, he bragged (though he had never experienced it himself). Then, after visiting Aspen twice, he ticked off a longer list of outdoor pastimes it might offer: horseback riding, hunting, camping, and fishing, to go along with winter sports. With such a variety of recreational amenities, he now envisioned Aspen becoming "a year-round vacation spot," perhaps "one of the great vacation spots in the world." He was moved by Aspen's scenery and by its splendid feeling of isolation, just as Elizabeth had been on her first visit. As the Paepckes were themselves tourists in Aspen, Walter's plans for developing the town quite naturally selected out those landscape qualities that a tourist would find most valuable.[21]

So why did Paepcke move so quickly to control so much property? Because tourists are not just interested in an attraction here, an attraction there. They are attuned to the overall atmosphere of the places they visit, the ambiance that distinguishes a nice vacation spot from a not-so-nice one. So even while Paepcke's plans for Aspen were vague at first, he already sensed that he would need to seize a great deal of control over the local landscape to create just the right atmosphere for visitors. As he told the *Denver Post*, "We want to rebuild or renovate the inherently good and throw out the bad," and in the process "preserve Aspen's own kind of local color." He even told an associate he was thinking of showcasing Aspen as an intact "frontier Victorian mining town" by undertaking a wholesale historic restoration, "as was done with Williamsburg in the east." That was quite suggestive, for in Williamsburg's historic town center, John D. Rockefeller Jr. had taken control of virtually everything—building design, land use, spatial arrangement, even the way locals made a living and the way they conceived of their community's past.[22]

Indeed, Paepcke toyed with the idea of putting locals to much the same use Rockefeller did: having them work as cottage craftspeople—silversmiths, weavers, leather toolers, and furniture and cheese makers—who would fashion things by hand, using the fruits of the local landscape, while visitors drank in the premodern rusticity of it all.[23] This plan never came to pass, but Paepcke did use people in another way, by personally recruiting select outsiders to move to Aspen to help enhance the local ambiance. First among them was Herbert Bayer, Austrian-born Bauhaus architect and graphic designer, whom Paepcke persuaded to move to Aspen to help physically renovate and culturally enlighten the town. Paepcke recruited other artistic and intellectual sophisticates to follow. He also got at least one entertainment icon—the stylish movie star and avid skier Gary Cooper—to build a home in Aspen, adding a bit of panache to Aspen's cachet (while unintentionally seeding its eventual notoriety as a celebrity stomping ground).[24] In effect, Paepcke was taking it upon himself to manipulate

1.2 Four faces of the new Aspen. Pompom neckties, modeled here for an Aspen ski shop, may not have caught on, but the changes these four men brought to Aspen were enduring indeed. *From left*: Friedl Pfeifer launched Aspen's rise as a ski resort; Walter Paepcke made Aspen a haven of summer seminars, concerts, and conferences in the arts and humanities; Herbert Bayer kick-started Aspen's historic restoration but also its image as a hotbed of modern design; and Gary Cooper embodied Aspen's emerging celebrity mystique. Photo taken at the Four Seasons Club, ca. 1955. Aspen Historical Society, Ted Ryan Collection.

Aspen's *human* scenery. The commodification of vacation ambiance, the packaging of a place for tourists to consume, could have powerful implications indeed.

Through the summer and fall of 1945, Paepcke asserted more and more control. A big step came on August 30, when he held a public meeting to reveal his plans for Aspen. Dozens of locals piled into the wood-paneled district courtroom, no doubt anxious to meet this rich newcomer who had spent the last few months buying up chunks of their town. Introduced by Judge Shaw, Paepcke straightaway took charge, lecturing the locals on what their town's chief assets were and instructing them on what they must do next: clean up vacant lots, tear down decrepit buildings, paint and prettify what was left. He introduced two architects, Chicago's Walter Frazier and

Bauhaus founder Walter Gropius, whom he had personally tapped to plan Aspen's reconstruction. At meeting's end, the locals were sent off to gather the data Gropius and Frazier would need for their master plan.[25] The whole meeting was a jaw-dropping display of effrontery—yet enough Aspenites seemed excited about Paepcke's plans to revive the town that they pledged their aid. Plans for a citywide cleanup got under way, and the next city council meeting buzzed with excitement over parks and master plans. For the first time, the council discussed the possibility of zoning and setting up a city park improvement fund.[26] At Paepcke's instigation, council members were already starting to see Aspen's rustic, small-town, Victorian ambiance as a marketable commodity, requiring conscious maintenance to attract visitors. In the not-so-long term, this way of seeing would have radical consequences for Aspen, reaching into every square inch of the local landscape and into almost every facet of daily life.

All the while, Paepcke kept acquiring property. He, along with others who had caught on to the coming boom, bought so many abandoned lots in fall 1945 that Pitkin County halted tax sales to allow the treasurer to catch his breath. (By that time, so wildly were rumors swirling that the *Aspen Times* saw the need to assure its readers: "Mr. Paepcke, contrary to popular belief, owns only a small part of Aspen.") In January Paepcke turned his attention back to buildings, buying two more downtown blocks and then, in his grandest gesture yet, signing a long-term lease with Laurence Elisha to renovate the Hotel Jerome into a luxury resort lodge. And he kept buying land in and around town. Each of his acquisitions, like each of Pfeifer's mining leases, was another step toward foreclosing the old mine and ranch economy—another step toward a new landscape of recreation and leisure.[27]

It might seem that Pfeifer's and Paepcke's plans complemented each other. In truth, Paepcke, whose proxies had apprised him of the Austrian's ski venture, feared what skiing might do to Aspen if not controlled. The sport's popularity showed signs of snowballing after the war, and Paepcke worried it would turn Aspen into a huge tourist mill—an outcome he emphatically did not want.[28] He assured locals that he had "no desire to build up a strictly resort town[,] for resorts cater to a mass influx of visitors and sightseers." You could almost hear his lips curl at the thought. Mass tourism went against everything this patrician wanted Aspen to be: small and quiet, not like a city; exclusive and refined, not crowded and commercialized; high-minded, not prostituted to superficialities like glamour and sport. "I'm interested . . . in providing more than a place for movie stars to ski," he told one reporter, in an unsubtle jab at Sun Valley. Nor would he let Aspen become like Coney Island, a tawdry tourist trap. "I would like to see us avoid the tourist tripper," he mused, "who litters the scenery with orange peelings and sardine cans." He was determined to prevent "unregulated growth," to keep "a rash of cabin camps, shooting galleries, roadhouses and other fly-by-night enterprises from breaking out."[29]

So fear of mass tourism was another reason why Paepcke sought such tight control over Aspen—and why he maneuvered to co-opt Pfeifer's ski development. At first, unbeknownst to Pfeifer, Paepcke tried to preempt the ski venture by leasing the Smuggler-Durant claim before the Austrian could.[30] But in fall 1945, after meeting with Pfeifer, Paepcke switched tactics. Instead of trying to thwart Pfeifer's project, he settled for simply monitoring its progress—probably because he had learned that Pfeifer's finances were too shaky to build a large ski resort. And indeed, before long, Pfeifer ran into money trouble. Unable to secure the loan he needed to build lifts, he was forced to beg Paepcke for help—which was likely what Paepcke had hoped for all along. The Chicagoan agreed to contribute some capital and to round up some of his wealthy friends to do the same. But the bailout bore a steep price: Paepcke insisted that Pfeifer relinquish control of the ski area. Left with no other options, Pfeifer agreed.[31]

So it was that in early 1946, the Aspen Skiing Corporation was born, capitalized by investors from Chicago, Denver, and the East. Immediately the firm announced plans to build lifts all the way to the summit of Aspen Mountain. And to clear the legal way, the firm assumed control of all the surface leases Pfeifer and his friends in town had worked so hard to secure. Pfeifer retained an executive position, twenty-five thousand shares of stock, and exclusive franchise for the ski school, but Paepcke had clearly seized control of the skiing side of Aspen. And he reminded his fellow investors why. "We don't want to make Aspen a mass skiing center," he wrote to one, expressing his hope that the ski area would remain "fairly selective and just large enough to make it entirely profitable, but not overrun."[32] He also found subtle ways to harness the energy of skiing to advance his more dearly held goals. For example, he required everyone who invested in the Aspen Skiing Corporation to also buy stock in the Aspen Company, the firm he had set up to handle the town's renovation and development as a cultural resort.[33] And he began talking up skiing as an enlightened pursuit, a form of Aristotelian leisure that cultivated the body even as artistic and intellectual endeavors cultivated the spirit and mind.[34]

To Paepcke's dismay, though, skiing hogged the headlines to the exclusion of everything else about Aspen, especially as work began on a two-part chairlift to the top of Aspen Mountain. The lower section, hyped as "the world's longest chair lift," rose 2,200 vertical feet from street level to Tourtelotte Park—an artificial clearing, a remnant of the Victorian minescape—where the Roch Run began its twisting, plummeting path back down. The lift's upper section would start at Tourtelotte Park and climb the final 1,200 feet to the summit.[35] At the lift's dedication on January 11, 1947, political and social luminaries, ski celebrities, and local residents cheered, and cameras snapped and whirred, as governor-elect Lee Knous smashed a champagne magnum across a lift tower. That kicked off a weekend-long "Grand Opening" gala, with ski races, daredevil displays, dances, and more. It was Aspen's flashy debut as a full-fledged resort, not just for the hundreds who had flocked to town for the event, but also for countless others across the country, who watched the revelry in the newsreels or read about it in newspapers and magazines.[36] One might think it a triumph for Paepcke, who let himself be photographed and interviewed that weekend as the "patron" or "founder" of Aspen skiing. But in fact the event left him perturbed. He was especially horrified when he saw press coverage of the Grand Opening, like the *March of Time* newsreel that showed revelers mindlessly skiing and partying the weekend away. It made Aspen look so vulgar and superficial that Paepcke personally apologized to the stockholders of the Aspen Skiing Corporation.[37]

Paepcke did not absolutely oppose skiing. He did like that it raked in winter revenue and lent name recognition to Aspen. But never again after the Grand Opening would he associate himself so closely with the sport. Instead, he focused his energy on Aspen's cultural offerings. Just a few weeks after the Grand Opening, feeling the need for some grand gesture to move the spotlight from skiing back toward Aspen's "serious" side, he hit upon the idea of having the town host a convocation honoring the two-hundredth birthday of the great German humanist Johann Wolfgang von Goethe. Paepcke envisioned the world's most eminent scholars, artists, and philosophers gathering in Aspen to discuss Goethe's teachings and ponder his legacy for modern times. The event would focus the world's attention on the urgent relevance of the humanities—and simultaneously on Aspen too. As always with Paepcke, entrepreneurialism and idealism went hand in hand. Having experimented with Aspen the vacation center, Aspen the living-history museum, and Aspen the ski resort, Paepcke was finally settling

1.3 Recreation overlays the land. In 1951, Aspen was small, surrounded by open space that had not yet been lost to resort development. But Aspen Mountain had clearly been repurposed for recreation. The telltale clear-cuts of ski runs dominate the mountain's face, covering old mining claims, and snow conceals most of the physical traces of mining, like shaft openings and haulage roads. The one conspicuous remnant is the derelict Veteran Mine ore bin, visible as a dark shape on the lower slopes at left center. Soon it too would disappear, demolished in 1953. Photo by Ferenc Berko / Courtesy berkophoto.com.

on what he really wanted Aspen to be: the home base for his cultural crusade, a refuge from contemporary troubles where visitors would rediscover high thinking and high art.[38]

Two frenzied years of preparation for the Goethe Bicentennial Convocation brought more striking changes to the local landscape, as more old land uses gave way to new. On a former mine site a few miles up Castle Creek, Paepcke's contractors built the posh Four Seasons Club, with tennis courts, a swimming pool, stocked fish ponds, and a lavish clubhouse to pamper the convocation's distinguished guests. No mining would ever take place on that land again. On the edge of town, in the meadow where rancher Johnny Hoaglund and his hired hands had once cut hay, Paepcke had up-and-coming architect Eero Saarinen design a giant dome-shaped tent, sheltering a two-thousand-seat Greek amphitheater, ready to host the convocation's lectures and music recitals. On another erstwhile ranch that Paepcke had bought a few miles downvalley, an airfield appeared, ready to spirit in Goethe celebrants and other future visitors.[39] Paepcke even exerted power over land not his own. Wanting Aspen to look rustic for the convocation, but not run-down, he prevailed on local landowners who had never fussed over weed lots to mow them, who had never minded junk heaps to clear them away. Scraggly trees got trimmed, tumbledown sheds demolished, sixty-year-old houses repainted—and the relaxed decrepitude familiar to all old mining towns gave way to a tidier aesthetic.[40]

Subtler changes crept into local people's lives. Because the Roaring Fork Valley had far too few hotel beds to accommodate three thousand convocation visitors, many Aspenites, at Paepcke's behest, rented out spare rooms and couches. For many, it was their first experience as workers in the tourist economy. And while the plan to have locals make cheese and leather goods thankfully did not resurface, Aspenites were exhorted to extend "western hospitality" to convocation visitors, and event publicity played up the colorful western characters—grizzled miners, strapping cowboys, pretty lasses—that Goethegoers could expect to encounter in Aspen. In other words, locals continued to be useful to Paepcke for helping to set the right atmosphere.[41]

A conference honoring a long-dead German author, whose works few Americans ever read, might seem a strange way to publicize a resort. But the Goethe festival did for Aspen just what Paepcke had hoped. He unleashed his public-relations team, lined up a bevy of intellectual celebrities (led by philosopher-physician Albert Schweitzer, who was persuaded to make his only trip to the United States for the event), and was rewarded with mounds of positive press coverage.[42] When the three-week convocation kicked off in July 1949, the newsreels returned, this time to portray Aspen as an ultraserious haven of high culture. The event was so successful that in its afterglow Paepcke and his friends began planning a permanent Aspen Institute for Humanistic Studies, which would host seminars, lectures, and concerts every summer starting in 1950. An annual Design Conference and Music Festival soon followed. And Aspen, so recently stereotyped as a hardpartying ski resort, found new repute for its sophisticated art, music, and intellectual scene—a sort of Rocky Mountain Athens.

It was not that everyone who flocked to Aspen shared Paepcke's esoteric tastes. In fact, if we read what Goethe Convocation attendees said about the experience, we find less about the lectures or concerts than about the setting itself. What attendees liked most about Aspen were the same qualities Elizabeth Paepcke and Friedl Pfeifer had noticed when they first saw the place: the rustic, small-town feel and spectacular mountain milieu. One after another, convocation guests gushed over Aspen's scenic majesty, the clearness of its air, the sense of remoteness from all things modern, the casual mood of the gathering places and streets. Even more, they marveled at the way this atmosphere had enabled them to relax, open their minds, and feel fulfilled. The "atmosphere of calm, majesty, and natural austerity and beauty" made Aspen the "ideal location," wrote one visitor. "At such altitudes," added another, "everything was a little sharper, in clearer focus, a little nearer the sky."[43]

The direct link these visitors drew between mountain setting and state of mind suggests that Paepcke had succeeded in his effort to evoke the right atmosphere (if not in his effort to overhaul American culture). Few visitors to Aspen ever became connoisseurs of screeching experimental symphonies or German Romantic thought. No matter. What Paepcke and Pfeifer did there carried broader historical significance: It set the blueprint for the wholesale remaking of the Colorado high country into a region of leisure. It showed how an old mining or ranching town could find new life, if one turned remoteness and rusticity into selling points and converted extractive landscapes to recreational use. At the same time, Aspen's example showed that once aura or atmosphere became itself the marketable commodity, virtually everything about a place was set for change. The way buildings looked and functioned, the way space was organized and used, the environmental values people applied to the surroundings—all of these got caught up in the effort to package and promote a town for tourism. Even the kinds of work people did, the ways they raised their children, and the ways they defined and circumscribed their community—who was included and excluded—came under the sway of tourist promotion.

In the coming years, boosters and business interests in communities throughout the high country followed Aspen's lead. They learned from Aspen that there was money to be made off atmosphere, off the location of a town and its unique qualities of place. They learned to manipulate and market these qualities to appeal to people's deep personal yearnings— for self-improvement, for emotional uplift, for respite from the humdrum world. And they sold the physical setting, the intangibles of "atmosphere," and the attendant emotional associations as a vacation package, sometimes with great success. As this happened, bit by bit, the Colorado high country became more than just a region for tourists to spend money. It became, itself, a product for consumption and an object of consumer desire.

TO GOVERNOR-ELECT LEE KNOUS, ASPEN'S NEW CHAIRLIFTS AND DOWN-hill runs looked like Colorado's future. Knous had won office in November

1946 largely by promising to energize the state's postwar economy, and now he pronounced Aspen "Exhibit 'A'" of what he had in mind. He hoped its success as a ski center would "encourage others . . . to develop other areas with equally as much promise." It "should mean the coming of great sums of new capital into Colorado at an otherwise quiet travel season," Knous predicted shortly before Aspen Mountain's Grand Opening in January 1947. "It [skiing] should prove of real benefit toward better balancing our seasonal economy."[44]

The new governor was not the only one thrilled by Aspen's revival. If anything, he saw its significance more narrowly than some. While he hoped skiing would even out seasonal fluctuations, many of his contemporaries saw it as the spark for a whole new boom, maybe even as rich as the gold and silver booms of yore. Not by coincidence did many headlines link Aspen's unfolding present to its epic past: "A Mining Town Is Reborn," "Money Fever Is Running In Aspen Again," "Bonanza Days Again for Silver Town." Paepcke thought Aspen was on the verge of something bigger than silver. "This town has struck it again," he declared at the Grand Opening. "But it won't be a short meteoric life like the last one." Like Knous, Paepcke hoped Aspen would set the pace for other towns. "We don't want Aspen to be the only spot in the state for skiing," he told one reporter. "The more places we have for skiing, the better."[45]

In Denver, the editors of the *Rocky Mountain News* heartily agreed. Long a cheerleader for development in Denver's mountain hinterland, the *Rocky* commended Aspen as a model for other depressed old mining towns to emulate. The influential daily lauded Aspen, along with Central City and Georgetown, for "adjusting themselves to the change in times" and declared itself "strongly in favor of such old mining camps as Aspen . . . being developed as sports communities."[46] In other words, Aspen's recreational rebirth should not be an isolated case. It should lead other high-country towns into a new era, when the tourist trade might sustain local economies as silver and gold no longer could.

In January 1947, there seemed good reason to hope for such a future. Travel for pleasure had taken a terrific upswing right after V-J Day, as millions of veterans and their families, reunited by rapid demobilization, jumped at the chance to reestablish family ties, relax, and recreate. They were flush with pent-up spending money, newly freed from gasoline rationing, and, with the conversion back to civilian manufacturing, able to buy sedans, station wagons, and campers once more. And by many predictions,

Colorado and the West sat directly in their path. Even during the war, a survey by the American Automobile Association had found that the West could expect to lure more postwar vacationers than any other region, and *Better Homes and Gardens* subscribers had ranked Colorado second only to California among states they most hoped to visit.[47] Peace had unleashed a tourist tidal wave. Already, in fall 1945, Colorado resort owners had reported they were booked to capacity for the following summer, and the State Advertising and Publicity Committee had warned that demand for lodging might badly outstrip supply. A few months later, the committee had thrown its own caution to the wind and launched an advertising blitz urging Americans to spend their "Victory Vacations" in Colorado. The results were instant and impressive. According to some estimates, visitors spent nearly $200 million in Colorado in 1946—65 percent more than they had in 1941 and an increase well above the national average.[48]

Looking at the numbers, the *Rocky Mountain News* editors made a bold statement: tourism, they declared, was now "by far Colorado's most important single activity." "We should, and must, foster agriculture, livestock and mining," they conceded, in a nod to the state's bedrock industries. "Other states have these resources, however. What we must do, likewise, is to develop the resources that are *unique*—our climate, our scenery, our place as the nation's playground."[49]

Words like these were more historic than they might seem. Yes, by 1946 tourism already had a long history in Colorado, and it was already a time-honored (and timeworn) tradition for boosters to tout the state's scenery, climate, and mountain "playground." But it was highly unusual, perhaps even unprecedented, for a voice as influential as the *Rocky Mountain News* to suggest that tourism should take precedence *above all other industries*. In the *Rocky*'s view, neither mining nor ranching could now match the money tourism brought in. And neither made Colorado "unique." Tourism did— or at least it could—so its promotion was paramount.

But the *Rocky*'s view was far from universal. Up in the high country, the long-established resource-based industries still anchored many people's identities, colored their views of the land, shaped their sense of history, and excited their hopes for the future. Mining and ranching rooted these people in the rugged terrain and remote communities where they lived. Mining, in particular, had sparked the booms to which towns like Leadville, Aspen, Georgetown, Central City, Idaho Springs, Empire, Frisco, Breckenridge, and Red Cliff owed their very existence. So it should not be surprising that in the late 1940s and 1950s, many people in the high country still saw mining as the best and most obvious use of the landscape. They fully expected—indeed, they thought it natural—that any future prosperity would hinge on it.

This view may have held greatest sway in Leadville, the two-mile-high "Cloud City," where many locals remained fiercely committed to mining and gouged their conviction into the land for everyone to see. Motorists driving up State Highway 91 saw it the moment they reached the top of Fremont Pass and the Lake County line. Immediately to the left loomed 13,550-foot Bartlett Mountain, its lower slopes crowded with the mills, crushers, hauling trains, and company-town houses of the giant Climax molybdenum mine, its upper slopes caving into a giant sinkhole because so much of the rock underground had been blasted away. In Leadville itself, fourteen miles farther down the road, the giant Arkansas Valley Smelter ruled the skyline, old miners' cottages shared neighborhoods with equally ancient headframes and rusting mounds of waste rock, and the surrounding gulches and mountainsides were a moonscape of gaping pits, eroded tailings piles, and acres upon acres of pitch-black smelter slag. That Leadville's history lay in the mines, these scenes left no doubt. That many Leadvillians kept their faith in the industry, and disdained a future built on tourism, would become abundantly clear in the late 1940s and 1950s. A *Denver Post* reporter summed up the stalwart attitude of Leadville's longtime residents: " 'This,' they remark with considerable acidity and pride, 'is a mining camp.' "[50]

Given hindsight—metal mining did *not* revive after the war, instead vanishing from most of Colorado within decades—we might be tempted to dismiss Leadville's postwar mine boosters as people behind the times, hopelessly clinging to a past forever dead. To do so would be more than uncharitable; it would be historically inaccurate. In fact, there were reasons to believe that mining would sustain Leadville for years to come. Zinc and lead mining had flourished during World War II and then boomed again during the conflict in Korea.[51] Most Leadville mines closed for good after that—but then the mammoth operation up at Climax picked up the slack. Through the 1950s Climax yielded more than $40 million worth of molybdenum per year, employing thousands of locals in the process. The jobs paid extremely well by rural western standards: many a visitor was impressed with the Climax parking lot, filled with miners' shiny new cars. Climax offered college scholarships for miners' children, and the company town boasted low rents, low crime—and, in 1953, the high country's first

CLIMAX MOLYBDENUM MINE

1.4 Mining's demise: greatly exaggerated. There was skiing up at Climax, as this postcard from 1956 shows, but the paramount use of this part of the high country was mining. Skiers gaze in apparent awe at the massive Climax molybdenum mining complex, with its cluster of mill buildings and its 1,500-inhabitant company town. Overhead looms Bartlett Mountain (*left*), its caving lower slopes hinting at the extent of blasting beneath the surface. Clearly, in the 1950s, the high country's recreational makeover was anything but a done deal. Courtesy Cooper Post Card Co. / Terrell Creative.

television service.[52] Not even sophisticated Aspen could claim that mark of modernity. So in the 1950s, when boosters in other towns looked for ways to revive their economies, Aspen was not the only model, nor tourism the only option they saw. Given the success of Climax and Leadville, mining struck many as an equally viable alternative.[53]

There was widespread belief—shared by many outside "experts"—that mining might revive on formerly worthless metals that society had only recently come to value. These included not just molybdenum but also uranium, the "yellow metal" of the atomic age, and its frequent companion, steel-toughening vanadium. The federal Atomic Energy Commission (AEC) began offering uranium-finding bonuses and other incentives in 1951, sparking a uranium frenzy in the Mountain West. According to the University of Colorado's L. J. Crampon, a leading authority on small-town economic development, the uranium rush showed "how an industry previously ignored" could burgeon "practically over night to the place where it is now an important segment of this Western Colorado economy."[54] Most of the uranium frenzy centered on the sedimentary canyonlands of the Colorado Plateau, but according to prospecting guides and maps issued by the AEC and the U.S. Geological Survey (USGS), veins also occurred in igneous formations of the high Rockies. In 1955 the AEC specifically targeted Eagle County as one of Colorado's next uranium hot spots, and the Eagle Chamber of Commerce was told to expect a "vast new population growth" from the imminent "uranium boom." Excited rumors lit up Clear Creek, Gilpin, and Grand Counties too, and many fortune seekers took their jeeps and Geiger counters right into the heart of the high country.[55]

And then there were fuel minerals: coal, petroleum, natural gas, and above all oil shale. Ever since the 1910s, experts and boosters alike had been predicting that the giant sheets of oil shale in northwestern Colorado—the world's largest high-grade deposit—would someday spark a resounding boom. As the State Bureau of Mines said in 1919, "The shale-oil industry seems destined to become one of the leading ones in Colorado." Historically, the "rock that burned" (actually not shale but a marlstone permeated with an oil-like substance called kerogen) had excited attention whenever conventional oil sources ran low, only to fade back to obscurity when new oil fields opened in California, Wyoming, Texas, or Oklahoma. The 1940s and 1950s saw very little shale oil produced in Colorado—but everyone seemed to think the boom was just around the corner. With America addicted to automobiles, and economies around the world thirsting for liquid fuels, oil shale waited, in one industry spokesman's words, like "an ace up Colorado's sleeve." Crampon thought it would make western Colorado a "powerhouse," even "the industrial center . . . of America's future," and would "sustain, both directly and indirectly, a large population." How large? He anticipated a shale-fueled explosion of nearly one million newcomers— a staggering figure given that the Western Slope had just 156,134 residents in 1950.[56]

Not all this growth was projected for the high country; oil shale was mostly in the state's far northwestern corner. But when boosters and experts fixated on shale as the inevitable next big thing, it revealed what they thought of the mountains in general: that they were first and foremost a storehouse of resources and that their future would probably look a lot like their extractive past. So when one historian predicted in 1959 that "each generation of people in Colorado will witness a new mining boom," two of his colleagues agreed, reasoning, "Nothing has yet happened to prove him wrong."[57] Of course the next boom would be rooted in resource extraction—because in Colorado, booms always had been. It was a deeply ingrained way of seeing the land and its future. It helps explain why so many people in places like Leadville stayed fiercely faithful to mining, even amid devastating downturns, and it helps explain why the Rocky Mountain News's idea of promoting tourism over mining was so controversial.

A similar attitude prevailed when it came to towns. The idea that tourism could sustain a town seemed, to many Coloradans, absurd. A town was supposed to be a place of production. It should *make* things, or at least sell them. All towns that existed in the high country in the late 1940s owed their creation and continued existence to such functions. Many processed crops or raw materials; most made items for immediate local use, like newspapers, bricks, or bread; all sold supplies to miners, ranchers, and others living and working in the area. So for boosters seeking to diversify the town economy, L. J. Crampon's advice was to *industrialize*. Likewise, when the Colorado Municipal League, a leading information source for town government, published an article titled "How Municipal Officials Can Promote Economic Growth," all its suggestions involved luring factories. Looking back from today, this might sound like pie in the sky for a small mountain community. But in an era that saw paved-highway and electric-power networks reaching for the first time into every corner of rural America, predictions were rife for manufacturing's wholesale decentralization, and landing a factory seemed possible even for smaller towns.[58] In any case, when Colorado's State Planning Commission, the agency charged with helping county officials draft local development plans, listed its areas of interest, it included farming, stock raising, mining, and manufacturing; tourism did not make the list.[59] Tourism, declared the chair of the Colorado Business Committee, might bring "desirable gains" to the state, "but it has long been recognized that the fundamental basis for Colorado's expansion and higher individual incomes is new industry." Even in Aspen, where tourism was starting to take off, many residents still sensed it was too slender a reed to lean the local economy on and felt mining would still make for a better economic base. "Skiing is fine and certainly has its place," editorialized the Aspen Times in 1947, "but 100 men on a steady payroll will *do* things for Aspen. . . . If and when the long overdue mining program starts . . . we are for it 100 per cent."[60]

And then there was the fact that many Coloradans did not particularly *like* tourists. Mocking "dudes" and "tenderfoots" from back East was an old sport, which is why mountainfolk found amusement in stories about the slide-rock bolter devouring hapless flatlanders. The derision persisted in the 1940s, when Thomas Hornsby Ferril, Colorado's future poet laureate, ridiculed the "miserable noncurious" tourists who flocked to the state each summer, bringing "the spewing of the carsick babes, the back-seat jangling, the inter-car cursing" to the crowded scenic drives outside Denver and Colorado Springs. Ferril actually cheered the war's curtailment of tourism, since "tourists always should have been rationed anyhow." Many fellow Coloradans agreed, or at least smiled in recognition of the sentiment.[61]

But if tourists still seemed more wretched than miners or manufacturers, proponents of tourism were beginning to gain their voice. Before World War II, tourist promotion had been mostly a piecemeal affair, with scattered interests—Denver boosters, outdoor-recreation enthusiasts, park proponents, resort owners, railroads—each pushing their pet forms of outdoor leisure in their pet places of concern. Now, in the war's aftermath, tourist promotion became increasingly integrated and coordinated. State government began to take the lead, promulgating a set of advertising themes that almost all other boosters soon parroted in their own literature. Advertising became more sophisticated, with vivid imagery and lively prose splashing across magazine pages, tourist brochures, and guidebooks. More and more high-country towns, valleys, lakes, peaks, fishing streams, and forests began to gain recognition as vacation destinations. It was not a zero-sum game: those who advertised for tourism often worked to boost mining, ranching, farming, or manufacturing at the same time. But the promotion of tourism was, quite literally, gaining ground fast.

The State Advertising and Publicity Committee (APC) did the most to get the momentum going. Established in 1941, the APC promoted Colorado's agricultural and industrial products, not just its recreational delights. But whereas earlier state booster agencies had seen tourism mostly as a vehicle for expanding those other economic sectors, the APC worked energetically to make tourism a thriving industry in its own right. It got off to a shaky start, as wartime travel restrictions and budget constraints kept it from advertising for tourism during the war. It briefly sprang into action with the Victory Vacation campaign in 1946 but then nearly starved for lack of funds over the next several years. The eminent journalist John Gunther, visiting Colorado after the war, heard widespread worry that the state was doing too little to "dramatize and buttress" its scenic appeal and had "missed the boat on tourism." State publicity director Lew Cobb begged state legislators for help, but they kept slashing the APC's allowance, down to a paltry $17,500 for fiscal year 1950–51.[62]

At that moment, state-sponsored tourist advertising seemed near extinction in Colorado—but it was about to gain new life. Cobb's lobbying played a key role. He did a statistical study, found that tourist spending in Colorado had crashed as the state advertising budget was slashed, and promptly forwarded these "disturbing" findings to reporters and legislators.[63] Then he hit the speaking circuit, warning anyone who would listen that fiscal stinginess was robbing Colorado of a tourist windfall. "Tourists . . . are going to the people that go after them," he told one audience. "This rich harvest of tourist dollars . . . cannot be reaped without . . . advertising and publicity."[64] Finally, his pleas fell on hearing ears. New Republican governor Dan Thornton, who entered office in January 1951, was convinced, as were the GOP majorities in the state senate and house. The APC got a more than elevenfold raise that year, and its budget swelled further as the decade went on.[65]

State-sponsored tourist promotion broke through in 1951, not just because of Lew Cobb, but because by that time an aggressive cohort of progrowthers had risen to power in Colorado. Besides Governor Thornton, their leading stars were Denverites: Quigg Newton, elected Denver mayor in 1947, and Palmer Hoyt, who took over the *Denver Post* the year before and used it to champion economic development in the wider Mountain West (which Hoyt called the "Rocky Mountain Empire"). A similar story was unfolding all over the Southwest, in cities like Phoenix, Albuquerque, San Antonio, and San Jose: powerful growth networks taking shape, alliances of metropolitan movers and shakers like bankers, developers, corporate executives, newspaper publishers, and upstart politicians. One after another, they toppled long-entrenched regimes that had resisted change and governed in a defensive crouch. (Newton ended the quarter-century reign of Mayor Ben Stapleton, who had grumbled that there would be no problem providing housing for Denver's postwar newcomers "if all these people would only go back where they came from.") The growth networks sought development through a mix of private investment and public funding, and they especially liked cutting-edge industries like aerospace, uranium mining, and electronics. And tourism. In their view, spending state money to attract tourists meshed perfectly with wider visions of postwar progress.[66]

So the APC budget battle of 1950–51 opened a dramatic expansion of state-sponsored tourist promotion in Colorado.[67] By the mid-1950s, ads touting Colorado's "magic" climate, its "riot" of autumn color, its "picturesque ghost towns," its "fighting rainbow trout," were popping up in *National Geographic, Holiday, Redbook, Collier's, Field and Stream*, and other travel, women's, sporting, and general-interest magazines. The APC began mailing thousands of brochures, "lure books," event calendars, hotel and motel listings, and colorful state highway maps to people all over the country. It also sent information packets to newspaper and magazine editors—a common practice in the travel industry that netted free publicity in the form of feature articles—and placed exhibits at major sports and vacation shows, so convention planners and travel agents, as well as recreational enthusiasts and prospective tourists, would learn what Colorado had to offer.[68]

Besides state government, many interest-group allies worked to lure tourists. Among the most active were the American Automobile Association (AAA) and the Denver Convention and Visitors Bureau (DCVB). The AAA's annual *Western Tour Book* oriented readers to the scenic and historic attractions of the high country, while the club's travel counselors and TripTik maps helped people plan their itineraries, making an unfamiliar region navigable. The AAA's state branch, Rocky Mountain Motorists, issued a yearly *Where to Vacation in Colorado*, which not only filled in more details about the high country but also sold ad space to small-town chambers of commerce and owners of motels, resorts, and other tourist businesses, enabling them to reach wider audiences.[69] As for the DCVB, while its goal was to build Denver's tourist trade, it did so largely by situating the city as the gateway to a mountain playground. That meant DCVB literature devoted many words and pictures to the high country—sometimes more than to Denver itself.[70] And like the AAA, the DCVB helped small-town, small-budget boosters reach wider audiences. Its downtown Hospitality Center, which opened in 1951 right on the main east-west route through Denver, stocked brochures from all over the state, giving modestly funded local chambers of commerce a highly visible place to display their literature. The DCVB would also mail local brochures to people planning their trips in advance.

Some of the most vivid tourist advertising of the 1950s came in forms other than brochures or lure books. Magazines were another medium western boosters used to build mystique around their home landscapes and generate interest in vacationing there. The pioneering examples were *Arizona Highways*, a state-funded periodical whose lavish color photography helped pique popular taste for desert scenery, and Bay Area–based *Sunset* magazine, whose lifestyle features helped mold impressions of California and the Far West as desirable places to visit or live.[71] Colorado's counterpart, *Colorado Wonderland* magazine, appeared in 1949 and depicted the state at its most inviting: big, friendly, casual, scenic, action-packed.[72] Articles, written in prose that seems painfully corny today, described rip-roarin' rodeos, pack trips into primeval wilderness, the fun of snagging a feisty trout or square dancing to a dude rancher's fiddle. Publisher-editor Raymond "Tex" Roberts said howdy in his folksy column, and readers wrote in to relate how happy they had been when they vacationed or lived in the Centennial State. But the highlight of each issue was the section of full-page, full-color photographs, depicting the most glorious of Colorado scenery. Expensive to print and thus fairly rare in the 1950s, such photographs recalled the older, better-known *Arizona Highways, Colorado Wonderland*'s obvious inspiration. Travel-lifestyle magazines like these pointed to important trends in tourist promotion and its cultural impact. Increasingly, as we will see, tourist promotion relied on vivid imagery and personal, emotional appeals to create demand for vacations. And increasingly, such advertising tactics shaped how people imagined, experienced, and valued the landscapes of tourist regions like the Colorado high country.

Also active in boosting Colorado tourism were airlines and railroads that served the state. The only railroad left in the high country after World War II, the Denver & Rio Grande Western, had been selling the scenery along its routes since the 1870s. Now, with auto, bus, and air travel cutting into its business, it redoubled its efforts. In 1949 the Rio Grande unveiled a specially designed passenger coach, the Vista-Dome, whose glass-enclosed rooftop observatory bubble let passengers stare straight up at sheer canyon walls or surround themselves with 360-degree panoramic views, open to the sun and turquoise Colorado sky. Vista-Domes were featured on the D&RGW's Denver-to-Grand Junction See-Liner trains, exclusively scheduled during daylight hours for optimum scenic viewing. Other railroads that advertised Colorado vacations included the Western Pacific and the Burlington, both of whose systems linked to the Rio Grande's.[73] Meanwhile, the railroads' upstart rivals, the airlines, joined the ranks of Colorado tourist boosters. They included the major carriers United, Western, Braniff, and Continental, all of which flew to Denver from outside Colorado, and Colorado's own Frontier Airlines, which flew smaller planes to several towns up in the mountains. Frontier's ads promised passengers the rare thrill of "Flight-Seeing"—looking down on the spectacular high country scenery from above.[74] Airline travel would become much more common, and airline advertising much more prolific, in the 1960s and 1970s, but already in the 1950s it was helping build the high country's recreational reputation.

All told, by the early 1950s an impressive range of interests were at work constructing Colorado's high country as a vacationland. Equally significant, they were beginning to consult with each other and coordinate their efforts to some degree. A major step in that direction came in May 1951, when Dan Thornton convened the first Governor's Travel and Hospitality Conference in Denver. Some 667 attendees came from all over the state to discuss ways of boosting the vacation trade. A second conference followed in 1952, and in 1954 it became a yearly event. The list of participants was a Who's Who of tourist promotion. Statewide interest groups like the Hotel Association, Dude and Guest Ranch Association, and Rocky Mountain Motorists sent delegates, as did local chambers of commerce and outdoor-sports clubs. Airlines and other big businesses were represented, while owners of small businesses, like motels and resorts, attended too. There were also officials from federal and state agencies: the Forest Service, Park Service, State Highway Department, Game and Fish Department, and of course the APC. At times, bitter divisions emerged, as at the 1954 conference when the chair of Rocky Mountain Motorists bashed the Highway 40 Association for promoting tourism along its own corridor at the rest of Colorado's expense. And certain subjects that pitted parts of the state against each other, like the endless battles over water rights and highway funds, had to be avoided altogether. Still, even if conference participants could not completely put aside their differences, they at least affirmed their shared interest in making tourism an ever-larger presence in Colorado.[75]

Even more importantly, they devised a basic set of strategies to reach that goal. An orthodoxy began to congeal on how best to present Colorado to tourists. Once tempers cooled at the 1954 meeting, for example, conferees agreed on a list of eleven "recommendations." Among them: Coloradans should cultivate a "genuine western atmosphere" through "apparel, architecture, food, cooking and entertainment"; should continue to work for highway improvements; and should mark scenic and historic spots with helpful signs.[76] Old West romance, scenery, convenient highways: if this list sounds like the talking points in the APC's "THIS is Colorado" advertisement—the one that appeared at the beginning of this book—that is no accident. The goal of such an ad was also the goal of the Governor's Conference: to develop a comprehensive, consistent, statewide strategy for building up the tourist trade.

The strategy took further shape through the work of tourist-industry analysts and other "experts" who conducted studies, issued reports, and traveled around the state talking to local chamber of commerce luncheons. In the 1950s, the most prominent such expert in Colorado was none other than L. J. Crampon, the same University of Colorado professor who had spent the late 1940s predicting a bright future for mining and urging local leaders to foster manufacturing. Now, in the 1950s, as director of the university's Bureau of Business Research, he emerged as the intellectual guru of Colorado tourist development. He issued his first full report on the subject in late 1953, followed by several others over the next several years.[77] Funded by the Colorado State Chamber of Commerce, the APC, and other tourist-boosting entities, Crampon conducted surveys to find out where visitors were coming from, how they got to Colorado, and what times of year they liked to come. He surveyed what they did on their vacations, how they spent their money, and what they thought of the state. He also tracked national currents in tourism and advertising. Then, based on his findings, he proposed "means by which tourist travel in Colorado might be increased."[78] Through reports, speeches, and presentations at the Governor's Conference, Crampon's "expert" ideas became widely held wisdom across Colorado, so that they, too, helped lend greater consistency to the business of boosting tourism.[79]

One should not overstate the degree of coordination that resulted. As discussed in the introduction, the tourist "industry" is really not a single industry, but a decentralized mix of interests and enterprises that are simultaneously in competition with each other and in need of each other's help. Tourist promotion in Colorado thus remained a haphazard business, with many free agents, many messages in the air all at once. Still, there can be no doubt that much about it was formulaic—and that the annual Governor's Conferences, the APC's outreach efforts, and Crampon's speeches and reports helped make it that way. They took the lead in spreading a set of strategies and selling points, so that even as different boosters fought for business, they often ended up echoing and reinforcing each other's pitches. Together, they built an increasingly recreational image of the high country, recasting a region that had once gone unnoticed, or had scared outsiders away, in a much more leisure-friendly light.

FOR ALL THE PROMOTERS' EFFORTS, THE BEST ADVERTISEMENT FOR HIGH-country tourism came through sheer luck—and for free. It happened when, for four summers running, Dwight Eisenhower made Colorado his summer vacation home. This was quite a publicity coup, for besides being president and war hero, Ike was an absolute avatar of 1950s leisure culture, with his well-known love for golf, fishing, bridge, backyard grilling, oil painting, and the like. Already a familiar figure in Denver (his wife Mamie had grown up there, they often visited her parents there, and he had several good friends there, especially real estate mogul Aksel Nielsen), Eisenhower headquartered his presidential campaign at the city's Brown Palace Hotel in 1952, then set up the Summer White House at Lowry Air Force Base for two months at a time in 1953, 1954, and 1955. Each stay involved almost daily rounds of golf at Cherry Hills Country Club and frequent fishing trips up in the mountains, many of them at the Byers Peak Ranch that Nielsen co-owned on St. Louis Creek near Fraser. There, Ike would while away the days fishing with "Aks" and other friends, working on his paintings of Colorado mountain scenes, and making pancakes for breakfast and bacon-fried trout for dinner. And the press corps covered it all. Wire photos of the president casting flies, teaching his grandson to ride horseback, dabbing at his scenic canvases, and flipping steaks showed up in newspapers and magazines around the country, together with descriptions of him looking happy, relaxed, and "deeply tanned," in the words of the Associated Press. "Ike has had a good rest, and shows it," observed *U.S. News and World Report* a month into Eisenhower's 1953 stay. For anyone with a stake in the high country vacation trade, this was free publicity of the most valuable kind. Indeed, many promoters tried to piggyback on the president's fondness for Colorado. The Highway 40 Association invited motorists to stop at "Ike's fishing hole," and Fraser boosters, who for some reason took pride in calling their town the "Icebox of the Nation," began pairing that nickname with a more inviting one: "Ike's Vacation Land."[80]

There are lots of ways to market a product. Linking it to a celebrity is one of the most obvious, and President Eisenhower was a better celebrity endorsement than most. But fundamentally, the process of branding and advertising Colorado's high country kept coming back to the place itself: its physical environment, its landscapes, its nature. To be sold on the high country as a vacationland, people had to be sold on these. So boosters sought to cement the high country in consumers' minds as an environment naturally suited for leisure. They played up its recreational amenities, its aesthetic qualities, its power to thrill people or put them at ease. Once again, there was nothing innovative in how the boosters did this. On the contrary, they tapped into deeply rooted cultural—particularly Romantic—notions about nature and distilled them down to the familiar, even hackneyed, vocabulary of modern advertising: colorful, high-contrast pictures; attention-grabbing slogans; and emotionally charged prose. And they recycled the same snippets of scenery and the same snatches of prose over and over, striving through repetition to ingrain a popular sense of the high country as a premier place for play.

It was not enough simply to play up the high country's appealing natural attributes. These also had to be linked to visitors' personal desires. The gist of branding and advertising is to make consumers want a product by playing to their innermost anxieties, aspirations, and emotional needs, by linking the product to their sense of themselves. Indeed, this is the very essence of consumerism: the idea that purchases carry powerful personal meanings, that we can define ourselves through what we buy. So the people marketing the high country sought to make it personally meaningful to potential visitors. They appealed to tourists' escapist fantasies; their yen for adventure; their desires to be glamorous or manly, renew family bonds, or just take it easy for a while.[81] All of these yearnings, and many others, resonated in Colorado tourist literature, in ad copy, the text of brochures and guidebooks, and the visual imagery that went with the words. Again, there was nothing original about this approach; tourist boosters everywhere else were doing it too. So, for that matter, were advertisers for cars, cigarettes, and bars of soap. But that was the point: experience and accepted wisdom said these tactics worked. And in Colorado's case they worked very well. They brought the once-obscure high country squarely into the realm of consumer culture—and, as a result, squarely into the tourist mainstream.

A vacation seems like a peculiar product, when you think about it. It is neither a good nor a service, as traditionally defined. Most tourists do buy plenty of goods (souvenirs, dinners, fishing bait) and services (guided tours, airplane trips, shelter for the night), but none of these is the point of the vacation. Instead, the point is the *experience*. Vacationers want to see new things, broaden their horizons, find adventure, relax, meet people, feel good about themselves, escape from the everyday. When they go on a trip, they are really buying experiences like these. Some authors have written of a recent shift toward an "experience economy," in which memorable and pleasurable personal experiences, rather than simple goods or services, are becoming more and more the focus of business practice and consumer desire. A chic coffeehouse is a good example: people patronize it not just for the coffee but for the feeling of being chic.[82] In reality, the idea of manufacturing, marketing, and consuming experiences has been around for quite some time. Americans have long "known" that you buy beer for sociability, sports cars for heart-pounding thrills and masculine prestige, roses and candlelit dinners for romance. To go on vacation has always been to buy experiences too, even if Victorian vacationers sought rather different experiences than did people in postwar America. In this sense, it is arguable that the vacation trade helped pioneer the experience economy that we know today.

But there is one major difference—an obvious yet crucial one—between vacations and most other marketed experiences: a vacation occurs in, and is utterly premised on, a *particular geographical setting*. The tourist pays to go to some specific landscape and spend time there; therein lies the desired experience. So the tourist promoter's task is to kindle in consumers a carefully crafted, marketable sense of that place. The promoter identifies certain distinctive features of the landscape, attributes emotional powers to them, and urges consumers to invest themselves psychologically in them. The implications are far-reaching. Even though tourists will not always relate to a setting exactly as its promoters had hoped, many people will still end up deriving their sense of certain places, in large part, from tourist advertising. Tourist advertising influences how they envision, value, and interact with those particular landscapes. And in a case like Colorado's, where tourist promotion became pervasive and ubiquitous, it could go further, affecting how people imagined and valued outdoor settings *in general*. In other words, it could shape—or reshape—people's environmental attitudes.

Of course, when it came to advertising the Colorado high country, the natural environment was the star attraction. By the time our loose coalition of tourist boosters was coalescing in the early 1950s, the tourist-drawing power of the Colorado Rockies—the so-called Switzerland of America—was already well established, thanks to the efforts of Victorian travel writers like Samuel Bowles (who may have been the first to make the Switzerland analogy), artists like Albert Bierstadt, boosters like William Byers, and developers like William Jackson Palmer and the Denver & Rio Grande Railway. They, in turn, had built upon an even older tradition of looking to rugged mountain settings for scenic splendor and spiritual and emotional uplift—a tradition rooted in Romantic thought and the Victorian American fascination with the aesthetics of the picturesque.[83] Post–World War II boosters did not have to persuade people to find mountains attractive and uplifting; by their time, that cultural inclination was already deeply entrenched.

But to capitalize on the tradition, promoters had to update it for modern times. They did so on two planes—one visual, the other emotional. Visually, nineteenth-century artists and theorists had applied a rigid set of standards for what constituted a picturesque landscape or picturesquely composed scene.[84] Postwar boosters used this same rigid formula to generate stock scenic images, endlessly reproduced until they became instantly recognizable and instantly identifiable with Colorado—logos, in effect, for Colorado tourism. Emotionally, nineteenth-century Romantics had held that immersion in nature could bring self-discovery, cultural uplift, patriotic awakening, and divine revelation.[85] Postwar boosters reasserted this link between nature and personal benefit, but they promised benefits more in keeping with twentieth-century American yearnings: happiness, a positive self-image, relaxation, escape, family togetherness, fun. In short, Romantic nature, refracted through the imagery and vocabulary of twentieth-century advertising, became the basis for a new view of the mountain environment and for a new and highly marketable sense of the Colorado high country as a place.

Consider how advertisers described mountain scenery. The long, florid passages of Victorian travel accounts were out; crisp, punchy prose was in. The allusions to literature, architecture, and antiquity that Victorian writers had loved gave way to simple sensory impressions and "action" words. (It is telling that the old "Switzerland of America" nickname, with its allusion to European aesthetic standards, all but vanished after the war, giving way to the splashier and more immediate "Colorful Colorado."[86]) And in place of Victorian character-building aspirations like enlightening and improving oneself and drawing closer to God, there were now immediate psychological rewards like rest or adventure. Read how a 1953 state publicity committee advertisement depicted the scenery—or, more precisely, the scenic *experience*—of the high country: "Romantic adventure trails in primeval forests, peaceful green valleys carpeted with wildflowers, . . . an enchanted world of white-robed peaks and candy-striped canyons." Or savor this 1952 pitch from the Denver tourist bureau: "Find peace of mind in this land of magnificent Rockies. Gain new vigor, new enjoyment in living, here among towering peaks, unspoiled forests, crystal streams, rich green valleys and jeweled lakes. Relax and refresh yourself under the blue sky, during golden days of Colorado sunshine."[87] Again and again, tourist literature of the 1940s and 1950s painted mountain settings in these same brushstrokes—as landscapes exploding with light and vivid colors, bursting with romance, relaxation, adventure, and other psychological delights. The prose was hardly less ornate than the Victorians', but now the ornateness stemmed from simple images strung together in list-like sentences. No effort here to describe whole landscapes by painting intricately composed word canvases. Instead, the latter-day tourist literature tossed out seemingly random visual elements and disconnected snippets of scenery, selected for their instant recognizability, visual impact, and emotional appeal.

The same snippets of scenery appeared again and again, to the point where they became predictable and familiar—*scenic clichés*, we might call them. Most common were snow-capped peaks, or some version thereof, but nearly as frequent were flower-carpeted meadows, pine-scented forests, golden aspens, cascading streams, turquoise skies, crystal lakes, and words echoing Romantic tradition, like "picturesque," "splendor," and "majestic." These clichés became the default vocabulary for marketing high-country topography, no matter the medium: brochures, magazines, guidebooks, postcard captions, print advertisements, radio spots. They also turned up in conversations with tour guides, waitresses, filling station attendants, and motel clerks, all of whom were encouraged to invoke the clichés too (recall the "sales training" ad at the beginning of this book and how it described scenery: "white-robed peaks . . . pine-scented forests . . . peaceful green valleys"). Indeed, so strongly did scenic clichés color people's consciousness of Colorado that it became difficult to talk about the landscape without using them. When reporters followed President Eisenhower on his fishing trips to Fraser, phrases like "the splendor of the mountains" and "Colorado's majestic Western Slope" crept into their dispatches, and their depictions of Ike's fishing spot—"cool, swift-running St. Louis Creek" burbling through a "pleasant valley with tall pines," rimmed by "snow-capped peaks" and a "skyline view of . . . America's greatest mountain range"—sounded like ad copy from the state publicity board.[88] Still more free advertising came when tourists themselves, trying to describe what they were seeing, resorted to the same scenic clichés. "Mary & I are really having a perfect time," gushed an Illinois man, writing home from his dude ranch vacation in 1946. "Yellow aspen, green firs & blue Colorado skies."[89]

Scenic photos of the high country were every bit as clichéd as scenic descriptions. Whether they appeared in ads, brochures, calendars, magazines, View-Master reels, or anywhere else, pictures of the high country overwhelmingly cleaved to a formulaic postcard style. That meant, first of all, a clearly defined foreground, middle ground, and background. Usually there would be one or more people posed in the foreground (fly fishermen and horseback riders were popular, or, for a bit of 1950s cheesecake, comely young women in western wear or bathing suits). Some feature in the middle ground (typically a lake, river, or gently curving highway) led the viewer's gaze toward a distant backdrop, almost always of soaring, snowy peaks. Tall pines, or some other view-framing device, edged the image on either side, and the figures in the foreground provided a sense of scale, emphasizing the grandeur of the scene. Most of all, there were theatrical contrasts of color and light. Color photos—which became much more common in the 1950s—exploded in a kaleidoscope of vivid hues. Deep-green forests, azure waters and skies, and gleaming white clouds and snowfields—the photographer's answers to the ad writer's scenic clichés—were in almost every picture, and there might also be the brilliant gold of aspen trees in autumn or perhaps some orange, pink, or purple cliffs, crags, or rocks. (For even greater color vibrancy, many photographers posed a person in the foreground in a bright red western shirt.) Yes, these compositional devices were almost painfully unoriginal. They were familiar to anyone who had ever received a postcard from anywhere. Most of them, in fact, would have been instantly familiar to a Romantic painter like Albert Bierstadt, as they were lifted directly from the nineteenth-century formula for composing the picturesque. But once again, the familiarity was precisely the point. By fitting the landscapes of the high country to long-standing conventions of what constituted "scenic-ness," promoters made it easy for consumers to find the region attractive. In this sense, scenic clichés did a great deal to bring Colorado's high country into the consumer mainstream.[90]

Yet as derivative as they were, scenic clichés also helped build a distinctive brand for the state and its landscapes (and some of its products too, notably Coors beer, whose sales region reached just eleven western states but whose postcardlike ads of peaks and waterfalls lent such a mystique that tourists would carry cases of the beer home in their car trunks). Colorado postcards and picture ads might be composed the same way as ones from Florida or Iowa, but no one was going to mistake cascading streams, abyssal canyons, or pine-girded alpine lakes for scenes from those states. This was especially true for pictures of snowy mountains. These, through endless reproduction, became like logos for Colorado, almost automatically calling the state to mind. In time it stopped mattering whether the picture was of any peak in particular. Colorado's 2006 state quarter used an idealized mountain, rather than any actual one, to stand for the state. So do the state's

1.5 The ultimate scenic cliché. No setting screams "Colorado tourism" quite like the Maroon Bells, southwest of Aspen. The classic view of these twin peaks has mirrorlike Maroon Lake at its center, framed by forested slopes. Pose a figure in the foreground, and you have the quintessential scenic cliché. Small wonder that this became one of the high country's most photographed scenes. It appears here (*clockwise from top left*) in an advertisement for Aspen's 1949 Goethe Convocation, the cover of the 1959 state lure book, the official state highway map for 1964, and a 1963 ad for the Burlington Route. Courtesy Aspen Institute, Colorado Tourism Office, Colorado Department of Transportation, and BNSF Railway.

license plates. It *does* seem to matter, though, if the mountain depicted is *not* in Colorado. There was a minor flap in 2008 when it was revealed that the peak pictured on the new Colorado postage stamp was actually in Wyoming. Similarly, a Colorado senate candidate in 2008 and a gubernatorial candidate in 2009 were embarrassed when it turned out that the mountainscapes displayed atop their campaign websites were, respectively, Alaskan and Canadian.[91] Mistakes like these happened because graphic artists and website designers saw stock images of snowy peaks and automatically assumed Colorado.

The association ran the other way too: the state came to be defined by its scenic clichés. In many people's minds, it just wasn't Colorado without them. When *Colorado Wonderland* ran cover shots *without* the usual alpine lakes or snow-robed peaks, readers took the magazine to task. Such covers did Colorado an "injustice," sputtered one. "I couldn't sell Colorado to any of [my New England friends] with those covers . . . they saw nothing uniquely Colorado in either photograph." "With all the beautiful scenery in Colorado," complained another, "it is a crime to waste color on . . . things [that] can be seen in any part of the country."[92] For his part, President Eisenhower resorted to all the same scenic clichés when painting his Colorado canvases: deep green forests and framing trees; lakes, streams, or fence lines leading the eye into the distance; snowy, craggy peaks towering over the scene. "He chose typical scenes that already existed in the popular imagination, which merely had to be recorded to be recognized," was how one art critic put it, and she might just as well have been explaining how postcard or advertising photographers chose their shots.[93] At one point Ike's dependence on the formula became embarrassingly clear. He gifted one of his Colorado paintings to Dan Thornton, a friend and former governor. But when Thornton excitedly wrote back that he planned to donate the painting to the State Historical Society for public display, Eisenhower sheepishly asked him to keep the gift private. He had plagiarized the scene, he admitted, from a calendar photo.[94]

The high-country climate was another environmental element that recreational promoters made into a "natural attraction." A 1957 report to the state's Department of Natural Resources called Colorado's climate "probably second only to its magnificent scenery in attracting tourists."[95] But just like scenery, it needed marketing to make it attractive. Weather in the high country is nothing if not mercurial. As nature writer Edwin Way Teale once observed on a visit, it is more accurate to speak of "mountain weathers" than

1.6 The high country through Eisenhower's eyes. Dwight Eisenhower, taking a break from his 1952 presidential campaign, pretends to put the finishing touches on one of his paintings of the Colorado mountains. The formulaic composition of the painting suggests that Eisenhower, too, had learned to see the high country landscape in terms of scenic clichés. This photo op took place at Byers Peak Ranch, owned by Eisenhower's close friend, Denver real estate mogul Aksel Nielsen. Courtesy Associated Press.

"mountain weather," because conditions change so drastically and so fast.[96] Especially at higher altitudes, your ideal hiking or picnicking day can turn sour in minutes, as the wind gusts up, clouds materialize out of nowhere, the temperature plummets, and suddenly you are caught in a blizzard or thunderstorm. Thin air, intense solar radiation, and the lack of large water bodies allow the mountain atmosphere to heat and cool rapidly, bringing these sudden shifts. Extreme variations in altitude and sun exposure make for a bewildering array of microclimates. Storms may repeatedly channel into a certain valley and stall at its upper end, dumping loads of rain or snow in just that one locale; and in winter, heavy, cold air sinks to the floors of valleys and mountain-ringed "parks" and becomes trapped, making for brutally frigid weather. Instability, unpredictability, and violent extremes: this is not the benign image of nature that typically lures tourists.

How, then, did promoters make this weather seem welcoming? Once again, they used the vivid imagery and unsubtle prose style of modern advertising. In photographs, every scene boasted bright blue skies; typically the only clouds were a fluffy, friendly white, not ominously gray. And in ad copy, every day in the mountains was a "sunny day" with "crisp, sparkling air"—clichés repeated again and again until they became, like "snow-capped peaks," catchphrases for Colorado tourism. As with scenic imagery, these climatic clichés were not just idealized but greatly generalized. They offered no hint of the weather's actual complexity—the fact, for instance, that it can be a gorgeous spring day on the Front Range while mountain towns just twenty or thirty miles away are getting buried by snow. That kind of information might scare vacationers away from the high country, at a time when entities like the state publicity committee were trying to build tourism there. So promotional literature made it sound like the weather was its same sunny, sparkling self all over the state, regardless of topography, altitude, or microclimate. As Denver tourist bureau ads cheerily proclaimed, "Every Day Is a Sunny Day," whether you spent it in Denver or in the "Rocky Mountain Wonderland" farther west.[97]

Sometimes, in their effort to make the weather seem tourist-friendly, advertisers engaged in outright lies. The best example is the oft-repeated claim that Colorado gets more than three hundred days of sunshine a year. Even today, many and perhaps most Coloradans proudly believe this to be true—yet it is not. The claim originated with territorial boosters in the 1870s and was repeated so many times that it took on the semblance of fact. While southern Colorado really does enjoy a surfeit of sunny days, almost no place in the state averages anywhere near three hundred days of sunshine a year, not even if you count partly cloudy days. But 1950s tourist boosters, especially the Denver Convention and Visitors Bureau, repeated the three-hundred-days claim in ad after ad, never letting on—maybe not even knowing for themselves—that it was false.[98]

Making the mountain climate seem hospitable did not always mean fudging facts. It was true, as 1950s ads often said, that average summer temperatures in the high country were cooler, and average humidity much lower, than in most of the East, South, or Midwest. In a time when air conditioning was still an uncommon luxury, these were big selling points for Colorado's summer tourist season. In the 1940s and 1950s, the state publicity committee often added "Cool" to the nickname "Colorful Colorado." Billboards showed polar bears trooping toward the "Playground of the Rockies," where summers were "Always Cooler." Slyly—some might say sadistically—the state placed these billboards in sweltering cities like Tulsa, Omaha, St. Louis, and Chicago.[99] And here again, the press corps covering Eisenhower echoed the message. "Having a heat wave back east?" a United Press International correspondent began his dispatch from a presidential fishing trip. "Not Fraser. It may go up to 80 in the daytime, but the mercury plunges below freezing at night. President Eisenhower and his ranking guest at Byers Peak Ranch, former President Hoover, have been sleeping under three blankets at night."[100] Imagine reading *that* while broiling in the oven that was the eastern seaboard. At a time when air-conditioning was still unusual in private homes, Colorado's cool summer temperatures resonated powerfully with popular notions of luxury and the postwar good life.[101]

If the Colorado summer carried obvious appeal, the other three seasons were a tougher sell. Here, unlike in their efforts to sell scenery, boosters had to battle *against* entrenched perceptions of mountains, namely the belief that they were too cold and snowy for most of the year. Winter was an especially tough sell. When it came to tourism in the Colorado Rockies, winter was, reported Crampon in 1957, "the low season"—as unbelievable as that may sound to us today. For the high-country tourist trade to break beyond what Crampon called a "ninety-day business," popular perceptions of inhospitable weather would have to change.[102] People would have to be taught that there was much to do in the mountains beyond summer. Skiing of course would become the leading nonsummer attraction, though in the 1950s many boosters placed great hope in fishing and hunting too. The State Advertising and Publicity Committee, under guises like the Sportsmen's Hospitality Committee and Winter Sports Committee, worked to promote all three. The Denver Convention and Visitors Bureau even organized its lure book by season, listing activities for each: golf and leaf peeking in the fall, skating and sleigh riding in the winter, tennis and flower watching in the spring.[103] But the favored approach to extending the season was to

Ski IN THE Sun IN COLORADO

COLORADO CLIMATE... The MAGIC INGREDIENT!

COLORADO WINTER SPORTS COMMITTEE
Capitol Building • Denver, Colorado

1.7 Climate also became a cliché. To get visitors to come to Colorado outside the summer season, state publicists had to overcome apprehension about the weather. Promises and pictures of sunshine reduced the high country's notoriously unstable winter weather to a happy cartoon and helped make every season appear as hospitable as summer. And as this brochure from the early 1950s shows, healthy-climate bromides mixed easily with skiing's mystique—its popular association with youth, health, athleticism, and sex appeal. Courtesy Colorado Tourism Office.

suggest that spring, winter, and fall weather in the mountains shared the best attributes of summer. That meant downplaying storms and freezing temperatures and playing up low humidity and sunshine. In the tourist literature, fall in the high country was full of "sunshiny days and crisp, sparkling air"; winter, despite the snow, had "clear blue skies" and "bright, warm sunshine"; and spring was crisp and sunshiny again, with snow giving way to flowers and new leaves.[104] As the state advertising committee chirped, "Vacation pleasures know no season in Colorful Colorado."[105]

As with scenery, a big part of the climate pitch was its alleged effect on the vacationer's personal happiness. Here was another notion with roots in the nineteenth century, when resort promoters in Manitou and Colorado Springs had touted the sunny, dry climate for its supposed medicinal qualities. So did Denver boosters, making their city a haven for sufferers of tuberculosis and other respiratory diseases. In the postwar era, medicinal benefits gave way to emotional and psychological ones. Mountain weather would energize and rejuvenate you, said the new generation of promoters. "The crisp, tangy air makes you feel years younger," claimed the Colorado Springs Chamber of Commerce. You "return revitalized," added the Denver tourist bureau, "with a new joy of living you found in the pure invigorating mountain air and sunshine."[106] Once again, these kinds of appeals made the high country not just a place but an emotional experience. A trip there became an entrée to personal renewal and happiness, even a better way of life.

It is difficult to overstate how crucial climate was to Colorado's leisure appeal. As noted earlier, the Department of Natural Resources deemed it "second only to [Colorado's] magnificent scenery in attracting tourists." The state publicity committee considered it such a powerful selling point that in the early 1950s it began running this slogan in all its ads and publications: "Colorado's Climate—The Magic Ingredient." It seemed a smart strategy, given the travel and migration trends of the 1940s and 1950s. Retirees, laborers, corporate executives, veterans, and many others were flocking from the East and Midwest to sunnier, warmer states like California, Arizona, Texas, and Florida, not just on vacation but often to relocate for a season or for good. In the 1970s, geographers, journalists, and others struggling to understand this westward-southward stampede would lump these states together in a newly invented region with a revealing name: the Sunbelt. Sunny weather, the name suggested, played a decisive role in defining this new "region" and shaping its appeal.[107] The problem for Colorado boosters was that their state—and especially its mountainous middle section—was popularly associated with the Snowbelt more than the Sunbelt. Colorado promoters urgently wanted to counter that perception, wanted to hitch their state to the same climatic mystique that fast-growing Arizona and California enjoyed. That helps explain why dry air and year-round sunshine featured so prominently in Colorado publicity. It was a key part of the wider effort to construct Colorado as an environment naturally suited for leisure. And it was quite successful—the proof lying not just in the many tourists but in the many permanent new residents who came to Colorado in postwar decades to live in or near the high-country vacationland.

But if popular images of the high country increasingly revolved around leisure, where did that leave the more traditional visions—the hopes for an oil shale boom, a metal-mining revival, or the growth of the manufacturing sector? As tourist boosters worked to turn topography and climate into amenities for recreation, how did they reconcile their efforts with the high country's extractive and agricultural past, a past that many Coloradans still hoped would be its future too?

Few if any boosters in the 1940s or 1950s predicted that tourism would ever replace mining, farming, or ranching. Indeed, advocates of tourism often seemed at pains to insist they were not trying to knock the old resource industries off the throne.[108] But there was another reason for tourist boosters to include mining and ranching in their visions for the future: mining and ranching helped sell vacations. Through their very presence in the landscape, these industries tinged the high country with an Old West mystique that tourists found alluring. Mining had given Colorado grizzled prospectors, wild boomtowns, and eerie ghost towns; ranching had brought rugged cowboys, rip-roaring rodeos, and wide-open ranges—iconic western images all. And in the context of the 1940s and 1950s, when Americans were flocking to Western movies, watching *Bonanza* and *Gunsmoke* on television, and decking out their little boys in fringed outfits, sheriffs' stars, and cap guns, it did not take a marketing genius to figure that western imagery might go a long way toward selling vacations too.[109] In the high country, that meant playing up the mining and ranching heritage that gave the region its tangy frontier flavor.

Honing Colorado's Old West appeal was a topic of much discussion in the 1950s. At the 1954 Governor's Travel and Hospitality Conference, L. J. Crampon passed around his latest survey findings, showing, among other things, that visitors wanted more "cowboy" activities (like square dancing) and more old mines and mining districts to tour. Conference participants agreed to make cultivating a "genuine western atmosphere" a top priority. By that time, the Old West was already a recurring theme in state-sponsored tourist literature, like the Highway Department's annual *Colorful Colorado* map-brochure and the state publicity committee's *Cool, Colorful Colorado* lure book. Remember that it was also one of the six themes the publicity committee highlighted in its sales-training ads for Colorado residents. "Many of our vacationists," the ads advised, "think of Colorado—or parts of it—as the last American frontier, the real Old West." For those visitors, the "romance" of "gold mines, prospectors, ghost towns, cowboys and Indians" carried "a powerful appeal."[110]

As with scenery and climate, the language used to paint these images became familiar to the point of cliché. In 1948, for example, the Advertising and Publicity Committee was hawking "picturesque ghost towns, gold mines, the storied cow country"; ten years later it was still promising "picturesque gold-rush towns" set amid a "romantic sage 'n' saddle land of song and story." In the same spirit, Denver's visitors bureau called the city a "portal to a paradise of western romance" and invited tourists to revel "in the atmosphere of once-bustling mining towns."[111] Visual imagery was just as formulaic, with image after image of tanned cowboys riding broncos, leading wilderness pack trips, or just gazing wistfully over the range. In scenic postcard-style shots, the requisite figure-in-the-foreground was often a person wearing cowboy duds. The Denver & Rio Grande Western Railroad added a family-friendly twist by having the cowboy wave to a delighted little boy—himself dressed in Roy Rogers finery and waving a pair of cap guns—as the boy and his family swept by in a Vista-Dome.[112] As for mining iconography, most common were images of abandoned, dilapidated mills or mines, clinging precariously to hillsides, but there was also the recurring image of the white-bearded prospector with rumpled clothes, floppy hat, and perhaps a burro. If you were lucky, hinted the ad copy, you might encounter one of these curmudgeonly old fellows, haunting the hills like a rare species of animal, "still hoping," in the words of the APC lure book, "to strike it rich."[113]

Words and images like these portrayed a landscape frozen in time, still peopled by the mythical cowboys and prospectors of yore, where the gold rushes and cattle drives lived on. Tourists were even told they could re-create the frontier experience for themselves. Mining imagery came in handy here, as much tourist literature drew a direct analogy between pleasure-seekers and gold- and silver-seekers. A day drive that circled from Denver

Travel to SEE in '53

on the *Vista-Dome* way thru the Rockies

4 Luxurious Vista-Dome Trains over 2 Glorious Scenic Routes...

1.8 Frontier flavor on a family vacation. In the fantasy world of this 1953 Rio Grande railroad ad, cowboy characters were just part of the scenery visitors could expect to see as they swept through Colorado in the comfort of a Vista-Dome. Courtesy Union Pacific Railroad.

through the historic mining towns of Black Hawk, Central City, and Idaho Springs was suggestively called the Prospectors' Trail, as if those who drove it were retracing the paths of the miners themselves.[114] Idaho Springs boosters invited visitors to explore the old mines and mills around town and "know the thrill of following the prospector, rediscovering old trails beckoning with new pleasures." One could even pan for gold—and possibly strike it rich, for in the same creek beds "from which MILLIONS in gold have been taken, lie MILLIONS of ounces of the precious metal, yet to be discovered by those that are willing to try. Just ask any old timer."[115] Probably very few tourists actually bought the notion that they might strike gold on their Colorado vacation. But the chance for a bit of Old West adventure was a powerful emotional lure. So mining, like scenery and climate, became another advertising theme—another way of visualizing and emotionally experiencing the Rockies, another element of the landscape that Colorado boosters crafted and sold to tourists.

Does that mean mining and tourism coexisted comfortably in 1950s Colorado? Not so much—because the kind of mining that tourist boosters "sold" to vacationers was not at all the same kind that the industry's actual advocates wanted. It was not the mid-twentieth-century version of mining, the full-blown industrial operation bustling with hundreds of workers, using electrical and gasoline-powered machinery to move tons of rock and spread vast tailings ponds over the earth—the kind of mining, for instance, that the Climax Molybdenum Company was doing up on Fremont Pass. Instead, it was mining made picturesque, even preindustrial—and above all, squarely relegated to a mythical past. It is still true that very few tourist boosters would have declared themselves opposed to a mining revival. Even so, when they promised scenery and Old West romance, they encouraged customers to envision the high country as a premodern, nonindustrial landscape. Whether they quite meant to or not, these boosters created an imagined space that, in order to live up to vacationers' expectations, almost *had* to preclude mining in its modern form.

Consider how mining towns were depicted in guidebooks. In Black Hawk, gateway to what was "once 'the richest square mile on earth,'" tourists could see "abandoned mine tunnels yawn[ing] beside the highway, [and] hillsides . . . pocked with prospect holes." Nearby Central City, with its grand Opera House and hotel, offered "a portrait of early mining days when fortunes were made and spent." On the other side of the mountain, Idaho Springs, "steeped in historic lore of the 1800's gold and silver mining era," had "evidence of the mining days linger[ing] on nearly every hillside" in the form of "old mine dumps, remnants of mine shafts and mills." Just up the road in Georgetown, elegant Victorian architecture "recall[ed] the bygone days of territorial wealth" and "the days when gold and silver were kings." Deeper in the mountains waited Leadville, a city that had "played an important role in Colorado's early history"; its old houses and abandoned mine structures "a must on the list of every visitor interested in Western history."[116] Different towns, described in different guidebooks, but they all conveyed the same message: *mining was a thing of the past.* Never mind that many people hoped or believed mining would revive in the near future or that several metals, including even gold, were still being mined (especially around Leadville and Idaho Springs). The way the guidebooks depicted these places, the work had long ago stopped, leaving only tumbledown shaft houses and headframes; and all the fabulous wealth had dried up, leaving only the faded gingerbread houses, grand hotels, and opera houses of an earlier day. No longer measured in profit margin, payroll, or annual ore yield, these minescapes' only remaining value lay in their power to conjure up a legendary, long-vanished past. From this perspective, the resumption of mining would *harm* a town like Georgetown, Aspen, or Central City by rupturing its quaint ambiance and undercutting its tourist appeal.

And then there was the ultimate example of placing mining in the past: the ghost town. Pictures of eerily silent, weather-beaten, remote, and lonely ghost towns were among the most frequently recurring images in Colorado tourist literature—so familiar that, like scenes of soaring peaks and crystal alpine lakes, they served almost as logos for Colorado tourism. But ghost town iconography, by definition, demanded the absence of mining in the present. Ghost towns were romantic for their dereliction, for the fact that they had supposedly been raucous and rowdy in their day, but no one lived or worked there anymore. In fact, some ghost town aficionados disliked having any people around at all. Muriel Sibell Wolle, a University of Colorado art professor who wrote ghost town guidebooks and illustrated them with her own paintings, never once showed a person in any of her pictures— even when she was painting towns that were still inhabited—and expressed regret whenever an old, abandoned building was removed or "restored to twentieth century needs." This put her at odds with many local residents, who saw collapsing buildings as symbols of failure, not allure.[117] Similarly, many locals bristled when a tourist guidebook made Breckenridge, a living town, sound like a ghost town, its "long-silent buildings, weathered and gray." Or when *Rocky Mountain Life* magazine ran a special "Ghost Town Edition," with the "ghost towns" being Aspen, Central City, Black Hawk, and Leadville—living, populated communities all.[118]

As the iconography of the ghost town suggests, the process of advertising high-country tourism was not as simple as it might seem. It involved much more than just pointing out the region's attractive natural features and waiting for the crowds to rush in. Rather, it meant selecting out certain elements of a complicated human and natural landscape and then having those select elements stand for, and simplify, the whole. Even those elements needed multiple levels of interpretation if they were to appeal to the masses of vacationers. Mountain settings had to be composed and cropped according to entrenched standards of the picturesque and then translated into the colorful, highly legible graphics of modern advertising. Ramshackle buildings were recast as romantic ruins and then depicted in brochures and guidebooks with all the people left out. The tremendous, even cultlike popularity of these ruins—in the 1950s and 1960s there were ghost town clubs, newsletters, and seemingly a whole publishing category of ghost town guidebooks—suggests that the process of interpretation served its purposes well. It really did succeed in fashioning a popular allure for the Colorado high country and in making the region the object of mainstream consumer desire. But this process privileged some landscape visions over others, and it left some pockets of the high country less loved than others. Tourist promotion was not so simple and predictable after all. Neither were its consequences.

THE FREE PUBLICITY THAT PRESIDENT EISENHOWER BROUGHT TO COLO-rado turned sour in September 1955. Just back from a Fraser fishing trip, in the middle of the night at his in-laws' house in Denver, Ike suffered a heart attack. He survived, recuperating for seven weeks at Fitzsimons Army Hospital in suburban Denver and then returning to Washington, DC. But the incident put an end to his long Colorado vacations, to his Summer White House in Denver, to the press pool trailing him up to his favorite high-country fishing spots. Worried about stress on his heart, the president's doctors forbade him from spending any more time at high altitude, which meant never again would he visit Fraser or anywhere else in the mountains—indeed, for the rest of his life, he would return to Colorado only for quick official appearances and brief visits with his in-laws in Denver.[119] It was a doubly bad blow for the high country's vacation image. Not only did tourist boosters lose their two months of free advertising every year, but also Ike's heart attack revived old fears about the perils of the mountain environment, contradicting efforts to recast it as healthful, safe, and mild.

In truth, the recasting was by that time well on its way. Though popular anxieties persisted about the high country's thin air, its weather, its challenging topography, and—as we will soon see—its driving conditions, the tourist boosters' image of a region ideally suited for recreation and relaxation now had the upper hand. Likewise, among those trying to chart the high country's economic development, the idea was gaining traction that the region's future lay primarily in the growth of tourism. To be sure, there was no unanimity on this point. Advocates of mining, ranching, and manufacturing continued to see those industries as the best uses of the land and the surest means to prosperity. But the coalition of tourist boosters that was coalescing in the 1950s called such assumptions into question. They focused not on minerals, water, timber, grazing land, or prime factory sites but instead on qualities of topography, climate, and historical color that, given Americans' prevailing ways of imagining nature and mythicizing the western past, seemed likely to strike cultural and emotional chords and lure lots of visitors. And the boosters became increasingly adept at translating these qualities into the highly readable imagery and vocabulary of modern advertising. Complicated topography became colorful, predictable, and scenic; a capricious climate became benign. Everything was painted in simple brushstrokes, reduced to formulaic images and repetitive, slogan-like clichés. Everything was packaged with the promise of emotional fulfillment: adventure, romance, relaxation, renewal, fun. Which is to say, the high country was remade to match the values, obsessions, and priorities of mainstream postwar consumers.

Again, it would be wrong to suggest that the tourist boosters of the 1940s and 1950s were necessarily hostile to a possible resurgence of mining. No doubt many of them, like L. J. Crampon and the *Rocky Mountain News*, believed tourism could coexist and thrive alongside mining, ranching, and the other traditional resource industries. But in reality, the images of the high country that vacation promoters popularized left little room for mining in the present day. Modern-day mining, ugly, gritty, and noisy, had no place in the scenic, relaxing, and romantic imagined landscape of the tourist brochures. That was why Walter Paepcke took care to erase the reminders of mining from the Aspen landscape. And that was why postwar tourist literature almost never depicted active mines (in stark contrast to the tourist literature of Victorian times, when boosters saw tourists as potential investors and urged them to visit places like Leadville to witness the working, prospering mines). The implications of this omission were powerful. People who came to the mountains to rediscover a mythical past, to escape modern industrial intrusions, would be deeply unhappy to find any. It was not so much that tourist boosters opposed the revival of mining or growth of manufacturing; it was that their lure books, advertisements, brochures, and magazines were creating a customer base that *was* so opposed. Again, as in Aspen, once tourism took root, it had a way of pushing aside and precluding other ways of valuing the land.

Aspen's example teaches another lesson: namely, that promoting tourism meant more than just constructing a new image for the high country.

It also meant physically modifying the landscape itself. Even as boosters advertised for prospective visitors, efforts were also under way to build the infrastructure needed to handle the hoped-for hordes of postwar leisure-seekers. Aspen's chairlift and Greek amphitheater got the media coverage, but scores of more mundane facilities—motels, ski hills, campgrounds, hiking trails, artificial fishing holes—were, bit by bit, changing the face of the landscape too, rendering it more usable for tourists. Most important was the building of new highways and upgrading of old ones, which remade the region, literally paving the way for more tourists to enter the once-inaccessible high country and explore its every corner.

2.1 Branding the road (badly). It is little wonder that this feeble 1956 branding effort by the Colorado Highway 6 Association failed to catch on. All the same, when postwar tourists organized their trips and made sense of their vacation space, they largely took their lead from modern paved highways like U.S. 6. Author's collection.

CHAPTER 2

The Roads Nature Made?

ONE OF THE WEIRDER MOMENTS IN COLORADO TOURIST ADVERTISING CAME in 1956, when the members of the Highway 6 Association—motel and gas station owners, chamber of commerce officials, small-town newspaper editors, and others along the Colorado portion of U.S. Highway 6—decided that what their road really needed was a mascot. It must have seemed like a good idea at the time. Ford had a dog, Hamm's Beer had a bear, Alka-Seltzer had Speedy the singing antacid tablet. Why not a cartoon character for a Colorado tourist highway? The highway association called in an ad agency, the ad agency put its artists to work—and thus was born Sidney Six.

Sadly, Sidney had a shaky debut. His first brochure, *Stick to 6 with Sidney Six*, was certainly cheery enough.[1] It showed our new friend smiling brightly, reveling in the delights along his namesake road. He fly-fished, panned for gold, and skied. He shot scenery with a Brownie camera, played tag with a friendly bear. But something was not quite right. Was it Sidney's goofy smile? His black horn-rimmed glasses? His drugstore cowboy garb? Or perhaps it was his not-so-fetching figure—simultaneously potbellied and hunchbacked, on account of his torso consisting of a big red "6"? Hamm's Bear charisma this was not. This looked more like runner-up in a grade-school "draw the mascot" contest. One wonders how much the ad agency (or the grade schooler) got paid. In any case, Sidney, unlike so many of his cartoon contemporaries, tragically failed to win the public's affection. Instead of enjoying a long, happy career of TV jingles and plastic figurines, his first appearance was his last.

Advertising does not always work. For every concept that catches the public fancy ("Cool, Colorful Colorado"), there are probably several that flop (Sidney Six). But simply to laugh Sidney off would be to miss what his creators were trying to do. Their aim was no less than to reshape consumers' sense of place, using a road to rearrange how the traveling public understood the geography of their own movement and their own leisure. In contrast to much more famous highways like Route 66, U.S. 6 was an uncelebrated road, squiggling through some of the least known, lightly populated, and economically stagnant counties of the Colorado Rockies. There was little reason for any outsiders to notice the area, much less go there. But Sidney Six tried to get tourists to see all of this in a new light: not just to know of Highway 6's existence, and all the towns and attractions it linked together, but to see them as a package, one that made for the perfect vacation. "Stick to 6," was the message, and you and your family, like Sidney, would find a wealth of outdoor activities all along the way. And all with a minimum of hassle—that too was an important part of the message. You might worry about driving in the mountains, but Sidney Six wanted you to know how easy it really was—how the road's "sound engineering" let you "sweep effortlessly along the broad, well-maintained miles" with no more trouble than "an average Sunday afternoon drive."

As it so happened, even as Sidney Six was touting the ease and convenience of his namesake route, the Highway 6 Association was scrambling to get the road itself to live up to the promises of the advertising. The mid-1950s saw the group frantically lobbying to get the route upgraded to interstate highway status, which would mean millions of federal dollars to turn a narrow, winding, two-lane road into a commodious four- and six-lane superhighway through the Rockies. Interstate status really would make U.S. 6 the smooth-sweeping boulevard that Sidney Six claimed it was—and mark it as the premier tourist corridor in Colorado, perhaps even the West. The problem for Highway 6's advocates was that boosters along other Colorado mountain routes were vying for the coveted interstate designation too—and federal highway planners seemed disinclined to designate any interstate through western Colorado at all. So Sidney Six stood for a political agenda as well as a promotional one—a campaign for the use of publicly funded infrastructure to succor private-sector tourist development and so breathe new life into Highway 6 communities like Georgetown, Dillon, Frisco, Minturn, and Eagle, old mining and ranching towns that badly needed an economic boost.

One cannot overstate how vital highways were to the making of the postwar vacationland. While very few postwar tourists would choose to "stick to 6" just because a brochure told them to, they did overwhelmingly stick to modern, paved roads. As such, the presence of such a highway did more than any advertising, more than any other type of infrastructure, to package a place for tourists. It gave people entrée into formerly inaccessible landscapes, guided where they went, and framed what they saw. Rarely do we stop to ask, though, how did this highway end up *here*? We have little historical memory of the political and promotional battles that determined where highways would go or which ones would become primary routes. The creation of the high country's main travel corridors—culminating in the 1960 decision to hand victory to U.S. 6 boosters and choose their route for Interstate 70—suggests that tourism could foster highways as much as the other way around. That is, the thirst for tourist dollars was the biggest single reason why promoters, public officials, and others fought so hard for highway funding, why they worked so hard to convince cold-eyed engineers to route the big roads their way.

Ultimately, highway improvement, culminating in the creation of Interstate 70, forged a new tourist corridor where none had existed before. In the process, it really did foster a new popular sense of the Colorado high country as a place, just as boosters had hoped. A public that had once seen the region as impenetrable and inhospitable—or ignored it outright—increasingly began to idealize it as a great place to enjoy the great outdoors. Yes, it was an outdoors creased by some of the heaviest-traveled highways in all of rural America, but this was not a contradiction for people living postwar America's automobile-obsessed way of life. For them, the presence of a major highway actually added value to the mountains of central Colorado. Thus could *Stick to 6*, a brochure premised on a massive artificial intrusion of asphalt and concrete, rhapsodize about an "unspoiled mountain wonderland" with plenty of "quiet areas far from civilization," and call Highway 6 the "scenic throughway to all of Colorado's true beauty spots." Such a description, smoothly blurring the artificial and the natural, begins to hint at how highways created new places—and new ways of understanding place—in the imaginations of postwar consumers. Promoters worked hard to convince planners that this really was a natural place for a highway. The highway, in turn, convinced consumers that it was a natural place for recreation. What ultimately resulted was not just more leisure-seekers but more leisure-seekers with a very auto-minded way of linking to the land.

BEFORE THE 1920S, MOST VISITORS TO COLORADO WENT NOT BY CAR BUT by rail. And railroads did more than any other entity to advertise Colorado tourism. They kept advertising after World War II, but by then it was less a matter of market leadership than of desperation. Rail's share of passenger traffic began plummeting in the 1920s, with especially steep declines for long routes across the plains.[2] That is why the 1940s and 1950s saw railroads like the Rock Island, Burlington, Missouri Pacific, and Union Pacific furiously flacking their Colorado-bound trains. Besides simply advertising these routes (using all the usual Old West imagery and scenic clichés), another way to market them was to make the trains themselves more luxurious. The much-loved Vista-Dome observation cars were part of this luxury offensive. So were air-conditioned coaches, reclining and rotating seats, ladies' dressing rooms, and lounge cars styled like English pubs—all of which appeared on Chicago-to-Denver trains after the war. Trains also became faster. The Burlington's sleek, stainless-steel Zephyrs could top a hundred miles an hour. The Union Pacific countered with its Streamliners, the Missouri Pacific with its Colorado Eagle, the Rock Island with the Rocky Mountain Rocket. All stressed modern luxury, a smooth ride, and above all speed.[3]

But despite the railroads' marketing blitz, it was becoming harder, not easier, for tourists in Colorado to take the train. Even as carriers promised better service, falling revenues forced them to slash the number of trains they ran each day and the number of towns they served. The latter was especially true in the Colorado high country. With so many mining districts in long-term decline, the Denver & Rio Grande Western and the Colorado & Southern (C&S) rapidly abandoned trackage in the decades after World War I. From 1915 to 1960, Colorado lost nearly a third of its railroad mileage, the highest abandonment rate of any state. Most of the mileage lost was in the mountains.[4] The casualties included the D&RGW spur up the Roaring Fork Valley; the C&S line up Clear Creek Canyon; and the C&S tracks over Boreas Pass, the last remaining railroad serving Summit County. Old mining towns like Aspen, Georgetown, Idaho Springs, and Breckenridge were left inaccessible by rail.

If by the 1940s railroads were looking like the vacationways of the past, airlines were starting to look like those of the future. Commercial air travel in the United States soared after the war, from 6.7 million passengers in 1945 to 55 million by 1959—a gain of over 720 percent.[5] Most of that was business travel, but big airlines like United and Western, and regional carriers like Denver-based Frontier, went after the tourist market too. Like railroads, they ran ads full of western "playground" imagery, and like railroads they emphasized convenience. It was not an easy sell. Flying was more expensive and less comfortable than riding the train. It also aroused fears that riding the train did not. (Many airports in the 1950s had vending machines where passengers could buy life insurance before boarding.) On the other hand, airlines could trade on the novelty, the thrill of flying. And what air travel lacked in lounge-car comfort, it recouped in sheer speed. Almost every airline ad sounded the same refrain: flying got you to your vacation destination fastest, which meant less time in transit and more time to relax.[6]

For boosters of Colorado tourism in the late 1940s, air travel seemed full of promise. Denver was a rising airline hub, thanks to its midcontinent location—a key consideration in those days when most airplanes had shorter ranges. A traveler in 1946 could fly to Denver on any of four major carriers (United, Braniff, Continental, Western) and from there hop on one of two feeder lines (Monarch or Challenger, soon to merge into Frontier) to reach several towns up in the mountains.[7] The nation's air network was growing, and civic leaders in the high country wanted to be a part of it. In 1945, within days of Japan's surrender, officials in Aspen, Glenwood Springs, and Eagle were already clamoring for public funds to build airports. The state legislature set up a State Division of Aeronautics later that year.[8]

Of course high-country airports would serve more than just tourists. But tourism was a big reason for building them. That was certainly true of Aspen's airfield, which opened in 1948. The two forces behind the facility—Walter Paepcke and Continental Air Lines—both had a strong stake in tourism. Continental wanted skiers to fly in on its DC-3s, and Paepcke (who actually bankrolled the airport) wanted to make his cultural retreat a little less remote for business leaders and cultural sophisticates.[9] By tying Aspen into a wider air network, he put the town where natural geography had not: much closer in terms of travel time to large population centers. In reality, it would be years before Aspen's airport could accommodate regular airline service.[10] But Paepcke's idea was pioneering all the same. Today, airports with direct service to major cities are considered crucial to the success of western mountain resorts like Sun Valley, Telluride, Jackson Hole, Steamboat Springs, and Vail.

But in the 1940s, those days were still a ways off. Boosters liked to dream of tourists swooping into the high country by the planeload, defying the earthbound barrier the Rockies had always posed to travel. In reality, though, the mountains hindered the airplanes of the era as much as they did cars or trains. High peaks play havoc with the flow of air, churning it into violent waves and eddies. Heated air boils up from mountaintops, erupting into sudden storms; cold air coursing over ranges spins into dangerous rotors on the lee side. Today's pressurized jets fly above all the commotion. But in the late 1940s and 1950s, the only airline serving the Colorado highlands was Frontier, and the only planes Frontier flew were unpressurized Douglas DC-3s—rugged and reliable but unable to go high enough to crest the weather.[11] Pilots had to detour around storms or plow grimly through, risking lethal icing in winter and sending passengers grabbing for airsickness bags. The limitations of the DC-3s also forced pilots to fly between or around the higher ranges instead of straight over them. That meant Frontier's westward flight paths did what the railroads and highways had long done: they avoided the Front Range and other high mountains directly west of Denver, instead swinging far to the north to cross over the easier terrain of southern Wyoming, or to the south to follow along river valleys and squeeze over the Continental Divide at some of the same passes motorists used.[12] Come landing time, Frontier pilots had to coax their craft onto airstrips, often gravel or dirt, set in valleys or on plateaus where turbulence roiled so violently that one pilot joked about monitoring it with a log chain instead of a windsock. This was not flying for the faint of heart. It certainly cannot be said that air travel freed tourists from the constraints of Colorado's earthly terrain.

Given the limitations of trains and planes, the transportation of choice for postwar tourists was the car. One study found that in 1948, 82 percent of all American vacationers went by automobile, and that by 1955 the number had hit 88 percent. In 1956 L. J. Crampon reported that over 89 percent of tourists coming to Colorado did so by auto.[13] So anyone hoping to profit off the tourist tidal wave would have to cater to the station-wagon and camper crowd. That explains why, when it came to transportation infrastructure, Colorado tourist boosters focused not on railroads or airports but squarely, even obsessively, on roads.

Good roads were a top selling point for state publicity bureaus and other tourist advertisers. Understandably so, for it was an article of faith among marketers that consumers craved convenience—and in postwar America, "convenient" and "drive-in" meant basically the same thing. Besides, "improved" or "modern" highways really were something to brag about: in the late 1940s many rural routes, especially in the West, were still gravel-surfaced or graded, not yet asphalt-paved. So Colorado promoters seized every chance to tout the "hard-surfaced thoroughfares," "broad, paved highways," and "wide, safe sky-reaching highways" that their state did have.[14]

All states bragged about their roads, but Coloradans had to brag louder than most, to overcome the Rockies' fearsome reputation in the minds of travelers. Many tourists were terrified by the prospect of mountain driving, conjuring visions in their heads of narrow, winding, cliff-ledge roads. When L. J. Crampon surveyed summer visitors to the state in 1953, many of them nervously asked for safety protections, like guard rails, on mountain roads, while others wanted special instructions on how to drive in the high country.[15] "There are people, it seems," remarked a *Holiday* magazine correspondent after a hair-raising drive to Central City, "who like to gape at the glories of nature while manipulating an automobile around hairpin turns on a narrow two-car road with nothing between them and the jagged rocks below but several thousand feet of invigorating mountain air." He concluded dryly: "I'm not one of them."[16]

Boosters tried to reassure the nervous that mountain driving was really not so bad. "Colorado has hundreds of miles of splendid highways," cooed one copywriter, "spectacular, comfortable and safe. Most of them are wide, plainly marked and well protected, with frequent switchbacks leading easily and smoothly to the highest summits."[17] In other words, modern roads made even the most vertical terrain easy to negotiate. Anxious vacationers could also pick up a State Highway Department brochure titled *Driving Our High Country* or consult the AAA guidebook on coping with sharp curves, vapor lock, and other quirks of high-altitude motoring. "If you can handle your car safely on the Pennsylvania Turnpike, Chicago's outer Drive, the coast highway in California or on Main Street, U.S.A.," the AAA reassured readers, "you'll have no trouble driving on the excellent highways through the Colorado Rockies."[18] The same message came in subtler forms too. Every year, the state highway map—the single most widely distributed piece of Colorado tourist literature—included a publicity shot of some "all-weather highway," in which the landscape was blanketed with deep, drifted snow, but the highway itself was bone dry and ice-free, plowed clear down to blacktop. The State Highway Department supplied similar pictures to magazines like *Colorado Wonderland* and *National Geographic*, trying to show that even wintertime driving was safe in the high country.[19] Such imagery paved the way for visitors who wanted spectacular scenery but did not want to inconvenience themselves or take serious risks.

Another way of highway-promoting the high country was to suggest "circle tours." These became staples of guidebooks and brochures. The Denver

2.2 The fear of mountain driving. This switchback on U.S. Highway 40 over Berthoud Pass—slushy, rutted, precipitous, vertiginous—illustrates what terrified so many visitors about driving in the high country and suggests the challenge Colorado boosters faced in making the mountain landscape seem hospitable. Highway improvements helped make the case. So did making sure that frightening pictures like this one never made it into the lure books and brochures. Courtesy Sanborn Ltd.

tourist bureau mapped out several Prospectors' Trails, including a "Leadville Trip" that led visitors into the mountains west of Denver, through several historic mining camps, and then back to Denver. The state tourist bureau outlined a similar tour (theme: "Gold and Silver Towns") in its colorful lure book, together with eleven other circle trips covering the entire state.[20] Scripted itineraries like these always served business interests: the Prospectors' Trails, for example, steered tourists back to Denver by the end of the day so they would eat in the city's restaurants and sleep in its motels. At the same time, circle tours organized Colorado's vast, bewildering mountainous region into discrete, thematically focused packages, making it more convenient and comprehensible for consumers.

But it all came back to this: the surest way to package a place for tourists was to pave its roads. Paved roads had a powerful channeling effect on the flow of tourists, because even as Americans celebrated the seemingly limitless freedom of automobility, they overwhelmingly confined themselves to roads that had been "improved." (You might say they forfeited some of their freedom for the sake of convenience.) Highway observers even had a saying that "tourists will drive a hundred miles out of their way to avoid five miles of dirt road." Or, as the *Colorado Information* newsletter warned local officials, "The most spectacular scenic wonder in the world will not lure many visitors if highways leading to it are rough and rocky trails." The newsletter noted an AAA study showing that 70 percent of motorists "go where good roads are found, even though scenery and recreation may not be exactly what they would like." The lesson was clear: "Travel naturally follows good highways."[21]

So local boosters lobbied vigorously for improvements to local roads. First they asked for oiling, then paving. Then they begged for the next step, like an added passing lane. Each successive improvement, went the thinking, would funnel more tourists, who would breed more gas stations, cafés, and cottage courts, which would lure still more tourists. And so in Colorado it became a ritual, every November, for local leaders from all over the state to troop down to Denver to lobby the State Highway Commission for road improvements. The commission would hold court for three or four days, and one by one, local delegations would enter the room to present wish lists of road projects for the coming year. It is striking how many of these delegations—particularly those from the high country—told the Highway Commission very frankly that the reason they wanted better roads was to foster tourism.

That was especially true of the most formidable delegation of all: the one from the "supralocal" organization called Club 20, so called because it claimed to speak for twenty or so counties on the Western Slope. A big reason for Club 20's founding was "to coordinate a broad program of tourist promotion, and highway improvement" for western Colorado.[22] Its president put the case bluntly: "Good roads are our lifeline. . . . Without good highways, tourist business just doesn't come and tourist business is all a lot of us [on the Western Slope] have left."[23] Armed with this logic—and with professionally printed brochures that wowed the highway commissioners—Club 20 quickly established itself as a group with real clout. A year after Club 20 began lobbying in 1954, the Western Slope's share of the state road-building budget jumped from 11 to 15 percent. Soon afterward it hit 25 percent.[24]

To be sure, Club 20 wanted highways for more than just tourism, and tourist boosters were not alone in their zeal for highways. In fact, by midcentury, highways were a matter of broad consensus—broader, perhaps, than any other policy issue in America. There was spirited disagreement over which roads should take priority and who should pay for them, but most agreed on the basic need for them. Planners, policy makers, public officials at all levels, business boosters of all stripes—seemingly everyone saw highways as "paths to progress," crucial to America's economic future.[25] In Colorado, the champions of mining, manufacturing, ranching, and farming found common ground with tourist boosters on the bedrock importance of high-ways. Many in that Cold War context also saw modern highways as vital to national defense—a matter that transcended petty interest groups. So it would be wrong to say that Colorado's postwar highways were built solely for tourism.

But they *were* built with tourism prominently in mind. As such, they ended up transforming how people idealized the high country and how people practiced and promoted leisure in its midst. The desire to lure vacationers became a leading rationale for building or improving highways, and in turn the existence of more and better highways deepened the popular impression that the high country was an attractive, accessible place to vacation. Eventually it became difficult for visitors, and even many local residents, to make sense of the region's geography without thinking of leisure, and it became impossible for them to understand the leisure landscape apart from its net-work of improved highways. The high country won repute as a wonderland of scenic routes, tourist towns, and recreation areas—all place perceptions that seemed to take their cues from natural features but that would have been inconceivable without paved roads.

To see that story unfold, we must first consider how traffic moved through the high country before World War II. The main-traveled road west out of Denver was U.S. Highway 40, and it was not exactly a straight shot. After heading directly west for the first 45 miles or so, it suddenly veered north, crossing the Continental Divide at Berthoud Pass and then tracing a wind-ing, generally northwesterly course for the next 115 miles. Only at Steam-boat Springs did it turn west again for the last 135 miles to the Utah line. By following this meandering path, U.S. 40 was able to make use of several river valleys and skirt most of the high ranges that ran north-to-south across Colorado's midsection, instead of slicing right through them as Interstate 70 later would.[26]

But U.S. 40 owed its crooked configuration to promotional consider-ations as well as practical ones. The 1910s and 1920s had seen boosters across the nation promoting automobile tourism by means of "named highways"—brand-named routes like the Lincoln or the Dixie Highway, which linked states and regions at a time when long-distance routes were rare.[27] U.S. 40's path was cobbled together from two such routes. From Denver to Kremmling it followed the old Midland Trail, dating from 1913. The rest of the route to Salt Lake City had its origins in the coast-to-coast Victory Highway, dating from 1921.[28] With the passage of the second federal highway-funding act in 1921 (an act championed by Colorado senator Lawrence Phipps), the Victory Highway became the first federal-aid road in western Colorado. And with the advent of the numbered U.S. highway system in 1925–26, it became U.S. 40. By the late 1930s, except for two short stretches, it was paved or oiled all the way from Denver to Utah, making it one of western Colorado's most "improved" roads. It also boasted the most cabin camps and cottage courts, reflecting its emerging status as a tourist route.[29]

And what of the route from Denver directly west, the one that is now Interstate 70? Simply put, it did not exist. Look at a road map from the 1920s and you will see not a single highway cutting straight across the high ranges west of Denver—nary a hint of I-70's future path, not even a gravel or dirt road. The two counties now at the heart of today's resort corridor, Eagle and Summit, were then some of the remotest places in the Rockies. Breckenridge, the Summit County seat, sat about 55 miles from Denver as the crow flew, but anyone wanting to get there had to take a circuitous route of more than 100 miles, first looping southwest of Denver for some distance and then making a sharp turn north to scale a timberline pass and descend into Summit County from the south. Eagle County was even harder to get to. Its eastern reaches lay just 70 miles from Denver, but getting there meant driving a staggering 170 miles, clambering over three passes and again descending into the county from the south.

The obvious reason for these roundabout routes was, once again, topography. The 14,000-foot peaks of the Front Range screened Summit County from Denver; beyond that, separating Summit from Eagle County, loomed the sawtoothed Gore and Tenmile chains. But a contributing factor was history. It was not just that these mountains posed daunting obstacles to travel; it was also that, historically speaking, there had never been enough economic incentive to take them on. During Colorado's mining heyday, the minescapes around Breckenridge and Red Cliff yielded decent quantities of gold and silver, but neither ranked among the top-producing districts in the state. So instead of beating paths directly west to these towns, the railroads raced southwest, toward booming Leadville. Later, when the first auto roads were built, they followed the old rail routes. Nineteenth-century history thus translated into twentieth-century remoteness for Eagle and Summit Counties.

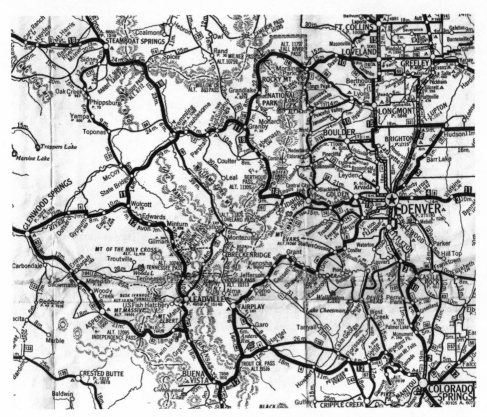

2.3 No natural corridor. Today, Interstate 70 follows a more or less direct line from Denver west to Glenwood Springs. But a highway map from the mid-1920s shows no hint of the path the road would eventually take. Instead, high ranges west of Denver deflect main routes (which were then gravel or graded dirt roads) to the north and south. Author's collection.

Only gradually, over decades, did access to this heart of the high country become more direct. It was not for lack of lobbying. For twenty years beginning in 1921, a highway association badgered the State Highway Department to build a paved road from Denver directly west to the Mount of the Holy Cross, ostensibly to allow religious pilgrimages to the storied peak.[30] This "Holy Cross Trail" was the first route proposal to approximate the path Interstate 70 would eventually take. Building it would have required improving the old wagon road over Loveland Pass, which separated Clear Creek from Summit County, and then building a new road from Summit County over Shrine Pass, descending into Eagle County at Red Cliff on the other side. Pilgrims would then use Red Cliff as a base for visiting Holy Cross itself, just a few miles away.

2.4 An "impenetrable barrier" before the interstate. In this 1946 scene, the sawtooth Gore Range stands like a fortified wall, sealing off the eastern end of Eagle County from Summit County and Denver beyond. Before modern highways, mountains like these isolated adjacent counties from each other and the outside world. But this oiled-gravel road hints at the future, when Eagle County would find itself on a direct superhighway link to Denver. This arcadian valley is now home to the resort complex of Vail. Courtesy Sanborn Ltd.

The Holy Cross Trail was the brainchild of Red Cliff newspaper editor Orion Daggett, and despite its pious-sounding intentions, it was first and foremost another tourist-boosting scheme. The faithful coming in on the highway, Daggett believed, could revive Red Cliff, which like so many mountain towns had gone into a steep decline with the silver market crash. (Indeed, the same year Daggett launched his highway association, Red Cliff lost the county seat to Eagle, thirty-five miles downvalley.) His crusade for the Holy Cross Trail won backing in other small, hard-hit towns in central Colorado, including Clear Creek County's Georgetown and Silver Plume; Summit County's Dillon; and Eagle County's Minturn, Wolcott, Gypsum, and Eagle. It even gained support in bigger towns like Glenwood Springs and Grand Junction, and from the influential *Denver Post*, and it got a big boost when President Hoover named the Mount of the Holy Cross a national monument in 1929. Eventually Daggett envisioned the Holy Cross Trail extending all the way to the Pacific. But the State Highway Department, while on record endorsing the route, never gave it more than a sporadic trickle of funds.[31]

Still, bit by bit, the department did bypass the long roads that looped around central Colorado's high mountain ranges with shorter, more direct roads that climbed right over them. First, in 1931, came a dirt road over 11,089-foot Shrine Pass. That same year, the state threw another dirt road over 11,992-foot Loveland Pass. And nine years later, with funding from the Public Works Administration, the state put a paved route over the southern tip of the Gore Range, naming it for the state's chief highway engineer, Charles Vail—thus, Vail Pass.[32] Much to Daggett's dismay, this last link supplanted Shrine Pass (which remains a dirt road to this day), and Red Cliff was left more isolated than ever. But by 1940 Denver finally had its direct link (if you could call the winding, switchbacking roads over Loveland and Vail Passes "direct") across the intervening ranges to Summit and Eagle Counties and points farther west—a rough precursor to Interstate 70.

In 1937 this route was made part of a coast-to-coast U.S. highway—U.S. Highway 6.[33] So it can truly be said that Colorado's stretch of U.S. 6 had its roots in tourist boosterism. But it was not the main corridor west of Denver when the postwar travel rush began. U.S. 40 was, handling almost twice as much traffic.[34] One reason was better surfacing: Highway 40 was by that time paved all the way from Denver to Utah, while Loveland Pass, Highway 6's key link, was still just a gravel road. Another reason was U.S. 40's mystique. Back east, it traced its origins to the National Road of Conestoga wagon days; out west, it included stretches traveled by Jim Bridger, John C. Frémont, and gold rushers on the Smoky Hill Trail. In the early auto era it had been one of the first coast-to-coast adventure trails, the Victory Highway. And it passed through a veritable cross-section of America, from big cities to small towns to pretty countryside to remote hinterlands. Small wonder that in 1950, when author and scholar George Stewart decided to drive across the nation, photographing and describing what he saw—ultimately creating a classic portrait of midcentury America—he chose U.S. 40. U.S. 6 he rejected with disdain. "Route 6 runs uncertainly from nowhere to nowhere," he wrote, "scarcely to be followed from one end to the other, except by some devoted eccentric."[35]

Trading on U.S. 40's mystique was the road's energetic booster corps. The National U.S. Highway 40 Association—whose members and contributors included thousands of local chamber of commerce heads; newspaper editors; politicians; and motel, restaurant, and gas station owners all along the route from Missouri to California, including an especially enthusiastic

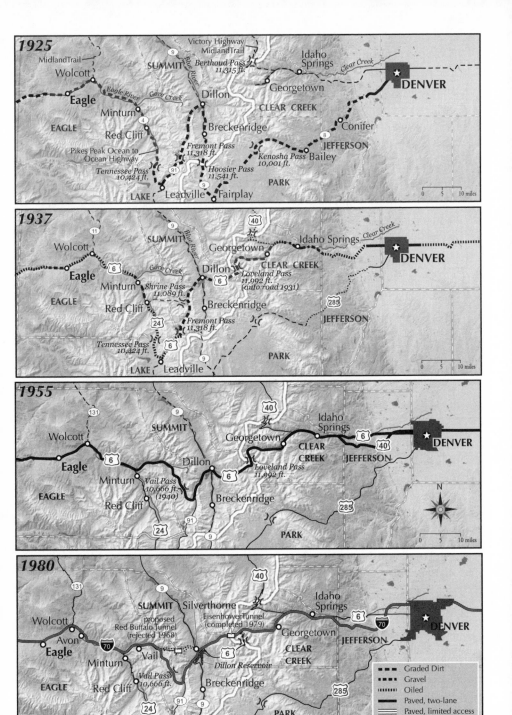

MAP 2. Evolution of the Interstate 70 corridor. These strips show how highway improvements made the high country less and less remote. As roads skirting the north-south-running mountain ranges were bypassed by more direct pass and tunnel routes, and as graded dirt and gravel roads gave way to paved highways (and eventually to a full-blown interstate), the effect was to bring high country towns like Eagle closer and closer to Denver.

Colorado contingent—was one of the most active highway associations of the numbered-highway era. It put up billboards to steer motorists toward Highway 40, sent salesmen to influence tourist-guide publishers and travel agents, and even (in the mid-1950s) dispatched "courtesy cars" to provide distressed motorists with gas, maps, tow chains, water, and first aid. But most of all it advertised. Its pictorial maps populated Highway 40 with the ghosts of Indian fighters and explorers; its copywriters dubbed the highway "the path of the pioneers," "the Main Line of America," or, in the group's favorite slogan, the "shortest and most scenic route" across the Rockies.[36] U.S. 40 never achieved the cachet of Route 66, but its boosters did succeed in establishing its brand—so much so that at one point the boosters of rival U.S. 30 in Wyoming tried to poach the number 40 for their own route.[37]

Meanwhile, U.S. 6 boosters were left struggling to establish their own brand. Highway 6 was then America's longest coast-to-coast highway but one of its more obscure. Oddly aimless, it had been pieced together in the 1920s and 1930s from existing roads in fourteen states, so that it ended up tracing a drunken diagonal from Cape Cod, Massachusetts, to Long Beach, California, managing to miss most major cities in the process. It was, in short, a tough sell. At the behest of a Civil War descendants' group, it became known as the Grand Army of the Republic Highway by the early 1940s, but the clunky name did not lend itself to much advertising. It was also called the Roosevelt Highway (after Theodore) before the war, and in 1948 a newly reorganized U.S. 6 Roosevelt Highway Association tried to revive that brand, but it did not really stick either.[38]

As with Highway 40, Coloradans took the lead in promoting Highway 6, often collaborating with Nebraskans.[39] But in Nebraska, U.S. 6's only real selling point was that it got you to Colorado, and in Colorado, boosters had trouble establishing a brand as strong as U.S. 40 or Route 66. It did not help that Highway 6 ran right through the highest Rockies, still an obstacle many cross-country travelers preferred to avoid, while Route 66 eased through New Mexico's gentler terrain. Highway 6 advertisers tried to defuse this disadvantage the same way Highway 40's boosters did: by claiming the most direct and scenic route. They also contrasted their refreshing high-altitude climate with Route 66's notorious desert driving conditions. As one brochure asked, "Why drive at night to avoid heat"—which many Route 66 travelers did in those days before air-conditioned cars—"when you can keep cool by day . . . while enjoying America's grandest scenery?"[40] But U.S. 6 never achieved the brand familiarity U.S. 40 did. Neither the Grand Army nor the Roosevelt name took root in the popular imagination, and a 1952 attempt to brand U.S. 6 as the "Pleasure Way Across the West" flopped too. Maybe this explains the decision to make a mascot out of Sidney Six: maybe by that time, Highway 6 boosters had simply reached the point of brand-name desperation.

Still, even as some brands caught on better than others, the very idea of building and advertising tourist highways had profound implications for the popular sense of place, even for popular environmental values. Marketing a highway as a vacation route in effect used road access to try to define a new region in the popular imagination. And if the marketing did not always succeed in doing this, the simple presence of the highway surely did. Alongside older ways of organizing space in their heads—by county or city lines, mining districts, river valleys, mountain ranges, opposite sides of the Continental Divide—people increasingly thought in terms of highway corridors too. Besides the "Front Range," the "Clear Creek valley," and the "Western Slope" there were now "U.S. 6," "U.S. 40," and eventually the "I-70 corridor"—geographic units that had not existed before those roads were built and advertised.[41]

Highway corridors had a powerful hold on people's movements and on the way tourists viewed and valued the land. Because few postwar vacationers dared to stray far from improved roads, they effectively let paved and promoted highways direct their way. They moved linearly over the land, stopping to savor certain places with supposedly superior scenic, recreational, historical, or cultural value, often learning of this value from brochures and guidebooks. Usually they skimmed past the places in between, and usually they never even saw the places *not* near the highway. They ended up experiencing the land in narrow strips, or like pearls on a string, the road linking one point of interest to the next.[42] Of course, tourists did not always pick the same pearls that tourist advertisers wanted them to. But their basic behavior—favoring some pockets of the countryside over others, and giving enormous primacy to those near paved roads—echoed the ways of seeing, valuing, and moving through landscapes that tourist advertising encouraged.

Moreover, not just tourists but many high country residents themselves began to organize their mental maps by highway corridor. Boosters and business owners in towns like Granby, Kremmling, Steamboat Springs, and Craig on U.S. 40, and Georgetown, Dillon, Eagle, and Glenwood Springs on U.S. 6, became so enthusiastically involved in their highway associations that their fierce allegiance to their respective corridors often cleaved their shared identity as citizens of the high country or the Western Slope. They fretted about losing business and political clout to each other and accused each other of conspiring to siphon off tourist traffic.[43] Even Club 20, purporting to unite the entire Western Slope against water- and power-hungry Denver, found it hard to heal these corridor-versus-corridor rifts—especially when boosters on rival corridors tussled for road funds, and *especially* when they competed for the favor of interstate highway planners.

Highway associations were not the only ones using roads to redefine regional geography. Many guidebooks and brochures grouped attractions into driving tours, or they listed motels and other accommodations, not by which town or county, but by which route they were on. Vacationers belonging to the AAA could get custom-made TripTiks, which presented the adventure ahead in a series of strip maps. TripTiks typically showed the territory within ten or fifteen miles of the highway—and nothing else. Then there were the ubiquitous state highway maps, distributed free at gas stations. Here, the strip-like sense of a region became a web, as the map unfolded to show a landscape latticed with multiple possible routes, expanding the vacationer's horizons beyond any one corridor. But even as the map opened up new possibilities, it limited them too, because once again, tourists overwhelmingly kept to where the map said the improved roads were. Thus state highway maps perfectly captured automobile tourists' paradoxical desire for both geographical freedom and geographical convenience. It was no coincidence that state highway maps were considered the most indispensable of all information available to tourists. No coincidence, either, that Club 20 lobbied hard for the Colorado Highway Department to show more roads on the official state highway map. Club 20 knew that big empty spaces on the map of western Colorado would scare travelers away—and, conversely, that filling in some of the empty spaces with highway lines would visually convey a more tourist-friendly sense of place.[44]

The road-centered sense of region could shape community identity too, as different towns took on different roles in relation to the road. Often the role was quite unglamorous. Many towns, for example, assumed the economic function of rest stops, with boldly painted signs or familiar oil-company logos alerting passing motorists that here was a place for gas, bait, a bite to eat, or (if misfortune called for it) a mechanic. Romantic these rest-stop towns were not, but they were essential to auto tourists. And judging from advertisements in guidebooks, boosters in such towns often accepted their communities' unassuming roles. In one 1949 example, the copywriter for tiny Frisco, in Summit County, made no claim for the town other than it being "a convenient place to stop" for travelers on U.S. 6. In the same guidebook, the ad writer for nearby Dillon modestly called that town "just the spot to stop" between radiator-taxing Loveland and Vail Passes.[45] Self-descriptions like these seem endearingly modest, compared to the inflated claims of so much twentieth-century advertising and traditional booster rhetoric.[46]

Boosters elsewhere tried to craft more alluring images for their communities. That was certainly so of Idaho Springs promoters, who boldly marketed their town as a "gateway" to all the attractions of the surrounding area. Idaho Springs was the "Gateway to Colorado Ski Areas," declared one ad; it sat "in the heart of the scenic Rockies," bragged a brochure; it was "Headquarters for Sportsmen," said the owners of a local lodge.[47] Roads defined this role too, for in a postwar cultural context that equated "convenient" with "car-accessible," a town could not be a gateway or a vacation headquarters without good roads linking it to its surroundings. Idaho Springs was well positioned in this respect. Straddling Highways 6 and 40, it enjoyed major-artery access to both Denver and the heart of the high country. (Postwar improvements—the paving of Highway 6 over Loveland Pass in 1950, and the completion of Highway 6 through Clear Creek Canyon in 1952, creating a more level and direct route to Denver—only enhanced the town's advantageous position.) Meanwhile, numerous side roads paved the way from Idaho Springs to nearby forests, fishing streams, ski areas, hiking trails, quaint old mining camps, and the picturesque Chicago lake-and-peak district that had inspired Albert Bierstadt. There was even a paved road from the west end of downtown to the summit of 14,264-foot Mount Evans. Not surprisingly, then, Idaho Springs tourist boosters made automobile access their central selling point, touting the "fine wide roads" leading to town and the "innumerable side roads branching off the main highways," which, it was claimed, allowed vacationers to "[use] Idaho Springs as headquarters" and "spend literally days taking short drives" to nearby delights.[48]

The same point was even more effective when made more subtly. Literature from the local chamber of commerce, for example, featured a map with Idaho Springs at center, roads snaking out in all directions, and vignettes of wild animals and outdoor pastimes scattered about the hills and dales. The map—captioned "Idaho Springs Region"—made the whole setting seem naturally suited for vacations.[49] But this was a "region" constructed by Idaho Springs's own advertising and defined by the reach of paved roads. By making the region look like a natural creation, the map tempted users to accept uncritically what Idaho Springs pitchmen were pitching: that the value of the "Idaho Springs Region" lay in leisure and that the defining quality of Idaho Springs itself was the recreational convenience of its surroundings.

The same geography lesson applied to any town advertised as a gateway, be it Grand Lake ("West Entrance [to] Rocky Mountain National Park"); Granby ("the south gateway to a resort district," sitting "in the heart of fine fishing and big game country"); or Glenwood Springs ("vacation hub of colorful Colorado" and "Headquarters of [the] Famous White River National Forest—Tops for Big Game, Fishing, Hiking and Alpine Scenery"). Denver's boosters went the furthest, capitalizing on western Colorado's expanding paved-highway network by claiming the entire high country as the "Denver Vacation Area."[50] Definitions of region, perceptions of place, notions of how towns relate to their surroundings—these are some of the most basic elements of geographical understanding. And highway-themed advertising redefined them all around the quest for outdoor leisure.

But advertising images that lived by the road could also die by the road. What if your competitors branded their road better than you? The creators of Sidney Six knew this pain. A bigger problem: what if your rivals got their road improved beyond yours? Here again U.S. 6 lagged. Even after Loveland Pass was paved in 1950, its sharp curves and steep drop-offs frightened many drivers away, and the pass was notoriously quick to close when the winter weather deteriorated. Farther west on U.S. 6, the route over Vail Pass was hardly any better. Widely considered Colorado's trickiest drive, its long, lulling straightaways ended in sudden twists, where motorists could find themselves suddenly plummeting off the road if they did not watch out. And all along Highway 6 there were pervasive maintenance concerns: the constant struggle to keep snow and ice off the roadway and to protect the pavement against the harsh high-altitude elements. U.S. 40 faced the same problems, albeit at mostly lower altitudes and lesser degrees. It made it that much harder for U.S. 40 and especially U.S. 6 to compete for cross-country tourist traffic against rival routes like U.S. 30 and Route 66. For all these reasons, despite all the efforts to hype Colorado's mountain highways as tourist corridors, most visitors well into the 1950s stuck close to Denver, Estes Park, and Colorado Springs, never venturing past the "impassable wall" of the Continental Divide into the heart of the high country.[51] Summit and Eagle Counties in particular remained backwaters when it came to tourism, obscure mountain fastnesses where few vacationers ever went.

We could simply say that Interstate 70 came along and changed all of that. But the story is not so simple. The emergence of interstate highways as a system—and its planners' embrace of high-speed, limited-access free-ways as a technology—had just as much potential to push the high country even farther to the fringes as it did to make the region a major vacationland. In the 1940s and 1950s everyone who saw roads in terms of tourism, as our Colorado boosters did, assumed that wherever interstates went, floods of leisure-seekers would follow. But it seemed just as certain that the interstates would leave everywhere else high and dry. No one knew yet which of those two fates would be western Colorado's. And the power to decide was not in tourist boosters' hands. It was left for professional highway engineers—men who thought very differently about space and place and the movement of people, and who dominated federal transportation policy at midcentury. Would they see fit to put an interstate highway through western Colorado? The boosters' frenzied campaign to sell the engineers on the idea was the next key step in moving the region from the margins to the mainstream of American leisure culture.

WHEN COLORADO'S CHIEF HIGHWAY ENGINEER CHARLES VAIL FIRST SAW what federal planners had in mind for the interstate highway system, he must have blanched from his bald pate down to his jowls. The feds were proposing to put every state on a transcontinental route—except Colo-rado. The tentative map the Public Roads Administration (PRA) circulated in January 1940 did show an interstate snaking west across the plains from Kansas, but it stopped short in Denver, as if afraid to venture into the Rock-ies. There hung Colorado: cul-de-sac of the nation.

Vail fired off an indignant protest. The map, he insisted, must be redrawn to put Colorado on a coast-to-coast superhighway, just like all the other states. But the PRA rebuffed him. Vail protested again four years later, again to no avail.[52] Over the next thirteen years, an increasingly panicky succession of Colorado politicians, business leaders, and highway officials begged fed-eral planners not to leave their state without a transcontinental throughway. But the planners, like the Rockies, put up a stone wall. When the interstate map became official in 1947, it still showed Colorado's interstate dead-ending in Denver. And when Congress passed the landmark Interstate Highway Act in 1956, setting the stage for the biggest road-building project in human his-tory, the plans still did not call for an east-west link across the Centennial State.

The disappointment for Colorado was all the worse because it recalled so many similar snubs in the past. Back in the 1860s, the first transcontinental railroad, the Union Pacific, had opted to go through southern Wyoming instead of Colorado. All the other transcontinentals had shunned Colorado too. Then, at the dawn of the auto age, the Lincoln Highway had skirted the state, following in the Union Pacific's path.[53] Now these historic letdowns seemed to be unfolding all over again. The specter that haunted Colorado's interstate dreams—the image of the Rockies as an impassable wall—was the same one that had scared away the railroads. Colorado officials certainly saw the parallel. It was no accident that they used terms like "Main Line" to describe the hoped-for interstate, and "sidetrack" to describe where they feared Colorado might end up instead.[54] They seethed when PRA officials rehashed the railroads' rationale that pounding a route through the Rockies would be "unreasonably costly." And when the PRA said an interstate across Colorado would needlessly duplicate the one planned for Wyoming, that was even more galling—for Wyoming's interstate was slated to follow the same path the Union Pacific and Lincoln Highway had used to circumvent Colorado all those years ago.[55]

The omission of Colorado from the original interstate plans reminds us that there was nothing historically inevitable about the superhighway that now transects the high country. In fact, there was nothing even historically *likely* about it. All prior history was on the other side: railroad and highway builders had always avoided this region. Now interstate planners seemed bent on doing the same.

Yet in hindsight it is tempting to see a superhighway like I-70 as a foregone conclusion. Modern highways, we tend to assume, grow inexorably from the well-worn paths of earlier times, in a process as organic as it is historical. Frederick Jackson Turner famously narrated, "The buffalo trail became the Indian trail, and this became the trader's 'trace'; the trails widened into roads, and the roads into turnpikes, and these in turn were transformed into railroads." George Stewart likened the progression from "packhorse trail" to "freeway" to a river cutting its canyon ever deeper "through the ages." Or, as one Colorado geologist put it, a highway system was "not designed, but inherited." In such tellings, the growth of roads is a story of natural evolution, of travel corridors taking shape from the land itself more than from a human master plan (and in Turner's case, not coincidentally, this was exactly how he explained the genesis of American civilization more broadly).[56]

Even today it is easy to envision highway history this way, not least because once a major road like I-70 is built it has a way of seeming integral to its setting. It creates its own region—"the Interstate 70 corridor"— and becomes central to our sense of geography, the way we think about the locations of places and our motion between them. People today say Vail is an hour and forty-five minutes from Denver, or one hundred miles; both measures, and the ease of travel over the intervening terrain that they imply, are premised on I-70's existence. So ingrained is this way of thinking that we cannot easily imagine the geography of that swath of Colorado before the interstate—or the roads that preceded it—existed. So it is worth reiterating: a highway is neither organic to its landscape nor inevitable in its origins. In Colorado, just as the builders and boosters of U.S. 40 and especially U.S. 6 fashioned new paths where none had naturally or even artificially existed before, reorganizing the spaces of the high country along new lines, so the creators of Interstate 70 came along and reorganized them again. How and why they did so—how this historically unlikely highway corridor came to be—is a story we must understand if we are to grasp the massive changes that followed along its course.

One way of explaining I-70's existence in western Colorado is to cast it like its earlier counterparts: it was put there for tourism. That is overstating the case, but not by much. Tourism was the single biggest reason state and local boosters wanted this highway in the first place. In the nascent interstate system, Coloradans saw an opportunity to take an old booster scheme—using roads to lure vacationers to places they had formerly avoided—and hook it up to a new technology—the high-volume, high-speed superhighway, the transportation system of the future. Indeed, the 1940s and early 1950s, when the interstate highway network was taking form on federal planners' drafting tables, were also the years when excitement was building in Colorado over dreams that tourism might become the next gold rush, the boom industry to bring the backward little towns and unsettled spaces of the high country into the modern age. Colorado boosters wanted a mountain interstate above all because they envisioned it becoming a conduit for large-scale tourism.

That was certainly true of the interstate's leading advocate, Governor Edwin C. Johnson, whom everyone called Big Ed. A conservative rural Democrat, he could play the honey-tongued charmer, outrageous maverick, or backcountry buffoon with equal ease. The 1950s found him near the end of a three-decade career as the biggest bull in Colorado politics, during which he had served two terms as governor in the 1930s, then three terms as U.S. senator, before returning for one last two-year gubernatorial term in 1955. Through it all, he had made highways a pet issue. It was partly personal: he hailed from northwestern Colorado, a lightly populated, economically iffy region that depended heavily on mine- and ranch-to-market highways. He had even worked in the transport business himself, at one point owning a small trucking firm.[57] But he was prohighway for political reasons too. After all, in the mid-twentieth century, championing highway improvement was about as controversial as supporting Mom and apple pie. A politician out front on the issue, as Big Ed always was, could count on a lot of goodwill and a lot of votes. Now, during his gubernatorial swan song, Johnson made the extension of the interstate through Colorado his highest priority. He declared it issue number one in his inaugural speech and told the State Highway Commission it was "the biggest job confronting the State."[58] From 1955 to 1957 he tirelessly lobbied federal highway officials, former congressional colleagues, and the White House, where Eisenhower's staff grew so sick of his incessant pleading that they finally ordered him to shut up.[59]

When he spoke to his constituents, Johnson openly acknowledged that his main reason for wanting the road was so Colorado could compete with other states for tourists. An interstate would put Colorado on "the most direct route between the West and East coast," he told a sympathetic editor in Steamboat Springs, "with side roads into the most scenic areas of these United States." That, he claimed, would bring $50 million in added tourist revenue every year.[60] On the other hand, if western Colorado went without a superhighway, vacationers would shun the region en masse. "How much will [tourists] spend," Big Ed moaned, "when Wyoming has a four and six lane boulevard and New Mexico has two such highways draining the huge volume of east-west traffic. These super highways to the North and South of us will be advertised nationally and will make Colorado's roads look like cow trails."[61]

These were compelling arguments in the hypercompetitive world of tourist boosterdom. The problem was, boosters did not have the power to decide on a new interstate. Only federal officials could do that. Tourist promoters and others with a stake in western Colorado's economic growth might dream of a high-country superhighway, but only the action of federal officials could move the dream to reality. And federal officials tended to see highways—their purpose, function, and design—in a very different light from local boosters. The gap on the interstate map west of Denver was graphic testament to that fact.

The federal officials in question were professionally trained highway engineers, working in the Bureau of Public Roads (or BPR, which replaced the Public Roads Administration in 1949). They were quintessential techno-crats—men who, on the basis of their expertise, claimed that they alone were qualified to plan the nation's highway system, free of petty biases and answerable only to the greater public good. The BPR technocracy had taken shape in the 1910s and 1920s, when federal road funding was just getting started and the Progressive Era faith in problem solving through professional expertise was in full bloom. Working closely with state-level highway engineers and private lobbies interested in good roads, BPR technocrats had quickly come to dominate U.S. highway policy, only to see their dominance erode some-what in the 1930s. But the interstate highway program revived their power—for they had final say over where this new generation of freeways would and would not go. And given their claim to impartial expertise, they were not going to yield to the clamor of tourist boosters in one state. Interstate plan-ning, they insisted, was not a political matter but a highly technical undertak-ing: topographical features must be surveyed; hydrological, pedological, and climatological conditions assessed; traffic patterns measured; demographic and economic statistics analyzed. The route-location decisions that resulted were supposed to carry the weight of scientific truth, undistorted by log-rolling, pork-barreling, or other political hijinks. In our more cynical times, authorities who claim absolute expertise and objectivity are automatically suspect. But the technocratic ideal still thrived in 1940s and 1950s America, and the federal highway technocracy was one of the most entrenched of all. Few dared openly challenge the authority of BPR engineers.[62]

The engineers did not shy away from tough topography. Really, the entire interstate program was an enterprise of breathtaking topographical hubris. Its goal, after all, was to make it possible for motorists to speed stoplessly from any corner of the country to any other, cruising over mountains, prairie loam, and alluvial plain without feeling any difference underwheel. Inter-state builders seemed almost omnipotent—capable, in the awestruck words of *National Geographic*, of "altering and circumventing geography on an unprecedented scale." At one point they seriously considered using nuclear explosives to annihilate California mountains in the way of Interstate 40.[63] But even for engineers this cavalier, the Colorado high country posed a big-ger obstacle than most. Blasting a four-lane boulevard straight through the Southern Rockies seemed almost impossible, even in the technologically brazen atomic age. Imagine the demons that might keep a highway engineer up at night: unstable soils, uneven drainage, flash floods, landslides, snow-slides, steep slopes and cliffs, faulted rock, and a neck-jerking freeze-thaw regime to turn even the sturdiest road into a crumbling, potholed mess. Put all those problems in one place, and there you have the Colorado high country. Historically, travelers avoided such refractory terrain by sticking close to rivers. But in Colorado even the riverways posed problems for road engineers. Tortuous, narrow, and steep, Colorado's river canyons might make for a nice "waterfall route," snickered the governor of rival Wyoming, but not a "watergrade" one.[64]

It is not quite right to say the engineers had finally met a part of the earth that humbled them. It was more that they saw no rational reason to take the challenge on. The sheer expense of laying a superhighway through such terrain would violate engineering rule number one: to build things as economically as possible. It would also offend the strongly utilitarian sensibility of highway technocrats in those days, their dogged belief that roads should serve demonstrated (as opposed to hypothetical) needs. Highways, in this mind-set, were not for social or economic engineering, not for redirecting the flow of people and commerce to empty or economically needy places like western Colorado. Instead, improvements should go where traffic already did, serving existing demand.[65] In this way of seeing, even if western Colorado were as flat as Kansas, it still might not merit an interstate. It was too lightly peopled, too far from major cities, too marginal in an economic sense.[66] So not just natural factors like rock, weather, and soil, but a host of human considerations too, argued against a Colorado interstate: location relative to commerce and population, technical calculations of cost versus benefit, and not least an engineering culture steeped in utilitarianism, narrowly defined. These artificial factors buttressed natural ones, making Colorado's ranges, forbidding enough as they were, seem bigger barriers than ever.

So Big Ed and his allies faced an intricate challenge: they would have to politick for their interstate without seeming political, and they would have to convince the technocrats on the technocrats' own terms. To do this, Coloradans ended up making a two-pronged case. First, they offered a utilitarian rationale based on natural resources. Western Colorado was a rich storehouse of strategic materials, they said, and not just Colorado but the whole nation would benefit by having access to it. Second, they made an engineering argument based on physical terrain. Despite the old notion that Colorado could not easily be crossed, they insisted, the landscape was in fact ideally suited for a modern freeway; and to the extent it was not, the state stood willing to make it so. In short, the Coloradans set out to make the high country seem both less remote and less rugged—a natural place for an interstate.

To make the utilitarian case, they played up the natural features that had lured people to Colorado as far back as the 1850s. Not scenery, fish and game, or recreation—but timber, farmland, rangeland, and above all minerals. It was ironic, to say the least: in their campaign to win the interstate, Coloradans who increasingly suspected that recreation was the resource of the future found themselves relying for rhetorical purposes on the resources of the past. In their entreaties to Congress, BPR technocrats, and the White House, Coloradans argued that the nation urgently needed the interstate for access to western Colorado's mineral riches: uranium, vanadium, molybdenum, coal, oil shale, natural gas, silver, copper, zinc, lead. Big Ed told President Eisenhower it was "the richest mineralized region in the world"; the State Highway Department called it "Our Nation's Greatest Storehouse of Mineral Wealth!" Once reached by a state-of-the-art superhighway, the region could get to work fueling America's postwar prosperity.[67]

It could also heighten national security. The Coloradans reminded everyone that Utah and Colorado's uranium was "strategic" (as were the two states' many military installations and defense-industry plants).[68] And they argued that the military needed an interstate across the Southern Rockies to ensure access to the West Coast in wartime. In one especially impassioned letter to Eisenhower, Johnson conjured up a nightmare scenario in which war broke out and the military found itself unable to move critical assets to the West Coast, due to "blizzards and drifting snow" blocking the interstates in Montana and Wyoming. An added interstate across Colorado would preclude this terrifying possibility, Johnson suggested.[69] Aside from his meteorological hypocrisy—a Coloradan criticizing other states for snow!—Big Ed actually made a powerful case. By the early 1950s, more and more opinion makers were talking about interstates as a national-security imperative, so Johnson was cleverly tapping into the jittery public mood. And he was appealing again to the technocrats' utilitarian mind-set by shifting the focus away from Colorado's parochial needs toward the needs of the nation as a whole. After all, in that time of the Cold War, nothing could be more nonpolitically a matter of national interest than protection from the Soviets.

By comparison, outdoor recreation seemed like a frivolous reason for an interstate. It excited local boosters, but to overstress it would sound too boosterish, risking alienating the federal technocrats who had the final say. For that reason, though Coloradans' talking points typically included some mention of scenery and recreation, they always tempered it in some way. For example, when Johnson listed recreation among western Colorado's natural resources, he gave it no more emphasis than water, timber, or farmland. Or he would grandly state that access to recreation was a matter of national interest—an argument that again downplayed the self-interest of Coloradans who hoped to profit off it.[70] All told, the dispassionately utilitarian way Coloradans talked about recreation to policy makers in Washington, DC, was markedly more restrained than the way they talked about it to each other or portrayed it in their tourist brochures. They were making the case for an interstate with their most passionately felt motive, and their most compelling advertising imagery, tied behind their backs. It must have been intensely frustrating for Johnson—all the more so because he knew President Eisenhower himself was an eager consumer of that very imagery. Here was a man who had loafed away summer days in Colorado just like the brochures advertised, whose scenic paintings took inspiration from tourist publicity shots—yet who refused to show any favoritism toward Colorado, insisting on staying above the fray.

Still, Big Ed thought maybe, just maybe, he could use Ike's love for the Colorado outdoors to get a foot in the door on the interstate issue. So at a White House photo op in May 1956, he presented Ike with two gifts: that year's honorary Colorado Fishing License No. 1 and a lavish coffee-table album making Colorado's case for the interstate. State officials had gone all out on the album, covering it in luxurious white cowhide, trimming it with hand-tooled leather accents, and silver-stamping the president's name on the front. Inside, they interspersed colorful, postcard-like photographs with maps and tables detailing Colorado's public lands and mineral deposits, crop yields, population growth, and tax revenues (statistics compiled by the quintessentially technocratic State Planning Commission). It was all very technical and utilitarian, in keeping with the technocratic mind-set. But it was no coincidence that the album included scenic images alongside the statistics, no coincidence either that Johnson gave Ike a ceremonial fishing license at the same time he presented this summary of Colorado's case. Perhaps these little reminders of what Ike loved about his Colorado summer trips would soften him up and incline him to do a little favor for the state.[71]

The strategy flopped. Eisenhower wrote a note a few days later, thanking Johnson for the fishing license but mentioning the album and the interstate not at all. One can imagine Big Ed reading the note, clutching at his thinning pompadour in utter frustration. The album got wrapped in kraft paper and dumped in a White House file room. The struggle for the interstate dragged on.[72]

Making the utilitarian case was not the Coloradans' only uphill battle. They also had to make the engineering case: to convince federal engineers that a superhighway really could fit through the high country. Interstate design standards called for at least four lanes, each twelve feet wide, with a minimum sixteen-foot median in most places; controlled access with no intersections at grade; and curves and slopes gentle enough for a cruising speed of fifty miles an hour.[73] None of this seemed realistic in a region where the topography forced even major routes like U.S. 40 to shrink to two narrow lanes, hairpin up and down high passes, and claw up grades as steep as 7 percent. How could such terrain accommodate the kind of high-speed boulevard the BPR had in mind?

Big Ed had an answer—a wildly audacious answer. He decided the boulevard should bore right *through* the mountains, by means of a tunnel under the Continental Divide. It was a stupendous notion: overcoming Colorado's greatest natural obstacle by undercutting it. And while it was not a new idea (dreams of a great tunnel under the mountains dated back to railroad days), it was Big Ed who made it his personal quest. Build a tunnel *now*, he believed, and the interstate would follow. The feds would surely decide in the state's favor if they saw a tunnel already in place. Fail to build it, and the interstate system would pass Colorado by. So Johnson spent his last term as governor stumping tirelessly for the tunnel, dogging state highway officials, the state legislature, and local civic leaders everywhere to support the huge, costly project. Only by building a tunnel, Johnson insisted, could Coloradans convince the feds, flatlanders, and *themselves* that the Rockies no longer posed a barrier. Only by building a tunnel could Colorado finally conquer its topography, change its fundamental nature, and secure its coveted interstate.[74]

Others in Colorado were not so sure. Many thought it unwise to gamble on building an interstate tunnel before the interstate itself was assured. Many others thought it unfair to splurge on one project to the detriment of road needs everywhere else in the state. These were political objections; there were also technical ones. Cost versus benefit became the sticking point for the state highway technocracy, with Mark Watrous, Charlie Vail's successor as chief highway engineer, repeatedly insisting that the marginal gains from a tunnel could not justify the massive expense. Some cost estimates ran well over $20 million, and when Watrous brought in a world-renowned tunnel engineer (Ole Singstad, mastermind behind New York City's famed underriver tunnels) to study the problem, Singstad determined that a tunnel at the cheapest location would still cost $15 million. Separately, a University of Colorado engineering professor pointed out that a tunnel at that site would bring only a slight reduction in altitude, driving distance, and weather exposure compared to existing pass roads. And so, rather ironically, the idea for a Continental Divide tunnel, which Big Ed hatched to please the experts in Washington, DC, ended up antagonizing the experts in his own state.[75] And much to his fury, the eight politically appointed members of the State Highway Commission sided with the technocrats, refusing to back the project.[76]

How did Big Ed react to the technocratic naysayers? By belittling their expertise and claiming some down-home expertise of his own. In a red-meat speech to a Denver civic club in March 1956, Johnson blasted Ole Singstad as a New York aesthete—a surefire way to discredit him in front of a bunch of westerners. Singstad's expertise might apply, Big Ed sniped, "if I were planning a tunnel under the Hudson River. . . . But he has had no experience in the mountains of the West." Singstad's $15 million tunnel design was "as much out of place in our hard rock mountains as a purple robe on a truck driver." For a real man's expertise, Johnson looked to real *western* experts. "Contractors who are at present building tunnels in the West," he claimed, had assured him a tunnel could be built far more cheaply than Singstad realized.[77] Why defer to effete eastern experts when Coloradans had their own native knowledge of the land? When it came to the highway readiness of the high-country landscape, scientific certainty was very much in the eye of the booster.

To Johnson and other tunnel advocates, the technocrats' caution was cowardice, a betrayal of Colorado's frontier heritage. Were highway "experts" going to be men enough to tackle the mountains as the pioneers had done? Or would they use their sissy scientific data to try to excuse inaction? Watrous, the chief highway engineer, took an especially brutal beating in the Colorado press for his timidity. He was "not man enough" to "take on a job as big" as the tunnel, railed a Georgetown newspaper editor in one furious polemic. He had hidden behind highway-engineering statistics for too long instead of taking the bold action worthy of a westerner. "Where would the . . . cities and states of the great western empire be now," raged the editor, "if our forefathers, leaders and men of great vision had taken a traffic count and went by their findings." What Colorado needed was not a pencil-neck like Watrous but "a man with the backbone to stand up and fight, to get in

2.5 The governor vs. the technocrat. Bullish Gov. "Big Ed" Johnson (*right*) towers over his nemesis, Chief Highway Engineer Mark Watrous, on a visit to a proposed highway tunnel site at Loveland Pass. To break the barrier of the Rockies and clear the way for an interstate, Big Ed determined to blast a tunnel beneath the Continental Divide. Watrous resisted the idea, questioning the project's considerable cost. His caution enraged Johnson and other tunnel advocates, who reviled the chief engineer as a pencil-neck, too timid to take on the mountains in the spirit of the pioneers. Courtesy Denver Public Library.

there and pitch with both fists" to get the "man sized project" done.[78]

Even with science and statistics backing it up—even with the midcentury American faith in expert authority on its side—technocratic prudence could not long withstand that kind of macho fury. So just days after his own fiery speech, with political pressure mounting to get the tunnel built, Governor Johnson ordered the Highway Commission into his office, sat them down, handed them a resolution he had drafted himself, and glared at them until they voted to approve it. The resolution ordered Watrous to solicit bids for construction of a tunnel under the divide. The very next month, in April 1956, the eight highway commissioners finally declared their own support for a tunnel. Again with Johnson in the room, breathing down their necks, they endorsed the project and authorized the bonds to pay for it.[79]

It is really not too surprising that they did. After all, the commissioners were not professional engineers like Watrous. They were petty political appointees, ambitious local businessmen and boosters from cities and towns across the state. As highway officials, they could be expected (and arguably were obligated) to bridle at the tunnel's giant price tag. But as boosters, they felt much the same impulse the governor did: they too were eager to foster local and state economic growth, and they too saw highways as a means to that end. Indeed, channeling tourists into the high country had been one of the Highway Commission's top objectives for decades. A tunnel might pose problems in terms of cost and logistics. But if building it would help lure vacationers to Colorado, then the Highway Commission was inclined to support it all along.

Even with the tunnel finally approved—even with Coloradans finally resolved to overcome their "impassable wall" for once and for all—there were still several more stages in the political process before the state could have its transcontinental route. Congress would still have to increase the total mileage of the interstate system, and then federal engineers would have to earmark those extra miles for a Denver-to-Salt Lake City extension.[80] Neither was a given. When Congress passed the Interstate Highway Act in June 1956, they added far fewer miles to the system than Colorado advocates had hoped. Worse, while Coloradans had always assumed the extra miles would be theirs, the legislation did not actually allot them. So now the Coloradans found themselves competing with forty other states that also petitioned the BPR for a share.[81] Which states would get more miles became a matter of jealous debate, and federal planners took an agonizing sixteen more months to decide.

Finally, in October 1957, the BPR made the announcement Colorado boosters had yearned for, allotting 547 of the new miles to Colorado and Utah.[82] But even this good news came with a catch. Coloradans had asked for an interstate from Denver to Salt Lake, but the BPR decided the route would instead link Denver to Cove Fort, out in the sagebrush of south-central Utah. Cove Fort, a historic Mormon way station, was not even a town, let alone a major city; it had never been publicly mentioned, much less lobbied for, as a possible interstate terminus. Its stunning selection—which blindsided Utah officials and must have had their puzzled Colorado counterparts reaching for maps—was proof that federal technocrats, even while granting the precious interstate, had hardly embraced all of Colorado's justifications for it. A key factor may well have been the army's desire to have a direct emergency route from Southern California to the major cities of the Midwest. Colorado just happened to lie in between. In any case, it seems clear that Johnson's talking points about his state's strategic natural resources and recreational lands had not exactly clinched the case for the BPR.[83]

But it did not matter that Big Ed had gotten his strategy all wrong. Colorado was going to have its interstate, and that was cause for joy. Up and down the valleys of the high country, people talked excitedly of a boost to industry, or a possible revival of mining, once the interstate came. But most of all they talked of tourism. Small-town newspaper editors wrote breathlessly of the floods of tourists who would seek instead of shun the high country once the interstate arrived, once there was a bold red line where the oil-company map used to show forlorn squiggles and empty space. They wrote of the interstate linking up with local roads to carry vacationers into the region's every corner, reinvigorating its small forgotten towns.[84] "Cross country travel will be almost exclusively on the highways in this [interstate] system," wrote one editor, expressing his faith in the superhighway's supreme channeling power. "Without a designation in Colorado we could have looked to a great loss in tourist travel, while now we can be assured of a continuing growth in the tourist travel."[85] This was no mere trucking route, mine-to-market highway, or military access road. In the minds of so many boosters, the interstate's higher purpose was to put a new vacationland on the map.

BUT WHERE EXACTLY WOULD THAT VACATIONLAND BE? THE BPR'S DECISION still did not settle the question. It granted mileage for the interstate and fixed the two termini, but how to get from point A to point B remained undetermined. Coloradans would have to decide, largely for themselves, what path their new superhighway would take. Which towns would end up on the main line? Which would be left off? Where exactly would the long-awaited flood of tourists go?

The obvious choice was to funnel the flood along either U.S. 6 or U.S. 40, the only two routes that reached all the way from Denver to the Utah line. But that choice was obvious only in the sense that it was inertial: the two routes already existed, and the rivalry between them was well entrenched. In fact, as we know, neither route lent itself to the kind of high-volume, high-speed passage an interstate was meant to be—which was a big reason why federal interstate planners had snubbed western Colorado in the first place.

Neither route had been designed for long-distance travel, having instead been cobbled together from shorter stretches of road. Each route threw mighty obstacles in the motorist's way: canyons, ridges, vertiginous pass roads dating from the days of stagecoaches and buckboards. Now Illinois families in station wagons were supposed to navigate such terrain?

But that was exactly the dream that captivated people living along each route: that their lonely two-lane road might magically become a high-speed tourist conduit, erasing the physical and psychological barriers that had scared so many flatlanders away. Conventional wisdom said that towns along the interstate could expect hordes of free-spending tourists thronging every motel, campground, curio shop, gas station, and café. "Yes, Tourist Business is big business," drooled one Summit County citizen in a letter to the local paper, "and anything that can be done to promote it means business." A tunnel built to bring the interstate through Summit would "pay for itself in business many times over in just a few years." People along U.S. 40 salivated at the same thought. An interstate would "be the route selected by thousands of tourists each year," gushed a Kremmling editor (in a prediction that actually underestimated I-70's eventual channeling power). "Too much emphasis cannot be placed on the importance of united action" to make that dream a reality.[86]

Backers of both highways—business owners, members of fraternal lodges and chambers of commerce, newspaper editors, state legislators, local government leaders—hurled themselves into what promised to be the final showdown in the long-running U.S. 6 versus U.S. 40 rivalry. They petitioned the Highway Commission, lobbied the state capitol, wrote letters to newspapers, bootlicked visiting dignitaries, even staged rallies and protest caravans to Denver. Those with financial stakes in tourism took especially active roles. Larry Jump, owner of Summit County's Arapahoe Basin ski area, was one of the most vocal advocates of sending the interstate along U.S. 6, and in a letter to Governor Johnson he forthrightly admitted favoring the route because it would channel skiers his way.[87] Farther west, Aspen businessmen also banded together for U.S. 6. Only that route, they claimed, would "take care of the many more thousands of visitors who want to motor through Colorado in the summer and other thousands who plan to drive to Colorado Ski resorts in the winter."[88] Along both U.S. 6 and U.S. 40, many people looked to their highway associations—veterans of the nonstop battle for tourist dollars—for leadership.[89] For a time, in fact, motel owners and tourist boosters from Colorado's stretch of U.S. 40 basically took over the National

U.S. Highway 40 Association, turning it into a vehicle for their interstate campaign.[90]

Any decision on where to route the new interstate would first have to go through State Highway Department headquarters in Denver. And the technocrats there, like their federal counterparts, did not seem swayable by local booster slogans or promotional schemes. Advocates of U.S. 6 and U.S. 40 would have to do what Big Ed had done in his appeals to federal officials: furnish statistics and scientific data to show that their route made the most sense. Matters of topography, geology, traffic flow, and economic activity thus took center stage in the debate. Boosters on each side tried to create the impression that their corridor was objectively, scientifically, and *naturally* best suited for a superhighway.

If you look at a political map of Colorado, you might wonder why there was ever any question which way the interstate should go. U.S. 6 looks like the clear choice. Draw a straight line from Denver through Grand Junction and on to Cove Fort, and it will closely approximate the path of U.S. 6. In fact, that is exactly how one Highway 6 backer made his case: he took a Colorado map, drew a straight line west from Denver, stuck it in an envelope, and mailed it to Governor Johnson.[91] What more needed to be said? U.S. 6 was by far the closest thing to a direct route, so for that reason alone, its boosters believed, it should get the nod. It was a strong argument, bound to appeal to the highway engineers, who worshipped efficiency and were taught that if a road must stray from a straight line, there needed to be a good reason for it.[92] U.S. 40 strayed a long ways. To follow it, the interstate would have to yaw far to the northwest before tacking back to the southwest toward Glenwood Springs and Grand Junction. It would look more like a circle route than a straight line.[93]

But U.S. 6 was not so obvious a choice as it might at first appear. After all, the earth is not flat and featureless, the way it appears on a political map—certainly not in the Southern Rockies. Swap the political map for a relief map, and suddenly U.S. 40's path starts to look more feasible for a freeway. U.S. 6 had to fight straight across central Colorado's north-to-south-running mountain ranges—precisely the prospect that deterred generations of travelers from venturing that direction. By contrast, Highway 40 had to scale only one high pass (Berthoud); then, it followed river valleys and kept clear of high mountains the rest of the way to Salt Lake City. Even after BPR nixed this route by deciding to aim Interstate 70 toward Cove Fort instead of Salt Lake, U.S. 40's advocates could still propose a path topographically superior to U.S. 6's. They suggested the interstate follow Highway 40 over Berthoud Pass and then settle into the valley of the Colorado River for the rest of the way to Utah—a "water-grade" route, a natural passageway through the Rockies. Here was a powerful counterargument to Highway 6's straight-line case. It even allowed U.S. 40's advocates to play the utilitarian card: since a Colorado River route would rejoin Highway 6 east of Glenwood Springs, U.S. 40's boosters could magnanimously claim that it would serve both corridors instead of just one. Efficiency, technical simplicity, utilitarian value—a U.S. 40–Colorado River passage carried obvious appeal for the highway engineer. No less than Chief Engineer Watrous called it the "natural route" for an east-west artery.[94] Highway 40's backers took the idea and ran with it, touting their single-pass, water-level route every chance they got.[95]

If lines on maps weren't enough to persuade the technocrats, U.S. 6 and U.S. 40 boosters offered other scientific-sounding rationales too. Both sides cited traffic statistics—and in fact these became a major bone of contention, with each side claiming its route was the most heavily traveled. Conventional wisdom said Highway 40 bore more traffic. So did Highway Department data—that is, until the Highway 6 Association triumphantly announced that traffic counts had tipped in their favor, a claim Highway 40's champions hotly denied.[96] The whole debate might seem arcane (or inane), but recall that for midcentury highway engineers, serving existing (as opposed to potential) traffic demand was always the first order of business. So in the great interstate battle, having the higher traffic count was like holding the ace of spades. Highway 6 backers went further, claiming their corridor also served a larger population and economic base.[97] And it was home to strategic assets like the army's Camp Hale, the Climax molybdenum mine, and the uranium deposits around Grand Junction, they pointed out—using the same national-interest rationale Big Ed and others had presented to the BPR.[98] Backers of Highway 40 disputed or downplayed these contentions, and they played a national-interest card of their own by insinuating that the commander-in-chief himself, President Eisenhower, preferred their route.[99]

While Governor Johnson is often credited with winning the interstate for western Colorado, in fact he vastly complicated the entire issue. For one thing, though he claimed to rise above regional rivalries, he badly wanted the interstate to follow U.S. 40. For his first year back as governor, he kept his preference to himself, but in spring 1956, with the issue headed for a showdown in the legislature, he came out with guns blazing for the U.S. 40–Colorado River route. (And behind the scenes, he relentlessly pressured the State

Highway Commission to endorse U.S. 40.) Big Ed's open favoritism toward U.S. 40—the result, critics charged, of his hailing from northwestern Colorado—roiled the debate, provoking Highway 6 partisans like irascible Breckenridge editor Robert Theobald and inflaming the already heated rivalry between the two corridors.[100]

Big Ed complicated the debate even more by insisting that Colorado had to build a tunnel to win the interstate. Some doubted this was really so. The tunnel was a "Red Herring," charged one critic; Big Ed only wanted it as "a monument to himself," fumed another. Some even began to accuse the governor, who fancied himself champion of Colorado's interstate dreams, of jeopardizing the chances of winning the interstate by bogging everyone down in endless debates over where to put a tunnel.[101] But Johnson insisted on linking the two. And so, from the moment he returned as governor, the quarrel over who had the best interstate route boiled down to which route had the best tunnel site. That brought a whole new set of scientific and technical variables into play. Suddenly people along U.S. 6 and U.S. 40, from newspaper editors to ordinary citizens, found themselves getting riled up over issues like avalanche dynamics, sun exposure, and subterranean rock faulting. It was as if all the boosters in the high country had had their cerebral cortices replaced with the brains of engineers.

Far from originating with Big Ed, the possibility of boring an auto tunnel under the Continental Divide had actually begun percolating in the 1930s. At that time it was not linked to the interstate system but to an old *intra*state dream of tying remote, thinly populated western Colorado more closely to the state's populous eastern half. In the 1940s the Highway Department's favored tunnel site—in fact, the only one it seriously considered—was on U.S. 6, under Loveland Pass between Georgetown and Dillon. In 1941 Charlie Vail ordered a test bore there, and in 1947 Vail's successor, Watrous, called for bids to drill the real thing.[102] But the Loveland site kept running into problems. Vail's test bore revealed unstable, fractured rock, spooking engineers, and Watrous's call netted just one unacceptably pricey bid. It was then that the cost-cautious Watrous cooled on the whole tunnel concept. U.S. 6 boosters fought to keep it alive, hastily assembling a Loveland tunnel lobbying group. Area mining companies donated expertise, putting their in-house engineers to work drafting new tunnel designs. But the unstable rock got the best of these experts too. When the Loveland Tunnel Association released its report in April 1948, the best it could propose was a one-lane tunnel with stoplights at each end. Lamely the group insisted that the single lane could handle the expected traffic until such time as the state could afford a second bore. But the one-lane configuration violated federal highway standards, and federal officials nixed the plan.

At that point, highway technocrats in Denver considered the tunnel idea dormant, if not dead. But up in the high country, the tunnel battle was just beginning. For the first time, the Loveland tunnel's apparent demise raised the possibility that U.S. 40 might get the coveted passage instead of U.S. 6. Alarmed, Highway 6's boosters scrambled to keep that from happening. Some clung to the Loveland Pass proposal: throughout the early 1950s, delegations from Highway 6 counties raised the Loveland tunnel issue repeatedly before the State Highway Commission.[103] Other Highway 6 backers looked for new sites, with most of them latching onto the Straight Creek location just north of Loveland Pass, so called because a tunnel there would take motorists under 12,477-foot Mount Trelease and disgorge them at Straight Creek's headwaters in Summit County on the other side.

Meanwhile, boosters along U.S. 40 started dreaming up tunnel plans that would channel travelers their way. Some wanted to take the Moffat Tunnel between Boulder and Grand County, built for trains in the 1920s, and expand it for cars and trucks. Another group fed off the hoopla surrounding the Denver-Boulder Turnpike, unveiled in 1952 as Colorado's first modern high-speed expressway. The group proposed to extend the turnpike beyond Boulder, burrow it through the Front Range under an obscure old wagon road called Devil's Thumb Pass, and have it dump drivers onto U.S. 40 near Granby (whose boosters, not coincidentally, hatched this particular scheme).[104] But the idea that won the most support among U.S. 40's advocates was to bore a tunnel somewhere around Berthoud Pass. In the 1950s, boosters proposed several different tunnel configurations in the general vicinity of the pass, each aimed at cutting off the highest, iciest part of the pass road. Of course, each of these proposed tunnels would steer the interstate along U.S. 40 instead of U.S. 6.

By 1953, prospective tunnel sites littered the mountains west of Denver like so many nineteenth-century mining claims. Each site had its ardent backers, who, like latter-day prospectors, told anyone who would listen that their hole in the ground held the key to the prosperity of the entire high country, even the entire state. But hype soon gave way to cold, hard science. Watrous slashed the list of locations down to the four most realistic and hired Ole Singstad to inspect them from the steely perspective of the civil engineer. Two of the tunnel sites Singstad analyzed (Loveland and Straight

Creek) would channel motorists along U.S. 6; the other two (Devil's Thumb and the Jones Pass site near Berthoud Pass) favored U.S. 40.

And so the battle lines were drawn: advocates of U.S. 40 closed ranks behind their two surviving possibilities; U.S. 6's champions lined up behind theirs. Each side called for a fair, objective analysis—while maintaining that such an analysis must inevitably favor them. U.S. 6 would be the clear choice, the Highway 6 Association predicted, so long as the decision was based on a "true and accurate" investigation "not dictated by any group or interests." Not so fast, answered Maurice Leckenby, editor of the paper in Steamboat Springs, a Highway 40 town. Once highway officials had "all the facts," and providing they did "not allow anything to sway the selection," they would surely conclude (as Leckenby had) that U.S. 40 was the "logical route."[105] Both sides seemed to be reading from the same playbook: accuse your rivals of pursuing a narrow booster scheme, while positioning yourself on the side of the objective, scientific truth.

This set a nasty trap for the technocrats. Even if they had been able to carry out a truly objective analysis of the tunnel sites, there was no way they could please both sides. Whenever the engineers publicized their findings, they faced charges of incompetence, bias, or both. Watrous, never popular to begin with, bore the brunt of it. When he bridled at the cost of a Loveland tunnel, U.S. 6 partisans impugned his manhood; when he refused to sign off on Straight Creek, the hot-tempered Breckenridge editor Robert Theobald called him a "complete and unanswerable dictator" in the mold of "Hitler, Mussolini, and Hirohito." On the U.S. 40 side, boosters seethed at the practice of investing first in roads with higher traffic counts—something they had favored when the counts favored U.S. 40—and Leckenby, the Steamboat Springs editor, dismissed the tunnel-site studies as "a waste of time" because "the mind of the highway department is made up beforehand."[106]

Even the nationally respected Singstad had his expertise second-guessed. When he completed his four-site study in January 1954, he delighted U.S. 6 backers by ruling out the two sites that favored U.S. 40—Devil's Thumb and Jones Pass—and declaring Straight Creek the best option, based on traffic volume, geological conditions, construction and maintenance costs.[107] U.S. 40 partisans responded by flinging out two more tunnel sites near Berthoud Pass. Singstad studied them and rejected them too. But instead of accepting Singstad's analysis, some U.S. 40 boosters faulted it, insisting that his data actually showed there should be no tunnel at all. Colorado would be better off, Maurice Leckenby wrote, if it took its $24 million (Singstad's cost estimate for a Straight Creek tunnel) and spent it on widening and straightening existing pass roads.[108]

Leckenby even began to question the basic assumption that a tunnel would boost tourism. "We don't believe tourists are going to get much excited about going several miles underground," he offered, "when they can cross a scenic mountain pass." It made no sense, agreed one of his readers, for Colorado to spend hundreds of thousands of dollars a year to advertise its scenery and then spend millions more to tunnel people beneath it. What sightseer would want to listen to a bus driver "expound the beauties of nature [the tourists] are missing while they ride through a hole in the ground under artificial light"?[109]

Sour grapes? Sure, but there was more to it than that. In fact, the U.S. 40 backers were broaching a potentially serious critique of the interstate juggernaut. Perhaps, they were suggesting, the brute-force approach to highway building might not be the best way to lure tourists after all. Perhaps it was wrong to assume, as rural western boosters and highway engineers usually did, that the most direct, highest-volume, highest-speed highway was always the best one. Perhaps such a road might clash in some ways with the scenic resources of the high-country landscape.

Leckenby was not the only one voicing concern. The leaders of two of Colorado's mightiest highway lobbies—Club 20 and Rocky Mountain Motorists, the state chapter of the AAA—questioned the brute-force approach too. In 1954 Club 20 chief Preston Walker suggested that "no tunnel"—no matter where it was driven—"will make the mountains look like Kansas flatlands to Kansas tourists." And in 1957 Rocky Mountain Motorists president Clarence Werthan went further, wondering whether an ultramodern superhighway might in fact "seriously harm" high-country tourism by tempting travelers to speed right through the region instead of stopping. Colorado, Werthan warned, would have "a major selling job on its hands trying to convince" passers-through "to leave the superhighway long enough to enjoy some of the state's travel attractions."[110] In the rural West of the 1950s, it was rare to hear such discouraging words—the nearly universal assumption was that highway improvements could do only good, never harm. (Indeed, many Club 20 members publicly repudiated Walker's remarks.)[111] But for a moment at least, two influential boosters had stopped to ask whether the heavy-handed highway-building approach was inevitably the way to go. And Werthan in particular, like Leckenby, had raised the possibility that such an approach might clash with efforts to package a scenic, recreational, relaxing tourist retreat. Tentative as they were, these questions prefigured a much broader and bitterer environmental critique of I-70 that would take shape as the interstate itself did over the next several years.

As late as 1957, though, it was still up in the air whether there would even be an interstate through the high country. In fact, given all their squabbling over when or whether to build a tunnel, and where, it is a wonder Coloradans ended up getting their road at all. The State Highway Commission finally caved to Governor Johnson in 1956, endorsing the tunnel project, only to see the state legislature refuse to fund it. The legislature reversed itself in 1957 (with Big Ed now retired from office, working the halls as a citizen-lobbyist), only to see all the construction bids come in unaffordably high. As of fall 1957, the Continental Divide still loomed, as enduring a barrier as ever.[112] But when the Bureau of Public Roads decided in October to give Colorado its interstate anyway, it also made a tunnel much likelier, since now the state would not have to shoulder the daunting cost. (Under the Interstate Highway Act, federal funding covered 90 percent of the construction costs for any road designated an interstate.)

Still, where exactly would the road go? Had Johnson still been governor, I-70's location might have been decided (or delayed) by more warring between Highways 6 and 40. But Big Ed's successor, Governor Stephen McNichols, was a different sort of politician. He hailed from Denver, so he had less truck with high-country booster rivalries. And he had made his name as something of a long-range planner and modernizer of state government. In fact, as a state senator in the early 1950s, he had chaired a high-profile commission to professionalize, systematize, and centralize Colorado's highway policy making.[113] Now, as governor, he applied that same technocratic inclination to the question of Interstate 70's location. Grandly declaring that the decision must be "completely free of bias" (and cleverly screening himself from the political fallout that would inevitably greet it), "Governor Steve" brought in another New York City engineering firm to study the options and decide where the tunnel, and the rest of I-70 west of Denver, would go.[114]

So in summer 1959 technicians from the E. Lionel Pavlo Engineering Co. fanned out along U.S. 40, U.S. 6, and some minor roads in between, measuring traffic flows, shooting aerial photographs, drilling rock samples, calculating slope gradients, and gathering other data to take back east for analysis. Rumors swirled about the route Pavlo would choose and where (or whether) he would agree a tunnel was needed. But if the calm that prevailed in the editorial pages is any indication, most local boosters had finally resigned themselves to a decision that was out of their hands. Even the strident Robert Theobald seemed tired of being strident. "An eastern engineering firm is going to approach the problem without sectional interests," he purred, "and is going to make a determination based on the shortest route which can be constructed at a cost that is not prohibitive."[115] (The words were as sanguine as they were sedate: Theobald remained confident that an objective, expert analysis would favor his route.)

Pavlo submitted his recommendations to the State Highway Commission in April 1960, and the commission endorsed them on the spot.[116] The winning route, which the BPR approved soon after, was indeed Theobald's U.S. 6. The new interstate would head almost directly west from Denver on Highway 6, burrow under the Continental Divide at the Straight Creek tunnel site, and then continue to parallel U.S. 6 west, through Summit and Eagle Counties and on into Glenwood Springs. Grand and Routt Counties, heart of the U.S. 40 corridor, were left entirely off the interstate.

The Pavlo route study, long buried in the footnotes of Colorado history, bears exhuming. In its pages we can see how the engineering mentality of the 1950s melded with the booster agendas of the day—and not least with the physical features of the land itself—to give shape to the Interstate 70 corridor, the high country as most visitors know it now. Not that Pavlo himself would have recognized his own work in this way. Shunning the hyperbolic slogans and splashy action words of the booster-advertiser, his report was coldly passive, its logic relentlessly methodical. Political and promotional considerations were ignored; conclusions were based on technical variables, like geological conditions, federally mandated highway standards, numerical measures of "user benefit," and projected construction costs. The report was structured so its conclusion seemed authoritative and inevitable: U.S. 6 was not just the better route, it was the only possible route.

On the first page, Pavlo settled the question of a tunnel under the Continental Divide. There must be one, he flatly stated, or the highway could not meet federal design standards for interstates. The logical next step was to narrow down the tunnel possibilities. Three of five proposed locations were quickly dismissed due to faulted rock, landslide and avalanche vulnerability, or both. That left one tunnel site for each corridor: Straight Creek for Highway 6, and the Vasquez or Stanley Mountain site near Berthoud Pass for Highway 40. The rest of the report assessed these two options and their corresponding corridors, weighing topographical, economic, demographic, and traffic-volume criteria. In the end Straight Creek and U.S. 6 prevailed for

MAP 3.

Routes studied for
possible interstate
location

Even after Cove
Fort, Utah, was set as
Interstate 70's western
terminus, the path
the interstate would
follow through the high
country was anything
but a foregone conclu-
sion. Engineer E. Lionel
Pavlo studied no fewer
than eight possible
routes, including seven
proposed tunnel sites,
all shown here. After
narrowing the choice
down to Route B (which
would favor U.S. 40
interests) and Route H
(which had I-70 mostly
following U.S. 6), Pavlo
recommended the latter
in his final report in
1960.

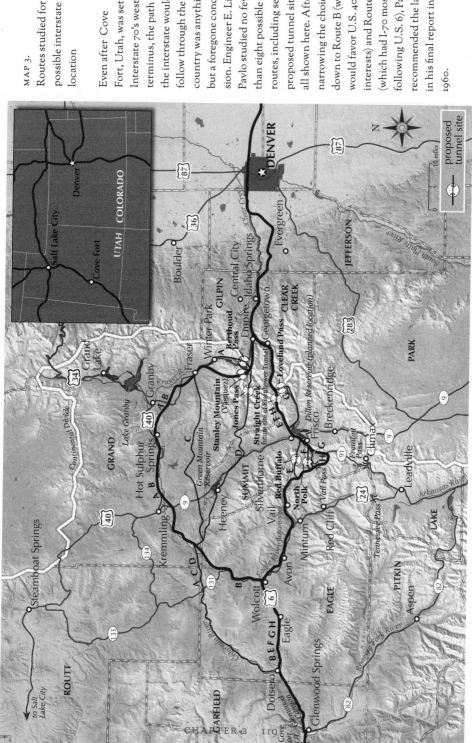

two reasons: an interstate along that route would cost about $55 million less to build; and it would yield a "road user benefit ratio" more than three times as large as an interstate along U.S. 40.[117]

This classically technocratic reasoning outweighed all the local social, economic, and environmental concerns that had filled the local newspapers for the past decade, to the point of ignoring them entirely. Small towns where high-country people made their homes and livelihoods, Pavlo coolly dismissed in a few lines, noting that "there are no large concentrations [of population or economic activity] to be served . . . which would have a significant effect on the location of the proposed Interstate Highway." Nor did mountain residents count for much when it came to the foremost consideration of the highway engineer: traffic demand. "It was concluded," stated the report in the scientific passive, "that there were no overwhelming local demands or conditions" that might sway the routing decision one way or another.[118] And so all the frantic lobbying by county commissioners, chambers of commerce, and Club 20; all the feverish editorializing by local advocates like Maurice Leckenby and Robert Theobald; all the impassioned fretting about the economic fate of Dillon, Eagle, Kremmling, Georgetown, Granby, Steamboat Springs—in the end the expert deciding the interstate route paid them no heed at all.

Pavlo was well aware that wherever the interstate went, economic and population growth would surely tag along. In fact, he forecasted I-70's mighty channeling effect with uncanny accuracy. His report included a map predicting the "areas of influence" that would result from the interstate following one route or the other. If it followed U.S. 6, Pavlo predicted, central Summit and eastern Eagle Counties would lie squarely in its area of influence; Jackson and eastern Grand Counties would be shut out.[119] Anyone who has seen condominium clutter around Breckenridge, Frisco, Silverthorne, and Vail—and contrasted it with the windblown sagebrush expanses of Middle and North Park—knows just how prescient that map turned out to be. But there is no evidence that this prediction factored at all into Pavlo's decision. He was an "impartial expert," not supposed to favor one county's booster dreams over another's—especially when, from his perspective as an engineer, all the counties in question were statistically insignificant.

But if Pavlo could ignore the local boosters, he could not ignore what made them so starry-eyed: the burgeoning tourist industry. His report acknowledged the industry's mounting importance, calling recreational amenities "probably Colorado's single greatest natural resource." (In contrast, he curtly dismissed the old extractive industries: mining, he said, had "diminished to a point where [it is] neither an economic nor transportation consideration insofar as this study is concerned.") Pavlo also made a point of tabulating skier-visit trends (with data supplied by the Forest Service) to show that more skiers would use the interstate if it followed along U.S. 6.[120] Ski areas and other tourist attractions were actually not major factors shaping Pavlo's route decision. But he did agree with the boosters on this basic idea: that meeting the demand for recreational access would be an important function of the new interstate.

Even more, he recognized that Coloradans would judge his report not just by its engineering expertise but by how well it meshed with their efforts to boost the tourist trade. After all, as the much-maligned Mark Watrous could attest, engineers could not count on unlimited public deference. Their authority still relied on the perception that their expertise was serving the ends of economic progress—which, in the Colorado high country, increasingly meant the growth of tourism. So Pavlo made a point of assuring Coloradans that the road he had designed would boost tourism by complementing the mountains' scenic grandeur. "Varying horizontal and vertical alignment and median," he wrote in the unpretty cant of his profession, "will preserve the natural beauty of the terrain and provide a route of exceptional recreational attraction." Interstate 70 would be "one of the most scenic roads in the nation."[121]

These were revealing words. They showed an engineer keenly aware that the highway had to fit into the political, not just physical, landscape. Pavlo's assurances that I-70 would augment the scenery and lure vacationers were aimed at all those local and state boosters who fetishized the interstate as a means to mass tourism. Significantly, these assurances appeared not in the dense, technical body of Pavlo's report but in the executive summary—the one section that reporters, boosters, and others looking for a quick overview were likeliest to read, react to, and mine for what we would now call sound bites. So even though scenery and other recreational considerations cropped up infrequently in the rest of the report, and seem not to have swayed the report's conclusions very much if at all, Pavlo used his executive summary to tell Coloradans what he figured they most wanted to hear: that if they followed his recommendations, their interstate would function brilliantly as a conduit for the vacation trade.

As for fitting into the physical landscape of tourism, Pavlo had that covered too. Not that he made special accommodations for scenic features—far from it. His plans called for altering the landscape more than working around it. If a creek meandered where Pavlo wanted the interstate, he proposed to straighten the creek; if a hill bulged into the right-of-way, he proposed to slice it off. This squared with the mantra of the midcentury engineer: safety and efficiency first. But engineers of the time also believed that a highway designed to be safe and efficient would by nature look nice. As one road engineering textbook put it, "Good appearance is . . . intimately integrated in almost every element of highway design, for whatever contributes to safety and efficiency becomes inherently more attractive." It is worth recalling that the immediate predecessor of the freeway was the parkway, the charming scenic pleasure drive of the early auto age. It has been said that freeways borrowed functional features from parkways (restricted points of access, separation of cross traffic by grade) and nothing else. But in the sweeping curves of a freeway and the framing of spectacular views along the right-of-way, men like Pavlo saw themselves perpetuating the aesthetic qualities of the old parkways. Later critics would vigorously disagree, but midcentury highway engineers felt supremely confident that their constructions actually enhanced the scenic value of the great American countryside.[122]

In any case, Pavlo struck exactly the right chords with his route study. Of course the friends of Sidney Six greeted it with particular jubilation. Some Highway 40 advocates were predictably bitter: in Kremmling, the *Middle Park Times* rather meanly pointed out that while the State Highway Commission had approved Pavlo's route, federal officials had not, and there was no money to build the interstate anyway. But others, like Maurice Leckenby in Steamboat Springs, bowed to the technocratic mystique. An impartial expert had made up his mind, Leckenby wrote, so Highway 40's backers must now accept it. It would only seem like "impeding progress to continue the fight."[123]

"Progress" did indeed begin to flow along U.S. 6—even before Interstate 70 took physical form. Federal funds were not appropriated for construction until 1962; the first two lanes of the Straight Creek Tunnel (by then renamed for Eisenhower) would not open until 1973, the other two (named for Big Ed Johnson) not until 1979. All the same, within two years of Pavlo's decision, two new resort projects were already under way in Summit and eastern Eagle Counties, exactly the area of influence Pavlo had projected for the new interstate. In Summit County, a Kansas City lumber company bought land around Breckenridge, laid out several second-home subdivisions, built rental properties, and, in December 1961, opened the first stage of a ski resort. The enterprise, reported the *Denver Post*, was premised on the knowledge that

2.6 Nestling into the natural setting. Boring the Eisenhower Tunnel beneath the Continental Divide took eleven years, cost the 2012 equivalent of nearly a billion dollars, took the lives of nine workers, and ripped nearly 2 million cubic yards of rock from the innards of Mount Trelease. It would be hard to find a more brazen assault on natural topography in the interstate highway system. Yet as this postcard view suggests, the completed tunnel quickly came to seem like part of the landscape, and it is difficult now to imagine the geography of the high country without the tunnel and Interstate 70. Courtesy Sanborn Ltd.

Interstate 70 would soon make it much easier for visitors to drive in from Denver.[124] Meanwhile, just over Vail Pass in Eagle County, a group of investors began drumming up capital to develop another ski area along a stretch of U.S. 6 where there was no existing town at all. It would be the largest ski resort in North America, they told prospective investors, and it would boast unmatched automobile accessibility via soon-to-be Interstate 70. That venture, of course, was Vail. More than just a ski area, it would quickly become the centerpiece of what a 1971 University of Colorado business-school study admiringly called "virtually a pilot program for a new concept," namely, "the conversion of an entire area into a balanced recreation region."[125]

If Interstate 70—or merely the promise of its future existence—could have that kind of transformative effect on Summit and Eagle Counties, it worked the opposite magic on counties along Highway 40. The same 1971 study that cheered the "recreation region" emerging around I-70 called the U.S. 40 counties "remote," noting that they "[could not] hope to compete successfully" when it came to visitor accessibility.[126] A significant new ski area did open near Steamboat Springs in 1963—Storm Mountain, soon renamed Mount Werner and now called Steamboat Ski Resort—but Steamboat Springs already enjoyed renown as a long-established ski town. Otherwise, the 1960s and 1970s, which brought several new megaresorts to the I-70/U.S. 6 corridor, saw no major new resorts spring up along U.S. 40.[127] Even today, while there are stirrings of Summit County–style development in eastern Grand County, Highway 40's corridor continues to draw far less tourist traffic and investment than I-70's. Ironically, another kind of traffic has gravitated toward U.S. 40: that in illegal drugs. Here the interstate's channeling effect worked in reverse: the more crowded I-70's corridor became, the more methamphetamine makers and drug runners were lured to U.S. 40 by its remoteness, lighter law enforcement, and abundant open space.[128] Not quite what Highway 40's boosters had in mind when they aimed to make the route western Colorado's main thoroughfare—but a poignant reminder of highways' power to rearrange geography all the same.

TODAY'S INTERSTATE 70 CAN SEEM STRANGELY NATURAL. THE WAY ITS sweeping curves trace the contours of slopes and valleys, and its rises and falls echo the relief of the Rockies themselves, it seems almost to fit itself to the land. We are lulled into forgetting the massive reordering it took to shoehorn this giant serpent of asphalt, concrete, rebar, and reflective paint into the mountainscape. Driving I-70 west of Idaho Springs, how many look up to see the artificial cliffs looming above the roadway, where the toes of mountains were amputated to make way for the highway, the exposed innards bandaged in steel netting to keep loose rock from raining down on motorists below?[129] Cruising through Tenmile Canyon west of Frisco, how many realize that the lovely creek cascading alongside has been relocated and forced through seven artificial channels, totaling three miles, to make room for I-70?[130] There are many other examples: shelves blasted out of mountainsides, wetlands drained or corseted by culverts, trees cleared and elk migration paths severed to make room for hundred-foot-wide rights-of-way. Such heavy-handed interventions obliterate natural obstacles to our motion, doing all the dirty work and excusing us from ever noticing it has been done. The highway builder's artifice obscures its own artificiality, freeing us to feel *closer* to nature. We follow the road's smooth, sinuous lead

Snowy Peaks of the Continental Divide   Photo by Bill Sanborn

2.7 High country entrée. Interstate 70 became part of the scenic clichés, nowhere so much
as this frequently photographed vantage point at Genesee Park, twenty miles west of
Denver. Having driven the engine-straining five miles up Mount Vernon Canyon, motorists
crested one final rise and were rewarded with this, their first panoramic view of Colorado's
trademark snow-capped peaks. I-70 curves enticingly off into the distance, looking every bit
the scenic, easy-to-drive superhighway, ushering visitors effortlessly (or so the advertising
had it) into the heart of the high country vacationland. Courtesy Sanborn Ltd.

deep into the once-impenetrable high country, where we find ourselves amid
forested slopes and soaring peaks. Assuming the traffic is reasonably light
and the road surface clear—admittedly, not givens on I-70—we can turn our
focus from the act of moving and lose ourselves in the natural grandeur gliding by.[131] By blurring the line between nature and technology, I-70 is doing
exactly what its creators intended it to.

Both key groups behind the interstate's inception—the boosters who
lobbied for it and the engineers who designed it—had strong reasons for
wanting the interstate to fit its natural setting. Engineers believed the design
of any highway should emerge scientifically—not just from traffic-flow numbers and other statistics, but also from careful analysis of the underlying and
overhanging soil, rock, vegetation, water, and weather. And though they
famously valued highways more on utilitarian than aesthetic grounds, it was
an article of faith among midcentury highway engineers that an expertly
designed road would be "inherently more attractive" as a matter of course.

That is certainly how Lionel Pavlo conceived of his I-70 design. Meanwhile, from tourist boosters' viewpoint, it is fair to say that having the interstate complement the mountains was the primary reason for having it at all. Instead of overwhelming its natural surroundings, boosters really believed it would enhance the landscape's recreational qualities, making scenery and recreational amenities more easily accessible and making the high country seem a natural place for a vacation.[132]

The parcelization of the landscape was one major legacy. More and more, the popular geography of the high country consisted of rest stops and gateway towns, recreation regions and tourist corridors, each set apart from its surroundings by the services or amenities it promised the vacationer, each defined by its position relative to the highway network. In this sense, perhaps it is not quite right to say highways packaged the high country for tourism. Better to say they created a patchwork of packaged landscapes, scattered across the wider mountainous expanse west of Denver. Just as advertising prodded tourists to value certain natural qualities over others, highways tempted tourists to value certain places over others. The upshot, once again, was a growing popular enthusiasm for the high-country environment—but an uneven and fragmented one. That would matter greatly as enthusiasm for the environment turned political.

Eventually the ultimate packaged landscape would be the Interstate 70 corridor itself—its backbone a superhighway that defied nature to put nature on display, that pushed aside forests and streams and sliced through some of Colorado's highest ranges to link valleys and watersheds formerly walled off from one another, stringing them together into a new tourist region where none had existed a quarter century before. And because tourist boosting was woven into this corridor's very conception and construction, Coloradans were committing that slice of the high country not just to large-scale tourism but to a type of tourist who was automobile-centered, who liked their scenic wonders and outdoor adventures to come with a dose of automobile-era comfort and convenience. It was not just a new physical landscape the highway builders and boosters were making. It was also a landscape of the popular imagination—one with a key role to play in defining new approaches to the tourist business, new lifestyles centered on outdoor recreation, and ultimately a new postwar culture of nature.

CHAPTER 3

Our Big Backyard

AS THE STORY GOES, EARL EATON, AN EAGLE COUNTY NATIVE AND SOME-
time ski-area, mine, and construction worker, accidentally "discovered"
the legendary mountain while prospecting for uranium. It was the mid-
1950s, and Eaton had heard the buzz that Eagle County might be the next
uranium hot spot. It wasn't, according to his Geiger counter. But while
traipsing around the White River National Forest on the west side of Vail
Pass, Eaton found something else: a sprawling, loaf-shaped mountain, its
north face wooded in lodgepole pine, aspen, and spruce, and its south face
sculpted into a series of spacious, sun-soaked basins, nearly bare of trees. It
suddenly struck Eaton that he had just stumbled across some of the world's
most spectacular ski terrain. So he shared his discovery with Pete Seibert,
his boss at a nearby ski area—and the vision for Vail was born.

The story is not entirely true. Eaton was not looking for uranium, he
later admitted, and the mountain was no sudden discovery; as a local, he
had known of it for years.[1] In fact Seibert was not even the first person
he told about it. By the time the two men met, Eaton had already tried to
interest several others in developing the mountain, including a Denver &
Rio Grande Western Railroad executive. It is true that Eaton showed the
place to Seibert in 1957 and that Seibert, a ski-area manager, former racing champion, and veteran of the Tenth Mountain Division, agreed it was
prime ski terrain. But even Seibert was not instantly sold on developing it.
He and Eaton scouted several other sites before deciding the first one was
best. After some difficulty, they got approval from the U.S. Forest Service,

which granted Seibert a use permit in 1959 and that same year put Eaton and Seibert's mountain toward the top of a thirty-year master plan for developing skiing in Colorado's national forests.[2] By that time Seibert was already on to the next step: raising capital and buying real estate. He recruited a small group of partners and began purchasing ranchland at the base of the mountain, along the banks of Gore Creek. Then he barnstormed around the country to drum up the money he would need to make Earl Eaton's mountain a resort.[3]

Here was a case study of what could happen when commercial leisure gave new value to nature and new identity to place. No one had ever paid much attention to this mountain before. No one had even bothered to give it a name. There was no gold or silver (or uranium) and not much marketable timber, especially on those treeless south-facing bowls. There *was* a lot of snow, but that only served to hinder human activity for most of every winter and spring. The mountain, in short, was close to worthless from a traditional resource point of view. But the postwar leisure boom made landscapes look different. Now snow was a valuable commodity, treeless bowls a potentially priceless asset. And with this newfound worth, an anonymous lump of topography finally merited a name. In 1959 Seibert and his partners decided to call the mountain after nearby Vail Pass, thinking the name short and catchy, the kind that would easily lodge in consumers' minds. In other words, Vail, more than just a name, was a brand name from the beginning, leisure marketing intertwined with the very labeling of the land.[4]

Vail's corporate vision, and its pitch to investors, emphasized "natural competitive advantages"—the foremost, of course, being ski terrain. Vail Mountain was a stupendous playground of powdery snow, with a north-side vertical drop of more than three thousand feet. Seibert envisioned a dazzling variety of ski trails on that side, snaking for miles through the trees, from "delightful bunny runs" to "heart-stopping vertical drops," in one reporter's words. On the south side, the "huge expanse of natural bowls" would give skiers "the primeval thrill" of plunging into "a vast alpine paradise" of untracked snow.[5] But topography and snow were not Vail's only "natural competitive advantages." Equally important, Seibert realized, was the resort's geographic location—namely, the fact that it sat right on U.S. Highway 6. The highway put the mountain just two and a half hours from Denver—and thanks to the Pavlo report, U.S. 6 was about to become Interstate 70, which would make the drive faster and easier still. Vail, in other words, was positioned for maximum automobile access. When Seibert and

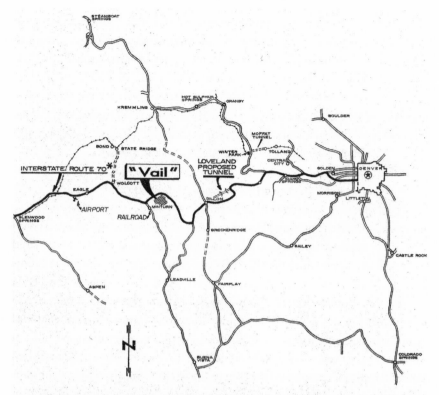

LOCATION of " VAIL"in COLORADO

3.1 The economic logic of the interstate. This map, which Pete Seibert and his partners
showed prospective investors in Vail, graphically connected the planned resort's profitability to its location on the future Interstate 70. Courtesy Vail Resorts, Inc.

his partners were going about the country drumming up investors, so crucial was this point to their sales pitch that they had little maps printed on
the flip side of their business cards, showing the future resort in relation to
the future interstate.[6]

To call Vail's advantages "natural" is misleading, though. Even with the
naturally occurring snow, glades, and bowls, it would take massive interventions—trail cutting, bulldozing, lift installing, snow grooming—to
make the mountain skiable by any but expert standards. And of course

there is nothing much natural about automobile accessibility. Highway 6 and Interstate 70 owed their locations not just to natural topography but to decades of lobbying and wrangling, surveying and engineering. Before the 1940 completion of Highway 6 over Vail Pass, the Gore Creek Valley had been one of the least accessible, remoter corners of the high country. But once in place, the highway became integral to people's sense of geography. So to Seibert, his investors, and eventual customers, it would define Vail's allegedly perfect location as surely as ski terrain and snow.

Natural features were not enough. As Vail's sudden, spectacular appearance shows, nature had to be enhanced, defanged, and rendered easily reachable if it were to appeal to most postwar leisure-seekers. As unlikely as it may seem, the die was cast by the massive proliferation of suburbia going on during those same years. Suburban settings were carefully constructed to appeal to mainstream, middle-class tastes in landscape. The ideal suburban landscape was open, anti-urban, pretty, and picturesque. It was a little bit Romantic, and maybe a little bit rough or rustic, but still fundamentally safe. And it lent itself to wholesome, all-family outdoor leisure that was casual, convenient, and accessible by car. Attracting the masses of (mostly) middle-class vacationers meant appealing to these essentially suburban tastes in outdoor leisure and landscape. This, then, became the task of tourist developers in Vail and everywhere else: to manufacture settings that were suburban in nature, that were *suburban nature*, so vacationers would feel at home.

That would become the defining nature of the vacationland: its suburbanness. And it took new infrastructure—like lodges and lifts at Vail or motels, restaurants, trails, and artificially improved fishing streams in other parts of the high country—to make it so. Just as Highways 6 and 40 and Interstate 70 put the high country on the main traffic line, Vail's development and thousands of smaller acts of infrastructure building brought the high country into the mainstream of postwar American recreational culture. Again, a variety of private- and public-sector actors at the local, state, and national levels were involved, collaborating and coordinating their efforts loosely or not at all, often competing with each other. But in practical effect, all their piecemeal efforts pointed toward a single goal: bit by bit, they all worked to make this rugged, remote, once-forbidding section of Colorado feel to middle-class tourists more like home. It was not a huge leap, then, for some visitors to actually *make* it home. The ultimate effect of building places like Vail was to lay the groundwork for some people to make the vacationland the basis for permanent living—living based on leisure-oriented ways of consuming the outdoors: a tourist way of life.

PROMOTIONAL BROCHURES MADE THE HIGH COUNTRY SEEM NATURE-made for recreation. It teemed with fish and game, sunny days, and scenic delights. It was a "playground," a "wonderland," a "vacationland"—words that conflated leisure with the landscape's very creation. Some promotional literature put it almost providentially. "Man could not ask," began one brochure, "nor Nature conceive a more glorious vacationland than Colorado."[7] (Or recall Friedl Pfeifer envisioning Aspen as a ski resort: "God must have created it just for this.") In truth, the playground was no more natural than the highway corridor. It too relied heavily on manipulation and outright manufacture. Attractions that seemed just to be "out there," furnished by nature for all to enjoy, had in fact been carefully packaged for tourists.

"Packaging" might seem a strange word in this context, but it underscores the essential connection between recreational development and the wider consumer culture. To make theirs a mainstream, mass-demand product, the producers and promoters of recreation adhered to the same basic strategy as their contemporaries who were busy making and marketing cars, kitchen appliances, cigarettes, or breakfast cereal: they tried to make their products seem exciting even while aiming them squarely at consumers' comfort zone. In modifying the landscape to make places for leisure, they enhanced what seemed thrilling about the outdoors, while making sure the thrill would demand little risk, inconvenience, or surprise on the consumer's part.[8]

Take fishing. Colorado was already known for trout fishing in Victorian times, but back then it was chiefly a connoisseur's sport. Boosters after 1945 made a concerted effort to broaden its appeal. It was not just more tourist dollars they were angling for; it was also the spread of those dollars into more remote, less prosperous parts of the state. Fishermen did not tend to cluster in already-developed resort centers, parks, and tourist corridors the way most other vacationers did. Instead, they dispersed more widely, stopping and staying in smaller, remoter towns, patronizing local businesses for food, gas, tackle, and motel rooms. So luring fishermen seemed a good way to bring tourist revenue to communities that might otherwise not see much of it.[9] Small-town boosters, sportsmen's clubs, local conservation groups, and federal agencies like the Forest Service all worked to promote fishing after 1945, but state publicists and state fish managers took the lead.

One way to popularize fishing was to distill it, like mountain scenery, into a set of easily digestible verbal and visual clichés. "Tumbling trout streams" and other stock phrases began multiplying in Colorado tourist literature after 1945, and so did pictures of people happily casting lines or reeling in fish. The State Highway Department ran such an image in every annual edition of the official state highway map from the 1940s through the mid-1960s. All the pictures were composed the same way: in the foreground, a brightly dressed fisherman (a red-checked shirt worked best, or white for high contrast); in the middle ground, sparkling sapphire water; and in the distance, a deep-green forest, rugged purple peaks, and the azure high-country sky. It amounted to another logo for the state, another instantly recognizable image that linked Colorado to leisure in consumers' heads. (And whenever newspapers and magazines ran wire photos of President Eisenhower casting flies in St. Louis Creek, it was like free product placement for the Colorado vacation trade.)

Another favorite tactic was to take nature ideals that anglers had long associated with their sport—ideals rooted in Romanticism and in the Rooseveltian quest for manhood in the wild—and translate them into the language of advertising.[10] So there was the feeling of tranquility at being outside, the "timeless serenity," as an AAA guidebook put it, "beneath a blue sky in pine-scented quiet." There was Romantic awe, the sense of being overwhelmed by settings "so picturesque," said Colorado Wonderland, "that 'fish taking' often becomes a secondary reward to the breathtaking scenery." And there was the virile thrill of the hunt itself. State publicity told of "the struggle between man and fighting trout," the adventure of testing oneself against nature. In brochures, lure books, and ads (the last usually appearing in magazines with strongly male readerships, like Field and Stream, Outdoor Life, and Sports Illustrated), copywriters bragged of Colorado's "lusty trout" (a phrase taken from Tennyson), its "Big, Scrappy, Mountain Trout," the "roughest, gamest trout you'll find anywhere." Snagging one of these "Fighting Rainbows" was "an experience you will always remember," promised one brochure: "A bolt of lightning strikes your line. . . . suddenly a flashing, twisting Rainbow breaks water in a spectacular leap and seems to hang suspended in mid-air before thrashing back into the churning stream. The battle has begun . . . a wild, exciting battle that you will relive many times."[11] If you asked Madison Avenue to rewrite one of Theodore Roosevelt's hunting stories, it would sound a lot like this. Indeed, the state publicity committee was playing on much the same urge for manly invigoration, for the "strenuous life," that had driven turn-of-the-century men like Roosevelt into the field. But in these ads, fly-fishing was not about combating "over-civilization" or struggling to save the Anglo-Saxon race, as Roosevelt and others had seen themselves doing. Instead, it fed postwar consumers' appetite for escape and emotional thrills—and postwar Coloradans' hunger for more tourist dollars.[12]

To market trout fishing to the masses, though, it was not enough to cast it in the colors and clichés of advertising. The sport itself, long the domain of connoisseurs, had to be transformed—made easier for nonexperts to enjoy. Sometimes that meant small changes, like relaxing state fishing rules.[13] But it also involved more far-reaching changes to the high-country environment itself. In particular, state and federal officials began manipulating aquatic ecosystems to manufacture more (and more convenient) places for visitors to fish. The U.S. Forest Service, for example, worked to "improve" fish habitat in the White River and Arapaho National Forests by dredging rivers to create fishing holes, lining banks with riprap to reduce turbidity, and removing snags and other woody debris to free up fish movement. The point of these practices—all of which would be discredited in later years—was to create more places where trout would thrive and thus to accommodate ever-larger crowds of fishing visitors. In some places the Forest Service and state Game and Fish Department built artificial lakes especially for recreational angling. The state also had an aggressive program to build roads to make remote fishing areas more easily accessible and to buy or condemn private land that was hindering access to fishing.[14]

At the same time, state and federal agencies were busy mass-producing—there is no other word for it—the fish themselves. Millions upon millions of rainbow, lake, brook, and brown trout and kokanee salmon were reared at the federal hatchery at Leadville and the two-dozen-plus hatcheries that the state owned and operated. Predictably, mass production and mass consumption spurred each other on. By 1954, for example, tourists were putting such pressure on fish populations in the White River National Forest, especially around Aspen and Glenwood Springs, that the state felt compelled to build a huge new hatchery—the largest state-run hatchery in the nation—west of Glenwood Springs, near Rifle. Trout from this and other fish factories wound up in waters throughout the mountains, forever changing the river and lake ecosystems of high-country Colorado. Exotic species all, the hatchery trout outcompeted or interbred with the native cutthroats, helping drive them to the brink of extinction. Voracious lake trout turned on their hatchery brethren, eventually crashing kokanee populations in some waters. Native suckers suffered too: considered "trash fish," they were often poisoned to make way for stocked species. Hatchery trout were even dumped in high alpine lakes where no fish had ever swum before, in wilderness areas where artificiality was not supposed to reach. Few visitors, enraptured by shimmering waters and the reflections of rock and sky—fancying themselves at the top of the world, far from any hint of civilization—probably suspected the intrusion of mass consumerism swimming right beneath the surface.[15]

The rationale for such aggressive stocking was tourism, pure and simple. The more fish, the easier the fishing, and easy fishing was a lot more marketable than the expert-only kind. Who would want to travel a thousand miles for the frustration of not catching anything? Tourists had to see Colorado as a failsafe place to fish. That is why state Game and Fish officials stocked St. Louis Creek just before President Eisenhower's visits: because they knew wire reports of a full First Creel made for great publicity. (For his part, Ike was not always so happy with the coverage. When reporters following him on one fishing trip reported that he had exceeded his bag limit, he angrily put an end to the daily body counts.)[16] The president got special treatment, of course, but he was not the only visitor to benefit from Colorado's heavy stocking. In lakes and rivers near resorts and population centers, the Game and Fish Department planted hatchery fish as often as every three weeks.[17] The practice was called put-and-take—that is, the fish were put there to be taken. They were mass-produced pleasure props, existing solely to swallow lures and please tourists. And that is how state fish managers understood their mission: "to provide good fishing to Coloradoans and visitors." They were not out to protect fragile ecosystems, perpetuate rare species, or the like. Instead, they aimed, through industrial trout production, to "spread the catch to as many fishermen's creels as possible."[18]

And so, as artificially propagated fish filled Colorado's waters, images of fishy abundance filled its ads and brochures. "In Colorado you can catch MORE of the world's gamest, tastiest, fighting Rainbow trout!" shouted one ad. "Millions of these scrappy, high-jumping beauties live in Colorado's snow-fed streams and high crystal clear lakes." They were so plentiful, prospective visitors were told, that "in some places you can depend on catching your legal limit almost every time you fish."[19]

Might that detract from the thrill? No, for according to state advertising, these were "the roughest, gamest trout you'll find." They had to be rugged, explained one brochure, "to live in the icy, fast moving, rock-strewn streams. They must constantly overcome formidable barriers—swimming against swift rushing currents and battling their way over waterfalls." Supposedly, this "hard active life" was what gave Colorado trout "their terrific fighting endurance."[20] It went unmentioned that most of the trout had been reared in concrete nurse ponds and raised to maturity in artificial raceways—a long way from icy torrents and rock-scouring rapids. Hatchery-bred fish were far from "scrappy," as fish managers secretly knew, and were relatively easy to catch.[21] But that was exactly the point. High-volume fish stocking indulged the lust for wildness while actually delivering mass-market convenience—just the formula for popularizing an outdoor sport. By 1964, Colorado's national forests were luring almost 2.5 million recreational anglers a year, second only to California.[22]

The formula worked just as well with other outdoor activities. In camping, for example, the postwar trend was toward roughing it in relative comfort. Gone were the days of "barbaric self-torture" by "hardy males who claimed to relish leaky tents, frequently sodden blankets, . . . and assorted hardships." With new techniques and cutting-edge equipment, "the average family" could "challenge the pioneer heritage in a modern way." Postwar campers were presumed to want the same qualities in a campsite that they liked in their suburban subdivisions: a benign outdoorsiness, apart from the city, but with comforts and conveniences close at hand. Appropriately, the same magazines that helped define postwar suburban living, like *Sunset* and *Better Homes and Gardens*, also helped popularize camping in this suburban style. In countless articles and how-to books, generally aimed at women, they detailed the latest in tents, car-top shelters, camp furniture, and cooking gear (because, it was assumed, "the lady of the tent" would want "protection from insects and 'crawly things,' a little comfort, and convenience in cooking").[23]

Alternatively, if you were skittish about fending for yourself so far from familiar turf, you could get professionals to organize and outfit a trip for you. A Colorado Springs company would pick you up at your motel, bus you to the Maroon Bells–Snowmass Primitive Area, and treat you to an "all-expense deluxe" camping trip, with "charming hostesses" and "he-man guides" leading the rides, staging the camps, and "feeding you royally" three times a day, with snacks in between, "any time . . . all you want. . . . You do no work, carry nothing . . . You're free, far from the confused clamor of the cities." The American Forestry Association, a nonprofit conservation group, ran a similar program in the early 1950s, taking tourists on horseback trips into the Maroon Bells, with crews riding ahead to set up each night's camp. Participants in this Trail Riders of the Wilderness program had only to point their horses in the direction of the lead guide and drink in the scenery along the trail.[24]

An even greater boon to camping came later in the decade, when federal agencies began beefing up recreational facilities on public lands. In 1956 the Park Service unveiled Mission 66, a ten-year push to expand visitor accommodations in national parks. The next year, the Forest Service launched Operation Outdoors, a five-year plan to double the supply of camping and other leisure facilities, and improve fish and wildlife habitat, in the national forests.[25] In Colorado's popular White River National Forest, for example, Operation Outdoors brought dramatic increases in the number of campgrounds and camping units, as well as new fireplaces, trash-disposal facilities, tables, toilets, hiking trails and access roads, and the damming of Black Gore Creek to create a new fishing lake next to Highway 6 atop Vail Pass.[26]

When it turned out that Operation Outdoors had badly underprojected user demand, the Forest Service stepped up its recreational development still further. The 1960s brought more trails and roads, and more campgrounds, some now with electrical and running-water hookups, showers, and laundry facilities. Parking lots were reconfigured with larger spaces, and scenic drives with wider turns, to accommodate motor homes. As these conveniences reveal, it was not just swelling demand that spurred Forest Service recreational development. It was not just that the public had come to see recreation as a primary purpose of the national forests (a shift in perception that the Forest Service recognized only reluctantly).[27] It was also that the public's taste in outdoor recreation had changed along the way. "Visitors," the Forest Service observed in 1965, "seem to be increasingly 'soft.' They don't venture far from their cars. Life in camp, in terms of creature comforts, is not much different from that at home."[28] In other words, Forest Service staff had noticed the same trend *Better Homes and Gardens* did. They may have viewed it more dubiously, and their agency culture may still have favored logging over leisure, but they ended up doing more than anyone else to make Colorado a favorite place for casual campers.

But when it came to readying the high country for recreation, the Forest Service's most critical contribution came in its decades-long effort to build up skiing. Even though skiing claimed fewer participants than camping or fishing, it grew more explosively, glittered more glamorously, and left starker marks on the landscape. And in the process, it became Colorado's signature outdoor activity, symbolizing the state's leisure allure like no other. State agencies certainly had a hand in this: the Advertising and Publicity Committee ran ads in ski magazines and yearbooks and handled inquiries from prospective ski visitors, while the Highway Department sent snowplows and road-building crews to make the glades, glaciers, slopes, and bowls of the high country more auto-accessible than before. But since most of Colorado's skiable terrain lay within the boundaries of national forests, it was the Forest Service that did the most to catalyze skiing's phenomenal postwar growth.

Before the war, Forest Service rangers had cooperated with ski interests like Denver parks manager George Cranmer, the Arlberg Club, and the Colorado Winter Sports Council to launch popular early ski areas like Berthoud Pass and Winter Park. After the war, collaboration between foresters and ski entrepreneurs grew even closer. Wilfred "Slim" Davis, the Forest Service winter sports administrator beginning in 1946, made it agency policy to "create business opportunities" for would-be ski-area operators in the national forests. To that end, the agency marked trails, certified ski instructors, offered technical aid for the construction of lifts and jumps, and, during the ski season, sent out "snow rangers" to help with slope and lift maintenance and avalanche control and rescue. Most importantly, Forest Service rangers kept up the work they had begun in the 1920s: identifying and surveying potential ski areas and then seeking private entities to develop them. In some cases the agency called for bids; in others it recruited developers individually. Either way, the work amounted to a major subsidy for the ski industry, analogous to the government doing exploration work for a mining company, at taxpayer expense, and then inviting the company to go at the vein. From the Forest Service perspective, identifying ski sites was simply part of the agency's responsibility to determine the "highest" use of each parcel of forestland and thus optimize the multiple-resource use of each national forest as a whole.[29]

By the late 1950s, with demand for Colorado skiing increasing even faster than the demand for other outdoor activities, the Forest Service took the next step and began master-planning the ski development of the entire state. Especially concerned about easing pressure on the crowded ski areas closest to Denver, in the Arapaho National Forest, the rangers fashioned a thirty-year plan in 1959 that called for more ski areas farther west. They compiled a list of twenty-one sites, scattered through all the national forests in Colorado, and set target dates for the development of each based on projected demand. Because one goal was to keep development as orderly as possible, and to avoid glutting the market in any one region, this schedule prevented some eager developers from receiving Forest Service permits as quickly as they might have liked. (Pete Seibert, for one, was initially denied a permit for Vail, because rangers wanted to ensure sufficient demand in light of the recently opened Aspen Highlands.) In many cases, though, the Forest Service ended up granting permits ahead of its own schedule. (Vail got its permit when its investors enlisted powerful, prodevelopment Congressman Wayne Aspinall and Senator Gordon Allott to pressure the Forest Service.) In the end, the most important legacy of the 1959 master plan was that it opened the way for ski development to reach ever deeper into the high country from Denver, especially along the U.S. 6/I-70 corridor. Within fifteen years of the plan's release, the western (Summit County) section of Arapaho National Forest would see big new ski resorts at Breckenridge, Copper Mountain, and Keystone, and the White River National Forest would see the meteoric rise of Vail.[30]

So the Forest Service made space for skiing to grow. But it would not have grown so fast without the efforts of ski enthusiasts in the private sector. They too scouted new sites—often with forest rangers in the lead or in tow—and when a promising site was identified and the Forest Service issued a permit (which it did with little hesitation, at least up to the late 1950s), these enthusiasts did most of the developing. Before World War II, there were two main groups doing this work: the members of ski clubs in small towns like Aspen, Steamboat Springs, and Hot Sulphur Springs; and business and professional elites from Denver, belonging to groups like the Arlberg Club. In the late 1940s two more groups joined the effort: college ski-team alumni, mostly from New England; and veterans of the army's Tenth Mountain Division, the soldiers-on-skis who had spent much of the war training at Camp Hale near Leadville and in the surrounding terrain. Once the war was over, both of these groups gravitated to Colorado in droves. They were part of a regionwide trend, a historic population influx that saw millions of people—workers who had sought wartime jobs in the West, military personnel who had been stationed there or passed through on their way overseas—decide to stay or return after the war, to build new families, homes, and lifestyles out West. These newcomers contributed to California's galactic growth in particular, but they poured into Colorado and other western states too.[31] And while Tenth Mountain veterans and ex-college ski racers made up a tiny part of the overall influx, they exerted an influence far out of proportion to their numbers. Tenth Mountain vets in particular developed several new ski areas, including Aspen, Arapahoe Basin, Buttermilk, and Vail, and they taught in scores of ski schools and added immeasurably to the publicity and glamour of their sport. They did not start the Colorado ski industry, but they did as much as anyone to build Colorado's new reputation as a ski state.[32]

Immediately after the war, Denver ski enthusiasts rekindled their prewar alliance with boosters who saw skiing as a way to lure tourists. Both groups turned out for the first Colorado Winter Sports Congress, convened by the Denver Chamber of Commerce in December 1945. Attendees packed the cavernous ballroom of the Cosmopolitan Hotel to discuss plans for developing, as one participant put it, "the state's great natural asset of winter sports into an economic and commercial asset." It would be a massive undertaking, involving not just boosters and ski clubs but also railroads, ski-equipment makers, department stores, ski shops, radio stations, college athletic departments, the Forest Service, and even the U.S. Weather Bureau, which would be asked to publicize Colorado's sunny skies and snow conditions. A speaker from Colorado Springs fantasized aloud that the winter tourist season might someday equal the summer. Friedl Pfeifer, two weeks from opening his new Aspen Ski School, talked of indoctrinating children to ski at an early age. And in an especially well-received speech, George Cranmer predicted there would someday be as many as seven ski areas in the five-mile stretch between Berthoud Pass and Winter Park.[33]

The idea that so many ski facilities would be needed so close to Denver suggests how Denver-driven the impetus for ski development was. Indeed, fully half of all Colorado ski areas operating in the 1950s clustered within a hundred highway miles of the Mile High City.[34] The two areas most popular with Denver skiers, Winter Park and Berthoud Pass, were also two of the most cutting-edge: Berthoud installed the nation's first double chairlift in 1947, while Winter Park in 1950 became the highest-capacity ski mountain in Colorado.[35] And the Denver Chamber of Commerce directly instigated the development of at least one major new mountain when it hired Frederick "Sandy" Schauffler and Larry Jump (both former collegiate racers, and Jump a Tenth Mountain veteran) to find the "best ski area in Colorado." The pair settled on a high glacial cirque in the Arapaho National Forest, sixty-six miles due west of Denver on Highway 6. Arapahoe Basin opened in 1946 with primitive facilities: an old military truck hauled skiers halfway up the mountain to a rope tow, which dragged them the rest of the way. But by 1948 Jump, Schauffler, and their partners had added two chairlifts, making "A-Basin" another favorite destination for Denver skiers. Thus did Denver boosters help make the high country even more "Denver's winter playground."[36]

One obstacle to skiing's becoming a mainstream, mass-demand activity was its reputation for extreme danger. This reputation originated in the days when jumping dominated the sport, and it persisted through the 1930s, when even the most skillful skiers expected someday to break an ankle or leg. A sense of excitement was needed to market an outdoor sport, as we have seen with fishing—but a sense of terror was another thing altogether. Somehow ski evangelists needed to dispel the fear that haunted their sport. A reader of *Ski Illustrated* suggested starting with the names of trails. "Look at these names," he chided: "*Suicide Six, Shincracker, Madman's Spin, John Doe's Misery, Slaughterhouse Slalom* . . . these are most likely to keep the less expert away in droves." They might as well call the trails "*Multiple Fracture . . . Mortician's Dish . . . Headlong to Hell . . . Hospital Highway*," he cracked. But his point was serious. Novices, he reasoned, would flock to skiing "if they could be persuaded that [it] is not just a sport for the most expert and daring. And their money makes just as merry a sound in the cash registers."[37] That, in a nutshell, was the formula that would power the postwar ski industry: even as the sport kept its adventurous reputation, its promoters worked to make it markedly easier and less risky, and thus much more welcoming of new enthusiasts.

With skiing, as with trout fishing, part of the thrill was a neo-Rooseveltian struggle against nature. Roosevelt's quest for the "strenuous life" found kindred spirit in skiing's Scandinavian pioneers, who believed that pitting the masculine body against the rugged outdoors would strengthen character and purify the soul.[38] By 1945 this link to self-purification had mostly gone, but there was still the exhilaration of testing oneself against the wilderness. "Alone, the skier pits his skill against nature," wrote one enthusiast, "in its most glorious setting—the high, wild solitude of the winter mountains." Racing across such a landscape brought "the sheer exultation of speed—skimming over clean snow with the wind tearing at your face." The thrill came not just from speed but the mastery of it: "speed under human control," as a Tenth Mountain veteran put it, "two mere strips of hickory winging you down in rhythmic turns through miles of white velvet." Trying to convey the sensation to the armchair adventurers who read

National Geographic, a newcomer to the sport described a "perfect run" in which "turning became effortless, and self-confidence soared as I suddenly realized for the first time I was skiing with both speed and control."[39]

This quest—for the mastery of terrain through mastery of technique—became an obsession for postwar skiers, novice and expert alike. Different schools championed different techniques. At Friedl Pfeifer's Aspen Ski School, the stem-turning Arlberg approach held sway; other resorts, notably Aspen Highlands, taught the new reverse-shoulder parallel technique called *wedeln*.[40] Some experts laughed at the fuss: "All this stuff about technique is bunk," remarked racing champion Dick Durrance. "Look, the whole idea is to have fun." But for many skiers, technique *did* make skiing more fun, because it allowed them fuller mastery over terrain. Paralleling in particular let skiers attack steeper slopes at higher speeds than before. One "could at last realize the skier's perennial . . . ambition," said one writer: "to go down the steepest slopes fast as hell, while still staying, at least theoretically, in control throughout." Aficionados likened parallel skiing to flying, which seems apt: both brought the same feeling of having transcended the limits of landscape.[41] And as technique was making skiing more exciting, the equipment innovations of the 1950s and 1960s, like shorter skis and plastic boots, were making it easier and safer.[42] Greater ease and safety plus greater thrills was a surefire formula for popularizing a sport.

Still, even with advances in equipment and technique, skiing would not have become so popular—in Colorado or anywhere else—if not for changes in the design of ski areas themselves. The most important innovations in postwar skiing came in the way ski landscapes were engineered. Technological and design manipulations became more elaborate and expensive, the goal being to reconfigure mountains for ever-larger numbers of less-expert skiers. As more and more terrain was remade in this way, the high country became "ski country"—not just in the popular imagination, but in physical reality too.

The experience of landscape had always been basic to skiing's appeal. Many skiers felt a kind of Romantic-era reverence at the magnificence of mountain settings that went beyond the rewards of mastering tough terrain. They skied not to conquer nature but to experience places where nature seemed pristine. "One of the very great joys" of skiing, wrote a devotee in *Holiday* magazine, was the feeling of "being alone in a wonderful, white, untouched, untraveled immensity." "The scenery is at its best," added another, "when the vast snow basins lay like white lace curtains stretched from peak to peak. A fairyland of shadows will greet you and even the most callous will find beauty in the snow-laden evergreens." Skiers' accounts in the 1940s and 1950s were full of passages like these, exulting in the silent beauty of snowy landscapes, expressing a powerful, even spiritual sense of serenity in nature's presence. Very often, skiers wrote of feeling physically dwarfed and emotionally overwhelmed by the sheer vastness of their surroundings—another Romantic trope. One *National Geographic* reporter saw the panoramic view atop Aspen Mountain and wrote that "the breath caught in my throat." When Friedl Pfeifer first came upon the same view, he marveled at the "endless rows of peaks running to the horizon."[43] There was no conquering spirit in reactions like these, just admiration, even humility, before nature's grandeur.

Predictably, ski promoters made this reverence for nature another marketing theme, distilling ideas with deep cultural resonance into simple slogans to make a sale. So, for example, the Idaho Springs Chamber of Commerce invited vacationers to "ride the [ski] tows to the 'top of the world' and revel in the panorama of Nature's wonderland." And the state publicity committee tempted winter visitors with images of "sparkling clear days white with mile upon mile of majestic unbroken snowfields waiting for you under bright blue skies."[44] Phrases like these became as slogan-like as the jagged peaks, primeval forests, and flower-carpeted valleys we encountered in chapter 1. And once again, there were visual clichés to accompany the verbal ones. Especially common in 1940s and 1950s ski advertising were images of tiny skiers, specks in their surroundings, tracking through vast, unblemished fields of snow or stopping to gaze at spectacular panoramas of snow-robed mountain ranges, receding into infinitude. (Having one of the figures point toward the infinitude with an upraised ski pole helped convey the proper sense of awe.) Albert Bierstadt and other nineteenth-century painters had often used the same device: placing tiny people or animals in the foreground to underscore the immensity of a landscape. Now this Romantic cliché found new life, reappropriated to sell postwar consumers on the appeal of skiing.

But even as ads promised skiers the experience of pristine nature, the actual landscapes most skiers encountered were more heavily engineered than ever before. With considerable capital from investors, and encouragement and aid from the Forest Service, postwar ski-area operators built lifts, trails, and other infrastructure, turning mountains into smoothly running machines, shuttling skiers up and channeling them back down, in effect mass-producing outdoor thrills for crowds of leisure seekers. The eminent western historian Earl Pomeroy once called postwar skiing "the ultimate in the mechanization of the outdoors for the multitudes."[45] He might also have called it the ultimate *packaging* of the outdoors, for ski mountains, even more than campgrounds or fishing streams, were scripted landscapes— elaborately orchestrated to indulge consumers' simultaneous desires for excitement and convenience. The engineering of these mountains made it easier than ever for people to access outdoor adventure with a minimum of effort or risk to themselves.

It all began with ski lifts. They came in many forms; some towed skiers and others carried them. But they all made skiing easier by eliminating the laborious slog uphill.[46] Interestingly, before the war many ski purists denied that this was a good thing. Friedl Pfeifer, for one, opposed lifts in his native Austria in the 1920s, because he felt the time skiers spent hiking up a mountain was invaluable for bonding with each other and learning the terrain. But by the mid-1930s, in both Europe and the United States, the clear trend was toward lifts. Even ski clubs in towns like Climax, Steamboat Springs, and Glenwood Springs were scraping together money to build tows. Then, in 1936, Sun Valley's grand opening introduced the world to the chairlift. Now skiers did not even have to support their own weight; they could sink onto padded seats, cover their laps with warm blankets, and let the lift spirit them up the mountain. When movie stars appeared in newsreels and magazines riding the Sun Valley chair, the contraption acquired an aura not just of convenience but of luxury and glamour too. Pfeifer was convinced, and when he began planning his skiing community in Aspen, he decided he needed a chairlift. Skiers were demanding them, he realized, and no ski area could afford to be without one. So in 1946 he one-upped Sun Valley by installing on Aspen Mountain the "world's longest chair lift"—a device as much marketing gimmick as means of conveyance. It worked famously in both respects, instantly placing Aspen in the top tier of ski resorts.[47] (Sixteen years later, Vail's founders would try the same strategy, making a splash by installing America's first gondola and meeting with similar success.)

When Aspen christened its chair, the race was on for other ski areas to upgrade their tows. So in 1947 Climax's ski club persuaded the mining company to replace the local rope tow with a T-bar. That same year, closer to Denver, Berthoud Pass unveiled the nation's first double chairlift, after Arlberg Club members raised the money and got Forest Service approval. The next season Arapahoe Basin replaced its jerry-rigged truck-and-rope-tow with two chairs that reached all the way to the top of the cirque, 12,500 feet above sea level. And two years after that, in 1950, a Glenwood Springs oilman converted Red Mountain's single chair to an expensive double. Winter Park, dependent on public funds, lagged a bit behind when it came to chairlifts, but in 1947 the City of Denver did install a T-bar to replace two rope tows on the upper slopes. Built on the cheap in city shops, the contraption never worked well and was dubbed "the Clunker." But within three years it gave way to a more reliable, manufacturer-made T-bar, making Winter Park the largest-capacity ski mountain in the state.[48]

Lifts not only made skiing less physically taxing, they also changed how skiers experienced nature. (This held true for summer tourists too, since many ski areas, like Aspen, Berthoud Pass, and later Vail, kept lifts running for summer sightseers.) Lifts opened more of the high country to recreation by reaching formerly inaccessible summits and slopes. They swept riders "easily and comfortably, sitting down, to new worlds with breath-taking vistas," marveled the *Ford Times*. An Austrian tourist, after riding the Aspen chair, told a reporter that "only a few years ago such beauty as she saw could only be experienced at great physical cost to the individual." Or, as another Aspen rider exclaimed, "Now I know how it feels to ride on air," so effortless was the ascent. And riders got a new perspective on the landscape—literally so, because lifts often ended in panoramic, peak-top views, the likes of which many visitors had never seen before.[49]

Now anyone could experience the awe Friedl Pfeifer had felt when he first scaled Aspen Mountain. Indeed, lift riders' reactions upon reaching the summit often sounded like Pfeifer's. "I felt pretty small and inconsequential," wrote one woman, "surrounded by that glorious magnitude of wide, deep valleys, mountain range after mountain range snow-tipped, high lighted with the lowering sun." It was nothing less than an experience of the sublime, achieved by mechanical means. So smooth and silent was the lift that it obscured its own obtrusion into the landscape, letting passengers feel like they were alone in nature. "I was wrapped in solitude," wrote a woman after taking Aspen's chair. "Below stretched wide slopes separated by stands of spruce. At times my skis . . . seemed to brush the treetops. Only the harsh caws of Rocky Mountain jays and the distant halloo of an early skier disturbed the stillness." Like eyes in the sky, lift riders could observe nature without disturbing it or being noticed in return. They could "spot wildlife and birdlife in their natural habitat," said the *Ford Times*. "Deer and elk, unmindful of the figures dangling like watch fobs in the air, amble along below."[50] For many vacationers, ski lifts actually enhanced the experience of the natural and the pristine.

By making skiing simultaneously less exhausting and more exhilarating, lifts contributed mightily to the sport's remarkable postwar popularity. Observers of the travel scene certainly noticed the trend, with *Holiday* magazine reporting in 1954 that "new mountain-climbing machines have made skiing one of the fastest growing sports in America."[51] And nowhere did it grow faster than in Colorado. In the ten years after the war, winter-sports visits to Colorado's national forests increased more than fourfold. In the next five years after that, winter visits to the two most popular national forests (Arapaho and White River) doubled again.[52]

The dramatic increase brought dramatic changes to the landscape. A ski mountain is instantly recognizable, even from miles away, for the tell-tale stripes cut into its forest cover. Not only did the ski boom leave these marks on more mountains than before, but the marks were more blatant than before. Prewar ski trails had traced thin zigzags through the woods, the "corkscrew" of Aspen's Roch Run being a classic example. The idea was to force the skier into a succession of controlled turns at controlled speed, in keeping with the Arlberg style. But while these thin, twisting trails worked well for the small ski parties of the 1930s, they could not handle the far bigger crowds that came after the war. Now skiers clogged the narrow old trails, colliding with each other and with trees. And because the zigzags forced everyone to turn at the same spots, the bends in the trail became hideously rutted. Lifts worsened the problem by letting each skier make more downhill runs per day, leaving still more ruts. So postwar ski operators devised a radically new kind of trail: wide swaths through the trees—clear-cuts, in effect—aiming more or less directly down the fall line. Wider slopes not only fit more skiers but also gave them more freedom to improvise their own ways down. Instead of everyone turning and carving ruts in the same places, skiers and their edge wear spread out more evenly over the slopes, keeping the snow in better shape.[53] So as skiing went from relative obscurity to mass popularity, more and more mountains in the high country—especially along the U.S. 6 and 40 corridors—began to bear unmistakable clear-cut scars down their sides.

Controversy swirled around these new runs at first. Traditionalists derided Vermont's Mount Snow, one of the first resorts to give itself over to wide slopes, as the "Coney Island of the Snow Belt." The epithet showed exactly what was at stake: whether skiing would stay clubby and elite or

MAP 4.
The spread of ski areas, 1934–1980

Ski areas with mechanical lifts proliferated rapidly after World War II. Before 1960, they appeared more or less equally along U.S. 40 and U.S. 6, but after the 1960 decision to route Interstate 70 along U.S. 6, new ski areas concentrated almost exclusively along that corridor. The post-1960 resorts were also markedly larger, premised as they were on the promise of high-volume interstate access.

Labeled ski areas were still operating as of 2013

3.2 The new landscape of skiing. Postwar ski mountains, designed for larger crowds and easier, safer skiing, looked very different from their prewar forebears. Narrow, twisting trails gave way to wide, spacious slopes, which fit more skiers and held up better under the wear. Mechanical lifts rendered the exhausting and time-consuming slog back up the mountain obsolete. With chairlifts like this one, skiers need not even stay on their feet for the ride up, as rope and bar tows had made them do. The scene is Buttermilk Mountain, the pioneering "teaching mountain" that Friedl Pfeifer opened in 1958. Photo © by Robert C. Bishop.

become an activity for the many. Mount Snow's wide runs were unabashedly meant to attract big crowds, including beginners and people who came to skiing casually, not with the purist passion of earlier devotees. The purists might not like it, but their sport was headed for mass-market appeal.[54]

By the mid-1950s nearly all new runs were of the wider design. In 1950, Winter Park area manager Steve Bradley introduced Denver skiers to the new design when he unveiled Bradley's Bash, a wide trail cut straight down the fall line. Many of Winter Park's existing runs were widened around the same time. Not to be outdone, Arapahoe Basin advertised its "rolling open slopes"; Loveland Basin bragged that "new, wide, rolling trails have been cleared to accommodate all classes of skiers"; and Glenwood Springs promised that its "steep slopes may be by-passed by gentle, open trails." Even Aspen's Roch Run was reconfigured to fit the new thinking. By the late 1950s its infamous corkscrew had been widened, the zigzags smoothed into a single sweeping curve.[55]

Bradley also helped pioneer another crowd-pleasing change in the ski landscape: mechanically groomed snow. In the early 1950s he tinkered around and invented the Bradley Packer, a device for smoothing out the moguls, or mounds of heaped-up snow, that accumulated as skiers curled and carved their way down slopes. The Packer looked like some kind of mutated farm implement—long yoke in front, five-foot-wide blade in the middle, slatted roller bringing up the rear. By towing it downhill, a patrolman could scrape the moguls off a run and roll out the loosened snow, leaving a smooth, easy-to-ski surface. That was a big step forward for ski promoters, for groomed slopes had the same effect as chairlifts and wide trails: they made mountains less intimidating, and thus more appealing, to greater numbers of inexperienced skiers. Grooming machines took a while to catch on—Bradley's Winter Park was years ahead in that respect—but eventually all ski areas would embrace them. So too, by the 1950s, most ski areas began hiring summer crews to rove over the mountainsides, removing logs, rocks, and underbrush and digging or blasting out stumps and roots, so when the snow fell the trails would be as even-surfaced as possible. The goal was to create so-called ballroom skiing conditions: broad expanses of smooth snow where skiers could frolic without fear.[56]

The very term "ballroom skiing" suggests how the sport had changed from the daredevil days before the war; how casual and lighthearted it was becoming; how much it now catered to dilettantes and newcomers, women as well as men, and families and children. With wide, groomed slopes and chairlifts already the norm by the late 1950s, the next step was to design entire ski areas expressly for intermediates and beginners. Colorado's first such area, Buttermilk Mountain, opened in 1958. Its founder was none other than Friedl Pfeifer, who, while still passionate about converting people to skiing, had become convinced that Aspen Mountain's precipitous slopes were scaring away novices and families. Two miles west of town, he found a gently sloping mountainside and decided it would make a perfect "teaching mountain." He bought three hundred acres of land at the base, sold his remaining stock in the Aspen Skiing Corporation, and used the proceeds to build a restaurant, install a T-bar, and cut miles of easy, rolling trails. To the Ski Corp.'s fury, Pfeifer also moved his famous Aspen Ski School to Buttermilk so it literally would be a teaching mountain. The concept worked. In four years, Pfeifer generated enough capital to build two chairlifts and add more trails. Novices were invited to cruise Buttermilk's "ultra-wide" runs, averaging a 34-degree grade, "considered ideal for pleasure skiing." The slopes were so easygoing, Buttermilk publicity claimed, that "beginners . . .

can ski from top to bottom [of the mountain] in class after a few lessons"—a thrill that would take far longer to achieve at other ski areas. "Ideal for family fun" was Buttermilk's slogan, a clear sign of the image and the clientele it sought.[57]

Buttermilk proved popular enough that in 1963 the Aspen Skiing Corporation bought Pfeifer out and took the teaching mountain for itself. The sale signaled a new era, when even the biggest and best-established ski resorts in Colorado would go aggressively after the beginner and family markets. Very soon Vail, which opened just a few months before Aspen absorbed Buttermilk, would take this marketing strategy to a whole new level.

As skiing got safer and easier, and less of its thrill came from risking life and limb, more came from the "ski scene," a concept almost incidental to slopes and snow. The ski scene was not a new idea. Skiing's pioneers had prided themselves not just on their daring and athleticism but on the convivial camaraderie they felt on the slopes—and, not least, around the fireplace at the end of the day. They liked to say skiing was "more than just a sport, a way of life."[58] That, it turned out, was yet another idea that lent itself to marketing. Indeed, skiing's link to a fun-loving, athletic, and social approach to life became essential to the sport's postwar popularity—especially when coupled with a dash of celebrity and sex appeal. Sun Valley pioneered the formula before the war, when its publicists used handsome models and Hollywood stars to turn a remote, windswept Idaho snowscape into a wonderland of glamour. Soon Sun Valley's image rubbed off on the sport. After the war, the idea of skiing as an alluring lifestyle intensified even further with the arrival of dashing European ski racers, heroic Tenth Mountain veterans, and, in the 1950s, stylish ski fashions. When photographs of Ingrid Bergman and Marilyn Monroe, wearing skis and form-revealing Bogner stretch pants, began appearing in mainstream magazines like *Life*, it did a great deal to elevate skiing's popular appeal.[59]

Colorado promoters did all they could to tap into this social and sexual allure. They illustrated ads and brochures with pictures of pretty women in stretch pants, and when Miss Colorado, Marilyn Van Derbur, won the Miss America pageant in 1958, they put her in the ads too.[60] When Friedl Pfeifer and Walter Paepcke persuaded Gary Cooper to come to Aspen in 1948, it was all about giving the upstart resort a bit of Hollywood sheen.[61] But the most common tactic was for a resort to import a male European racing champion to run its ski school. Aspen Highlands founder Whip Jones scored a coup in 1958 when he landed Stein Eriksen, a blond Norwegian whose ballet-like *wedeln* and electrifying somersaults on skis had made him unquestionably the top ski celebrity of the 1950s.[62] Soon other resorts had Europeans-in-residence of their own: besides Eriksen, Switzerland's Fred Iselin played the part for Aspen Highlands; Norwegian Trygve Berge attracted attention to the new ski mountain at Breckenridge; and Austria's Pepi Gramshammer and the Swiss Roger Staub helped glamorize Vail.

Significantly, one did not have to ski to share in the chic. Much of the ski scene mystique swirled not around the mountain but the village below, where après-ski socializing, drinking, and dancing began as soon as the lifts stopped running for the day. Aspen became especially infamous for costume parties, bar-to-bar revelry, and other hijinks (dismaying Paepcke, who, again, wanted the town to cultivate a more serious image).[63] In an era that found more humor in hard drinking than Americans generally do today, images of attractive young revelers sloshing down beers at the Red Onion or some other watering hole helped mold Aspen's reputation for boisterous spirits and bacchanalian fun.[64] There and at other resorts, après-ski became as big a part of a stay as skiing itself. A 1957 survey found that more than half the skiers visiting Colorado or New Mexico liked to go dancing at day's end, while nearly as many enjoyed going to a tavern or lounge. Ski movies and parties were popular too. Promoters learned to play on these preferences. You could enjoy a Colorado ski vacation, said the state publicity committee in a 1961 ad, "whether you want the unmatched thrill of skiing" or simply "the light-hearted fun of dancing and relaxing in the gay and sparkling atmosphere of a ski resort."[65] Living the resort life was reason for even nonskiers to make the trip. And that was the ad's intent: to expand skiing's appeal beyond skiers, to lure people who otherwise would never have considered a ski vacation in the high country.

By the mid-1960s skiing had become Colorado's marquee attraction, even more than fishing, which many boosters had once thought would play that role. Every time another high-country mountainside got striped with those unmistakable clear-cuts and strung up with lifts, skiing became more conspicuous on the land—and more etched into the popular image of it. In 1963, the Rocky Mountain Ski Area Operators Association trademarked a new nickname for Colorado: borrowing a slogan from Vail's earliest advertising, they branded the state Ski Country USA.[66] The name soon passed into popular parlance, another case of marketing shaping people's sense of place. Of course, the nickname would not have rung true were it not for the reshaping of the land itself—the efforts of ski-area managers, trail crews, local boosters, Forest Service rangers, ski evangelists, and others, all working to modify the mountain landscape and manufacture places for skiing.

Nor would it have been possible to market Ski Country USA so successfully had ski settings scared people away. Ski enthusiasts and entrepreneurs did not just make places for skiing; they made them make sense to the mainstream. The end result of carving up forests, recontouring slopes, smoothing snow cover, and mechanizing uphill movement was to turn daunting topography and a dangerous sport into much less intimidating, much more inviting versions of their former selves. The same was true of Forest Service crews who built hiking trails and campgrounds; fish and game workers who modified riparian habitats and stocked millions of hatchery-raised fish; and, for that matter, highway builders who pounded superhighways through formerly impassable terrain. Taken together, their interventions brought the once-marginal Colorado high country into the American mainstream—literally, in the sense that much more tourist traffic now flowed there, and figuratively, in the sense that the high country became much better suited to mainstream tastes in outdoor recreation. If the postwar obsession with suburban living connoted a craving for easy-access, casual, and comfortable interaction with the outdoors, then in that realm the high country began to seem, like the ads suggested, an absolute natural.

IT MIGHT SEEM QUESTIONABLE TO SUGGEST THAT TOURISTS LIKED THE vacationland for its suburbanness. Aren't tourists supposed to want to *escape* the suburban and other humdrum settings of their everyday lives? Maybe so. But that does not mean they also leave behind their worldviews, their core values, their ingrained tastes. When the great crowds of midcentury Americans took to the highways and airways on vacation, the preponderance carried with them fundamentally suburban ways of idealizing the outdoors. Suburban dreams conjured up landscapes of open space and picturesque prospects; landscapes where city elements vanished and work gave way to play; landscapes where one could relax, recharge, and find wholesome and healthy outlets for the kids—and all this without too much exertion or incommodity. Postwar vacationers looked to outdoor settings for the same things. To put it another way, the suburban boom and the vacation craze sprang from essentially the same environmental vision. If we follow the road from the high country back to the suburbs—and this time pay attention to the built environment, the townscapes, along with their recreational surroundings—we can see how vacation spaces borrowed from suburbia and how suburbia borrowed right back, so that the vacationer's way of consuming nature and landscape shaded ever more into everyday life.

Inevitably, tourism rearranged townscapes, because tourists needed lots of special establishments: motels, cafés, gas stations, information booths, and shops that sold groceries, equipment, and souvenirs. Such structures proliferated after the war, in the high country as across the nation. Clustering especially along the main roads through town, usually sporting eye-grabbing signs, they remade the outward face of many mountain communities. In some places, the change went far deeper. Consider again Aspen, which sold visitors not just services but an entire "scene." There, efforts to create the right atmosphere touched everything about the townscape, from main street to back street, from the uses of land to the appearances of buildings, outbuildings, yards, vehicles, and even people.

Even in communities less resortified than Aspen, the more tourist establishments that sprouted, the more closely the town became tied to a surrounding leisure landscape. In part that was because a town with more services could attract and accommodate more visitors, and more of its local economy came to feed off recreation. But it was also because a town with tourist infrastructure became, in effect, a mediator between consumers and the local environment. Its business became to frame local nature according to prevailing consumer tastes—which in the postwar context meant making it easy for consumers to enjoy scenery and outdoor adventure with a minimum of discomfort or inconvenience. In this sense, tourist infrastructure not only tied towns more closely to their recreational surroundings but also tugged town and surroundings together into the wider leisure culture of America. And in a time when millions of Americans were migrating to the Sunbelt or the suburbs, seeking out idealized living environments with outdoor-oriented lifestyles, some would start to see Colorado and its high country not just as a vacationland but as a place to pursue more permanent dreams of the good life.

Any town with a restaurant, gas station, or tackle shop might find a place in the vacation landscape, as we saw with the "rest-stop" towns in chapter 2. But aside from the route decisions made by highway planners—decisions that were ultimately out of locals' hands—policy and planning played only a small role in making any given community into a "tourist town." Most towns that found their way onto tourists' mental maps did so through the unplanned accumulation of small businesses aimed at leisure seekers. Georgetown, for example, sat on the road to several ski areas, so many of its business start-ups tried to tap into the lucrative skier traffic. One woman advertised guesthouses with "plenty of hot water" (a key consideration after a day on the slopes) and "large living rooms . . . for games and cards" (ideal for après-ski parties). Georgetown's Red Ram tavern catered specifically to skiers, and it became one of the state's best-known après-ski hangouts, a favorite place to stop for a few rounds on the drive back to Denver (in a time when drunk driving was less frowned upon than now). Especially in the world of skiing, where sociability was a top priority and word of mouth the best advertising, a single establishment like the Red Ram could be enough to put a town on the map.[67]

In warmer months, Georgetown began to take on a different identity: it was becoming a popular day-trip destination. It had played the same role back in Victorian times, when each summer thousands of tourists would take the daylong railroad outing from Denver to ride the spectacular "Georgetown Loop." The excursion lost popularity when automobiles entered the scene, and the Colorado & Southern Railway abandoned the route in 1939. But about that same time the State Highway Department improved U.S. 6 through Clear Creek valley, paving the way for day-trippers after the war. This time, instead of the rail loop, the main attraction was Georgetown's Victorian ambiance: its charmingly restored and repainted old houses, tucked photogenically among trees and flower beds, and its elegant little downtown, seemingly frozen in the time of buggies and gaslights. Georgetown owed its tourist-pleasing appearance in part to history and in part to local pride, but members of the Denver leisure class also played a key role. In the 1930s, well-to-do Denverites began buying derelict houses in the Gothic Revival, Italianate, and Second Empire styles, once home to mine owners and merchants, and rehabilitating them as summer homes. By the late 1940s, the number of second-home owners stood somewhere between three hundred and five hundred, doubling Georgetown's population every time June rolled around.[68]

The most significant of these seasonal denizens was the remarkable James Grafton Rogers, who bought a house in Georgetown in 1941. Rogers was part of the true power elite: an eminent Denver attorney who had also been a professor, law school dean, state official, civic leader, diplomat (Herbert Hoover named him assistant secretary of state in 1931), and spymaster (Franklin Roosevelt appointed him deputy director of the Office of Strategic Services during World War II). He was also a keen outdoorsman, having cofounded the Colorado Mountain Club in 1912, and an acolyte of

Colorado history who would go on to head the State Historical Society for two decades.[69] When he and his wife, Cora, arrived in Georgetown, they did not spruce up a modest little cottage like most other summer residents; they purchased one of Georgetown's highest-style houses, a Victorian Gothic beauty that an English mine promoter had built amid terraced gardens on a hillside above town. Jim Rogers would quickly enter Georgetown's power circles as he had in Denver and Washington, DC, twice winning election as mayor in the 1950s and using his historical society and legal community connections to spearhead a vigorous local preservation movement.[70] Late in life he wrote a book about the natural history of the area, titled, a bit imperiously, *My Rocky Mountain Valley*. Yet as singular a path as Rogers blazed through life and through Georgetown, the yearnings that lured him there were typical—and suburban. Like the hundreds of other second-home owners who settled in Georgetown after the war, Rogers relished the chance to get back to a neighborly small-town setting and back to nature—in his book he wrote lovingly of local bird life, wildflowers, and seasonal weather patterns—while still having (though his nature writing never mentioned this) an easy auto link back to his business in Denver via Highway 6.

Rogers and most other summer transplants came to Georgetown for quaintness and quiet, not profits. Yet the Victorian houses they rehabilitated became a major draw for tourists. And it did not take long for other newcomers to begin to see dollar signs in Georgetown's gingerbread ambiance. Benjamin Draper, an economist who like Rogers hailed from Denver, was the first to turn Georgetown's preservation into a business venture. He traced his interest in the town back to his own tourism: he had ridden the Georgetown Loop in 1921, and the experience had so piqued his interest in the area's history that he went on to restore a local Victorian home, help with the reopening of the historic opera house in nearby Central City, and write a master's thesis on theater culture in boom-era Georgetown. Through it all, he became convinced that the local history he found so fascinating had great potential for luring tourists. Like Friedl Pfeifer and other Tenth Mountain veterans; like members of the Denver ski clubs, the Colorado Mountain Club, and the Izaak Walton League; and like the early advocates of mountain parks, ski hills, and scenic highways, Draper was yet another recreational enthusiast who himself became an energetic promoter of recreational development.[71]

Though military service delayed Draper's project, he, like Pfeifer, returned immediately after the war, partnering with another veteran to

Picturesque
GEORGETOWN
Colo.

3.3 The value of Victorian ambiance. First Denverites looking for quiet summer homes and then Highway 6 tourists searching for a bit of Old West flavor found what they wanted in Georgetown. In silver-mining days, these commercial blocks on Alpine (6th) Street had housed assay offices, mining suppliers, and general stores. Now, with their original reason for existing mostly vanished, these buildings took on new value as architecture and ambiance, evoking for visitors a romantic vision of yesteryear that all but precluded mining in the present. Courtesy Roach Photos, Inc.

launch Georgetown Enterprises Inc. Already by June 1946 they had bought and restored four commercial buildings on Alpine Street, the main street downtown. With the Denver papers gushing positive publicity and Georgetown's new chamber of commerce supporting him too, Draper announced plans to restore all buildings on Alpine Street "to 1880 style" and use them for "businesses that will cater to growing needs of tourists, campers, fishermen, hikers, skiers, and thousands of motoring visitors." He also planned to build a hundred-room hotel and rebuild an opera house that had burned in 1892. Soon, he predicted, Georgetown would become "a showplace of authentic historical interest" and would "again feel the heavy tramp of boots—vacationers' boots."[72] And its success, he hoped, would inspire the conversion of other historic mining towns into tourist attractions. Post-war America had gone crazy for the Old West, he wrote in the *Denver Post* in 1947, immodestly citing the "tremendous interest in the restorations at Central City, Aspen and Georgetown" as proof that this mania for things western could be harnessed to lure the traveling hordes to Colorado. It was time, Draper concluded, to "develop to the fullest" the profit potential of Colorado's "romantic background," to "co-ordinate our efforts and begin to expand our tourist business."[73]

Draper, lacking capital, never realized his grand plans. But others continued the process he started of turning Georgetown into a place whose primary identity lay in charming tourists. In 1954 the Colonial Dames of America acquired the faded old Hotel de Paris on Alpine Street and made it a museum, showing off its diamond-dust mirrors, elegant walnut furniture, and silver and Haviland china. The hotel became a marquee tourist draw.[74] Soon after, Mayor Rogers put forth his "Georgetown Plan" for making historic preservation a matter of town policy.[75] He envisioned Georgetown becoming a quasi-official monument to Colorado's mining history—and he had the clout to make it so. In 1959 he persuaded a fellow Denver lawyer to donate to the State Historical Society several old claims around the abandoned railroad loop right-of-way for use as a mining and railroad history park. In 1966 this land would become part of a National Historic Landmark, and in the 1980s the State Historical Society would use the same land to rebuild the storied loop—the attraction that had lured so many sightseers to Georgetown in pre-automobile days.[76] The rebuilt loop brought Georgetown full circle in its identity as a tourist town. Except this time, instead of mining and tourist landscapes coexisting as they had in Victorian Georgetown, the latter now operated to erase the former. Much as in Aspen, tourist rights-of-way covered the former sites of mines and mills, and gift shops replaced assay offices in downtown storefronts. Recreation even erased hints of the labor that had gone into blasting rock and hauling ore, as Lower Town, where Georgetown's miners had once made their modest homes, was largely flooded by an artificial fishing lake. Georgetown, originally founded to extract silver, was taking on a wholly new role in the landscape of post-war leisure.

Thirteen miles downvalley, Georgetown's old rival, Idaho Springs, also found a place in the emerging tourist landscape, albeit of a different sort. Idaho Springs boosters did not have Georgetown's elegant mansions to show off, but they did have excellent highway access; so, as we saw in chapter

2, they hyped their town less as an attraction in itself and more as a gateway to other attractions in the surrounding area.[77] That did not mean tourist infrastructure was any less important, though. To fulfill the gateway role, Idaho Springs needed a wide range of basic services like gas stations and garages, groceries and gift shops, cottage camps and motels, and restaurants and cafés that catered to visitors instead of just locals. Idaho Springs offered them all—in particular, more motels and restaurants than any other community in the area.[78] There was nothing planned about this: such establishments accrued as entrepreneurs more or less independently anticipated or reacted to tourist demand. But the presence of so many tourist businesses, lined up along U.S. 6-40 as the two highways ran together through the long, narrow valley town, gave Idaho Springs an unmistakable look and identity in the eyes of the vacationing public. The same was true of other mountain towns—like Granby, Dillon, Kremmling, and Glenwood Springs—where motels and other tourist businesses lined the highway through town, and promoters played on the gateway theme.

But Denver was the city that played the gateway role to greatest effect, and it was not even in the mountains. If Denver's location on the plains surprises many first-time visitors, that is largely because the city's tourist boosters have long marketed the mountains as a part of the city—its backyard, its playground.[79] The claim was not just a figment of advertising. It was also a product of infrastructure. Rail lines, then scenic drives, and then oiled and paved highways linked flat Denver to its backdrop of foothills, valleys, peaks, and canyons well before World War II. The city's unusual collection of municipal "mountain parks" beckoned to picnickers and hikers beginning in the 1920s, while ski hills and jumps drew the winter carnival crowd. And Denver offered a wealth of tourist accommodations, including what was, in the heyday of the tin-can tourist, probably the nation's biggest and best-known autocamp, Overland Park. Again, no one entity built or planned all this infrastructure; it accumulated from the efforts of city officials, state and federal government, business owners, and recreation and booster groups. By the 1950s Denver could boast another infrastructural advantage: a great multitude of motels, which made it easy to use the city as a jumping-off point to the high country. A great many motels mushroomed along Colfax Avenue in particular, the boulevard that carried U.S. 40 through Denver.[80] After a long, numbing drive across the plains, many tourists were happy to stop at a motel on Colfax instead of pressing on another hour to stay the night in Idaho Springs.

To cement Denver's status as a western vacation headquarters, the city's Convention and Visitors Bureau unveiled another key piece of infrastructure in 1951: a gleaming, streamline moderne–style Hospitality Center, eye-catchingly located right where Colfax Avenue curved and slowed traffic on its way through downtown. The Hospitality Center, as we have seen, stocked brochures from all over the high country, underscoring Denver's position as a launchpad for mountain leisure.[81] As it turned out, that concept, meant to attract people on vacation, would also end up attracting a lot of people looking for a permanent place to live.

Not just rival community boosters but also rival motel owners were locked in constant competition to make their place the home base of choice. Motels had famously unsubtle ways of grabbing motorists' attention, like colorful signs and fanciful design schemes. In Colorado, not surprisingly, the scheme often had something to do with the Old West. Denver boasted the Brandin' Iron, Sand & Sage, and Wagon Wheel motels; Granby offered the Broken Arrow, Frontier, and Thunderbird; and Glenwood Springs tempted tired vacationers with the Silver Spruce, the Westerner, and the Trail. One can easily imagine the corral-style fence around the parking lot, the faux-log walls, or the smiling cowboy or perky pine tree on the neon sign.

But beneath their kitschy exteriors, motels were peddling something more mundane. With postwar vacationers hailing largely from middle-class suburbia, a big part of motel marketing was to mimic the comforts and conveniences of the modern suburban home. That is why the word "modern" appeared on so many motel signs, ads, postcards, and brochures. "Modern," wrote one motel owner, was one of those "simple sure-fire words" that "must be pointed up."[82] It signaled that guests could expect a full complement of domestic amenities: brand-name mattresses; clean, private bathrooms; oftentimes kitchenettes; wall-to-wall carpeting; and up-to-date house technologies like telephones, (increasingly) televisions, and year-round climate control. Of course, motels did not always live up to such promises, as veterans of lumpy motel mattresses and malfunctioning motel toilets could attest. But at the very least, the *image* of modernness that motels put forward aimed to resonate with expectations of suburban domestic cleanliness and convenience. "Combining the Modern with the Western": that was how one Glenwood Springs motel ad described the ideal balance between frontier vacation thrills on the one hand and, on the other, the contemporary comforts that suburbanites had come to expect back home.[83]

It is equally significant that motel owners tried to make their properties

3.4 Suburban nature on vacation. In Denver, where U.S. 40 became Colfax Avenue, motels tried to lure passing tourists with ranch-house or cottage-style architecture, lawns, flowerbeds, and trees—a vision of suburban home-away-from-home. And it was not just the motels. The entire postwar vacationland was constructed around the promise of suburban nature—the chance to escape to attractive, healthful, wholesome environs with outdoor leisure always in sight, while sacrificing none of the familiar comforts or modern conveniences. Lake County Museum / Curt Teich Postcard Archives

look suburban. The likeness was most evident in the 1930s and 1940s motel forebears called cottage courts, which scattered small private houses (and their attached carports or garages) among grass, flowers, shrubs, and trees. By the 1950s, cottage courts had evolved into motels, which fused the cottages into a single long, usually one-story building. But motels continued to give off a strongly suburban air. A broken roofline might sustain the impression of separate single-family houses, or a continuous long, low roof might echo the ranch-house profile so popular in 1950s suburbia. Other clues also would have looked instantly familiar to suburban families on vacation: knotty-pine paneling, which gave motel interiors a rustic rec-room feel; picture windows and patios, which casually blurred indoors and out, as the archetypal ranch house was supposed to do; and swimming pools, which beckoned from in front of many motels like billboards for backyard-style leisure. And then there was that signature symbol of suburbia, the lawn:

a "neat lawn" with "carefully tended flower beds, shrubs, and beautiful trees," as one motel owner proudly described hers.[84] It was no accident that lawns and plantings fronted so many motels, including many along Denver's Colfax Avenue, creating residential oases in an otherwise relentlessly commercial landscape. So eager were motel owners to evoke the suburban lawn that even if they lacked space for a large one, they usually still found room for little scraps of yard-like greenery. In Idaho Springs, where tourist businesses crowded unprettily into a narrow strip along U.S. 6-40, mom-and-pop motels like the Sleepy U, the Krenzel, and the Rest Haven gamely cultivated little patches of grass, complete with lawn chairs, while the nearby Peoriana and H&H were trimmed with topiary and ornamental trees. The H&H had what might have been the only flowering hedges on the Highway 6-40 strip.[85]

Of course, what most commended a motel was its proximity to tourist attractions. Motels in Denver and along Highways 40 and 6 scrambled to position themselves as the take-off point for tourists exploring the high country. With the motel serving as "your headquarters," suggested the Pig'n Whistle on Colfax in west Denver, "you can make thrilling one-day circle trips to Grand Lake and Estes Park . . . up Mount Evans over the highest highway in America. . . . You'll spend lazy, fun-packed days exploring the old ghost towns, fishing the well-stocked mountain streams, or in winter, skiing the trails through untouched wilderness where big game hunting abounds." The Pig'n Whistle, it was claimed, "makes all these fascinating places readily accessible." Combine this pitch with the "comfort and convenience" of the rooms and the "artistically landscaped" grounds, "with outdoor tables and chairs for fun in the sun," and it becomes evident that a motel like the Pig'n Whistle was trying to do more than just look suburban.[86] It was, more broadly, trying to tap into its customers' fundamentally suburban way of relating to nature. Like a suburban house, the motel promised a modern dwelling with all the latest technological comforts, set in an environment where green spaces, recreational amenities, and pretty views awaited right outside your picture window—or, at most, a short drive from your door. All the thrills of the high-country environment, packaged so as to obviate any dangers, difficulties, or inconveniences—that was the formula that motel owners, whether in Denver, Idaho Springs, Granby, or Glenwood, used to lure customers.

And if that, in turn, sounds like the formula that was also being used to market skiing, camping, and trout fishing, then you begin to grasp the

3.5 Make your home in vacationland. Sometimes it was hard to distinguish a pitch to prospective homebuyers from a tourist brochure. This early-1960s example came from Jefferson County, which extends from Denver's western edge up into the foothills and low mountains. Author's collection.

significance of motels in the Colorado landscape: namely, that motels were part of a much wider effort to construct Colorado as *suburban nature*. Like stocked trout streams, groomed ski slopes, Forest Service campgrounds, and paved highways, motels helped remake the Colorado environment into one akin to what middle-class suburbanites valued and felt comfortable with back home. Suburbanites sought landscapes that were fresh, green, open, and pretty; that felt like escapes from the city; that excited or soothed the emotions and bolstered one's sense of self; that were good for the kids. Suburbanites liked to live in landscapes with nature close at hand, so long as the "nature" was wholly benign: fun and uplifting, yet utterly unthreatening, and conveniently accessible by car. Suburbs were designed to be such settings. So were vacationlands. In Colorado we can see how the two blurred together, tourism building off suburban ideals for the good life.

The blurring went the other way too. The suburban ideal, as it turned out, borrowed a lot from tourism. Suburban boosters in metro Denver never missed the chance to talk up their suburbs' mountain views, abundant sunshine, and nearness to recreational amenities. When the chamber of commerce for Denver's western suburbs in Jefferson County set out to recruit new residents, its brochure included some images of schools, churches, and shopping centers but even more pictures of people skiing, boating, fishing, hunting, and golfing. The brochure brimmed with slogans like "Hub for Year Around Activity" (the vacation-headquarters theme); "Rough It in Style" (a slogan fit for a dude ranch); and "climate at its very best . . . the famed Colorado magic ingredient" (a catchphrase lifted straight from state tourist advertising). Developers used the same tropes to market new subdivisions. When the Bow-Mar development in Denver's southwest suburbs opened for lot sales in 1947, the cover of its promotional pamphlet echoed the motels' western-yet-modern theme: a western-dressed couple on horseback in the foreground, scenic foothills in the background, clean-lined ranch houses in between. The pamphlet gushed vacation clichés that were emotionally and environmentally charged. In Bow-Mar, it said, "you may fully enjoy the invigorating Colorado climate . . . blue skies, glorious sunshine and inspiring views . . . the wide and magnificent panorama of the snow-capped Rockies." Prospective residents learned that Bow-Mar had been planned, resort-like, around two lakes: "great glittering jewels" reserved for residents' exclusive fishing, swimming, boating, or skating use. There were bridle paths for riding, and traffic-free highways let residents "quickly drive to any of the recreational facilities of Denver's Mountain Parks System." All told, bragged the pamphlet, Bow-Mar was "a perfect design for living."[87]

Bow-Mar's pitch makes clear what the suburbs were really selling. It was tourism become lifestyle: a *tourist way of life*. The fleeting pleasures of a Colorado vacation, Denver-area suburbanites could enjoy on a permanent

3.6 Living the tourist way of life. The sales pitch for living in Denver, especially its spreading suburbs, began to look like advertising for the vacationland. Here, the new suburb of Bow-Mar (1947) promised mountain recreation right in the backyard. Author's collection.

basis—so went the pitch. Every day they could soak in Colorado's sunshine and crisp air and find inspiration in its celebrated mountain views from their picture windows, patios, and backyards. Every weekend, if they wanted, they could take paved highways up to the high country for some fishing, hiking, or skiing. Just as a motel in a gateway town gave tourists ready access to recreation, so too did a ranch house in a Front Range subdivision, except its "tourists" lived there full time. And with both tourist and residential landscapes constructed as suburban nature—scenic, spacious, uplifting, unthreatening, recreational, and of course auto-accessible—the high-country vacationland became an extension of every Front Range suburbanite's backyard. That was the promise of living in Bow-Mar—or in Columbine Valley, Pinehurst Estates, Palos Verdes, Bel-Vue Heights, Dream House Acres, Ken-Caryl Ranch, Southglenn, Stony Creek, Cherry Knolls, Greenwood Hills, Walnut Hills, or any of the many other middle- to upper-middle-class subdivisions that sprouted from the rolling grasslands around Denver in the decades after 1945.

By no means did Colorado pioneer this tourist way of life. In fact, the popular imagination of the 1940s and 1950s already associated it with vacationlands farther south, like Florida, Arizona, and Southern California—the Sunbelt states, as many would call them by the 1970s. They, even more than Colorado at the time, carried a powerful allure for postwar Americans. In part this was because their economies were booming bigger, their populations exploding faster than anywhere else. But it was also because they epitomized the new leisure-centered, automobile- and outdoor-oriented lifestyle. This lifestyle was suburban, yes, but so much more than that: it was the chance to flee the tired old cities of the East and Midwest, to start anew in vibrant young metropolises with plentiful sunshine, close by some of the most magnificent scenery and recreation-friendly settings the nation could offer. Many observers believed that westward lifestyle migration was opening a whole new chapter in human history. The nation was now "so prosperous and so mobile," wrote California journalist Neil Morgan, "that its people are free to go in search of a more luxurious way of life. The Westerners of today are the first people in world history to attain that freedom in the mass." Moving not for stodgy old reasons like jobs but instead for pleasures like outdoor recreation, "scenic extravagances," a sense of "escape from conventional urban crowding," and a more "leisurely pace," the new migrants were "moving West to build their future, and they have dreams of the super-life."[88]

Without question Southern California was this aspiration's ultimate exemplar. It also had a long history of luring tourists. But it was famous long before 1945 as an idyllic place to live, an image glamorized in Hollywood movies and endlessly reproduced in the form of California bungalows, which had spread from the Golden State to become the most popular house

style for suburbanites in the Progressive Era. After 1945, Hollywood, Disneyland, the Los Angeles freeway system (which at first was much admired,
only later reviled), and Palm Springs renewed Southern California's reputation as a pacesetter for the good life. And the ranch house, another California native, became the new bungalow—the architectural expression of
the postwar suburban ideal.[89] Southern California, the "golden magnet,"
led the way in making escapist fantasy into everyday life, merging suburban
paradise and vacationland into one.[90]

So when Colorado partisans reached out to newcomers, this Southern
California or Sunbelt mystique was what they tapped into. Again, that is
why they hyped the sunny climate: to rid Colorado of its Snowbelt image
and persuade people to see it as a Sunbelt state. And that is why they talked
endlessly about the "outdoor living," the "healthful, informal living," the
"new joy in living" that putatively made Colorado, like California, more
than just a place to live: "It's a Way of Life."[91] Especially telling is how eagerly
Coloradans laid claim to the California ranch house. When *Rocky Mountain
Life*, a magazine of the 1940s, profiled a family's new house in the Denver
suburb of Cherry Hills—complete with built-in back-patio grill, spacious
yard, knotty-pine rec room, and big windows for expansive mountain
views—the headline, "Design for Western Living," echoed what California
tastemakers like *Sunset* called ranch houses. *Colorado Wonderland*, the colorful booster magazine of the 1950s, went further, all but claiming the ranch
house as a Colorado invention. In Colorado, reported *Wonderland*, houses
were being specially designed "for a way of life"'—for "Colorado's experiment in an all-weather life"—"instead of for shelter." Readers were invited
to mail-order plans for the "Colorado Wonderland Home," a rambling one-
story house with relaxed multipurpose rooms, kitchen oriented to serve
the patio, and generous picture windows to "bring outdoors inside." Never
mind that these features made the "Wonderland Home" really just a typical
ranch house; never mind that these ideas about architecture for outdoor living actually came from California. In *Colorado Wonderland*, Colorado was
the one setting the pace, innovating the ranch house and its exciting new
way of relating to nature. Colorado was the one making "rapid progress"
toward casual, vacation-like "outdoor living"—the "future way of life" for
all Americans.[92]

And, the pitch continued, all the same environmental delights that suited
a Colorado vacation also made Colorado a perfect place to make a home. "In
this big country every home has its trees, lawn and flowers—with plenty of

room for children to play in fresh air and sunshine," gushed the state lure book, seamlessly meshing tourist and suburban clichés. Prospective visitors and armchair travelers learned that people were flocking to Denver to make their homes by the mountain playground and that "heading for the hills" was part of the weekly rhythm for people lucky enough to live there. "Being part of the every-day life of the Coloradan taught us the full meaning of the relaxed life," marveled one author after visiting friends. "Our friends had their work, but they also had other things . . . picnics enjoyed on a mountainside . . . only an hour's drive from the front door . . . equally informal patio parties, delicious food cooked out-of-doors." In the same vein, a man who had moved from New Jersey raved about the "staggering scenery to look at even driving to work. Gobs more in the hills for my exclusive use. . . . Polly and I and the kids can fish and hunt and dig for gold and picnic and camp and hike and horseback until we get looking real rugged and ruddy-weathered like the pioneers." There were thousands of people like this, boosters would have you believe: "thousands," claimed Denver's tourist bureau, who "have found in the Centennial State the achievement of a permanent home in an environment that fulfills their fondest dreams." The Advertising and Publicity Committee put it most succinctly: "For Coloradoans, this all-year vacationland is home!"[93]

More than just a way to lure new residents, the blurring of tourism with everyday life became a new economic development strategy too. Boosters learned that vacation amenities could also attract new businesses and industries. After all, businesses were becoming almost as mobile as people. The postwar decades saw dizzying economic decentralization, as droves of footloose firms deserted cities for suburbs and fled the Midwest and Northeast for the South and West. And executives (re)locating their companies were, in Neil Morgan's words, more and more "oblivious to the traditional industrial requirements of location," like nearness to major population centers, markets, or stores of raw materials.[94] Instead, they showed more and more inclination to choose places with vacation amenities and a high quality of life. Why? In part because that was where the CEOs themselves wanted to live; but also because, according to the new thinking, that was where the best employees were headed too. As one real estate analyst explained, "Talented, creative people," like professionals, administrators, scientists, and technicians, were "basically interested in a good place to live . . . pleasant physical surroundings . . . recreational facilities and climatic conditions that permit both outdoor and indoor activities." So employers who set up shop in vacationland stood to reap outstanding talent. There was a lesson here for boosters too: use the lure of amenities to "relocate these [talented] people in the area," and "the industrial plants will follow."[95] The very phrasing represented a radical new way of thinking about economic development. Instead of the old idea that people followed jobs, the new thinking had jobs following people—and people following the qualities that made places nice to vacation in. In short, it was becoming increasingly accepted that environmental amenities could generate economic growth on their own.[96]

As a result, the late 1950s and 1960s saw a whole army of Colorado boosters working to lure new firms: state publicists, local officials, chambers of commerce, utility companies, banks, real estate brokers, *Colorado Wonderland*. And all of them dangled the temptation of scenery, outdoor fun, and sun. *Denver Post* editor Palmer Hoyt, a leading regional cheerleader, proclaimed that Denver sat on the cusp of greatness not just because its "Rocky Mountain Empire" was rich in minerals and other resources but also because the city was a "desirable place to live," with a lovely climate and "nearness to mountain refuge and playground." Tapping this same theory, the Advertising and Publicity Committee, under Governor Steve McNichols, began courting footloose firms by issuing industrial relocation guides with colorful postcard scenery—and nary a hint of industry—on the cover. "Pleasant Living," promised the agency's industrial-development ads. John Love, McNichols's successor in 1963, kept up the same strategy. On Governor Love's frequent missions to "Sell Colorado"—which saw him leading delegations of Colorado businessmen to cities like New York and Chicago, where they would wine and dine executives and try to persuade them to move their companies to the Centennial State—the tourist lifestyle was always a big part of the pitch. Attendees at a Sell Colorado event could count on lots of scenic lighted displays, scenic slide shows, and colorful, tourist-style information packets.[97]

Executives were told that once their business settled in Colorado, the year-round recreation would make it easy to recruit personnel. (Indeed, one Colorado businessman attested that he had found "some of his best men" by running recruitment ads "in the ski magazines.") And surely executives themselves, as card-carrying members of the leisure class, would like working where they could also play. But the pitch went still further: outdoor amenities, boosters claimed, actually made a business more profitable. Colorado's wide-open spaces offered "room to grow"; its scenery stimulated creative thinking; its salutary climate meant "minimum time lost for illness."

And best of all, vacation surroundings made employees more productive. "A fly rod, a golf club, a boat, a horse, high country family camping, great weather and climate . . . it's important to have something *extra* to work for," explained one ad. "Because [when] a man wants to enjoy these things, he gets to work on time and works a little harder."[98] A wonderland where both boss and worker could find happiness, where miracles of productivity and prosperity unfolded amid scenery and sun—by the boosters' accounts, it really was the California dream all over again, just at higher altitude and farther inland.

The marketing of Denver's suburbs shows how deeply the lifestyle mystique surrounding the postwar Sunbelt and West drew from tourist fancies, how visions of these places as vacationlands morphed into dreams of a modern, leisure-centered good life. In many ways the dream was simply the latest version of the old middle-class suburban ideal. It offered the exhilarating prospect of living in material comfort after years of the Depression, in security after years of war; of finding a sanctuary to shield the family from outside threats and a refuge to rediscover oneself amid an effacing, alienating world. Basic to these middle-class suburban dreams was an even older, Romantic idea that in nature and the outdoors—even if just a park, an open space in the city, or a backyard—one might find relaxation, regeneration, and revelation. But even though these visions of nature and suburbia were far from new, they did take on a new twist in postwar vacationlands like California, Arizona, and now Colorado. Here, the backyard reached far beyond the fence line. Homes sat close to famous tourist destinations, and residents enjoyed easy access to some of the nation's most popular playgrounds. That, as much as anything, was what made western metropolises like Denver, Phoenix, and Los Angeles so different—at least in the popular imagination—from older eastern cities. Here, like nowhere else, work seemed to blur with play, vacation time with everyday life, and with them the settings where each took place.[99]

The surest way to see the blurring was to look at the landscape itself. Outside Denver and in parts of its hinterland, a striking new development pattern was taking shape. It washed around the city's outermost edges, spread northward and southward along the Front Range piedmont, crept into the foothills just west of the city, and drove deeper into the mountains along Interstate 70. Development was advancing not along a solid line but in much patchier fashion, with resorts, suburbs, exurbs, and other clusters popping up in scattered, highly dispersed, often surprising locations, separated by stretches of open land. Tract-house subdivisions hopscotched across the hilly plains around Denver, competing for the best mountain views. Exurban pockets dotted the forested foothills, where homeowners woke up to deer in their backyards. Farther west, seemingly random trailer parks appeared along I-70 and master-planned resort complexes at the bases of mountains, while weather-beaten old mining towns suddenly sprouted modernistic condominium blocks and A-frames. Neither suburb nor exurb, city nor small town, the new regional landscape blurred these conventional categories and many others too: rural and urban, natural and artificial, settled and wild—and, it bears repeating, vacations and everyday life. The landscape was none of them alone, all of them at the same time.

Similar landscapes were taking shape in other parts of the country— clusters of new growth beyond the traditional metropolis, scattering widely across otherwise open rural space. This was not just urban agglomeration, not just suburban sprawl; it had elements of both and of neither. Geographer Peirce Lewis would later call it the "galactic city," arguing that it was best seen not as a mess of separate clusters but as a single system with multiple nodes. And what tied the system together was a web of paved highways. So it was in Colorado. After decades of road building, modern highways now radiated in every direction from Denver, snaking through the foothills and up into the high country. And every day, thousands of people coursed along these roads, circulating among suburbs, small towns, exurbs, resorts, rural areas, and Denver itself, for work, business, errands, and entertainment—and, of course, for outdoor leisure. That this same galactic pattern appeared in Illinois, Pennsylvania, and other nonvacation states signals that historical causes besides tourism were at play. But Colorado's experience suggests that the large-scale promotion and development of tourism could be a potent shaping force too. Without question, encouraging this kind of landscape was one of tourism's most significant legacies.[100]

Even as this landscape blurred all the familiar categories, it was, once again, very suburban—even the parts of it located far from the suburbs. A trip along the nascent I-70 corridor is revealing. If you drove west from Denver in the 1960s, you would see suburbia's unmistakable influence in the foothills exurb of Evergreen, where the new subdivision called Hiwan Village was growing around a supermarket complex, golf course, and for the first time in that area, a full complement of modern utilities, ready for hookup before the first home lot was sold. Farther west in Georgetown, you would see The Meadows development taking shape, whose plans called for contemporary houses (a departure from Georgetown's Victorian look) and for buried utilities, protective covenants, greenbelts, and an artificial lake.[101]

You would even see the suburban look starting to spill over Loveland Pass, into long-isolated Summit County. There, the catalyst was the construction of a giant new reservoir for the city of Denver, which forced the abandonment and flooding of the old Highway 6 town of Dillon. The Denver Water Board's condemnation of Dillon, and the resulting displacement of some four hundred people, was a wrenching and embittering experience for such a small rural county.[102] But some locals saw it as a chance to build a new community more in keeping with latter-day landscape and lifestyle ideals. Boulder planner Trafton Bean, hired to design the new Dillon on the north shore of the new reservoir, crafted a suburban-looking plan of curving roads and circle drives, artfully fitted to the land contours, the shoreline, and a pretty grove of pine trees. There were separate zones for residences and resorts, all arranged around a large shopping center. Design rules called for low-rise buildings clad in natural materials, while sights that had been common in Old Dillon, like garish signs, trailers, and tar-paper shacks, were strictly forbidden.[103] Many locals scorned the new Dillon for its high land values (which made moving there too costly for many Old Dillonites, especially pensioners) and for its implicit denigration of the rough-edged townscape they had known. But for others, New Dillon was "the chance of a lifetime," as one woman put it. Instead of "a Stringtown, an old fashioned hick town, the same as our old Dillon," locals could live in "a new modern up-to-date planned town" with a shopping center in the middle. And there would be vacation amenities for residents and visitors alike, especially sailing, motorboating, and fishing on Lake Dillon itself, right in residents' backyards.[104] New Dillon began construction in summer 1961, bulldozers and bonfires demolished Old Dillon that fall, and the reservoir inundated the old townsite two years later. In this case, the shift from small-town to suburban landscape was forceful and absolute.

Meanwhile, over the next pass in Eagle County, perhaps the ultimate enclave of suburban nature in the mountains—and the ultimate example of a landscape packaged around the tourist way of life—was taking shape. That would be Vail.

VERY FEW COLORADANS HAD HEARD OF VAIL BEFORE DECEMBER 1961, when the *Denver Post* revealed plans for the resort. Even then, readers could be excused if they missed the significance. Outdoor recreation reporter Cal

Queal got just two hundred words to tell the story, and he spent most of it on statistics: how many acres of ski terrain Vail would cover, how high the vertical drop, how many lifts were planned, how long the runs. He offered no hint that Vail was going to be anything but a big new ski area.[105] It took a longer article, a week later, for the rest of the story to surface. This time business editor Willard Haselbush focused not on ski facilities but on the development planned for the foot of the mountain: a five-million-dollar "complex of hotels, lodges, shops and private dwellings," complete with golf course, prime trout fishing tracts, a gondola for summer sightseeing, and other attractions. Now it was becoming clear. Vail's founders envisioned far more than a ski area. They had in mind an entire new town, devoted to year-round leisure.[106]

Vail's oft-told creation myth tells of an instant genesis: a fabulous resort that suddenly materialized alongside U.S. 6 at the western foot of Vail Pass, in a quiet valley where only a sawmill and sheep pasture had been. This part of the myth, it turns out, is not far from reality. Vail really did go from sheep pasture to ski resort in a matter of months. Construction began in spring 1962, with opening set for December 15. After workers spent a frantic summer and fall cutting ski trails; installing a gondola and two chairlifts; laying gas, sewer, water, and electrical lines; and building a luxury lodge; developer Vail Associates managed, incredibly, to open the resort on schedule. Other businesses open in time for the inaugural 1962–63 ski season included a motel, restaurant, ski boutique, gas station, liquor store, drugstore, and delicatessen. Several vacation houses, and two dormitories for employees and visitors, were also built or near completion on opening day.[107]

The abruptness of Vail's appearance awed observers. It was "a miracle out of a meadow," wrote one travel writer, "a magician's trick." "Motorists traveling Highway 6," marveled a local reporter, "have seen before their eyes one town [Old Dillon] disappear and another [Vail] come to being in a matter of months." *Rocky Mountain News* editor Jack Foster likened Vail's birth to the overnight boomtowns of gold- and silver-rush days. Foster often wrote about hiking to ghost towns, ruminating wistfully amid the ruins on the lost glory of Colorado's past. Now, in Vail, he saw glory returning. "For the first time I can write of the birth of a city," Foster rejoiced. "I had lain on my back many a time beside a crashing stream, gazing at the grass-grown streets and fallen cabins of the days when yellow gold made a city. Now in another day a new city is rising of far greater splendor than that of the past. . . . White gold has made Vail City!"[108]

Evoking the gold-rush camps made Vail seem all the more romantic, but it was not the most accurate historical analogy. Vail's sudden appearance bore stronger similarity to another, more recent and much less romantic place creation: suburban development—or, more precisely, the particular species of suburban development that western urban-cultural historian John Findlay has termed the "magic land." A magic land—Findlay's examples include Disneyland, Stanford Industrial Park, and the original Sun City—was planned as a unit, built and controlled by some corporate or central authority, as were many if not most suburban developments after World War II. But a magic land was also elaborately scripted around some distinctive unifying design theme, giving it greater spatial and visual coherence than the typical suburban enclave and setting it starkly apart from the surrounding metropolis. Indeed, magic lands were meant as middle-class havens from the explosive growth and attendant visual and social confusion that roiled western cities like Los Angeles and Phoenix in the 1950s and 1960s.[109] Vail was no suburb, but it sprang from this same historical context, and its carefully orchestrated, corporate-controlled, thematic plan fits Findlay's concept to a T. That such a magic land would materialize a hundred miles from the nearest metropolis, in the midst of a tourist region, is yet more evidence that suburban sensibilities were powerfully shaping postwar vacationlands. The result, in Vail as in the Denver suburbs, was a landscape that blurred tourism and everyday living, laying the literal groundwork for a tourist way of life.

Pete Seibert, who did more than anyone else to create Vail, was tapped into every facet of the ski world. A child of New England's thriving prewar ski scene, he had joined the ski troopers of the Tenth Mountain Division in 1943, trained at Camp Hale, and suffered near-fatal wounds in Italy (just weeks after Friedl Pfeifer did). After miraculously recovering, he had pursued a racing career in Europe and then returned to Colorado in the early 1950s to work a series of ski-area jobs, leading up to a position as manager at Loveland and then assistant manager at Aspen Highlands, helping to lay out lifts and trails. Like the "discoverer" of Vail Mountain, Earl Eaton—really, like many ski-area employees in skiing's postwar boom years—Seibert dreamed of someday starting up his own ski resort. But he was better prepared than most. Besides his experience managing Loveland and planning Aspen Highlands, he had also, while racing professionally in Europe in the early 1950s, studied at Switzerland's top hotel school to learn the art of managing luxury accommodations.[110]

He had some financial savvy and good business contacts too. Needing money to develop his ski resort, he was able to convince several investors, mostly Denver lawyers and oilmen, to join him in a limited partnership—a common way of raising capital in the oil business. Then he and one of the partners, oilman George Caulkins Jr., began driving around Texas, the Midwest, and the Northeast, recruiting more investors. They came armed with a sales pitch and a fifteen-minute silent film with spectacular footage of Seibert and friends cavorting in the deep powder of Vail Mountain's back bowls. At first they offered each new partner four lifetime lift passes at the future ski resort, but that generated little interest. So they started dangling a more conventional carrot: real estate. They promised each investor a homesite in Vail Village, and that did the trick. By late 1961 they had raised the capital they needed to begin building Vail.[111]

Again, they never meant Vail to be just a ski area. Seibert and his company, Vail Associates (VA), planned to push business beyond one season and make a real "year-round resort" (as the *Post*'s Haselbush labeled it), competing with established four-season destinations like the venerable Broadmoor in Colorado Springs.[112] The business plan that Seibert shopped to investors called not just for ski lodges, lifts, and trails but also for a nine-hole golf course, swimming pools, a skating rink, a curling pond, tennis courts, a stocked fishing stream, a trap and skeet field, and a stabling area with facilities for riding, rodeos, and equestrian events. When skiing was not in season, the gondola would be open for scenic rides, the hotels for conventions; and the resort would also serve as a jumping-off point for nearby summer attractions like the planned Dillon Reservoir, with its fishing, sailing, and water skiing. Vail would be no one-season wonder. It would be a year-round vacation mecca, "a fully integrated resort with all facilities necessary for summer and winter recreation."[113]

VA's "total resort concept," as marketing director Robert Parker called it, also meant providing services to meet visitors' every conceivable need. By its third year, according to VA, Vail Village already boasted several "modern" hotels and motels; "restaurants featur[ing] a variety of cuisine and decor"; the gamut of shopping and services, including "barber and beauty shop, book and novelty store, gift shop, fashion boutique, ski and sports shop . . . drugstore-pharmacy, photo shop, grocery and delicatessen, and liquor store . . . physician, post office, sauna baths, coin laundry, garage and service station, Hertz and Budget Rent-a-Car, Ski Desk, and travel agency"; and in-town diversions like "a new nightclub-restaurant . . . folk music,

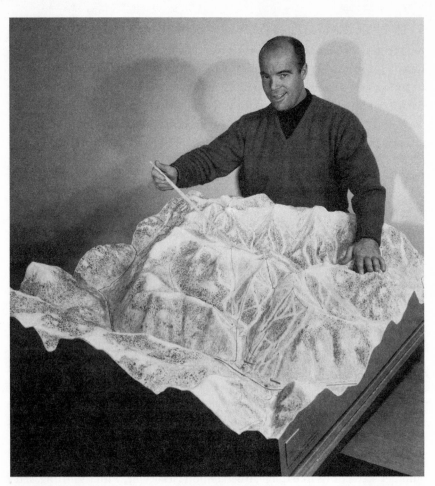

3.7 The original Vail plan. In the midst of crisscrossing the country to recruit investors, Pete Seibert takes a moment to pose with his three-dimensional scale model of Vail. He is pointing to the mostly treeless "back bowls," where he imagined expert skiers gliding down vast, untracked fields of snow. For the front side of Vail Mountain, he envisioned miles of ski trails for all skill levels, converging on a "total resort" village at the base (*lower right*). The future Interstate 70, tracing the deep valley at the front of the model, would link Vail to Denver and beyond. Courtesy Vail Resorts, Inc.

sing-alongs, a Parisian 'discothèque,' movies, ice skating, sleigh rides, and swimming in three heated pools."[114] And this list didn't even mention the nursery, masseuse, dentist, tailor shop, and chapel that would come along within a few years.

Reading all this, it becomes clear that Vail's "total resort concept" hinged less on recreational facilities than on the resort village itself. And while those who value Vail's sophistication might bridle at this association, it was the little village that embodied Vail's fundamental suburbanness—and by extension, the suburbanness of the postwar vacationscape. This suburbanness began, as suggested above, with a strong emphasis on convenience. Convenience was the controlling principle of Vail's physical layout. It dictated the auto-accessible location right next to the future Interstate 70 and ran through the layout of the village itself. The basic village plan was Seibert's, working with architects Fitzhugh Scott Jr. (an early VA partner from Milwaukee) and Fritz Benedict (the Tenth Mountain veteran who had settled in Aspen and also invested in VA). Working with a narrow strip of land, hemmed in by U.S. 6 on the north and the steep lower face of the ski mountain on the south, Seibert, Benedict, and Scott penciled in a parking lot next to the highway, a gondola terminal at the foot of the mountain, and a compact village core in between. This layout would allow visitors to walk from their lodges to the lifts in the morning, ski right back to their hostels at day's end, and stroll easily from restaurant to nightclub, boutique to masseuse, lodge back to car. Convenience truly was, as one travel writer observed, "the key to the Vail master plan."[115]

The village made it easy not just to move around but to spend money too. In other words, Vail—in another stroke of suburbanness—was designed to induce people to consume.[116] Seibert and Scott accomplished this by making Bridge Street, the pedestrian passage that led from the parking lot to the gondola, the main shopping street. To get from their cars to the lifts, visitors *had* to use Bridge Street, which meant they *had* to walk by all the boutiques, bistros, and other businesses along the way. And Scott threw in another sly twist—literally: he made Bridge Street bend gently to the left as it sloped uphill to the gondola. From the vacationer's viewpoint, the bend added a bit of charm. But from the shop owner's perspective, it was another subliminal way of encouraging spending. Scott realized that a bend in Bridge Street would pique visitors' curiosity; they would want to walk up the street to find out what lay around the curve. And as they did, they would pass shops and cafés and presumably succumb to the temptation to spend.[117]

As carefully as VA choreographed the village layout, the design feature that drew the most attention was Vail's faux-Alpine theme, variously described by admirers and detractors as "neo-Salzburgian," "New World Kitzbühel," "Hansel-and-Gretel-Contemporary-Howard-Johnson," or "Wisconsin Swiss."[118] Whatever one called it, it reflected the personal taste

3.8 The bend in Bridge Street. Architect and Vail Associates partner Fitzhugh Scott Jr. designed Bridge Street, in the heart of Vail Village, to curve gently as it ushered visitors from the parking lot up to the ski slopes. The curve made a planned village look unplanned, like an old Swiss hamlet with quirky chalets and picturesque lanes. But the bend also revealed Vail's essential commercialism. Scott knew the curve would pique pedestrians' curiosity and make them want to walk up the street to see what lay around the bend, leading them past shops and restaurants along the way. Photo © by Robert C. Bishop.

of Seibert, who had been charmed by Alpine burgs since his boyhood days spent poring over pictures in ski annuals. Scott had also traveled widely in Europe and fallen in love with the agricultural and recreational hamlets of the Alps. So the two men mapped out a village core they hoped would call Zermatt or St. Anton to mind. Shunning the grid pattern of Colorado's older mountain towns, Scott sketched out a tangle of crooked streets and lanes, some invitingly wide and some cozily narrow, in keeping with the popular image of a rustic European town. And Scott and Seibert decided that all buildings in Vail should conform to an Alpine architectural theme. Anyone wanting to buy a lot in the village would have to clear building plans with an Architectural Control Committee before VA would grant title to the land. The committee encouraged the kinds of design features one might find on a Swiss chalet: gabled roofs with heavy overhangs; an emphasis on "natural," earthy, or subdued colors; and liberal exterior use of stone, stucco, brick or wood. Most of all, the committee decreed that all buildings must be modest in scale so as not to dwarf passers-by and overwhelm the village's cozy feel.[119]

What actually resulted was a weird mix of Continental clichés. Seibert and Scott mostly had Switzerland or Austria in mind, and they did indeed get a lot of Alpine-looking buildings with German-sounding names—the Gasthof Gramshammer, the Sitzmark, the Edelweiss, the St. Moritz. But they also ended up with all the rest of Europe crammed into their village. Builders went wild with the European trappings, and the travel press delighted in trying to describe them. Some second-home owners competed to build "the most authentic Swiss house in Vail," while others tried to outdo each other's Spanish-style interiors. Private homes, according to one reporter, "[ran] the gamut from Bavarian hunting lodges to . . . Normandy chateaux." A columnist claimed to find a house "in Japanese simplicity, another a Swiss chalet, and another a villa from the Italian hill country." Eating and lodging places ranged from a Scandinavian-style inn to restaurants serving Basque food and fondue, from an English-style hunting lodge to an exact replica of a Kitzbühel casino, right on Bridge Street. Sometimes the Euromania got downright bizarre. It is not exactly clear, for instance, what the owners of the Valhalla at Vail meant when they touted their "design and decor . . . in the early Viking tradition." And the writer who called Fitzhugh Scott's Mill Creek House "a combination of Norman castle and Florentine palazzo" might not have been praising it.[120]

Vail's Europretensions struck some as hokey. "The village looks like a Hollywood set of a tiny Austrian ski city," sneered one columnist. "All the exposed beams are in the right places, but you can still smell the sawdust." But for many others, the Old World atmosphere, though contrived, worked anyway. For all one writer cared, "Bridge Street, Vail, U.S.A., could just as well be Brucken Strasse, Kitzbuhel, Austria." "Nobody is speaking Schwyzer [sic] Deutsch for heaven's sake," admitted another, "but from a hundred yards away you could swear you're looking at Yodel-am-Alp." "You halfway expect Heidi to appear in stretch pants," gushed a third, getting into the spirit. VA actively encouraged these kinds of escapist fantasies. "The moment you set boot in Vail," the company promised in one 1968 ad, "you've crossed an ocean. . . . Come to Vail. It's where Europe is."[121]

At first blush, this thematic design does not seem very suburban. Escapism was basic to the suburban ideal, but the exotic brand of escapism Vail was peddling might appear to have little in common with the mundane, ranch-house-and-backyard version that prevailed in postwar suburbia. Yet beneath all its fondue stubes and Swiss chalets, Vail was designed around the same escapist yearnings as the "magic lands" of suburbia. Most fundamentally, it catered openly to anti-urban escapism: the desire, so central to the suburban dream, of leaving behind the troubles of the city and getting back in touch with nature. That is why Vail's designers strove to keep reminders of city life out of their village. Shopping malls, buildings more than four stories tall, noisy vehicles, rooftop TV antennas, overhead wires, parking meters, traffic lights, neon signs, and "diners that come in the shape of frankfurters" were just some of the citified trappings banned first by VA policy and later by town ordinance. In the very beginning, VA even banned automobiles from the village core, leaving Bridge Street and the other narrow lanes to pedestrians and horse-drawn sleighs. Restricting cars seems a bit ironic, given that VA's business model was so heavily premised on ready auto access via Interstate 70, but the idea stemmed from the overarching desire to make Vail feel like a refuge from urban ills.[122]

Little known today, the original Vail concept explicitly envisioned a resort in harmony with its natural setting. Fritz Benedict seems to have been the chief influence here. His 1960 village plan, which Seibert used to recruit investors, proposed some nature protections that were cutting-edge for the time, such as hiding construction in wooded areas to preserve viewsheds and banning construction outright along the banks of Gore Creek. Benedict imagined the golf course not just as a sporting facility but also as a means to "preserve much of the charm of the open parks" on the valley floor, and he urged that tree cutting on the mountain's forested lower reaches be tightly restricted, again to "preserve the natural character."[123] It is true that no one in 1960 could have happened across this secluded vale, tucked among steep wooded slopes and sheer cliffs and spectacular sawtooth crags, and mistaken it for a suburb. Yet Benedict's ideas for harmonizing a new resort into this space were wholly consistent with suburban yearnings: for comfortable contact with nature, for attractive greenery and open space, and especially for refuge from the city. As VA marketing guru Bob Parker explained, Vail's founders "predicted . . . that Americans would be delighted to *get away* from smog and noise and speed and the frantic bustle of our modern urban existence." Indeed, in the mind of Vail's first mayor, the chance to "escape asphalt jungles" and other city worries was "Vail's very excuse for existence."[124]

The same could be said of the social scene Vail cultivated. On the surface it looked exotic and chic. Following ski-industry practice, VA provided bars and "brau hauses" for après-ski revelry, clustered buildings close together to appeal to skiers' "gregarious" nature, and stocked the ski school with handsome foreign instructors to "add to the social life and atmosphere of the village." The company ran ads depicting blonde Eurobeauties like "Ingrid," bragging that the resort was full of people like her: "fun people, exciting people; the young in heart, the daring—leaders in sport and fashion who never settle for less than the best."[125] Again, though, beneath this glamorous veneer, Vail was actually appealing to another suburban ideal: the desire for social exclusivity, for an enclave safe from society's unsavory elements, a place where middle-class respectability (and perhaps whiteness) reigned supreme.[126] Denizens of Vail took pride in it being "square, four corners," as Parker put it, "middle-of-the-road as far as lifestyle is concerned." Indeed, even as VA advertised Vail's "young, vibrant, exciting" spirit, it made a point of adding that the place was "wholesome" too. Few if any Vail investors, business owners, or residents saw themselves creating a scene like Aspen's, notorious by the 1960s for its raucous bars, door-to-door parties, and hectic, hedonistic lifestyle. Instead, the people of the village, bragged the weekly *Vail Trail*, "start out and end up with just good, clean fun."[127]

The claim to wholesomeness suggests another suburban obsession at work in Vail: child raising, or more precisely, the quest for safe places for kids. VA went out of its way to color Vail child- and family-friendly; in fact, it is no exaggeration to say that Vail marketing helped remake skiing into a family sport. Older resorts like Aspen and Sun Valley, with their glamorous auras and steep slopes, catered to adult, expert skiers; when Friedl Pfeifer opened Buttermilk in 1958, it was one of the few ski areas to emphasize easier terrain for "family fun." Now Vail, with its much larger mountain and greater variety of terrain, took Buttermilk's approach to a new level. Indeed, one reason Seibert seized upon this mountain was that its vast surface encompassed plenty of easy slopes, not just difficult ones, with terrain for every skill level, every member of the family. This would prove one of Vail's top selling points—not just for guests but for investors too. Parker later recalled that many of VA's original investors were lured to the enterprise because, in his words, "they'd been scaring themselves and their wives and children on the steep slopes at Aspen and Sun Valley for years," and they wanted "to get involved in a mountain that had plenty of gentle slopes." So VA went after the family market from the start. A typical 1963 ad depicted a freckle-faced pixie named Karen and promised that "a special concern for people like Karen—and you—makes Vail the place for this winter's ski vacation."[128] This might seem unremarkable today, but in the early 1960s, when ski advertising fixated on downhill die-hards and après-ski party animals, Vail's kid-centered pitch stood out boldly.

Vail might be even better for children than suburbia, suggested the resort's propagandists. In logic that revealed Vail's essential conservatism, marketing director Parker reasoned that children who skied would have "no time or inclination for marijuana, LSD, beat-the-draft demonstrations, or other youthful escapism." Instead, at Vail, "the kids will go out and play in the snow for a change" and then "leave for home, tanned, refreshed, calmed and cleaned, for the moment, of their ingrained compulsion to turn on the tube." Not just the kids, but the entire family would benefit. Indeed, the *Vail Trail* recommended skiing for any "family who enjoys being together and reaping the rewards—sound bodies, appreciating the outdoors and most important, solidifying the family unit."[129] Restoring health, contact with nature, and the family bond—skiing, in this vision, brought the same benefits as suburban living was supposed to. Perhaps, in the mid-1960s context, Vail even offered a *post*suburban solution, picking up where many were beginning to realize the suburban dream had fallen short.

Marketing a family-friendly Vail also meant attracting the right kinds of people and excluding the wrong kind. Some worried that Vail's roadside location might open it to "shoddy customers" or "undesirables," in the words of *Trail* editor George Knox, and turn it into a crass, Coney Island tourist trap. Efforts to avoid that fate—to keep Vail exclusive—were built into the original resort concept and intensified as the village evolved. Fritz Benedict's initial plan would have separated motels along the highway from more luxurious lodges, chalets, and vacation homes set back from the road; Fitzhugh Scott's plan, supplanting Benedict's, simply eliminated almost all of the motels. Similarly, Benedict's plan to segregate "transient guests" and "summer tourists" from longer-staying visitors gave way to a policy of discouraging the short-term, off-road crowd altogether.[130] VA deliberately spent its summer advertising budget on "high-class convention and group meetings" instead of "off highway tourism" or "strictly tourist appeals," because the Vail business community preferred the people who came to conventions: "intellectual, elite groups," members of "professions such as law, engineering, medicine, education." That was how one Vail booster characterized them, and she might as well have been describing the social standards of any affluent suburb in America.[131]

Meanwhile, VA made no bones about barring another kind of "undesirable": hippies. In a rule known to all in town, VA barred its workers from

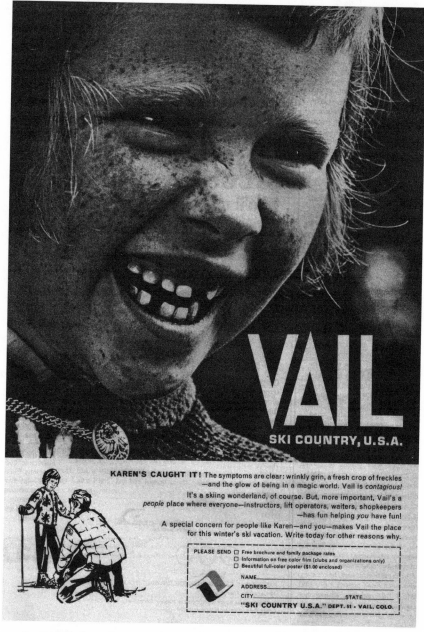

3.9 Family-friendly marketing. In the early 1960s, Vail was a pioneer of marketing ski vacations to families. Ads like this 1963 example offered skiing for beginners and promised wholesome activity for the kids. Courtesy Vail Resorts, Inc.

wearing beards (putting Vail "off limits to Jesus Christ, Abraham Lincoln, and other Subversive Employees," deadpanned one VA hireling). Seibert urged other employers in Vail to do the same. "When the long hair starts to turn off the guest," he explained, "I feel that we owe it to our stockholders and our own jobs to toe the line." The bottom-line rationalization was revealing. So was Seibert's further explanation: "Most of the people who go on vacation are more or less my age group [forties], and . . . when we go on vacation, we often like to see things the way we expect them and not too far out." The words suggested, once again, how much the vacation trade depended on keeping visitors in their comfort zone.[132]

For Seibert and Parker, pursuing "high-class" customers made sense because it would lead to a larger market share. Seibert liked to say that "mass follows class": if trend-setting elites came to Vail, other visitors would follow, and business would flourish.[133] But others in Vail wanted to attract high-class people as an end in itself; they did not want the mass to follow. They wanted Vail to stay an elite enclave, "sort-of-a snooty village," as the Vail Trail's Knox put it unapologetically. And indeed that was the image Vail acquired. It quickly became known as a haven for the rich, but less the celebrity rich than the CEO kind. "You may rub ski poles with the presidents of IBM, Motorola, Sundstrand, and other large corporations," according to one travel writer. "Everyone around you looks contagiously rich and competent," said another.[134] Like the affluent suburbs that yielded most of its visitors, Vail's appeal lay less in glitz or glamour than in its orientation toward family, exclusivity, respectability, and upward mobility—packaged together, of course, with the charming village setting, nonurban atmosphere, and conveniently accessible recreation.

To say the package sold well would be an understatement. Vail in its first decade thrived far beyond its founders' dreams. VA had expected to reach 100,000 skier visits in the fifth season, but that year Vail drew nearly a quarter million. In the tenth season well over a half million lift tickets were sold. By that time there were eleven lifts up on the mountain and an annual bloom of new inns, shops, condos, and houses in the village below. Breathless business reporters supplied the numbers: *$8 million worth of construction has been completed in Vail's first two summers, with $4 million more planned for summer 1964. A whopping $12 million will be spent in 1969, making this year's building season the busiest yet. A $2.25 million luxury condominium complex is under construction just east of the village. Homes of $100,000 are now common. Building sites that went for $3,500 in 1960 sell for $15,000 in 1969.*[135] Bridge Street filled in by 1965, and many business owners began moving on to second projects. One, Ted Kindel, sold his cozy Christiania lodge in 1968 and started work on a mammoth shopping center on the village's north edge.

More development mushroomed outside the village, spreading up and down the long, narrow Gore Creek Valley along Highway 6. In 1963 the Eagle County Development Corporation (ECDC) broke ground for Bighorn, Vail's first "suburb," three miles east of the village. Suburbanization spread the other direction in 1970, when ECDC launched Lion's Ridge, a "high-density condominium area" west of Vail on the opposite side of the highway. Other subdivisions sprang up nearby: Sandstone 70, Buffer Creek, Vail Village West, Matterhorn, Vail Das Schone. Helping facilitate such resort sprawl was the passage, in 1963, of a state law giving legal recognition to the newfangled concept of condominium ownership. The opportunity to own a unit in the mountains without having to maintain the building, utilities, or grounds, at about the price of renting but with the possibility of appreciation on the investment, made it possible and desirable for many more people to acquire second homes. The Condominium Ownership Act, then, helped open the way for new residential complexes to proliferate in towns and resorts throughout the high-country vacationland. And the first places it caught on were Summit County and Vail. Almost all of Vail's new "suburbs" were anchored by condominium complexes, supported in some cases by shops, athletic clubs, and other amenities.[136]

A powerful entrepreneurial zeal—"blind enthusiasm and blind optimism," as one town resident remembered it—permeated Vail in its early years. This was no stereotypical company town, in the sense that the company owned all the land and all the businesses. Instead, VA's strategy was to sell village lots to entrepreneurs and then rely on them to start their own businesses. Together they would make Vail a "total resort."[137] That meant Vail business owners, even while competing with each other for customers, also felt a shared commitment to VA's grand vision. Ted Kindel, the innkeeper-turned-shopping-center developer, called Vail "a place for the 'fighter' where 'the battle is to literally get visitors away from other resorts.'" George Knox, who had worked as an ad-agency man before coming to Vail to found the *Trail*, exhorted every Vailite to become a walking chamber of commerce, ready to pump the nearest visitor's hand, help him find his hotel, and ply him with information about Vail's attributes. "Tell [visitors] about Vail's growth," Knox urged. "Point out to them things they'd probably like to know—how we got started, what our long-range planning is—get in a plug for . . . a summer vacation." For those who did not feel up to the task, the Vail chamber offered sales-training seminars, which, like the newspaper ads the state publicity committee had run in the 1950s, taught locals talking points to pass on to tourists. The goal was to "bring about 100% saturation of all people in Vail who have contacts with our guests," explained the *Trail*, "so that the wonderful, magical, interesting story of Vail can be passed on with complete authenticity."[138] In short, to be a citizen of Vail was to sell it, using Vail's magical origin story and other prepackaged selling points. It seems fitting that Vail's first "unofficial town government" was really a promotional association—the Vail Resort Association, cofounded by VA and various village business owners in 1964.[139]

For people who had pulled up roots to start anew in Vail, working to build a business and a resort economy could be all-consuming. But the hope of profits was not the only reason people relocated to Vail. Many also liked the idea of living in a small town. They craved neighborly familiarity and relished the chance to participate in the creation of a new community—sitting on town committees, volunteering for the fire department, starting up a school. "Unlike city dwellers who specialize within their own vocations," wrote one woman rather smugly, "we at Vail . . . find ourselves involved in every phase of [the town's] operations."[140] Many also idealized Vail as a wholesome place to raise children. They felt it insulated youngsters "from the realities of war, pollution and the major world crises," as one resident put it, and they were convinced their kids were better for it. "It's a pleasure to watch the children in Vail," wrote a *Trail* columnist—"how much enjoyment they extract from the surroundings . . . how mature their thinking . . . how aware they are of every aspect of life and their future responsibilities not only to Vail, but to their roles as good citizens." There was more than just small-town nostalgia to such sentiments, for these were same benefits that children were presumed to get from growing up in the suburbs. So too the joys of neighborliness, community involvement, and institution building were all ones that many Americans in those years associated with suburbia.[141]

And of course there was the environmental side of the suburban dream: the promise of an informal lifestyle of leisure, in a pleasant climate and in close touch with the recreational outdoors. Vail took that promise and planted it amid one of postwar America's most sought-after vacationlands. In other words, even as they hoped to make money off tourists, Vail business owners also hoped to live the tourist way of life themselves. Not surprisingly, skiing was the draw for many of them. Rod Slifer arrived in 1962, a middle-class Colorado kid not long out of college, hoping to spend a few years ski bumming before leaving the mountains to go on to a business career. But like a striking number of the ski bums who arrived in Vail in the 1960s, he ended up staying permanently, becoming one of the area's most successful real estate agents and a local political fixture. It was not just the skiing that drew permanent transplants to Vail. Early residents seemed sincerely to buy into the broader product VA was packaging: an environment where all kinds of outdoor recreation were readily available and where reminders of the city were few. There were many "people who were escaping from cities, from corporate situations," remembers one early comer. "I happen to prefer spruce to smog," wrote another in the *Trail*, explaining why she had made the move. "Year round mountain living offers something more than life in the cement canyons of a smog-smothered city."[142]

And so the settlers of Vail made themselves at home in their anti-urban paradise. On the banks of Gore Creek, around the edges of the golf course, and along intimate lanes that curled up the forested lower slopes overlooking Vail Village, Vail's business class built their high-country sanctuaries, hidden amid lodgepole pines and aspen trees. The house exteriors used stained wood, stucco, and shake shingles to harmonize with the natural environs. The interiors borrowed from ranch-house design—informal, flowing floor plans, and extensive use of patios, decks, and picture windows to bring the outdoors in. Vail houses adapted these ideas to the alpine setting, often by stacking the living and dining spaces atop the bedrooms, opening the upper stories to dramatic panoramas of the ski slopes and the distant, awe-inspiring Gore Range.[143]

For all its European styling and ski-resort glitz, Vail ended up, more than anything else, epitomizing the suburbanness of the high-country vacationscape. Its houses sought the casual marriage of everyday life with the outdoors, while its carefully planned and packaged village facilitated consumerism and indulged escapism from the proverbially troubled city. Its predication on an umbilical highway link back to Denver underscored how indispensable automobility was to the profitability and practicality of suburbia, while its close-at-hand recreational facilities, headlined by one of the world's largest and most cunningly engineered ski mountains, catered to the suburban yearning for conveniently accessible outdoor leisure. To say Vail tapped into suburban sensibilities is not to diminish it—if anything, it helps explain why so many people found Vail so easy to like. But most importantly, when we look closely at the leisurely outdoor lifestyle that was being packaged in a rarefied resort like Vail, and see its essential likeness to the lifestyle that suburban developers were manufacturing and marketing in subdivisions all across the country, we can better see how the line was blurring between tourism and suburbia, as vacation-like ways of valuing the outdoors insinuated their way into more and more Americans' daily lives.

IT IS WELL TO REMEMBER AT THIS POINT THAT THE TOURIST WAY OF LIFE was not available to all Coloradans. If the affluent suburbanites of Bow-Mar could enjoy bridle rides, water sports, and weekend jaunts up to the mountains, those options were a lot less accessible to the poorer residents of inner-city neighborhoods like Five Points, Globeville, or Denver's West Side; working-class suburbs like Commerce City; or for that matter even many of Denver's more middle-class outskirts. Even in Vail, there was a large underclass of locals who could not afford view-commanding houses among the aspens and who had little free time for the golf course or ski slopes. These were the wageworkers who bused tables in the fondue stubes and made beds in the inns. Some of them were ski bums who chose poverty for a few years after college so they could live in a ski resort. But for many others, wage work in Vail was a long-term proposition and a matter of economic necessity, not choice. And it was difficult for them to make ends meet in a town with a cost of living like Vail's. "Since $2 per hour is the standard starting wage," explained one worker in 1971, "take $80 or $100, deduct Income Tax, go food shopping, pay your rent, and then see how much you have left over for clothes, auto and hospital insurance, and other necessities." He added bitterly, "If many of Vail's first families had been asked in 1962 to make the same sacrifices that many young people make here each year, Vail would still be a Hay Ranch."[144]

Housing was a particular worry. With pricey homes and condominiums predominating in Vail Village, employees were forced to live somewhere else—which often meant substandard old houses in nearby Minturn or the mobile homes or cheap apartments that straggled several miles downvalley, along Highway 6. "People who are supposed to be our friendly, courteous, congenial, guest-pleasing employees have been forced to live six, eight, ten and more to an apartment," wrote a sympathetic shop owner, putting his finger on the essential irony of a premium-service resort. In this case, the problem was Vail's own success. The tremendous demand for real estate in Vail Village translated into astronomical land values, which discouraged developers from building cheap housing there. (Not until 1970 would the village's first sizable employee housing project, Apollo Park, get under way.)[145]

But blaming unaffordable housing on the "logic" of the market is too facile. There was a deeper cause, and it cut to the heart of how tourism and the tourist lifestyle were marketed and consumed. Vail, for its part, had been packaged as a place apart from the masses, a refuge from the undesirable elements of the outside world. So it not only excluded but was *premised* on excluding things like low-income apartment buildings and the kinds of people who needed them. Certainly, VA seemed in no hurry to make space for such things. For example, Pete Seibert suggested that voting in Vail be restricted to property owners because "we don't want a local bartender to be mayor"; and VA board member Dick Hauserman urged the company to discourage undesirables by making a point "not to allow very cheap housing to be constructed or operated at Vail."[146] The elitism in such statements is easy to see. But anyone tempted to single out Vail—or Aspen, another easy target—should remember that they were not the only settings styled and sold as places apart. So were other less elite tourist destinations. So were suburbs around Denver. So, really, was Colorado as a whole. The entire concept of the state being a vacationland and lifestyle haven hinged on the idea that it was far removed from the crowds and cares of everyday life.

That idea profoundly changed Colorado. Not only did it lure millions of tourists and tourist dollars, but it also became the impetus for an untold number of permanent new residents to come to the state. Reports in the late 1950s suggested that as many as three-quarters of the state's new residents had first seen Colorado on vacations or convention trips. "It was the outdoor life that brought many of us," agreed Dick Lamm, who himself made the move in the early 1960s, and who would go on to become governor in 1974. "The skiing. The mountain climbing. The white-water trips. Hunting and fishing. . . . You could escape the regimentation and restrictions of a civilized world. . . . The mountains were a refuge from the noise and stench of the city."[147] Not by coincidence, the same polls that found Colorado to be one of the most desirable states for a vacation also found it to be one of the states where Americans most yearned to move.[148] And many did. Colorado's population swelled by nearly a third in the 1950s, and by *two-thirds* from 1950 to 1970.

The outdoor lifestyle allure was not the only reason for the influx. Employment opportunities, above all, were the leading driver of population growth in Colorado and the rest of the booming postwar West. But lifestyle allure was also an important reason for many companies to move to Colorado and start hiring there. In any case, census numbers certainly bear out the notion that many people were coming to live the suburban-tourist way of life. Consider, for example, that the percentage of Colorado's population living in what the Bureau of the Census called the "urban fringe"—meaning mostly suburbia—surged from 7 percent in 1950 to 28 percent by 1970. And consider that the center of Colorado's suburban explosion, the Denver metro area, accounted for three-quarters of Colorado's total population growth in the 1950s and two-thirds of its growth in the 1960s. In the 1960s, of the ten fastest-growing counties beyond the Front Range metropolitan corridor, six of them were the six tourist-booming counties along I-70.[149]

Tourist promoters had succeeded beyond their wildest dreams. All marketing encourages consumers to develop a personal connection to the things they are purchasing. In this case, tens of thousands of consumers had gone well beyond that, rearranging their entire lives around the places and pastimes tourist promoters had packaged for them. That in itself was an unexpected consequence of tourist development in Colorado. But there was about to be an even more unexpected consequence, as consumers' personal investment became political too. Already by the 1960s, more and more Coloradans were developing, through their interests in outdoor recreation, a newfound concern for the fate of the landscapes where they lived or played or both. A popular environmental movement would become the latest legacy of the making of the Colorado vacationland.

CHAPTER 4

Blueprints for Action

DECADES BEFORE YOU COULD SET SAIL IN SUMMIT COUNTY OR TIME-share a condo in Vail, you could find yourself a cabin up in some piney corner of the high country and live a modest version of the tourist lifestyle. That is what Arthur Carhart did when he bought a cabin in Hot Sulphur Springs, right on the Colorado River, in the early 1940s. An alpine retreat must have sounded good to a man as busy as he was. In the two decades since his stint as the Forest Service's first recreation engineer, Carhart had worked as a landscape architect, outdoor writer, Western pulp novelist, and director of wildlife research for the Colorado Game and Fish Department. He churned out articles and books promoting recreational pleasures like fly fishing, campfire cooking, and dude ranching—especially in Colorado. And he became a prolific writer on recreation and resource issues, emerging by the early 1950s as one of the nation's most respected conservationists.[1] But on summer weekends Art and his wife, Vee, were no different than thousands of other Denverites who hopped in their cars and headed west on Highway 6 or 40 for some down time in the mountains.

But on one such sojourn in summer 1948, something horrible happened. Art and Vee were loafing at their riverside cabin, when they began to notice mud wisping downstream. It swirled, then thickened, then covered the aquatic plants with a heavy layer of slime. It settled on the gravel riverbed, smothering the insect hatchery and dooming the local trout—an environmental nightmare unfolding right before Art and Vee Carhart's eyes. The culprit? A sediment release from several miles upstream, where the federal

Bureau of Reclamation was building Granby Dam. Carhart complained vehemently. So did state Game and Fish officials, local dude ranch owners, and the Izaak Walton League. But it was too late. In fact, it was about to get even worse.[2]

Two years later, with the dam finished, renewed disaster befell the same stretch of river. The Bureau of Reclamation reneged on the minimum flows it had promised, choking the river from 322 cubic feet per second to just 30—a near-total dewatering. The ecological impact, Carhart later recalled, was "ghastly." For miles below Granby Dam, "the Colorado River was no longer a clear, rolling, cool trout stream. It was no longer something to give pleasure in its laughing rapids or quiet pools. It was a sun-baked, stinking little trickle." A scenic and recreational resource whose worth Carhart pegged at more than twenty million dollars was utterly ruined. It was, he charged, "common murder!" And it could happen anywhere. "Sooner or later," he warned his fellow sportsmen, "they'll deal the same dose to your favorite fishing stream if they are not brought to account for their acts at Granby Dam. . . . It's YOUR fight, brother."[3]

Angry words. The sliming and strangling of the Colorado clearly offended Carhart, not just professionally, as a conservationist who felt that the Bureau of Reclamation should have heeded expertise like his, but *personally*, as a sportsman who loved fishing in the river the agency had ruined. And he wanted others to take it personally too. Though he did not use this language, he was calling on his fellow leisure consumers—people who, like him, had bought into the recreational qualities of rivers—and he was asking them to make their personal investment the basis for political action. It was no coincidence that Carhart described what he had lost—"a clear, rolling, cool trout stream . . . laughing rapids . . . quiet pools"—in vivid yet clichéd words that sounded remarkably like lines from a tourist brochure. It was no coincidence because those were the terms in which he and his fellow sportsmen had learned to envision a recreational environment like the Colorado high country—to desire it, value it, consume it. Now those were the terms Carhart used to urge people to care about it and fight for it.

Recreational consumerism changed how people dreamed of the natural environment, profited off it, moved through it, and molded their lifestyles around it. But as Carhart's outrage suggests, it also changed how they acted politically about it. The recreational connections that people felt toward certain places became the basis for their taking action to defend them. At first, this action was limited to a narrow cohort of outdoorsmen-conservationists,

4.1 A Colorado conservationist. By the time of this portrait in the early 1960s, Art Carhart's career was winding down. For over forty years he had worked and written on conservation issues, championing the cause of science-based professional resource management. He had worked almost as long to publicize and popularize outdoor recreation, especially in Colorado. These sides of his career came together in his work on recreation planning, a field he helped invent—and one that became a founding cause of the emerging popular environmental movement in Colorado. Courtesy Denver Public Library.

like Carhart. But as they fought in the 1940s and 1950s against the dam-building juggernaut in particular, these conservationists realized they were overmatched and needed allies. The most obvious candidates were recreational consumers themselves. But in a booming tourist state like Colorado, another promising possibility was to align conservation with business interests in the tourism and outdoor-recreation industry. Colorado conservationists like Carhart ended up doing both, and their strategy met with real success. By the mid-1960s they had built momentum for a new conservation agenda, one that sought to protect the scenic and leisure qualities of the mountains by zoning recreational landscapes and planning for recreational growth on a large scale. In the ensuing years it would become clear that this agenda was fraught with environmental dilemmas of its own. But at the time it was an agenda that growing numbers of leisure promoters and consumers found they could rally around. Their faith in recreational development as the means to environmental progress was the founding principle of the popular environmental movement in Colorado.

THERE WAS NO SUCH THING AS AN "ENVIRONMENTAL MOVEMENT" WHEN the river outside Art Carhart's cabin got slimed. There was only "conservation." All problems concerning natural resources or the outdoors—whether they involved timber, water, minerals, soil, scenery, wildlife, pollution, or recreation—got lumped under that one word. It came from the turn-of-the-century Progressive conservation movement, which also gave Americans their default strategy for dealing with such problems: turn them over to foresters, wildlife managers, and other professionally and scientifically trained experts. Experts, the Progressives held, were best qualified to manage resources impartially, guard against waste, guarantee America's natural bounty for the long term, and ensure that it was put to the greatest public good.[4]

Not until the 1960s did environmental issues become matters of widespread popular worry and mass political action, and that is when Americans began talking of "environmentalism" and an "environmental movement." It was a convergence of historical circumstances that brought this movement about, including the rise of affluence and automobility; the inspiration of the civil rights movement and other mass protests in its wake; creeping anxieties over atomic and chemical technology, pollution, and their effects on public health; the efforts (and affronts) of government agencies involved with dam building, public-lands management, and other resource matters; and environmental disasters and other watershed incidents that grabbed headlines and galvanized popular concern.[5] But the rise of the environmental movement also had a lot to do with outdoor recreation. On a societal level, booming participation in outdoor recreation was a leading reason why more Americans began to feel a personal stake in the management of public lands and the wider national landscape. And at an organizational level, recreational interest groups often took the lead in both popularizing and publicly critiquing the work of expert resource managers, opening once obscure environmental issues, long considered strictly technical or bureaucratic affairs, to wider public view.

The relationship between recreational enthusiasts and resource managers—between the conservation profession and the outdoor-loving public—had long been mixed. In the early twentieth century, the most ardent advocates of conservation, outside conservation agencies themselves, had been recreational enthusiasts—especially sport hunters and anglers.[6] But they did not like all conservation equally. They applauded the kind that fish and game managers practiced, but they bemoaned the way the Bureau of

Reclamation, Forest Service, and other nominally nonrecreational conservation agencies seemed so often to develop timber, water, and other resources at the expense of hunting and fishing. Groups like the National Wildlife Federation and Izaak Walton League sprang up in the 1920s to defend sportsmen's interests against such threats. By the late 1940s these groups began allying with other recreation-minded organizations like the Wilderness Society and Sierra Club, and they tried, Art Carhart-like, to curry public support by appealing to the broader—and ever-broadening—population of leisure consumers. What resulted by the late 1950s was a nascent environmentalism that never totally abandoned older conservation ideals. Its adherents purported to be populist but still looked to expert resource managers, decried extractive greed but held fast to the notion of nature's bounty, and professed faith in cold, hard science even as they exalted the emotional and transcendent benefits of leisure time spent outside.

The Sierra Club usually gets the most credit for catalyzing this movement, but in Colorado the initial catalyst was the Izaak Walton League of America (IWLA).[7] Nationally, the IWLA in the 1940s had more members and more pull with policy makers than any other outdoor group, and in Colorado its brand of conservation played especially well. Colorado's outdoor leisure scene was largely middle class and casual, and so was the Izaak Walton League; it resembled, in historian Stephen Fox's words, "a Rotary Club that liked to go fishing." Founded by businessmen and professionals in Chicago in 1922, it caught on quickly in cities and small towns across the Midwest and then did the same in Colorado. Perhaps because several of its founders were salesmen and advertising men, the league had a flair for publicity that fit well with Colorado's culture of outdoor boosterism. (Indeed, in some locales, like Summit County, IWLA chapters actually issued tourist brochures.)[8] It did not hurt that the league's primary focus—fishing— was also Colorado's signature sport in those days before the ski boom. Yet the league's vision went well beyond one pastime. Its magazine, *Outdoor America*, ran not just fishing stories but stories on hiking, shooting, auto camping, bird-watching, and women's outdoor activities, evoking less a cult of fishermen than an entire recreational lifestyle.[9]

League members called themselves Waltonians or Ikes. They also called themselves "Defenders of Soil, Woods, Waters, and Wildlife" and strode forth to fight for the natural elements of their recreational world. This struck a chord in Colorado, a state with a long history of sportsmen appointing themselves enforcers of conservation principles. As early as

1882, members of the Colorado Game and Fish Protective Association were patrolling rural areas to catch poachers, fish dynamiters, and other scofflaws. The 1910s saw the association calling for a nonpartisan commission of sportsmen to oversee state game and fish policy—another point of congruence with the IWLA, which in the 1920s advocated the commission model for other states. Indeed, so simpatico was the Game and Fish Protective Association with the Waltonian spirit that in 1925 it converted itself into a chapter of the IWLA, Colorado's first.[10] Thereafter the Ikes thrived in the state, especially in the late 1940s and early 1950s.[11] Colorado even became a breeding ground for IWLA leaders, most notably William Voigt Jr., who rose from head of the Denver regional office to national executive director; and Voigt's successor in Denver, Joseph Penfold, who became the league's conservation director, its leading voice in Washington, DC.

Still, sportsmen-activists could take the conservation cause only so far. As they faced their first postwar battle, some Colorado Ikes could already see the need to enlist broader popular support. The battle erupted in 1946, when western stockmen and their allies in Congress began pushing to privatize public grazing lands. Ikes in Colorado and Wyoming were outraged by this "land grab," as they called it, but they felt terrifyingly alone. Even their brother Waltonians seemed uninterested, as most of them lived in the Midwest, far from the scrublands and forests under threat. So Colorado Waltonians took their case to a wider audience. Voigt and Art Carhart, a devoted Ike, began feeding on-the-ground information to *Harper's Magazine* columnist Bernard DeVoto, who fulminated against the land grab in a series of fiery articles. Carhart himself wrote several articles for sportsmen's magazines, and he fantasized about launching a glossy new magazine, "on the lines of *Look* or *Life*," that would appeal beyond the die-hards to the masses of more casual sportsmen—the "9,000,000 fishermen and 6,000,000 hunters" across the nation who were conservationists' natural allies. "If ever they could be reached en mass [sic] and get moving," Carhart mused, "nothing could hold them."[12]

But Carhart had an even greater force in mind. He also hoped to rally the even vaster masses of casual recreational enthusiasts who did *not* belong to elite fraternities of rod or gun. Significantly, one of the first places he submitted an anti–land grab article was the magazine of the Colorado Mountain Club (CMC), an organization of climbers, hikers, and skiers. Founded in Denver in 1912, the CMC was as much social as sporting club, welcoming outdoor novices as well as experts and taking pride in not taking itself too seriously. It did have a history of fighting for nature protection; most notably, it had lobbied in the 1910s for the creation of Rocky Mountain National Park. But like California's Sierra Club, the CMC's activism had waned, so that by the time of the land grab few members were even aware of their club's fighting past.[13] Carhart urged them to fight again. If the land grabbers succeeded in privatizing national forest lands, he warned CMC members, it would imperil the great Rocky Mountain commons where Coloradans went to play. "Practically every foot of ski territory in the high country" was at stake, he claimed, and so were many favorite climbing and hiking areas: "the Maroon Basin, even Snowmass, the Gore country, the Holy Cross area, the San Juans." All might "be closed to you and me . . . if this scheme works." Surely CMC members would not want to pay a fee to climb a peak, see their campsites posted for no trespassing, or "find that when they ski in the high country they suddenly are on some private sheep range." If club members wanted to keep their Rocky Mountain backyard open for recreation, it was now "time to act."[14]

As it turned out, the time for a mass movement of recreational consumers was still some years off. "We are reading all we can on both sides of the question," was all CMC's Conservation Committee would say about the land grab.[15] But beneath that tepid response, there were rumblings of an uprising to come. At least one member of the Conservation Committee did endorse Carhart's view. "Our immediate and selfish interest is to preserve recreational values," agreed Marjorie Peregrine. "We want to know no one can put a new fence across a favorite trail, post a keep-off sign on a now open fishing spot or take over a potentially fine ski slope for the benefit of a favored few." And Peregrine reported another intriguing development: up in Casper, Wyoming, the Dude Ranchers' Association, representing mostly Wyoming and Montana dude ranch owners, had come out against the land grab.[16] For them it was a business decision: dude ranch visitors expected horseback rides to pretty meadows, forests, and lakes, and most of those rides depended on free access to public lands.[17] The dude ranchers thus stood for another constituency whose support Carhart coveted: in this case, not recreational consumers, but the people who made money off them.

The more people saw profits in recreation, Carhart reasoned, the more they would favor conservation of the resources recreation relied upon: fish, game, forest habitat, fresh water, scenic beauty, open space. Thus Carhart took an especially keen interest in documenting the economic benefits of outdoor recreation. He wrote a series of pioneering articles in the 1940s and 1950s that attempted to quantify the surprisingly vast—yet, Carhart insisted, statistically verifiable—sums that recreational hunters and anglers were pouring into the American economy. Counting bait, ammunition, gas, meals, motel rooms, club dues, clothing, and all other purchases sportsmen had to make, Carhart reported "almost unbelievable" total expenditures: $2 billion a year during the war, $4 billion in 1947, more than $9 billion by 1950.[18] These were splashy numbers, which Carhart hoped would help sell business interests on the profit potential of conservation. Over the next two decades, he would spend much of his energy trying to make the sale.

He and his fellow recreational conservationists would need all the economic data they could muster to fight their stiffest postwar challenge: the Bureau of Reclamation's seemingly insatiable push to build ever more dams. Already by 1945 there were so many western water projects in the works, including in Colorado, that Carhart was predicting dams would be *the* environmental issue of the coming years. "The engineers have their plans ready; they have their plans approved; they have the go signal," he told listeners to his *All Outdoors* radio show in January 1945. The situation had to be met by "a strong, militant informed body of sportsmen."[19] A few years later, when the federal agency moved forward with plans to dam the Colorado, six miles upstream from the Highway 40 town of Granby, Carhart found himself in his first big water fight.

Granby Dam was the keystone of the Colorado–Big Thompson Project, or C-BT. Authorized in 1937, C-BT marked a critical divide in Colorado history: it was the first project to suck water from the Western Slope and send it to the Front Range, opening the floodgates for many transmountain diversions to come. To Carhart, C-BT smacked of "super-engineering": it was a costly Rube Goldberg contraption that piped, pumped, and siphoned away water that could have gone to better use "within its natural watershed."[20] Bureau of Reclamation engineers and "concrete mixers," he felt, should have worked with "foresters, land management planners, wildlife authorities, [and] recreation planners" to develop "a total watershed program" instead of one that fixated so single-mindedly on diversions and dams.[21]

Carhart's reaction to Granby Dam was a snapshot of American environmental advocacy in transition. In many ways his critique harked back to the core principles of early twentieth-century conservation, particularly its faith in resource management by experts. Never did Carhart question the value of expertise; instead, it was the failure of federal engineers to consult with *other* experts—especially ones who knew about fish—that infuriated him. His preferred scenario—in which engineers, fish managers, foresters, and recreation land planners would collaborate on a multiple-use plan for *all* of the river's resources—was a classic vision of Progressive-style conservation at work. But in other ways Carhart's response to Granby Dam anticipated the popular environmentalism of the 1960s and 1970s. Consider his anguished appeal to fellow sportsmen, quoted at the outset of this chapter. The emotionally charged rhetoric, the imagery of mankind's cruel violence against nature, and the cry for popular protest against the powers that be would all have been at home in the early 1970s environmental movement. So too would Carhart's underlying plea: that people's personal interests as consumers must become the basis for political action. This was how mid-century environmental advocates like Carhart, the IWLA, and the Sierra Club began to update conservation for the postwar era. They recast their appeals for old-fashioned expert resource management in newly personal terms. They spoke directly to the growing masses of Americans who went on family vacations or weekend trips. Conservation became a fight for one's favorite campsite, streamside cabin, or fishing hole—a cause, that is, for every consumer of outdoor leisure.

What of the other constituency Carhart coveted, the *providers* of outdoor leisure? Could the burgeoning recreation trade turn them into conservationists too? In one booming high-country resort town—Aspen—there was evidence that it could. And once again, the catalyst was a Bureau of Reclamation project. This time, the agency was proposing to take water from the Fryingpan and Roaring Fork Rivers and smaller creeks around Aspen and pipe it under the Sawatch Range for distribution to the cities and farms of the Arkansas River valley. Aspenites denounced this Fryingpan-Arkansas, or Fry-Ark, project, and local boosters began mobilizing against it even before the plans were formalized. Already in 1948 the *Aspen Times* was railing against rumored diversions from the Roaring Fork, and in 1949, when Western Slopers organized the Western Colorado Water Planning Association to fight Eastern Slope water greed, it was Aspen that hosted the meeting and an Aspen Chamber of Commerce official who was elected president.[22] Over the next several years, the list of Aspenites who joined the fight against Fry-Ark read like a Who's Who of the local business and political leadership. They denounced Fry-Ark's hefty price tag and its threat to area ranching and to the future development of Western Slope oil shale. But most often, and in the most urgent terms, they raged that the loss of water would dry up the local tourist trade. "Our economy," argued *Aspen Times* editor Verlin Ringle in 1948, "is based partially upon people coming to this area to enjoy the scenic beauty, of which the streams are an integral part." People also came to fish, Ringle noted, but "if there is no water [anglers] will go elsewhere and the residents of the district will suffer financial loss."[23]

Ringle's logic seemed simple enough, but in fact it rested on a notion radical for its time: that in some cases water carried more economic value if left in place, if allowed to remain visually and ecologically a part of its landscape. That notion flew in the face of Colorado water law, which blessed as "beneficial use" the removal of water for agricultural or industrial uses but accorded no legitimacy to leaving the water in its natural channel for the sake of, say, scenery or trout. The Fry-Ark project sprang from this same assumption: that water, if undiverted, went to waste.[24] "Diversionists think water is useless unless it is flowing down a muddy irrigation ditch," Ringle charged, and the charge was not entirely unfair.[25] That Ringle, hardly a trained conservationist or die-hard recreationist, preferred the tumbling creek to the muddy ditch suggests how tourism had already begun to reshape the environmental values of some boosters. Before long, in fact, Aspen's boosters found themselves at odds with their counterparts elsewhere on the Western Slope. Initially the opposition to Fry-Ark was regionwide, but in 1951 the state water board struck a deal, promising that Fry-Ark would be the last federally funded diversion from the Western Slope until the region's future water needs could be fully assessed. The deal mollified boosters of Western Slope agricultural, industrial, and oil shale development.[26] But it did nothing to save Aspen's scenic trout streams, and suddenly Aspenites found themselves fighting Fry-Ark alone.

They reacted by resorting to Carhart-style conservation. They set up the Pitkin County Water Protection Association, which, like Carhart, used the language of tourist advertising to press its case. "Pitkin County, Colorado, is the nation's most beautiful playground," pleaded one association flyer. "Its scenery is unsurpassed and its beauty is irreplaceable."[27] The Aspenites also built a Carhart-style coalition of local businessmen, sportsmen, and the IWLA. A local IWLA chapter appeared in 1953, fifty-plus members strong, including officers from the Aspen Chamber of Commerce and the water-protection association and owners of local motels, restaurants, and ski shops. The national IWLA responded by taking up the fight against Fry-Ark.[28] Art Carhart got involved, working his contacts in Congress, the New York Times, and other influential outlets to draw attention to Aspen's plight.[29]

Meanwhile, local boosters tried to mobilize the many people who looked to Aspen for pleasure. The water-protection association issued a brochure, *The Rape of the Roaring Fork*, and mass-mailed it all over the country to people who had vacationed in Aspen. Later the brochure was updated to appeal to skiers, who made up the biggest bloc of Aspen visitors but who might not see why stream water was so important. "Dear Skier and Visitor to Aspen," began the brochure. "You may want to return to Aspen sometime during the summer, . . . and you may wish to do some fishing." Imagine, then, finding "dry river beds and the mountainside desecrated with tunnels and canals." Readers moved by such a scenario were asked to write to their members of Congress to voice their outrage.[30] As Verlin Ringle explained, "If you are in Aspen . . . because you think it is a pleasant place to live, water makes it so. If you love to fish—abundant water makes it possible. If you love to picnic beside a dashing, tumbling mountain stream—brother or sister, you won't unless you have abundant water."[31] It was exactly the same case Carhart made to his "brother" sportsmen after Granby Dam: to protect your place of leisure, you must get personally involved.

The appeal made sense only because so many vacationers had, in fact, come to feel a personal stake in Aspen. Had boosters in some lesser-known burg faced the same threat, they would not have found so many "friends" around the country to help them out. Even in Aspen, personal appeals would have flopped in the "quiet years" before the town gained fame as a resort. But by the early 1950s, resort development had made Aspen into a popular product, and in a consumer society products take on powerful personal meanings. That is why Aspen had so many friends eager to defend it. And in this sense, the Fry-Ark battle, though mostly forgotten today, helped pioneer a new phenomenon in the high country: consumers of leisure getting politically involved to preserve the places promoters had sold them.

The backlash could be furious, though. Aspenites were accused of standing in the way of progress and of placing the vacation fancies of wealthy outsiders over the needs of fellow Coloradans. Aspen visitors came to Colorado "for the sole purpose of buying land for summer homes," snarled one Western Slope booster; they opposed "our water development program" entirely "for selfish reasons" and had "no interest in the state's welfare."[32] Aspenites also stood accused of letting themselves become overly emotional, of putting personal passions above rational, technical expertise and the broader public good. The applicable epithet was "nature lover," which carried the same connotations in the 1950s that the coded insult "tree hugger" does today: a person so smitten with leafy, furry, or finny things that he was willing to sacrifice human welfare for their sake. (Actually, the pronoun would be "she," since "nature lover" also implied an unmanly sort of sentimentality.)

This unflattering caricature had long bedeviled advocates of wildlife, wilderness, and scenic preservation. Infuriating enough to Aspen boosters, it was even more galling to someone like Art Carhart, who had fought for years to get recreational resource conservation accepted as a legitimate professional pursuit and who had pioneered the use of cold, hard economic statistics to justify it. For this reason, even as Carhart sided with the Aspenites against Fry-Ark, he disowned some of their more impassioned rhetoric. Reacting to *The Rape of the Roaring Fork*, he wrote disapprovingly that "the Aspen people have gone at this rather emotionally," and his colleague, Sierra Club president Dick Leonard, apologized to the Bureau of Reclamation that the "adjectives . . . are rather strong in this particular pamphlet."[33] When Fry-Ark proponents called Carhart a "nature lover," he bristled—and shot back with a statistic: "The $250,000,000 state tourist business can't continue to thrive as it has without natural water in stream beds."[34]

Carhart's defensiveness highlighted a basic dilemma for postwar conservationists. With millions of Americans joining in the recreation boom, it made sense for conservationists to build support for their cause by playing on the passions of outdoor consumers. But the cause risked losing legitimacy—even, Carhart's reaction suggests, in the eyes of some conservationists themselves—if it started to seem too impassioned, too emotion-based or sentimental. So conservationists also worked to make the "hard-facts" case for recreation, citing statistics and scientific and technical data. In a region like the Colorado high country, a flourishing tourist trade meant conservationists could credibly base their hard-facts case on profits—on the economic gains to be had from safeguarding recreational resources. And that is exactly what Art Carhart did. Understanding that tourism fostered both emotional and entrepreneurial attachments to the high country, he built a case that combined the two, an approach that in turn influenced the kind of environmental movement that took shape in Colorado.

Consider how Carhart and other Colorado conservationists fought the greatest environmental battle of the 1950s: the effort to stop the Bureau of Reclamation from damming the scenic Colorado canyon called Echo Park. This fight has achieved near-mythical status as a founding episode of the American environmental movement. Echo Park in the 1950s became a "symbol of wilderness," in historian Mark Harvey's words, the place where conservationists first convinced great numbers of Americans to care about wilderness protection and the episode that launched the nation on its path to the Wilderness Act.[35] But for Carhart and many others in Echo Park's home state, the place meant something different. Instead of setting it aside as wilderness, they imagined packaging it for mainstream, even mass recreational use, the way a developer or tourist booster might. And they saw the possibility that such place planning and packaging might become the basis for a popular conservation agenda—one that both business interests and outdoor consumers could get enthusiastically behind.

Hidden in the mazelike canyonlands of northwestern Colorado, Echo Park is the spot where the Green and Yampa Rivers wash out of their gorges, flow together, and trace a lazy hairpin around the base of a monumental, prow-shaped promontory called Steamboat Rock. In the 1940s, the Bureau of Reclamation made plans to dam the Green River two miles downstream and inundate Echo Park—with its sandbars, box elders, and spectacular cliff walls—under five hundred feet of reservoir water. It would be part of the Colorado River Storage Project, a five-state, ten-dam effort to turn the raw torrent of the upper Colorado and its tributaries into irrigation water and hydropower for a new era of western progress. Most of the project's other dam sites were noncontroversial, and Echo Park itself was little known. But the plans to flood it roused a mighty furor. Why? Because Echo Park sat inside a unit of the national park system—Dinosaur National Monument— and conservationists worried that damming it would open the door to resource development in all the national parks. So they mounted a desperate six-year campaign to save Echo Park. In congressional hearings, public meetings, mass mailings, movies, books, newspapers, and magazines, they made this obscure place famous, rallying support in Congress and the wider public, and, in 1956, finally forcing the Bureau of Reclamation and its allies to abandon plans for the dam.

Nationally, the Sierra Club spearheaded the campaign, casting it as a crusade for nonmaterial values—"the delights we have clung to, in our civilization, for the good of our soul, even if those delights don't affect the Dow Jones average."[36] But conservationists based in Colorado, a state that figured to benefit economically from the water-storage project, seemed reluctant to stand on such principles. The home-state opposition to Echo Park was mostly orchestrated by Art Carhart and his close associate Joe Penfold, the Denver-based western representative for the IWLA. Both were science-minded sportsman-conservationists who hated being tarred with the "nature lover" brush. So instead of professing their love for pristine wilderness, they staked their case on environmental values that were much more mainstream in 1950s Colorado: the cult of casual nature that was gripping growing numbers of leisure consumers and the chamber-of-commerce dream of making nature pay by packaging it for tourists.

Carhart and Penfold made a hard-facts business case against the dam to "stress the loss of . . . economic value" if Echo Park was flooded.[37] Carhart predicted that a Dinosaur National Monument left undammed would generate fifteen million dollars a year in tourist revenue. Penfold, too, pointed out the economic value of recreation, calling it "a major industry in Colorado," but warned that "day by day, [water] project by project, we are diminishing the resource values which support it."[38] The two men organized a citizens' group against the dam and made a point of getting businessmen to lead it, so there would not be (in Carhart's words) "a 'professional nature lover' heading the deal."[39] The group's objective was to create the impression that Colorado's economic elites were lining up against the dam, and to this end group members wrote letters, news releases, and radio spots and recruited fellow businessmen (and the leaders of Front Range women's clubs) to the cause. One of their most interesting recruits was Denver motel owner Eddie Bohn, who headed the National U.S. Highway 40 Association. Bohn became intrigued by the idea that if Dinosaur were left in its natural state, scenically intact, it might merit upgrading to a national park. That would give Highway 40 a new tourist attraction of national renown—and would give Bohn and other U.S. 40 boosters a lift in their rivalry with Wyoming's Highway 30 and Sidney Six's Highway 6. Older efforts to promote tourist corridors and newer efforts to preserve recreational landscapes thus converged in the battle for Echo Park.[40]

Carhart and Penfold's strategy—stressing Dinosaur's tourist potential— fit somewhat awkwardly with wilderness values. Few tourists sought true wilderness experiences; most wanted leisure settings that were auto-accessible, close to modern conveniences, and "thrilling" (to use the advertising word) without actually being dangerous. Carhart knew this—which is why, when describing Dinosaur, he often *downplayed* its wildness. Consider how he wrote about river rafting there: the thrill of bobbing along the Yampa, slipping past sculpted sandstone walls soaring hundreds of feet straight up on either side. It was exhilarating—but, Carhart insisted, not at all dangerous. You need not be a "rugged, hairy-chested outdoorsmen" to raft the Yampa; "anyone physically able to sit in a jeep" could do it. Dinosaur

National Monument offered a rare chance to run real western rivers "with all reasonable safety," but if a dam were built, "that chance will be lost."[41] In short, it was Dinosaur's capacity to thrill visitors without threatening them that made it such a terrific tourist draw.

Significantly, dam advocates were busy arguing the exact opposite. A dam would *enhance* Dinosaur's tourist appeal, they contended, because the free-flowing rivers were too wild for tourists. In the pro-dam *Denver Post*, the Yampa was "beautiful but treacherous," its rapids so "terrifying" that "few people will risk" rafting there. And since "the canyons can be explored no other way by the average tourist," that meant an undammed Dinosaur would be useless for large-scale visitorship.[42] In short, dam *proponents* were the ones stressing Dinosaur's wildness, while dam *opponents* insisted it was really quite tame. This was no minor point; it was crucial enough that Carhart got into a heated argument over it. Invited to address a meeting of Denver Waltonians, he seethed as another guest, a dam backer, falsely claimed that several rafters had drowned on a Sierra Club–sponsored float trip. Carhart leapt to his feet and denounced this "'scare' stuff." In fact, he retorted, rafting in Dinosaur was no more dangerous than driving a car—an analogy any postwar tourist or suburbanite could easily understand.[43]

Carhart and Penfold's unwild way of depicting Dinosaur extended to the future landscape they envisioned there. In effect, they proposed making it into what more and more of the Colorado high country was becoming: a setting specially packaged for tourism. Carhart declared that Dinosaur, without a dam, could be "comparable to the best of our national parks" in its range of scenic, recreational, wildlife, and geological attributes. There was just one rub: "It lacks only use facilities." So he and Penfold called for something that any local booster would have found logical but that wilderness advocates considered anathema: a network of paved, all-weather roads to give tourists access to several spots at river level. Carhart insisted (citing his expertise as a landscape architect and recreation engineer) that these improvements could be made "without losing much of the pristine conditions." Dinosaur's wide benches and snaking canyons made it "physically ideal" for accommodating large crowds of visitors without having to cram them all into one small space, as was done in Yosemite. All in all, Carhart concluded, Dinosaur possessed great "service value," a "use-capacity of the highest potential."[44] That kind of thinking, that kind of language, was not going to make wilderness advocates too happy. But it seemed likelier to resonate with the tourist boosters and casual outdoor consumers of 1950s Colorado.

None of this is to suggest that Colorado lacked wilderness advocates (both Carhart and Penfold, in fact, counted themselves as such). Nor is it to suggest that Colorado conservationists were alone in talking about tourist profits and auto access. But in the fight for Echo Park, Colorado conservationists relied on these arguments more heavily than did other groups, like the Sierra Club, that came to the battle from out of state. Echo Park was a slice of *Colorado* real estate, so home-state conservationists had to speak to the ways their fellow Coloradans viewed their land. And in the 1950s, dreams of large-scale tourist development and enthusiasm for the nascent tourist way of life were increasingly coloring the view.

Ultimately, when we look at the way Art Carhart, Joe Penfold, and the Izaak Walton League fought the battles of the 1940s and 1950s, we can see emerging in Colorado an early version of environmentalism. And we can see it taking its cues from Colorado's recreational culture. Sportsmen-conservationists led the way, but increasingly they sought and got support from Colorado's swelling ranks of tourist boosters and recreational consumers. As a consequence, this emerging environmentalism fixated not just on raw, remote nature, as the movement after Echo Park is often thought to have done, but more on those thrilling but unthreatening kinds of settings that promised easy enjoyment for car-dependent leisure-seekers. In other words, this environmentalism focused on the landscapes of travel guidebooks and tourist brochures.

COLORADO'S ENVIRONMENTAL MOVEMENT GOT A RUNNING START AT Echo Park, but where was it headed next? As the story is usually told, after winning the Echo Park battle, conservation leaders turned next to the campaign for a federal Wilderness Act. But in Colorado, Joe Penfold and Art Carhart, together with allies like Jack Wagar, forestry professor at Colorado A&M, set their sights on a different goal.[45] To them, wilderness protection alone was too narrow. With the American population booming, its appetite for outdoor leisure ballooning, the next pressing need was to ensure that the supply of recreational settings kept pace. That meant land managers of all sorts—at the federal, state, and local levels and even the managers of privately owned lands—would have to start seriously planning for recreation. They would have to apply the same approach that Progressive-style conservation applied to other natural resources. They would have to gather data on leisure trends, tastes, amenities, and facilities, and use that data to plan for recreation of all sorts. Comprehensive recreation planning: this became

Carhart and Penfold's pet cause in the post–Echo Park 1950s.

Recreation planning did include wilderness protection. But it placed no higher priority on wilderness than on car campgrounds, roadside picnic areas, ski mountains, or marinas. As Jack Wagar memorably put it, it covered everything "from the flower pot at the window to the wilderness."[46] In this sense, recreation planning continued the quest to make conservation more relevant to consumers of mainstream leisure. But at the same time, it showed the Colorado conservationists making a subtle shift in emphasis. In early battles like Echo Park and Fry-Ark, Carhart and Penfold had sought support from recreational consumers and recreational business interests alike. But now, knowingly or not, they were gravitating toward the latter. Many basic goals of recreation planning—increasing the "supply," asserting a central role for the private sector, catering to the most popular kinds of leisure, and statistically documenting recreation's value to the wider economy—could have easily come from a chamber of commerce, a business consultant like L. J. Crampon, or a publicist like Lew Cobb. This was a key reason recreation planning caught on in Colorado: because it put the venerable Progressive tradition of expert, data-based conservation at the service of the state's tourist businesses and boosters. If the rise of recreation planning gave conservation new legitimacy in Colorado, it also tied that legitimacy more closely than ever to how well conservation could advance the tourism and recreation trade.

The late 1950s and early 1960s brought major new initiatives to increase recreational supply. The National Park Service launched Mission 66, the Forest Service unleashed Operation Outdoors, and the state parks movement was in full swing. All of these drew on the tradition of technocratic resource management, and all strongly favored easy-access recreation for the masses.[47] But the ultimate example of this approach was the one Carhart and Penfold championed: the federal Outdoor Recreation Resources Review Commission (ORRRC), which began its work in 1958.

Penfold was widely recognized as the father of ORRRC, and he came to that role through his time in the trenches in Colorado. He had headed the Izaak Walton League's Denver office from 1949 to 1957, arduous years for Colorado conservationists. Echo Park, Fry-Ark, Granby—it seemed like one dam battle after another. Penfold came away convinced that conservationists suffered from two grave weaknesses. First, they had failed to establish recreation as a public good on a par with traditional resource uses like mining, logging, irrigation, or hydropower. And second, they had precious little data to back themselves up. "When the chips were down," Penfold later recalled, "the [dam] developers could talk about future needs in kilowatts of power and acre feet of water. . . . They could point to money in the till, economic advantages from what they wanted to do. Conservationists could not." Conservationists needed statistics on what leisure-seekers liked to do and what they contributed to the economy, Penfold believed, so they could start winning debates on technocratic and utilitarian terms.[48]

If that sounds like Art Carhart, it should: Penfold took direct inspiration from Carhart's pioneering efforts to measure spending by sportsmen.[49] His idea also resembled L. J. Crampon's surveys of Colorado tourism, in which Crampon had amassed data on tourists' behavior and spending and used it to argue that recreation was badly undervalued and deserved a boost. Now Penfold wanted to expand such studies to the nation as a whole. He hit on the idea of having a presidential commission survey all the nation's recreational resources, compile data on current and future demand, and craft a master plan to meet America's recreational needs. With help from a publicist in the Colorado Game and Fish Department, Penfold drafted a bill to create the commission; then, with the IWLA's blessing, he began working his contacts in Congress. After some effort to line up sponsors, he saw the bill sail through both houses. And thus, in June 1958, was born ORRRC.[50] President Eisenhower named philanthropist and national parks advocate Laurance Rockefeller to chair the commission. Of the fourteen other members, eight came from Congress, three from the private sector, and three from the world of conservation—including Joe Penfold.

Today, most see the Wilderness Act as the crowning environmental achievement of the early 1960s. ORRRC is a footnote, if it is remembered at all. But back then many considered ORRRC a landmark of equal if not greater stature. Its work took three years and a passel of agencies, institutes, academics, and consultants. It culminated in 1962 with a monumental report titled *Outdoor Recreation in America*, together with twenty-seven "study reports" on various facets of the subject. And it had a very real impact. Of ORRRC's sixty-odd policy recommendations, most eventually became reality, including creation of a federal Bureau of Outdoor Recreation, passage of the Wilderness Act, designation of new national parks, and funding for states and localities to build recreational facilities and buy open space. Most important of all was the core principle ORRRC championed: that nature's recreational potential—no less than its resource potential—was vital to Americans' health, cultural identity, social harmony, and national security.[51] (Indeed, when ORRRC called for all metropolitan Americans to have "Sunday outing" access to nearby recreation, "a place in the sun for their families on the weekend," it effectively made the casual leisure lifestyle of Colorado and other western vacationlands an ideal for the nation as a whole.)[52] These principles, which had moved Penfold to dream up a commission in the first place, were not original to him or to ORRRC. But as a blue-ribbon presidential panel, ORRRC stated them more authoritatively than ever before. In so doing, it helped refocus environmental debate in the early 1960s. And as more than one historian has noted, its proposals set the environmental agenda for Lyndon Johnson's Great Society.[53] So Joe Penfold's brainstorm, born amid Colorado's 1950s water wars, ended up having quite a national impact indeed.

Not all conservationists cheered ORRRC, though—especially not those whose primary passion was wilderness. They fumed when foes of the wilderness bill, led by Colorado senator Gordon Allott and aided by powerful Western Slope congressman Wayne Aspinall, used ORRRC's unfinished work as an excuse to delay the bill's consideration.[54] Then, when ORRRC finally came out for wilderness protection, some advocates thought the endorsement too tepid—"anemic," said the Sierra Club.[55] To be fair, the very fact that a presidential commission endorsed the wilderness bill at all, anemically or not, struck a serious blow to the bill's enemies.[56] But the critics were right that wilderness was never ORRRC's chief concern. By Penfold's design, ORRRC studied all types of recreational lands, with wilderness just one part of the picture.

Nowhere did ORRRC make this clearer than in its call for "recreation zoning." As one of its core recommendations, the commission urged that all recreational lands, public and private, be classified into six zones, each allowing certain recreational uses while excluding certain others. It would work like zoning in cities and suburbs, but instead of "Mixed Use" or "Large Lot Residential," ORRRC's zones carried tags like "High-Density Recreation" and "Unique Natural Area." The most restrictive zone was the "Primitive Area," or wilderness by a less politically charged name.[57] Primitive areas, ORRRC stipulated, should be free of "commercial utilization," "mechanized transportation," and permanent structures of any kind—almost exactly what the 1964 Wilderness Act would later mandate.[58] But while wilderness devotees saw such restrictions as a moral imperative, in ORRRC's report they became just another set of management criteria, couched in the matter-of-fact language of the city planner.[59] ORRRC gave no sense that planning for primitive areas held any higher purpose than planning for public beaches or campgrounds—or any other easier-access and heavier-use facilities in the other five zones.

The Sierra Club's David Brower blamed Penfold for leading ORRRC down this errant path.[60] Whether or not one agrees that the path was errant, it is true that ORRRC's approach had a lot of Joe Penfold in it—and a lot of what he had learned from his conservation work in Colorado. Especially Penfoldian was ORRRC's broad bent toward mainstream recreational settings: places where, unlike wilderness, some commercial development was allowed or even encouraged and where visitor presence was relatively heavy. This certainly reflected how Penfold and his closest ally, Art Carhart, had argued for Echo Park—by stressing less its wildness than its value to ordinary leisure-seekers and tourist entrepreneurs.[61] Indeed, if ORRRC had a lot of Joe Penfold in it, it had a lot of Art Carhart too. Consider again ORRRC's call for recreation zoning. For more than forty years, Carhart had been touting a similar sort of zoning as the best way to plan recreational facilities and protect recreational resources. In fact, when conservationists thought of recreation zoning, they thought of Art Carhart: as the Wilderness Society's Howard Zahniser put it, "We all look upon him as a pioneer and authority" in the field.[62] Carhart had practically *invented* the field. Working in Colorado in the early 1920s as the Forest Service's first-ever recreation engineer, he had hit on the idea of zoning forests the way planners were just then beginning to zone cities and suburbs, dividing them into districts by function and allowable building type.

Here again it is crucial to see how Colorado shaped Carhart's thinking. In the early 1920s Colorado's national forests were facing mounting demand from car-driving leisure-seekers; that was why the Forest Service felt it needed a recreation engineer in the first place. Residents of Denver and other Front Range cities were acquiring a taste for the tourist way of life, looking more often to the mountains for weekend leisure. They sought not so much backcountry "wilderness" as scenic drives; day hikes to pretty vistas; places to fish, ski, picnic, and camp; and spots to build summer homes. It was the summer-home-building rush in particular that had spurred Carhart to invent the idea of zoning for wilderness, when in 1919 he recommended that the Forest Service ban cabins and access roads from a buffer zone around scenic Trappers Lake in the White River National Forest. Significantly, though, he never saw this action as a goal in itself. Instead, it was part of his wider effort to zone Colorado's national forests for all intensities and

SIX CLASSES OF OUTDOOR RECREATION RESOURCES AS PROPOSED AND ILLUSTRATED BY THE OUTDOOR RECREATION RESOURCES REVIEW COMMISSION—I, HIGH-DENSITY RECREATION AREA (A SWIMMING BEACH); II, GENERAL OUTDOOR RECREATION AREAS (A SKI SLOPE, A PICNIC GROUND); III, NATURAL ENVIRONMENT (A FOREST); IV, UNIQUE NATURAL AREA (A SPECTACULAR WATERFALL); V, PRIMITIVE AREA (A WILDERNESS AREA); VI, HISTORIC SITE (AN OLD CHURCH).

4.2 Recreation zoning. To address the burgeoning demand for outdoor leisure, the Outdoor Recreation Resources Review Commission proposed classifying recreational amenities into six zones, schematically depicted here in an illustration from ORRRC's final report in 1962. Wilderness was simply one of the zones.

varieties of recreational use. Undeveloped, roadless space (Carhart did not actually use the term "wilderness" in his Trappers Lake recommendation) was just one of the zones.[63] Four decades later, with the recreational pressure Colorado had experienced in the 1920s now a nationwide concern, ORRRC took the concept Carhart had innovated in Colorado and applied it to the whole country. ORRRC, too, wanted zoning for all kinds of recreation. And ORRRC, too, treated wilderness as simply one of the zones.

Carhart wore many hats in the forty-plus years after his Forest Service stint, as we saw at the outset of this chapter. But one thing never changed: he continued to live and work out of Denver, and conditions in Colorado continued to shape how he thought about recreational lands and wilderness. A case in point came in the late 1950s and early 1960s, as he wrote a handbook on recreation and wildland zoning called *Planning for America's Wildlands*. A capstone to Carhart's four decades of work on such issues, the handbook was originally intended as an aid to ORRRC.[64] But it may also be seen as Carhart's attempt to master the core problem of the Colorado-style vacationland: the way it blurred together the country with the city, the residential with the recreational, the developed with the wild. In keeping with his long experience, Carhart struggled to define zones that would impose order on this confounding landscape so planners could control it.

The struggle was especially evident in his efforts to define "wilderness" itself, this category he had helped invent. He found himself disagreeing with the Wilderness Society's Howard Zahniser, the author and leading champion of the wilderness bill, over what wilderness really was and how it should be managed. The dispute took shape in letters between the two conservationists, as Carhart drafted his manuscript and Zahniser offered feedback. Friends and mutual admirers, the two men agreed on the need to preserve "true wilderness," settings that seemed untouched by humans. They also agreed that "wild" qualities could exist in other settings—like suburbs—and that these other "wildlands" needed care too. But they disagreed over which deserved top priority. Zahniser firmly believed that protecting "true wilderness" was paramount. Carhart, on the other hand, thought comprehensive planning of *all* wildlands, ranging from "semi-suburban" zones to "true wilderness," must take precedence, or efforts to preserve the "true wilderness" would fail.[65] He also clashed with Zahniser over how wilderness should be managed. Carhart suggested that some wilderness zones—which, in unromantic planner-speak, he labeled "Wilderness B" and "Wilderness C"—should allow human intrusions, like logging, jeep roads, or rustic cabins. Zahniser, reading Carhart's draft, strongly demurred. Any landscape with roads, cabins, or logging was not "wilderness," he argued. Calling it that would only undermine efforts to protect wilderness in its pure form.[66]

Carhart did yield on some points. Most importantly, even as he remained sure of the need for "all-use" wildland planning, he decided to support Zahniser's wilderness bill, which concerned itself with "true wilderness" alone. He also agreed to relabel his Wilderness B and C zones "Wilderness Buffer" and "Primitive Camping" to appease Zahniser's belief that only "true wilderness" should carry the "wilderness" name.[67] But it was clear from the final wording of *Planning for America's Wildlands* that Carhart still considered Zahniser's archetypal wilderness too rarefied. To fixate on the remotest landscapes with no hints of human influence, Carhart wrote, was to miss the point that wilderness was a matter of the mind, not any particular place. It was a spirit-restoring sense of escape from the city, a feeling of returning to nature, an emotional reconnection with the universe. And while one person might need to retreat deep into a primeval forest to find it, another person might experience it just off a highway or at a dude ranch. Carhart wrote of meeting a New Jersey tourist who, having never left the big city before, found wilderness in a Colorado resort village. He even contended that the mere sight of faraway wilderness, viewed from the suburbs, could evoke a wilderness experience—which meant that semi-suburban settings, no less than remote mountain retreats, must be zoned and managed for their wildness. So should places that had once borne a heavy human imprint but were turning wild again: an abandoned mining town, for example, whose ghostly ruins were slowly collapsing back into the loam.[68]

Here, again, Carhart's ideas oozed Colorado. Not by coincidence did it occur to him to use iconic Colorado tourist settings—the dude ranch, the scenic highway, the resort village in the mountains, the ghost town—to illustrate the varieties of wildland or wilderness experience. And when he described the thrill of standing in the suburbs, gazing at distant wilderness, it called to mind another scenic Colorado cliché: the Denver metro area's dramatic view of the Front Range, which was not just a recurring image in Colorado tourist iconography but the one that for many Denverites epitomized (as it still does today) their cherished outdoorsy quality of life. More broadly, when Carhart insisted that tourist facilities need not detract from the wilderness experience, but could in fact enhance it, he echoed a core theme of Colorado vacation advertising. For nearly a hundred years the state's tourist boosters had been saying that the emotional benefits of the outdoors—the sense of adventure, escape, inspiration, rest—could be had without forgoing comfort and convenience, without really having to rough it. Judging from *Planning for America's Wildlands*, Carhart (who, it is worth reiterating, had spent much of his own career writing guidebooks and articles to promote outdoor leisure in Colorado) had thoroughly internalized that pitch.

Of course Colorado was far from the only state to market the outdoors this way. But because it was Carhart's home, and had so powerfully molded his professional life, its marketing found expression in the recreation planning and zoning techniques that he helped invent—and that ORRRC then inherited. Consciously catering to mass use, privileging pure wilderness no higher than picnic areas or playgrounds, ORRRC's was a conservation agenda that made many wilderness-first advocates nervous. But it was tailor-made for a vacationland like Colorado, where so many had worked so hard to nurture a recreational reputation and a big-market tourist industry.

Recreation planning did not just serve the needs of tourist boosters; it was in large part a product of their values.

Not surprisingly, recreation planning caught on in Colorado. In the late 1950s, Colorado officials began experimenting with it as a way to enhance the state's visitor appeal. In 1957, the State Park and Recreation Board began inventorying Colorado's leisure facilities and planning a system of state-operated fishing, boating, swimming, hiking, and picnic areas. Booster motives were behind this work. At the time, though Colorado was billed as "tops in all things recreational," it was the only state without a state park, and boosters feared that embarrassing fact might harm its reputation as a vacation state.[69] The park board's long-term goal—to put parks in all parts of the state, for residents and tourists alike—shared ORRRC's premise that all Americans should have convenient access to outdoor recreation. And the first round of parks the park board created in 1959–60 were the same kinds of facilities that ORRRC ended up devoting much of its attention to: not mountain fastnesses or wilderness enclaves but rest areas along highways, marinas, beaches, and picnic areas around reservoirs—facilities meant for automobile accessibility and heavy visitor use.[70]

Truth be told, by the late 1950s, the use of zoning to conserve tourist-pleasing landscapes was already a familiar idea in some corners of the high country. In this case, the idea had come not from ORRRC or Art Carhart but from the evolution of zoning as a municipal practice. When zoning first caught on in American cities and suburbs in the 1910s and 1920s, it was primarily used to protect property values. But over the ensuing decades it became local officials' go-to strategy for all kinds of other land-use objectives, like regulating growth around the edges of a town or protecting green space and scenic views. Zoning was not originally designed to do such things, but it was the one major power that local officials wielded over land use, so they bent it to these ends anyway.[71] That was what happened in the high country in the 1940s and 1950s, when officials in a few aspiring tourist towns began using zoning to conserve scenery, architectural character, rural ambiance, greenery, and open space—in short, the landscape qualities that lured vacationers, investors, and entrepreneurs.

Aspen again led the way. Walter Paepcke, almost as soon as he began buying Aspen property, began pushing for zoning to protect his investment. In his very first meeting with locals, in August 1945, Paepcke brought along his architect friends Walter Gropius and Walter Frazier to press the need for a "comprehensive city plan," including zoning. The three Walters offered the classic rationale, that planning and zoning would bolster property values.[72] In those days zoning was rare in towns as small as Aspen; most locals hadn't the foggiest idea how it was even supposed to work. (The city council had to ask the Colorado Municipal League to explain it to them.) But Aspenites seemed to react positively to Paepcke's idea, and the process of gathering data and consulting experts got under way. A citizens' committee set out to gather data on "population, weather, educational and social groups, geography of the area and historical background, and a list of projects that the people feel might be desirable." Then the "experts," Frazier and Gropius, would use the data to design a zoning map and master plan.[73]

The process did not go so smoothly. For one thing, Gropius and Frazier were architects, not really the planning experts Paepcke portrayed them as.[74] And they were in Aspen (at Paepcke's invitation) for pleasure, not work, so they treated the planning and zoning project as a diversion. For a while they had fun dabbling in it. Gropius, Paepcke reported, was "pleasantly amused" by the challenge of restoring Aspen's Victorian charm, and Frazier was "terribly enthusiastic about the whole idea" of doing "some city planning, rehabilitation, tearing down shacks, dressing up other buildings, etc." But when it came time to do real work, Gropius dished the job to one of his protégés, who proceeded to ask too high a fee—and there the planning part of the project died.[75] The zoning part survived, as Paepcke kept pursuing it with the city council. But the draft zoning ordinance that the city floated in spring 1947 flopped. At a town forum, when asked who objected to the draft, nearly the entire audience surged to their feet. The loudest outcry came from people who feared that the residential zone would restrict them from building motels on their property and profiting from the tourist trade. In other words, if zoning acted in any way to hinder business in Aspen, it was not going to fly.[76]

But Verlin Ringle, the *Aspen Times* editor and reliable Paepcke ally, insisted that business would actually benefit if it were barred from Aspen's historic mansion district. Many people were drawn to Aspen "to live without the necessity of a job for livelihood," Ringle pointed out, picking up on the rise of the tourist way of life. Unless the town set aside residential zones, growth would overwhelm the "pleasant and congenial surroundings" that lured these newcomers to build or restore their "nice homes." And that would hurt business, for "business cannot live where there are no people living." Protect the living atmosphere and landscape qualities that lured the leisure-minded, Ringle was saying, and Aspen would reap dividends: more people and more profits.[77]

This was the spirit in which Aspenites finally embraced zoning. In summer 1947, the city called in two new experts (this time from the State Planning Commission and the Colorado Municipal League) to engineer a compromise. The experts met with locals to explain the concept of zoning and discuss amendments to the draft ordinance. This meeting went much better, and two weeks later the city council at last passed the high country's first small-town zoning measure.[78] It did what Paepcke and Aspen officials had originally proposed and the motel owners opposed: it banned almost all business from Aspen's West End, where the silver elites had once built their gabled mansions and latter-day elites like the Paepckes were now restoring or building theirs. But the ordinance also created a compromise zone at the base of the ski mountain and along the path that State Highway 82 traced through town. Here, tourist businesses like motels and gas stations would be allowed alongside houses and recreational facilities like parks and playgrounds.[79] In other words, this "B–Residence" zone blended the lucrative tourist trade with the leisurely tourist way of life—not a bad metaphor for the mix of interests that had led Aspenites to this, their first effort to legislate the local landscape.

More and more of that landscape came under zoning in the following years. Advocates of "businesslike" planning swept the 1953 city council elections and then joined the chamber of commerce in urging that some unincorporated, rural parts of Pitkin County be zoned the way Aspen was.[80] Economic benefits continued to be the rationale: zoning would raise property values and "benefit . . . the [county's] future development," the commissioners predicted. And again an expert was brought in: Trafton Bean, former planning director for Boulder, a city already known around the state for cutting-edge planning. (This was the same Trafton Bean who, soon after, would design the new, relocated lakeside resort town of Dillon.) By summer 1955 the meadows and mountainsides fringing Aspen were covered by brand-new Pitkin County zoning rules.[81] And in summer 1956 the city—also drawing on Bean's expertise and on input from lodge owners, the chamber, and other business interests—revised and expanded its own zoning ordinance.[82]

Significantly, as regulation of the local landscape became more expansive, it also became more *environmental*—more concerned with attractiveness, cleanliness, and healthfulness. Paepcke's vision for Aspen had always placed a premium on such qualities. He, Gropius, and Frazier had made this clear in their first meeting with locals, in 1945. So had Herbert Bayer in 1951, when he called for a bold initiative to plant trees and flowers, install fountains and playgrounds, and impose strict architectural controls to protect Aspen's "esthetic qualities."[83] By the mid-1950s, these environmental goals were finding their way into official policy. Aspen restricted tree cutting along city streets, regulated the appearance of new buildings, and moved to replace the city's ancient wooden sewer with a new one, so as not to pollute the Roaring Fork River as it ran through town. Pitkin County also got into the environmental act; its 1955 zoning rules tried to keep Highway 82 scenic by banning billboards and mandating setbacks for buildings along the road. Such rules made Pitkin seem even more a place apart. Travelers were used to visual pollution along the American roadside, but when travel writer Kent Ruth drove Highway 82 in the late 1950s, he was wowed by the "remarkable" lack of billboards along this particular road.[84]

That was the point of all the environmental measures: to make Aspen more attractive to leisure seekers like Ruth. Even the new sewer was sold to local voters as a way to "prove to potential visitors" that "we are serious in seeking their trade."[85] Notably, these were the same years Aspen boosters were fighting to save their local river recreation industry from the "Rape of the Roaring Fork," as threatened by the Fry-Ark diversion project. It was clear by the late 1950s that Aspen's civic and business establishment had embraced Verlin Ringle's basic insight: that the more local prosperity depended on luring leisure-seekers, the more profitable it became to protect the quality of the local environment.

Planning and zoning advocates wanted other communities to embrace the same insight. Aspen's consultant, Trafton Bean, emerged as a leading proponent of local planning in Colorado, but he was not the only one. Business and law professors, officials from bigger cities that had their own planning departments, consultants-for-hire like Bean—the 1950s found all of them preaching the economic benefits of planning and zoning. They wrote countless articles for the State Planning Commission newsletter and the magazine of the Colorado Municipal League, trying to convert the small-town, rural-county officials who read these publications to the religion of local planning. They launched an outreach organization, the Colorado Coordinating Committee for Planning and Zoning, to spread the word. Committee sponsors included not just business and travel boosters but also gardening, recreation, and conservation groups, including the Izaak Walton League—another reflection of zoning's ability to appeal to economic and environmental interests at the same time.[86] In 1951 the committee took its message up to the high country, convening a series of meetings with business and local-government representatives in Eagle, Summit, Pitkin, and nearby counties. The meetings yielded a set of planning principles, and many of these—including the suggestion that counties zone along highways to protect against sprawl—were eventually enshrined in zoning measures in Aspen, Pitkin County, Summit County, and elsewhere.[87]

This proselytizing for planning was going on in many parts of the country in the 1950s. But it is revealing that among Colorado's small mountain towns, the tourist-luring ones like Aspen were the first converts. Elsewhere, recreational growth lagged, and planning and zoning did too. Reining in rampant development was simply not an issue yet in slow-growing counties like Summit, Eagle, or Grand—frankly it was a problem many locals in those places would have loved to have. In Summit County, locals resisted planning and zoning for the same reason Aspenites initially did: because after decades of economic stagnation, they yearned for some way, *any* way, to turn a profit off their property, and they were loath to accept limits on their freedom to do so. The mere hint of planning or zoning could send them into a rage. When Summit County set up a planning commission in 1956, local landowners suspected a secret plot to impose "absolute control" over local land use in "true totalitarian fashion." The commission "savored of Russia," charged one man, invoking a Cold War stereotype that dogged planning and zoning throughout the 1950s.[88]

But before long Summit County followed Aspen: recreational development took off, and planning and zoning gained favor. In Summit's case, the landscape began shifting in the late 1950s. Anticipating Denver's dam construction and the inundation of Old Dillon, plans for a new Dillon took shape two miles to the north. Next to that, the new settlement of Silverthorne arose, filling with displaced Dillonites (in some cases they actually moved their houses and stores) and with the trailer homes of construction workers and their families who had come to work on the water-diversion tunnel and dam.[89] But these developments were nothing compared to what happened in Summit County in the early 1960s. First, in April 1960, came the Pavlo report and highway officials' decision to route Interstate 70 through this long-overlooked pocket of the Rockies, putting it directly on the tourist pipeline. Then, in the next several months, work finally got under way on Dillon Reservoir (soon to be Summit County's premier summer attraction) and the Peak 8–Breckenridge ski area (a major winter lure). Add the news that the nation's largest ski resort was under development just over Vail Pass, and suddenly Summit was, in one local reporter's words, "the growingest county in the state."[90]

Subdividers began selling homesites in the forests and meadows around Breckenridge and on the hills around the future reservoir. Restaurants, cocktail lounges, and specialty shops started popping up in Breckenridge and along the roads into town. Plans were made for an airstrip that could handle commercial planes.[91] The county commissioners found themselves reviewing new subdivision plats almost every month—in some cases, two or three in a single meeting. It was in that context that they decided, in April 1962, to hire Denver consultant Sam Huddleston to craft a county master plan. And this time there was no outcry, no Red Scare, in response. "The present mushrooming growth of the county has made this new planning very necessary," declared the *Summit County Journal*, reversing its own strident opposition from six years earlier. Public hearings on Huddleston's efforts were well attended and revealed the "vast majority" in favor of his proposed plan, according to the *Journal*. By late 1963, the *Journal* was reporting that "the entire county is vitally interested in planning."[92]

The tilt toward planning in Summit County stemmed from the same fear many in Aspen felt: that growth might swamp the environmental qualities—scenic views, rustic charm, open space—that made the place pleasant and had begun to make it prosperous too. Open-space loss was a paramount concern. Given all the new subdivisions, all the stringing of new businesses along the roadsides, it might "soon be impossible to tell where one town stops and the other begins," fretted one local reporter. (She added darkly: "I only hope the tops of the mountains will remain vacant.") Another reporter eyed the "startling" growth around the new ski area and wondered if the county could continue to live up to its own tourist advertising—if it could remain "the wonderful unspoiled recreational area which they tell us it is." The plans she had seen "make it sound like a suburb of Denver."[93]

Words like these echoed a creeping national nervousness in the 1950s: that America was losing too much of its open space to suburban sprawl. In retrospect, this worry was a watershed in American environmental thinking. Anxiety over open space alerted people to a host of related issues, like pollution, overpopulation, and loss of wildlife habitat. Loss of open space laid bare the dark side of the suburban dream, forcing many Americans to consider for the first time, right in their own backyards, the notion that "progress" might carry environmental costs.[94]

There was revolutionary potential in such reckoning, a chance that new worries about the fate of the landscape might prod people to renounce old orthodoxies about the goodness of growth. But in Summit County, the open-space issue led in a very unrevolutionary direction: it buttressed ongoing efforts to *boost* growth, especially that of the county's budding tourism-recreation trade. The land-use plan that Huddleston crafted and the county adopted in 1963 did not rein in recreational growth in order to save open space. Instead, it saved open space to spur further recreational growth. Tourism and recreation were "the key to economic rejuvenation of Summit County," the plan asserted, which meant "the County's splendid scenic and recreation resources [must] be maintained." Chief among these "resources," in Huddleston's expert view, were the open meadows along the Blue River and its tributaries, which lent a spacious ranch-country feel to drives between Dillon, Frisco, and Breckenridge and opened up postcard-pretty views of the mountains ringing Summit County all around.[95]

What tool did Huddleston have to keep these meadows open? Once again, it was his profession's stock-in-trade: zoning. As the centerpiece of his plan, he proposed a zoning map that would clump commercial development in Summit County's towns instead of letting it string out along the highways and that would hide vacation homes in the forests instead of letting them clutter the meadows on the valley floor. The meadows themselves would be zoned for ranching, reservoirs, parks, and golf courses—land uses that would preserve openness and mountain views. But the goal was not to limit growth; it was just the opposite. Huddleston insisted that such zoning would actually attract more real estate investment (by protecting property values) and more tourists and seasonal residents (by preserving scenic vistas and the "sense of rural open space"). Indeed, zoning to save open space was "*the* most critical element of economic improvement," Huddleston's plan declared.[96] This was not sacrificing booster values for the sake of sentimentality, aesthetics, or the quality of life. This was, instead, boosterism retooled: a new generation of environmental-protection measures put to work serving the familiar old goals of tourist growth.

By the time of Huddleston's Summit County master plan, recreation planning and zoning was in full swing throughout Colorado—and everywhere in the United States. The Outdoor Recreation Resources Review Commission had issued its report, and the states were in the process of drafting their own comprehensive outdoor recreation plans. A major incentive was money. Congress, acting on ORRRC's recommendation, had set up a Land and Water Conservation Fund to help state and local governments

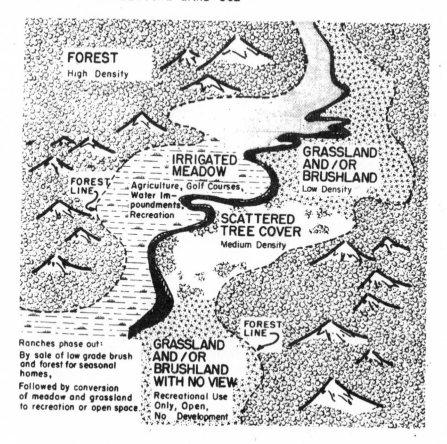

SCENIC RESOURCE PROTECTION PLAN

4.3 Zoning for scenery and prosperity. In his 1963 master plan for Summit County, Denver-based consultant Sam Huddleston identified scenic views as one of the county's key economic assets. To conserve them, he proposed keeping meadows open, restricting denser development to forested land where it would be screened from view.

acquire and develop recreational lands, and each state had to complete a recreation plan to become eligible. But Coloradans' enthusiasm for recreation planning seemed to go beyond the thirst for federal funds. Right after ORRRC released its report—still two years before the conservation fund was established—Governor Steve McNichols was already launching an ORRRC-style recreation steering committee. The committee convened the first annual Governor's Conference on Parks and Recreation in October 1962, inviting the head of the new U.S. Bureau of Outdoor Recreation (another ORRRC offspring) as keynote speaker and framing the agenda around ORRRC's recommendations. The conference, which drew local officials and organizational leaders from all over the state, was meant to help Colorado get a handle on the same issues ORRRC had studied at the national level: what kinds of recreation Coloradans and their guests needed, what facilities existed to meet the need, and how best to plan for the explosion in demand over the decades to come.[97]

Other ORRRC-inspired changes quickly followed. In 1963 the state legislature merged the young, underfunded state parks board with the older, better-funded Game and Fish Department. The merger was widely seen (and widely resented by hunters and anglers) as a move to divert funding from old-fashioned outdoor sports toward a wider diversity of recreation, in keeping with ORRRC's mass-leisure message.[98] Another item on ORRRC's action list—charging user fees for public recreation areas, to raise revenue for more such areas—found favor when the commission in charge of the new Game, Fish and Parks Department endorsed the idea in 1963. It was not an entirely popular stand, but the state Izaak Walton League lent crucial support, and in 1964 attendees at the Governor's Third Annual Conference on Parks and Recreation did too. Colorado state parks began charging user fees in 1965.[99]

The state's deepest foray into ORRRC-style planning came that same year, when the Game, Fish and Parks Department unveiled Colorado's first comprehensive outdoor recreation plan. A state-level clone of *Outdoor Recreation for America*, the plan quantified recreational demand from residents and tourists, inventoried existing facilities "by classification and activity," and outlined an "action program" to meet future demand. It dutifully broke down the numbers by ORRRC's six-zone system and further echoed ORRRC by placing highest priority on heavy-use facilities near population centers. And it got results: its proposals for 14 state and 27 local recreation projects netted two million dollars in federal conservation grants. Meanwhile, as soon as the 1965 plan was out, state staffers from the Game, Fish and Parks Department and the Division of Commerce and Development got busy updating it, seeking more detailed data on tourist demand, private recreation areas, and the "carrying capacity" of existing leisure facilities, public and private.[100]

If all of this sounds exceedingly bureaucratic, it was. The flurry of recreation planning that swept Colorado and the rest of the nation in the early 1960s lacked the drama of the popular environmental movement soon to come. Its protagonists were technicians and administrators, not concerned citizens or grassroots activists. It yielded maps, reports, and statistical tables, not rallies, teach-ins, or boycotts. But as unflashy as it may seem to us today, the institutionalization of recreation planning marked an exhilarating triumph for conservationists in the Carhart-Penfold mold. Finally, they had managed to establish outdoor leisure as a vital public good and a pressing policy concern. And finally, they had a robust bureaucracy to back them up. For the moment, at least, the wide-ranging federal- and state-level recreation planning machines taking shape in the early 1960s seemed much more muscular than the politically weak park, game, and fish agencies that had been recreation's main government allies in the past.

What is more, conservationists now found themselves closer than ever to Art Carhart's dream: a mighty alliance with recreational moneymakers. Recreation planning blurred the line between protecting and promoting outdoor leisure, in many ways putting conservationists in the business of boosting recreation. True, recreation planning was designed in part to protect against crass commercial clutter: the roadside blight, the tacky tourist traps. But these planners also had much in common with those who made and marketed outdoor recreation. Both reacted, fundamentally, to market demand: studying what kinds of fun people wanted and then seeking ways to provide it—in ever-larger amounts, with the easiest possible access. And as we have seen, Carhart's influential model for recreation zoning even drew on tourist advertising imagery to explain and frame the zones.

Perhaps the surest vindication of Carhart's approach—at least from Carhart's perspective—was that recreation planning was becoming a tool for boosters. In aspiring resort areas like Aspen and Summit County, booster-minded officials, with backing from local business, were experimenting with planning and zoning as a way to make local landscapes more attractive to visitors. Likewise, at the state level, recreation planning won broad support in large part because it promised to raise Colorado's vacation-market profile.[101] Carhart was right: the closer conservation bound itself to the outdoor leisure industry, the more momentum it gained. And the momentum went beyond the booster crowd. There were strong signs that the final piece of Carhart's dream coalition—the mass of recreational consumers—was also coming around.

HISTORICALLY, CONSERVATION HAD FOCUSED MOSTLY ON RAW MATERI-
als at the front end of the production process, far from the point of consumption: timber, water, minerals, soil. But the goal of recreation planning
was to provide end "products"—parks and playgrounds, pretty views, green
and open space, resort and recreational facilities—for consumers to consume firsthand. As such, recreation planning gave more people reason to
feel a direct personal stake in conservation. This was especially true in the
1950s and 1960s, when more and more Americans were either moving to the
leafy, leisurely spaciousness of suburban nature, or were yearning to. And
it was *especially* true in a state like Colorado, where such leisurely interaction with the outdoors had come to define so many people's sense of self
and sense of place. In such a context, recreation planning became a critical, if now largely forgotten, bridge from Progressive-style, expert-centered
conservation to popular environmental concern.[102] Simply put, it helped set
the stage for the postwar environmental movement. It also helped shape the
form the movement took on. That was certainly the case in Colorado, where
recreation planning was particularly popular, and where environmentalists took on certain core tendencies in common with it: an abiding faith in
technical solutions, a hopeful optimism that recreational development itself
would pave the way to environmental quality, and an obsession with proving that environmental protection could pay.

A key moment in the rise of Colorado environmentalism came when
the Colorado Mountain Club, that fun-loving crowd of hikers, climbers,
and skiers, began to take a more activist role. The CMC had a history in
this arena, having pushed hard for park designation and other preservation
causes in the 1910s. Then, like its California counterpart the Sierra Club,
its advocacy had lapsed. Despite Art Carhart's pleas, the CMC had stayed
mostly silent during the fight for Echo Park. But in the late 1950s the club
rediscovered its voice over the issue of wilderness. The battle for the federal wilderness bill struck a powerful chord with club members—people
who regularly escaped to the high country's remotest corners; who had
"climbed, hiked and camped in every Colorado wilderness proposed," as
one member said; and who saw the terrain in an almost proprietary light.
For them the wilderness experience was social, but also, as one wrote, it "is
esthetic; it is physical; it is spiritual and it is sensual." And it was deeply personal. It had come to define their very identities. The club's Denver chapter
explained, "We are secretaries and clerks, surgeons and students, technicians and teachers. . . . [But] wilderness and wilderness use have become a

part of our outlook on life and a part of our personal values." So the thought of losing the high-country wildlands to logging, damming, mining, or highway building horrified them. The wilderness bill sprang from such fears: that if government did not take action, there would soon be nowhere left to rediscover the personal and primeval, to take refuge from everyone else.[103]

So in 1958, soon after Congress began debating the wilderness bill, the CMC revived its Conservation Committee and sent representatives to testify on the bill's behalf. It was a gingerly first step; club leaders still hesitated to launch into full-bore advocacy. But in 1961, with the bill stalled in Washington, DC, they finally resolved to "take a more active role in conservation" and to push the wilderness measure "in any way possible." The decision fired up the whole club. Members' interest in environmental issues experienced "a pronounced upswing," the conservation chair reported, and the CMC began reaching out to other groups to coordinate wilderness advocacy statewide. A shining moment came in January 1964, when the CMC mustered supporters from all over the state to stack a congressional hearing in Denver in favor of the bill. At a similar hearing a few years earlier, in the Western Slope city of Montrose, foes of the bill had far outnumbered friends, sending a message that Coloradans were hostile to wilderness. But at the 1964 hearing the CMC and its allies swamped the naysayers 3 to 1—"the most vocal support" for wilderness that the congressional committee had "encountered to date anywhere in the country," claimed club officer Estelle Brown. It was, she rejoiced, a "giant step forward in conservation." To many in the CMC, the Denver hearing revealed an enormous potential to be tapped, an entire stratum of ordinary Coloradans who felt a powerful personal stake in the outdoors but had been excluded from debates surrounding it. It was time to rally these "informed, but as yet, unorganized conservation amateurs," Brown wrote—to "work out their similarities and strength and to promote unified action."[104]

In the movement building that followed, CMC member Edward Hilliard Jr. would take center stage. He came to the job naturally, for his own blend of identities made him something of a walking outdoor coalition unto himself. As an expert hunter and climber, he belonged to two of the most elite outdoor fraternities; yet as a camper and skier, he consumed mass-market leisure in a more casual way too. He invested in recreation as a lifestyle, he and his wife, Joy, having moved to Colorado in the early 1950s largely to pursue their outdoor pastimes. But he also invested in recreation as a business, as owner of a company that manufactured high-end hunting riflescopes.[105]

All told, Ed Hilliard was exceptionally well positioned to bring together disparate recreational stakeholders. In fact, he already had a history of doing just that. In 1959 he had cofounded the Conservation Council of Colorado, recruiting members from the Colorado Wildlife Federation, the Izaak Walton League, and other sportsmen's groups.[106] Then, in 1962, he had moved to expand the council beyond the rod-and-gun crowd. Seeking "state level coordinating" of Colorado's myriad "recreational conservation groups," he invited more than twenty such groups to confer, representing campers, climbers, hikers, hunters, anglers, skiers, gardeners, bird-watchers, photographers, white-water rafters, even history buffs, Boy and Girl Scouts, archers, and skeet shooters.[107] He hoped to build a grand alliance among—though he never used this language—all the different consumers in Colorado's bustling outdoor-recreation scene.

At the time, CMC leaders were consumed with the battle for the wilderness bill. But once that battle was finally won—the bill cleared Congress in July 1964—the club threw its weight behind Hilliard's coalition-building efforts. In September the CMC hosted a conference in Breckenridge, inviting outdoor lovers from all over the state to hobnob with the Sierra Club's Dave Brower, the Izaak Walton League's Joe Penfold, the Wilderness Society's Stewart Brandborg, and other luminaries. The goal, explained CMC officer Hugh Kingery, was to "have conservationists and outdoor lovers talking to each other—the fisherman to the climber, the garden club lady to the timberman." For two days they discussed wilderness, wildlife, recreation planning, roadside blight, and more. Then, in the closing speech, Roger Hansen, a young lawyer and conservationist in Sam Huddleston's Denver land-planning firm, laid out a "Blueprint for Action." He called on outdoor devotees of all kinds to join together in a "Colorado Outdoors Coordinating Council," defending Colorado's "priceless scenic and outdoor recreational resources." The idea electrified the audience and generated rapid results. By spring 1965, the group envisioned by Hansen (and Hilliard)—the Colorado Open Space Coordinating Council (COSCC)—was up and running, with Hansen as executive director, CMC members prominently and energetically involved, and the original driving force, Hilliard, lending a hand with funding and logistics.[108]

COSCC (which dropped the "Coordinating" in late 1967 to become COSC) was successful enough that it soon inspired similar umbrella organizations in other states. In Colorado, it quickly became the preeminent environmental advocacy group, spearheading the state's popular environmental movement in the 1960s and 1970s. And that meant the movement, like COSCC itself, had its roots deep in recreational consumerism. Recreational consumerism gave COSCC its energy. Almost all of the groups that joined the council did so out of passion for some outdoor pastime: the Colorado White Water Association (rafting), the Colorado Federation of Garden Clubs (gardening), Denver Field Ornithologists (bird-watching), the Colorado Wildlife Federation (hunting), Trout Unlimited (fishing), and of course the Colorado Mountain Club (climbing, hiking, and skiing), just to name a few.

But if recreation made these groups care, it did not make them all care in the same way. Skiers, bird-watchers, hunters, and horticulturists had very different ways of consuming the high country. They represented not just outdoor pastimes but outdoor niche markets. That is why COSCC was set up as a loose confederation—an umbrella group really—with each member group assured autonomy and the freedom to disavow any COSCC position it disliked.[109] Organizing this way recognized the reality that recreation was an inherently segmented market and that people whose politics stemmed from personal consumer preferences were often going to disagree. The list of priorities that came out of the Breckenridge conference—wilderness, billboard control, water, wildlife, air pollution, outdoor education, parks, zoning—further spoke to the variety-pack nature of a movement built on outdoor consumerism.[110] Each of these priorities became the basis for a "workshop," or issue-focused subsidiary of COSCC, and over time some of the workshops matured into semiautonomous organizations of their own. It was not exactly a recipe for a tightly unified movement.

Paradoxically, though, even as recreational consumerism fragmented the movement, it also imparted an essential underlying unity. The groups that joined COSCC differed in which amenities they cared most about, but they shared a concern for the visual, spatial, and experiential elements of place: the way high-country settings looked and what it felt like to spend time in them—the same qualities of landscape that tourist boosters promoted. Most of the priorities that came out of the 1964 Breckenridge conference revolved around such concerns. So did COSCC's mission statement, written in 1965. It committed COSCC to the care of "scenic, historic, open space, wilderness and outdoor recreational resources," which we can translate into advertising language and say that COSCC wanted to keep Colorado scenic, thrilling, wide open, western, and wild. And when the COSCC mission linked these resources to the "cultural, educational, physical, health, spiritual and economic benefits of our citizens and our visitors," it drew the same connection between product and personal well-being that drove not just tourist advertising but advertising in general—indeed, the consumerist mind-set in general.[111] COSCC thus took the key step that Art Carhart had been begging leisure-seekers to take since the late 1940s: it made product and personal well-being the basis for unified political action.

Perhaps surprisingly, another element that unified COSCC's disparate constituencies—for the moment, at least—was a shared enthusiasm for ORRRC-style recreation planning and zoning. Of all COSCC's agenda items, this one seemed to participants to hold the most promise for serving all the recreational niches at once. Roger Hansen focused much of his "Blueprint for Action" on it. Other states had moved forward with recreation planning, he reported; Colorado should too. The state should execute a comprehensive recreation plan (in fact, Game, Fish and Parks officials were working on one even as Hansen spoke), and counties should use their planning and zoning powers to protect scenic and leisure resources and buy up open space, with funding assistance from the state. Hansen had some self-interest in the matter, since his boss, Sam Huddleston, was a local planner (recall that he had designed the land-use plan for Summit County). But Hansen was not the only one who favored this approach. The CMC's Hugh Kingery was another who thought ORRRC-style planning should be Colorado conservationists' "next objective" and that zoning should be the centerpiece. There were many demands on Colorado's open space, Kingery realized, but he professed faith in the gospel of ORRRC: "By using the concept of zoning, all these needs can be met." The attendees at Breckenridge seemed to agree, voting at the end of the conference to make rural zoning one of the top priorities going forward. In the coming years, COSCC would keep up the drumbeat for recreation planning and zoning, pushing for upgrades to the state's comprehensive outdoor recreation plan and urging local efforts along the same lines.[112]

Why would these pioneering environmentalists get excited about something so technical, so bureaucratic, as recreation planning? About something so *pro-development* as recreation planning? Their enthusiasm suggests that even for people building an ostensibly bottom-up movement, the technocratic approach to environmental problem solving had an enduring appeal. It also suggests that for people who came to environmentalism through recreational consumerism, as so many in Colorado did, the commercial development of recreation could seem compatible with, even essential to, the protection of leisure amenities. From today's perspective, when large-scale recreational development has achieved an environmental reputation almost as bad as logging or mining, it might be hard to accept that environmentalists ever thought this way—especially wilderness advocates, who were supposedly dead-set against commercializing nature (and who were well represented in COSCC). But recreation planning, in keeping with its Carhartian roots, held wilderness "zones" to be part of the wider, all-purpose recreational landscape. So it was possible to love wilderness and still feel common cause with people invested in other recreation zones, including commercialized, heavy-use ones. For a hopeful moment in the 1960s, then, tourist-industry interests, wilderness advocates, and consumers of more commercial forms of outdoor leisure were able to rally around the flag of recreation planning. In Colorado, recreation planning, rooted in Progressive-style conservation by technical experts, became an unexpected popular cause, one of the first agenda items of the emerging environmental movement. And for the moment, at least, it forged a bond between those who valued the vacationland for lifestyle and those who valued it for livelihood.

Colorado environmentalists also had a tactical reason for allying themselves with the tourist industry: it shielded them from the self-indulgent, emotional, impractical "nature lover" stereotype. Roger Hansen clearly had this in mind when he warned his Breckenridge audience against acting "on the basis of esthetics alone, or our physical and spiritual need alone." Yes, he allowed, "we are Emersonians or Izaak Waltons or Audubons or followers of Muir and Thoreau. But this 'Ah, wilderness' attitude alone will NOT help develop a recreation-conservation program for Colorado." Recreational advocacy would achieve legitimacy only if it mixed "the idealistic with the practical." And the way to be practical was to talk like a tourist booster. "The *practical* justification for an action program revolves around cold, hard economic facts," Hansen lectured, channeling Art Carhart. "Income, jobs and building permits is a language most people understand." So outdoor enthusiasts must make sure their recreation-protection efforts "dovetailed with . . . economic development efforts, notably tourism." And they must constantly repeat: "There is *business* in beauty, *opportunity* in open space, *economic rewards* in recreation."[113]

Rhetoric like that was not going to remind anyone of Aldo Leopold or John Muir. But it made sense in a state as bullish on tourism as Colorado. In fact, by the time Hansen spoke, environmental advocacy in Colorado had long since appropriated the language and logic of tourist boosters. Carhart and Penfold had set the tone in their defense of Echo Park. Colorado backers of the wilderness bill had followed suit. The leader of the state's Izaak Walton League warned that to forsake wilderness "would be short-sighted and irresponsible toward [Colorado's] future" because such settings "bring us millions of visitors every year." An Aspen man urged recalcitrant Western Slope congressman Wayne Aspinall to back the wilderness bill because "beauty and solitude themselves have become an industry" of major import in Aspinall's district. And Ed Hilliard predicted that wilderness designation would spur lucrative "fringe development" like that around national parks.[114]

Even before COSCC, statements like these gave environmental advocacy in Colorado a strongly pro–tourist industry tone. And COSCC itself went even further, sometimes casting itself almost as an accessory to the booster machine. In its mission statement, COSCC listed "economic benefits" as a core objective and resolved to serve both "our citizens *and our visitors*."[115] In a 1966 resolution, it declared that a "Quality Colorado Environment" would be "a major attraction for new industry to our state" and would maintain "tourism and recreation as a vital factor in our economy." COSCC director Hansen sounded even more boosterish: an "irreplaceable treasure chest of open space and outdoor recreation opportunities," he proclaimed, was "the *economic* giant of Colorado's future."[116]

COSCC also took pains to operate in a way that put businesspeople at ease. Hansen wanted it known that "we don't just sit around the campfire and read Thoreau to each other"; under his direction COSCC won plaudits for its "business-like approach."[117] Hansen, and especially the well-connected Hilliard, made great efforts to reach out to executives and boosters, including many in the leisure sector. Hansen hoped to bring the Colorado Dude and Guest Ranch Association, the Colorado Motel Association, and the various highway associations into COSCC (which never happened) and struck up a friendship with Robert Parker, Vail Associates marketing chief, after Parker wrote to the *Denver Post* about the need to protect scenic resources.[118] Much of Hansen's outreach to business interests took place under the aegis of the Colorado Open Space Foundation (COSF), a 1966 spin-off from COSCC that focused on research and education instead of lobbying. Hansen and Hilliard hoped that businesspeople who balked at working with an overtly agenda-driven ecogroup like COSCC might feel cozier with a nonpartisan one like COSF. In 1968 COSF became the Colorado branch of the new Rocky Mountain Center on Environment

(ROMCOE), an environmental-consulting nonprofit set up with a Ford Foundation grant. Under the directorship of Roger Hansen (who moved over from COSCC), ROMCOE pointedly shunned "policy-making or position-taking," instead offering research, informational, and educational services to government agencies, academia, citizen groups, and—significantly—business clients.[119] In this role, ROMCOE nudged tourist entrepreneurs to embrace green ideas. For example, the center advised developers on zoning and architectural controls for a ski resort near Steamboat Springs, and consulted with the American Hotel and Motel Association on how that industry might contribute to a "quality environment for benefit of the tourist trade."[120]

It would be a mistake to write this off as environmentalists selling out to business interests. In fact, the line often blurred between entrepreneurial and environmental thinking, because when it came to an interest in outdoor amenities, they did have a lot in common. Consider the case of Bob Parker, the Vail Associates marketing chief, who became one of COSCC's earliest and staunchest business allies. On one level, he saw environmental quality as a matter of dollars and cents. "We are not only selling a service," he bluntly said of the recreation business. "We're selling the environment." And that meant "our product is only as valid as the environment which surround[s] it."[121] It was said with profits in mind, but it was also exactly what Colorado's coalescing environmental movement wanted to hear: confirmation that business and environmental advocacy really could find common cause. When Parker told the 1966 Colorado Open Space Conference, "We are out of business in the recreation business if we lose our scenic resources," Hansen reported that the speech "brought applauding conservationists to their feet." Parker did agree with Hansen that "conservationists will carry the day only if they speak in economic as well as esthetic terms," but he did not dispute that aesthetics counted too. In fact, Parker was not just a marketer of the outdoors but an avid skier, hiker, horseback rider, and outdoor lover who was known to rhapsodize sincerely on the emotional, noneconomic benefits of recreation in the Rockies.[122] In complicated ways, then, the economic and emotional, promoters' and consumers' ways of valuing the recreational outdoors intertwined, and the affinity environmentalists found with some tourist boosters in the 1960s was more than just a cynical ploy.

So when Colorado's newly organized environmentalists waded into their first big battle, they did so with significant backing from tourist boosters. The battle erupted over highway officials' plans to route Interstate 70 through a wilderness area. In the past, boosters had cheered almost any kind of highway improvement. But now many of them, seeing a stake in the economic value of wilderness, sided with the environmentalists. Together they thwarted the road builders—a triumph that marked the environmentalists' arrival as a political force in the state.

For years, state highway officials had sought to shorten and straighten the drive through the high country, plowing through pretty much any obstacle in the way. In the early 1960s, they fixed their sights on one of the last obstacles left: the Gore Range, a dramatic ridge of Precambrian granite about seventy miles west of Denver. Walling off eastern Eagle County, the future home of Vail, from Summit County on the other side, the range had long posed problems for travel. No railroad ever pierced the precipitous Gores, nor did any highway, until 1940, when crews threw a road over 10,666-foot Vail Pass—but the road dodged the main part of the range, looping around its southern end. That might work for a U.S. highway, but once the 1960 Pavlo report chose U.S. 6 as the future route of Interstate 70, state highway officials determined that the loop must go. Vail Pass marked one of the largest deviations from straight on the entire 2,150-mile path I-70 followed from Baltimore to Utah, which did not sit well with Colorado engineers. So with typical hubris, they decided to slice off the Vail Pass loop and save 10.8 miles of driving distance, by tunneling I-70 straight through the Gores. The problem was that gouging I-70 through the Gores would also mean gouging it through the Gore Range–Eagles Nest Primitive Area, one of the most scenically spectacular tracts of wilderness in the high country.[123] The tunnel proposal thus put highway engineers on a collision course with Colorado's increasingly spirited environmental movement.

In 1960, E. Lionel Pavlo had studied the tunnel route—called "Red Buffalo" because it would cut between humpbacked Buffalo Mountain and knife-ridged Red Peak—and advised against it. The tunnel would be too long and too high, Pavlo said, and drivers too vulnerable to avalanches thundering down the steep sides of the Gores.[124] But state highway officials clung to their tunnel vision. Even four years later, when the wilderness bill, nearing passage, threatened to close all primitive areas to road building, the highway officials still did not relent. Instead, they prevailed upon a powerful ally, Congressman Aspinall, to slip a little-noticed clause into the final version of the Wilderness Act, empowering the U.S. secretary of agriculture (in his role as overseer of the national forests) to remove up to seven thousand acres from the southern end of the Gore Range wilderness.[125] The deletion, of course, would allow Red Buffalo to go through. No other primitive area in the country was subject to such a clause.

But Colorado's outdoor advocates refused to go along. They erupted in protest when the State Highway Department resurrected the Red Buffalo proposal in 1965 and especially when the U.S. Bureau of Public Roads endorsed it the next year. COSCC and CMC began organizing a campaign against Red Buffalo; other groups like the Colorado Wildlife Federation joined in voicing displeasure. The case also drew national attention, with the Wilderness Society, the Sierra Club, the *New York Times*, and others speaking out against the tunnel plan. For a time in 1966–67, Red Buffalo became a battle for environmentalists everywhere, saving the Gore Range–Eagles Nest Primitive Area a national cause.[126]

The environmentalists attacked Red Buffalo on economic and engineering grounds. COSCC's Roads Committee touted a report by CMC member Dick Guadagno that debunked the cost estimates highway officials were using to justify Red Buffalo. Guadagno drew on his day-job expertise as an engineer to show, among other things, that the route would have to be encased in snowsheds for much of its length to protect against avalanches—increasing the construction cost by two-thirds, he claimed. COSCC also presented a report by Dennis Neuzil (a civil-engineering professor and former Coloradan who had been active in the Sierra Club's regional chapter), exposing several illogical assumptions highway officials had used to inflate Red Buffalo's "user benefit." Guadagno and Neuzil were using the same tactic employed by Echo Park's defenders a decade earlier: mustering what Art Carhart would call "cold, hard" data to discredit the technocrats on their own terms.[127]

But the environmentalists' real objection was the threat Red Buffalo posed to wilderness and recreational values. CMC considered the Gore Range "one of the most rugged and most beautiful of the Colorado wildernesses," while the Wilderness Society noted its value for hiking, climbing, and the study of high-altitude plant and animal communities. The proposed I-70 route put all of that in peril. If the interstate went through, warned the U.S. Bureau of Outdoor Recreation, it would "destroy wilderness values" by shattering the calm, dirtying the air, and disrupting wildlife habitat and drainage patterns. The reverberations would echo beyond the high country. "The issue is a national one," said the Sierra Club, because it came down to whether economic concerns like highway "user savings" would be allowed to trump wilderness values.[128]

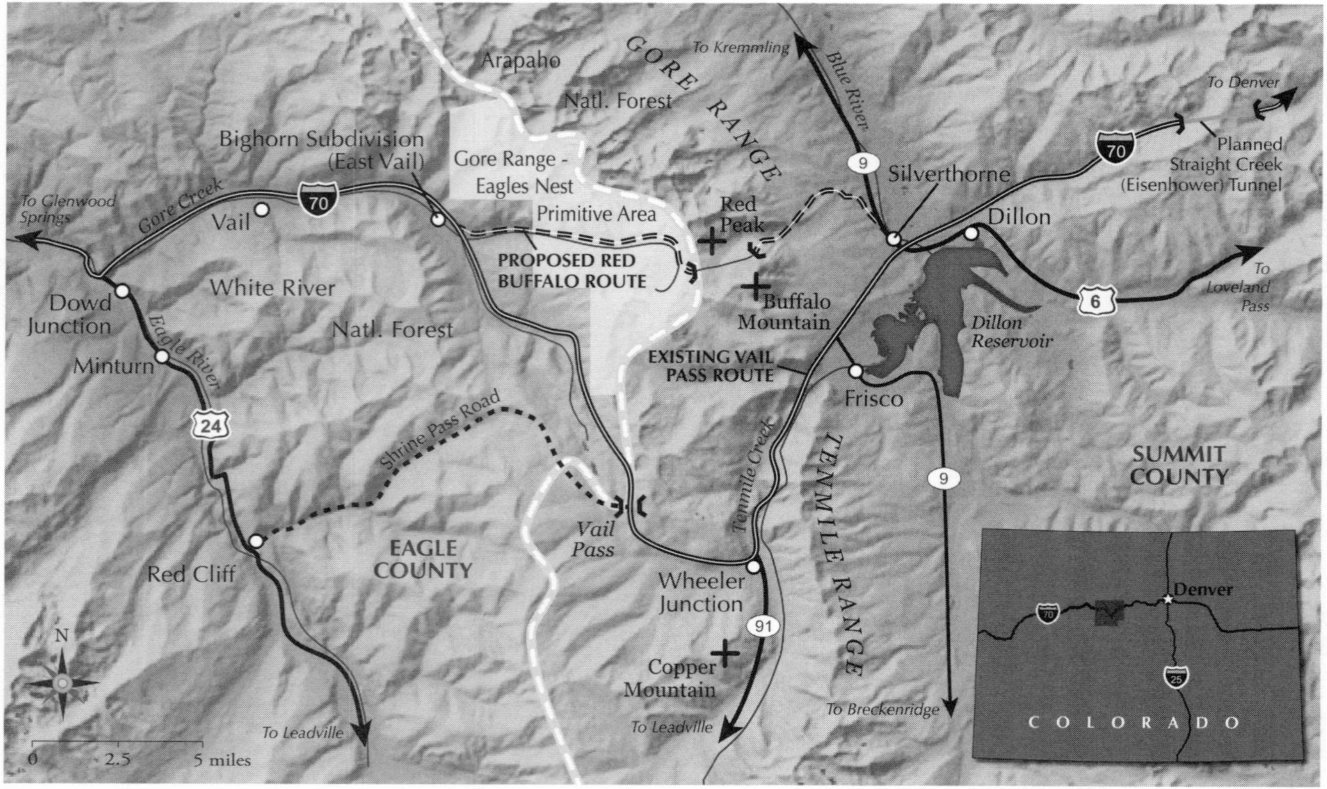

MAP 5.
Proposed Red Buffalo tunnel route, 1960s.

Even beyond wilderness, the broader issue of recreation was at stake. As the Bureau of Outdoor Recreation reported, Gore Range–Eagles Nest was "very popular with recreationists" like hikers and horseback riders, accounting for 11 percent of all wilderness visits in Colorado, "principally because of its accessibility to Denver." (The agency failed to note the irony that this accessibility came thanks to the same highway that engineers now wanted to ram through the primitive area.) Hikers, climbers, and horseback riders would lose their backcountry experience if the interstate tunnel was built. Hunters stood to lose too: according to state Game, Fish and Parks director Harry Woodward, Red Buffalo would cause a "serious decline in hunting opportunities" by severing a major wildlife migration route and closing thirty-six thousand acres of summer range to elk and deer.[129] So the Red Buffalo battle did not just belong to wilderness advocates. Like the push for recreation planning, it drew many recreational niche markets together in common cause.

And in this cause, once again, wilderness advocates found common ground with Coloradans who counted on outdoor recreation as a business. For if Red Buffalo threatened recreational values, it stood to reason that it also threatened the value of recreation—the economic value, that is. That was how many people in the high country saw it, especially those in the region right around the primitive area: Summit and Lake Counties immediately to the east and south and Vail to the west. The Summit County Citizens Committee and Vail Wilderness Workshop began coordinating with COSCC to defeat Red Buffalo. The Vail town council passed a resolution declaring that the route would harm "the residents of and visitors to Vail."[130] Local officials, business owners, ordinary citizens—many in the immediate vicinity were convinced that blasting an interstate through the wilderness would devastate their local tourist economies. And they were furious that the State Highway Department seemed not to care.

The locals vented their anger at a meeting in the I-70 town of Frisco in October 1966. It was the only public hearing on Red Buffalo that highway officials ever agreed to—and they probably wished they hadn't. Some three hundred people, mostly locals, packed into Frisco's school gym that night, and Dick Guadagno, who was there to present his report, estimated that Red Buffalo critics outnumbered supporters 4 to 1. Emissaries from COSCC and the Colorado Federation of Garden Clubs spoke for the sanctity of wilderness; other speakers raised cost and engineering concerns. But the crowd's anger was best captured by the stream of local citizens and officials—from

Breckenridge, Leadville, Frisco, and Lake and Summit Counties—who decried the economic damage Red Buffalo would do.

In effect, they admitted, the Summit and Lake County economies now depended on luring tourists. That was what their consultants had told them; that was what their newly adopted land-use plans (the ones executed by Sam Huddleston) were designed to do. These plans and forecasts had been approved and partially funded by state and federal agencies. Now Red Buffalo was ignoring them all. Red Buffalo, predicted the locals, would degrade local *amenity* by ruining one of the area's premier tourist draws, its wilderness. It would hamper local *accessibility* by slashing Summit County's interstate mileage and leaving Summit and Lake Counties with just one I-70 exit between them—and that one located far from the local business centers of Breckenridge and Leadville. And it might cripple local *advertising* by bypassing the area's best "billboard": the dramatic roadside view of Dillon Reservoir, studded with piney islands and surrounded by magnificent mountain skylines. Tourists drove right by this tempting view on the existing highway, as it swung south on the way to Vail Pass. But future travelers driving the more northerly Red Buffalo route might not see the lake at all.[131]

In retrospect, these contentions might have given environmentalists pause. While COSCC worried primarily about the primitive area being put *on* the interstate; Summit and Lake County locals seemed most upset that they were going to be left *off* it. Indeed, on balance, the value of wilderness was a small part of their overall case—and what they did say about wilderness had to do mostly with its use as a tourist magnet. Here was a sign that, despite agreement on Red Buffalo, there was a basic difference between the environmental values of environmentalists and tourist boosters. Before long this divergence would jeopardize the alliance between the two camps and with it the momentum of Colorado's environmental movement.

But not yet. In 1966 hostility between boosters and environmentalists was not a foregone conclusion. Talking about wilderness's power to lure tourists was consistent with the way many Colorado advocates had sold the wilderness concept in the first place. So the locals' talk did not alarm environmentalists. That a bunch of western small-town boosters were seeing any value at all in wilderness—and, despite their ancient animosity toward federal land managers, were arguing for the need to respect the Wilderness Act—seemed to environmentalists a sign of real progress. So in 1966, those Red Buffalo foes whose chief concern was wilderness did not worry about (perhaps did not even notice) that they were arguing from a different set of priorities than many of their allies up in the high country. All that mattered was that all their arguments ended on the same note: Red Buffalo must not go through.

Highway officials did have their backers, including chambers of commerce in Denver, Grand Junction, and a number of smaller cities in far western Colorado. Former governor Big Ed Johnson weighed in for Red Buffalo too, reminding everyone how hard he had fought for I-70 in the 1950s, imploring Coloradans not to abandon his dream for the shortest and fastest route. "Colorado cannot tolerate being handicapped now with 10 extra and unnecessary miles of winding mountain trails," Big Ed said, dredging up the same rhetoric he had used in the 1950s. "That magic word 'shortest' has terrific appeal to tourists. I believe that one word is worth a hundred million dollars to Colorado a year."[132]

But this assumption, which Coloradans had accepted ten years ago, was on the defensive now. The sense was spreading that the better way to serve the industry was to rein in the road-building machine. Many heavy hitters in Colorado tourism came to this conclusion, including veterans of the Tenth Mountain Division, who had done so much to build the ski industry. They decried Red Buffalo as a group, and two of them became especially outspoken critics: Vail's Bob Parker, who felt conservation was basic to good business; and *Skiing* magazine founder Merrill Hastings, whose new venture, *Colorado Magazine*, was devoted to marketing the high-country lifestyle. Hastings urged his readers to write to public officials in protest of Red Buffalo, and his readers responded in droves.[133] Concerned citizens wrote to the State Highway Department or the Denver dailies (letters to both ran heavily against the tunnel), and though few of these writers were themselves involved in the tourist trade, a striking number cited concern for the industry as a reason for their opposition. ("The enormous tourist industry of Colorado is based almost exclusively on wilderness appeal," said a typical letter.) Charles Shumate, the chief highway engineer, still insisted that highway experts need not listen to popular pressure: "It's none of their business," he growled of the letter-writers bombarding his department.[134] But many people clearly felt protecting the wilderness *was* their business, and beyond that, the business of Colorado.

By late 1967 more prominent figures were siding against Red Buffalo. State legislators, the lieutenant governor, and the state Game, Fish and Parks director swore their opposition. So did two of Colorado's four congressmen and one of its senators, Republican Peter Dominick. Dominick drew attention to the cause when he and Hastings took a pack trip through the primitive area, with a *Rocky Mountain News* reporter and photographer in tow. The reporter might well have been a mouthpiece for COSCC. He breathlessly described mammoth trees, glorious vistas, and windswept tundra. He deepened the area's wild mystique by alluding to legends that a mysterious giant bear lurked up there. And he speculated that Chief Engineer Shumate would relent if only he experienced this place for himself.[135] The Bureau of Outdoor Recreation, that child of the Outdoor Recreation Resources Review Commission, came out against Red Buffalo, proving itself the friendly agency that outdoor advocates had hoped it would be. COSCC also found allies in President Lyndon Johnson's cabinet: the secretaries of transportation and commerce expressed qualms about the tunnel; and Interior Secretary Stewart Udall, who in another high-profile dispute was trying to keep a highway from going through a recreation area on the Oregon coast, hinted he would kill Red Buffalo if it were up to him.[136]

Under the clause Congressman Aspinall had added to the Wilderness Act, the final decision lay with Agriculture Secretary Orville Freeman. And though Freeman was not exactly known as a friend of environmentalists, he ended up, in May 1968, taking their side. Not only did he veto Red Buffalo, putting the primitive area off-limits to road building, but he justified his dramatic decision with a ringing defense of recreational values. A population exploding in numbers and wealth, he observed, was already putting terrific pressure on the nation's outdoor spaces. Yet "we have all the land now that we will ever have." So wilderness had to be protected wherever possible. Red Buffalo might save motorists money, but "economics *alone* is not a sufficient basis for determining whether wilderness shall survive or die." Weighing economics against the expanding masses' outdoor needs, Freeman concluded that it was "in the interest of the greatest number of people in the long run" to spare Gore Range–Eagles Nest.[137] And with that rationale he affirmed the core tenets of COSCC's brand of environmentalism: that open space was a scarce and precious resource; that it must be managed to meet recreational market demand; that lifestyle values must be weighed alongside economic ones in gauging a landscape's utility; and that the more Americans looked outside for fun and fulfillment, the more the public interest was served by favoring the former values over the latter.

As the first great victory for environmentalists in Colorado—one Summit County man called it "the first time that public officials had truly been forced to submit to the will of the people"—the Red Buffalo decision also seemed to vindicate COSCC's tactics: reaching out to business interests and emulating conservationists' expert, "practical" approach. In the afterglow, Roger Hansen proudly recalled every step in the strategy. How COSCC had stood with Lake and Summit County locals "on a nippy fall evening . . . at the little red schoolhouse in Frisco." How COSCC's Roads Committee had built "a powerful case" against Red Buffalo, using engineering data and expert legal analysis to argue "not only from a wilderness standpoint but legally and economically as well." And how COSCC had rallied the grassroots, "hundreds of private citizens," to send letters and telegrams, even as it also worked the halls of power, meeting with federal officials and forging alliances with "powerful forces" like Sen. Peter Dominick and the *Rocky Mountain News*. All told, Hansen predicted, COSCC's multilayered coalition building would "serve as a model to citizens everywhere" in the environmental battles of the future.[138]

OVER AT *Colorado Magazine*, IN HIS EDITORIAL INTRODUCING THE SUMmer 1968 issue, Merrill Hastings hailed the victory too. Red Buffalo marked the dawn of a new era, he wrote excitedly, a new "movement . . . to preserve the natural grandeur of Colorado."[139] Then he turned the rest of the issue over to the magazine's usual business: a guide to Colorado's "camping hot spots," pleas for companies to relocate to the state, a feature on a new vacation house in Vail, and ads for rental cars, four-wheel-drives, outdoor equipment, and everything else to make the high-country experience more pleasant and convenient for visitors and residents alike.

Hastings saw no contradiction between his environmentalist convictions and his magazine's promotion of mass outdoor leisure. Neither did Bob Parker. The Vail Associates marketing maven felt sure that a thriving tourism and recreation business was the key to preserving the fragile high-country environment. And he seized every opportunity to make the case to anyone who would listen: local chambers of commerce, fellow skiarea operators, *Denver Post* readers, attendees at the Colorado Open Space Conference. With the right backing, tourism could become the state's top industry "in a very short time," he told one booster group. "Think of what that might imply! Not less trout water, but more! Not more freeways, but more ski trails! Not carelessly slaughtered game, but carefully harvested game! Not tarpaper shacks and trailers, but attractive, planned resorts!" It might sound too good to be true, Parker admitted, but "Many of us believe that all this is not only possible, but is the only future for Colorado, if we are to preserve the environment that makes Colorado such a marvelous place to live and recreate!"[140] In this vision, recreational development and environmental quality were not only compatible, they absolutely depended on each other. Environmental utopia could be Colorado's if Coloradans opted for the "attractive, planned" Vails of the future over the destructive, dirty industries of the past.

Of course, it served Vail Associates' interests for Parker to say such things. But Parker was sincere, and truth be told, Colorado's environmental movement was born of hopes like his. Art Carhart in the 1950s, and COSCC's founders in the 1960s, expressed essentially the same hope: that the emerging recreational economy would counterbalance the old extractive industries. The rise of recreation vested economic value in open meadows, unobstructed views, wilderness enclaves, and clean water left in streams. And that gave Coloradans—including powerful boosters and business interests—incentive to side with COSCC in saving them. That is why COSCC, again like Carhart a decade earlier, spent so much time asserting recreation's economic value and courting allies in the business world. That is why they embraced Carhart's Progressive-style recreation planning and zoning: because it legitimized recreation's presence in the landscape and promoted its ever-wider spread.

But if recreational growth gave outdoor advocates the practical and political means to protect their amenities, it was the advocates' own recreational consumerism that made them care so deeply about those amenities in the first place. This is not to say they were dupes of tourist advertisers. But outdoor advocates *did* live by the basic premise of tourist advertising: they found pleasure and personal meaning in the leisure settings of the high country. Yes, different consumers fixed on different settings—the wilderness trail, the mountain resort, the fishing river purling past Carhart's cabin. But they all felt personally, not just financially, invested in the recreational outdoors. That meant they all had a personal stake in conserving recreational resources. As more of them discovered such a stake, recreational conservation gained popularity and became the environmental movement, vacationland style.

The momentum from Red Buffalo would build into the early 1970s, when the influence of environmentalism in Colorado would reach its peak. But even as it did, the limitations of a movement built on consumerism would become clear. The environmental utopia Bob Parker promised would prove as elusive as a drive on I-70 without traffic or a lift in Vail without a line.

CHAPTER 5

The John Denver Tenor

A LOT OF COLORADANS WILL CRINGE AT THIS, BUT BACK IN THE 1970S the leading symbol of their state was John Denver. Yes, he of the toothy grin, blond mop, and granny glasses, who lived near Aspen and sang of sunshine and soaring eagles and needing nothing more than mountains to get high.[1] For the rest of the country—and for a great many Coloradans too—this shy but strangely ebullient former folkie absolutely embodied Colorado's recreational-environmental ideal. His songs and TV specials were calls for caring about nature, his concerts multimedia celebrations of the Colorado lifestyle. You could count on lots of strumming, picking, and harmonizing up on stage, while a screen overhead showed movies of Denver, his wife and friends hiking in the high country, skiing, climbing, and roasting marshmallows over the fire. Other screens flashed postcard images of peaks and sunsets, bighorns and birds of prey. "We've got a far-out show for you tonight!" Denver would happily shout to the sold-out crowd. "Make believe you're in the Rocky Mountains . . . sitting around a campfire!"—as much as that was possible for sixteen thousand fans packing an arena in Los Angeles or New York.[2]

The music critics ripped him. They called him hypocritical for selling outdoor solitude to a mass audience and saccharine for fixating on only happy things. "It's nice to sing about the Rocky Mountains and sunshine," grumped one reviewer, "but what about the troubles of the cities and the despair that surrounds so much of modern life?" But John Denver's huge fan base would not hear it. After a negative review, one Los Angeles critic found himself flooded with indignant letters. "Rock music has a proliferation of darkness in it already," said one Denver defender. "Let's have peacefulness, serenity, love, beauty without having always to be cynical." "If only more people could hear what John Denver sings," mused another, "maybe I could find a place to walk and view the stars unobstructed by city lights and building heights."[3]

Escaping from the city, returning to nature—the yearnings that made John Denver so popular were the same ones that sold Colorado vacations. Like a vacation, Denver offered to steal you away from the everyday and make you happy by placing you in the high country. His lyrics, like the pictures flashing on the screen during his concerts, worked on audiences because they traded on the familiar (detractors would say hackneyed) high-country imagery that tourist boosters had long since ingrained in the popular imagination. (At least one critic spotted the connection, likening Denver to "an undercover agent for the Rocky Mountain tourist bureau.")[4] But Denver's appeal went well beyond the fact that he confirmed Colorado tourist clichés. His fans seemed really to love not just his songs but *him*. Even one of his most persistent critics conceded he was "one of the few pop figures able in recent years to forge a sociological—rather than simply entertainment—bond with a vast mid-America audience."[5]

A big reason for this was that he embodied a still deeper postwar yearning. Denver was not just a tourist but a full-time liver of the tourist lifestyle, a man who found in Colorado's wide-open spaces fun, fulfillment, a new home, and a new meaning in life. Colorado literally gave him a new identity; his old one was the less poetic Henry John Deutschendorf Jr.—something most of his fans probably did not know. But they did know his life story of feeling lonely and rootless until he discovered Aspen. He confessed it in interviews, lyrics, and between-song patter, and he made it the basis for his signature song, the autobiographical "Rocky Mountain High." "He was born in the summer of his twenty-seventh year," it began, "Comin' home to a place he'd never been before / He left yesterday behind him; you might say he was born again / You might say he found a key for ev'ry door."[6] This may have been the language of 1970s self-discovery, but it drew on much the same emotional-environmental association that had been the stock-in-trade of Colorado tourist boosters since at least the 1940s.

But if John Denver crystallized Colorado's outdoor mystique, he also hinted at how that mystique was changing by the early 1970s. Beyond his endearing (or cloying) "Sunshine Kid" image, there was a nagging sense that not all was well in the "sweet Rocky Mountain paradise." Denver composed many bittersweet songs about personal longing and loss and, most significantly for our story, about his fear that his beloved high country was under threat from overdevelopment and overpopulation. To Denver that fear was acute, especially in 1971–72, when business and political leaders were working to bring the 1976 Winter Olympics to Colorado—a blockbuster event they anticipated would draw worldwide attention to the state but that Denver and other opponents feared would trigger an influx of population and development that the high-country environment could not possibly withstand. It was in furious protest against the Winter Olympics that Denver wrote the last verse to the otherwise exultant "Rocky Mountain High": "Why they try to tear the mountains down to bring in a couple more / More people, more scars upon the land." Here was Colorado's most famous permanent tourist crying out against tourist development itself—against the seemingly endless quest to lure more newcomers to Colorado and spread them over the most beautiful and delicate landscapes in the state.[7]

The Olympics became the defining environmental debate in early-1970s Colorado, but even more important was the broader shift in popular attitudes the controversy signaled. In chapter 4 we saw how recreational values became the basis for environmental activism in the 1960s, as outdoor enthusiasts touted the continued growth of tourism and commercial recreation as the antidote to environmental decline. In the early 1970s, popular interest in environmental issues broadened further still. But now many were beginning, like John Denver, to see tourism, commercial recreation, and development that catered to the leisure lifestyle as environmental problems unto themselves—and the need to curb them as the state's most pressing priority. This was the John Denver tenor: an exuberant and deeply personal pride of place, coupled with an urgent sense that the landscape and the recreational lifestyle it supported were fragile and in danger of imminent destruction.

This tenor, this anxious mood, resulted in an outpouring of popular support for environmental reform in the early 1970s. But it remained to be seen whether people who had learned their environmental sensibilities through recreation would actually be able to reform the recreational growth machine in any significant way.

THERE WERE EARLIER HINTS OF SECOND THOUGHTS ABOUT FULL-BORE recreational growth. One came in 1960, from the widely respected Steamboat Springs newspaper editor Maurice Leckenby. Most of his fellow U.S.

40 boosters were deeply embittered at the time by the decision to route Interstate 70 along the path of U.S. 6. But Leckenby suggested that Highway 40 towns like Steamboat Springs might actually benefit by being left off the interstate. They could offer a slow-paced, scenic alternative to I-70's traffic, speed, and smog, Leckenby reasoned; they could give refuge to "those who want leisurely travel and . . . a chance to enjoy Colorado hospitality."[8] By decade's end, many along I-70's path would pick up on Leckenby's premise: that as recreational traffic and development exploded, they showed a disturbing tendency to erode the scenic and atmospheric qualities that made the high country so relaxing and refreshing—and so marketable.

Were tourism and recreation becoming environmental problems in their own right? It was an awkward question, not just for boosters who had coveted the interstate and the hordes of visitors it would bring, but even more for conservationists who had held up recreational development as a buttress against the destruction of wilderness, scenery, historic character, and open space. By the late 1960s, the kind of large-scale leisure development that Interstate 70 both promised and symbolized was already looking a lot less benign, a lot more pernicious to the very environmental sensibilities that made people seek out the high country. In many of the towns along I-70's planned path, people began asking, Is there such thing as too much tourism?

Georgetown was one of the first places the question cropped up. Tucked into its narrow, deep valley, hugged by steep mountains on three sides, this picturesque former silver camp had become one of the high country's first successful tourist towns in the 1940s, when Ben Draper and others began restoring its gingerbread charm. But by the mid-1960s locals were starting to worry that tourism might go too far, overwhelming the scenic and historic qualities of the place. The catalyst for these worries was the impending arrival of Interstate 70. Its tourist-channeling power, cheered just a few years before, now struck some Georgetowners as a monster in the making.

To see how fast attitudes were shifting, consider how people in nearby Idaho Springs reacted less than a decade earlier when Interstate 70 construction reached their community. The interstate was controversial here, too, but for different reasons. Highway officials planned a four-lane freeway on the hillside above Idaho Springs, bypassing the town's two-lane Highway 6-40 tourist strip, and locals worried it would devastate the town's motel, restaurant, and gas station trade. How to entice motorists to stop and spend money? Local leaders haggled with the Highway Department for an additional off-ramp and set about making their town look nicer from the new hillside bypass. A revelatory moment came in February 1958, when local business owners toured the almost-completed bypass to see the new "tourist-eye view" of Idaho Springs. They were aghast to find themselves looking down at the backs of their buildings, unkempt and piled high with junk. The view made Idaho Springs look like "a ghost town . . . in the process of decay," wailed the local newspaper.[9] In Idaho Springs in the 1950s, then, locals worried about the interstate on mostly economic grounds, and they saw fit to change their town's appearance to fit the new interstate landscape.

By the time I-70 reached Georgetown, thirteen miles upvalley, in the mid-1960s, the reaction was a bit different. Here again, highway planners opted for a bypass, a shelf road blasted out of the mountainside above the town. Here again, tourists would form their first impressions of the community by glancing down at it. A typical driver would have "just about seven seconds to decide if he wants to pull off and visit," figured a visiting highway engineer. His advice to Georgetowners—"You had better paint your church steeples"—sounded like the lesson that Idaho Springs had already learned. But the engineer had another warning for Georgetown: "Do everything you can to hold on to the character of the town."[10] Those words hinted at a creeping anxiety of the mid-1960s: that interstate highways were starting to degrade and homogenize the American landscape, making every place look like everyplace else. Already by 1965 this anxiety had inspired several initiatives from Lyndon Johnson's administration, including the presidential Task Force on the Preservation of Natural Beauty, a landmark speech by LBJ on the subject, and Lady Bird Johnson's high-profile crusade for a Highway Beautification Act.[11] Basically, by the time I-70 reached Georgetown, the uglifying power of interstates had become something of a national obsession.

Eight years earlier, Idaho Springs residents had worried I-70 would steal their town's business; now Georgetown locals feared it would steal their community's soul. Since Victorian times, Georgetowners had fancied their village prettier and more refined than the average mountain town, with its spectacular setting and elegant charm, its tastefully designed mansions and sophisticated touches like the Hotel de Paris. Since World War II, this superior self-image had paid dividends, luring sightseers, weekenders, and summer residents from Denver. But now a superhighway was about to slice off one side of the valley and bring hordes of tourists pouring through. Would Georgetown's special charm survive?

Profits and personal attachments were both at stake. From the profit-making point of view, more tourists would certainly be welcome. But boosters feared the interstate would bring *too* many, and with them a mass, crass commercialism that would ruin Georgetown's lucrative charm and reduce the place to just another roadside tourist trap. So it was critical, in local boosters' minds, to "keep the honky-tonk out," as one businesswoman put it; to discourage the "bigger and bolder bunch of hoodlums ... and bigger and brassier hot dog-eaters" that flocked to so many other tourist towns. By preserving its gingerbread ambiance, Georgetown could continue to bring "the more desirable visitor to our town."[12] Elitist? No question. But these thoughts showed how ideas were changing, as the old gung-ho booster mind-set gave way to new concerns that too much success at luring tourists might undermine efforts to maintain an exclusive, high-class brand.

It is also true that, in Georgetown, bracing for the I-70 tourist influx was never just a question of business or branding strategy. A genuine pride of place was also involved. When the local paper reported that many "worried folks in town" feared "the new highway might be disastrous to our historic spots and natural landscaping," it was clear that they cared about more than just marketable amenities. They feared losing the qualities that made the area pleasant and personally meaningful *for them*. Many people—longtime locals and recently arrived second-home owners alike—felt a powerful bond with the landscape of Georgetown and the upper Clear Creek valley. The newspaper lauded the valley's "mighty heritages": a powerful sense of place and identity, rooted in the remnants of nineteenth-century boom days. Preserving this historic landscape might attract tourists, wrote one local columnist, but that would happen "incidentally ... not necessarily." What *was* necessary was to protect the setting's special character for its own sake, and with it the essence of the community. "History is its own reason for being," mused the columnist, so preserving history meant not just educating and entertaining guests but protecting "our own Clear Creek County pride."[13] In Georgetown, then, not just business owners and boosters, but also old-timers and more recent newcomers, had reason to fear what too much tourism might do to the local landscape. And because the historic landscape in particular figured so centrally in both local marketing and local identity, these fears fixated most on historic-preservation concerns—saving the physical remnants of Georgetown's past from the tidal wave of billboards, neon signs, and roadside kitsch that, it was assumed, would follow wherever an interstate highway went.

If historic preservation became the obsession of anxious Georgetowners, then in Aspen, zoning and open-space protections became the environmental crusade. The motivating factor in Aspen was also the fear of too much tourism, but the fear focused less on the potential damage to the local tourist economy and more on concern for the local lifestyle—to use the term just then becoming popular, the "quality of life." Aspen, of course, was home to many more permanent tourists who had moved there to consume some version of the lifestyle, from John Denver, purveyor of Rocky Mountain highs, to Hunter S. Thompson, the infamous "gonzo" journalist who was well known for getting high on lots of other things. Thompson, in fact, would find himself leading the charge against continued development in his adopted corner of Colorado.

Aspen's first stalwart against too much tourism was Walter Paepcke himself. He and the many newcomers he attracted in the 1950s wanted to believe that Aspen was governed by human, not commercial values, and in fact Paepcke so feared mass tourism that he took over Aspen's ski business—something he had no prior interest in and did not even particularly respect—just so he could control its growth. But as much power as he wielded in Aspen through the 1950s, Paepcke could not keep the lid on growth forever. He died of cancer in 1960, and many locals sensed a dramatic speedup in development immediately afterward. Part of that was perception, stemming from the shock that Aspen's patron was no longer there to protect the community. But part of it was reality. Growth in Aspen really did pick up in the 1960s, whether measured by population gain, acreage of land converted to second homes and condominiums, or the temperature of the rhetoric as Aspenites debated what was happening to their town. Saying Aspen politics got a little heated in the 1960s would be like saying Hunter S. Thompson dabbled in drugs. A town best known for skiing and summer philosophizing gained a new reputation for dramatic politics, as Aspen's quality-of-life connoisseurs resisted what they saw as the greed-driven destruction of their leisurely lifestyle.

They got an important ally in 1956, when former ski-magazine editor and Tenth Mountain Division veteran Bil Dunaway bought the *Aspen Times*. Unlike his predecessor, the mostly sunny Verlin Ringle, Dunaway did not hesitate to use the paper to rail against the powerful in town, even if it brought Aspen a little bad publicity. He helped incite one of the earliest and oddest protests against overcommercialization: the Mothers March of 1960. It began when the Aspen Skiing Corporation decided to charge local children two dollars a day to ski, instead of the former seventy-five cents, pricing the sport beyond the means of many families in town. When a group of mothers complained, Dunaway began hyping their cause in the *Times*. The next thing anyone knew, a hundred mothers and children were marching in the streets, waving signs with slogans like "Kids vs. Profits" and "It Used to Be Aspen's Mountain"—with, of course, *Times* cameras capturing the whole scene. ("Incidentally, who telephoned the Denver Post suggesting that they send a reporter and photographer?" groused an Aspen Ski Corp. executive, knowing full well who had.) The whole incident was tongue-in-cheek—it ended with the mothers laughingly burning a Ski Corp. director in effigy— but the women's grievances were dead serious. To them, skiing had become an integral part of growing up in Aspen, and the mountain really belonged to the townspeople, not the company. The company countered that it had to care for its bottom line, but as *Times* columnist Peggy Clifford shot back, "Life is not a business and a town is not a corporation." The quest for profits should not be allowed to rob locals of the recreational lifestyle that was rightfully theirs.[14]

More at issue than lift-ticket prices were the changes taking place in the local landscape. The 1960s real estate rush forever changed the Roaring Fork Valley. Aspen's lifestyle refugees watched in alarm as mountainsides and meadows gave way to subdivisions; tall, boxy condominiums began to wall off scenic views; and real estate agents even began pressing for strip development along State Highway 82. Open-space proponents won a key battle in 1960 when Pitkin County upheld the 1955 anti-strip setback requirement along the highway, but they sensed a worrisome precedent later that same year when Aspen approved investor Teno Roncalio's plans to erect a thirty-eight-foot hotel in the middle of town. The permit "shook the very foundation of Aspen's zoning concept," wrote Clifford in the *Times*, echoing the fears of many. In fact the city's 1956 zoning ordinance had placed no height limits on buildings. Clifford conceded that but felt it shouldn't matter: "it should not be necessary," she inveighed, "for Aspen residents to make all their communal aspirations into laws in order that they be honored."[15] All the same, that was a lesson that many Aspenites drew from big new real estate developments like Roncalio's hotel: anyone who wanted to save the landscape for Aspen's distinctive lifestyle was going to have to legislate it. So that is what consumed politics in Pitkin County for the next fifteen years: debates over how local government could, or whether it should, be used to control the physical spread of recreational development and so protect the Aspen lifestyle.

Though these debates would soon give Aspen a reputation for divisive

5.1 What Aspen stood to lose. This cartoon, which appeared on the front page of the *Aspen Times* in February 1960, suggests how fear of overdevelopment had already gripped many in town. Along with the fright of rampant real-estate speculation, open-space loss, and scenery-destroying sprawl, the cartoon is noteworthy for its nightmare vision of over-commercialization, suggesting that Aspenites' anxiety was about not just environmental degradation but also the erosion of Aspen's high-class cachet and its potential slide into "honky-tonk" or "Coney Island" crassness. Courtesy *Aspen Times*.

and downright surreal politics, there was an early glimmer of consensus in the form of the 1966 *Aspen Area General Plan*. Drafted by San Francisco consultants, the "Master Plan," as everyone called it, was an earnest attempt to find common ground between lifestyle and business concerns. The plan expressed the by-now familiar anxiety about overgrowth, warning of development spilling beyond Aspen into the rest of the valley, blurring the line "between urbanization and the natural landscape." And too much tourism took the blame: "the impact of continuing growth in the recreation industry"; "the heightened sense of aesthetics which encourages people to select homesites with scenic advantages"; "an accelerating trend of . . . intensive urban and recreation use." But the Master Plan was no anti-growth screed. Instead of slowing future growth, it proposed, through zoning and other legal means, to cluster it in Aspen and around the valley's three other ski areas, sparing the open space everywhere else. Within the urbanized clusters, pedestrian streets and building-density controls would help offset the impact of development. Eventually, light rail and a system of parks and trails would tie together clusters and open spaces, country and city. Commercial, residential, and recreational settings would form a unified whole, and the Roaring Fork Valley could continue to grow and prosper, all the while keeping its small-town ambiance, majestic views, and rustic ranchland feel. Or so the Master Plan promised—and so, judging from its broadly positive reception, locals seemed to hope.[16]

But within a year, any good feelings surrounding the Master Plan were lost to Aspen's next bizarre episode: the battle over how to treat the town's newest, youngest lifestyle refugees. Aspen was used to young ski bums, as much as it was to tourists, artists, and musicians—but by 1967 a new youth contingent was finding its way there. So-called hippies, whom San Francisco's Summer of Love was just then bringing to the national spotlight, began flocking that same summer to Aspen. And while townspeople had by this time seen some pretty strange things, for many of them this latest was too much to take. In a sense, the hippies were wholly in sync with Aspen's Paepckean spirit: escaping to a remote and rustic place to find enlightenment and chase something other than material ends. But since hippies allegedly did not meet the Paepckean standard of elevated taste, many longer-standing locals cast them as an alien species: "longhairs" in urgent need of showers, in various states of shabby (un)dress, smoking pot, acid tripping, loitering in the parks and streets. Reversing the charges that the resort business was eroding Aspen's lifestyle, many now decided this new lifestyle was eroding the resort business. So at the behest of businesspeople who wanted to clean up Aspen's image, the city began cracking down on hippies, using an old vagrancy law to fine them and toss them in jail. The heavy-handedness split the community deeply.[17] Never before had the clash between Aspen's leisure economy and leisure lifestyle seemed so embittered. And all the while development continued to transform the landscape: new condo projects in Aspen, more subdivisions in the outlying areas, the first of eight new resort villages planned for Snowmass-at-Aspen. Anger over how the valley was changing even boiled over into a string of arsons and dynamite explosions, culminating in 1970 with someone's decision, at once symbolic and weird, to bomb a fake windmill advertising the (oxymoronically named?) subdivision of Holland Hills.[18]

This was the state of things that compelled Hunter S. Thompson to emerge from his secluded house in Woody Creek, a wide spot in the valley six miles downstream from Aspen, and turn local politics into a theater of the absurd. Thompson had first visited Aspen in 1960, lived there briefly in 1963–64, and then returned to settle in Woody Creek in 1968. He would probably spit expletives at being called a "permanent tourist," but that is what he was. He relished that in Aspen people could "walk out our front doors and smile at what we see," and he appreciated that Aspen left people mostly alone to live the way they liked. Thompson himself liked loud music, hallucinogenic drugs, and firearms. "I like to wander outside, stark naked," he wrote, "and fire my .44 magnum at various gongs I've mounted on the nearby hillside. . . . Which," he admitted, "is not entirely the point." The point, in Thompson's mind, was that resort profiteering was ruining the Aspen area, its landscape and lifestyle alike; that "the sub-dividers, ski-pimps and city-based land-developers . . . had come like a plague of poison roaches to buy and sell the whole valley out from under the people who still valued it as a good place to live, not just a good investment."[19]

So when a "united front" of Aspen businesspeople put forth Eve Homeyer, a shop owner active in the state Republican Party, to run for mayor in 1969, Thompson decided "the fuckers had gone too far this time." He recruited Joe Edwards, a young lawyer who had successfully sued the city over its crackdown on hippies, to run against Homeyer as an antigrowth insurgent. Thompson steered the campaign, issuing furious polemics against the "greedheads" and calling on countercultural youths—whom he termed "Freak Power"—to overthrow them. Peggy Clifford wrote campaign ads in the *Aspen Times*, illustrated with images of freeways and suburban sprawl, stark warnings of the valley's fate should the greedheads go unchecked. On election day Edwards came within six votes of victory, and growth-wary liberals won half the city council seats, sending shudders through the local political establishment. It was enough to convince Thompson to run for office himself the following year. So he declared himself an "outlaw" candidate for sheriff and went on to wage one of the most surreal campaigns in American history. He chose as his logo a double-thumbed fist with a peyote button; he shaved his head and chain-smoked with a plastic cigarette holder during debates; he railed against "cowboy cops" and "rapists" of the land.[20]

While opponents treated Thompson's campaign, in Clifford's words, like "a bad joke," it actually sprang from a serious critique of what the resort economy was doing to the community and the land. Take two of Thompson's campaign promises: to sod Aspen's streets and to legally change the town's name to Fat City. Both were patently ridiculous. But the first dramatized the failure to fulfill the Master Plan's call for a car-free downtown. And the second was a clever jab at the "human jackals," like the developers of the big new Vail-like resort Snowmass-at-Aspen, who had reduced the community's identity to a brand name. No one would be able to use Fat City as a brand, Thompson smirked. In the end, he lost. But his theatrical campaigns in 1969 and 1970 riveted local, statewide, even national attention on Aspen's struggle with growth and stoked local determination to somehow rein it in.[21]

Aspen was, shall we say, its own place. Did its anger against the resort machine simply spring from its weird mix of Paepckean ideals, cartoonish personalities, and deeply entrenched exclusivity—with perhaps some chemicals stirred in? Or did it really reflect a wider shift in environmental thinking?

Consider that at exactly the same time Hunter S. Thompson decided he just couldn't take it anymore, people in both of the major resort areas right on I-70—Vail Valley and Summit County—were also starting to raise questions about whether recreational development had gone too far, too fast. Vail's case is of particular interest. A community of its corporate origins and proudly buttoned-down identity was not going to explode in Freak Power the way Aspen did, but in the early 1970s Vail nevertheless did see a real backlash against rapid resort growth—the very thing that had brought the community into being. The story bears telling, not just because it signals that a broader shift in attitudes really was under way, but also because it lays bare, more so than anywhere else, the degree to which environmentalist ideals in Colorado were drawing inspiration from advertised qualities of place.

When growth seemed to erode these qualities in Vail, it was nothing short of an existential crisis. For Vail was as much marketing concept as community. Its residents were there to profit off the concept—and profit they did, as shown by the town's dramatic expansion. But they were also there to live the concept for themselves. So they were used to accepting a sort of seasonal trade-off: work to exhaustion during ski season and then spend the off-season acting like people in Vail Associates ads, relaxing, recharging, and enjoying a respite from city-like stress. Already by the late 1960s, though, off-season quietude was giving way to the clamor of construction ("the sound of saws and hammers drowns out the sound of rushing water in Gore Creek," wrote a reporter) and the swelling summer convention trade ("it seems the locals' last bit of refuge is about to vanish," mourned a worker in town).[22] Meanwhile, in wintertime, crowding in the village worsened with each new skier-attendance record. Traffic clogged the narrow streets as drivers searched in vain for parking spaces: these, like peace and quiet in the Vail summer, were getting harder and harder to find.

The crowding looked to get worse once I-70 arrived. Ironically, in the early 1960s, Vail Associates had touted interstate highway accessibility as one of the factors favoring the new resort. Pete Seibert and his fellow founders, barnstorming to recruit investors, had even highlighted I-70 on the backs of their business cards. But in 1966, before construction of the interstate had yet reached Vail Valley, Seibert was already worrying that I-70 might "destroy scenic values and otherwise reduce the desirability of the Vail resort location." George Knox, the normally optimistic *Vail Trail* editor, worried too. "We've heard highway engineers predict that the traffic . . . could easily double, or triple or even quadruple," he fretted. "Could it become a monster?"[23]

Vail was starting to see the same dilemma that Aspen had and that Coloradans elsewhere would soon confront too: what happened when mass-marketing a place for tourists made it harder for residents to enjoy the marketed qualities themselves? The question gripped Vail as early as 1966, during the town's first-ever political campaign. Many Vailites, like the bullish businessman Ted Kindel, insisted that boosting tourism must take precedence. But a rising number felt it was time to prioritize the lifestyle interests of locals instead. When Kindel, running for mayor, lectured that town officials must make sure that visitors' needs were met, because "all of us who reside here are 'investors,'" his fellow local businessman John McBride retorted that local government's "first obligation" should be "establishing a pleasant, efficient, and protective community *for the people living here*." When Kindel declared that "Vail is much more than a community. It is in the most important sense a product," McBride again objected: "To me, Vail . . . is first and foremost a community. Secondly, and only secondly, it is a product."[24]

It might have been more accurate to say the product had become the community. In the same 1966 campaign, when Kindel accused the growth critics of "selfish escapism," of wanting "to see Vail become a quiet little community with interminable play hours for its residents," those on the other side protested that they had every right to stand up for their leisurely way of life. Vail, wrote three local men, rebutting Kindel in a letter to the *Trail*, "should be represented not just as a product that is to be sold, but as a place to raise families and lead the good life that our brochures so attractively promise."[25]

They could not have been franker than that. The same character of setting and quality of life that Vail Associates advertised to its customers, these townspeople felt belonged to them too. The place that began as a product was becoming a home. Kindel won the 1966 election, but it was clear that his brand of business-at-all-costs politics was no longer the unanimous view, even in entrepreneurial Vail.

The centerpiece of Vail Associates' product—the carefully planned and packaged village itself—also anchored how locals defined their lifestyle. How can we know this? Because it was when growth began to alter the village's physical appearance that Vail residents became most upset. There was an outcry in 1968, for example, when a Holiday Inn went up. It was not the building itself that angered locals; the chain had taken pains to abide by the Alpine theme—stucco walls, heavy beams, pitched roofs, overhangs. (The inn was even christened "Chateau Vail" for an added Continental touch.) No, what angered locals was that the chain insisted on installing its trademark "Great Sign," with lighted arrow and neon star—and that Vail Associates, which had always kept flashy commercial trappings out of town, agreed to it. "Now this perfect setting is marred with a crass 'neon-type' sign," wailed one local. "WHY?" George Knox, the former adman, conceded the marketing strategy behind the logo, but even he criticized VA for allowing it.[26] "One of these days," he warned after another 1968 design dispute, this one over a gaudy spire on Bridge Street, "we're going to wake up and discover . . . a bunch of neon-lighted hamburger stands in amongst a conglomeration of lighted billboards."[27] This again was elitist anxiety, to be sure, but it suggested how crucial the absence of overt commercialism, a core principle of VA's original village plan, had become to townspeople's sense of finding sanctuary there.

Even more basic to the village's escapist mystique was its small scale, its lack of city-sized buildings. Yet Vail began to lose this quality too. Just like in the downtown of a major city, the surging demand for real estate, coupled with limited availability in the compact village core, drove up values, spurring landowners to build higher and higher. As early as 1965, some critics panned John McBride's austere, three-story Clock Tower Building. But it would soon look small. Ted Kindel completed his Crossroads of Vail in 1968, touting it as "fantastic and huge . . . Vail's largest building project to date." Seven stories tall, it housed a shopping center, theater-auditorium, and condominiums. But it was one-upped the following year, when the Lodge at Vail (which VA had sold to new owners) announced expansion plans, including an *eight*-story Lodge Tower.[28] Though these projects adhered to the Alpine design theme, they stretched it to its absolute limit. How many Swiss chalets are eight stories tall?

A worse architectural obscenity, in the minds of most, was the one that appeared on the lot next to the Covered Bridge, right where visitors walked into the village. There, in 1969–70, Gaynor Miller tore down the Night Latch dormitory he had built back in Vail's earliest days—by the logic of the market, it no longer made sense to operate a small, budget-priced hostel on such a valuable piece of real estate—and built in its place a three-million-dollar, 120,000-square-foot deluxe condominium complex called the Mountain Haus. The new building's gabled roof and top-story overhang hinted at the chalet look, but its stark modern lines, looming six-story hulk, and massive footprint made a mockery of the town's pedestrian scale. It engulfed passersby in its shadow; it blocked scenic views from the village and postcard views of the village from the highway; it was, one part-time resident said, "grotesquely out of scale in Vail." And it provoked "community wrath," in the town manager's words. "If we have any consideration for aesthetics and human sensibilities we should condemn buildings such as these," raged a second-home owner, couching the Vail ideal in the rhetoric of environmentalism. "They shut off people from their environment and create an urban atmosphere which most people want to avoid in Vail."[29]

And then came the capper. Just west of Vail Village, also in 1969, construction began on a whole new town core, slated to be as big as the original one. (It would serve as the base area for a major expansion of ski terrain up on the mountain.) Brand-named LionsHead after a nearby rock formation, this second village was jarring not just for its size but for its utterly un-Vail-like design. Instead of little storybook lanes, LionsHead had concrete malls and plazas; instead of funky little chalets, it had giant edifices, coldly angular and symmetrical and up to eight stories tall. The first two buildings—a shoebox-shaped gondola terminal and a sprawling "redwood contemporary" condominium complex—set an architectural tone that alarmed locals who liked Vail Village's Swiss look.[30] Most perplexing of all, the developer behind LionsHead, this seemingly complete contradiction of the landscape and lifestyle ideal that was Vail, was the same developer that had invented the ideal in the first place: Vail Associates.

Why did VA abandon its original village formula? One reason was VA founder Pete Seibert's changing taste. Seibert had fallen in love with the new generation of French luxury ski resorts—Flaine, Avoriaz, La Plagne,

Les Menuires—where somber, high-rise towers, devoid of exterior embellishment, were regimented around central squares. Always attentive to European precedents, and looking to keep Vail on the cutting edge, Seibert felt these resorts "were in vogue" and would prove popular in Colorado. So he worked with Denver planner George Beardsley to re-create the look.[31] Money considerations played a major role too. Property values in Vail Valley had skyrocketed, and demand for condominiums was red-hot. These market pressures favored high-rise development, and VA, cash-poor from spending so much on its ski mountain, was in no position to resist. Badly needing to sell land in LionsHead to pay for the expanded ski facilities, VA sweetened the deal for developers by allowing them to build much bigger buildings than in the original village.[32]

Developers took advantage. After the $7 million in construction leading up to LionsHead's opening in December 1969, another $3.2 million worth went up the next summer, including another condominium complex, "the first completely prefabricated building in Vail," with "prestressed concrete, [and] vertical simulated wood exterior panels." New buildings for 1971 included a pile called Treetops, which lived up to its name by soaring eight stories high. Vailites were horrified. "How or what happened that these concrete monsters were allowed to be built?" asked one in disbelief. "Doesn't the architectural control board control that area?"[33]

The twin shocks of LionsHead and the Mountain Haus seemed to upset locals more than the crowds, traffic, shortage of parking spaces, or anything else that afflicted boom-time Vail. They were "the two things that got people thinking about density and about growth," Rod Slifer later recalled. "All of a sudden, they saw these big buildings going up, and everybody said, 'Wait a minute, this isn't what we perceived Vail to be.'" Changes in Vail Associates' carefully packaged townscape suggested to residents that the entire lifestyle they had bought into was under siege. Even VA could no longer be counted on to defend it. "These recent [building] developments," wrote a Bighorn resident, "give the impression that those who originally conceived of Vail, and did such an excellent job in implementing their concept, are now marching to a different drummer or are no longer playing leadership roles in planning."[34]

So the early 1970s saw townspeople trying to pick up where VA had left off: trying to establish control over the physical setting in order to protect the original Vail "concept" against the pressures of growth. Managing the townscape became a major focus of local government, more so than in any

5.2 Forsaking the Vail vision. LionsHead, the new town center that opened in late 1969, shocked Vail residents not just with its sheer size but with its abandonment of Vail Associates' Swiss-chalet marketing formula in favor of modern, severe architecture. Many locals reacted to the stark angularity of LionsHead by calling for a return to the original Vail formula—and to the original strict design controls. (The heavy double-line in this view from around 1973 is the cable of the LionsHead gondola.) Photo by Peter Runyon.

other high-country community besides maybe Aspen. And Vail's political culture, like Aspen's, took on a John Denver tenor: it celebrated the tourist landscape and tourist lifestyle but exuded constant anxiety that either could be lost at any time.

When Vailites chose John Dobson to succeed Ted Kindel as mayor in 1968, they replaced an aggressive pro-growther with a voice of reflection and restraint. Dobson and his wife, Cissy, New England expatriates who built a Vermont-style general store at the foot of Bridge Street, typified Vail's business establishment: they had come for enterprise as well as enjoyment and, arriving relatively early (1965), had quickly made themselves fixtures in the local business, social, and political scenes. They raised funds to build Vail's interfaith chapel, and John got elected to the town council when Vail incorporated in 1966. Well-liked for his humor—he drew cartoons and wrote consciously corny summer melodramas lampooning life in a resort town—Dobson was nonetheless very serious about the problems facing Vail. Blending the perspectives of a businessman, environmental-ist, and consumer of the Vail ideal, he defined the challenge facing the town: "how to accommodate this demand for more skiing facilities, more summer recreational facilities, and still maintain as much as possible the natural resources, the beauty, and the charm of the area in which we live." To meet the challenge, Dobson sought to centralize control over the look and lay of the land, by means of planning, zoning, and other regulations—an approach that put him squarely in the mainstream of environmentalist thinking at the time.[35]

Colorado law would not let town government exercise the kind of benevolent dictatorship Vail Associates had enjoyed in the early 1960s. But it did allow the usual municipal powers over land use and development: zon-ing, building, and subdivision codes. In Dobson's first year as mayor, 1969, the Town of Vail began flexing these powers for the first time, passing its first zoning ordinance and enacting subdivision standards. It also annexed LionsHead and proceeded over the next few years to annex land up and down Gore Creek, aiming to control condominium sprawl in the East and West Vail "suburbs" and bring the entire valley's development under a uni-fied zoning code.

Another key change came in 1970, when the town hired its first town manager, bringing to Vail a resourceful and articulate advocate of growth control. Terry Minger had been assistant city manager in Boulder, another fast-growing community with the Rockies in its backyard, and one with a decades-long reputation for its efforts to protect scenic beauty and guide growth. Boulder was even better known (in municipal-government circles, at least) for its efforts to *limit* growth. In 1959 its citizens had voted for a "blue line" to stop view-degrading development on ridges and mesas, and in 1967 they voted for a sales-tax hike so the city could preempt sprawl by buying up open space.[36] Learning from his time in Boulder, Minger pushed Vail toward some growth-limiting policies of its own. He became the leading local voice for annexing the entire valley so it could be subjected to stringent zoning.[37] He also championed new recreational facilities and a Boulder-like effort to acquire open space. To pay for it all, he seized on a new Colorado law that for the first time allowed small towns to declare "home rule," raise their level of indebtedness, and pursue new sources of revenue.[38] With Minger's urging, locals voted overwhelmingly in fall 1972 to make Vail the first small home-rule municipality in Colorado—and thus the one best equipped to pay for ambitious efforts to save open space.[39]

Another Minger brainchild was the Vail Symposium, an effort to get Vailites, like Boulderites, intensely engaged in the issue of growth. For two days each summer, starting in 1971, the Symposium gathered speakers from a range of perspectives—politicians, planners, developers, foresters, architects, environmentalists—to talk to each other and to locals about growth and its consequences. The keynote speakers were big names: maverick New York City mayor and rumored presidential candidate John Lindsay in 1971, ex–interior secretary and conservation hero Stewart Udall in 1972. They lured hundreds of listeners to the mountaintop lodge high above Vail Village and LionsHead. There, more than ten thousand feet above sea level, swirled and jelled the ideas that guided the local environmental movement in Vail.

Some of these ideas bore the imprint of the national movement, as when Lindsay counseled his audience to think globally about local issues, or when Udall called for a *"value* revolution" (a favorite rallying cry for environmentalists) and urged Vailites to identify their "limits to growth" (the title of a bestselling environmental jeremiad the year Udall spoke).[40] But once again, Vail Associates' marketing also shaped much of what was said. Many Symposium speakers in both 1971 and 1972 lavished praise on Vail Village's main selling points: its "human scale," its attempt to "keep the people and cars separate," its use of "wood and natural building materials," and its ban on the kind of "ticky-tacky, unattractive, uncoordinated" growth that might result in a "second-rate valley."[41] A consensus emerged that VA's original vision— low-rise, clustered, tightly controlled development, with an insistence on high class and on integrating the built landscape with its recreational surroundings—was the best recipe for growth in a fragile environment like the high country. What had begun in the early 1960s as a frankly profit-minded business model for frankly elite recreational living was now the inspiration for an ethics of environmental protection.

The Symposium speakers took this a step further still. Vail, a striking number of them suggested, represented one of the last places where one could escape the urban hubbub and find a sense of serenity and harmony with nature. Far from being frivolous, Vail served an essential human need: the need to "find areas of natural beauty, new strength spiritually and emotionally, physically and intellectually," as Dobson put it; the need to "remain in harmony with nature and not in competition with it," added the mayor of Boulder; the need to "participate in outdoor recreation in an unpolluted natural environment," said a member of the VA board. And because those needs were so vital, and places like Vail so imperiled, it was critical that such

5.3 Sprawl in the high country. By the late 1960s, not only had the original Vail Village grown larger and denser but the resort had expanded well beyond its original footprint, spreading up and down Interstate 70 and the narrow Gore Creek Valley, even spawning its own suburbs. (In this early-1970s aerial view, looking east, Vail Village is at center and the second, more angular village cluster of LionsHead is at bottom.) The resort's rapid growth sparked a local outcry, spurring town government to annex most of the valley floor with the intent of managing future growth. Courtesy Sanborn Ltd.

places be saved for nothing less than the sake of humankind. The people of Vail and other mountain recreation communities, Minger admonished, bore "an enormous responsibility as the trustee of the last remnants of our natural heritage." Or, as Dobson pointedly ended his speech, "We are fortunate enough to live in some of the most beautiful areas of our country. They are endangered and they are irreplaceable. The challenge is obvious and it is ours."[42]

Vail as a place of natural harmony? Guarding the last remnants of the true outdoors? On behalf of all humankind? To Vail's detractors today, this must sound laughable. Isn't Vail the hometown of artificiality, exclusivity, and environmentally destructive sprawl? But if we accept that the speakers at the Vail Symposium were serious and sincere, we gain a key insight into the environmentalist imagination of early-1970s Colorado: it held fast to the environmental ideals that tourist promoters had long encouraged and instilled. People speaking out against rapid growth in Georgetown, Aspen, and Vail in the late 1960s and early 1970s had a clear sense of the kind of nature and recreational landscape they wanted to get back to: very few of them would have put it this way, but what they wanted was to preserve their places as they had originally been packaged and promoted for tourists. When they pushed for carefully planned development, building on a small scale, or safeguards for open spaces and scenic views, when they fought to keep out city-style trappings, city-style problems, and city-style masses of people and preserve an aura of taste and escapist charm, they were harking back to the same selling points that tourist boosters had been using to market high-country places for decades. Far from being on the fringe, then, the brand of environmentalism emerging in Colorado carried broad appeal. It had the potential to resonate with anyone who had ever spent leisure time in the high country, ever bought into the vacation product, whether on weekend getaways or as a permanent new home. To grasp this is to grasp why environmentalism found such broad popularity in Colorado by the early 1970s—the years when it reached its peak influence in the state.

WHAT MADE THE GRASSROOTS DISCONTENT IN GEORGETOWN, ASPEN, and Vail ironic, of course, was that the grassroots were drawing many of their environmental ideals from the ways those places had been marketed to tourists—and then using those ideals to critique tourist development itself. In effect, tourism both caused environmental problems and helped sensitize Coloradans to them. It drummed into their heads the value of scenery, greenery, open space, human-scale buildings, and the like, but it also changed the landscape in ways that threatened those very same qualities. For people who had fashioned their lifestyles around such attributes of place, the result was a sense of ambivalence, even crisis, that was not just political but deeply personal.

Thus the late 1960s and early 1970s saw more and more Coloradans politically and personally consumed with the question of how much tourist and recreational growth was too much. There was mounting indignation, not just locally in places like Aspen but statewide, toward what we might call *big recreation*: the increasingly large-scale, capital-intensive, corporate development and mass-marketing of trademark Colorado pastimes like skiing and fishing. Pillars of both the Colorado lifestyle mystique and the Colorado vacation trade, these pastimes came under fire from growing numbers of people who thought such diversions were being oversold, damaging the landscape and detracting from the quality of life. This critique reached fever pitch in the statewide debate over the Winter Olympics, ultimately dealing tourist-development advocates a stunning defeat and vaulting environmentalism to its pinnacle of political influence in Colorado.

One pillar of Colorado tourist development—the state's relentless promotion of fishing—had actually been under fire since the late 1950s. Controversy swirled around the Game and Fish Department's policy of stocking millions of hatchery trout each year to meet the tourist demand, a policy Colorado shared with other states where fishing was big business. The Izaak Walton League expressed concern about heavy stocking as early as 1959, and that same year, trout fishermen in Michigan founded Trout Unlimited specifically to fight the practice. The group caught on quickly in the West, especially in Colorado—so much so that it moved its offices to Denver in 1969, in part because the state's hatchery policy was considered especially egregious. Colorado was notorious in fishing circles for the mass scale of its stocking, which made fishing "a farce rather than a sport," complained one unhappy angler who had moved from Michigan in vain hopes of finding better fishing out West.[43]

The anglers' objection was that mass-producing trout for tourists took the wildness out of fishing, and with it the sport. They cited research by fish biologists, who were themselves often sport fishermen. Hatchery trout were "spoon-fed, and accustomed to an easy life," said the biologists; they had "never been required to swim fast or vigorously . . . to escape predators, search for food, or endure environmental extremes." Instead of hiding from sight like wild trout, hatchery fish lolled in open water and chomped any food they saw. Instead of engaging in lusty battle once hooked, they gave up without much of a fight. "In Colorado, if your timing is sharp, you can sometimes catch your limit of trout as fast as you can get your line in the water," wrote one angler—and he did not see this as a good thing. The fish, he lamented, could "hardly . . . tell a No. 12 Rio Grand King [fly] from a gob of liver."[44] Expert anglers wanted not just to catch fish but to be tested while doing it; they wanted a quarry they could respect, so they could prove their mettle against a worthy foe. This was the stuff of Victorian gentlemen's sporting codes, and it lent a strongly elitist tone to misgivings about mass-produced fish. Some anglers took this elitism further by disparaging those who did not know the expert techniques or complaining about the crowds that turned out to fish heavily stocked waters. "To fish elbow to elbow with hordes of fishermen," sniffed one ichthyologist and Waltonian, "is not high quality sport."[45]

To be fair, the anglers would have denied that they stood only for their own privilege. They saw themselves as guardians of far greater things: the fate of the environment and of the nation's outdoor heritage. So, for example, they often argued that the enormous sums spent on hatcheries left too little for broader needs like improving water quality and riverine habitat. They saw game fish and their habitats as barometers of water quality and environmental health: "When trout are threatened," wrote the national director of Trout Unlimited, "so is man." And they worried that when Americans were forced to fish for tame hatchery trout, they lost yet another way of connecting to wild nature. Wild trout fishing instilled a "love of outdoors," said one fishing group, and "knowledge of plants, flowers, birds, trees, [and] insects." "It's communing with nature," said Trout Unlimited's statement of philosophy, "where the chief reward is a refreshed body and a contented soul." Trout-fishing devotees had been saying these things for centuries—there is hardly a pastime more shrouded in Romantic mystique—but the sentiments took on new urgency in the postwar context, when conservationists were battling to save what they saw as the last vestiges of the American wild. Hatchery foes envisioned themselves at the forefront of this battle, just like advocates of the Wilderness Act.[46] That is why Trout Unlimited's Colorado chapter joined the Colorado Open Space Coordinating Council in the fight for wilderness and recreation planning in 1966 and why it fought to save fishing from the tourist free-for-all. And the group had some success: by the early 1970s it had persuaded Colorado's Game and Fish Department to set aside some waters for wild trout and "quality" fishing.[47]

By that time another backlash was brewing against an even bigger outdoor industry. Skiing, which had eclipsed fishing to become Colorado's signature pastime, was on its way to environmental pariah-hood too. At issue was the speed of new ski development, as the sport exploded into the mainstream in the 1960s and as the Forest Service, acting on its 1959 master plan, spent the decade approving new ski areas at a rapid clip. It was not just the carving up of more mountainsides in national forests that piqued popular concern but the semi-urban clusters that sprang up in the valley beneath each ski mountain, on privately owned, largely unregulated land. Colorado was not alone in facing this issue. In Vermont, ski-resort sprawl was a matter of such intense debate in the 1960s that in 1970 the state passed a pioneering law holding developers responsible for sewage, air quality, and other environmental problems. In Montana, controversy bedeviled the huge Big Sky resort, proposed by retired television anchor Chet Huntley. And in California, the Sierra Club was locked in battle against a giant resort project in a scenic subalpine valley called Mineral King. Walt Disney Enterprises, with Forest Service backing, planned this $35 million ski complex, including accommodations for fourteen thousand visitors and a twenty-mile access highway through adjacent Sequoia National Park. The battle over Mineral King, which ended in 1978 with Disney's defeat, did more than anything else to make ski development into a heated environmental issue in the late 1960s.[48]

In Colorado, for many people, Vail became the symbol of ski development run amok. The same Denver papers that had so breathlessly covered its early years—VAIL WILDERNESS BECOMING SKI PARADISE; WHITE GOLD MAKES A GLEAMING CITY; FABULOUS RESORT AREA TAKING SHAPE; SKY IS THE LIMIT FOR HIGHLAND JEWEL—were by the early 1970s running far less flattering descriptions: "a developmental brushfire," "a crowded urban condition," "instant Tyrolia," "plastic Bavaria," "a California-type strip city." One reporter wrote of people in Eagle, the county seat, trying to ward off the downvalley creep of the "Vail Syndrome," as if it were a contagious disease. "People come here for the openness and the beauty of the valley," said Eagle's town manager, himself a recent transplant (and Vail Village shop owner). "They come to live and enjoy it and they have got to make sure they don't ruin it."[49]

Well beyond Eagle County, Vail opened the floodgates for a new era of ski development on an unprecedented scale. Even in the early 1960s, when Vail was still in the planning stages, rumors of the gargantuan resort-to-be were already inspiring other entrepreneurs to imagine their own dream resorts. Over in Summit County, for example, Bill Rounds, a Wichita businessman with stakes in lumber, oil, and real estate, began exploring the possibility of putting a ski resort on Peak 8 above Breckenridge. As the Vail partners had done just a few years earlier, Rounds's group began quietly buying land at the base of the mountain and consulting with national forest rangers about a permit. Local business interests voiced strong support.[50] But even as Peak 8 opened in December 1961, some locals were already worried about how big it might grow and how much it might change Summit County. Seemingly trivial criticism of the company for using Swiss names for the ski facilities, instead of names suited to the county's mining heritage, revealed locals' fears that ski growth might cost their community its identity.[51]

Breckenridge, as the Peak 8 resort became known, did indeed grow through the 1960s. And Vail's influence kept rearing its head. In 1969, the Eagle County Development Corporation, which had cut its teeth building the sprawling Bighorn development in East Vail, came over the pass and started work on three big subdivisions. Then, in 1970, the Aspen Skiing Corporation bought the Peak 8 resort and began expanding it onto adjacent Peak 9. Predictably, the influx of Aspen capital sparked more construction in the valley below, including a $52 million "luxury, total vacation community," designed by Aspen's Fritz Benedict, with lodges, condos, restaurants, shops, convention facilities, and a twenty-story "European-style hotel."[52] Many hated it, like the second-home owners who lamented in the local paper that "the commercialism of an Aspen or Vail" was ruining the "rustic character" that had once set Breckenridge apart.[53]

Beyond Breckenridge, the 1960s and early 1970s brought one new ski development after another: Crested Butte, Indianhead (later Geneva Basin), Lake Eldora, Storm Mountain (later Mount Werner, then Steamboat Ski Resort), Sunlight, Purgatory, Powderhorn, Meadow Mountain, Telluride. Perhaps most significant were the new resorts that directly imitated Vail, like Snowmass, Keystone, and Copper Mountain. These were not just ski mountains. They were Vail-style megacomplexes, corporate-financed, built-from-scratch resort "villages" with condominium towers, hotels, shopping centers, town squares, and parking lots.

Disgust with ski-resort sprawl stemmed from hopes of saving "openness and beauty" (as Eagle's town manager had put it) and other landscape qualities essential to the tourist lifestyle. Interestingly, though, avid skiers did not lead the protests the way avid anglers did on the issue of hatchery trout. While a conservation-minded group like the Colorado Mountain Club counted many skiers as members, there was no analogue to Trout Unlimited, no entity specifically dedicated to conserving ski resources. To be sure, by the early 1970s avid skiers could find fairly regular coverage of environmental issues in a periodical like *Ski* magazine, much of it critical of what was happening in Colorado. In 1971, editor Morten Lund contrasted

Colorado's resort boom with the French Savoie's, lauding how the French had kept their base villages compact and deploring the tendency of Colorado resorts to "grow like crabgrass"—a phrase that slyly linked ski expansion to popular anxiety about suburban sprawl. But even as he mourned the high country's "traumatic exploitation" and "despoliation," Lund had little praise for environmentalists who were fighting it. In his mind, they mindlessly opposed *all* ski growth. "Almost every proposal for a new or expanded resort," he griped, was "met with a savage attack by Sierra Clubbers, Friends of the Earth, and a whole latter-day zodiac of amateur ecologists . . . armed with publicity, petitions and the ear of a liberal Congressman."[54] Disparaging words like these hinted at a problem that would soon haunt Colorado's environmental movement: people who came to environmentalism from one pastime, like skiing, did not always see common cause with people who came to it from other directions.

Still, the environmental critique of skiing gained traction and by the early 1970s was changing the face of ski development. Keystone, Summit County's third big winter resort, opened in 1970 with ski trails aesthetically sculpted to fit the mountain's natural contours. Copper Mountain, which opened as Summit's fourth big resort in 1972, was also designed with appearance in mind. Instead of slashing the usual clear-cut stripes straight down the mountainside, Copper's designers scalloped the trail edges and selectively thinned the timber to create natural-looking stands and glades, so motorists whizzing by on I-70 would have a scenically pleasing view. Copper's "precise planning," its ads bragged, paid "meticulous attention to the needs of both man and nature. Copper Mountain—it's a natural."[55] The Forest Service advanced the cause of aesthetically and ecologically sensitive ski-mountain design when it issued a handbook on the subject in 1973. Pete Wingle, of the agency's regional office in Denver, illustrated the handbook with examples from Colorado's recent past, including horror stories of badly planned trails, lifts, and base villages that had unleashed congestion, erosion, wind scour, soil instability, and plain old ugliness. Wingle's manual, Morten Lund wrote, was "well-thumbed" by developers planning new resorts in national forests. "It *is* a new era," Lund observed.[56]

Why were forest rangers and ski developers suddenly paying such heed to popular environmental concerns? Mostly because they had to. Beginning in 1970, the landmark National Environmental Policy Act required any federal agency mulling an action with potentially major environmental impacts—like the Forest Service issuing a permit for a ski area—to first assess these impacts, consider alternatives (such as *not* issuing the permit), reveal these findings in an "environmental impact statement," and allow the public to comment. The legislation not only forced the Forest Service to think more environmentally but also opened the entire planning and permitting process to public scrutiny, giving citizens leverage to demand mitigations—and in some cases to stop new resorts from being built at all.

Environmentalists in Colorado used this leverage to great effect. When developers in 1970 began planning a sizable new ski resort near the Pitkin-Gunnison county line, around the tiny town of Marble, not only did the state Game, Fish and Parks Department cry foul, citing adverse impacts to wildlife, but so did the Rocky Mountain Center on Environment, the Colorado Open Space Council and its Wilderness Workshop, and assorted Pitkin County citizens' groups. The Marble project was utterly defeated, shelved in 1974. By that time, environmental groups had turned their attention to another ski area in the works: Beaver Creek, a luxury resort that Vail Associates wanted to develop in a side valley eight miles west of Vail. The debate over Beaver Creek quickly escalated into the bitterest ski battle Colorado had yet seen, as the state sided with environmentalists against VA and the Forest Service; studies, negotiations, lawsuits, and appeals dragged on for years. VA eventually prevailed, but it was an enormously time-consuming and expensive victory. No major new ski area has been built in Colorado since Beaver Creek, and that in itself is one major legacy of Colorado's backlash against big recreation.[57]

The backlash went beyond ski-resort sprawl and mass-produced trout—beyond even big recreation. The backlash was really against the attitude that underlay all of these: the long-standing assumption that growth was always good. Greater numbers of Americans found themselves seriously questioning this assumption by the early 1970s.[58] The questioning, the brewing national backlash against growth, took on different forms in different parts of the country. It is telling that in Colorado it focused most of all on the environmental amenities that recreational promotion had promised and on the problems it had helped cause. These included the loss of scenic views, air and water quality, and open space, but above all, worry fixated on population growth in certain alluring parts of the state. To boosters, population growth had always meant progress. But to many Coloradans now, "more people," as John Denver sang, meant "more scars upon the land"— the destruction of qualities that made the state such a pleasant place to live. Some had been fretting about this for years, like the young Denver lawyer

5.4 Ski mountain with scenery in mind. The environmentalist critique of big recreation did not halt the production of massive new ski resorts, but it did affect how they were designed, forcing more attention to variables like wind, water drainage, and scenic impact. These images, taken from Pete Wingle's 1973 Forest Service manual on environmentally sensitive ski-area design, show Copper Mountain, which opened that year. Seen in aerial view (*top*), the mountain shows the familiar clear-cut stripes. But the stripes were cut with scalloped edges and free-standing glades of trees, so that when seen from Interstate 70 (*below*), Copper appeared more natural. Courtesy U.S. Forest Service.

and Colorado Mountain Club member Richard Lamm, who in 1963 called population growth "the ultimate problem" and darkly warned that before it exhausted the earth's resources it would crowd out all the recreational spaces. "None," he told his fellow mountain lovers, "will feel it as acutely as those who depend on wilderness . . . to survive the stresses of the twentieth century."[59]

At that time there was still optimism that the expert planning and promotion of recreation—in the style of the Outdoor Recreation Resources Review Commission—would save special settings like wilderness from the population wave. This had been a founding tenet of COSCC. But by the late 1960s the optimism had dissolved, not least because recreational growth itself now seemed a big part of the problem. By decade's end, someone like *Denver Post* outdoor writer Cal Queal, who a few years earlier had cheered

Vail's expansion, was spinning dystopian imagery of a paradise lost to big recreation: "The stand of spruce that once marked the edge of a forest now screens a mountain subdivision. The aspen grove where deer used to bed down in the afternoon is split by a ski lift." The cause, Queal declared, was "population gain . . . compounded, paradoxically, by the American thirst for the 'good life.'" The restless quest for leisure was helping drive Colorado's population wave, and the state was getting swamped.[60]

So the late 1960s saw overpopulation joining open-space loss—two issues closely linked to recreational growth—as Colorado's most-discussed environmental anxieties. Not all the proposed solutions involved reining in recreation. There was also strong support for birth-control measures (which led to Colorado passing the nation's most liberal abortion-rights law in 1969) and regulations to steer population growth away from Denver and the rest of the fast-growing Front Range. (Some wanted to settle new residents in small "new towns" in rural Colorado—another case of the Vail business model turned environmental ideal?) Governor John Love faced heavy pressure to suspend his "Sell Colorado" shtick, which held out scenery and recreation as incentives for executives to relocate themselves, their firms, and employees to Colorado. Among those urging Love to stop selling Colorado were COSC and Dick Lamm, who had won election to the state legislature in 1966 and sponsored the 1969 abortion bill. Love experienced a partial conversion on the issue, agreeing to refocus Sell Colorado on environmentally friendly industries and to steer them away from the Front Range toward less populated parts of the state.[61]

Still, nothing—not Sell Colorado, not Marble or Beaver Creek—made the splash that the plan to host the 1976 Winter Olympics did. This mother of all publicity schemes, meant to seal Colorado's status as a world-class vacationland, instead incited the fiercest backlash yet. The opposition stunned supporters of the Olympics, like Governor Love, but in hindsight it was unsurprising. The prospect of the world rushing to Colorado for the Olympic Games churned up fears of big recreation, overpopulation, and open-space loss all at the same time—a perfect storm that swept environmentalists to their most dramatic victory and marked the crest of environmentalism's influence in the state.

The dream of hosting the Olympics had kicked around Colorado ski circles for some time, and Aspen had submitted little-noticed bids in 1949 and 1956. But then in the 1960s, skiing became big business, "Ski Country U.S.A." a bankable brand, and the governor a self-appointed salesman for the state—all of which positioned Colorado to mount a more coordinated, corporate Olympic bid. Governor Love recruited interested businessmen, including many from the ski, resort hotel, airline, outdoor gear, real estate, and banking industries, to do the planning. (*Colorado Magazine*'s Merrill Hastings and Vail Associates' Pete Seibert were among those involved early on.) A Denver Organizing Committee (DOC), again made up mostly of executives, put together the official bid. It promised Olympians everything Colorado tourist ads promised: world-class ski terrain, abundant snow and sunshine, glorious scenery, western charm, a relaxed atmosphere, and friendly natives eager to share their state. So effective was this pitch that international Olympic officials started quoting Colorado tourist clichés back to the DOC. "Colorado certainly has the mountains and the men to match them," remarked one, "but it is your clear blue skies and fresh, crisp air that make me the most enthusiastic about holding the Winter Olympics here."[62]

The pitch paid off in May 1970, when the International Olympic Committee (IOC) chose Denver to host the 1976 Winter Games. The state's business and political establishment exulted. So did everyone else—at least that was how the ever-boosterish *Denver Post* made it sound. "It's everything everybody wanted," the *Post* quoted one woman. "It'll bring a lot of people here and that'll be good for the economy." "This will mean a lot to Denver," agreed a man-on-the-street, "and it'll have a big impact on the resort areas.... People coming to the games will return."[63] But was that a good thing? Even as the IOC news reached home, there was already grumbling that Olympic-scale growth would make living in Colorado less pleasant—lengthening lift lines, dirtying the high-country air, attracting undesirable people, and uglifying mountain towns. Already there were scary predictions of what the I-70 corridor might become: "a solid line of phony Alpine motels and condominiums from Denver to Loveland Ski Basin," a "big traffic jam ranging from Denver to Grand Junction." The *Post* tried to marginalize these critics, calling them "killjoys," but as it turned out, they were just the start.[64]

In fact, beyond just grumbling, there was already a grassroots anti-Olympics insurgency under way. It began in the foothills just west of Denver and south of I-70, where Denver's historic mountain parks mingled with exurbs like Evergreen and Indian Hills and rising numbers of lifestyle refugees lived in secluded beauty, their houses screened from each other by ponderosa pines. Some were second-home owners, some professionals who commuted to Denver, some retirees. In late 1967 they discovered that the

DOC, without bothering to consult them, had decided to put the Nordic skiing, biathlon, bobsled, and luge events literally in their backyards. The locals were horrified. No way, they thought, could their scenic refuge and placid quality of life withstand a fifty-two-mile ski course, a ski-jump complex, refrigerated concrete bobsled runs, artificial snow machines, access roads, parking lots, tens of thousands of spectators, and "millions of toilet-goings" polluting their streams and wells. So in 1968, twenty-seven area homeowners wrote to the DOC asking that the events be moved. When the DOC brushed them off, they wrote more letters, held public meetings, and appeared on local television and radio with their concerns. In 1970 they set up a group called Protect Our Mountain Environment (POME) to coordinate their efforts. By 1971 it claimed five hundred members, some of whom now wanted the games moved not just out of the foothills but out of Colorado altogether. Still the DOC refused to take them seriously. But *Newsweek*, *Sports Illustrated*, and newspapers as far away as England began picking up on the story of these grassroots environmentalists who were taking on the mighty Olympics establishment.[65]

The Olympics were drawing fire from other quarters too. Anger was mounting over how much the games were going to cost taxpayers. Estimates kept ballooning, and no one could get a straight answer out of the DOC. Some accused the DOC of secrecy, others of outright lying. It did not help when it came out that the DOC had, shall we say, stretched the truth in making its pitch to the IOC. For example, it had claimed that the ski venues were short drives from Denver, when any local could have told you that was only true if I-70's notorious traffic magically vanished. The DOC had also shown misleading photos to the IOC, in one case airbrushing an aerial shot of a ski mountain to cover up snowless spots, in another case carefully selecting a picture of downtown Denver that made the Rockies look much closer to the city than they really are. In a weird way, shenanigans like these simply perpetuated the tourist advertiser's tradition of glossing over nature's complexities to make it seem naturally suited for leisure. But many Coloradans, tired of big-recreation boosterism, seemed unwilling to go along with the ruse now. Least of all the people of Evergreen, who pointed out that their area was not the Nordic ski paradise the DOC had claimed it was—that in fact a typical February in Evergreen saw little if any snow on the ground. Soon it came out that the DOC had also ignored on-the-ground realities—poor snow and severe wind scour—at Mount Sniktau, the undeveloped peak near the Eisenhower Tunnel where Alpine skiing was planned. As the

DOC fumbled to find new venues for these marquee events, besides seeming imperious and duplicitous it looked incompetent too.[66]

There now seemed plenty of reasons to resent the Olympics. But high on many people's list was the fear of losing Colorado's amenities—fear that the worldwide publicity surrounding the games would start a new spiral of growth and wipe out all that was scenic and leisurely about the state. As Dick Lamm wrote, "There are an awful lot of us who don't like seeing our Garden of Eden turned into a commercial playground." Lamm, who became the games' most vocal critic, was himself a permanent tourist: an avid skier, climber, and kayaker who had moved from Wisconsin to Denver after falling in love with the mountains during an army stint in the late 1950s. But to say he opposed the Olympics merely out of touristic self-indulgence misses much of what motivated him and the rest of the opposition. Lamm saved his fiercest anger for the Olympics' fiscal, not ecological, cost. The games were a boondoggle, he charged; a diversion from pressing needs like affordable housing and health care; a giant subsidy for developers, bankers, and resort operators who were already prospering quite well, thank you very much. Why pay them to profit while the rest of Colorado suffered economic and environmental disaster? Why pay them to bring more people to the Front Range and the I-70 corridor, already the most overstressed parts of the state? It was time to "stop 'selling' Colorado," Lamm declared, "stop the mindless promotionalism and the Chamber of Commerce boosterism, exemplified by the Olympics."[67]

Popular anxieties about big recreation, open-space loss, overpopulation, and the fragility of the Colorado landscape and lifestyle came together in a single, scathing critique. In hindsight, unease had been brewing for years and went well beyond the Olympics. But now the Olympics became the target, and Lamm became the leader. He kept hammering away in the legislature, urging his fellow lawmakers to cut off state funding for the games, and he helped set up citizens' advocacy groups to leaflet, canvass, petition, and keep the issue in the public eye. Environmental groups jumped in: the state chapters of the Sierra Club and Zero Population Growth fought alongside Lamm, and the Colorado Open Space Council opposed further state funding until pressing ecological issues were addressed. (The Rocky Mountain Center on Environment, again cautious about alienating business and booster interests, declined to take a side, but it did urge careful environmental planning in preparation for the games.)[68]

The debate began to roil not just the Denver metro area and the foothills

5.5 Deceptive twist on a trademark scene. This clever take on Denver's famous mountain view appeared in the DOC's winning "bid book." Shot from a distance-compressing vantage point on a morning when fresh snow made the close-in foothills look almost indistinguishable from the distant peaks, the photograph made the city look closer to the mountains than it actually is. Courtesy Colorado State Archives.

but the high country too. The influential Club 20, ever eager to boost Western Slope tourism, came out strongly for the games. But opinion elsewhere was mixed. In Georgetown, located right on I-70 near where the Alpine ski events were planned, part of the reason the community's groundbreaking 1970 historic preservation ordinance passed when it did was because locals feared the Olympics visitor influx would overrun their town. Mayor Jim Abbott fired a shot across the DOC's bow: if "they come in and run all over us," he growled, "and make us a 10,000-car parking lot . . . why, we'll make Evergreen's fight look like nothing. . . . They'll find a bunch of s.o.b.s up here." The DOC found itself even less welcome in Aspen, where it considered moving the Alpine events after Mount Sniktau proved unworkable. The Aspen Skiing Corporation and some area politicians seemed receptive to the idea, but local protest—by then a fine Aspen tradition—scotched it. (It was at this time that John Denver, fearful of the games invading his own backyard, wrote the protest verse in "Rocky Mountain High.")[69]

Vail Associates then offered the use of Beaver Creek, the new ski area it had been planning to develop anyway, and the desperate DOC seized on the offer. Local sentiment in Vail was generally favorable, though some raised concerns about crowds, sprawl, and the fact that Beaver Creek would abut a wilderness area. (Local resistance would prove the least of VA's worries as the fight to get Beaver Creek through the permit process dragged on for the next several years.) Steamboat Springs was still another town that entered the Olympics fray, when the DOC, drummed out of Evergreen, decided to move the Nordic events there. Many in Steamboat Springs welcomed the distinction. But not all did. At one point, someone burned down the town's ninety-meter ski jump in apparent protest. "The Olympic Torch has been lit in Steamboat Springs," deadpanned the local paper.[70]

By 1972, the Olympics were on a downhill slide—pun intended. Lamm almost managed that spring to get the legislature to end state funding, which emboldened one of his grassroots groups, Citizens for Colorado's Future (CCF), to petition to put the question to a popular vote. Games backers tried to stem the tide, but everything they tried backfired. They howled that yanking funds would ruin Colorado's international image, but that argument was unlikely to sway anyone sick of Sell Colorado. They insisted that, despite their own gleeful predictions a few years earlier, the Olympics would *not* attract more permanent residents. But many Coloradans were themselves tourists turned permanent, and everyone could see how powerfully tourism's allure had driven Colorado's population growth. As one observer put it, "The trouble with tourists is that, having looked around, many wish to return. To stay."[71] Equally futile were games supporters' efforts to debunk environmental fears. The fears were "ridiculous," railed the *Rocky Mountain News*, since "environmental-conscious experts" had done all the planning. Winter sports were "near-perfect types of commercial activity," added the *Denver Post*, "for a state which wants to keep its scenic beauties and its recreational opportunities intact." But faith in experts, and in the environmental goodness of tourism—two of COSCC's founding principles back in 1965—carried a lot less weight now. Now popular opinion seemed closer to what an Indian Hills man had to say: the so-called "experts," he sneered, were just

5.6 Environmentalist icons. In the 1970s, no one embodied Colorado's outdoor-living mystique more than John Denver (*right*), and no one symbolized its complicated political legacy better than Dick Lamm (*left*). The two men, both attracted to Colorado by the recreational lifestyle—and worried about the environmental impact of too many others doing the same—became allies, with Denver giving free concerts to rally voters for Lamm during the gubernatorial campaigns of 1974 and (here) 1978. Courtesy Richard D. Lamm.

people "whose job it is to twist ideas and facts to suit the [DOC's] monetary needs."[72]

One intriguing part of the argument centered on who could claim roots in Colorado. Games supporters often scorned environmentalists and CCF staffers as newly arrived, carpetbagging, hippie-living "professional agitators" (one ad called them "dangerous hitch-hikers") who claimed to care about the land but really only came to raise left-wing hell.[73] But then it was revealed that some DOC staffers had arrived in Colorado even more recently. Equally damning, most DOC members and state Olympics officials had business ties that situated them to profit off the games, casting doubt on their loyalty to the land and people of the state. (For example, the chair of the state Olympics oversight commission, who also sat on the DOC, *also* sat on the Vail Associates board, making the late choice of Beaver Creek for Alpine events look fishy.) When Governor Love announced a statewide citizens' "Committee of '76" to rally support for the games, but the committee turned out to consist largely of bank executives and other corporate leaders, it only deepened suspicions that the games were a giant profit-making scheme for fat cats.[74] In the end, that was the conclusion many Coloradans drew—and on election day they voted by a thumping 60–40 margin to kill public funding for the Games, effectively kicking them out of the state.[75]

As it turned out, then, it was not just environmental anxiety that doomed the Denver Olympics. Disgust with the DOC, and with the idea of them and their corporate cronies profiting while taxpayers footed the bill, seems to have done even more than open-space concerns to sour Coloradans on the games. Or did it? Dick Lamm, in a major speech meant to clarify his position to the press, called state-sponsored booster schemes like the Olympics "promotional pollution."[76] He meant that they were fiscally objectionable, but his choice of words showed how even these objections were informed by environmental sensibilities. Never far beneath the surface in the Olympics debate lay fears about the fragility of the land and the leisurely way of life. In any case, Coloradans' ringing rejection of the Olympics, whether cast in overtly environmental terms or not, pointed to a clear end: that blind faith in boosters was dead and so too blind faith in the goodness of growth.

Is that too much to read into the Denver Olympics' demise? Not when you consider how many other symbols of big recreation and boosterism were under fire by 1972. Or, especially, when you consider the tidal wave that swept through Colorado politics that year. The casualties included not just the Olympics but some of Colorado's longest-entrenched champions of growth.[77] The Denver Water Board suffered a major defeat when city voters, concerned about more sprawl in the metro area and more amenity loss up in the mountains, rejected a $200 million bond issue for new water projects. Three-term senator Gordon Allott, an old foe of wilderness and other environmental causes, lost his reelection bid in a stunning upset to little-known Floyd Haskell, who hammered the incumbent's environmental record. Twelve-term Western Slope congressman Wayne Aspinall, another bête noire of environmentalists, with close ties to Club 20 and mining, ranching, and dam-building interests, lost his primary to Alan Merson, an environmental-law professor and Breckenridge second-home owner active in Protect Our Mountain Environment and Citizens for Colorado's Future. The district had just been redrawn, cutting out part of Aspinall's Western Slope power base and bringing in some of Denver's northern suburbs. Aspinall, having spent his career catering to extractive industries, found himself needing to appeal to much more environmentally minded voters. It did not work. Merson, himself a lifestyle refugee (he had lived in Colorado just a few years), trounced Aspinall in the suburbs and in Aspen, providing the margin he needed to win.[78] And if the election shocks of 1972 were not sea change enough, the biggest antibooster, pro-environmentalist wave of all hit in 1974, when Dick Lamm, vaulted to prominence by his campaign against the Olympics, was elected governor. He ousted incumbent Republican John Vanderhoof, another stalwart of the pro-growth Club 20 crowd.[79]

The fact that environmentalism flexed such political muscle in the early 1970s did not make Colorado unique. If anything, it made Colorado typical, for those years saw environmental concerns spreading across the country. Nor were Coloradans alone in rebelling against growth. That too was a broader phenomenon of the 1960s and 1970s, a seismic shift in thinking that was linked to environmentalism but was not limited to it: the spreading sense that postwar economic expansion, even while generating wealth, was undermining people's quality of life. But the specifics of both environmentalism and the turn against growth differed in different parts of the country. In a state like Colorado, where tourism had done so much to shape people's visions of the land, mediate their ties to it, alter the landscape itself, and fuel the population boom, tourism figured centrally in environmental disputes and the wider debate over growth. Tourist development and promotion came under heavy fire, with permanent tourists doing much of the firing. Their choice of targets—whether hatchery trout, ski-resort sprawl, or Sell Colorado and its progeny, the Winter Olympics—reflected their fear of the same promotional forces that had made Colorado such a popular vacationland. They were passionate about fun and fulfillment in the mountains, and now, with their electoral victories in the early 1970s, it seemed they had the political clout to match their passion.

SOMEHOW, THOUGH, MOMENTUM FALTERED. THE DEFEAT OF THE booster politicians and the banishment of the Olympics did not, in fact, bring about the environmentalist millennium that many in Colorado had hoped for (or feared). There would be no sweeping reform to reverse the tide of tourist development or turn back big recreation. Big recreation would have to get used to new political obstacles and procedural delays, yes. But there was no fundamental transformation of values, no permanent power shift. By the 1980s the business of packaging high-country places for pleasure continued to flourish pretty much as it had before.

Much has been said about why the American environmentalist

revolution—if "revolution" is really the right word—fell apart in the mid-1970s. The oil crisis and recession hit in 1973–75, which made environmental quality seem an unaffordable luxury to many Americans. Business interests and the New Right mounted an organized backlash to demonize environmentalists as druids, doomsayers, and foes of free enterprise, private property, and the American way of life. And public support for environmentalism, while broad for a time, never ran very deep. It was fashionable to talk of "the ecology" in the early 1970s, but Americans who measured their happiness and higher living standards by what they consumed were not inclined to make personal sacrifices for "the ecology's" sake. In Colorado and the rest of the country, economic, political, and cultural pressures seriously limited the impact of the environmental movement.

But so did the nature of the movement itself. Consumerism was not external to environmentalism—it was woven into its very fabric. And this is what we so vividly see in Colorado's case: recreational consumerism, even while galvanizing impressive popular support for environmentalism, also shaped it in ways that severely impeded its success. In other words, another reason why the environmental movement faltered lies in recreational consumerism itself.

Serious environmental reform seemed well on its way in January 1970, when it got a big boost from an unexpected ally: Governor Love. Opening the new legislative session in a reelection year, the usually low-key Republican, whose pet issue had been economic development, surprised everyone by making an impassioned plea for bold action to protect the environment. Never before had a Colorado governor put such issues at the top of the agenda. In response, not only did the Republican-majority legislature pass bills on air and water pollution, water rights, and billboard control, but also—by authorizing a statewide environmental resources inventory and a blue-ribbon Colorado Environmental Commission (CEC)—they signaled that more environmental measures were on the way. The resources inventory was meant to set the stage for future planning, while the CEC, after surveying all the state's environmental problems, was expected to recommend a raft of policy responses.[80]

Both the resources inventory and the CEC reflected the influence of ecology—especially its core lesson that all organisms and processes were interconnected and that environmental problems must thus be studied and solved in relation to one another rather than in isolation.[81] After years of scattered efforts to stand up for the scenic, wild, and recreational in Colorado, followed by efforts to forge a broader recreation-conservation movement in the state, it seemed that Love had finally tugged Colorado into the age of ecology. In the state legislature, environmental problems that stemmed from recreational growth and the recreational mystique remained high priorities, but the fixes legislators debated were more sweeping, more systemic, more *ecological* than ever before. To steer Coloradans away from their overreliance on cars and interstates, for example, legislators considered diverting funds earmarked for highways to build an integrated, multimodal transportation system for the entire state. To deal with the relentless flood of lifestyle refugees, lawmakers talked about retooling the Sell Colorado motif, devising "population dispersion" policies, and even overhauling century-old state water law, all to channel growth away from places that were already at "carrying capacity"—another ecological concept.[82]

But in a state where so much revolved around landscape imagery and the recreational and real estate value of land, the reform proposals that generated the most interest were those that would have the state do more to control and coordinate land use. As it stood, most public controls on the use of private land came at the town or county level, through local permitting, planning, and zoning. In light of problems like scenic degradation and sprawl, though, a surprisingly wide consensus began to emerge that local officials could no longer be entrusted with the landscape's fate and that the state must step in. Love, a moderate Republican, began urging state land-use controls; so did Democrats like Dick Lamm; so even did some conservatives, like state and future U.S. senator Bill Armstrong. "Sound land use planning is the heart and soul of preserving quality living in Colorado," agreed the state's biggest business lobby.[83]

State-level land-use controls were gaining favor in many parts of the country in the early 1970s, including in states where tourism and lifestyle migration were driving landscape change. State government in Hawaii, Vermont, Oregon, and Florida, to name a few such places, variously claimed the power to veto local development projects, restrict them in zones of "critical concern," or in Hawaii's case, zone the whole state. Grounding all of these initiatives was the ecological principle of interconnectedness. Ecology taught that what happened to one piece of land affected the area and the people all around it. Development in any one jurisdiction could reverberate throughout a state, sucking up water and energy resources, spilling pollution, traffic, and population across town and county lines, damaging scenery, leisure, public health, and quality of life for everyone. Making land use even more ecological was the fact that postwar people did not tend to stay on any one piece of land: they were constantly moving, commuting, vacationing, crossing political boundaries and staking claims to places not their primary homes. It was just such ecological reasoning that led Governor Love to conclude that "some 99 per cent of our environmental factors depend on how land is used" and the Rocky Mountain Center on Environment to call land use "the key to many other environmental problems," including air and water pollution, "community quality," and the loss of wildlife, scenic and historical resources, and open space.[84]

At the same time that sweeping land-use reform seemed well suited for the ecological 1970s, it also fit comfortably into Colorado's past. For all its new-era ambition, land-use reform sought to do pretty much what Boulder, Aspen, Art Carhart with his wildland planning, and recreation planners after the Outdoor Recreation Resources Review Commission had tried to do in decades past: turn the old idea of zoning land into a primary strategy for maintaining an amenity-rich landscape. Colorado's lifestyle-minded environmental culture, and Coloradans' familiarity with zoning for environmental quality, made the state a natural for sweeping land-use reform. Or so it seemed.

As it turned out, though, despite a seemingly optimal public mood and political climate, serious land-use reforms kept hitting a brick wall in the legislature. The most ambitious proposal, to have Colorado enact statewide zoning in the Hawaiian style, enjoyed substantial support entering the 1970 session, with Love placing it atop that year's agenda. But legislators balked, and Love backed off. The lawmakers did agree to create a state Land Use Commission (LUC) but refused to give it anything more than advisory powers.[85] Above all, the legislators reasserted the principle that planning and zoning should take place primarily at the local level—which is to say, they rejected the notion that protecting landscape amenities demanded an integrated, ecological approach.

From that point on, reform advocates struggled to get the state to assert even minimal land-use controls. Every year from 1971 to 1974, land-use bills came before the legislature—with backing from environmental interests like ROMCOE, COSC, and the Sierra Club—only to be eviscerated by hostile legislators or killed outright. Some of the bills would have given the LUC review authority over major landscape-transforming projects like new resort towns, subdivisions, and ski areas and other recreational facilities. A 1972 measure went further: it would have created a state "environmental council" with power to require environmental impact studies before big projects could go ahead. Bills introduced in 1971, 1973, and 1974 would have let the state designate certain "areas of state concern"—especially "conservation and recreation areas" like the I-70 corridor, where not just locals but many Coloradans felt a strong lifestyle stake—and require local officials in those areas to enact strict landscape protections, subject to LUC review.[86]

Any of these bills would have given the state strong powers to regulate land use. But lawmakers rejected them all. With few exceptions, the only land-use reforms enacted between 1970 and 1974 were ones that offered aid to local planners, thus reasserting the principle that planning and zoning should remain local, not state, prerogatives.[87] These were supposedly the salad days of environmentalism, and land-use reform was supposedly the key to solving all of Colorado's environmental problems at once. Environmentalists seemed to have public opinion on their side and the support of many well-placed politicians too; for the first time they had a professional lobbyist representing them in Denver, and the anti-Olympics campaign was building momentum for their cause.[88] Yet none of it was enough to push serious state-level land-use reform over the hump.

Why not? Because the debate over land-use reform, like the Olympics furor raging at the same time, exposed a bedrock incompatibility between consumers' and promoters' ways of valuing the outdoors. Just a few years earlier, many had hoped for an alliance between the two: recreational enthusiasts and environmentalists on the one hand; tourism-happy boosters, business interests, and local officials on the other. But when the former vested their hopes in sweeping land-use regulation, the latter refused to go along. Town and county officials did not want the state usurping their power to control land within their jurisdictions; they bridled when reformers called for local authority to give way to planning by region, watershed, or ecosystem.[89] Recreational developers did not want the state curtailing their right to develop their holdings; they recoiled when a reform advocate like ROMCOE and former COSC director Roger Hansen urged Coloradans to take on "the great bawling, sacred cow called 'private property.'" Local boosters did not want limits on local growth; they rejected Hansen's plea for Coloradans to "abandon traditional and entrenched economic thinking" and halt the endless quest for more consumers so "*existing* consumers" might enjoy "higher standards of living."[90]

Rhetoric like Hansen's challenged basic principles of land ownership, boosterism, and economic and political localism. Which is why boosters, business interests, and local officials—whom environmentalists had hoped would be their allies, and many of whom had expressed initial support for land-use reform—instead unleashed their muscular lobbies in Denver to crush it. The influential Colorado Municipal League, representing local governments, acted with particular force; so did the state's top business lobby, the Colorado Association of Commerce and Industry (CACI). Both insisted that any land-use planning "be effected at the lowest possible level of government," and they worked to enfeeble or kill any bill that violated that principle. And they were successful: in 1971, when ambitious land-use reform still seemed a possibility, CACI proposed several amendments to weaken it—and every single one prevailed.[91] The consequences went well beyond a bunch of defeated or watered-down bills. Truly, the early 1970s battles over land use ruptured any real chance of alliance between those Coloradans whose personal or nonmaterial ways of valuing nature led them to seek sweeping environmental reforms, and those whose chiefly profit-minded environmental values were much better served by something close to the status quo. After the early 1970s, it would be much harder to find tourist boosters and business interests and environmentalists making common cause.

But it is too simple to say that business lobbies doomed land-use reform. For if reform seemed too radical to investors in the tourist industry, it also seemed that way to many consumers of the tourist lifestyle. Did Colorado's lifestyle consumers really want to reject the value of growth, reorder the relationship between state and local government, or rethink the notion of private property? The last in particular was a revolutionary idea, and con-sumerism, when the chips are down, is not a revolutionary mind-set. Nor is the defense of "lifestyle." Think again of the Vail residents who made Vail Associates' original resort concept the basis for their transplanted personal lives, their pursuit of happiness, and their newfound identities—and then made it the basis of their politics too. They could hardly be called radical for rallying behind the banner of a marketing formula. They were hardly challenging the system when they spoke up to protect their preferred way of life. Nor were the many other Coloradans whose "environmentalism" meant standing up for the landscape qualities in which they had person-ally invested themselves as consumers of leisure and the tourist lifestyle. Consumerism, which literally teaches people to buy into the system, did not incline these Coloradans toward the kind of systemic transformation that the most ambitious land-use reforms would have entailed. Nor did the

1970s concept of lifestyle, which by its very nature emphasized the freedom of individual choice, not the imposition of society-wide change.[92]

In short, consumerism and the love of lifestyle discouraged "big-picture" thinking, the sort of holistic, ecological vision needed to follow through on the more comprehensive land-use reforms. Decades of tourist marketing had taught recreational consumers to see different parts of the high country separately and unequally, not as constituent parts of an interlinked whole. We have seen how tourist promoters packaged pieces of the environment and landscape, set them apart from their surroundings and their ecological context, and marketed them to demographic and psychographic niches. As ROMCOE's Bert Melcher mused mournfully in 1971, "Hundreds of years of geological history, of biological evolution, all woven together in an intricate web of life" had a way of becoming just so many pieces for "man's auction block." "Multiply [the] sales pitch by several tens of thousands," Melcher wrote, "and there you had the present-day "picture of earth."[93] Insofar as this endless place packaging instilled environmental values in consumers, it did so by encouraging them to become attached to particular places, and to particular ways of relating to them, that resonated with consumers' particular personalities. These attachments could be extraordinarily strong—strong enough for some consumers to refocus their lives and become permanent tourists. But they tended to be specific to the person and the location, not generic to "nature," "the environment," or even Colorado or the high country as a whole. So even as outdoor-loving Coloradans became familiar with the insights of ecology, most only halfheartedly supported ecologically inspired reforms, like regional planning or statewide zoning, that challenged them to care about every place as much as they cared about their personal favorites.

If the segmented nature of recreational consumerism made it hard for Coloradans to think in terms of sweeping environmental reforms, it also made it hard for them to forge a unified environmental movement. Many of the state's earliest outdoor-advocacy groups, like the Pitkin County Water Protection Association and chapters of the Izaak Walton League, had been staunchly local in focus, born of their founders' attachments to those specific settings. An even greater number of early environmental groups sprang from specific outdoor pastimes—hunting, fishing, climbing, gardening, bird-watching, rafting, jeeping. That segmented the environmental movement even more, because each of these pastimes had its own subculture, its own ways of relating to nature, and its own set of sacred places, be they trails, peaks, rock faces, rivers, wildlife habitats, or wilderness areas. It was going to be difficult for niche groups like these to agree on a shared set of environmental values and priorities.

Still, for a time in the 1960s, it looked like they might. The emergence of the Colorado Open Space Coordinating Council provided an organizational umbrella, while the spread of ecological ideas gave the otherwise single-focus groups a shared language and a logic for concerted action. By dint of their membership in COSCC, groups like the Colorado White Water Association and Colorado Mountain Club found themselves engaged in an ever-wider range of outdoor issues, many of which lay well beyond their recreational niches.

But niche thinking died hard. Any group that broadened its focus was likely to hear grumbling from members who could not see why, say, a club founded around rafting should concern itself with air pollution or zoning. One of the first to face such complaints was the Izaak Walton League, which, while rooted in sport fishing, had long committed itself to the broader conservation agenda of defending "Soil, Woods, Waters, and Wildlife." In 1960, new IWLA president George Jackson suggested that this agenda was alienating rank-and-file Ikes. As former head of the league in Colorado, Jackson may have had Colorado Ikes specifically in mind; in any case, he called for rededicating the IWLA to "sport fishermen and their interests."[94]

Similar misgivings compelled the Colorado Mountain Club to dial back its activism in the early 1970s. By then the CMC had become a major player in environmental debates from wilderness to nuclear energy, population control to the Olympics, Grand Canyon dams to supersonic airplanes (SSTs). Yet many of its own members seemed unimpressed. Instead of hurling itself into "all of the far-flung subjects which can be labeled 'Environment,'" a Denver member scolded, the club should "focus its efforts on mountaineering and hiking" and "limit conservation efforts to assuring that we will have a place to carry on our mountaineering activities." In 1972, CMC members directed their leadership to do just that. It may have been the age of ecology, but the ecological ethos that connected all environmental concerns lost out to the narrower niche mentality of the recreational consumer.[95]

Recreational market segmentation also got in the way of building broad environmental coalitions. Especially noticeable was the difficulty COSCC had in getting hunters and anglers on board. Ed Hilliard had envisioned these groups as the vanguard of the movement—indeed, the idea for COSCC had grown out of the sportsman-dominated Conservation

Council that Hilliard helped found in the late 1950s. But once COSCC got up and running in the mid-1960s, it quickly became clear that people primarily interested in outdoor beautification (such as antibillboard, gardening, and women's clubs) and in outings (such as the Colorado White Water Association and the CMC) were participating much more energetically than sportsmen's groups like Ducks Unlimited, Trout Unlimited, or the Colorado Wildlife Federation. COSCC's Roger Hansen went so far as to beg the state Game, Fish and Parks Department for help in getting sportsmen more involved.[96] Part of the problem was the generational torch passing that was happening nationwide, as the older "conservationists" gave way to younger "environmentalists." But powerful consumer currents were also at play. Hansen himself realized that sportsmen tended to see COSCC as a group more interested in the *preservation* of amenities, like scenic beauty and wilderness, than in the *conservation* of extractable resources, like fish and game. By that way of seeing, COSCC had little to offer anyone whose idea of enjoying the outdoors was to take fish and game from it.

Another crowd that did not cotton to COSCC were the "jeepers"— people who, on weekends, loved nothing more than to bump around the high country in their four-wheel-drives. Unlike most tourists, they sought out Colorado's *least*-improved roads, following them to ghost towns, hidden lakes, high meadows, and abandoned passes. Four-wheeling enabled "marvelous inspiration to be found in that special world of the high mountains," wrote one jeeper, but "with a bit more comfort than non-motorized travel"— which is to say, four-wheeling was in many ways the quintessential activity for the tourist way of life. Tens of thousands of jeepers lived in the Denver area, and hundreds joined the Mile-Hi Jeep Club, founded in 1956. The club itself was divided into "patrols," each a niche market unto itself: some patrols were for older jeepers, others for couples or families; some took day outings, others overnight trips; some favored scenic jaunts to ghost towns, while others sought out technically difficult trails. In the 1960s the Jeep Club got increasingly involved in environmental matters. Patrols planted trees, cleaned up rivers and campsites, and tried to set a good example for all jeepers by spreading the message to stay on the trail instead of leaving ruts in fragile meadows, riverbeds, and mountainsides. Club leaders even petitioned four-wheel-drive manufacturers to stop glorifying off-trail driving in their advertising. And in 1964, the Jeep Club enthusiastically joined the Colorado Outdoor Roundtable, the immediate ancestor of COSCC. But when COSCC itself launched in 1965, the Jeep Club steered clear of it.[97]

The sticking point was wilderness. There was no cause COSCC fought harder for—and none that made jeepers angrier. Understandably so, for under the terms of the Wilderness Act, once an area received wilderness designation, it was off-limits to motorized vehicles. Many jeepers became convinced that the wilderness "purists" wanted to close the entire high country to four-wheelers. "They won't give up until practically all public lands are put into the wilderness condition," the Jeep Club warned its members. For the club, this was nothing short of a "survival situation," and it was a deal breaker when it came to associating with the likes of COSCC.[98]

Making an alliance even harder was the way these different tastes in outdoor leisure came to stand for deeper social divisions. Many jeepers saw wilderness acolytes as rich snobs: an "elitist minority," wrote the head of the national four-wheelers' association, intent on an "elitist system of playground." Wilderness outings excluded "the too-old, the too-young, the timid, the inexperienced, the frail, the hurried, the out-of-shape or the just-plain lazy." In contrast, jeeping was for "ordinary Americans" who liked "driving, sightseeing, easy walking and camping." The typical wilderness acolyte was "a college graduate," had "an advanced degree," and sat "in the upper-income brackets." Jeepers, on the other hand, had "regular jobs," if one believed the Jeep Club newsletter (and if club leaders' home addresses are any indication, Denver-area four-wheelers did tend overwhelmingly to come from neighborhoods of modest single-family homes).[99]

Jeepers resented any implication that their motorized way of enjoying nature was less enlightened or less legitimate than wilderness lovers'. But there was no denying it was different. One can hardly imagine the Colorado Mountain Club calling its chapters the Roughriders, the Stump Thumpers, or Rugged Rock & Roll, as Jeep Club patrols named themselves. Jeepers saw no conflict between loving their brawny machines and loving the high-country landscape, but every hiker had seen ghost towns vandalized and streams and meadows torn up by telltale tire tracks. Privileged snob, destructive meathead: ultimately, the pejorative image each side held of the other, based on their different means of recreation, made it almost impossible to forge an environmental alliance. "We could classify ourselves as environmentalists," mused the Jeep Club's leader in 1974, "but it has become a bitter-tasting word."[100]

Without question, niche-market schisms like these hindered the environmental movement. But that did not mean environmental reform failed completely in Colorado. It just meant that narrow, modest reforms had a better chance than sweeping, ambitious ones. Between 1970 and 1974, even as big land-use measures kept failing in the legislature, many smaller environmental bills did get through: controls on air, water, and noise pollution; aid for local sewer upgrades; a directive to the Division of Commerce and Development to refocus its Sell Colorado campaign away from the crowded Front Range toward less populated parts of the state. Some of these smaller measures (billboard removal, designation of scenic mountain highways) sought to enhance Colorado's recreational allure; while others (regulations on off-road vehicles, stiff penalties for abuse of recreation areas) reflected the creeping concern that the biggest threat to that allure was now recreation itself.

As the jeepers well knew, another niche environmental cause that flourished in the early 1970s was wilderness protection. The Forest Service and other federal land agencies were busy studying old "primitive" and "wild" areas for possible protection under the 1964 Wilderness Act, which meant groups like COSC's Wilderness Workshop were busy issuing proposals and testifying at hearings to try to make that protection happen. Certain pockets of the high country became causes célèbres for wilderness lovers, including the Flat Tops (the maze of uplands, lakes, scarps, and spruce forests in northwestern Colorado where Art Carhart had innovated his early version of wilderness protection) and the Indian Peaks (a serrated, glacially sculpted granitescape in Denver and Boulder's backyard, which some U.S. 40 boosters wanted to bisect with a tunnel and four-lane highway).

It may seem unfair to call wilderness a niche cause when in many ways it was a founding ethic of the entire environmental movement. But there can be no doubt that wilderness protection catered to a subset of recreational consumers—the Jeep Club's anger reminds us it did not cater to all of them—and that its object was to package certain places in that group's image of outdoor enjoyment. If it sounds odd to refer to wilderness designation as "packaging," consider the case of the Gore Range–Eagles Nest Primitive Area, where the State Highway Department had sought to build its Red Buffalo interstate link. Having fended off that intrusion, recreational-environmental groups like CMC and COSC next moved to get the primitive area designated a wilderness. In this effort they were joined by some interesting allies: boosters and business owners in nearby Vail, who thought that protecting the primitive area was vital to Vail's continued marketability. A spokesman for the Eagles Nest Wilderness Committee made the case directly: "Much of Vail's success is because of the beauty of our natural surroundings and use of the land for outdoor recreation."[101] And it would be endangered if Eagles Nest were opened to logging (as a lumber company was demanding) or water development (the Denver Water Board wanted to put a diversion project inside the primitive area).

So Vail business owners found themselves leading a wilderness campaign. When the Forest Service drew the wilderness boundary too narrowly, the Vailites fought to expand it; when the Forest Service moved to allow logging *next* to the primitive area, the Vailites sued to stop it (with none other than Bob Parker, Vail Associates' marketing director, acting as lead plaintiff). Logging, the Vailites argued, would "jeopardize the businesses and economic welfare of residents and investors in the Vail area."[102] As these words suggest, while it would be terribly unfair to write off wilderness advocacy as just a cynical promotional ploy, it would also be wrong to assume it was too pure to have anything to do with the consumer and market dynamics of outdoor recreation.[103]

Consumers' and promoters' continuing interest in protecting their favorite places of leisure also helps explain why, even as ambitious environmental reforms faltered at the state level in Colorado, they continued to thrive at the local level—and why they especially thrived in recreational and lifestyle enclaves, like Boulder, and up in the high country, like in Aspen and Vail.[104] Aspen's reforms were the most ambitious. After years of trying, slow-growth advocates won majorities on the county commission in 1972 and the city council in 1973, and a flurry of growth-control measures ensued. To stop the trend toward ever-larger buildings, Aspen officials slapped a moratorium on building permits and raced to pass strict new zoning rules. To halt open-space loss, they began buying up land for a planned greenbelt around town. And to combat city-like traffic and noise, they turned two blocks of downtown into a pedestrian mall—a radical solution for the time. Meanwhile, Pitkin County officials fought sprawl by downzoning much of the county, mandating house lots as large as thirty acres in some areas. The city and county jointly undertook trail and light-rail projects and then, in 1977, collaborated on the most aggressive measure of all, a new master plan that capped annual growth at 3.4 percent. The unintended consequence was inflated land and housing prices well beyond the means of most mortals, including most of the workers who made the resort economy hum. Sadly, even as Aspen's 1970s growth-control efforts reflected the exuberant environmental idealism of the tourist lifestyle, they also replicated one of its most glaring blind spots.

In Vail, too, local officials pressed ahead with substantive growth-management measures. Spring 1973 saw the Town of Vail using its new home-rule power to levy a fee on new building projects, with the revenue going to buy open space and build recreational facilities on it: tennis courts, bike paths, playgrounds, and parks.[105] Town officials especially set their sights on a thirty-eight-acre meadow, tucked into a curve of Gore Creek, that was the largest remaining parcel of undeveloped land near Vail Village. In a sign of how aggressively they were now willing to act in defense of amenities, when the developer who owned the meadow refused to sell the whole parcel, the town council, with strong support from the townspeople, went ahead and condemned it.[106] Then the council enacted a sweeping zoning ordinance, including a requirement that most new construction projects undergo environmental impact reviews. Environmentalists had tried but repeatedly failed to get the state to enact such a requirement—but in Vail, it seemed, the environmental decade was alive and well.[107]

The spirit of environmentalism shone even brighter in Vail's 1973 master plan. Drafted by a team of San Francisco planners and landscape architects, whom the town had hired at town manager Terry Minger's urging, *The Vail Plan* cast the community's history, identity, and destiny in vivid shades of green. It began by retelling Vail's remarkable history, not as the "fulfillment of a dream," as developer Vail Associates liked to tell it, but as a declension, a fall from grace. A once-cozy hamlet, where small, earth-toned buildings clustered in a single, manageable core, had grown over time into a "confused and urban" mess with multiple centers and tall, hard-edged towers that were "higher than the trees." Vail had grown out of scale with nature, and the solution was to invite nature back in. Enact zoning and architectural controls to keep new buildings small in harmony with the surroundings. Construct a giant underground parking garage and use it to banish cars from sight. Cover the garage with an earthen berm, contoured to look like natural terrain and planted with grass, flowers, and trees, to separate and insulate the village from the exhaust fumes and engine noise of I-70. Add more recreational facilities: parks, playgrounds, tennis courts, an aquatic center, and a network of greenbelts, bike paths, and walkways. And landscape every part of Vail with rock walls, pedestrian plazas, log benches, and above all, thousands of trees. The desired effect was to have "the adjacent forests creeping in from the hillsides, over the roadway, into the village itself." Thus would "the impact of man within the Valley of Vail be softened," the plan concluded. "The time in Vail for man to work in harmony with nature is now."[108]

On the surface *The Vail Plan* looked like a redefinition of the resort, a declaration that environmental values, not profits, would guide its future. But in fact the plan was yet another reassertion of the marketing formula Vail Associates had devised in the early 1960s. Environmentalism had given Vailites new ways of understanding and articulating their interests, but the interests themselves had not changed much. Locals still wanted to live Vail's trademark leisure lifestyle, and the way they thought best to preserve it was to put it back in its original package: the intimate and convenient little resort village that had always been the core of Vail's appeal. Most of the qualities *The Vail Plan* sought to revive—the small-scale architecture and Alpine ambiance, the pedestrian streets and compact town core, the feeling of escape from urban ills, the appearance of harmony with nature, and the ready access to open space and outdoor recreation all around—are ones we have by now heard many times before, because they were the same qualities that had always defined Vail's marketing and Vail's mystique. That helps explain why, despite early objections from developers who feared that it would slow growth and depress property values, the plan ultimately won almost universal local support.[109]

Above all, the plan reaffirmed Vail's original reason for being: making money off visitors. By opting for the Vail Village aesthetic over that of LionsHead, for example, or by keeping traffic out of the town core, the plan catered to visitors' demonstrated preferences as much as locals'. Likewise, by calling for more recreational facilities like bike paths and tennis courts, the plan aimed not just to please residents but also to boost Vail's summer trade. The plan even had its own Bend in Bridge Street, its own landscape flourish to induce visitors to consume. Its version was the "Window on Vail," a series of steps and terraces cascading from the top of the berm-covered parking garage down into Vail Village. Visitors would pause here, the plan's authors explained, getting an overview of the shopping, entertainment, and other options spread out before them. The terraces would function like a department-store display window: orienting consumers to what awaited inside, tempting them to indulge.[110] Like the rest of Vail's 1973 master plan, the Window on Vail showed that there were limits to the rethinking of boosterism and big recreation. Even as it embraced environmental values, Vail as a community remained committed to an ever-expanding tourist trade.

And here we can see another reason why environmentalism, seemingly so ascendant at the decade's outset, ended up having only a limited impact

5.7 Hiding Vail's dependence on automobiles. The 1973 *Vail Plan* sought to reduce the visual impact of cars and bring "nature" back into the resort. In this illustration, the old surface parking lot is replaced by a giant underground parking structure, screened from Vail Village by a lavishly landscaped berm. At center, the "Window on Vail," a multi-terraced stairway, leads from the top of the structure down to a circular plaza at the village entrance. Interstate 70 runs along the top of the picture, almost entirely hidden from view by trees. Courtesy Town of Vail.

on the fate of the landscape in 1970s Colorado. Yes, environmental reforms faced stiff resistance from powerful pro-growth pressure groups like the land developers, highway users, and the Colorado Association of Commerce and Industry. But Vail's example suggests a deeper limiting factor: the kind of environmentalism that gained popular favor in Colorado owed too much to tourism itself to fundamentally challenge tourism's continued growth. Popular environmentalism in the state rested so squarely on the outdoor values that tourist marketing had taught, and esteemed so highly the recreational landscape the tourist industry had fashioned, that even as environmentalists recoiled at the scale and appearance of latter-day tourist development, they could not let go of the values that had given it rise.

The proof was in the landscape. Consider how the map of the high country changed from the late 1970s through the 1980s. Several new wilderness areas appeared: the Flat Tops (which, after years of urging from COSC and others, Congress designated in 1975); Eagles Nest (1976); Hunter-Fryingpan and the Indian Peaks (both in 1978); and the Collegiate Peaks, Mount Massive, and Holy Cross (all in 1980). But a big high-end ski resort appeared in the late 1970s too, butting up against the Holy Cross Wilderness. And not just any resort: it was none other than Beaver Creek, the hugely controversial Vail Associates venture that had arisen out of the Olympics flap and that foes of big recreation had resolved to defeat. Dick Lamm, elected governor in 1974, had all but sworn to kill it. Yet it went ahead. Why? In part because some environmentalists decided it was in fact compatible with their values. Most notably, the Rocky Mountain Center on Environment, practicing its business-collaborative brand of environmentalism, signed on to help Vail Associates integrate wildlife, air, and water protections into its plans for the resort. (ROMCOE's Roger Hansen even ended up representing VA in talks with state officials.) There was also the simple fact that skier demand was exploding, and with Colorado now firmly branded as Ski Country, many thought it was the state's responsibility to meet the need. "Doesn't Gov. Lamm realize," wondered the Vail Trail, voicing a popular view, "that Colorado has an obligation to the rest of the country to provide adequate ski and recreational facilities?" Certainly the Forest Service never questioned this premise, never questioned that skier demand, however meteoric, must be met. And that was the agency's basis for approving Beaver Creek in 1975.[111]

At that point, with the legislature having ruled out serious state-level land-use controls, the Lamm administration had no means to stop the resort. State officials did manage to exact some concessions, getting VA to cap the size of the ski mountain and Eagle County to regulate the density of the new residential development that everyone knew would mushroom in the valley below. For its part, the Sierra Club persuaded the Forest Service to reevaluate the rugged Holy Cross terrain immediately south of Beaver Creek for classification as wilderness.[112] So by 1980, the high country had a new wilderness area—right next to a new corporate ski resort. The jarring juxtaposition epitomized how piecemeal environmentalism was in Colorado and how easily it existed alongside, even accepted, and in some ways even encouraged, the juggernaut of recreational growth.

Environmental sentiment proved equally unwilling, equally unable to stop the ultimate high-country juggernaut—Interstate 70. Though environmentalism did make a difference in how parts of the interstate look. Today if you drive I-70 through the mountains, you can see which stretches were designed before environmentalism gained traction. They are the ones where the raw power of road building is most visible. I-70 begins its ascent to the high country by barreling straight through the ridge called the Dakota Hogback, gouging out a giant, terraced V, laying bare ancient layers of sandstone and shale like a cross-section drawing in a geology textbook. Several miles on, on either side of Idaho Springs, where I-70 shares a narrow valley with Clear Creek, the highway shears entire shoulders off mountains, leaving exposed rock and gravel to glare in the sun, never to revegetate but to crumble slowly (or sometimes suddenly and violently) into the cut. You may notice vertical drill marks scoring a rock face, wire mesh swathing a blasted-away mountainside, or overhanging grass where a slope stripped down to dirt is eroding away, undermining the turf.

This section of I-70, built from 1957 to 1966, is the oldest west of Denver, and to design it, State Highway Department engineers relied on calculations of projected cost, user benefit, and scientific-sounding "priority ratios." There is no evidence that they gave a thought to aesthetic or ecological considerations. In fact they seemed quite cavalier about moving a stream to make room for the road, turning a pretty little canyon into a transcontinental traffic artery, or boring a tunnel straight through a mountain that loomed in the way.[113] Their mentality was typical of their profession at the time. As we have seen, highway engineers of the late 1950s admitted few topographical limits—and as for concerns about beauty, those were a distant afterthought, if they were brooked at all. Any roadside landscaping had to be justified on functional or utilitarian grounds, and the idea of, say, revegetating a road cut to cover the scars was derided as "pansy planting," unworthy of the highway engineer's time and expertise.[114]

But already by the mid-1960s, environmental concerns were prompting small changes in highway design. Some of the clues on I-70 are subtle: slight curves built into the interstate to avoid wiping out historic structures, slopes replanted to cover construction scars, a deer passage built beneath the highway west of Vail.[115] At Georgetown, where I-70 arrived in 1966–67, crews rather clumsily decorated the exit with chunks of native moss rock, an earnest if fumbling effort to address local residents' concerns about the interstate's visual impact. Other clues are more striking, like the vintage-1970 steel box-girder bridge that arcs elegantly over I-70 at Genesee. Positioned at the point where a long incline suddenly gives way to the westbound motorist's first glorious view of the snowy Continental Divide, the bridge was built in one long span, without a center pier, specifically to frame the sweeping mountain panorama—a "welcome to the high country" moment for vacationers, a bit of aesthetic packaging that engineers would not have bothered with just a half-decade earlier.[116]

In the 1970s, engineers moved beyond such window dressing to make environmental concerns a central determinant of highway design. They had to, because by then popular environmental sentiment was taking on the force of law. Most notably, the National Environmental Policy Act (NEPA), enacted in 1970, required the weighing of environmental impacts before any big federal action—like building a stretch of interstate—could forge ahead. So to see how environmentalism at its peak affected Interstate 70, look at segments that were not just built but designed in the 1970s, after NEPA took effect.

Vail Pass is one example. This fourteen-mile meander around the southern tip of the Gore Range—which state highway officials were stuck with after citizen protests thwarted their first choice, the bluntly direct Red Buffalo tunnel route—was upgraded from the old two-lane U.S. 6 roadway to the divided, four-lane interstate highway configuration in the late 1970s. But first it underwent years of impact studies, public comments, partial redesigns, and input from engineers, planners, landscape architects, biologists, ecologists, the Forest Service, the state Division of Wildlife, even architects from the Frank Lloyd Wright Foundation. It was indeed a new era in highway planning—and in this case it yielded a showpiece of environmental design. Unusual for an interstate, Vail Pass's eastbound lanes split from the westbound ones for much of the way, with trees, rocks, and rises screening one direction from the other; the impression is of driving along a two-lane road instead of a superhighway. For many stretches, instead of blasting shelves into mountainsides or wiping out swaths of forest, engineers ran the road atop viaducts, which not only spared unstable slopes, wildlife passages, stream banks, and mature trees, but also gave motorists the very un-interstate-like feeling of floating above the terrain, gliding between the spruces, firs, and pines. All along the route, curves and clearings were scripted with scenic views in mind, and road cuts were contoured, revegetated, and scattered with boulders, stumps, and logs, visually blending the right-of-way into the surrounding landscape—at least that was the intent. Completed in 1978, Vail Pass is not successful in all design respects, but there is no doubt it looks quite different from the rest of I-70.[117]

The ultimate artifact of post-NEPA highway design—not just in Colorado but arguably in the entire nation—comes some fifty miles farther west,

5.8 The blunt-force era of highway design. Stretches of Interstate 70 built in the 1960s reflect a time when highway builders sought to conquer topography more than work around it. A striking example occurs immediately west of Denver, where I-70 plows directly through the Dakota Hogback (ridge), laying bare tilted layers of Mesozoic sandstone and shale. Completed in 1969, the gaping road cut saved about a half-mile's driving distance compared to U.S. 40, which skirted the hogback to the north. Courtesy Sanborn Ltd.

where I-70 wends its way through Glenwood Canyon. Here, the Colorado River has worked its way down through 1.4 billion years of limestone, dolomite, quartzite, granite, gneiss, and shale, cutting a narrow, winding gorge where multicolored cliffs and promontories rise high above the roaring waters. The idea of hammering a superhighway through this canyon was bitterly controversial from the start, and the public passions the project aroused powerfully shaped this stretch of I-70. You can see the results today in Glenwood Canyon's terraced and cantilevered roadways, sinuous segmental bridges, landscaped rest areas, and earth-toned building materials. They are concrete monuments to the popular environmental values of the 1970s.

When the Glenwood Canyon project started, it looked like those values would fall by the wayside. In the late 1960s, crews built the first two miles of I-70 east of Glenwood Springs in the old cut-and-fill manner, dumping rock and earth in the river and leaving hideous scars on the north canyon wall. Moved in part by that horror, a citizens' committee (which Charlie Shumate, the chief highway engineer, had reluctantly convened at the state legislature's request) urged the Highway Department to consider alternatives to the canyon route. Shumate's response? He told the committee to go home. Highway technocrats did not like laypeople second-guessing them. But in a post-NEPA world, Shumate's kind of imperiousness did not fly anymore. NEPA meant that technocrats like him had to weigh environmental concerns and solicit citizen feedback. And *that* meant, despite the initial disdain of many in the highway hierarchy, that the popular interest in protecting Glenwood Canyon's beauty would figure vitally in the design process.[118]

Over the next decade, this interest found voice in a new citizens' advisory committee, impaneled by Governor Lamm in 1976; in a numbing series of draft, final, and revised design proposals and impact studies; in countless public comments and letters to the editor; and in the protests (and sometimes lawsuits) lodged by, among others, COSC, ROMCOE, the Colorado White Water Association, the Sierra Club, the Environmental Defense Fund, and a group called Citizens for a Glenwood Canyon Scenic Corridor, whose "honorary directors" were Stewart Udall and John Denver. All of these groups, and others, spoke out for the scenic splendor of Glenwood Canyon, and together they succeeded in getting the highway builders to go to unprecedented lengths to craft the road with that scenery in mind. That is why this twelve-mile stretch of I-70 was so long in the making (the permit process took until 1976, the design process until 1981, and the construction process another dozen years after that)—and why it ended up looking so different from any other interstate.[119]

But the bottom line is, the interstate still went through. There was never much question that it would—or debate whether it should. Very few Coloradans ever aggressively questioned the need for completing a superhighway all the way through the high country. Even many environmentalists, while pleading Glenwood Canyon's case, took it as a given that a four-lane limited-access artery had to go *somewhere* in the area. As ROMCOE declared, "There will be an Interstate 70 highway through Colorado; the 'no Interstate highway' option is no longer available."[120] The only question was what path it should take.

There was a small minority who challenged this consensus, who dared to ask whether a superhighway was actually necessary, why the existing two-lane road would not suffice. John Denver's group, for one, fought well into the 1980s for the canyon road to remain just two lanes. But for their efforts,

VAIL PASS ENVIRONMENTAL STUDY

INTERSTATE HIGHWAY 70 · COLORADO DIVISION OF HIGHWAYS

5.9 Environmentally sensitive superhighway? Unlike the interstate engineers of the 1950s and 1960s, who prioritized functionality above all else, interstate designers in the 1970s had to weigh aesthetic, ecological, and other environmental considerations, even as the goal of high-speed, high-volume access remained paramount. Here, the designers of Interstate 70 over Vail Pass idealize the four-lane freeway fitting unobtrusively into its scenic setting of lakes, peaks, and trees—a "highway in harmony with its environment," as one engineering journal admiringly put it. Courtesy Colorado Department of Transportation.

they were mercilessly marginalized. Proponents of the canyon interstate cast them as selfish elitists, enemies of the public interest who stood in the way of a safe, modern superhighway that would serve the ever-growing demand for access to high-country recreation. There were mountains of money to be made off that demand, of course, which was why this argument was a favorite among tourist boosters, including local officials, local chambers of commerce, and Club 20 and their long-standing enablers in the Highway Department, the Division of Commerce and Development, and other state agencies. But there was another reason for this particular argument: because it effectively split the opposition to the canyon interstate. To oppose it outright, went the message, was to oppose convenient, nonthreatening, automobile-accessible recreation. Given that this was easily the most popular kind of recreation, most Coloradans, rather than joining the battle to stop the interstate, settled for the more modest goal of making it look nicer.

An environmental movement that might have forced fundamental change—in this case by halting the interstate highway juggernaut, the ultimate driver of big recreation in the high country—instead splintered according to its sympathizers' disparate recreational interests. Interstate 70 in Glenwood Canyon is a marvel of environmental design, yes. But the very fact that there *is* an interstate in the canyon is a monument to the limitations of an environmentalism grounded in recreational consumerism.

AS COLORADO'S MOST FAMOUS MOUNTAIN LOVER, JOHN DENVER OFTEN tried to use his stature to win support for environmental causes, but in the Glenwood Canyon case it did not work so well. At one point he arranged a media event that had him hurling a rock across the river to dramatize that the canyon was too narrow for a four-lane interstate. Embarrassingly, though, as the cameras clicked and whirred, his first several throws fell short, the rocks plunking in the water. Not until his sixth try did he manage to get one all the way across. (Perhaps he should have stuck to his strengths, as in 1977 when, testifying before Congress in support of a wilderness bill, he pulled out his guitar and sang a song about wild places into the witness table microphone. The performance won loud applause. The bill sailed out of committee.)[121]

Truth be told, Denver's effectiveness as an environmental advocate was often hampered by the way he marketed himself. Determined to appeal to middle-America audiences and not seem like, in his words, "a long-haired, obscenity-shouting weirdo," he stuck to mostly cheery songs and apolitical commentary in his concerts. Cautious about angering corporate sponsors, he admitted to pulling his punches during his nature specials on TV. But most importantly, even though he was deeply, personally alarmed by the population growth and development he saw in Colorado, his songs about fun and freedom and self-discovery in the high country fit comfortably with efforts to sell more and more consumers on the region and the lifestyle. In 1973, Denver was horrified to find that "Rocky Mountain High"—a song he had written in part to protest growth—was being used in television commercials for a Colorado Springs land developer. Probably he should not have been surprised: just a few years earlier, he had written an ode to a subdivision ("Starwood in Aspen") of his own.[122]

We could call John Denver a hypocrite—plenty of his critics did. Or we could see in him the same environmental ambivalence that so many Coloradans seemed to feel in the 1970s: on the one hand, a genuine joy in their state's celebrated outdoor lifestyle, on the other, a fear that the celebration was getting out of hand, bringing too many people and too much development to high-country landscapes that seemed too fragile to withstand it. This anxiety brought an outpouring of support for environmental protections—but that meant people were decrying the selling of a product even as they consumed the product for themselves.

And that, fundamentally, was what it came back to: consumerism, and the peculiar ways it attached people to nature and place. Consumers of leisure and lifestyle often invested themselves deeply in the places that had been advertised and packaged for them, which goes a long way toward explaining both the popularity of environmentalism in the 1970s and the personal, passionate stake so many individual Coloradans felt in it. But the kinds of attachments that grew through consumerism tended to militate against environmentalism achieving a truly broad, transformative impact. Instead of inspiring a strong and unified movement, consumerism created many niche ones, corresponding to the niche recreation markets that had sold consumers on the outdoors in the first place. Instead of getting people to care about the total environment in all its ecological interconnectedness, consumerism encouraged them to care more about the particular places where their leisure and lifestyle interests were located. And instead of instilling concern for the underlying and often invisible processes that determined environmental health, quality, or decline, consumerism focused people primarily on surface impressions and appearances, the way a landscape looked and made one feel. In the end, then, consumerism, which did so much to energize popular support for the environmental movement, also saddled it with its most critical limitations. The movement's rise in Colorado, but also its frustration, must be seen as products of recreational consumerism, just as surely as the tourist accommodations and leisure facilities of the high country; just as surely as the area's vacationland or Ski Country image; just as surely as Interstate 70 itself.

CONCLUSION

How Tourism Took Place

THE EERIE ORANGE GLOW THAT LIT THE PREDAWN SKY OVER VAIL MOUN-
tain made sickeningly clear just how fraught an issue big recreation had
become. When morning came on October 18, 1998, the smoke still pouring
from the shambles of Two Elk Lodge made the point clearer still. The massive log, glass, and stone structure, which had commanded a grand prospect
of Vail's back bowls, lay in smoldering ruins; so did a chairlift terminal and
the ski patrol headquarters. Five other buildings had burned too. It took a
few days for someone to claim responsibility. The arson, declared the shad-
owy Earth Liberation Front (ELF), was a protest against Vail Associates'
plans to develop 885 acres of ski terrain off the back bowls, on national forest land believed to be the last Colorado habitat for the Canada lynx. "Vail,
Inc. is already the largest ski operation in North America and now wants to
expand it even further," said ELF in its communiqué. "Putting profits ahead
of Colorado's wildlife will not be tolerated."[1]

In the lead-up to the fires, a lot of people, especially in the Vail Valley
itself, had been angry at Vail Associates (which is what most locals still
called it, even though it had just changed its name to Vail Resorts). Besides
environmentalists—nonviolent environmental groups unconnected to
ELF had been fighting the proposed ski-area expansion in the courts for
months—the company also faced the fury of local workers who accused
VA of neglecting the need for affordable housing; local business owners
who felt threatened by VA's push into retail and restaurants; and other valley residents who felt that VA, recently bought by a New York investment
group, was generally putting moneymaking too far above the needs of the

community. Yet an intriguing thing happened after the Two Elk arson: area residents forgot their anger and rallied around VA. Where ELF saw itself targeting a corporate behemoth, locals on all sides of the debate saw outsiders targeting the entire community. "It's been a catalyst for all of us to take a step back," said a VA spokesman, "and remember that we all need each other." A village shopkeeper and usually vocal critic of VA agreed. The arson, he declared, was "an attack on everybody and on the lifeblood of all in the valley."[2] People might not like what the company was doing to the landscape and the community, but they could not imagine the landscape or community without it. So fundamentally did recreation define this place, so fully was it ingrained into the ways people viewed and valued the local environment, lived there, and made their living, that ELF's ecoterrorism harmed more than just VA property—it posed an existential crisis for the people and their place.

The Two Elk fire sent shock waves throughout the recreational West. It came at a time when the region was already on edge. The 1990s had brought a new blitz of residential and commercial development, an explosion of the galactic pattern more extensive than anything the 1960s or 1970s had ever seen.[3] Certainly not since the 1970s had popular concern over land use been so acute. It seemed like every issue of every western newspaper carried a story about some new subdivision or ski-area expansion tearing into another mountainside, chopping up another expanse of desert, meadow, or sage. Much of the coverage sounded like war reportage: stories of hard-working rural citizens battling desperately to keep hard-playing, citified invaders from seizing the western landscape and stealing its very soul. INVADING THE WEST, blared the headlines. THE WEST AT WAR. CATTLEMEN VS. "GRANOLA BARS." CORRALS VS. COUNTRY CLUBS. YUPPIE SPRAWL. PARADISE PAVED. PARADISE LOST.[4] And every war story told how this "culture clash" was ravaging the land. How more roads meant snarled traffic and smog, polluted runoff and the shattering of the country quiet. How sprawl was cutting into wildlife habitat, ruining views, and making the rural West look more like everyplace else. How the new land uses conspired with newcomers' environmental values to crowd out traditional resource-based livelihoods, while spiraling real estate values pushed residential and recreational space beyond the means of longtime locals, service workers, and even many in the middle class. In an ironic recycling of regional lingo, some invaded communities were termed "ghost towns," where neighborhoods full of seasonal residents' "trophy homes" sat empty much of the year.[5]

Many took to calling this war zone the New West.[6] It was a useful short-hand but misleading too. The New West was not really all that new.[7] As far back as the 1940s and 1950s, western journalists, boosters, and scholars had seen ranches convert to dude operations, an old mining town like Aspen suddenly celebrate Goethe, gravel roads change to asphalt—and they had wondered at a New West apparently in the making. The cover of the federal Works Progress Administration's 1941 guide to Wyoming carried the richly symbolic image of an old-time cowboy watching an airplane fly overhead. Right after the war, Palmer Hoyt's *Denver Post*, self-anointed champion of a modern "Rocky Mountain Empire," began sending writers and photographers for its newly launched *Empire Magazine* to catch "revealing glimpses of the West in transition from old to new." And in the 1950s, California-born historian Earl Pomeroy wrote of pampered tourists and recreationists pouring into the West, "filling up the wide-open spaces" and weakening what made them western.[8]

By calling it the New West, then, we forget that we are not the first to find it. We also risk forgetting the long-wave historical transitions that went into its making. These transitions were certainly at work in Colorado's high country, from the migrations of postwar resettlers and vacationers to the mainstreaming of suburban lifestyle and landscape ideals; from the construction of the U.S. and interstate highway systems to the growing sense by boosters, business leaders, planners, conservation advocates, public land managers, and others that promoting tourism and recreational development could help them achieve their various goals. Americans' embrace of auto-mobility was another essential precondition to the "New West's" formation, and that dated all the way back to the early twentieth century. Other foundations were laid even longer ago, by territorial boosters and railroad promoters; Victorian sportsmen, sightseers, and health-seekers; and not least the artists and writers who pioneered and promulgated Romantic ways of looking at landscapes. They all helped set the stage for the New West of our own time, generations in the past.

But most importantly for our story, the idea of a New West obscures the reality that the dynamics in question are far from just western. They are national, even international, in scale. Yes, they have sometimes played out differently in the West than elsewhere, given the region's distinctive land-scapes, ecologies, and climatic extremes; its mix of cultures and peoples and landownership patterns; and its peculiar place in the national imagination. But in the boom-boom 1990s, as the war stories made it sound like the entire rural West was under siege, surprisingly similar dispatches were pouring in from rural areas in almost every other section of America, from northern Michigan to central Florida, Iowa to upstate New York, the Texas hill country to coastal Maine. On South Carolina's Sea Islands, descendants of slaves took seminars in zoning law, land-use planning, and economic development so they could protect their Gullah culture and landscape against resort development by whites. On Minnesota's Lake Superior North Shore, locals lamented that Twin Citians were rushing in for quick golf, kayak, or biking weekends and shunning the older, slower tradition of loafing at lakeside cabins for longer stays. Vermonters drew national attention for struggling to keep Wal-Mart out of their state, for fear that big-box sprawl would destroy the iconic Vermont countryside of open farmland and tightly clustered church-and-commons villages. And in Key West, a longtime resident and former local official went so far as to strap on dynamite and plant himself in the middle of a construction site, hoping to stop a townhouse complex from filling one of the island's last scraps of open space.[9]

What did all these vignettes have in common with each other and with similar stories coming out of the so-called New West? Each involved a landscape so heavily layered with tourist infrastructure and tourist imagery that for many people it was no longer possible to see the setting through a different lens. The ways the place had been packaged dominated their sense of the place and their personal attachment to it. That is why so many conflicts centered on threats to easy recreational access, scenic vistas, a small-town atmosphere, a sense of stepping back in time, or a slow pace of life. It is not that all of these qualities were mere inventions of tourist promoters. It is more that these qualities' persistent promotion helped cement them in the popular imagination of a place, so that many people came to view and value a place primarily in those terms and had a hard time imagining or accepting it in any other way.

Even that is not the whole picture, though. In the broadest terms, stories of change and conflict in settings like the Colorado high country are really stories of how the triumph of consumerism has revolutionized the culture of place. After all, vacationlands are far from the only settings that are packaged and promoted to us as consumers. There are also suburban and exurban housing developments of seemingly endless variety: gated, golf course, and retirement communities; New Urbanist projects; New Towns; and many more. There are rehabilitated and gentrified neighborhoods in the older parts of our cities. There are small towns with their own logos, slogans, and promotional websites. There are entire regions that did not exist in the popular consciousness until professional marketers dreamed up brand names and identities for them. And there are office parks, indus- trial parks, theme parks, research parks, "transit villages," exposition cen- ters, "lifestyle centers," college campuses, historic districts, arts districts, shopping districts, sports complexes, and "festival marketplaces." Branded, themed, and packaged places are now all around us, and they powerfully influence not just where we choose to go on vacation but also where we choose to shop, meet fellow singles, raise our kids, spend our older years, search for work, celebrate special occasions, go to school, go to eat, spend a night out, locate our businesses, convene with colleagues, and on and on and on. We have gotten in the habit of shopping for such places much as consumer culture has ingrained it in us to shop for other goods: that is, we seek out not just—or not necessarily—the places that are the most practical but the ones that seem the best fit for our personalities, aesthetic sensibili- ties, ideals, and aspirations, and maybe also for the reputations we hope to cultivate and the self-images we want to project.

The places we choose for vacation might be the baldest examples of all, because in their case our choice is completely and consciously about the place itself and the personal experience we expect to have there. To explore the history of vacation spots and vacationlands is therefore to confront head-on the question of how consumerism has played out on the land. It throws into the starkest possible relief how consumerism spawned a new economy of place making and encouraged in us new ways of connecting to our surroundings, our environment, and our natural and physical world. This is the key lesson to be learned from our historical look at the high country: that place making yielded far more than tourist traffic and tourist dollars—it helped create a new kind of environmental consciousness. For a great many consumers, nature came to stand for pleasure and personal ful- fillment, and landscapes took on meaning according to the aesthetic, atmo- spheric, and recreational qualities they offered. Places became products for people to bond with and define themselves by, like the cars they drove, the fashions they wore, and the houses they made home.

Yet it is too simple to call these the new environmental values. For one thing, not all Americans had equal access to the packaged places and expe- riences that gave rise to these values. Yes, one can certainly encounter the increasingly ubiquitous place-marketing imagery, and even come to care about some faraway vacationland as a result, without actually having the means to vacation there. But it would be foolish to forget that recreation-minded environmental values did not apply equally to all classes of American society—that in fact they could have starkly exclusionary connotations and consequences. Even among those who *were* recreational consumers, to talk of new environmental values is still problematic because it implies that all such consumers were learning to value the environment the same way. In fact outdoor leisure was and is a kaleidoscope of niche markets, demographics and psychographics, shifting trends and tastes. Each niche fixed on its own set of environmental qualities; each connoted a different way of relating to nature. A group like the Colorado Open Space Council, which struggled to bridge such differences, knew all too well that there was no one set of environmental values, even among those who might share a generally recreation-centered way of knowing and loving nature.

There is another reason it is overly simple to talk of place packaging bringing about new environmental values: because it implies that people learned to apply the same new values consistently across the entire environment. In fact, the opposite was true. Place packaging taught consumers to relate to different bits of land and nature in radically different ways, to care about them to radically different degrees—indeed, this has turned out to be one of consumerism's most critical environmental legacies. It happened that way because place packaging, by its very nature, unfolded unevenly across the earth. It parcelized nature and the land, picking out some settings to package and promote while ignoring others. And that is really how most postwar people learned to love "the environment." They bonded with places they had personally bought into but not so much with ones they had not—and even less with the settings, the parts of the world or of nature that went unpackaged altogether. (Even the species: the conservationists who humanized cetaceans and made a catchphrase out of "Save the Whales" in the 1970s understood this extraordinarily well.) The resulting environmental consciousness focused narrowly and intensely on certain places and pieces but paid too little attention to the wider web of connections that tied one piece to another and wove them all together into an integrated environmental whole. The consumer's way of valuing nature and place got squarely in the way of consumers developing an ethic of ecological interdependence.

This is a worrisome prospect for anyone convinced that such an ethic is needed to make real, broad-based environmental progress. Yet there is still this: the consumer's way of valuing nature and place did get a great many Americans to *care*. The practice of shopping for places that met one's

6.1 Place as consumer product. Rarely do developers or promoters admit it so openly as in this 1970 magazine ad, but the practice of packaging and marketing landscapes as consumer goods has become ubiquitous—with profound consequences for the ways we relate to nature, environment, and place. Courtesy Western Sugar Cooperative.

dreams and matched one's personality gave people a greater personal stake in environmental quality and protection than all but a very few of them had ever had before. We might wish that they cared about more than just their own personal pieces of the earth. But is there not something to be said for the fact that they cared at all? Some might scorn their consumerism as shallow or self-centered. But with consumerism so thoroughly embedded in our culture, our society, the way we understand ourselves and our relations with others, even our sense of such things as faith and health and love—is it possible to forge a bond with *anything* anymore, without resorting to consumerism, at least in part? The history of land and leisure in the high country certainly makes one wonder, can popular environmental concern rooted in consumerism ever be truly ecological? But it equally begs the question, could environmental concern *not* rooted in consumerism ever be truly popular?

Whatever our suspicions, it is also worth remembering that everything happens in environmental context, and as environmental context changes, it can rock the most basic rules of the game. At this writing, it is easy to accept that the spread of recreational development, recreational values, and recreational consumers into ever more rural areas is the "new normal" for regions like the American West. But will it be so for long? Anyone who assumes so should remember that recreation's remarkable growth relied on a very specific set of environmental conditions that prevailed in the postwar period. What happens if those conditions change? What do we make of the fact that many of them already *are* changing? We know, for example, that fossil fuels are becoming more difficult and expensive to extract. What will befall our freedom to drive or fly seemingly anywhere we want to live, work, or play when the era of cheap oil comes to an end? We know that our spreading recreational-residential development has cut deeply into wildlife habitat and might be affecting animal behavior. What will happen if more frequent and perhaps more violent encounters with species like bears and mountain lions make the outdoor lifestyle seem less risk-free and benign?[10] There is mounting evidence that electronic and other technologies are fundamentally changing the landscapes of child's play from nature-based to virtual. Will children with bodies and brains molded by the new playscapes show any grown-up interest in wilderness, national forests and parks, wildlife preserves, or even mass-use recreation areas?[11] Perhaps most basically, we know the world is warming and weather patterns changing. How will the vacation lifestyles and vacationlands that are popular today fare if faced with a future of droughts and water shortages, low snowfall, fiercer storms, rising sea levels, withering heat waves, out-of-control insect infestations, radical changes in flora and fauna, or more frequent and catastrophic wildfires?[12]

This is not to suggest that amid such changes recreation is the only thing at stake—or that it is remotely the most important thing at stake. But it is to ask: If environmental change renders our vacationlands or outdoor living patterns less desirable or recognizable, will it also render obsolete the environmental sensibilities those landscapes helped instill? Will consumerism still condition how people relate to nature and place? If it does, how well will it inspire and guide us in facing the challenges of a new environmental age? And if it does not, what new inspiration and guide might we find?

NOTES

INTRODUCTION: SEEING LIKE A TOURIST

1. Colorado State Advertising and Publicity Committee, ad in *Aspen Times*, May 24, 1956, 2.

2. Hafen and Hafen, *Our State*, esp. chap. 1 (textbook quotation p. 25); T. K. Kelley, *Living in Colorado*, esp. chaps. 9 and 10; Athearn and Ubbelohde, *Centennial Colorado*; Bancroft, *Colorful Colorado*.

3. The "Colorado" entry in the *Book of the Year*, an annual supplement to the *Encyclopædia Britannica*, was written by Pearl Anoe, feature writer for the state publicity office, every year from 1948 to 1952, and by Hal Haney, assistant state advertising and publicity director, from 1954 to 1963. From 1941 to 1946, the director of the State Planning Commission wrote the entry, the commission being in charge of publicity before the legislature established the separate Advertising and Publicity Committee. See Walter Yust, letters to Hal Haney, 1953–56, FFs 1 and 2, Box 1, Hal Haney Papers. By the early 1960s, the annual *Colorado Year Book*, the definitive reference for information about Colorado government, demographics, resources, counties and towns, business, and the like, had also adopted a much more vivid, promotional tone than in the past, in part because some of its material was submitted by local chambers of commerce (Colorado State Planning Division, *Colorado Year Book, 1962–1964*, iv).

4. In Gallup polls in 1948, 1950, and 1956, Colorado ranked third, fourth, and third as the state where respondents would most like to take a summer vacation. It ranked a bit lower for winter trips (warm-weather states being the most sought-after winter destinations), but still finished sixth in that category in 1954, eighth in 1955, and seventh in 1956. Occasionally Gallup also surveyed Americans' scenic preferences: in 1948, respondents named Colorado the second "most scenic" state, and in 1956 Colorado ranked as the second "most beautiful" state. Gallup polls no. 414T (March 5–10, 1948), questions 4b and 4c; no. 456 (June 4–9, 1950), question 1a; no. 541 (December 31, 1954–January 5, 1955), question 1; no. 557 (December 6, 1955), question 14c; no. 575 (November 20, 1956), questions 55a and 56b; all data on Gallup Brain website, www.institution.gallup.com (accessed March 12, 2009).

5. The phrase "republic of consumers" is inspired by L. Cohen, *Consumers' Republic*.

6. See World Tourism Organization, *Resolutions of International Conference on Travel and Tourism*. Textbooks encourage the next generation of tourism professionals to

embrace these same rigid definitions; see, for example, Nickerson, *Foundations of Tourism*, 2–3.

7. At least since the 1980s, geographers of leisure have recognized that tourism and recreation could not be neatly separated, that they had similar social and spatial effects and should be subjected to similar theoretical analyses. See, for instance, Jansen-Verbeke and Dietvorst, "Leisure, Recreation, Tourism: A Geographic View on Integration"; and Carr, "Tourism-Leisure Behavioural Continuum." Yet geographers, like policy makers, still tend to define tourism in ways that stress its distinctiveness from other kinds of recreation and leisure. See, for example, Hall and Page, *Geography of Tourism and Recreation*. The authors note the growing realization that tourism, leisure, and recreation are overlapping categories (3–5), but in the next chapter (58–61), they propose structural, technical definitions of tourism that differentiate it from other types of leisure, again based on the notion that tourists are temporary visitors and seek leisure in places spatially separated from where they ordinarily live and work.

8. Rugh, in *Are We There Yet?*, comes to a similar conclusion, arguing that Americans went on family vacations to realize everyday aspirations: strengthening family bonds, cementing middle-class status, and forging a stronger sense of American citizenship.

9. For an interesting effort to delineate the "industry," see S. L. J. Smith, "Tourism Product."

10. In this sense, vacationlands like Colorado's arguably pioneered the phenomenon that is at the heart of today's "New West School" of thinking. The New West School is geographer William R. Travis's name for a cohort of economists, geographers, demographers, and others who argue that footloose individuals and companies, who choose their locations largely on the basis of quality of life and environmental factors, instead of traditional considerations like nearness to resources, have increasingly come to drive the West's economic growth. See Travis, *New Geographies of the American West*, 22–32, 44–67, 137–39; Gober, McHugh, and Leclerc, "Job-Rich but Housing-Poor"; Snepenger, Johnson, and Rasker, "Travel-Stimulated Entrepreneurial Migration"; Power, *Lost Landscapes and Failed Economies*; Nelson and Beyers, "Using Economic Base Models to Explain New Trends in Rural Income"; Rudzitis, "Amenities Increasingly Draw People to the American West"; Vias, "Jobs Follow People in the Rural Rocky Mountain West"; Jobes, *Moving Nearer to Heaven*; Beyers and Nelson, "Contemporary Development Forces in the Nonmetropolitan West"; Rasker, "Your Next Job Will Be in Services"; and Power and Barrett, *Post-Cowboy Economics*.

11. Scholarship on the social and cultural consequences of tourism, already prodigious, continues to mushroom. Very much ahead of its time, Earl Pomeroy's 1957 *In Search of the Golden West* argued that efforts to serve and meet the expectations of eastern tourists ended up transforming the West and westerners themselves. More recent works build on Pomeroy, for example, Hal Rothman's study of tourism's colonial tendencies, *Devil's Bargains*. Rothman argues for a recurring pattern in which residents of western towns lost political and economic power when tourist-industry capitalists and corporations arrived and, more insidiously, lost control of their local cultures and community identities to "neonatives" who settled seasonally or permanently in tourist towns and claimed them as their own. Other insightful books on tourism's social and cultural

effects include Schwartz, *Pleasure Island*; Blackford, *Fragile Paradise*; B. Christensen, *Red Lodge and the Mythic West*; Souther, *New Orleans on Parade*; Halseth, *Cottage Country in Transition*; Norris, *Discovered Country*; and Wrobel and Long, *Seeing and Being Seen*. Anthropologists have a longer history than historians of studying these issues; see V. L. Smith, *Hosts and Guests*; and D. Nash, "Tourism as an Anthropological Subject," a useful overview of the early anthropological work on tourism. Literary critics have taken up these matters too; see, for example, Pratt, *Imperial Eyes*.

12. This last insight borrows from Dean MacCannell, perhaps the most thoughtful and influential critic of modern tourism. In *The Tourist*, he argued that the experience of tourism not only influenced participants' attitudes but figured centrally in the emergence of modern subjectivity. Ellen Furlough has argued persuasively that tourism is an important means by which consumers construct personal and collective identities. See her "Making Mass Vacations"; and Baranowski and Furlough, *Being Elsewhere*. Cocks, *Doing the Town*, shows how tourists' visits to cities helped them rethink their gender and class identities at the close of the Victorian era.

13. Roland Marchand grapples with this question—to what degree can advertising be said to reflect the popular attitudes and values of its time?—in the introduction to *Advertising the American Dream*. My own claims lean heavily on his thoughtful analysis.

14. On elite travel to picturesque settings in the early nineteenth century, see Huth, *Nature and the American*, esp. chaps. 5–9; McKinsey, *Niagara Falls: Icon of the American Sublime*; Sears, *Sacred Places*; D. Brown, *Inventing New England*, esp. chap. 2; Purchase, *Out of Nowhere*; and Conron, *American Picturesque*, xix, 10–12. Itineraries that collected picturesque settings were the early republican counterpart to the classic British "grand tour," which had young Englishmen touring Europe to develop their cultural literacy and sense of British identity; on this connection, see Withey, *Grand Tours and Cook's Tours*, chaps. 1–4. For an example of early nineteenth-century travelers visiting landscapes that did *not* live up to standards of the picturesque, see Dunlop, *Sixty Miles from Contentment*, chap. 3.

15. On the pursuit of scenery in the nineteenth-century West, see Pomeroy, *In Search of the Golden West*, chap. 2; and Hyde, *American Vision*. Another useful treatment is Sears, *Sacred Places*, chaps. 6–7. On the emergence of middle-class tourism and its nationalistic underpinnings, the definitive treatment is Shaffer, *See America First*. Pomeroy, *In Search of the Golden West*, chap. 4, is useful here too. On the culture of middle-class tourism in the nineteenth and early twentieth centuries, see Aron's indispensable *Working at Play*. While there was also a strong nineteenth-century tradition of vacationing for personal benefit—such as health seeking at mineral spas, self-improvement at temperance resorts, and the Romantic notion of finding spiritual uplift in God's natural creation—even these activities had overtones of the individual meeting some collective moral or cultural standard.

16. On the rise of consumerism in the United States, see Cross, *All-Consuming Century*; Lears, "From Salvation to Self-Realization"; Marchand, *Advertising the American Dream*; Strasser, *Satisfaction Guaranteed*; Leach, *Land of Desire*; Lears, *Fables of Abundance*; Glickman, *Consumer Society in American History*; Hine, *I Want That!*; and Susan Strasser's aptly titled *Commodifying Everything*, esp. the opening essays by Strasser and

Jean-Christophe Agnew. On links between leisure and consumerism, see Butsch, *For Fun and Profit*. For the post–World War II period, see L. Cohen, *Consumers' Republic*.

17. This contention builds on Jennifer Price's argument in *Flight Maps*: that consumer culture tends to vest natural things with meanings that have almost nothing to do with the natural things themselves and everything to do with consumers' cultural obsessions and personal anxieties. On how natural things have been refracted through the lens of consumerism, see S. G. Davis, *Spectacular Nature*; Mitman, *Reel Nature*; Dunaway, *Natural Visions*, esp. chap. 5; and Rollins, "Reflections on a Spare Tire."

18. Ellen Furlough has made a similar argument about the idealism of tourism; see esp. "Making Mass Vacations." See also Cross, *All-Consuming Century*; Campbell, "Consuming Goods and the Good of Consuming"; and Belk, Wallendorf, and Sherry, "The Sacred and the Profane in Consumer Behavior."

19. On the allure of, and concomitant boom in, the West and the so-called Sunbelt after World War II, see Pomeroy, *Pacific Slope*; G. D. Nash, *American West in the Twentieth Century*; R. G. Athearn, *Mythic West in Twentieth-Century America*; Abbott, "Metropolitan Region"; Mohl, *Searching for the Sunbelt*; Schulman, *From Cotton Belt to Sunbelt*; Findlay, *Magic Lands*; Abbott, *Metropolitan Frontier*; Moore, *To the Golden Cities*; Culver, *Frontier of Leisure*; C. Davis, "From Oasis to Metropolis"; Faragher, "Bungalow and Ranch House"; May, *Golden State, Golden Youth*; Cullen, *American Dream*, esp. chap. 6; and Mormino, *Land of Sunshine, State of Dreams*. Also relevant are Kevin Starr's books on the "California dream": see esp. *Americans and the California Dream, 1850–1915*; *Inventing the Dream*; *Material Dreams*; *Embattled Dreams*; and *Golden Dreams*.

20. Outside of Colorado, the term "high country" is especially well entrenched in Arizona, where it refers to eastern and northern parts of the state above the Mogollon Rim. Outside the West, the term might be most common in North Carolina, where it describes that state's westernmost reaches, in the Appalachians. A similar phrase in French, *pays d'en haut*, refers not to altitude but to remoteness: historically, it applied to the fur-trading interior of North America, while now it is heard in reference to lightly populated northwestern Quebec.

21. Bowles, *Switzerland of America*. See also B. Taylor, *Colorado: A Summer Trip*. For the story of Byers and Bierstadt's outing, which yielded one of the artist's most famous paintings (*Storm in the Rocky Mountains—Mount Rosalie*), see Byers's retelling in "Bierstadt's Visit to Colorado"; and Trenton and Hassrick, *Rocky Mountains: A Vision for Artists in the Nineteenth Century*, 141–44. The painting, reproduced on pp. 136–37, shows one of the Chicago Lakes, near Idaho Springs, with Mount Rosalie in the distance, soaring above the menacing thunderheads. Bierstadt named the mountain after a friend's wife, whom he later stole away and married. The peak, next to the more famous Mount Evans, was later renamed Mount Bierstadt. On the ways that visual images of the western landscape shaped people's preconceptions of the region, see Hyde, "Cultural Filters," 366–73; and Sandweiss, *Print the Legend*, chaps. 3–5.

22. Pomeroy, *In Search of the Golden West*, esp. 131–32.

23. On nineteenth-century tourism in Manitou and Colorado Springs, and the ways it reflected elite leisure tastes, see Hyde, *American Vision*, 148–54, 159–61, 174–83; Pomeroy, *In Search of the Golden West*, 20–21; and Wyckoff, *Creating Colorado*, 135–43. Two helpful

local histories are Cunningham, *Manitou, Saratoga of the West*; and Sprague, *Newport in the Rockies*. These last two titles explicitly tie the Pikes Peak resorts to their fashionable forebears in the East.

24. W. T. Cox, *Fearsome Creatures*, 20–21; Wyman, *Mythical Creatures*, 80–81.

25. Gillette, *Idaho Springs*, 151–57; G. Morgan, *Rails around the Loop*, 21–25.

26. On western spas, see Hyde, *American Vision*, chap. 4. On the eastern prototypes the western resorts were emulating, see Sterngass, *First Resorts*; Corbett, *Making of American Resorts*; and Boyer Lewis, *Ladies and Gentlemen on Display*. On these spas' middle-class counterparts, see Aron, *Working at Play*, chap. 3.

27. J. Nelson, *Glenwood Springs*, chaps. 6–8; Urquhart, *Spa in the Mountains*, parts 1–2.

28. Here, I borrow from the insights of Anne Hyde and John Sears. Sears argues that tourist spots like Niagara Falls became "sacred places" in the pantheon of nineteenth-century American nationalism: icons of the young nation's distinctiveness but also, because they lived up to European standards of scenic beauty, conferrers of cultural legitimacy. Hyde too explains how Victorian Americans applied European standards to their own nation's landscapes (for instance, exalting the Rockies as the American version of the Swiss Alps), and she describes how they created islands of Europeanness (like Colorado Springs) so the West would seem as culturally advanced as Europe. But Hyde finds that Americans grappling with the strange and sometimes terrifying landscapes of the West (especially deserts and canyonlands) had to come up with new aesthetic standards and descriptive strategies, planting the seeds of an independent American culture. Sears, *Sacred Places*; Hyde, *American Vision*.

29. This point borrows from Ogden, "From Spatial to Aesthetic Distance in the Eighteenth Century."

30. On the western tourist's view from the railroad-coach window, see Hyde, *American Vision*, 107–46; T. G. Andrews, "'Made by Toile?,'" 848–50; and Schivelbusch, *Railway Journey*, 64–66.

31. J. Nelson, *Glenwood Springs*, 129–32; D. A. Smith, "'The Bulliest Time,'" 13–15. See also T. G. Andrews, "'Made by Toile?,'" 853–54. Roosevelt's account of the hunt appeared in *Scribner's Magazine* and then in *Outdoor Pastimes of an American Hunter*, 68–99. On changing views of nature and changing tastes in outdoor leisure around the turn of the century, see Schmitt, *Back to Nature*; and R. F. Nash, *Wilderness and the American Mind*, chap. 9. Higham, "Reorientation of American Culture in the 1890s," and Lears, *No Place of Grace*, place these changing tastes in the broader context of "antimodernism," as Lears calls it.

32. The idea that skiing could not only strengthen the body but also build character and purify the soul dated back to nineteenth-century Scandinavian pioneers of *ski-idræt* (skisport). The idea resonated with the recreational sensibilities of Americans like Roosevelt—which, according to John Allen, was a major reason why skiing began to catch on in the United States just after the turn of the century. See E. J. B. Allen, *From Skisport to Skiing*, esp. 5, 10–12, 48–49; and E. J. B. Allen, *Culture and Sport of Skiing*, 41–42. Allen argues that by the 1920s and 1930s American ski culture increasingly forsook the old idea of self-improvement through skiing, substituting a new emphasis on competitive speed (in racing) and distance (in jumping). In turn, this evolved into a fixation on fashion and glamour.

33. Hafen, "The Coming of the Automobile and Improved Roads to Colorado," 8, 10–16; Noel, "Paving the Way to Colorado," 43; Wyckoff, *Creating Colorado*, 85–87. On early twentieth-century automobile tourism and links to road building, see Shaffer, *See America First*, esp. 130–69; and Sutter, *Driven Wild*, esp. 19–53.

34. Kingery, *Colorado Mountain Club*, 11, 21–23, 28–30, 51–53, 65, 89, 111.

35. A. G. Coleman, *Ski Style*, 34–40, 56–59; Fay, *History of Skiing in Colorado*, 31–41; Kingery, *Colorado Mountain Club*, 96–7, 103–7.

36. Noel, "Paving the Way to Colorado"; Bradley, "Origin of the Denver Mountain Parks System"; W. H. Wilson, *City Beautiful Movement*, 184–87; W. H. Wilson, "New Wine in Old Bottles"; Wyckoff, *Creating Colorado*, 85.

37. Buchholtz, *Rocky Mountain National Park*, chap. 5; Wyckoff, *Creating Colorado*, 85–86, 98–99; Kingery, *Colorado Mountain Club*, 71.

38. Arthur H. Carhart, *Report on Preliminary Study of the Mount Evans Recreation Area, Pike National Forest, Colorado* (June 1919), in FF "Reports: Recreation Plan, Mount Evans Area [Preliminary Report]: 1919," Box 20, Arthur Hawthorne Carhart Papers. On Carhart's work for the Forest Service, see Wolf, *Arthur Carhart*, chaps. 2–7; and Baldwin, *Quiet Revolution*, 17–79, 100–24.

39. Jim Wier, "In the Beginning," in Miller and Wier, "A Mountain, a Dream, a Train—Winter Park," 3–24; Jean Miller, "The Early Birds," and Jim Wier, "The Winter Park Ski Area," in Miller and Wier, "1859–1950 Skiing in Middle Park," 25–33; Patterson and Forrest, *Ski Train*; Fay, *History of Skiing in Colorado*, 35–44; A. G. Coleman, *Ski Style*, 91–93.

40. Young, *Opera in Central City*, 6–21; Sprague et al., *Enchanted Central City*; Bancroft, *Gulch of Gold*, 334–51; Bancroft, *Historic Central City*, 27–36.

41. See especially the "ghost town" guidebooks produced by artist and writer Muriel Sibell Wolle in the 1930s, *Ghost Cities of Colorado* and *Cloud Cities of Colorado*; and the Colorado Writers' Program's 1941 opus *Colorado: A Guide to the Highest State*, which comprised a treasure trove of local history and folklore. The Writers' Program also compiled mining-camp lore in *Ghost Towns of Colorado*. On the Federal Writers' Project's efforts to preserve and celebrate local and regional folklore, history, and culture, see Hirsch, *Portrait of America*; and Schulten, "How to See Colorado."

42. Fay, *History of Skiing in Colorado*, 21–29, 44–45, 49–55; A. G. Coleman, *Ski Style*, 32–40, 73–74, 77–81, 94–97; Whiteside, *Colorado: A Sports History*, 91–105; Jim Wier, "Skiing at Hot Sulphur Springs," and Jean Miller, "Skiing at Grand Lake," in Miller and Wier, "1859–1950 Skiing in Middle Park," 13–24; Barlow-Perez, *History of Aspen*, 37–43.

43. The literature on the Tenth Mountain Division is voluminous. On the time the trainees spent in Colorado, their hijinks in nearby towns, and their interactions with the high-country environment, see J. A. Benson, "Skiing at Camp Hale"; Shelton, *Climb to Conquer*, chaps. 3–6; Leich, *Tales of the 10th*, 43–72; Dusenbery, *Ski the High Trail*; Coquoz, *Invisible Men on Skis*; Cassidy, *Off Limits*; A. G. Coleman, *Ski Style*, 97–107; Whiteside, *Colorado: A Sports History*, 105–10; Fay, *History of Skiing in Colorado*, 57–65; and Barlow-Perez, *History of Aspen*, 43–46.

44. On the practice of branding places, see Hankinson, "Relational Network Brands"; Blain, Levy, and Ritchie, "Destination Branding"; and Cai, "Cooperative Branding for Rural Destinations."

45. On the idea of consumers developing personal bonds or "relationships" with brands and branded goods, including branded places, see Olins, *On Brand*; Power and Hauge, "No Man's Brand"; Hankinson, "Relational Network Brands," 110–11; and Sirgy and Su, "Destination Image, Self-Congruity, and Travel Behavior."

46. Since place is a core concept for geographers, there is a bewilderingly large body of literature on it. Cresswell's *Place: A Short Introduction* is an excellent guide. I have also found Yi-Fu Tuan's ruminations very useful: see "Space and Place: Humanistic Perspective"; *Topophilia*; and *Space and Place: The Perspective of Experience*. Historical geographers have a long, rich history of studying place making. A thought-provoking survey of the field is Baker, *Geography and History*; and a good, brief (if now outdated) retrospective is Dennis, "History, Geography, and Historical Geography." On place making as an exercise of power, again there is an overwhelming literature, but one might start with Lefebvre, *Production of Space*; Pred, "Place as Historically Contingent Process"; and D. Harvey, *Justice, Nature, and the Geography of Difference*.

47. Then again, this is only surprising if we accept the dismissive view of tourists as superficial "collectors of gazes." Julia Harrison, in probably the most thoughtful effort to discern the true motivations of tourists in our own time, finds that they usually choose their destinations in hopes of being emotionally moved, of finding personal resonance and meaning on a deeper symbolic, not just surface, level; see J. Harrison, *Being a Tourist*, 97–99, 104, 131–23 (quotation p. 99). Rudy Koshar comes to essentially the same conclusion; see *German Travel Cultures*, x, 5, 12, 18. If this is true of many or most tourists, we should not be shocked that some of them would forge genuine, lasting, even life-changing bonds with the temporary or permanent places of their leisure.

48. This insight ties in to an emerging body of scholarship on environmental identity, or the ways our interactions with landscapes and the natural world shape our senses of self, in turn influencing how we respond to environmental issues. An excellent introduction to this scholarship is Clayton and Opotow, *Identity and the Natural Environment*. Also relevant here are political scientists' efforts to understand the political and policy implications of different environmental cultures, or of different groups' ways of relating to nature. See, for example, Fischer and Hajer, *Living with Nature*. See also Greider and Garkovich, "Landscapes: The Social Construction of Nature and the Environment."

CHAPTER I. SELLING THE SCENE

1. This account of the Tenth Recon's march on Aspen is derived from Pfeifer, *Nice Goin'*, 111; O'Rear and O'Rear, *Aspen Story*, 68–69; and Bowen, *Book of American Skiing*, 148–50.

2. Pfeifer, *Nice Goin'*, 111. See also Bowen, *Book of American Skiing*, 149–51.

3. Friedl Pfeifer, interview by Annie Gilbert, Aspen, July 21, 1994, transcript at the Aspen Historical Society (hereafter AHS).

4. The idea that World War II marked a watershed for the West, reviving and diversifying the regional economy and sparking a new westward rush, is most closely associated with Gerald Nash. See his *American West Transformed*; *Federal Landscape*; and *American West in the Twentieth Century*, esp. 191–209, 229–43. See also Pomeroy, *Pacific Slope*, 297–303; and Malone and Etulain, *American West: A Twentieth-Century History*,

107–15, 219–24. For a revision of Nash's thesis, see Lotchin, *Fortress California*; for a rejection, see Rhode, "Nash Thesis Revisited."

5. Pfeifer, *Nice Goin'*, 1–129 (quotation p. 129).

6. The three men, respectively, were Billy Fiske, Ted Ryan, and T. J. Flynn. They formed the Highland-Bavarian Corporation in 1936, bought land at the base of Mount Hayden, around the old ghost town of Ashcroft, and began planning an Alpine-style ski village there. Highland-Bavarian got a permit from the Forest Service, favorable press coverage, excited interest from the Colorado Mountain Club and other ski groups, and even a bond issue from the state legislature for construction of an aerial tram. But all that ever got built was a lodge; the venture was slow to raise capital and then got derailed for good by World War II. Convery, "Ski Heil!"; Paul Hauk, "Hayden Peak," in *Ski Area Chronologies, White River National Forest*, Ring Binder 3, Box 1, Paul I. Hauk Papers, Denver Public Library; Barlow-Perez, *History of Aspen*, 37–43; "Aspen Developing into Leading Winter Resort," *Rocky Mountain News*, December 19, 1937, sec. 3, 6; Louisa Ward, "Aspen Antics," *Trail and Timberline*, no. 221 (March 1937): 31, 35.

7. Barlow-Perez, *History of Aspen*, 37–43; A. G. Coleman, *Ski Style*, 55, 74, 77–78, 97; Fay, *History of Skiing in Colorado*, 49–51; Bowen, *Book of American Skiing*, 151; "Ski Heil to Aspen," *Trail and Timberline*, no. 232 (March 1938): 31.

8. On the idea of a skiing community, see Pfeifer, interview by Gilbert, AHS; Pfeifer, *Nice Goin'*, 115; and Barlow-Perez, *History of Aspen*, 44. On the idea that skiing could strengthen character and spirit along with the body, see note 32 in the introduction to this book. On the revival of St. Anton, see Pfeifer, *Nice Goin'*, 4–6, 10, 13–14, 16, 19, 23. On the cult of the Arlberg technique, see A. G. Coleman, *Ski Style*, 43–50; E. J. B. Allen, *From Skisport to Skiing*, 96–98; Fry, *Story of Modern Skiing*; and Pfeifer, *Nice Goin'*, 19.

9. Elizabeth Oblock Sinclair, interview by Annie Gilbert, Aspen, July 26, 1994, transcript at AHS; Steve Knowlton, interview by Gilbert, Denver, October 19, 1994, transcript at AHS; John Litchfield, interview by Gilbert, Denver, September 29, 1994, transcript at AHS; Barlow-Perez, *History of Aspen*, 43; Pfeifer, *Nice Goin'*, 111–14; O'Rear and O'Rear, *Aspen Story*, 67–68. On the camaraderie of American ski culture at the time, see E. J. B. Allen, *From Skisport to Skiing*, 75, 81–84, 107, 117–18. On Pfeifer's sense that Aspenites would support his plans for ski development, see Pfeifer, *Nice Goin'*, 115.

10. Pfeifer, *Nice Goin'*, 113, 115; Barlow-Perez, *History of Aspen*, 44; Bancroft, *Famous Aspen*, 40–41; City of Aspen, City Council, minutes, June 3, 1944 (quotation). Caroline Bancroft, author of many popular booklets on Colorado history, purports to quote what Pfeifer said to the council: "I'm coming back after the war—this town's going to be my home. I want to start a ski school here and I'll give the local children free lessons so that we can develop a real skiing community. People will be interested in expanding commercial possibilities, and we'll get enough money to build more adequate tows and lifts." Bancroft, *Famous Aspen*, 41. Historians Sally Barlow-Perez and James Sloan Allen both repeat this quotation in their books, and it does largely fit with the gist of Pfeifer's plans. However, we have no evidence that Pfeifer actually said this, certainly not in the city council minutes. Bancroft provides no citation for Pfeifer's words, and given her reputation as a creative embellisher of Colorado history (and admitted user of invented quotations), it seems likely that she made them up. See M. G. Riley, "Sin, Gin, and Jasmine."

11. Pfeifer, *Nice Goin'*, 111, 113 (quotation), 114–15.

12. Pfeifer, *Nice Goin'*, 129–30, 136; William V. Hodges Jr. to Bruce Cole, October 20, 1947, "Aspen Skiing Corporation—Titles to Properties" folder, Aspen Skiing Corporation/William V. Hodges Jr. Papers (hereafter ASC-Hodges Papers); Pitkin County, Board of Commissioners, minutes, August 6, 1945; "Construction of Chair Tow on Aspen Mt. Starts This Spring," *Aspen Times*, January 3, 1946, 1; William V. Hodges Jr., "Report to the Directors of the Aspen Skiing Corporation," May 22, 1962, typescript in Box 1, ASC-Hodges Papers. Another who helped Pfeifer was his father-in-law, a well-connected Utah banker, who put him in touch with Wilson McCarthy, president of the Denver & Rio Grande Western Railroad, who in turn recommended two lawyers to help Pfeifer untangle the mess of mining claims. McCarthy himself declined to invest in Pfeifer's ski venture, but that did not stop the Austrian from reporting to the Aspen City Council, rather misleadingly, that the D&RGW was interested. Impressed, the council agreed to help. In winter 1944–45, even as Pfeifer left for Europe, Mayor Gene Robison and other Aspen officials kept his project alive by inquiring around town about rights-of-way on the mountain. City of Aspen, City Council, minutes, November 3, 1943, and January 5, June 3, September 5, and November 3, 1944; Pfeifer, *Nice Goin'*, 113–14, 116, 119, 126; Cal Queal, "Past Decade Has Seen Aspen Ski Center Grow Tenfold," *Denver Post*, December 7, 1956; Harry Brown to D. R. C. Brown Jr., August 16, 1945, "Bio: Brown, D. R. C., Jr." folder, Aspen Historical Society Written Material Files (hereafter AHS-WMF); D. R. C. Brown Jr. to Harry Brown, August 7, 1945, "Envelope 1952–12: Ski Corp.—Corporate Minutes," Box 2, ASC-Hodges Papers. The city clerk recorded that ski club member Laurence Elisha spoke before the city council, apparently about Pfeifer's venture, on November 3, 1943. Pfeifer himself "reported [that] the R R was interested" at the council's June 3, 1944, meeting.

13. Harry Brown to D. R. C. Brown Jr., August 16, 1945, "Bio: Brown, D .R. C., Jr." folder, AHS-WMF; D. R. C. Brown Jr. to Harry Brown, August 7, 1945, "Envelope 1952–12: Ski Corp.—Corporate Minutes," Box 2, ASC-Hodges Papers; Pfeifer, *Nice Goin'*, 136; "Construction of Chair Tow on Aspen Mt. Starts This Spring"; City of Aspen, City Council, minutes, December 4, 1945, and January 3, February 4, February 18, and March 18, 1946.

14. O'Rear and O'Rear, *Aspen Story*, 69–70, 72; Pfeifer, *Nice Goin'*, 111, 126–27, 129; Litchfield, interview by Gilbert, AHS; Elizabeth Forbes, "Ghost-Town Aspen Lives Again," *Ski Illustrated*, March 1947, 19, 38; Wylie, "Ghost Town on Skis," 25; Barlow-Perez, *History of Aspen*, 44–45. Virtually all of the Tenth Mountain veterans who returned to Aspen after the war got involved in some way with skiing (by teaching in the ski school, opening ski shops, working for the Aspen Skiing Corporation, or writing about or promoting the sport) or with the resort business more broadly (by opening or working in a restaurant, lodge, dude ranch, or the like). Sally Barlow-Perez lists sixteen Tenth Mountain veterans who fit this pattern, and there were certainly many others. Barlow-Perez, *History of Aspen*, 44–46. See also Wylie, "Ghost Town on Skis," 25.

15. "Magnifico, Pfeifer Form Partnership," *Aspen Times*, January 3, 1946, 1; "Pfeifer Ski School to Operate Tows," *Aspen Times*, October 25, 1945, 1; Pfeifer, *Nice Goin'*, 129–30.

16. Myrtle S. Nord, "Friedl Pfeifer: Errant Knight of Skiing," *Western Skiing*,

September 1946, 11. Steady coverage in the ski magazines, beginning during the war, described Pfeifer's evolving plans for Aspen, helping mold the old town's new image (at least among ski enthusiasts) as a "hot skispot." See, for example, Ethel Severson, "Friedl Pfeiffer [sic]," *Ski Illustrated*, February 1944, 14–15, 32; Ski-torials column, *Ski Illustrated*, March 1944, 9; Betty Hosburgh, "So. Rocky Mountain," update in Parade column, *Ski Illustrated*, January 1945, 26; Western Ski Slopes column, *Western Skiing*, November 1945, 5 ("hot skispot" quotation); Western Ski Slopes column, *Western Skiing*, December 1945, 3, 6; Jerry Hiatt, "Colorado Winter Sports Congress," *Western Skiing*, January 1946, 24; and Betty Hosburgh, "So. Rocky Mountain," update in Winter Sports Parade column, *Ski Illustrated*, December 1946, 46–47. On at least one occasion, Pfeifer wrote his own publicity; see Sgt. Friedl Pfeiffer [sic], "American Skiing Comes of Age," *Ski Illustrated*, January 1945, 17, 32.

17. The word "type" here echoes Theodore Roosevelt's classic discussion of "frontier types," like the hunter, Indian fighter, and cowboy, who supposedly embodied essential qualities of the West. See especially the chapter "Frontier Types" in Roosevelt, *Ranch Life and the Hunting-Trail*, 80–100.

18. For a detailed explanation of the University of Chicago's "Chicago Bildungsideal" and a narrative of Walter Paepcke's early involvement with it, see J. S. Allen, *Romance of Commerce and Culture*, chap. 3. In chapter 2, Allen describes the so-called New Bauhaus and explains how Paepcke became its leading patron and a close friend of its founder, Hungarian designer László Moholy-Nagy, in the late 1930s.

19. Typifying this two-prong strategy were the eye-grabbing ads that the art department of the Container Corporation of America (CCA) began issuing in the late 1930s. Paepcke hired avant-garde artists from all over the world to create the ads, which featured colorful, innovative, often abstract images, and a minimum of text. Part of the point was to market CCA products; indeed, around this same time, Paepcke's in-house designers were devising a clean-lined CCA aesthetic and a brown-and-tan CCA color scheme, for integration into everything from the company's stationery to its delivery trucks. But Paepcke, like his friends in the New Bauhaus, also had a more idealistic goal in mind: to promote art by putting it to modern-day use. J. S. Allen, *Romance of Commerce and Culture*, 26–34; "Advertising Eye-Catchers," *Time*, April 30, 1945; "Container Corp. Builds Ahead," *Business Week*, April 24, 1948, 94, 97–98.

20. J. S. Allen, *Romance of Commerce and Culture*, 114–15, 121, 125–27, 129–33; Barlow-Perez, *History of Aspen*, 41–42, 46; "Industrialist Has Big Plans for Old Aspen," *Denver Post*, August 26, 1945, 1; "Pioneer Park Sold," "Graves House Sold," and "Hendricks House Sold," all *Aspen Times*, July 12, 1945, 1.

21. Walter P. Paepcke to Albin Dearing, May 3, 1945, quoted in J. S. Allen, *Romance of Commerce and Culture*, 127; "Industrialist Has Big Plans for Old Aspen," *Denver Post*, August 26, 1945, 1; Jack Foster, "Aspen to Re-Live Days of Gay '90s," *Rocky Mountain News*, September 26, 1945, 13.

22. "Industrialist Has Big Plans for Old Aspen" (first and second quotations); Paepcke to Dearing, May 3, 1945, and June 23, 1945, quoted in J. S. Allen, *Romance of Commerce and Culture*, 127 (third quotation), 133 (fourth quotation). See also Hal Boyle, "A Mining Town Is Reborn: Aspen May Become 'Athens of the Rockies,'" *Denver Post*,

January 15, 1947, 10. On the ways John D. Rockefeller Jr. rearranged life and the local landscape in Williamsburg, see Kammen, *Mystic Chords of Memory*, 361–68; Yetter, *Williamsburg Before and After*, esp. 52–55, 67; and Handler and Gable, *New History in an Old Museum*, 31–35. Besides Williamsburg, another model for Paepcke was the centuries-old silver-mining town of Taxco, Mexico, which had undergone a wholesale historical restoration under the leadership of American entrepreneur Bill Spratling. Paepcke was so impressed with Spratling's efforts in Taxco that he passed a *Reader's Digest* article about Spratling around Aspen. The article discussed the "rigid code . . . sternly enforced" that Taxco locals, acting at Spratling's behest, had adopted to protect the town's character. "All designs for new buildings must be in harmony with the old colonial architecture," reported *Reader's Digest*. "No building may be torn down or used without approval. . . . Even the color schemes must be harmonious." J. S. Allen, *Romance of Commerce and Culture*, 137; McEvoy, "'Silver Bill'" (quotations). On Spratling and Taxco, see Mark, *Silver Gringo*.

23. Jane Nes, "Old Aspen to Get Face Lifting," *Denver Post Rocky Mountain Empire Magazine*, June 23, 1946, 4; Boyle, "Mining Town Is Reborn"; "Ghost on Skis," *Time*, January 20, 1947, 83–84; Lee Callison, "Aspen Booms Again," *Denver Post Rocky Mountain Empire Magazine*, March 2, 1947, 2. Here again Paepcke learned from what Bill Spratling had done in Taxco, Mexico. In 1930, Spratling, charmed by the Taxco's rusticity, bought a house and opened a silversmithing shop, hiring locals to handcraft "traditional" items (actually items Spratling had designed himself, using pre-Columbian motifs) from native silver. From there, the enterprise grew into a wider project to restore Taxco's architecture and attract tourists. Nes, "Old Aspen to Get Face Lifting"; Mark, *Silver Gringo*; McEvoy, "'Silver Bill.'"

24. J. S. Allen, *Romance of Commerce and Culture*, 128–29, 145; "Hideaway—In Aspen," *Aspen Times*, November 18, 1948, 1, 8; "*Life* Visits Gary Cooper: The Film Star Haunts an Abandoned House on a Trip to Aspen," *Life*, March 7, 1949, 128–30, 133.

25. "Cooperation Assures Aspen's Future," *Aspen Times*, August 30, 1945, 1; "Citizens Meet to Discuss City Planning," *Aspen Times*, September 6, 1945, 1. For other descriptions of the August 30 meeting, see J. S. Allen, *Romance of Commerce and Culture*, 135–36; and Barlow-Perez, *History of Aspen*, 51.

26. The council seemed markedly more energetic, and more optimistic about Aspen's future, than they had been before Paepcke publicly announced his plans. At the September 4 meeting alone, besides discussing parks and planning, council members also talked about funding for a proposed Aspen airport and resolved to fight the Denver & Rio Grande Western Railroad's recent decision to end passenger service to Aspen. The D&RGW should wait at least six months, the council contended, because business in Aspen might "pick up by such time." "Citizens Committee Meets, Talks, Acts," *Aspen Times*, September 13, 1945, 1; "Plans Completed for Aspen's Fall Cleanup," *Aspen Times*, September 20, 1945, 1; City of Aspen, City Council, minutes, September 4, 1945.

27. "Tax Sale Draws Record Crowd," *Aspen Times*, September 6, 1945, 1; "Cooperation Assures Aspen's Future" (quotation); Jack Foster, "Aspen to Re-Live Days of Gay '90s," *Rocky Mountain News*, September 26, 1945, 13; Jane Nes, "Money Fever Is Running in Aspen Again," *Denver Post Magazine*, March 17, 1946, 3; "Notice to the

Public Concerning Sale of Tax Sale Certificates," *Aspen Times*, October 11, 1945, 8; Pitkin County, Board of Commissioners, minutes, October 3 and 18, 1945; "Long Time Lease on Hotel Jerome Taken," *Aspen Times*, January 24, 1946, 1. For a sense of the land-buying frenzy that gripped Aspen in fall 1945, see "Tax Sale Draws Record Crowd," *Aspen Times*, September 6, 1945, 1; V. E. Ringle, Aspen Quakings column, *Aspen Times*, September 13, 1945, 4; Pitkin County, Board of Commissioners, minutes, October 1, 1945; and the many notices of tax-sale transactions that appeared in the *Times* from August through early October. County commissioners ordered a tax-sale moratorium at an emergency meeting on October 3.

28. Chapter 3 discusses the burgeoning postwar popularity of skiing in more detail. See also Morris, "So You Want to Go Skiing!," 7.

29. V. E. Ringle, Aspen Quakings column, *Aspen Times*, July 12, 1945, 4 (first quotation); Boyle, "Mining Town Is Reborn" (second and third quotations); "Citizens Meet to Discuss City Planning" (fourth quotation); Nes, "Money Fever Is Running in Aspen Again" (fifth quotation).

30. During his second trip to Aspen, in July 1945, Paepcke paid a visit to Harry Brown, Darcy's elderly uncle, declared himself "very much interested in skiing and winter sports," and asked if the Browns might lease him the Smuggler-Durant claim. Harry, needing to clear any lease with Darcy, did not commit to Paepcke, but he did assure the Chicagoan that "we were thoroly in accord with what he [Paepcke] was doing." And in a letter to Darcy, Harry cast Paepcke in a far more favorable light than Pfeifer. The Austrian's ski-area project seemed "very doubtful," Harry warned his nephew, but the wealthy Chicago industrialist "looks all to the good!" Despite his uncle's endorsement, Darcy offered the Smuggler-Durant lease to Pfeifer, not Paepcke, in late 1945. Exactly how this happened is unclear. Given Paepcke's superior financial resources and legal counsel, it seems unlikely that Pfeifer outmaneuvered Paepcke. More likely, Pfeifer and Paepcke came to a tacit agreement during their October 1945 meeting that they would continue to work separately from one another but not at cross-purposes. Harry Brown to D. R. C. Brown Jr., August 16, 1945, "Bio: Brown, D. R. C., Jr." folder, AHS-WMF (all three quotations); Pfeifer, *Nice Goin'*, 136.

31. Pfeifer, *Nice Goin'*, 127, 129, 139.

32. Pfeifer, *Nice Goin'*, 139; "Incorporation Articles for Tow Recorded," *Aspen Times*, May 16, 1946, 1; "Denver Men Backing Aspen," *Denver Post*, May 12, 1946, 5; "Denver Capital Joins in Developing Aspen as Recreation Spot," *Rocky Mountain News*, May 12, 1946, 5; William V. Hodges Jr., "Report to the Directors of Aspen Skiing Corporation," May 22, 1962, typescript in Box I, ASC-Hodges Papers; J. S. Allen, *Romance of Commerce and Culture*, 140; Paul Nitze, interview by Annie Gilbert, Aspen, July 20, 1994, transcript at AHS; Barlow-Perez, *History of Aspen*, 47; Walter P. Paepcke to Paul Nitze, January 30, 1946, quoted in J. S. Allen, *Romance of Commerce and Culture*, 140–41 (quotation). Paul Nitze, a well-connected Washington, DC, investment banker and defense official, was the largest (by far) investor in the new skiing corporation and a close ally of Paepcke— his brother-in-law, in fact.

33. Dick Durrance, interview by Annie Gilbert, Aspen, July 8, 1994, transcript at AHS.

34. Barlow-Perez, *History of Aspen*, 46, 51; Boyle, "Mining Town Is Reborn"; Nitze, interview by Gilbert, AHS; O'Brien, "Skiing: Aspen Holiday," 82.

35. "Construction of Ski Lift to Start Next Monday," *Aspen Times*, June 20, 1946, 1; William V. Hodges Jr., "Report to the Directors of Aspen Skiing Corporation," May 22, 1962, typescript in Box I, ASC-Hodges Papers; Pfeifer, *Nice Goin'*, 138–39; Barlow-Perez, *History of Aspen*, 49. The upper lift segment was itself a relic of mining. Many of its parts were cannibalized from an old mine tram elsewhere on the mountain, a shrewd bit of recycling necessitated by the scarcity of building materials right after the war.

36. Coverage of the Grand Opening weekend included O'Brien, "Skiing: Aspen Holiday"; "Ghost on Skis"; "Bonanza Days Again for Silver Town," *Business Week*, January 18, 1947, 18; Lee Callison, "2,000 Ski Fans Make Aspen Gay," *Denver Post*, January 11, 1947, 1; Dick Smith, "Gala Opening of Aspen Ski Capital Is Hailed as Sensational Success," *Rocky Mountain News*, January 13, 1947, 12; Jack Foster, "Aspen Takes on a Gleaming New Existence," *Rocky Mountain News*, January 13, 1947, 11; Lee Callison, untitled article accompanied by photo essay, *Denver Post*, January 13, 1947, 26; and Dick Smith, "Aspen Proves Claims as Top Sports Center," *Rocky Mountain News*, January 14, 1947, 6. The Denver dailies covered not just the big event but also the weeks of preparation leading up to it. The sense of breathless anticipation seemed to intensify with each story: "National Figures to Attend Aspen Sport Center Opening," *Denver Post*, December 29, 1946, 2; Pasquale Marranzino, "Trainloads of Celebrities Will See Aspen Sport Debut," *Rocky Mountain News*, December 29, 1946, 5; "Notables Take Train for Aspen Ski Celebration," *Denver Post*, January 10, 1947, 1. Local Aspen reporters got into the spirit too; see, for example, "Aspen Formal Opening Jan. 10–11–12; Creates Much State-wide Interest," *Aspen Times*, January 2, 1947, 1; and "Aspen Grand Opening: Governor-Elect Lee Knous to Dedicate Ski Lift Saturday A.M.," *Aspen Times*, January 9, 1947, 1, 5.

37. J. S. Allen, *Romance of Commerce and Culture*, 144. We can only imagine Paepcke's reaction weeks earlier, when he read a *Denver Post* feature that described an entire Aspen neighborhood descending into après-ski drunkenness. "Unlike most other ski resorts, where guests live in one big lodge," reported the *Post*, "Aspen skiers party from house to house. A drink of gluehwein at Friedl's, toddies at the Litchfields', a call at the Browns' for a highball. . . . At each stop the typical party grows like a rolling snowball. The songs get louder and longer. . . . By then somebody's tap dancing on a table." This was not the image Paepcke hoped to cultivate for Aspen. S. Elizabeth Forbes, "Ski Heaven," *Denver Post Rocky Mountain Empire Magazine*, December 1, 1946, 2.

38. The idea of organizing a convocation in honor of Goethe's bicentennial was one Paepcke and some of his fellow cultural reformers had been kicking around for a while. The idea of having Aspen host it came during a lunch conversation between Paepcke and Robert Hutchins, president of the University of Chicago, in February 1947. See J. S. Allen, *Romance of Commerce and Culture*, 146.

39. Jane True, "Festival in the Mountains," *Denver Post Rocky Mountain Empire Magazine*, June 12, 1949, 2; "Huge Tent for Goethe Convocation Being Built," *Aspen Times*, May 12, 1949, 1; J. S. Allen, *Romance of Commerce and Culture*, 58, 60–61; Barlow-Perez, *History of Aspen*, 54. The Four Seasons Club occupied the site of the old Percy La Salle mine, property that Paepcke had bought in summer 1945; he bought Hoaglund's ranch in

early 1946. See "Newman Property to Be New Club," *Aspen Times*, April 3, 1947, 1; John-nie Hoaglund Sells," *Aspen Times*, January 24, 1946, 1.

40. Paepcke had first suggested a townwide cleanup campaign in 1945.To renew the idea, he had his ally at the *Aspen Times*, editor Verlin Ringle, exhort townspeople to participate, and he recruited Mayor Gene Robison and the Aspen Lions Club to the cause. "Aspen Clean-Up Day Set for Wednesday, Aug. 25," *Aspen Times*, August 12, 1948, 1; "City Clean-Up Starts Wednesday, August 25," and A. E. Robison, "Proclama-tion," both *Aspen Times*, August 19, 1948, 1; "Clean-Up Day Is Successful," *Aspen Times*, August 26, 1948, 1; "Aspen Lions Discuss Goethe Celebration," *Aspen Times*, January 6, 1949, 1; "What Can We Do?," *Aspen Times*, March 3, 1949, 1; "Get Ready Folks for Full Harmony," full-page ad, *Aspen Times*, April 7, 1949, 7; and "Clean-Up, Paint-Up, Fix-Up, Starts Saturday," *Aspen Times*, May 5, 1949, 1.

41. "Goethe Bicentennial Possible for Aspen," *Aspen Times*, October 21, 1948, 1; "Aspen Lions Discuss Goethe Celebration"; "What Can We Do?," *Aspen Times*, March 3, 1949, 1; Loudon Kelly, "Aspen Folk Can Take Goethe or Leave Him," *Rocky Mountain News*, June 28, 1949, 10; "Get Ready Folks for Full Harmony"; J. S. Allen, *Romance of Com-merce and Culture*, 170–71.

42. For a detailed and amusing look at the Goethe Convocation marketing efforts, including efforts to hype Goethe's life and work in a "newsworthy style," see J. S. Allen, *Romance of Commerce and Culture*, chap. 5. As Allen points out, the publicity blitz was wholly consonant with Paepcke's commercial-cultural crusade, especially his adeptness at selling cultural uplift through sophisticated marketing techniques.

43. William Longmaid, "Scholars, Artists Claim Festival Greatest Ever," *Aspen Times*, July 7, 1949, 1, 8 (first quotation); Barlow-Perez, *History of Aspen*, 56–57 (second quotation). See also J. S. Allen, *Romance of Commerce and Culture*, 202.

44. "Aspen Formal Opening Jan. 10–11–12; Creates Much State-Wide Interest," *Aspen Times*, January 2, 1947, 1. Some of these same comments by Knous appeared in Pasquale Marranzino, "Trainloads of Celebrities Will See Aspen Sport Debut," *Rocky Mountain News*, December 29, 1946, 5. On Knous's enthusiasm for recreational devel-opment, see also Phil Kerby, "The Man with the Bright Bow Tie," *Rocky Mountain Life*, November 1948, 38.

45. Boyle, "Mining Town Is Reborn"; Nes, "Money Fever Is Running in Aspen Again"; "Bonanza Days Again for Silver Town"; Walter Paepcke, quoted in Dick Smith, "Aspen Proves Claims as Top Sports Center," *Rocky Mountain News*, January 14, 1947, 6; Paepcke, quoted in Lee Callison, untitled back-page article and photo essay on the Grand Opening, *Denver Post*, January 13, 1947, 26.

46. "Colorado Looks Ahead," editorial, *Rocky Mountain News*, April 21, 1946, 14 (first quotation); "Aspen Is NOT Decayed," editorial, *Rocky Mountain News*, January 16, 1947, 12 (second quotation).

47. "Postwar Travel Will Help This Section," *Aspen Times*, January 4, 1945, 1; L. J. Crampon, *The Tourist and Colorado*, 12.

48. "Colorado's Resort Business Booms," *Denver Post*, September 23, 1945, 2; "State Must Have Added Tourist Facilities or Shoo Off Visitors," *Rocky Mountain News*, Sep-tember 23, 1945, 5; Colorado State Advertising and Publicity Committee (hereafter

APC), *Making the World Colorado Conscious*. Some years later, L. J. Crampon of the University of Colorado used a different metric for calculating tourist expenditures and came to a 1946 figure of less than $93 million. That represented a 52 percent gain over his new number for 1941—not so spectacular as 65 percent, but a steep increase nonetheless. Crampon, *The Tourist and Colorado*, 42.

49. "Colorado Looks Ahead," emphasis added.

50. Jane Nes, "New Millions for Leadville," *Denver Post Rocky Mountain Empire Magazine*, July 14, 1946, 5.

51. Circumstances well beyond any Leadvillian's control—namely, war overseas— helped spark both of these lead-zinc booms. But the efforts of local boosters—specifically, their twenty-year campaign to get federal funding for a Leadville mine drainage tunnel—played a key role too. In 1943 the town got $1.7 million for the project, but the end of World War II left the tunnel unfinished and unfunded. Against the backdrop of the Korean War, federal funding was restored and construction resumed in summer 1950, and the tunnel reached its final 12,000-foot length the next year, draining many mines and opening the way for Leadville's brief, final hurrah as a lead-zinc producer. On Leadville's long, frustrated love affair with drainage tunnels, see Blair, *Leadville: Colorado's Magic City*, 216–17, 227–28, 229, 236–37; and Voynick, *Leadville: A Miner's Epic*, 92, 105, 114–16. See also "Governor Vivian Visits Aspen," *Aspen Times*, August 23, 1945, 1; "Gov. Sees Future for Western Slope," *Aspen Times*, August 30, 1945, 1; Robert H. Hansen, "New Boom for Leadville," *Denver Post*, December 27, 1950, 36; and Don Sterling, "Tunnel Held Key: Leadville Sees Second Boom," *Denver Post*, October 21, 1951, 21A. Klucas, *Leadville: The Struggle to Revive an American Town*, describes how later Leadville residents struggled to deal with the environmental devastation the drainage tunnels left behind.

52. Blair, *Leadville: Colorado's Magic City*, 237; Voynick, *Climax*, esp. 202, 212–17, 220–21, 226–28, 237–38; Coquoz, *Leadville Story*, 32–36; Ruth, *Colorado Vacations*, 165. For a delightful account of life in the Climax company town, see Vincent, *Climax Kids*, 1956.

53. Not just booster fantasies, these hopes were echoed by many outside experts. When the *Aspen Times* predicted a local mining revival in the late 1940s, no less than the state's top authority on small-town economic development, L. J. Crampon of the University of Colorado, backed it up. Crampon reported that copper giant Anaconda was poking through ore dumps, buying old claims, and readying to build a concentration mill, making it "reasonably certain" that "a new period of mining activity" was afoot in Aspen. Crampon predicted it would reverse the town's population decline and allow local merchants to challenge the retail dominance of nearby Glenwood Springs. Similarly, in 1959 Harvard geologist Hugh McKinstry predicted that new prospecting technologies might soon yield significant strikes in Lake, Eagle, and Pitkin Counties and that tax breaks and favorable metal prices could induce mining to spread more widely across the area than ever before. Crampon, *Glenwood Springs Business Report*, 5–6, 11, 15; McKinstry, *Future of Mining in Colorado*, esp. 13, 14, 19–21, 25–28. See also Crampon, *Business in the Small Cities of Colorado*, 13; and Frush, "Century of Mining in Colorado." Even experts who offered less rosy views of Colorado mining often insisted that it could and should be revived. Yale economist Olin Glenn Saxon, warning that mining had become

a "marginal industry" in Colorado, added that "attempting to solve this problem should logically be one of [Coloradans'] primary concerns." Saxon, *Colorado and Its Mining Industry*, 17 (quotations), 27, 49, 67, 73–74. As late as 1960, the two counties at the heart of today's Interstate 70 vacation corridor—Summit and Eagle—still counted mining as the first (Summit) or second (Eagle) most important industry. "Mining Important to Local Areas," *Colorado Business Review*, July 1963, 3.

54. McKinstry, *Future of Mining in Colorado*, 15; Oliver C. Ralston, "Mt. Region Can Look to 'New' Mineral Resources," *Colorado Business*, September 1947, 7, 10, 13–14; Frush, "Century of Mining in Colorado," esp. 5–6; Crampon, Lawson, and Ellinghaus, *Report on the Economic Potential of Western Colorado*, iii (quotation), 124.

55. "High Grade Uranium Ore in Holy Cross District," *Eagle Valley Enterprise*, October 28, 1954, 1; "Uranium and Titanium Sought in Eagle County," *Georgetown Courier*, January 20, 1955, 1; "Eagle Told to Expect New Boom," *Denver Post*, March 17, 1955; "Rich Ore Reported on Vail Pass," *Eagle Valley Enterprise*, September 1, 1955, 1; "Vail Pass Center of U Ore Search," *Eagle Valley Enterprise*, September 9, 1956, 1; "Richest Uranium in Clear Creek, Gilpin?," *Georgetown Courier*, April 30, 1953, 3; "Uranium Strike Seen Certainty," *Georgetown Courier*, June 4, 1953, 8; "Troublesome Uranium Find Starts Claim Staking Rush," *Middle Park Times*, December 10, 1953, 1. For an overview of the 1950s uranium boom on the Western Slope, see Ringholz, *Uranium Frenzy*; Vandenbusche and Smith, *Land Alone*, 234–36; and Mehls, *Valley of Opportunity*, 242–44.

56. State of Colorado Bureau of Mines, *The Oil Shales of Northwestern Colorado*, Bulletin no. 8 (August 1, 1919), quoted in Gulliford and the Grand River Museum Alliance, *Garfield County, Colorado*, 40 (first quotation); F. J. Taylor, "Colorado's Fabulous Mountains of Oil"; Henry W. Hough, "Colorado Oil Fields," *Colorado Wonderland*, Development Issue, 1952, 18 (second quotation); Crampon, Lawson, and Ellinghaus, *Report on the Economic Potential of Western Colorado*, 143 (fifth quotation), 146, 147 (third and fourth quotations), 263–64; L. J. Crampon and Donald F. Lawson, "Summary of the Report on the Economic Potential of Western Colorado," p. 4, Denver Public Library Government Documents Collection. The words about western Colorado becoming a "powerhouse" and an "industrial center" were not Crampon's—he quoted them from a report by the Bituminous Coal Institute—but he endorsed the prediction. For a highly readable and ultimately heartbreaking history of oil shale in Colorado, see Gulliford, *Boomtown Blues*. Scamehorn, *High Altitude Energy*, 143–64, 180–85, and Mehls, *Valley of Opportunity*, 244–53, offer succinct surveys of the subject.

57. Athearn and Ubbelohde, *Centennial Colorado*, 65. This brief history, aimed at a popular audience, was written for the yearlong Rush to the Rockies celebration, commemorating the centennial of the first Colorado gold rush.

58. Crampon, *Business in the Small Cities of Colorado*, esp. 15; Crampon, *Promoting Colorado's Industrial Potential*; Victor Roterus, "How Municipal Officials Can Promote Industrial Growth," *Colorado Municipalities*, March 1960, 60–61, 70; "Industry Looks West and South for Sites," *CRDC Progress*, May 1948; "C.D.C. Sparks Industrial Dispersion Policy," *Colorado Development Council, Inc., Newsletter*, September 1951, 1; "Why Industries Have Selected a Colorado Site," *Colorado Business Review*, April 1956, 1–4.

59. Colorado State Planning Commission (hereafter SPC), *State of Colorado Year*

Book, 1951 to 1955, 78. Created in 1935, the State Planning Commission inherited its priorities from its predecessor, the old State Board of Immigration (BOI). The BOI's job had been to boost agriculture, mining, and manufacturing. It also worked to promote tourism, but mostly as a way of recruiting new residents and investors in business and industry. The other statewide booster organization of the early 1930s, the private Colorado Association, took the same approach: it titled its lure book *Opportunity's Playground*, expressing hope that people who came to play would find investment and employment opportunities and come back to live. This same sense of tourism's subsidiary importance guided the SPC. When it described its own work, the SPC focused on mining, manufacturing, and farming, not tourism. Though the SPC did decide in 1945 to have its committee on public lands and recreation cover "tourist travel" too, SPC reports of the 1940s and 1950s mentioned tourism very rarely. In 1951, Governor Dan Thornton ordered the SPC to organize the first of several statewide travel-industry summits, but even then, state planners never seemed to warm to the vacation trade. In 1957, when the SPC became the State Planning Division, with an "expanded program of planning, development and public works services," its list of priorities made no mention of tourism at all. BOI, *The Northwest Plateau*; Colorado Association, *The Colorado Association: Its Policies, Work and Organization*, brochure (Denver, [1929?]), Norlin Library Pamphlet Collection; Colorado Association, *Colorful Colorado: Opportunity's Playground*, lure book (Denver, 1931); SPC, *Report of the Colorado State Planning Commission to the Governor and the Thirty-Fifth General Assembly*, vol. 2 of *Suggested Outline for Economic Development in Colorado*; SPC, *Ten Years of State Planning in Colorado*; SPC, *Year Book of the State of Colorado, 1945–1947*, 66; SPC, *State of Colorado Year Book, 1951 to 1955*, 78, 473; "An Expanded Program of Planning, Development and Public Works Services," *Facts from the State Planning Division*, September 1957, 1.

60. Charles B. Roth, "Building Colorado," *Colorado Business*, September 1946, 12 (first quotation); V. E. Ringle, Aspen Quakings column, *Aspen Times*, February 20, 1947, 8 (second quotation, emphasis in original). Ringle, the *Times* editor, was a vocal supporter of Walter Paepcke's resort-building efforts, which makes his suggestion that Aspen still needed mining all the more noteworthy.

61. Thomas Hornsby Ferril, "Bless the Absent Tourists," *Rocky Mountain Herald*, June 16, 1942, reprinted in R. C. Baron, Leonard, and Noel, *Thomas Hornsby Ferril and the American West*, 140–41 (all quotations). See also Ferril, "Tourists, Stay Away from My Door."

62. Colo. Stat. Ann. chap. 158A; APC, *Telling the World About Colorado*; APC, *Making the World Colorado Conscious*; SPC, *Year Book of the State of Colorado, 1945–1947*, 122; Gunther, *Inside U.S.A.*, 214; "Tourists, Markets, Industries Go to States That Advertise, Says State Director Cobb," *Aspen Times*, September 21, 1950, 1; Colorado Advertising and Publicity Department [sic], *Annual Report, Fiscal Year 1950–51* (1951), Box 10223, records of the Colorado Department of Local Affairs (hereafter DOLA Records). Cobb asked the legislature for $150,000 in 1950. The APC's budget for the 1947–49 biennium had been $50,000.

63. APC, "Analysis of Colorado Tourist Industry, 1947 through 1950" [ca. 1951], Box 10223, DOLA Records. Cobb found that from 1947 to 1950, as the state advertising budget

shrank by two-thirds, tourist spending in Colorado had dipped more than 7 percent—nearly 30 percent if calculated on a per person basis. Interestingly, the number of tourists in Colorado had risen by almost a third during these same years. Cobb's concern, then, was not that tourists were avoiding Colorado but that they were spending too little once they got there.

64. APC, "Fact Sheet on State Advertising and Publicity" [1951], Box 10223, DOLA Records; "Tourists, Markets, Industries Go to States That Advertise, Says State Director Cobb," *Aspen Times*, September 21, 1950, 1. Cobb complained, in the *Times* article, that the legislature had given the APC "barely enough [money] for a skeleton payroll, postage and curtailed publicity activities." He pointed out that at $17,500, Colorado's advertising budget ranked forty-first in the nation—just ahead of tiny Delaware, whose publicity department had existed for only one year. The other six states that ranked lower had no publicity programs at all. On the opposite end were states like Missouri, which, Cobb claimed, had recently started spending more money on tourist advertising and had immediately seen rises in tourist spending. Cobb cited studies indicating that every dollar's worth of publicity brought back $300 in new tourist spending and $12.50 in new tax revenues.

65. APC, *Annual Report, Fiscal Year 1951–52* (1952), Box 10223, DOLA Records. Also in 1951, the legislature increased the APC to five members, one from each congressional district and one at large. Colo. Rev. Stat. 53 § 134-1-1.

66. Abbott, *Metropolitan Frontier*, chap. 2 (Stapleton quoted p. 41); Wiley and Gottlieb, *Empires in the Sun*, part 2; Fleischmann and Feagin, "Politics of Growth-Oriented Urban Alliances"; White, *"It's Your Misfortune and None of My Own,"* 541–46; Leonard and Noel, *Denver: Mining Camp to Metropolis*, chap. 20; G. V. Kelly, *Old Gray Mayors of Denver*, 23–54; Hornby, *Voice of Empire*, 29–38.

67. The matter of state advertising, and the branding of states for tourism and other purposes, has received little attention from historians, but a recent exception is Rugh, "Branding Utah." See also Knobloch, "Creating the Cowboy State"; and Hinrichs, "Consuming Images." For a regional example, see Gómez, *Quest for the Golden Circle*, chap. 6; for a Canadian example, see Dawson, *Selling British Columbia*. On the broader history of state-level economic development initiatives, see Eisinger, *Rise of the Entrepreneurial State*.

68. APC, *Annual Report: July 1, 1953–June 30, 1954* (1954); *Annual Report: July 1, 1955–June 30, 1956* (1956); *Annual Report: July 1, 1956–June 30, 1957* (1957); and *Annual Report: July 1, 1959–June 30, 1960* (1960); all in Box 10223, DOLA Records.

69. Rocky Mountain Motorists' annual guidebook was originally titled *Rocky Mountain Travel Directory* and covered Wyoming, New Mexico, and Colorado. It narrowed its focus to Colorado in the late 1940s, changing its title to *Where to Vacation in Colorado* in the early 1950s. The publication consisted largely of half-, full-, or facing-page ads submitted by local chambers of commerce, resorts, motels, and dude ranches. The *Western Tour Book* was more of an actual guidebook, sprinkled with ads. Both publications were available only to AAA members, but there were a lot of those—around 4 million in the mid-1950s; more than 5.5 million by decade's end. American Automobile Association, *Western Accommodations Directory*, 1954–55 ed., 11, and 1958–59 ed., 6.

70. For example, the Denver lure book that the Denver Convention and Visitors Bureau (hereafter DCVB) published in the 1950s packed seventy-three photographs into forty pages—and thirty-five of the pictures depicted places in the mountains, not in the city. All four of the cover photographs showed high-country scenes. DCVB, *Come to Denver, Capital City of Colorado*, lure book (Denver, [ca. 1951]). Around 1954, the DCVB gave the lure book a more evocative title, *Denver—Colorado: Vacation Land in the Rockies*, suggesting how much the city's visitor appeal continued to rely on the appeal of the mountain hinterland.

71. For more on these magazines, see Zeman, "High Roads and Highways to Romance"; and Kevin Starr, "Sunset Magazine and the Phenomenon of the Far West," in *"Sunset" Magazine: A Century of Western Living, 1898–1998*, 31–75.

72. The title *Colorado Wonderland* originally belonged to a picture book, published annually by the Colorado State Junior Chamber of Commerce, beginning in 1939. After the Jaycees suspended this nonprofit project in early 1949, Tex Roberts of Colorado Springs picked up the title for his new magazine. Roberts's *Colorado Wonderland* absorbed a similar but less picture-oriented magazine, *Rocky Mountain Life*, in early 1950. See "Legislature Commends *Colorado Wonderland* Magazine," *Colorado Wonderland*, March 1952, 23.

73. Colorado-themed ads from the Western Pacific and the Burlington Route appeared frequently in national magazines, including *Collier's, Life, National Geographic*, and *Holiday*, the leading travel-interest periodical of the day. The D&RGW, a more narrowly regional line with a far smaller marketing budget, placed far fewer ads in national magazines; for an exception, see *National Geographic*, August 1954, 148. Rio Grande ads did appear in almost every issue of *Colorado Wonderland*.

74. Some airline ads focused in whole or in part on Colorado and emphasized high-country scenery and recreation: Frontier Airlines, ad in *Colorado Wonderland*, Summer II, 1952, 39, and Fall 1952, 10; United Air Lines, ad in *Holiday*, May 1946, 16; and Western Air Lines, ad in *Holiday*, April 1946, 2. By the early 1950s, United and Continental were also issuing colorful posters with Colorado themes for display in travel agencies, airports, and other spots frequented by tourists. For a map of early 1950s airline routes in Colorado, see *Colorado Wonderland*, Development Issue, 1952, 22.

75. SPC, *State of Colorado Year Book, 1951 to 1955*, 473; SPC, *Colorado, 1956–1958*, 645; APC, *Annual Report: July 1, 1956–June 30, 1957* (1957), and *Annual Report: July 1, 1957–June 30, 1958* (1958), Box 10223, DOLA Records; "Better Service Urged at Tourist Parley," *Rocky Mountain News*, May 12, 1954, 23.

76. "Better Service Urged at Tourist Parley."

77. Crampon's interest in tourism dated back to 1945, when he surveyed the travel desires of *Better Homes and Gardens* subscribers. But during his early years at the University of Colorado, from the late 1940s to 1953, he mostly monitored other Colorado industries and wrote no reports about tourism. After he released his 1953 *Colorado Statewide Summer Tourist Survey*, however, he focused his studies almost exclusively on this topic. By the late 1950s, his expertise on tourism had won recognition beyond Colorado, and he would go on to work for the Hawaii Visitors Bureau, the U.S. Department of Commerce, and the Stanford Research Institute. See Crampon, *Tourist Development Notes*, vol. 2, p. i,

and vol. 3, pp. ii–iii. Crampon authored or coauthored numerous reports on Colorado tourism; see "Other Reports and Plans" in the bibliography.

78. From the title page of Crampon, *The Tourist and Colorado*.

79. Crampon gave more than a hundred speeches during his eighteen years at the University of Colorado. Some are anthologized in the three volumes of *Tourist Development Notes*. A speech he delivered at the 1954 travel conference, titled "The Colorado Tourist Business," is reprinted in volume 2. To supplement that speech, he passed out a digest of his 1953 summer travel survey: see *Summary of 1953 Colorado Statewide Tourist Survey*.

80. "Eisenhower Signs Social Security Bill," *Roanoke Times*, September 2, 1954, 1; "When Ike Takes a Vacation . . . Golf, Fishing, Painting—but the Work Goes On," *U.S. News and World Report*, September 11, 1953, 21; National U.S. Highway 40 Association, *New! US 40: Mainline of America*, brochure (Lakewood, CO, 1959); "This Is Fraser, Ike's Vacation Land . . . the Coldest Spot in the Nation," [1950s] postcard in author's collection. On Eisenhower's long association with Colorado, see Pasquale Marranzino, "Ike: Favorite Son-in-Law," *Rocky Mountain News*, April 17, 1959, 73; and M. Benson, "Dwight D. Eisenhower and the West," 60–64.

81. On tourists' yearning to find emotional involvement and personal meaning in the places they visit, see J. Harrison, *Being a Tourist*, 95, 97–99.

82. The idea of an "experience economy" succeeding the earlier industrial and service economies originated with business consultants Joseph Pine and James Gilmore; see Pine and Gilmore, *Experience Economy*. For an important precursor to this argument, see Holbrook and Hirschman, "Experiential Aspects of Consumption." For an example of the new thinking in Pine and Gilmore's wake, see Sundbo and Darmer, *Creating Experiences in the Experience Economy*.

83. The definitive history of how Anglo-American culture came to view mountains this way is Nicolson, *Mountain Gloom and Mountain Glory*.

84. On nineteenth-century standards of the picturesque, and the composition of picturesque paintings and other scenes, see Novak, *Nature and Culture*; and Conron, *American Picturesque*. John Conron contributes the key insight that the distinctive aesthetic categories of the sublime, beautiful, and picturesque, so firmly established by eighteenth-century English theorists, blurred together in the work of American artists and theorists contemplating their young nation's landscape in the early to mid-nineteenth century. For an important case study of how the picturesque was broadly applied to the Victorian American scene, see Rainey, *Creating Picturesque America*.

85. There is literally a mountain of scholarship on Romantic notions of nature. On the Romantic relation between the individual and nature, excellent introductions include Gatta, *Making Nature Sacred*; Cherry, *Nature and Religious Imagination*; Albanese, *Nature Religion in America*, chap. 3; Huth, *Nature and the American*, chaps. 3, 5, 6; R. F. Nash, *Wilderness and the American Mind*, chaps. 3–5; Worster, *Nature's Economy*, chaps. 3–5; and Buell, *Environmental Imagination*. On the connection between tourist landscapes, cultural uplift, and the consolidation and celebration of American national identity, see especially R. F. Nash, *Wilderness and the American Mind*, chap. 4; Sears, *Sacred Places*; Hyde, *American Vision*; and Shaffer, *See America First*. On the broader tradition of vacationing for self-improvement, see Aron, *Working at Play*.

86. "Colorful Colorado," the most successful brand ever devised for the state, seems to have been a product of the punchy new ad-writing style of the 1920s. It appeared as an incidental phrase in mid-1920s ads for the Missouri Pacific Railroad (MP); see, for example, ads in *Times-Picayune* (New Orleans, LA), June 22, 1923, 18, and June 24, 1926, 24. But the first to turn it into an intentional brand was the Colorado Association, a booster group founded in 1929. Casting around for a catchy state nickname, the association considered the forgettable "High Colorado" but by 1930 settled on "Colorful Colorado" instead. A nationwide newspaper and magazine ad campaign ensued, with "Colorful Colorado" as the verbal and visual centerpiece. The association's tourist literature highlighted it too: *High Spots of Colorful Colorado*, brochure (Denver, [ca. 1930]); *Colorful Colorado: Opportunity's Playground*, lure book (Denver, 1931); *Roads to the Clouds in Colorful Colorado*, brochure (Denver, [1932?]). And it caught on: the nickname appeared increasingly often in promotion and press coverage of Colorado in the later 1930s, and by the 1940s it was well entrenched. The state began using it on the annual state highway map in 1942 and on license plates in 1950. On the ill-fated "High Colorado" brand, see Conner Advertising Agency, *Plan for Advertising Colorado by the Colorado Association* (Denver, 1929), 61–64 and appendix.

87. Sample ad reproduced in APC, *Annual Report: July 1, 1953–June 30, 1954* (1954), Box 10223, DOLA Records; DCVB, ad in *Holiday*, March 1952, 19.

88. "President Ike's Fishing Retreat . . . a National Home," *Your National Homes Magazine*, 1956, 56; Andrew Tully, "When Ike Comes to Fraser He's Gotta Meet the Folks," *Rocky Mountain News*, August 17, 1955, 5; Marvin L. Arrowsmith, "Ike and Hoover to Fish Together in Colo. Rockies," *Times-Herald* (Newport News, VA), August 26, 1954, 20 (an Associated Press story that ran in newspapers around the country); "When Ike Takes a Vacation . . . Golf, Fishing, Painting—but the Work Goes On"; Virgil Pinkley, "Bulletins" broadcast, October 26, 1955, transcript in FF "Nielsen, Aksel 1952 thru 1956 (2)," Box 23, Name Series, Dwight D. Eisenhower: Papers as President of the United States, 1953–61, Ann Whitman File (hereafter DDE-Whitman).

89. "Stanbrough," postcard to Jamie Davis, postmarked September 13, 1946, from Fraser, CO, author's collection.

90. On the composition of picturesque landscapes, see Conron, *American Picturesque*, chap. 5; and Novak, *Nature and Culture*. Hoelscher, in "Photographic Construction of Tourist Space in Victorian America," argues that despite their superficial similarities, landscape photography represented a different aesthetic than landscape painting, was more a product of the market, and thus played a vital role in creating landscapes as tourist places.

91. Jim Hughes and Annette Espinoza, "Images on State Coins Say a Lot," *Denver Post*, March 10, 2005; "Exclusive: Wyoming Mountain Depicted on Colorado Stamp?" KMGH 7News, June 26, 2008, www.thedenverchannel.com/news/16722424/detail.html (accessed June 27, 2008); John C. Ensslin, "Schaffer's Ad Moved Mountains," *Rocky Mountain News*, May 14, 2008; Lynn Bartels, "McInnis Campaign Has Its Own Mountain Misstep," *Denver Post*, July 6, 2009.

92. Norman A. Hartford, letter to the editor, *Colorado Wonderland*, Christmas 1954, 6; A. J. Lechner, letter to the editor, *Colorado Wonderland*, Summer I, 1952, 40.

93. Davis and Fall, *Eisenhower College Collection,* 155.

94. Dwight D. Eisenhower to Dan Thornton, September 16, 1953, FF "DDE Diary—Aug.–Sept. 1953 (1)," Box 3, DDE Diary Series, DDE-Whitman.

95. Colorado Department of Natural Resources, *Climate as a Natural Resource,* 15.

96. Teale, *Journey into Summer,* 312.

97. This was a slogan the DCVB used in the mid- to late 1940s. See, for example, the DCVB ads in *Holiday,* October 1946, 156; and *Ski Illustrated,* January 1947, 39.

98. On the falsity of the three-hundred-days claim, see Nelson and the 9News Weather Team, *Colorado Weather Book,* 57–58, 71; Nolan Doesken, "For Fun: Questions and Answers," Colorado Climate Center, http://climate.colostate.edu/questions.php (accessed July 12, 2010); Robert Baun, "40 Northern Colorado Icons: 300 Days of Sunshine," *Northern Colorado Business Report,* October 28, 2005; National Atmospheric and Oceanic Administration, "Ranking of Cities Based on % Annual Possible Sunshine in Descending Order from Most to Least Average Possible Sunshine," table at www.ncdc.noaa.gov/oa/climate/online/ccd/pctpos.txt (accessed August 19, 2010).

99. Beginning in the late 1940s, the APC began referring to "Cool, Colorful Colorado" in many of its print ads, and its annually updated lure book carried the title *Cool, Colorful Colorado Invites You!* On the billboards, see APC, *Telling the World About Colorado.*

100. Merriman Smith, "Temperature Dips Low at President's Fishing Camp," *Bend Bulletin* (Bend, OR), September 2, 1954 (a United Press story that ran in newspapers around the country).

101. On the midcentury cultural appeal of air-conditioning and coolness, see Ackermann, *Cool Comfort,* chaps. 5–6.

102. Crampon and Lemon, *Skiing in the Southern Rocky Mountain Region,* 1 (first quotation); Crampon, *Business in the Small Cities of Colorado,* 19 (second quotation). In *The Tourist and Colorado,* 15, Crampon offered statistical proof of this seasonal imbalance. Some 60 percent of Colorado tourism took place in July and August, he pointed out, while for the nation as a whole, only 39 percent of all tourism occurred during those months. In summer, 1 out of every 25 tourist parties in the United States visited Colorado, but in winter only 1 of every 250 did so. All told, while tourism in most parts of the country peaked in summertime, Crampon found that the disparity between summer and winter was much greater in Colorado.

103. DCVB, *Come to Denver, Capital City of Colorado* [ca. 1951]. This booklet included five pages under the title "Variety for Denver's Spring Visitors," nine pages of "Summer-Time Fun . . . a Mile in the Sky," six pages explaining that "Fall in Denver Holds Endless Fascination," and seven pages of "Snow-Season Pastimes . . . Indoors and Out."

104. Fall examples: DCVB, ad in *Holiday,* August 1948, 20 (quotation); DCVB, ad in *Holiday,* October 1946, 156; APC, ad in *Holiday,* September 1948, 19; Colorado Springs Chamber of Commerce, ad in *Holiday,* September 1948, 123; APC, dba Department of Public Relations, *Enjoy Summer Fun This* FALL *in Colorful Colorado,* brochure (Denver, 1951); sample ads in APC, *Annual Report: July 1, 1953–June 30, 1954* (1954), Box 10223, DOLA Records; APC, dba Department of Public Relations, *Cool, Colorful Colorado Invites You!,* lure book (1959), 4; DCVB, *Denver Welcomes You to Colorado,* brochure (Denver, [1950s]);

APC, dba Department of Public Relations, *This Fall—Summer* FUN *in the* SUN *in Colorful Colorado*, brochure (Denver, [1950s]); sample ads in APC, *Annual Report: July 1, 1962–June 30, 1963* (1963), Box 10223, DOLA Records. To further blur the distinction between summer and fall, the APC recommended the same activities in autumn—hiking, golfing, horseback riding, ghost-town exploring—as in summer. See APC, *Enjoy Summer Fun this* FALL *in Colorful Colorado* (1951); sample ads in APC, *Annual Report: July 1, 1953–June 30, 1954* (1954), Box 10223, DOLA Records; APC, ad in *Holiday*, September 1955, 82; and APC, *This Fall—Summer* FUN *in the* SUN *in Colorful Colorado* [Denver, 1950s].

Winter examples: APC, dba Colorado Winter Sports Committee, *Ski in the Sun in Colorado*, brochure (Denver, [1950s]) (quotation); APC, ad in *Ski Illustrated*, January 1947; DCVB, ad in *Ski Illustrated*, January 1947, 39; "Year Round Vacation Land," in APC, *Colorado: Top of the Nation*, booklet (1948); Colorado Springs Chamber of Commerce, ad in *Holiday*, February 1948, 8; APC, ad in *Holiday*, October 1948, 92; Rocky Mountain Motorists (hereafter RMM), *Rocky Mountain Travel Directory: Colorado*, 1949 ed., 44; DCVB, *Come to Denver, Capital City of Colorado* [ca. 1951]; APC, *Cool, Colorful Colorado Invites You!* (1959), 4; DCVB, *Denver Welcomes You to Colorado*; APC, dba Colorado Winter Sports Committee, *Ski Colorado*, brochure (Denver, [1950s]); sample ads in APC, *Annual Report: July 1, 1961–June 30, 1962* (1962), Box 10223, DOLA Records.

Spring examples: APC, "Year Round Vacation Land," in *Colorado: Top of the Nation* (1948); DCVB, ad in *Holiday*, May 1948, 126; RMM, *Rocky Mountain Travel Directory: Colorado*, 1949 ed., 44; DCVB, *Come to Denver, Capital City of Colorado* [ca. 1951]; APC, *Cool, Colorful Colorado Invites You!* (1959), 4. In 1950s Colorado, the spring season—"mud season" in high-country parlance—was less heavily promoted than winter or fall.

105. APC, *Cool, Colorful Colorado Welcomes You!* (1959), 2.

106. Colorado Springs Chamber of Commerce, ad in *Holiday*, September 1948, 123; DCVB, ad in *Holiday*, April 1952, 72.

107. Mohl, *Searching for the Sunbelt*; Meyer, *Americans and Their Weather*, chap. 5.

108. For example, when Ben Draper, leader of the effort to restore historic Georgetown, urged the private sector to pay more attention to tourism, he denied wanting "to build the tourist industry up as Colorado's greatest." Instead, tourism should expand "along with new developments in . . . manufacturing, farming, revived mining and cattle." Similarly, when the *Rocky Mountain News* editorialized that Colorado's future greatness lay in "our climate, our scenery, our place as the nation's playground," it tempered the message by acknowledging that "we should, and must, foster agriculture, livestock and mining" together with the vacation trade. Benjamin Draper, "Survey of Tourist Industry Advocated: Interest in Colorado Shown by Mining Camp Revivals," *Denver Post*, September 29, 1947, 10; "Colorado Looks Ahead."

109. On the powerful resonance of western and frontier imagery in postwar American popular culture, I have found these studies most helpful: R. G. Athearn, *Mythic West in Twentieth-Century America*; Slotkin, *Gunfighter Nation*; Hausladen, *Western Places, American Myths*; Tompkins, *West of Everything*; Aquila, *Wanted Dead or Alive*; and M. L. Johnson, *New Westers*. On the link between kiddie westerns and tourist marketing, see Rugh, *Are We There Yet?*, chap. 4.

110. "Tabulation of Comments," in *Summary of 1953 Colorado Statewide Tourist Survey*,

esp. 6–7; "Better Service Urged at Tourist Parley," *Rocky Mountain News*, May 12, 1954, 23; APC, ad in *Aspen Times*, May 24, 1956, 2.

111. APC, ad in *Holiday*, March 1948, 120; sample ad in APC, *Annual Report: July 1, 1958–June 30, 1959* (1959), Box 10223, DOLA Records; DCVB, ad in *Holiday*, September 1948, 133.

112. Denver & Rio Grande Western Railroad, advertisement in *Colorado Wonderland*, Fall 1952, 3.

113. APC, *Cool, Colorful Colorado Invites You!* (1959), 35; see also p. 6. For other examples of the old-prospector icon, see Mark U. Watrous, "Colorado's Million Dollar Highways Follow the Gold Trail," *Colorado Wonderland*, Fall 1952, 34; and Revis, "Colorado by Car and Campfire," 215, 218, 227.

114. The Prospectors' Trail name seems to have been devised by the DCVB before the war, and various itineraries evolved over the course of many bureau-issued brochures in the 1940s and 1950s. See DCVB, *Adventure Map: Prospectors Trail*, brochure (Denver, [late 1940s]); DCVB, *Denver and Its Mountain Playgrounds*, brochure (Denver, [ca. 1948]); DCVB, *Prospectors' Trails*, brochure (Denver, [early 1950s]); and DCVB, *Come to Denver, Capital City of Colorado* (Denver, [ca. 1951]), 16. By the late 1950s, the APC was promoting the concept too, offering a "Prospectors' Trail" as one of the eleven suggested driving tours in its lure book. APC, *Cool, Colorful Colorado Invites You!* (1959), 6–8. See also DCVB, ad in RMM, *Rocky Mountain Travel Directory: Colorado*, 1949 ed., 47; and Gray Line Sight-Seeing Companies, *Sightseeing in Denver: The Mile Hi City*, brochure (Denver, [1950s]). Prospectors' Trails found their way into guidebooks aimed not just at tourists but at Coloradans too; see, for example, Talmadge and Gilmore, *Colorado Hi-Ways and By-Ways*, vol. 1.

115. Idaho Springs Chamber of Commerce (hereafter ISCC), ad in RMM, *Rocky Mountain Travel Directory: Colorado*, 1949 ed., 32; ISCC, *Introducing Colorado's Famed "Gold Rush" City, Idaho Springs*, brochure (Idaho Springs, [late 1950s]) (emphasis in original). See also DCVB, *What to See and Do*, brochure (Denver, [1950s]).

116. APC, *Cool, Colorful Colorado Invites You!* (1959), 7, 35 (Black Hawk and Georgetown); RMM, *Where to Vacation in Colorado*, 1963–64 ed., 69 (Central City), 145 (Georgetown and Leadville), 150 (Idaho Springs); DCVB, *What to See and Do* [1950s] (Leadville).

117. Some Central Citians decried Wolle's fixation on their local ruins, pointing out that many of the buildings she depicted as derelict had in fact been rehabilitated for modern use. Reacting to Wolle's first book, *Ghost Cities of Colorado*, a local editor huffed that "we hardly approve of the title of the book.... [Central City and Black Hawk] are far from being 'Ghost Cities' as the young lady [Wolle] well knows through her many visits here." Wolle dismissed these critics; they were, she said, "completely unaware that my whole thesis was to preserve the past rather than record the present." Wolle, *Stampede to Timberline*, 39–40. See also J. T. Coleman, "Prim Reaper." Wolle's other Colorado ghost town books were *Cloud Cities of Colorado* and *Timberline Tailings*.

118. APC, *Cool, Colorful Colorado Invites You!* (1959), 35; *Rocky Mountain Life*, July 1947. On the different cultural meanings that ghost towns took on—some celebratory and some condemnatory of the past, some hopeful and some pessimistic about the future—see Poff, "Western Ghost Town in American Culture"; DeLyser, "'Good, by God,

We're Going to Bodie!'"; and Glotfelty, "Riddle of Ghost Towns in the Environmental Imagination."

119. On Eisenhower's heart attack and its aftermath, see Secrest, "Picture That Reassured the World"; and M. Benson, "Dwight D. Eisenhower and the West," 63–64.

CHAPTER 2. THE ROADS NATURE MADE?

1. Colorado Highway 6 Association, *Stick to 6 with Sidney Six*, booklet (Grand Junction: Advertising Associates, for the Colorado Highway 6 Association, 1956). All quotations from the "Stick to 6" campaign are from this booklet.

2. In 1916, before America entered World War I, trains had virtually monopolized commercial passenger traffic between cities. By 1950, they had lost more than half of their share, carrying just over 46 percent. Even that number was misleading, because if one considered total intercity passenger traffic—meaning not just commercial but private too—the railroads' share had collapsed from a near-monopoly to less than 4 percent in those thirty-four years. Stover, *American Railroads*, 219.

3. On the wave of new passenger-train comforts, see Schafer and Welsh, *Classic American Streamliners*; and Stover, *American Railroads*, 215–18. For examples specific to trains that served Colorado, see railroad-issued guidebooks like Burlington Route, *Colorado: The Perfect Vacationland*, lure book ([Chicago], various years), esp. 52–54; and Union Pacific Railroad, *Colorado*, lure book ([Omaha?], various years), 36–37. The new comforts figured prominently in railroad advertising; see, for example, Burlington Route, ad in *Holiday*, May 1952, 167; California Zephyr (Burlington–Rio Grande–Western Pacific), ad in *Holiday*, February 1959, 23; and Union Pacific, ad in *National Geographic*, March 1951.

4. Colorado counted 5,604 miles of track in 1915 but just 3,772 by 1960, a decrease of 32.7 percent. On cutbacks in service and track abandonment in Colorado and the nation, see Stover, *American Railroads*, 203, 221–22. Statistics on track losses in Colorado specifically appear in Colorado State Planning Commission (hereafter SPC), *Year Book of the State of Colorado, 1937–1938*, 190; and Colorado State Planning Division (hereafter SPD), *Colorado Year Book, 1962–1964*, 320, 336. For proof that Colorado's mountain section was hardest hit, consider that from 1935 to 1960, the trackage loss in Colorado's thirty-five westernmost counties—an area that excludes the large Front Range cities and extends from the easternmost chain of mountains west to Utah—was 42 percent, compared to 23 percent for the state as a whole. The state lost 1,137 miles of track from 1935 to 1960, of which 847 miles, or nearly three-quarters, came out of those thirty-five westernmost counties.

5. Heppenheimer, *Turbulent Skies*, 124, 170.

6. See, for instance, Western Air Lines, ad in *Holiday*, April 1946, 2; United Air Lines, ad in *Holiday*, May 1946, 16; Continental Air Lines, ad in *Colorado Wonderland*, June 1956, 4.

7. American Airlines' coast-to-coast flights also landed regularly in Denver in the early 1950s—not because it was a scheduled stop, but because the turbocharged engines of the day had difficulty making it across the country without mechanical problems and frequently failed midway through the trip. American had so many unplanned landings

in Denver that it began keeping a store of spare engines there, underscoring the importance of Denver's midcontinent location in the early days of coast-to-coast air service. Heppenheimer, *Turbulent Skies*, 157–58.

8. "Gov. Sees Future for Western Slope," *Aspen Times*, August 30, 1945, 1; SPC, *Year Book of the State of Colorado, 1945–1947*, 364–66; "Colorado's Economic Frontiers," *Colorado Wonderland*, Development Issue, 1952, 22; SPD, *Colorado, 1956–1958*, 571–75.

9. The Aspen airport was laid out a few miles west of town, on ranchland that Paepcke and Jack Spachner, vice president of Paepcke's Container Corporation of America, had purchased in May 1948. For local involvement and local media coverage, see City of Aspen, City Council, minutes, April 19, 1948; "Aspen May Get Modern Airport This Summer," *Aspen Times*, April 22, 1948, 1; "Chicago Men Purchase Ranch," *Aspen Times*, June 3, 1948, 1; "Work on Aspen Airport to Start Immediately," *Aspen Times*, September 30, 1948, 1; "First Planes Land at New Aspen Airport," *Aspen Times*, November 11, 1948, 1; "Airport Co. and Aspen Air Service Inc. Formed," *Aspen Times*, December 9, 1948, 1; "Aspen Plans for Big Weekend With Official Opening of Airport and Winter Season," *Aspen Times*, December 16, 1948, 1. See also J. S. Allen, *Romance of Commerce and Culture*, 158.

10. As originally built, Aspen's gravel-runway airport could not accommodate larger passenger aircraft like the DC-3s that Continental had hoped to fly in. In fact, despite the Aspen Company's goal of getting a commercial airline to establish scheduled service, the airport would be limited to private planes and charter service for many years. Pitkin County took over the airport in 1956 and built a paved runway the next year, but not until the 1960s, after further improvements, did the new owners of Aspen Airways (which Paepcke had founded in the early 1950s as an air taxi for Aspen Institute participants) schedule service to Denver and other cities. For its first decade and a half, then, the airport made Aspen more accessible, but only for guests and staff of the institute and affluent visitors who owned or could charter planes.

11. The discussion of the DC-3's capabilities, and the hazards that pilots faced in flying it over the Rockies, is derived from the reminiscences of former Frontier pilots compiled in Searle, *Golden Years of Flying*, esp. 3–4, 37, 39, 43, 74, 92–93, 105, 125, 148, 189, 216.

12. Frontier Airlines' service to western Colorado followed such a track. Instead of heading directly west from Denver, Frontier DC-3s flew more than one hundred miles south to Pueblo and then followed the Arkansas and Gunnison river valleys west to Grand Junction. This flight path crossed the Continental Divide at Monarch Pass, just as U.S. Highway 50 did. In contrast, when United Air Lines introduced service from Denver to Grand Junction in 1947, its planes followed a straight-line flight path, right over the Front Range and other high mountains. United could do this because it flew high-altitude, pressurized DC-6s. Frontier did not acquire its first pressurized planes—Convair 340s—until 1959.

13. The nationwide figures appeared in *The American Magazine Travelogue*, no. 8 (New York: Crowell-Collier Publishing Co., 1955), and were cited in Crampon, *The Tourist and Colorado*, 32 (the figure specific to Colorado is from p. 33).

14. Denver Convention and Visitors Bureau (hereafter DCVB), *Come to Denver, Capital City of Colorado*, lure book (Denver, [ca. 1951]); sample ads in Colorado State Advertising and Publicity Committee (hereafter APC), *Annual Report: July 1, 1958–June*

30, 1959 (1959), Box 10223, records of the Colorado Department of Local Affairs; APC, dba Department of Public Relations, *Cool, Colorful Colorado Invites You!*, lure book (Denver, 1959), 5.

15. "Tabulation of Comments . . . ," in *Summary of 1953 Colorado Statewide Tourist Survey*, 1–2.

16. Debs Myers, "Colorado," *Holiday*, September 1952, 42. This particular article, with its less-than-reassuring depiction of mountain driving, got added exposure when it appeared in a popular travel anthology eight years later: *American Panorama West of the Mississippi: A "Holiday" Magazine Book.*

17. Burlington Route, *Colorado: The Perfect Vacationland* (1948), 2. That such a passage appeared in a railroad guidebook suggests that auto travel was already so popular by the late 1940s that even the railroads had to accede to it. Burlington sought a happy medium: persuade tourists to travel by train across the plains and then rent a car to satisfy their automobile-age wanderlust once they arrived in Colorado. "To enjoy these scenic highways to the utmost," the same guidebook suggested (p. 4), "it is neither necessary nor particularly advisable to drive one's own car over a long, hot tiresome route to Colorado. It is far more comfortable, and much faster to go in the coolness and comfort of a modern, air-conditioned Burlington train, availing oneself of motor transportation on arrival in the West."

18. The *Driving Our High Country* brochure was announced in the Highway Department's weekly press release, *Over the Highways*, March 27, 1969, 3. For mountain driving tips in the annual guidebook published by Rocky Mountain Motorists (hereafter RMM), the AAA's Colorado branch, see *Rocky Mountain Travel Directory: Colorado*, 1949 ed., 40; *Where to Vacation in Colorado*, 1953–54 ed., 18; *Where to Vacation in Colorado*, 1957–58 ed., 173, 175; and *Where to Vacation in Colorado*, 1963–64 ed., 161. The comparison to driving on Main Street appeared in the 1957–58 and 1963–64 editions.

19. A photograph of a snowplowed "all-weather highway" appeared in the official state highway map, *Colorful Colorado*, every year from 1949 through the mid-1960s (when the map went to a smaller format with fewer pictures). In the early 1950s, this photograph usually showed a plowed but snowpacked road, but starting in 1954 the highway in the picture was always plowed down to bare pavement—which, the State Highway Department surely realized, was more reassuring to tourists who were afraid to drive on snow or ice. Publicity photographs that the Highway Department distributed to the press not only showed the all-weather highways but often depicted hard-working road crews in the act of plowing them. See, for example, "Snow Plow," *Colorado Wonderland*, Christmas 1952, 14, 16; and Revis, "Colorado by Car and Campfire," 242–43.

20. DCVB, *Prospectors' Trails*, brochure (Denver, [early 1950s]); APC, *Cool, Colorful Colorado Invites You!* (1959). See also chapter 1, note 114. Circle tours were also familiar to tourists in the railroad age, with the Denver & Rio Grande's "Around the Circle" itinerary through southern and western Colorado enjoying particular renown; see Hooper, "Around the Circle" (1892); and Sabin, "Around the Circle" (1907).

21. "Burn the Maps," editorial, *Summit County Journal*, September 5, 1958, 4; "AAA Says Tourists Won't Leave Paved Roads for Scenery," *Middle Park Times*, August 22, 1957, 5; "Colorado Needs More Highways in Every County to Attract Tourists," *Colorado*

Information, April 25, 1946, 4; P. T. Thompson, *Use of Mountain Recreational Resources*, 158.

22. "Club '21' Organized," *Rangely Driller*, April 16, 1954 (quotation); "Entire West Slope Responds in Enthusiastic Meet of Club 21 in Ouray Last Saturday," *Ouray Herald*, April 16, 1954; and "Recommendations for Gunnison County Chamber of Commerce to Club Twenty," [June 1954], typescript, all in the scrapbook "Club 20 News Artc. from Mar 1954 to Nov 1964," in the historical files of Club 20 (hereafter Club 20 Files). On Club 20's origins, see Pollard, "Birth and Early Years of Club 20." On its pinnacle of power in the 1970s, see R. Martin, "Johnny Van and Club 20"; and Wiley and Gottlieb, *Empires in the Sun*, 128–30. The catchy name "Club 20," still in use today, reflected the public-relations savvy of the group's founders. They sensed, wrote one reporter, that "titles such as 'Western Colorado This or That Chamber of Commerce' [were] already overworked and that another such monikered association would only get lost in the shuffle." The name also fit easily into headlines, winning free publicity for the organization and making it seem more powerful than it actually was at first. Early on, the name fluctuated from Club 19 to Club 21, depending on how many counties were participating at any given time. "All for One, One for All," *Delta County Independent*, April 12, 1954 (quotation); and Preston Walker, untitled typescript [1954], both in the scrapbook "Club 20 News Artc. from Mar 1954 to Nov 1964," Club 20 Files; Greg Walcher, interview, Grand Junction, CO, July 7, 1997.

23. L. W. Parcell, quoted in "Club 20 Urges Road Improvements," *Durango Herald*, November 13, 1961, clipping in the scrapbook "Club 20 News Artc. from Jan 1960 to Feb 1964," Club 20 Files.

24. "A Powerful Influence," *Cortez Sentinel*, June 30, 1955, clipping in the scrapbook "Club 20 News Artc. from Mar 1954 to Nov 1964," Club 20 Files. After one year's presentation, Charles Shumate, the second-in-command at the State Highway Department, gushed, "There is no group in Colorado that meets with the Highway Commission . . . that can even compare with your Club 20." Quoted in "Club 20 Seeks More Road Funds for West Slope," *Steamboat Pilot*, August 15, 1957, clipping in ibid.

25. This characterization owes a debt to Mark Rose's *Interstate: Express Highway Politics, 1939–1989*. Owen Gutfreund offers an interesting explanation for how highways became a matter of such broad public consensus. In the early twentieth century, he argues, private pressure groups pushing for "good roads" forged tight alliances with public agencies like the federal Office of Road Inquiry and its successor, the Bureau of Public Roads. These agencies spread information that was, in effect, propaganda for the private lobbies and was sometimes even drafted by them. But because the information came from public officials, it carried "the seemingly apolitical stamp of 'expert' approval." Deepening this impression, Gutfreund adds (drawing from an earlier argument by Bruce Seely), was the fact that federal and state highway agencies were dominated by professional highway engineers, at a time when many Americans regarded professionally trained "experts" with great deference. The highway engineers were thus able to seem apolitical and authoritative—even as they actually worked to further their own narrow professional interests. Gutfreund, *20th-Century Sprawl*, esp. 12–13 (quotation p. 13), 16; Seely, *Building the American Highway System*. See also T. Lewis, *Divided Highways*, 12–16.

26. U.S. 40 reached its highest point (11,315 feet above sea level) at Berthoud Pass, on the Continental Divide. It actually crossed the divide two more times before reaching Utah, but at far lower altitudes: over Muddy Pass (8,772 feet) and Rabbit Ears Pass (9,426 feet). These two passes took advantage of an area where the Park, Gore, and Rabbit Ears Ranges met and flattened out a bit. Elsewhere, all three ranges were higher and, especially in the case of the jagged Gores, much less conducive to crossing.

27. Some of the earliest named highways, like the Lincoln, had to be built from scratch, mostly by private initiative. Later named highways, like the Victory, were usually pieced together from roads that already existed. Most famously, in 1917, publisher Rand McNally began selling maps and atlases that showed scores of "blazed trails" crisscrossing the country. Each was really just a string of shorter, local roads, brought together under a catchy name and marked by Rand McNally employees and volunteers with color-coded blazes on trees, telephone poles, and fence posts. Most of these blazed trails gave rise to highway associations, made up of business owners and boosters working together to promote travel on a given road. See Jakle, "Pioneer Roads"; Jakle and Sculle, *Motoring*, 43–53; Hokanson, *Lincoln Highway*, 5–21; Davies, *American Road*, 24–39; Liebs, *Main Street to Miracle Mile*, 17–18; Akerman, "Selling Maps, Selling Highways," 77–89; Yorke, Margolies, and Baker, *Hitting the Road*, 19, 40–41; and Ristow, "American Road Maps and Guides," 404–5.

28. The Midland Trail ran from Norfolk, Virginia, to Los Angeles. Its passage through Colorado spurred improvements to Berthoud Pass and to the crude, narrow shelf road along the Grand (Colorado) River below Kremmling. The Victory Highway incorporated the 114-mile stretch of the Midland Trail from Denver to Kremmling, but whereas the Midland headed southwest from Kremmling down the Colorado River toward Glenwood Springs, the Victory Highway continued northwest toward Steamboat Springs and Salt Lake City beyond. The Denver–Kremmling road was also part of the Grand Valley and Hot Springs Scenic Route, an intrastate named highway that linked Denver to scenic attractions on the Western Slope, including the Eagle River valley, Glenwood Canyon, and Glenwood Springs. M. C. Wiley, *High Road*, 19; Black, *Island in the Rockies*, 316–18, 356.

29. The state highway map for 1939 shows U.S. 40 "oil process and paved" all the way from Denver to the Utah state line, except for a brief stretch of gravel road through Byers Canyon, immediately west of Hot Sulphur Springs, and a section slated for oiling on the eastern approach to Muddy Pass. Colorado State Highway Department (hereafter SHD), *Travel Colorado Highways*, 1939 ed. For a list of tourist accommodations, which shows them concentrating more along U.S. 40 than any other road in western Colorado, see Continental Oil Company, dba Conoco Travel Bureau, *Conoco Travel Bureau Hotel and Cottage Camp Directory: List No. 3, Rocky Mountain and Central Plains Section*, booklet (Denver, [1935]).

30. The mountain first won renown when William Henry Jackson's famous photograph and Thomas Moran's famous painting of it went on display in 1876. The religious ferment of the 1920s revived interest, and area boosters, working with the *Denver Post*, began sponsoring annual summer pilgrimages to the peak. President Hoover designated Holy Cross a national monument in 1929, and in the 1930s Civilian Conservation Corps

crews built roads, trails, campgrounds, and rest houses. But interest in the snowy cross declined in the late 1930s (as did the cross itself: shifting rock partially collapsed one arm of the formation). In 1950 the Park Service decommissioned the national monument and returned the land to the White River National Forest. See R. L. Brown, *Holy Cross*, 29–50, 65–86; Szasz, "Wheeler and Holy Cross," 133, 140–44; Gallegos et al., *From County Seat to "Charlie" Vail*, 35–36; and Eagle Chamber of Commerce, *Western Colorado: The Playground of America*.

31. R. L. Brown, *Holy Cross*, 87–102; Gallegos et al., *From County Seat to "Charlie" Vail*, 12, 35–36; Colorado State Highway Advisory Board, minutes, November 3–10, 1921, December 13, 1922, December 12, 1924, November 10, 1925, November 29, 1932.

32. M. C. Wiley, *High Road*, 26–27; R. L. Brown, *Holy Cross*, 95, 99.

33. U.S. 6 as originally designated in the 1920s ran from Provincetown, Massachusetts, to Erie, Pennsylvania. In 1931 it was extended west to Greeley, Colorado. In 1937 it was extended the rest of the way through Colorado and on to the Pacific, ending in Long Beach, California. Shrine Pass, being unpaved, was not included on this route. Instead, U.S. 6 got from Summit County to next-door Eagle County by going south over Fremont Pass to Leadville and then swinging back north to cross Tennessee Pass into the upper Eagle River valley. Federal officials planned to cut out this long southward loop and incorporate Shrine Pass into the route once the pass was paved, but Colorado never paved it. When Vail Pass opened in 1940, U.S. 6 was rerouted there instead. See Richard F. Weingroff, "U.S. 6—The Grand Army of the Republic Highway," Federal Highway Administration, "Highway History" webpage, www.fhwa.dot.gov/infrastructure/us6.cfm (accessed December 19, 2009).

34. In 1948, by the State Highway Department's count, every day almost twice as many cars took U.S. 40 over Berthoud Pass as drove on U.S. 6 over Loveland Pass. SHD, Planning and Research Division, *1948 Traffic Volume Map, State of Colorado* (Denver, 1949), Box 10140, records of the Colorado Department of Transportation.

35. Stewart, *U.S. 40*, 8.

36. *Romance of the Old West along US 40 thru Utah–Colorado–Kansas* [ca. 1950], booklet in "Roads. Colorado. US Highways. #40" folder, Denver Public Library Clippings Files, Western History and Genealogy Department (hereafter DPL Clippings); National U.S. Highway 40 Association, *New! US 40: Mainline of America*, brochure (Lakewood, CO, [1950s]); *Take US 40 Denver–Salt Lake City: Winter and Summer . . . Summer and Winter* [1954?], brochure in "Roads. Colorado. US Highways. #40" folder, DPL Clippings.

37. See "Highway 40 Proud of Name," *Steamboat Pilot*, March 11, 1954, 2; and coverage from the *Middle Park Times*: "Plans Announced to Steal Hiway 40 From Colorado," February 25, 1954, 1; "Highway 40 Move, Design to Serve Selfish Interests," March 4, 1954, 1; "Sulphur Lions Club Joins Battle to Protect Highway 40 from 49er Steal," April 1, 1954, 1, 7; and "'Travel Pirating' Main Theme of Highway 40 Meet in Denver Friday," April 22, 1954, 1.

38. On the Grand Army of the Republic naming effort, see Weingroff, "U.S. 6"; and Brian Churchill and Joanne Churchill, "History of US Route 6—1937–1940," Discovering the 6 website, www.discoveringthe6.com/1937-1940.htm (accessed June 15, 2005). On the reorganization of the highway association, see "U.S. 6 Roosevelt Highway Association," *Colorado Information*, April 1, 1948, 2.

39. In 1951, for example, the Highway 6 Association began presenting westbound motorists passing through Omaha with a packet of colorful brochures advertising the Colorado towns along U.S. 6. The packet included "a personal letter of welcome from Governor Dan Thornton," the *Georgetown Courier* reported approvingly. "Tourist Packet Aid to Visitors," *Georgetown Courier*, March 29, 1951, 1, 4.

40. *Pleasure Ways Across the West*, brochure [1952?], author's collection. This brochure, advertising both U.S. 6 and U.S. 50, was jointly published by fifteen local service clubs and chambers of commerce (including the Glenwood Springs Chamber of Commerce) along the two routes in California, Nevada, Utah, and Colorado.

41. On the cultural construction of new regions, a theoretical overview is Paasi, "Place and Region"; and an excellent historical case study is Morrissey, *Mental Territories*. For a region whose construction was heavily premised on tourist promotion, see Gómez, *Quest for the Golden Circle*, esp. chap. 6.

42. As Yi-Fu Tuan explained it, people move through *spaces* and pause at *places*. Tuan, *Space and Place*, 6. The idea that automobile sightseers learned to see the landscape as a series of discrete interest points, strung out along a highway, also resembles part of Gabrielle Barnett's argument in "Drive-By Viewing," esp. 38–47. Also germane is David Louter's analysis in *Windshield Wilderness* of how, in the early twentieth century, the Park Service used roads to frame scenic spots and "wilderness" experiences for tourists; see esp. chaps. 1 and 2. As for the areas tourists shun, thinking them uninteresting and inaccessible, Julia Harrison has an apt term for them: "black holes" on the tourist map. J. Harrison, *Being a Tourist*, 171, 173.

43. The accusations could reach paranoia levels. In 1949, crews began paving U.S. 6 over Loveland Pass—a major improvement that Highway 6 boosters had long clamored for. Yet some in the nearby U.S. 6 community of Georgetown accused highway officials of secretly favoring U.S. 40. Their evidence? The crews had put up signs warning westbound motorists of closures ahead while Loveland Pass was being paved. "Motorists are thereby 'frightened' into driving west over highway 40" instead of staying on U.S. 6, the *Georgetown Courier* fumed. Georgetowners also accused the AAA of "actively campaigning" to divert tourists to U.S. 40, a conspiracy theory the AAA had heard many times before. "It is about time . . . that the business men of this state quit baiting each other over the routing of traffic," responded the head of AAA's Colorado chapter, sounding tired of the whole thing. "We should all work together to improve our highway system and to encourage more travel to the state." "Georgetown Merchants Suffering Loss of Business as Result of State Highway Sign," *Georgetown Courier*, July 26, 1949, 1; C. W. Werthan, letter to the editor, *Georgetown Courier*, August 23, 1949, 1, 4.

44. Before 1955 it was department policy to show only state and federal roads on the official state highway map. So when a streamlining program remanded a number of state highways to county status, those routes were removed from the map, and the 1954 edition showed Western Slope counties with far fewer roads. Club 20 protested, and in 1955 the Highway Department began showing county highways along with state ones. See clippings in the scrapbook "Club 20 News Artc. from Mar 1954 to Nov 1964," Club 20 Files; and compare the *Colorful Colorado* official state highway maps (Denver: Colorado Department of Highways) for 1953, 1954, and 1955. Boosters also fretted about tourists

who carried outdated maps that did not show the latest road improvements. One Dillon café owner noticed tourists using old maps that, among other things, showed U.S. 6 over Loveland Pass—the main entrance into Summit County from the east—not even oiled, when in fact it had been paved eight years earlier. It was "downright discouraging," said the *Summit County Journal*, "to a man who depends on tourists for the bulk of his business." "Burn the Maps," editorial, *Summit County Journal*, September 5, 1958, 4. On highway maps' power to direct tourists' movements, see Rugh, *Are We There Yet?*, 43–45, 66.

45. *Rocky Mountain Guide Book: Colorado and Wyoming Edition*, May 1949, 15, 17. See also Frisco's very similar ad in *Colorado United Travel Guide*, October–November 1954, 56: "it is an ideal rest stop between Vail and Loveland Passes."

46. Dillon's and Frisco's modest self-descriptions were also honest, corroborated by traffic-flow studies. Given that the preponderance of tourists entered the high country from the east, from Denver, we would expect "destination" towns to stop significant numbers of these people, hold them for a while, and then send them back east toward Denver—so that traffic volume should be markedly higher on the east side of a destination town than the west side. For "drive-through" towns, on the other hand, the traffic should be essentially the same over long stretches of road on either side. Sure enough, in traffic-flow studies from the late 1940s and 1950s, Frisco and Dillon fit the latter pattern. So did Empire in Clear Creek County, Eagle and Avon in Eagle County, and Fraser and Kremmling in Grand County. See SHD, *1948 Traffic Volume Map, State of Colorado*; and Crampon and Lawson, *1953 Colorado Summer Tourist Traffic Flow Study*, 18–21.

47. *Rocky Mountain Guide Book: Colorado and Wyoming Edition*, May 1949, 11 (first quotation); Idaho Springs Chamber of Commerce (hereafter ISCC), *Introducing . . . Colorado's Famed "Gold Rush" City: Idaho Springs*, brochure (Idaho Springs, [late 1950s]) (second quotation); Hanson Lodge (Idaho Springs), ad in *Rocky Mountain Life*, October 1948, 6 (third quotation).

48. ISCC, *Suggested Trips and Drives in and around Idaho Springs, Colorado*, booklet (Idaho Springs, [ca. 1947]); ISCC, *Introducing . . . Colorado's Famed "Gold Rush" City: Idaho Springs* [late 1950s]; *Rocky Mountain Guide Book: Colorado and Wyoming Edition*, May 1949, 11; *Colorado United Travel Guide*, October–November 1954, 66; ISCC, ad in RMM, *Where to Vacation in Colorado*, 1963–64 ed., 150. Also helping to further Idaho Springs's gateway image was the AAA, which in the early 1950s expanded the town's entry in its annual *Western Tour Book* to list several scenic drives. AAA, *Western Tour Book*, 1954–55 ed., 100.

49. See, for example, ad in *Rocky Mountain Guide Book: Colorado and Wyoming Edition*, May 1949, 10–11; Clear Creek County Chamber of Commerce (hereafter CCCCC), *Idaho Springs, Colorado, and Vicinity*, booklet (Idaho Springs, [ca. 1952]); CCCCC, *Introducing You to Clear Creek Canyon in the Heart of the Scenic Rockies*, brochure (Idaho Springs, [ca. 1954]); and ISCC, *Introducing . . . Colorado's Famed "Gold Rush" City* [late 1950s].

50. Grand Lake Chamber of Commerce, ad in RMM, *Rocky Mountain Travel Directory: Colorado*, 1949 ed., 52–53; "Granby, Colorado," *Rocky Mountain Guide Book: Colorado and Wyoming Edition*, May 1949, 19; Glenwood Springs Chamber of Commerce, *Glenwood Springs, Colorado: Vacation Hub of Colorado's Mountains and Lakes at Their Best!*, brochure (Glenwood Springs, [ca. 1954]); Glenwood Springs Chamber of Commerce, ad in RMM, *Where to Vacation in Colorado*, 1963–64 ed., 125; DCVB, *Come to Denver, Capital*

City of Colorado [ca. 1951]. Later in the decade, this Denver lure book got a new title that expressed the city's gateway status even more clearly: *Denver—Colorado: Vacation Land in the Rockies.*

51. This was one of L. J. Crampon's more striking findings when he conducted his survey of tourism patterns in Colorado. See Crampon and Ellinghaus, *1953 Colorado Statewide Summer Tourist Survey*, 21–22.

52. M. C. Wiley, *High Road*, 37; "Vail Protests Interregional Highway System," *Denver Post*, January 5, 1944, 3. In 1940, the "interstate" moniker was not yet universal; the PRA instead called them "interregional" highways.

53. Wolfe, "How the Lincoln Highway Snubbed Colorado."

54. Mark U. Watrous, in a speech to a gathering of Denver civil engineers, quoted in "Need for Federal Aid, Interstate Designation Cited in Address," *Colorado Information*, February 24, 1956, 13. Watrous was Charles Vail's successor as chief highway engineer.

55. A. V. Williamson, PRA district engineer, quoted in Ed C. Johnson, "Governor Johnson Gives History of Efforts to Get Colorado on Important Interstate System in Letter to Editor of Steamboat Pilot," *Summit County Journal*, March 9, 1956, 7; M. C. Wiley, *High Road*, 39.

56. F. J. Turner, "Significance of the Frontier in American History," 14; Stewart, *U.S. 40*, 21; Charles S. Robinson, "Environmental Aspects of Colorado Streets and Highway Engineering," in Colorado Department of Natural Resources, Geological Survey, *Governor's Conference on Environmental Geology*, 56. For a later expression of the idea that travel corridors emerge through an organic process, see Clay, *Close-Up*, 88–97.

57. Lamm and Smith, *Pioneers and Politicians*, 126–27. See also McCarty, "Big Ed Johnson of Colorado: A Political Portrait," esp. 6–7. Johnson was not a Colorado native; like many others in the state at the time, he was a "lunger," having originally come for respiratory health. Raised on a Kansas farm, he was stricken with tuberculosis at age twenty-five, whereupon he moved to Colorado with his wife, homesteading near the Moffat County seat, Craig.

58. Shortly after his inauguration in January 1955, Johnson summoned the State Highway Commission to meet with him in his chambers, to underscore his strong personal interest in the issue, and it was there that he made these comments. Colorado State Highway Commission, minutes, February 7, 1955. On the emphasis Johnson gave to the interstate in his inaugural speech, see "The Courier Viewpoint," *Georgetown Courier*, January 13, 1955, 2.

59. White House chief of staff Sherman Adams sent this not-so-subtle request through a mutual friend of Eisenhower's and Johnson's, Denver real estate magnate Aksel Nielsen. Johnson, with only the tiniest hint of sheepishness, dashed off a cheery handwritten reply to Adams, agreeing, "I will try to keep all of our folks quiet with respect to the Interstate Highway and await developments without pushing. . . . From now on the word is *mum* from this end!" Ed. C. Johnson to Hon. Sherman Adams, January 29, 1957, FF "141–B Highways and Thoroughfares (Roads) (7)" (emphasis in original), Box 729, Official File, White House Central Files, Dwight D. Eisenhower: Records as President of the United States, 1953–61 (hereafter DDE-WHCF).

60. E. C. Johnson, "Governor Johnson Gives History," 7. See also "State Legislature

Now in Session with Proposed Toll Tunnel Likely to Result in Long and Bitter Fight," *Steamboat Pilot*, January 5, 1956, 1; Bill Brenneman, "Gov. Johnson to Ask Ike for Tunnel Aid," *Rocky Mountain News*, March 25, 1956; Edwin C. Johnson to David Clarke, April 20, 1956, quoted in T. A. Thomas, "Roads to a Troubled Future," 206. Johnson frequently cited this $50 million statistic but never said where it came from.

61. Edwin C. Johnson to David Clarke, April 20, 1956, quoted in T. A. Thomas, "Roads to a Troubled Future," 206.

62. On the BPR technocracy, see Seely, *Building the American Highway System*. Seely later condensed his analysis and placed it in the wider context of American public-works history in "Saga of American Infrastructure," esp. 29–31. For another account of the BPR's rise, focusing on the pivotal role played by Thomas MacDonald, BPR chief from 1919 to 1953, see T. Lewis, *Divided Highways*, 5–17. On the rise of "experts" and Progressive technocracy more generally, the best introduction remains Wiebe's *Search for Order*, esp. chaps. 5, 6, and 7. Another good overview is Fischer, *Technocracy and the Politics of Expertise*, chap. 4.

63. Jordan, "Our Growing Interstate Highway System," 195 (quotation); B. Kelley, *Pavers and the Paved*, 13–14; Howard Wilshire, "Building a Radioactive Highway," *Desert Report* (Spring 2001): 9, 14; T. Lewis, *Divided Highways*, 170–71. The Interstate 40 idea was part of Project Plowshare, an Atomic Energy Commission initiative exploring the use of nuclear explosions for harbor and canal construction, mineral extraction, water projects, and other peacetime purposes.

64. Milward L. Simpson to Dwight D. Eisenhower, May 17, 1956, FF "141–B Highways and Thoroughfares (Roads) (6)," Box 728, Official File, DDE-WHCF.

65. A leading highway-engineering textbook of the time put it succinctly: "The end product of any transportation system is to provide service for which there is a demand." Harmer E. Davis and Richard M. Zettel, "Highway Administration and Finance," in Woods, Berry, and Goetz, *Highway Engineering Handbook*, sec. 1, p. 6. For more on the narrowly traffic-focused, anti-social-engineering mind-set of postwar highway engineers, see Rose, *Interstate*, esp. 59–60, 65–66, 96; and J. Brown, "Tale of Two Visions." Louis Ward Kemp, in "Aesthetes and Engineers," explains how this mind-set evolved in the decades after World War II—but always stayed true to the core belief that highways should serve existing traffic rather than redirect it.

66. Granted, Wyoming and New Mexico, where the PRA *did* plan interstates, were geographically remote and economically marginal too. But Wyoming already had a highway, U.S. 30, that handled much more traffic than did any east-west route across Colorado. New Mexico had two corridors, U.S. 70–80 and Route 66, that were busier still. In the late 1940s, summer traffic peaked at more than 2,600 vehicles a day on U.S. 30 in Wyoming and 3,000 vehicles a day on Route 66 in New Mexico. By comparison, the number for U.S. 40 in Colorado was only about 1,700 vehicles a day. See Lackey, "Mountain Passes in the Colorado Rockies," 214. To an engineer, these statistics meant that it made more sense to route the interstates through Wyoming and New Mexico, where the heaviest traffic already ran, than to add an expensive and redundant interstate over the rugged Colorado Rockies in between. And that, in fact, is what the BPR told Colorado; see M. C. Wiley, *High Road*, 38–39.

67. Aksel Nielsen, Dan Thornton, and Governor Edwin C. Johnson to Dwight D. Eisenhower, December 17, 1956, FF "141–B Highways and Thoroughfares (Roads) (7)," Box 729, Official File, DDE-WHCF; Colorado Department of Highways, *Major Link in America's Interstate Highway System* (Denver, 1956), Package 10 [oversized], in the series "Large Items from Top of Cabinet, Cupboard, Rooms 65, 68, 71, 74, and 98," DDE-WHCF.

68. See, for example, Governor Dan Thornton to Sherman Adams, December 16, 1954, FF "141–B-1 $50 Billion Highway Program (1)," Box 730, Official File, DDE-WHCF; Nielsen, Thornton, and Johnson to Eisenhower, December 17, 1956, FF "141–B Highways and Thoroughfares (Roads) (7)," Box 729, Official File, DDE-WHCF; E. C. Johnson, "Governor Johnson Gives History," 1.

69. Nielsen, Thornton, and Johnson to Eisenhower, December 17, 1956, FF "141–B Highways and Thoroughfares (Roads) (7)," Box 729, Official File, DDE-WHCF. Though this detailed, ten-page letter was cosigned by three men, it is apparent that Johnson wrote it. It rings truer to his writing style than Thornton's, and it rehashes Johnson's favorite talking points, using many of the same phrases. As for Nielsen, Eisenhower's personal friend, business partner, and sometime fishing buddy, we know he did not write the letter, because he telephoned the president's secretary and told her he had been "caught in the draft" between Johnson and Thornton and felt compelled (by implication, against his better judgment) to cosign the letter. See Ann Whitman, undated memos to Eisenhower and Col. Andrew J. Goodpaster, attached to the letter. In general, Nielsen was reluctant to use his friendship with the president for political ends—much less allow others, like Johnson, to use *him* for such ends.

70. For example, in the long letter to the president in December 1956 (see the prior note), Johnson, former governor Dan Thornton, and Aksel Nielsen devoted just two paragraphs to recreation. In the first, they argued recreation in Colorado was a matter of national interest: since so much of it occurred on public lands, "all of the people of the United States have a tremendous stake in its development." In the second paragraph, they candidly admitted Colorado's "desperate" need to compete for tourism, pointing out that it was "Colorado's second largest industry" and the state "[could not] afford to have prospective tourists shunted around Colorado to the north and to the south." But they tempered the point by casting it as a call for impartiality. Colorado asked for no special favors, they assured Ike: "We think the Federal Government should give us an equal break with our neighbors. We do not ask for an advantage. We only seek equal treatment." Johnson took a similar tack when he appeared before the Senate Subcommittee on Roads in 1955. This time, he complained bitterly that Colorado would lose tourists to neighboring states if they had interstates and Colorado did not. "You are going to build a four-lane highway through Wyoming," he railed. "You are going to build two 4-lane highways through New Mexico and Arizona. Colorado needs to be able to compete with our neighboring States." But then he again spun his remarks as a nonpolitical call for fair play. "We do not want to take anything away" from other states, he insisted. "We want to be able to compete with them on even terms." U.S. Congress, Senate Committee on Public Works, *National Highway Program: Hearings*, 838 (statement of Hon. Ed Johnson, April 13, 1955).

71. The album was Colorado Department of Highways, *Major Link in America's*

Interstate Highway System. Record of the ten-minute photo op, crammed in just before a National Security Council meeting, appears in "The President's Appointments, Thursday, May 3, 1956," typescript in FF "May '56 Miscellaneous (5)," Box 14, DDE Diary Series, Dwight D. Eisenhower: Papers as President of the United States, 1953–61, Ann Whitman File (hereafter DDE-Whitman). See also Ed C. Johnson, telegram to President Eisenhower, April 29, 1956, FF "[PPF]: 52–A: Fishing (2)," Box 898, President's Personal File, DDE-WHCF. The brief May 1956 meeting was not the only time Johnson appealed to Eisenhower's love for Colorado. On at least two occasions he reminded the president of traffic congestion on Berthoud Pass, which Ike had seen firsthand while motoring to his fishing retreat near Fraser. In an August 1956 letter, Johnson fawned that "no one in Washington, as do you, knows and understands so well" the need to ease traffic over the pass. Then again, in the long letter of December 1956 (see note 69 in this chapter): "Mr. President, no one knows this traffic snarl [on Colorado's high passes] better than you and no one knows better than you how it can be cured." But if Eisenhower was ever inclined to favor the interstate for the convenience of his own vacations, that incentive vanished with his 1955 heart attack. In April 1957 he confided to Colorado senator Gordon Allott that he personally favored a Colorado interstate "but he doubted whether he would ever use the route because his doctors keep cautioning him about high altitudes." Indeed, after 1955, Eisenhower never again visited the high country. E. C. Johnson to Eisenhower, August 27, 1956, in FF "Johnson, Edwin C.," Box 1593, Alpha File, DDE-WHCF; Ann Whitman, memorandum on "Conference between the President and Senator Gordon Allott," April 16, 1957, FF "Apr '57 Diary—Staff Memos (1)," Box 23, DDE Diary Series, DDE-Whitman.

72. Dwight D. Eisenhower to Ed [Johnson], May 7, 1956, FF "[PPF]: 52–A: Fishing (2)," Box 898, President's Personal File, DDE-WHCF. Adding to the album's pathetic ineffectiveness, White House staff filed the records of its presentation not under "Highways," "Transportation," or the like but under the throwaway category "Fishing." I am deeply grateful to Jim Leyerzapf at the Eisenhower Library, whose detective work unearthed these obscure records, which in turn led to the rediscovery of the leather-bound album, still wrapped in its kraft paper and forgotten from almost fifty years ago.

73. These were the design standards as revised in 1956; the original standards, adopted in 1945, did not specify lane or median widths. On both sets of standards, see Richard F. Weingroff, "Target: $27 Billion—The 1955 Estimate," Federal Highway Administration, "Highway History" webpage, www.fhwa.dot.gov/infrastructure/target.cfm (accessed May 31, 2012).

74. Johnson explicitly linked the tunnel concept to the winning of the interstate in his January 1955 inaugural address; see "The Courier Viewpoint," *Georgetown Courier*, January 13, 1955, 2. By early 1956, the governor was regularly casting this argument in do-or-die terms, warning that the feds would never grant an interstate until and unless a tunnel was already in place. See, for example, "State Legislature Now in Session with Proposed Toll Tunnel Likely to Result in Long and Bitter Fight"; and item on Johnson's speech to the Denver City Club, *Colorado Information Newsletter*, March 8, 1956, 2.

75. "Actual Counts Prove Highway 40 the Best Traffic Route in Colorado," *Middle Park Times*, June 10, 1954, 1; Howard, Needles, Tammen & Bergendorff and Singstad &

Baillie, *Continental Divide Tunnels*. Singstad had won renown for directing the design and construction of New York City's Holland, Lincoln, Queens-Midtown, and Brooklyn-Battery tunnels. In his report on four proposed tunnel sites in Colorado, he collaborated with Howard, Needles, Tammen, & Bergendoff, a Kansas City firm that had worked on the planning and design of the Denver–Boulder Turnpike in the late 1940s–early 1950s.

76. In 1954, the commission endorsed the tunnel in principle but declined to authorize bonds to fund it. In 1955 and 1956, the commission openly defied Johnson by recommending against tunnel construction "at this time," based on the technocratic reasoning that the benefits would be too small to justify the cost. Colorado State Highway Commission, minutes, July 31–August 2, 1954, March 12, 1955, and January 10, 1956; "Resolution Adopted by the Colo. Highway Commission Regarding the Proposed Tunnel thru the Divide," *Middle Park Times*, August 12, 1954, 1, 6, 8.

77. Edwin Johnson, speech to the Denver City Club, quoted in *Colorado Information Newsletter*, March 8, 1956, 1–2; and in "Governor Has New Tunnel Site," *Steamboat Pilot*, March 15, 1956, 6. The week after his speech, Johnson summoned the State Highway Commission to his office and pointedly rehashed these same comments. Colorado State Highway Commission, minutes, March 11, 1956.

78. E. C. Johnson, "Governor Johnson Gives History," 7; Milt Andrus, "Good Roads Assn. Director Expresses His Views on a Continental Divide Tunnel," *Colorado Information*, January 26, 1956, 6; "Editorial," *Georgetown Courier*, August 20, 1948, 1. On the western tradition of invoking pioneer heritage to try to control the terms of political debate, see Wrobel, *Promised Lands*, chap. 6.

79. Colorado State Highway Commission, minutes, March 11 and April 26, 1956. The April resolution was necessary because the commissioners' March 11 resolution had stopped short of endorsing the tunnel concept. Instead, the commissioners had carefully declared that they were ordering the calling of bids only to gauge the project's "cost and practicability."

80. In the Federal Aid Highway Act of 1944, formally establishing the interstate highway system, Congress capped the system at 40,000 miles and did not include an interstate west of Denver. Under fiscally cautious Republican control, Congress seemed unlikely to increase the overall mileage, but fortunately for Colorado's interstate ambitions, public-works-friendly Democrats regained control of Congress in 1954. After much haggling between the House and Senate, the Federal Aid Highway Act of 1956 (better known as the Interstate Highway Act) included a provision expanding the system by 1,000 miles. See Richard Weingroff, "Why Does I-70 End in Cove Fort, Utah?," Federal Highway Administration "Highway History" webpage, www.fhwa.dot.gov/infrastructure/covefort.cfm (accessed December 19, 2009); Lee Mertz, "Origins of the Interstate," at the same site, www.fhwa.dot.gov/infrastructure/origin.htm (accessed December 19, 2009); T. Lewis, *Divided Highways*, chap. 5; and Rose, *Interstate*, 26, 92.

81. T. A. Thomas, "Roads to a Troubled Future," 206–7.

82. "Denver-Utah Link OKd," *Denver Post*, October 18, 1957, 1; "Western Colorado Finally Selected for Part of Interstate System," *Steamboat Pilot*, October 24, 1957, 1. "You have the gratitude of the State of Colorado and me," an elated Ed Johnson wired Ike upon hearing the BPR's decision. "May God bless you." Ed C. Johnson, telegram to

President Eisenhower, October 18, 1957, FF "141–B Highways and Thoroughfares (Roads) (7)," Box 729, Official File, DDE-WHCF.

83. In "Roads to a Troubled Future," 210–41, Thomas A. Thomas argues that the deciding factor was the behind-the-scenes influence of Aksel Nielsen, who had secretly involved the president in several real estate ventures in the Denver metro area, so that Ike stood to profit financially if a new interstate brought a boom to Colorado. Thomas claims that after Nielsen made his support for the interstate clear (by cosigning the long letter that Ed Johnson sent to Ike in December 1956), Eisenhower shifted from a neutral stance to a position favoring Colorado's case. But remember that immediately after signing the long letter, Nielsen effectively disavowed it in a call to the president's office (see note 69 in this chapter). Thomas does show that Eisenhower was heavily invested in Denver suburban and mall development while still in the White House, but there is no direct evidence that his investments influenced his judgment on the interstate or that Nielsen played a deciding role (or, for that matter, that Eisenhower himself did—no document, public or private, shows him endorsing or even favoring Colorado's case). On the other hand, the Federal Highway Administration's in-house history, while acknowledging that the exact reasons for the BPR's decision are unknown, points to army approval as a critical factor and also to congressional intent—that is, the BPR's sense that when Congress voted the additional interstate mileage in 1956, it had the proposed Colorado–Utah link in mind. See the quoted documents in Weingroff, "Why Does I-70 End in Cove Fort, Utah?"

84. See, for example, "Western Colorado Finally Selected for Part of Interstate System," and the accompanying editorial, "Pilot Opinion," *Steamboat Pilot*, October 24, 1957, 1, 2.

85. "Our Interstate Highway Designation," *Summit County Journal*, October 25, 1957, 4.

86. Anonymous reader, quoted in "Highway 40 Logical for Network," *Summit County Journal*, February 4, 1955, 4; "Meeting to Be Held in Craig to Support Berthoud Tunnel," *Middle Park Times*, April 26, 1956, 1.

87. Laurence Jump to Edwin C. Johnson, March 5, 1955, cited in T. A. Thomas, "Roads to a Trouble Future," 191–92. For more on Jump's involvement, including his chairing Georgetown's ad hoc Tunnel Committee, see Town of Georgetown, Board of Selectmen, minutes, July 13, 1953; "Burwell Blasts Highway Dep't," *Georgetown Courier*, May 14, 1953, 1; and "Governor Johnson Will Be Greeted by Citizens on Loveland Tunnel Trip," *Georgetown Courier*, February 3, 1955, 1.

88. "Association Will Work for Improved Roads," *Aspen Times*, January 29, 1948, 1. The business owners founded the Highway 82 Association, named for State Highway 82, which ran from Aspen northwest to junction with U.S. 6 at Glenwood Springs and was the main route through Aspen's Pitkin County. The association was cofounded by *Aspen Times* editor Verlin Ringle and Aspen banker W. Lucas Woodall at a January 1948 meeting called by the local Lions Club (the leading booster group in Aspen before the founding of the chamber of commerce in 1949). The Highway 82 Association pledged to work closely with the newly created Loveland Tunnel Association in pushing for a tunnel under Loveland Pass on U.S. 6. See ibid. and "Important Mass Meeting of Citizens Called," *Aspen Times*, January 22, 1948, 1.

89. On the efforts of the Colorado Highway 6 Association and its national counterpart, the U.S. 6 Roosevelt Highway Association, see *Colorado Information*, April 1, 1948; "Straight Creek Pushed for Tunnel Site," *Eagle Valley Enterprise*, January 5, 1956, 1; "Meet with Governor to Discuss Tunnels," *Clear Creek Mining Journal* (hereafter CCMJ), April 27, 1956, 1; and "Bryant Re-Elected Highway 6 President," CCMJ, December 6, 1957, 1. The *Middle Park Times* in Kremmling regularly covered the National U.S. Highway 40 Association's efforts to win the interstate designation for 40: see, for example, "Inter-State Designation of Highway 40 thru State Sought by Assn.," December 30, 1954, 1; "National U.S. Highway 40 Officials Report Satisfactory Tour Results," February 24, 1955, 1; and "US 40 Improvements Outlined at Meeting," November 22, 1956, 1.

90. The National U.S. Highway 40 Association was headquartered in Lakewood, the suburb immediately west of Denver. Though the organization, as of 1954, counted 5,700 members (including individuals and businesses) from six states along the highway (Missouri, Kansas, Colorado, Utah, Nevada, and California), its 1954 convention saw Coloradans winning five of six elected leadership positions. The new president, Clarence Reiff, was a motel owner from Kremmling; he succeeded Eddie Bohn, a motel owner from Denver. The unelected executive secretary was also from Denver. See "Reiff Named U S Highway 40 Assn. Head Tuesday," *Middle Park Times*, November 18, 1954, 1. At least one earlier president of the association, Ed Harding of Craig, also hailed from Colorado.

91. "Hiway 6 Tunnel Promoted by Buckley Letter," *Georgetown Courier*, January 20, 1955, 1. The man, Ron Buckley, sent an identical map to Chief Highway Engineer Watrous. Buckley, who was active in the Colorado Highway 6 Association, hailed from Silver Plume, a small former mining community on U.S. 6 about two miles west of Georgetown, where Highway 6 began its long, winding climb to the summit of Loveland Pass.

92. A widely used highway-engineering textbook of the day began its discussion of route selection this way: "Since a straight line is the shortest distance between two points, the engineer must determine what, if any, intermediate controls exist which would tend to bend the location away from a straight line." J. C. Young, Robert D. Miles, and C. L. Miller, "Route Selection, Airphoto Interpretation, Photogrammetry, and Digital Computers," in Woods, Berry, and Goetz, eds., *Highway Engineering Handbook*, sec. 5, p. 6.

93. At one point, U.S. 40 advocates had also been able to claim theirs was the most direct route—that is, the most direct route from Denver to Salt Lake City. But the BPR's surprise decision to aim the interstate southwesterly toward Cove Fort rendered that argument obsolete and left U.S. 40 advocates scrambling for new selling points.

94. Mark Watrous, quoted in *Colorado Information Newsletter*, March 20, 1952, 1. Later, engineers studying the Colorado River route would find that it was not such a natural passage after all. Fitting an interstate into the winding, often narrow canyon between Kremmling and Dotsero would require several tunnels and "frequent crossings of the river . . . to occupy first one side of the valley, then the other." E. Lionel Pavlo Engineering Co., *Interstate Highway Location Study*, 38. To this day, there is still no road all the way down the Colorado River from Kremmling to Dotsero, despite the widespread

assumption in the 1950s that with or without an interstate, one would surely be built.

95. Examples of this rhetoric include Grand County, Board of Commissioners, minutes, April 5, 1954; "Vasquez Creek Tunnel Site on Highway 40 Favored," *Middle Park Times*, March 24, 1955, 3; "Meeting to Be Held in Craig to Support Berthoud Tunnel," *Middle Park Times*, April 26, 1956, 1; and "Berthoud Tunnel Will Give Pass-Free Route between East-West Slopes," *Middle Park Times*, May 3, 1956, 1.

96. See, for example, "A Tunnel . . . to Serve All Colorado," *Summit County Journal*, January 13, 1956, 4; "Actual Counts Prove Highway 40 the Best Traffic Route in Colorado"; and "Straight Creek Pushed for Tunnel Site." For its part, the National U.S. Highway 40 Association asserted (dubiously) that U.S. 40 in Colorado handled more traffic than any other three highways in the state combined. Bob Campbell, a representative of the association, made this claim on more than one occasion; see "C of C Hears Hiway 40 Representative," *Middle Park Times*, April 8, 1954, 1; and "Actual Counts Prove Highway 40 the Best Traffic Route in Colorado."

97. See, for example, "Highway Tunnel Prospects Brighten with Opening of Bids by Highway Department," CCMJ, April 20, 1956, 1; "Straight Creek Pushed for Tunnel Site"; and "A Tunnel . . . to Serve All Colorado." Like traffic numbers, these claims were debatable. The numbers said that U.S. 6 had a much larger population and economic base—but that came from counting Lake County (home to Leadville and the giant Climax molybdenum mine); Garfield County (home to major coal-mining operations and Glenwood Springs, the Western Slope's biggest resort town); and Delta and Mesa Counties (the latter the home to Grand Junction, the economic hub and largest city in all of western Colorado). But Lake County was actually not on U.S. 6—it was twelve miles away, on the other side of Fremont Pass, and in any case Climax shipped its product by rail, not road. As for Garfield, Delta, and Mesa Counties, once the BPR fixed Cove Fort as the interstate's western terminus, it guaranteed that all three counties would end up on or near the interstate no matter which path it took over the Continental Divide—so U.S. 40 backers could justifiably have counted Mesa, Delta, and Garfield Counties in their economic and population statistics too. A fairer comparison would have been to juxtapose the areas U.S. 6 and U.S. 40 ran through between Empire Junction (the point where the two routes diverged) and Dotsero (the point where they came back together). For U.S. 40 that meant Grand County and northern Eagle County; for U.S. 6 it included western Clear Creek County, Summit County, and southern Eagle County. Given that comparison, the choice was essentially a wash. There were no sizable industrial or mining operations and no large or particularly prosperous towns along either route—which is precisely why business and civic leaders in those towns were so desperate to get on an interstate in the first place.

98. "Highway 40 Logical for Network," *Summit County Journal*, February 4, 1955, 4; "Loveland Tunnel Most Feasible of All Routes," *Eagle Valley Enterprise*, March 17, 1955, 1; "Straight Creek Pushed for Tunnel Site"; "Eagle-Glenwood Area Unites for Tunnel Fight," *Eagle Valley Enterprise*, March 8, 1956, 1; "Wanted—Empire Builders," *Georgetown Courier*, May 10, 1956, unpaginated insert.

99. This talking point originated with Governor Johnson, who revealed that Ike had once told him something should be done to ease the traffic over Berthoud Pass. See

"Titanic Struggle Being Waged before Special Legislative Session over Selection of Site for East-West Tunnel," *Steamboat Pilot*, May 10, 1956, 1; and "Good Treatment in Highway Budget," *Steamboat Pilot*, May 24, 1956, 2. Johnson wanted Coloradans to infer that the president favored the U.S. 40 route, which must have seemed plausible to many Coloradans because Eisenhower had to take U.S. 40 whenever he went to Grand County to fish. But the president was careful never to express a preference for either side in the Colorado interstate debate, and there is no evidence, in his correspondence with Johnson or anywhere else, that he favored U.S. 40.

100. For Theobald's accusation that Johnson harbored a bias toward his home region, see "Phoney Tunnel Bids," *Summit County Journal*, March 23, 1956, 4. See also "Eagle-Glenwood Area Unites for Tunnel Fight," *Eagle Valley Enterprise*, March 8, 1956, 1; and John Leuthold, letter to the editor, *Rocky Mountain News*, April 8, 1956. Johnson indignantly denied he had a hometown bias in an open letter to the *Rocky Mountain News*, reprinted locally as "Governor Johnson Rises to Mr. Leuthold's Bait," *Summit County Journal*, April 20, 1956, 3. On Johnson's public pronouncements for Berthoud Pass, see *Colorado Information Newsletter*, March 8, 1956, 1–2; "Governor Has New Tunnel Site," *Steamboat Pilot*, March 15, 1956, 6; "Meet with Governor to Discuss Tunnels"; "Legislators to Take Look-See at Site for Divide Tunnel," *Rocky Mountain News*, May 8, 1956, 5; "Legislators Visit Here on Tour of Tunnel Sites," *Middle Park Times*, May 10, 1956, 1; and "Titanic Struggle Being Waged before Special Legislative Session over Selection of Site for East-West Tunnel". On the governor's behind-the-scenes efforts to sway the Highway Commission, see Colorado State Highway Commission minutes, March 11, April 26, May 14–15, and July 20, 1956. See also "Legislators to Take Look-See at Site for Divide Tunnel"; and T. A. Thomas, "Roads to a Troubled Future," 192–94.

101. "Around Town," *Eagle Valley Enterprise*, May 10, 1956, 1; "Former Editor of Journal Writes Of 'Johnson's Folly,'" *Summit County Journal*, March 30, 1956, 4; "Johnson Accused of Hampering Federal Designation," *Eagle Valley Enterprise*, January 24, 1957, 1. The first charge was from the iconoclastic *Enterprise* editor, Marilla McCain; the second from John Leuthold, former editor of the *Journal* in Breckenridge; and the third from state senator Vernon Cheever of Colorado Springs and state representative John Vanderhoof of Glenwood Springs.

102. Wiley, *High Road*, 48; "Loveland Pass Tunnel Project to Start Soon," *Georgetown Courier*, July 18, 1947, 1; "Loveland Pass Tunnel to be Started Soon," *Georgetown Courier*, August 15, 1947, 1. Both of these *Courier* articles were reprinted from the *Denver Post*.

103. The commissioners from Clear Creek and Summit Counties pushed especially persistently for Loveland; see Colorado State Highway Advisory Board, minutes, November 22–4, 1948, November 26, 1951, November 2–4, 1953.

104. Items in *Colorado Information Newsletter*, January 17, 1952, 4, May 29, 1952, 3, and November 27, 1952, 2; Grand County, Board of Commissioners, resolutions, November 3, 1952, and October 5, 1953; "Proposed Devil's Thumb Highway Route to West Slope," *Middle Park Times*, April 16, 1953; "Devil's Thumb Road Given Added Impetus," *Middle Park Times*, October 8, 1953, 1.

105. "Highway Six Asks Fairness in Tunnel Investigation," *Eagle Valley Enterprise*, May 21, 1953, 1; "Highway 40 Logical Route," *Steamboat Pilot*, June 28, 1956, 2.

106. Editorial, *Georgetown Courier*, August 20, 1948, 1; "Our Views on the Tunnel," *Summit County Journal*, January 20, 1956, 4 (Theobald quotations); "Highway Problem Is Serious," *Steamboat Pilot*, October 7, 1954, 2; "All Colorado Passes Need Improvement," *Steamboat Pilot*, March 1, 1956, 2; "Mapping Highway Improvement," *Steamboat Pilot*, November 24, 1955, 2 (Leckenby quotations).

107. Howard, Needles, Tammen & Bergendorff and Singstad & Baillie, *Continental Divide Tunnels*; "Engineers Also Recommend Straight Creek Tunnel," *Denver Post*, January 11, 1954,1; "Straight Creek Gets Tunnel Nod," *Georgetown Courier*, January 14, 1954, 1; "Straight Creek Proposed for Tunnel Site," *Eagle Valley Enterprise*, January 14, 1954, 1; "Proposed Tunnel Data Is Outlined," *Georgetown Courier*, January 28, 1954, 1. See also "Watrous Gives Tunnel Data at Lawson Meeting," *Eagle Valley Enterprise*, November 5, 1953, 1.

108. In the two-plus years after Singstad's initial "consolidated" report came out, Leckenby repeatedly used his *Steamboat Pilot* editorial column to make this case: see esp. "Not Too Fast on Tunnel," March 11, 1954, 2; "Time Not Ripe for Tunnel," March 18, 1954, 2; "More Knockers Than Defenders," April 29, 1954, 2; "A Practical Highway Tunnel," June 10, 1954, 2; "Sure We Want a Tunnel," August 12, 1954, 2; "Passes Must Be Improved," March 17, 1955, 2; "We Want Tunnel That Will Work," December 22, 1955, 2; "An Important Session," January 5, 1956, 2; and "All Colorado Passes Need Improvement," 2. Citizen groups and local officials from all along the U.S. 40 corridor made a similar argument to Leckenby's; see, for example, "Three Lane Berthoud Pass Route Suggested by Commissioners as Doing Away with Need of Tunnel," *Steamboat Pilot*, December 2, 1954, 1; "The Reasons a Tunnel Shouldn't Be Considered at the Present Time," *Middle Park Times*, January 19, 1956, 1; and Ted Schefler, "Toll Tunnel Would Be Fizzle but Better Highways Are Necessity," letter to the editor, *Steamboat Pilot*, February 23, 1956, 9.

109. "Not Too Fast on Tunnel"; Schefler, "Toll Tunnel Would Be Fizzle." Leckenby's comment was hardly an isolated one; at least two other times he voiced his concern that scenery-seeking tourists might actually shun a tunnel. See "All Colorado Passes Need Improvement"; and "Good Treatment in Highway Budget."

110. Preston Walker, quoted in "Club 20 Asks Better Passes," *Salida Daily Mail-Record*, November 30, 1954, clipping in the scrapbook "Club 20 News Artc. from Mar 1954 to Nov 1964," Club 20 Files; Clarence Werthan, paraphrased in "New Highway Assures Future Travel," *Eagle Valley Enterprise*, October 31, 1957, 1.

111. "Tunnel Fight Splits West Slope Leaders," *Rocky Mountain News*, December 5, 1954.

112. Colorado State Highway Commission, minutes, March 11 and April 26, 1956; "Compromise Tunnel Bill OK'd; Ed Claims Partial Victory," *Rocky Mountain News*, May 13, 1956, 5; "Legislature Approves Tunnel If and When Route Is Approved for Part of Federal Interstate System," *Steamboat Pilot*, May 17, 1956, 1; "Location of Tunnel Waits on Federal Action," *CCMJ*, May 18, 1956, 1; Ed Harding, "New Law Tells How Tunnel Can Be Built," *Middle Park Times*, March 28, 1957, 8.

113. On the Long-Range Highway Planning Committee that McNichols chaired, see Wiley, *High Road*, 33–34; Colorado Department of Highways, *Paths of Progress*, 14; and

SPC, *State of Colorado Year Book*, 1951 to 1955, 113–15, 426–28. One of the quintessentially technocratic reforms to come out of McNichols's committee was a new way of deciding which roads most urgently needed improving: sufficiency ratings, in which each road was graded from 1 to 100 based on quantifiable variables like surface condition, traffic volume, and anticipated remaining life. Devised in Arizona in the 1940s and championed by the National Research Council's Highway Research Board, sufficiency ratings were supposed to be impartial and to "render ineffective, individual or group pressure." Colorado Highway Planning Committee, *Committee Reports to John Q. Public*, 4, 7 (quotation); Colorado Department of Highways, *Colorado's Annual Highway Report for 1955* [1956], 16; Rose, *Interstate*, 42–43.

114. Colorado State Highway Commission, minutes, August 28, 1958. The engineer hired to conduct the study, E. Lionel Pavlo, took the job only after discussing with the commission the "desirability of preserving complete objectivity"; "only in such a climate would his firm be willing to undertake the work." Colorado State Highway Commission, minutes, February 20, 1959. See also the commission's minutes for August 4, September 6, and November 17–19, 1958; and E. Lionel Pavlo to Mark U. Watrous, January 16, 1959, transcribed in Colorado State Highway Commission, minutes, Book 3, 484–86.

115. "An Outside Firm Was Hired," *Summit County Journal*, February 20, 1959, 4. For some of the rumors surrounding Pavlo's ongoing survey, see "The Highway Tunnel," *Summit County Journal*, January 9, 1959, 4.

116. Colorado State Highway Commission, minutes, April 18, 1960.

117. E. Lionel Pavlo Engineering Co., *Interstate Highway Location Study*, i, 3, 5, 6–14, 17–25.

118. Ibid., 7, 9.

119. Ibid., 14 and figure 25.

120. Ibid., 7–9. In the 1954–55 and 1955–56 seasons, the two largest ski areas on U.S. 40 (Winter Park and Berthoud Pass) had received more skier-visits than the two largest on U.S. 6 (Arapahoe Basin and Loveland Basin). But then Loveland's numbers had soared and Berthoud's fallen, so by 1958–59 the ski areas on U.S. 6 were a bigger combined draw. Visits to Winter Park had continued to climb, but Pavlo noted that Winter Park was served by the Moffat Tunnel from Denver, so by implication many of its customers took the train and would not use an interstate. As for extractive industries, Pavlo mentioned the giant Climax molybdenum mine near Leadville but noted that it shipped almost all of its yield by rail, so it did not need interstate access and should not influence the route location. Finally, Pavlo called ranching a "large activity" and logging "an important industry" in the study area but gave no sense that either one swayed his route choice. In fact, he observed that the timber reserves along U.S. 40 were three or four times larger than those along U.S. 6—but he chose U.S. 6 anyway.

121. E. Lionel Pavlo Engineering Co, *Interstate Highway Location Study*, iii.

122. Nelson M. Wells, "Landscaping," in Woods, Berry, and Goetz, *Highway Engineering Handbook*, sec. 28, p. 5 (quotation). On parkways as precursors to freeways, see Brown, "Tale of Two Visions," 7–8, 20; and T. Lewis, *Divided Highways*, 28.

123. "Spending Freely; Not Wisely," *Middle Park Times*, April 21, 1960, 2; "Improve Highway 40 Now," *Steamboat Pilot*, April 28, 1960, 2 (quotation). See also "Eagle Valley

Selected for Interstate Highway Route," *Eagle Valley Enterprise*, April 21, 1960, 1; "Straight Creek Tunnel–Highway 6 Win Acceptance for Interstate Route," *Steamboat Pilot* (April 21, 1960, 1; "Now That We Know Where . . . WHEN . . . is the Next Big Question," *CCMJ*, April 22, 1960, 1; and "Berthoud Pass Improvement Planned," *Steamboat Pilot*, April 28, 1960, 1.

124. According to the *Post*, the investors "believe[d] Breckenridge—less than 100 miles from Denver over what eventually will be a four-lane interstate highway with an auto tunnel penetrating Loveland Pass—and the area around it is destined to become one of Colorado's top year-around resorts." Willard Haselbush, "$3 Million Brecken-ridge Spa Taking Shape," *Denver Post*, January 3, 1963, 3D.

125. P. T. Thompson, *Use of Mountain Recreational Resources*, 93.

126. Ibid., 94.

127. Towler, *History of Skiing at Steamboat Springs*, 108–19. Besides Steamboat, the only other big new ski development to open along U.S. 40 during the era of I-70 megar-esorts—Mary Jane, in 1975—was really just an expansion of adjacent Winter Park. Two more ambitious resort ventures popped up near Steamboat Springs in the early 1970s, but both closed within two seasons. Del Webb, famed developer of Sun City, Arizona, was involved in a 1968 land purchase near Granby that was supposed to yield a ski-golf resort, but that vision did not materialize until another developer took over the land and opened Silver Creek in 1982.

128. Jim Hughes, "DEA coming to Steamboat: U.S. 40 a growing drug corridor," *Denver Post*, May 21, 1998, 8B.

129. These mountains have been known to strike back, though. In August 2005, after heavy rains triggered three especially large rockfalls along this stretch of the inter-state, a Colorado Department of Transportation spokesperson noted, not very reassur-ingly, "When you look up at these mountainsides, and look at the fatigue and how old these rocks are, it's kind of a scary thing to think that we're driving under them." "I-70 Reopens after Crews Clean Up Three Rock Slides," *Summit Daily News*, August 15, 2005.

130. It should be said that before this intervention the creek had already been rechanneled in places by railroad construction, heavily sedimented by tailings, and pol-luted by acid drainage from the old Tenmile mining district upstream. The I-70 stream relocation actually restored the canyon as a trout habitat. "Tenmile Creek: A Case Study in Stream Relocation," Federal Highway Administration, "Environmental Review Tool-kit" webpage, http://environment.fhwa.dot.gov/ecosystems/wildlife/fish8.asp (accessed June 8, 2012).

131. I am indebted to Gregory Summers, who comes to a similar insight in *Consum-ing Nature*, esp. 140–49, and who has helped me hone my own thinking about highway artifice and the experience of scenery.

132. On midcentury boosters' and highway designers' optimism that roads could be made to blend with topography and enhance motorists' experience of nature, see Louter, *Windshield Wilderness*, chaps. 1, 2.

1. Hauserman, *Inventors of Vail*, 16. Dick Hauserman (who was one of the original investors in Vail Associates) reported that Eaton had known of the snow bowls since childhood and had probably first seen them while hunting with his family. That said, it is true that in adulthood Eaton was known to prospect for uranium in the area. His hometown newspaper reported as much almost a year before Vail opened and well before its creation story took shape. "Nation's Largest Ski Area for Eagle County," *Eagle Valley Enterprise*, January 4, 1962, 1.

2. Hauserman, *Inventors of Vail*, 18–22; "Forests Draw Ski Boom Plan," *Denver Post*, October 4, 1959, 7E; "Winter Sports Business Boom: Two $1 Million Ski Sites Planned West of Denver," *Cervi's Journal*, March 8, 1961; Paul Hauk, interview, Glenwood Springs, CO, August 5, 1993. Hauk, a Forest Service ranger, toured the mountain with Eaton and Seibert in summer 1957. He had just been named the White River National Forest's staff officer in charge of recreation, lands, watershed, and mineral management (a position he would hold until 1977), so it was his responsibility to review ski-area permit applications and survey proposed sites to assess their feasibility. Hauk also played a key role in the development of the Forest Service's 1959 master plan for ski development in Colorado's national forests. That plan called for Vail to open in 1962—as in fact it would.

3. Simonton, *Vail: Story of a Colorado Mountain Valley*, 61–65, 67; Seibert, *Vail: Triumph of a Dream*, 84–93; Hauserman, *Inventors of Vail*, 64–71; George Caulkins Jr., interview, Denver, January 12, 1994; Robert Parker, telephone interview, January 12, 1994.

4. On the choice of Vail as a name, see Simonton, *Vail: Story of a Colorado Mountain Valley*, 66; Seibert, *Vail: Triumph of a Dream*, 38; and Hauserman, *Inventors of Vail*, 13. Some of the original Vail partners wanted to use an old Ute name for the Rockies: Shining Mountains. But others, including Seibert, worried that "shining" might suggest the ski trails were icy—anathema to lovers of powder or "ballroom" skiing. So "Vail" prevailed.

5. Vail Associates Ltd., prospectus, August 14, 1961, 5–6, 8, Box 1, Vail Associates Papers (hereafter VA Papers); Seibert, *Vail: Triumph of a Dream*, 84–93; Vail Associates Inc., Board of Directors, minutes, October 5, 1968, Box 3, VA Papers (first quotation); Mike Erickson, "Vail Well-Named as 'Ski Country, USA,'" *Los Angeles Times* [December 1963?], in "Vail—1963" folder, historical clippings file, Vail Public Library (second and third quotations); George Bushnell Jr., "Vail: A Ski Resort Designed to Satisfy Any Guest," *Chicago Tribune*, February 7, 1965, G3 (fourth quotation); "Thrills of Powder," *Skiing*, February 1962, 22–5 (fifth quotation); Vail Associates Inc., annual report, 1973, Box 1, VA Papers (sixth quotation).

6. George P. Caulkins Jr.'s Vail Associates Ltd., business card, in George P. Caulkins Jr. private papers (hereafter Caulkins private papers). The map also marked the future site of the Continental Divide tunnel, which would make the drive faster still, by cutting out Loveland Pass. A similar, larger map ("Location of 'Vail' in Colorado") appeared in the green ring binder that Seibert and Caulkins took around the country to show their plans for Vail to potential investors. A replica of this ring binder, including the map, is on exhibit at Vail's ski museum: "The Vail Project: Real Estate Development" (1960),

ring binder at Colorado Ski and Snowboard Museum and Hall of Fame, Vail. Prospectuses issued by Vail Associates also made prominent mention of the future I-70 (and the tunnel) and noted that anyone driving from Denver to Aspen would have to pass Vail on the way—an unsubtle hint that Vail would be more auto-accessible than its older rival. Vail Associates Ltd., prospectus, April 25, 1961, 6, and prospectus, August 14, 1961, 7, both in Box 1, VA Papers.

7. Opening sentence of Burlington Route, *Colorado: The Perfect Vacationland*, lure book ([Chicago?], various years), 1. The railroad distributed this booklet from the late 1940s through the early 1960s, revising it each year but leaving the introductory section (including the sentence quoted here) unchanged.

8. This pitch fit not just with tactics of product packaging but also with time-honored traditions of western boosterism. See Wrobel, *Promised Lands*, chap. 1, on how nineteenth-century promoters lured settlers by portraying western places as frontiers of opportunity while downplaying how difficult it would be to actually live there.

9. Colorado Department of Natural Resources, *Fish and Wildlife Resources*, 3. Business owners in smaller, more obscure communities competed keenly for fishermen, erecting signs by the highways and running ads in guidebooks, local newspapers, and anywhere else they could afford. For example, the Summit County commissioners used some of their paltry budget to take out an ad for local fishing in the 1947 AAA guidebook, and in the *Rocky Mountain Guide Book* (a periodical whose ad rates were low enough for small businesses like cafés and gas stations to afford), almost all the Summit County advertisers made sure to mention that they sold fishing licenses, stocked fishing equipment, or welcomed fishermen. Summit County, Board of County Commissioners, ad in Rocky Mountain Motorists (hereafter RMM), *Official Rocky Mountain Travel Directory: Colorado, New Mexico, Wyoming*, 1947 ed., 72–73; *Rocky Mountain Guide Book: Colorado and Wyoming Edition*, May 1949, 15–17. Some Summit County promoters saw a new opportunity to attract fishermen when Green Mountain Reservoir, nineteen miles down the Blue River from Dillon, was completed in 1943. (The reservoir was the first component of the U.S. Bureau of Reclamation's Colorado–Big Thompson Project; see p. 196.) Green Mountain did lure enough anglers to spawn a cluster of motels and fishing camps in the new lakeside hamlet of Heeney, but because the Bureau of Reclamation was slow to develop recreational facilities on the reservoir, it took decades to become the kind of visitor draw that Summit's boosters had hoped.

10. On the evolution of fly-fishing culture in the United States, especially its connections to notions of Romantic nature, gentility, masculinity, and the frontier, see Washabaugh, *Deep Trout*, chaps. 3–5; Halverson, *An Entirely Synthetic Fish*, chap. 6; Schullery, *American Fly Fishing*, chap. 12; and Waterman, *Fishing in America*, chap. 3. Reiger, *American Sportsmen and the Origins of Conservation*, chap. 1, is also helpful, though it is more about sport hunting.

11. "Colorado—the Land of Trout Waters," in RMM, *Where to Vacation in Colorado*, 1957–58 ed., 57; Tim K. Kelley, "Hook, Line and Sinker," *Colorado Wonderland*, May–June 1959, 13; Colorado State Advertising and Publicity Committee (hereafter APC), dba Department of Public Relations, *Cool, Colorful Colorado Invites You!*, lure book (Denver, 1959), 15; APC, dba Sportsmen's Hospitality Committee, Department of Public Relations,

Come to Cool, Colorful Colorado . . . Catch Fighting Rainbows!, brochure (Denver, 1953). The phrase "lusty trout" originated in Tennyson's 1855 poem "The Brook."

12. According to Charles Hjelte, editor of the Colorado Game and Fish Department magazine, *Colorado Outdoors*, the earlier yearning to escape from cities had been replaced in postwar times by the yearning to escape from Cold War fears. "Today," he suggested, "fishing is largely a sport enjoyed by people who want to escape the nervous tensions of a new way of life"—by which he meant life under an atomic cloud. Charles Hjelte, introduction to Seaman, *Fishes of Colorado*.

13. For example, the state lengthened nonresident permits (to encourage out-of-staters to stay longer); shifted the fishing season to always start on a Saturday (to better fit vacationers' travel schedules); and then abolished the season altogether (so anyone could fish at any time of year). These reforms occurred in 1949, 1953, and 1962, respectively. Another change, in 1957, gave violators of game and fish laws the option of paying their fines on the spot instead of having to travel out of their way to a court, making even Colorado's fishing penalties friendly to out-of-staters. "Good News for Sportsmen," in *Rocky Mountain Guide Book*, May 1949, 23; "Spring Means Fishing," in RMM, *Where to Vacation in Colorado: Rocky Mountain Travel Directory*, 1953–54 ed., 7; [Feltner], *A Look Back*, 34.

14. On Forest Service efforts to improve fish habitat, see U.S. Department of Agriculture (hereafter USDA), Forest Service, *Outdoor Recreation in the National Forests*, 15, 76, 80–82. Much of this work was done as part of Operation Outdoors, a five-year initiative launched in 1957 to build new recreational facilities in the national forests and rehabilitate old ones. State Game and Fish Department efforts to improve fishing waters and create new ones are summarized in Seaman, *Fishes of Colorado*, 4–5. On more recent changes in fish habitat restoration practices, and a critique of the traditional emphasis on stocking, an accessible (if agenda-driven) introduction is Jim Yuskavitch, "Taking Stock of Stocking," *Trout*, Winter 1999, 16–26. *Trout* is the magazine of Trout Unlimited, a group that concerns itself with the health of riparian habitats and watersheds and that opposes what it considers a long-standing overreliance on hatcheries for improving fish stocks.

15. Martinez et al., "Western Lake Trout Woes."

16. Gordon G. Gauss, "President Finds Little Time for Fishing at Fraser," *Denver Post*, September 2, 1954, 3; "Not Even Fishing's Sacred Now, Hoover Complains," *Portland Press Herald* (Portland, ME), September 2, 1954; Jean Miller, "Welcome, Friend," in Miller and Wier, "A Dude Ranch Is . . . , 1874–1986," special issue, 61.

17. [Feltner], *A Look Back*, 34–35; Seaman, *Fishes of Colorado*, 1–2; Waterman, *Fishing in America*, 126. For a brief overview and statistical profile of Game and Fish's hatchery operations in the 1950s, see Colorado State Planning Commission (hereafter SPC), *State of Colorado Year Book*, 1951 to 1955, 383–84; and Colorado State Planning Division (hereafter SPD), *Colorado, 1956–1958: Year Book of the State of Colorado*, 452–53.

18. SPC, *State of Colorado Year Book*, 1951 to 1955, 383 (first quotation); SPD, *Colorado, 1956–1958: Year Book of the State of Colorado*, 452 (second quotation).

19. Sample ad in APC, *Annual Report: July 1, 1953–June 30, 1954* (1954), Box 10223, records of the Colorado Department of Local Affairs (hereafter DOLA Records) (first

, quotation); Union Pacific Railroad, *Colorado*, lure book ([Chicago?], 1957), 4 (second quotation).

20. APC, *Come to Cool, Colorful Colorado . . . Catch Fighting Rainbows!* (1953).

21. This was never acknowledged in mainstream promotional literature, but state publications aimed at knowledgeable anglers admitted it openly. See, for example, Seaman, *Fishes of Colorado*, 1, 7. Indeed, expert fly fishers were already inclined to scorn hatchery trout, believing them to be duller and less attractive and to put up less fight than wild fish. See Halverson, *An Entirely Synthetic Fish*, 114–15, 122–23, 184; and Sternberg, *Trout*, 29. Worth mentioning, about a quarter of the trout caught in Colorado were brook trout, a species notorious among experienced fly fishermen for grabbing almost any lure and giving up without much of a fight. Seaman, *Fishes of Colorado*, 8.

22. In 1964 the number of fishing visits to California national forests was 2,458,000; Colorado was close behind with 2,429,000. The third-place state, Oregon, trailed well behind at 1,589,000 fishing visits. USDA, Forest Service, *Outdoor Recreation in the National Forests*, 45.

23. *"Better Homes and Gardens" Family Camping*, quotations from pp. 8, 10, 11. See also *"Sunset" Ideas for Outdoor Family Fun in the West* and *"Sunset" Ideas for Family Camping*.

24. Starlite Campers of the Rockies Inc., *Starlite Campers of the Rockies, Inc. . . . 'Where Daydreams Meet Moonbeams,'"* brochure (Colorado Springs, 1948); William J. Barker, "Star Dust Is Pay Dirt," *Rocky Mountain Life*, May 1948, 30–31, 37; Weldon F. Heald, "Trail Riders of the Wilderness," *Colorado Wonderland*, Early Summer 1951, 27–30. The Maroon Bells–Snowmass Primitive Area, designated in 1933, was reclassified as a "Wild Area" in 1956 and then as a "Wilderness" with the passage of the 1964 Wilderness Act.

25. Operation Outdoors sprang in large part from the Forest Service's longtime rivalry with the Park Service. It was not that Forest Service officials wanted to emulate the Park Service in its recreational orientation; it was more that they wanted to keep the latter agency from encroaching on their turf. Park advocates had long sought the transfer of some national forest lands with scenic or recreational value to the Park Service, and indeed Mission 66 proposed such transfers. Forest Service officials hoped Operation Outdoors would deflect the threat by making their agency appear equally committed to recreation—even though, in reality, Forest Service culture still ranked logging as the highest use of the forests and tended to see recreation as an insidious threat to it. As Edward Cliff, assistant Forest Service chief, former Rocky Mountain regional chief, and soon-to-be chief forester, warned fellow foresters in 1961, "We had better be prepared, ready and willing to [manage the forests for recreation] because if we are not, we can expect that someone else will take over the forest recreation job, which rightfully belongs to foresters, and deprive us of the opportunity to produce wood and other resources." See Hirt, *Conspiracy of Optimism*, 157–59; Edward P. Cliff, "The Role of Forest Recreation in Forest Land Management," speech to the Third Annual All-Day Meeting of the Washington Section, Society of American Foresters, Washington, DC, February 16, 1961, typescript in FF "Volume I [Folder 2]—Speeches," Edward Parley Cliff Papers.

26. See, for example, "Deep Lake Object of Operation Outdoors," *Eagle Valley Enterprise*, August 7, 1958, 1; untitled photo feature on new developments in the White River National Forest, *Eagle Valley Enterprise*, February 19, 1959, 5; APC, dba Colorado

Department of Public Relations, *Colorado Camp Grounds within National Forests, Parks, and Monuments*, booklet (Denver, [early 1960s]). The proliferation of new facilities in the White River National Forest can be tracked through the periodically updated map guides that were distributed to visitors. USDA, Forest Service, *White River National Forest, Colorado, Forest Visitors Map* (1955–79).

27. Besides Operation Outdoors, another sign of this dawning recognition was the Multiple Use-Sustained Yield Act of 1960, which reasserted the importance of logging and other traditional resource uses in the national forests but also, for the first time, listed recreation as a primary use too, ostensibly on a par with the others. The early to mid-1960s also saw the Forest Service moving aggressively to build more access roads, supposedly in response to the finding by the federal Outdoor Recreation Resources Review Commission that driving for pleasure had become America's favorite recreational activity. While the new roads gave leisure-seekers better access to the national forests, though, they gave loggers better access too—something not lost on Forest Service officials like Chief Forester Edward Cliff, who continued to favor logging above other forest uses. Steen, *U.S. Forest Service: A History*, 297–307, 311–13; Hirt, *Conspiracy of Optimism*, 182–92, 220–29; USDA, Forest Service, *Outdoor Recreation in the National Forests*, 1–3, 14–16, 27.

28. USDA, Forest Service, *Outdoor Recreation in the National Forests*, 29.

29. W. S. Davis, "How the Forest Service Aids Winter Sports," *Colorado Business*, December 1946, 15; Wallace Taber, "Uncle Sam's Forest Rangers Unsung Heroes of Skiing Areas," *Denver Post*, March 27, 1949; A. G. Coleman, *Ski Style*, 140–41; USDA, Forest Service, *Public Lands and Private Recreation Enterprise*, 15–17.

30. "Arapaho National Forest Reports All Time High Winter Ski Use in Season Just Past," *Middle Park Times*, June 12, 1958, 2; "Forests Draw Ski Boom Plan," *Denver Post*, October 4, 1959, 7E; "R-2 Winter Sports Master Plan," August 1959, document in Ring Binder 1, Box 1, Paul I. Hauk Papers, Denver Public Library (hereafter Hauk Papers-DPL); Seibert, *Vail: Triumph of a Dream*, 85–87; Hauserman, *Inventors of Vail*, 61–64. As of 1958, the four existing ski areas in Arapaho National Forest—Winter Park, Berthoud Pass, Arapahoe Basin, and Loveland—were handling nearly two-thirds of all skier demand in Colorado.

31. On the postwar return of veterans to the West, and the resulting growth of cities and suburbs, see especially G. D. Nash, *American West in the Twentieth Century*, 193, 216–17, 219–22.

32. Many postwar ski entrepreneurs, like Larry Jump, Johnny Litchfield, and Percy Rideout, fit both categories, having raced in college and then volunteered for the Tenth. A few, like Friedl Pfeifer, had been racing champions in Europe before joining the Tenth.

33. Jerry Hiatt, "Colorado Winter Sports Congress," *Western Skiing*, January 1946, 17, 24, 26 (quotation p. 17). See also Betty Hosburgh, "So. Rocky Mountain [Update]," *Ski Illustrated*, February 1946, 26, 38.

34. For the 1952–53 ski season, the APC mapped thirty-two ski areas in Colorado; nearly half were within a hundred driving miles of Denver. See the map titled "Skiing Centers in Colorado," *Colorado Wonderland*, Christmas 1952, 37. (The map was credited to the Forest Service and the Colorado Winter Sports Committee, a pseudonym for the

APC.) See also Denver Convention and Visitors Bureau (hereafter DCVB), dba Colorado Ski Information Center, *Manual of Colorado Skiing: At the Top of the Nation!*, 1957–58
ed., 2; and "Ski Colorado," in RMM, *Where to Vacation in Colorado*, 1963–64 ed., 191. The
1957 map showed seven of the state's fifteen ski areas located within a hundred miles of
Denver; in the 1963 map the ratio was twelve of twenty-five.

35. Jean Miller, "The Early Birds," in Miller and Wier, "1859–1950: Skiing in Middle
Park," special issue, 27–28; Fay, *History of Skiing in Colorado*, 81; Jean Miller, "The Transformation," in Miller and Wier, "A Mountain, a Dream, a Train—Winter Park," special
issue, 45.

36. Paul Hauk, "Arapahoe Basin," in *Ski Area Chronologies, White River National Forest*, Ring Binder 1, Box 1, Hauk Papers-DPL; "Jack Groutage, "Skiing the Continental
Divide," *Western Skiing*, January 1948, 12–13; Fay, *History of Skiing in Colorado*, 79–80;
A. G. Coleman, *Ski Style*, 122; "Denver's winter playground" quoted from DCVB, *Come
to Denver, Capital City of Colorado*, lure book (Denver, [ca. 1951]). Jump and Schauffler
initially flirted with a spot in the San Juan Mountains of far southwestern Colorado,
but in keeping with the chamber of commerce's desire to have the new ski area enhance
Denver's tourist business, they rejected that site as "inaccessible" (meaning too long a
drive from Denver).

37. James Albert Wales, "Ski Letter Box: No More 'Horror Names' for Slopes and
Trails!," letter to the editor, *Ski Illustrated*, January 1946, 6, 37.

38. See introduction, note 32.

39. Revis, "Skiing in the United States," 218 (first quotation), 220 (third quotation);
Jay, *Skiing the Americas*, 13 (second quotation).

40. The venerable Arlberg approach, invented by Friedl Pfeifer's boyhood mentor,
the Austrian Hannes Schneider, taught skiers to stem-turn back and forth across the
fall line. In contrast, the parallel method had skiers keep their skis close together and
take a more direct, albeit still undulating, path down the hill. *Wedeln*, new in the 1950s,
modified the parallel technique by having skiers twist their shoulders opposite their
feet. The owners of Aspen Highlands made their resort the leading place to learn *wedeln*
when they hired Stein Eriksen, a glamorous Norwegian Olympic champion, to run the
ski school. Eriksen's graceful "reverse-shoulder" or "delayed shoulder" skiing style did
more than anything else to popularize *wedeln*, and "to ski 'Stein's way,'" writes ski historian Richard Needham, "became a national obsession" in the mid-1950s. For detailed
descriptions of these techniques (and the debates that raged around them), see Fry, *Story
of Modern Skiing*, chap. 5; and Needham, *Ski*, 28–29, 47–48, 53, 60.

41. Dick Durrance, quoted in Bowen, *Book of American Skiing*, 71; Robert M. Coates,
"Winter Sports," *Holiday*, December 1948, 47. On skiing as flying, see, for example, the
anonymous Tenth Mountain veteran quoted in Bowen, *Book of American Skiing*, 294.
Durrance, in his own racing career, became famous for throwing the niceties of technique completely out the window, rocketing madly down the slope—usually faster than
anyone else.

42. Metal skis, introduced in the 1950s, took so much less effort to turn than wooden
skis that they were called "cheaters." The 1960s brought flexible fiberglass skis, which
absorbed bumps better, reduced leg and knee wear, and helped skiers "grip" uneven

terrain. As skis became shorter and leather boots gave way to plastic, controlling one's turns became easier still. The new equipment made skiing safer too. Plastic boots, for example, gave better ankle support, reducing the fear of breaks; new bindings were designed to release a boot under sudden strain, guarding against spiral leg fractures and severe knee sprains. For the first time, one could say with a straight face, as *Today's Health* did in the mid-1950s, that "skiing is less dangerous than football or boxing." Yet for all the safety improvements, the sport lost none of its reputation for thrills. In fact, safer equipment allowed skiers an even greater sense of daring. The quick-release bindings imparted "a false sense of security," warned one expert. "I would be too prone to take chances and rely on the binding to see me through!" The logic made ski patrollers and orthopedic surgeons nervous, but it was music to ski promoters' ears. *Today's Health* quoted in Needham, *Ski*, 73. For more on equipment innovations, see Fry, *Story of Modern Skiing*, chap. 4; Needham, *Ski*, 52–53, 56–57, 62–63, 70, 73, 74, 86; A. G. Coleman, *Ski Style*, 125–26; and Jay, *Skiing the Americas*, 42.

43. Coates, "Winter Sports," 83 (quotation in *Holiday*); Myrtle S. Nord, "A Tour-N for the Better," *Western Skiing*, February 1946, 16; Revis, "Skiing in the United States," 234 (quotation in *National Geographic*); Pfeifer, *Nice Goin'*, 113.

44. Idaho Springs Chamber of Commerce (hereafter ISCC), ad in RMM, *Rocky Mountain Travel Directory: Colorado*, 1949 ed., 32–33; APC, dba Colorado Winter Sports Committee, sample ad in APC, *Annual Report: July 1, 1957–June 30, 1958* (1958), Box 10223, DOLA Records.

45. Pomeroy, *In Search of the Golden West*, 209.

46. Without tows or lifts, skiers had to spend hours climbing long, steep slopes just to get in one or two downhill runs a day. As ski lifts proliferated, a magazine like *Sunset*, famous for teaching people how to dabble in casual western hobbies, could assure its readers that "most skiing is downhill" and that "endurance isn't called for." *"Sunset" Ideas for Outdoor Family Fun in the West*, 104. Besides saving a great deal of effort, lifts spared the skier from needing as much expertise. Before lifts, a skier had to master both Alpine skills (to get down the slope) and Nordic techniques (to climb back up again). For most skiers, the lift made the Nordic skills obsolete.

47. Pfeifer, *Nice Goin'*, 24, 29, 39; Oppenheimer and Poore, *Sun Valley*, 57–75; Needham, *Ski*, 18–21. Another important pioneer in this area was Fred Pabst, an heir to the Milwaukee brewing fortune, who in the 1930s became the first to make lift building a bona fide business strategy. Convinced that more people would ski if they did not have to climb hills, Pabst bought seventeen small ski areas in the Midwest, Canada, and the East and installed rope tows and J-bars at all of them. His business model was a bit ahead of its time—his sprawling enterprise would fail during the war—but the connection he drew between lift building and mass-market skiing came to dominate the ski industry after the war. On Pabst's idea of "skiing for the masses," see Bowen, *Book of American Skiing*, 162–63; and Needham, *Ski*, 31.

48. Voynick, *Climax*, 199; "Climax Ski Area Has Had a Lively, Exciting History," *Summit County Journal*, March 11, 1960, 4; "Glenwood Springs Ski Course," *Colorado Wonderland*, Development Issue, 1952, 37; Nelson, *Glenwood Springs*, 187; J. Miller, "The Early Birds," 27–28; Fay, *History of Skiing in Colorado*, 80–81; Jean Miller, "Cranmer's

Dream in Action," in Miller and Wier, "A Mountain, a Dream, a Train—Winter Park," special issue, 37, 44–45.

49. Frank Elkins, "Summer Ski Lifts," in Ford Motor Co. Publications Department, *Ford Treasury of the Outdoors*, 93; Herta Glaz, paraphrased in William Longmaid, "Visiting Artists Like Aspen Scenery, Climate," *Aspen Times*, June 30, 1949, 5; The Aspen Bark(ess) [pseud.], "Impressions on Riding Chair Lift for First Time," *Aspen Times*, January 2, 1947, 6. *Ford Treasury of the Outdoors* was a compilation of articles that had originally appeared in *Ford Times* from 1946 to 1952.

50. The Aspen Bark(ess) [pseud.], "Impressions on Riding Chair Lift for First Time"; Revis, "Skiing in the United States," 234; Elkins, "Summer Ski Lifts," 94.

51. Ray Duncan, "California's Snow Boom," *Holiday*, February 1954, 64–65, quoted in Pomeroy, *In Search of the Golden West*, 209.

52. In 1946 the Forest Service counted 83,055 visits to winter-sports areas in Colorado's national forests. In 1956 the number hit 355,550—an increase of 428 percent in ten years. For Arapaho, 166,878 lift tickets were sold in the 1956–57 ski season; 327,013 in 1961–62. For White River, 84,550 lift tickets were sold in 1956–57; 193,442 in 1961–62. Beginning in the 1962–63 season, when Vail opened for business, lift ticket sales for White River increased even more rapidly. Crampon and Lemon, *Skiing in the Southern Rocky Mountain Region*, 32; SPD, *Colorado Year Book, 1962–1964*, 628.

53. See Sepp Ruschp, "Modern Trail Planning," *Ski Illustrated*, March 1945, 17, 33. Ruschp, a former Austrian ski champion who coached racers and ran a ski school in Vermont, was an influential early advocate of the new trail design.

54. Mount Snow's brash owner, Walt Schoenknecht, made no bones about creating a skiing "supermarket," as he called it. Besides his outrageously (for the time) wide runs, he also packed his base village with all kinds of amenities, including a heated pool, indoor ice rink, giant fireplaces and cafeterias, and an unending schedule of après-ski events, from fondue parties to dog-sled rides. It worked, making Mount Snow, as of the early 1960s, the world's busiest ski area. Bowen, *Book of American Skiing*, 166–67; Needham, *Ski*, 51; B. Harrison, *View from Vermont*, 180.

55. J. Miller, "Transformation," 37–38, 45; Arapahoe Basin, Aspen ski area, Loveland Basin, and Glenwood Springs ski area, ads in DCVB, *Manual of Colorado Skiing*, 1957–58 ed., 4, 6, 12, 16.

56. J. Miller, "Transformation," 45–48; Fry, *Story of Modern Skiing*, 51–55; Needham, *Ski*, 51–52; A. G. Coleman, *Ski Style*, 131.

57. Pfeifer, *Nice Goin'*, 183–92; Paul Hauk, "Buttermilk Mountain," in *Ski Area Chronologies, White River National Forest*, Ring Binder 2, Box 1, Hauk Papers-DPL; Barlow-Perez, *History of Aspen*, 64; Fay, *History of Skiing in Colorado*, 75. The quotations are from Buttermilk Mountain Skiing Corp., *Buttermilk Mountain*, brochure (Aspen, [1962]).

58. Otto Schniebs, legendary ski instructor and coach of the Dartmouth team, was known for repeating this slogan, though it is unclear whether he coined it.

59. Bowen, *Book of American Skiing*, 270–75; Needham, *Ski*, 64–65; Jay, O'Rear, and O'Rear, *Ski Down the Years*, 249; A. G. Coleman, *Ski Style*, 185; Fry, *Story of Modern Skiing*, 37–38. On the beginnings of this glamorization before the war, see E. J. B. Allen, *From Skisport to Skiing*, 143–44, 156–58.

60. See, for example, sample ads in APC, *Annual Report: July 1, 1953–June 30, 1954* (1954), Box 10223, DOLA Records; APC, dba Colorado Winter Sports Committee, ad in *Holiday*, November 1955, 151; and the photograph that ran on the cover of the DCVB's annual *Manual of Colorado Skiing* during the mid- to late 1950s. A sample ad featuring Marilyn Van Derbur appears in APC, *Annual Report: July 1, 1957–June 30, 1958* (1958), Box 10223, DOLA Records.

61. Pfeifer describes his role in recruiting Cooper, whom he had gotten to know on the slopes at Sun Valley, in *Nice Goin'*, 149–50. See also J. S. Allen, *Romance of Commerce and Culture*, 145. For coverage of Cooper's arrival in Aspen, see "Hideaway—In Aspen," *Aspen Times*, November 18, 1948, 1, 8.

62. On Eriksen's star quality, see esp. A. G. Coleman, *Ski Style*, 167–68; Needham, *Ski*, 57, 60–62; and Fry, *Story of Modern Skiing*, 225–26.

63. See, for example, S. Elizabeth Forbes, "Ski Heaven," *Denver Post Rocky Mountain Empire Magazine*, December 1, 1946, 2; and Tukey Koffend, interview by Annie Gilbert, Aspen, June 30, 1994, transcript at the Aspen Historical Society.

64. See, for example, Evan M. Wylie, "Ghost Town on Skis," *Collier's*, February 7, 1948, esp. the photograph on p. 24.

65. Crampon and Lemon, *Skiing in the Southern Rocky Mountain Region*, 23–24; APC, dba Colorado Winter Sports Committee, sample ad in APC, *Annual Report: July 1, 1961– June 30, 1962* (1962), Box 10223, DOLA Records.

66. Rocky Mountain Ski Area Operators Association, minutes, February 13, 1963, and April 19, 1963; and "Report by Committee: Ski Country U.S.A.," all in untitled folder, no. 79.90.27, Box 1, Aspen Skiing Corporation/William V. Hodges Jr. Papers; "Ski Country U.S.A. Formed by Area Operators," *Colorado Host*, September 1963, 1; Parker, telephone interview, January 12, 1994; Seibert, *Vail: Triumph of a Dream*, 120. The nickname was coined by Vail Associates marketing director Bob Parker and first appeared in magazine advertisements for Vail in 1963.

67. Georgetown Guest Houses, ad in DCVB, *Manual of Colorado Skiing*, 1957–58 ed., 5, 17. On the Red Ram, see Mike McPhee, "A Jolly Sendoff," *Denver Post*, November 13, 1997, 1E, 2E. By the early 1950s, the Georgetown Civic Association listed four eating places and eight lodging facilities where skiers could stay; see Georgetown Civic Association, *The Silver Queen: A Good Place to Live and to Play*, and *Georgetown, Colorado*, brochures (Georgetown, [ca. 1953]).

68. "Booming Georgetown Is All Set for 'Big Do' on Saturday Night," *Denver Post*, June 8, 1946, 3; Betty Jean Lee, "'Likker, Grub' Signs Recall Georgetown's Silver Days," *Denver Post*, June 12, 1949, 7B.

69. For a synopsis of Rogers's protean career, see his obituary, "James Grafton Rogers Dies at 88," *Denver Post*, April 23, 1971, 2.

70. Technically, Rogers was elected "police judge." Georgetown's 1868 charter, instead of providing for an elected mayor, quaintly calls for the person elected as police judge to serve as mayor ex officio.

71. On Draper's personal and professional background, see "Draper of Georgetown Runs for Nomination," *Aspen Times*, August 29, 1946, 1. Draper explained how he had become interested in Georgetown's history in the foreword to his booklet, *Georgetown*

Pictorial. He self-published an abridged version of his master's thesis in 1940, titled *Georgetown: High Points in the Story of the Famous Colorado Silver Camp.*

72. "New Firm Plans on Restoration of Georgetown," *Denver Post,* March 27, 1946, 24; "Plan to Restore Historic Town," *Colorado Municipalities,* May 1946, 82; Ben Draper, "Georgetown—1880 Style: Colorado's Newest Tourist Attraction," *Trail and Timberline,* no. 329 (May 1946): 74–75; "Booming Georgetown Is All Set for 'Big Do' on Saturday Night"; Jane Nes, "Gala Festival Breathes New Life into Old Georgetown," *Denver Post,* June 9, 1946, 6B; "People around the Mountain Region," *Rocky Mountain Life,* July 1947, 11; Draper, *Georgetown Pictorial.* Both quotations are from Draper, "Georgetown—1880 Style."

73. Benjamin Draper, "Survey of Tourist Industry Advocated: Interest in Colorado Shown by Mining Camp Revivals," *Denver Post,* September 29, 1947, 10.

74. Riddle, *Louis Dupuy and His Souvenir of France.* See also the amusing details about the Hotel de Paris in Noel, *Buildings of Colorado,* 204–5; and "Museums," in Draper, *Georgetown Pictorial.*

75. A synopsis of the Georgetown Plan appeared in "Municipal News from around the State," *Colorado Municipalities,* February 1957, 44. When the town passed its pioneering historic preservation ordinance in 1970, participants and observers traced the idea back to these late-1950s policies; see, for example, Chuck Green, "Past Spared in Georgetown," *Denver Post,* June 14, 1970, 61.

76. On the land donation by lawyer Stanley Wallbank, the National Historic Landmark designation, and the Georgetown Loop Historic Mining and Railroad Park, see Walter R. Borneman, "A Centennial Bridge to the Past," in [Halaas and Borneman], *Story of a Valley.*

77. See, for example, ISCC, *Suggested Trips and Drives in and around Idaho Springs, Colorado,* booklet (Idaho Springs, [ca. 1947]); Clear Creek County Chamber of Commerce (hereafter CCCCC), *Idaho Springs, Colorado, and Vicinity,* booklet (Idaho Springs, [ca. 1952]); CCCCC, ad in RMM, *Where to Vacation in Colorado,* 1953–54 ed., 9; CCCCC, *Introducing You to Clear Creek Canyon in the Heart of the Scenic Rockies,* brochure (Idaho Springs, [ca. 1954]); ISCC, *Introducing . . . Colorado's Famed "Gold Rush" City: Idaho Springs* (Idaho Springs, [late 1950s]); and ISCC, ad in RMM, *Where to Vacation in Colorado,* 1963–64 ed., 150.

78. One early 1950s pamphlet ran ads for twelve motels in Idaho Springs and twelve dining establishments—quite a lot for a town of fewer than 1,800 people. CCCCC, *Idaho Springs, Colorado, and Vicinity* [ca. 1952].

79. See esp. Noel, "Paving the Way to Colorado," 42–49. The image of the mountains as Denver's recreational backyard took hold especially in the automobile era. In railroad days, Colorado Springs was actually better known (and more aggressively promoted) as a jumping-off point for tourist excursions into the mountains, at least the mountains immediately west of the city. See Brosnan, *Uniting Mountain and Plain,* chap. 4.

80. On the evolution of Colfax Avenue as a tourist strip, see Wyckoff, "Denver's Aging Commercial Strip," 282–94.

81. On the Hospitality Center's opening, see "Denver Hospitality Center," *Colorado Wonderland,* Early Summer 1951, 11; on its helping to cement Denver's status as a gateway

to the vacationland, see Ruth, *Colorado Vacations*, 19. Through the 1950s and into the early 1960s, the DCVB and its successor, the Colorado Visitors Bureau, included a line drawing of the Hospitality Center in most of its ads and publications, and on the decals that members displayed in the windows of their establishments, suggesting that the bureau considered the Hospitality Center an especially valuable promotional tool.

82. Graf, *No Vacancy*, 148.

83. Spruce Motor Lodge (Glenwood Springs), ad in *Colorado Wonderland*, May 1950, 33. See also Jakle, Sculle, and Rogers, *Motel in America*, 136, 231–40.

84. Graf, *No Vacancy*, 35.

85. Descriptions of the motel and strip landscape of Idaho Springs derive from post-cards in author's collection. On the history of motel architecture, room design and decoration, and landscaping, see Jakle, Sculle, and Rogers, *Motel in America*, chaps. 2 and 8; and L. Miller, "The Hi Ho, Lucky U, Bugs Bunny, and Sleepy Hollow," esp. 9–15.

86. Ranch House Motor Hotel (Denver), ad in *Colorado Wonderland*, Development Issue 1952, 6; Westerner Motel (Granby), ad in RMM, *Where to Vacation in Colorado*, 1957–58 ed., 87; *Eddie Bohn's Pig'n Whistle Village*, brochure (Denver, [ca. 1950]).

87. East Jefferson County Chamber of Commerce, *Rough It in Style . . . in Jefferson County, Colorado*, brochure (Lakewood, CO, [early 1960s]); E. E. Ambrose and Sons, Realtors, *Bow-Mar*, booklet (Denver, [ca. 1947]). Bow-Mar, named for the two lakes it abutted (Bowles and Marston), was developed by entrepreneur Lloyd King around the same time he founded the Front Range supermarket chain King Soopers.

88. N. Morgan, *Westward Tilt*, 5.

89. On Southern California's almost magical lifestyle allure after World War II, see Starr, *Golden Dreams*, esp. chaps. 1 and 2; and Culver, *Frontier of Leisure*. Culver traces this allure back to the Gilded Age, notably emphasizing its roots in tourist promotion and in resort development at Catalina Island and, later, Palm Springs. May, *Golden State, Golden Youth*, is also helpful, as is Avila, *Popular Culture in the Age of White Flight*, which argues that the Southern California suburban lifestyle was a critical influence in shaping postwar white identity. On the California origins of the bungalow and ranch house, see Faragher, "Bungalow and Ranch House."

90. The quotation is from Graves, "California, the Golden Magnet." See also G. W. Long, "New Rush to Golden California."

91. DCVB, *Come to Denver, Capital City of Colorado* [ca. 1951] (first and third quotations); Marshall Sprague, "The Coloradan," in *Colorado: The Colorful Centennial State*; Mountain States Telephone, "Colorado . . . It's a Way of Life," advertising insert in *Colorado Business*, June 1965 (fourth quotation).

92. Elizabeth Berg, "Design for Western Living," *Rocky Mountain Life*, September 1948, 13–6; "Outdoor Living in Colorado," *Colorado Wonderland*, Fall 1952, 20–2. To see how *Sunset* promoted ranch houses and proclaimed their suitability for "western living," see esp. Sunset Magazine editors, *"Sunset" Western Ranch Houses*; and Sunset Magazine and Books editors, *Western Ranch Houses by Cliff May*. Or see the many articles listed under "ranch houses" in the magazine's centennial index, *"Sunset" Magazine: A Century of Western Living, 1898–1998*, 287.

93. APC, *Cool, Colorful Colorado Invites You!*, 48 (first quotation); Revis, "Colorado

by Car and Campfire," 224; RMM, *Where to Vacation in Colorado, 1963–64* ed., 85 (second quotation); Dabney Otis Collins, "The Mountains and Fun," in *Colorado: The Colorful Centennial State* (third quotation); Sprague, "Coloradan" (fourth quotation); RMM, *Where to Vacation in Colorado, 1957–58* ed., 140–41, 185; DCVB, *Come to Denver, Capital City of Colorado* [ca. 1951] (fifth quotation); APC, dba Colorado Department of Development, *Know How, Know Where: An Analysis of Industrial Colorado and Its Potential for Industrial Development*, booklet (Denver, [1950]), 31 (sixth quotation).

94. N. Morgan, *Westward Tilt*, 5.

95. B. E. Tsagris, "Regional Growth Inducements," *Colorado Business Review*, April 1967, 4.

96. On this new way of understanding economic development, see introduction, note 10.

97. Palmer Hoyt, "Forecast for the Future," *This Is Colorado: Special Centennial Magazine Section of the Denver Post*, June 21, 1959, 307; Hornby, *Voice of Empire*, 32–33; APC, dba Colorado Department of Development, sample ads in APC, *Annual Report: July 1, 1956–June 30, 1957* (1957), Box 10223, DOLA Records; Ronald D. Lemon, "The 'Sell Colorado' Ambassador Program," *Colorado Business Review*, August 1967, 3–4, 8; "Second 'Sell Colorado' Mission to New York Highly Successful," *Colorado Development Digest*, September 1967, 1–3; John A. Love, "'We Have Room for a Few More Good Ones . . . and Then, We'll Close the Borders!" *Coloscope*, July 1969, 1–2; "Los Angeles Industry Invited to Explore Colorado West," *Colorado Development Digest*, July 1970, 1–2.

98. James R. Quinn, "The Economic Environment," in *Colorado: The Colorful Centennial State* (first quotation); APC, dba Colorado Department of Development, *Colorado: Capital of the Industrial West*, folder (Denver, [late 1950s]), Box 10223, DOLA Records (second quotation); Denver Technological Center, ad in *Colorado Magazine*, Summer 1965, 36; APC, *Cool, Colorful Colorado Invites You!* (1959), 49 (third quotation); Forward Metro Denver, ad in *Colorado Magazine*, Fall 1966, 9; CF&I Steel, ad in *Colorado Magazine*, Summer 1966, 111 (fourth quotation, emphasis in original).

99. On the particular allure of western cities, see Findlay, *Magic Lands*, and, for Los Angeles's allure, Culver, *Frontier of Leisure*. On nature as the antidote to middle-class anxieties, see Price, *Flight Maps*, chap. 4.

100. P. Lewis, "Galactic Metropolis"; P. Lewis, "Urban Invasion of Rural America." An excellent study of this landscape pattern, as it occurs in the American West in our own time, is Travis, *New Geographies of the American West*. Travis helpfully groups the West's "development landscapes" into four categories, but each of the four transcends traditional definitions of urban, suburban, exurban, small-town, rural, and so forth. Other useful treatments of this low-density, multicentered development pattern are Flint, *This Land*; Cutsinger and Galster, "There Is No Sprawl Syndrome"; Knox, *Metroburbia, USA*; Lang and Knox, "New Metropolis: Rethinking Megalopolis"; D. G. Brown et al., "Rural Land-Use Trends in the Coterminous United States"; and R. B. Riley, "Thoughts on the New Rural Landscape." On the specific phenomenon of exurbia, see Herbers, *New Heartland*; Berube et al., *Finding Exurbia*; and Travis, *New Geographies of the American West*, chap. 5.

101. Sternberg and Sternberg, *Evergreen: Our Mountain Community*, 213–15;

Georgetown Associates Inc., ad for The Meadows at Georgetown, in Allen, Baehler, and Simonds, *Historic Georgetown*, 24–27; Joan White, "Georgetown Rumblings Portend Growth," *Denver Post*, July 31, 1971, 31, 44.

102. Pritchard, *Dillon, Denver and the Dam*, tells this story in some detail. Especially poignant are photographs, on pp. 30–35, of the demolition of the old town. See also Pritchard, *Southern Summit*, 35–46.

103. See these articles in the *Summit County Journal*: "Denver Advances Dillon, County $10,000 For Town," September 6, 1957, 1; "Proposed Plans For New Dillon Now Available," June 13, 1958, 3; "Only 22 Dillonites Attend Meeting on New Dillon," December 19, 1958, 1; Gordon Goodridge, "Southeast Leg Gets Majority Support as Meeting Discusses Water Board Pact," April 8, 1960, 1; "Building Restriction for the New Town of Dillon," September 30, 1960, 3; and Mrs. Walter Byron, "Saunders' Pledges Fade In Face of Denver Grab," November 18, 1960, 1. See also Bert Hanna, "Dillon Relocation Stirs Feud of 'Oldtimers' vs. 'Newcomers,'" *Denver Post*, May 21, 1961, 32C; Greg Pearson, "Bulldozer Deals Death Blow to Town of Dillon," *Denver Post*, November 15, 1961; Fred Baker, "Dillon, Tomorrow's Old Town," *Denver Post Empire Magazine*, April 7, 1963, 3–4; Willard Haselbush, "Dillon—The Town That Would Not Drown," *Denver Post*, January 9, 1967, 43; Town of Dillon, Ordinance no. A-12, "Official Zoning Ordinance," August 7, 1967; and Pritchard, *Dillon, Denver and the Dam*, 36–39.

104. *Summit County Journal*, July 4, 1958, 1, quoted in Pritchard, *Dillon, Denver and the Dam*, 36.

105. Cal Queal, "Good News Today: Huge Vail Pass Ski Area Set," *Denver Post*, December 28, 1961, 1. Queal's column on Vail the following day waxed more descriptive but still focused on ski facilities, not the ambitious plans for the base village. Queal, "Huge New Ski Area in Works," *Denver Post*, December 29, 1961, 24. The first Denver daily to break the story of Vail was actually not the *Post* but *Cervi's Journal*, in March 1961. But *Cervi's*, specializing in business news and local politics, had a far smaller circulation than the *Post* or the *Rocky Mountain News*. Nello Cassai, "Two $1 Million Ski Sites Planned West of Denver," *Cervi's Journal*, March 8, 1961, 1.

106. Willard Haselbush, "New Vail Pass Ski Area to Be a Major Resort," *Denver Post*, January 7, 1962, 1D. While Haselbush's story, like most early press on Vail, featured a photograph of the ski mountain, it also, for the first time, depicted architect Fitzhugh Scott's model of the elaborate resort village planned for the base of the mountain.

107. Simonton, *Vail: Story of a Colorado Mountain Valley*, 67–75; Hauserman, *Inventors of Vail*, 47; Casewit, "Victory at Vail," 43; Rod Slifer, interview, Vail, August 30, 1993; Hauk, *Chronology of the Vail Ski Area*, 1, 6; Pasquale Marranzino, "Vail Ski Pass Starts Fast," *Rocky Mountain News*, January 8, 1963, 29; Parker, telephone interview, January 12, 1994.

108. Casewit, "Miracle out of a Meadow," 7, 10; "Vail Gondola Operating," *Eagle Valley Enterprise*, December 13, 1962, 1; Jack Foster, "White Gold Makes a Gleaming City," *Rocky Mountain News*, March 10, 1963, 53. Jack Foster's ghost town columns are anthologized in *Adventures at Timberline*.

109. Findlay, *Magic Lands*, esp. 5–6.

110. Pete Seibert, interview, Vail, January 6, 1994; Parker, telephone interview,

January 12, 1994; Seibert, *Vail: Triumph of a Dream*, 45–49, 52, 58–60, 64–71, 74–75, 78–81. L'École Hôtelière de Lausanne, where Seibert studied from 1950 to 1952, is the oldest hotel school in the world and is widely regarded as one of the best.

111. Caulkins, interview; Hauk, interview, August 5, 1993; Seibert, *Vail: Triumph of a Dream*, 84–93; Hauserman, *Inventors of Vail*, 64–71; Simonton, *Vail: Story of a Colorado Mountain Valley*, 61–65; Vail Associates Ltd., prospectus, August 14, 1961, 5–6, 8.

112. Vail Corporation, memorandum, November 1960, Caulkins private papers; Vail Associates Ltd., prospectus, August 14, 1961, 13. See also "Vail Ski Area Competitive to Aspen," *Eagle Valley Enterprise*, February 1, 1962, 1.

113. "The Vail Project: Real Estate Development" (1960), 7–9; Vail Associates Ltd., prospectus, April 25, 1961, 11, and prospectus, August 14, 1961, 13, Box 1, VA Papers. Seibert, for one, thought the summer appeal should focus on golf. Along with VA board member Dick Hauserman, Seibert "fought like hell" to lease a large parcel of land just east of Vail Village to the citizen-run Vail Recreation District for a golf course. The first nine holes opened in fall 1966, giving Vail its first major attraction outside the ski season. The recreation district later added nine more holes and several tennis courts, all on VA-leased land. Seibert, interview; Parker, telephone interview, January 19, 1994; Vail Corporation, Executive Committee, minutes, August 10, 1964, Box 1, VA Papers; Vail Corporation, Board of Directors, minutes, June 5, 1965, Box 3, VA Papers; "Vail Summer Season Opens," *Eagle Valley Enterprise*, June 16, 1966, 1; Willard Haselbush, "Resort Construction Booms in Vail," *Denver Post*, July 31, 1966, 4I; Charlie Meyers, "Skiing, Golfing 'Linked' at Vail," *Denver Post*, October 2, 1966, 71; Rod Slifer, interview, Vail, August 30, 1993. (Slifer was an early president of the Vail Recreation District.)

114. Sharon Brown, "Profile: Image Maker, Bob Parker," *Vail Trail*, April 16, 1971, 7; Vail Associates Ltd., ads in *Skiing*, October 1965 and November 1964; Vail Associates Ltd., brochure, 1964–65 ski season, Paul I. Hauk private papers (hereafter Hauk private papers); Jay, O'Rear, and O'Rear, *Ski Down the Years*, 253.

115. Seibert, interview; Roger Ritchie, "A Cozy Place to Ski . . . Vail," *Flightime: The Air Travelers Magazine*, January–February 1968, 16. Benedict and Scott drew up separate preliminary plans for the village, and the actual village grew more out of Scott's plan; see Hauserman, *Inventors of Vail*, 44–45. Seibert saw the integration of mountain and village as a key feature setting Vail apart from Sun Valley. The Union Pacific Railroad, which owned Sun Valley, had built its resort village from scratch, much like VA. But at Sun Valley, some three miles separated the village from the ski facilities, meaning visitors had to rely on cars or buses to get from their accommodations to the slopes.

116. John Urry, a British sociologist of tourism and leisure, has termed such a setting, structured to facilitate or encourage spending, as a "consuming place." See Urry, *Consuming Places*, esp. 1–2.

117. Seibert, interview; Fitzhugh Scott Jr., interview, Vail, August 27, 1993. Seibert later hinted that Bridge Street was his idea, and that he got it from Zermatt, the Swiss ski hamlet. "You get off the train in Zermatt," he told me, "and then to go to the mountain you have to walk up this main street. It was obvious that there were important commercial advantages to having kind of a dog bone [Bridge Street, bent like a dog leg] and having the shaft of the bone be the shopping area." But Scott claimed *he* had designed

Bridge Street, and his account has been corroborated by VA's early marketing director, Bob Parker, and by Dick Hauserman, another early VA partner. Parker, telephone interview, January 12, 1994; Hauserman, *Inventors of Vail*, 39.

118. Judith Axler Turner, "One Vail of No Tears," *Washington Post*, January 24, 1974, D11; Morten Lund, "Vail: Wave of the Future," *Ski*, October 1969, 67; Belle Forrest, "Happy Vail Pass: Our Never Land," *Rocky Mountain News Festival*, February 19, 1967, 1; Dallas, *Vail*, 24. "Wisconsin Swiss" referred to the Milwaukee origins of architect Scott.

119. Seibert, interview; Seibert, *Vail: Triumph of a Dream*, 98–99; Scott, interview; Parker, telephone interview, January 12, 1994; Slifer, interview; David Sage, interview, Vail, July 22, 1993; Hauserman, *Inventors of Vail*, 47. Fritz Benedict, the third collaborator in the original village design, parted ways here. He "pushed for something like a new indigenous architecture," according to Parker, "taking off from mine buildings and ranches." Parker, telephone interview, January 12, 1994. VA's original business plan, before Fitzhugh Scott came on board, incorporated Benedict's idea for a western architectural theme: the main lodge, it said, would evoke "the spirit of the western mountains" and thus set the tone for the rest of the village. "The Vail Project: Real Estate Development" (1960), 9. But, Seibert later claimed, "It certainly didn't make sense to me to . . . put in buildings that were faux-mining buildings, because this was not a mining community." As for an "indigenous architecture," Seibert contended, "there may have been here in Colorado, but it was log cabins; it was pretty limited. Gay Nineties was [the prevailing architectural style in] Aspen, so we needed to do something different. Alpine architecture made sense." So Seibert and Benedict, according to Parker, came to a "parting of ways on philosophy of design, . . . and when Fritz left the project, Fitzhugh [Scott] took over the overall planning." Seibert, interview; Parker, telephone interview, January 12, 1994.

120. Lois Hagen, "'We've Always Wanted a Swiss Chalet,'" Women's Section, *Milwaukee Journal*, January 30, 1969, 3 (first quotation); Hagen, "Vacation House Steps Down the Mountain," Women's Section, *Milwaukee Journal*, February 6, 1969, 6; Forrest, "Happy Vail Pass: Our Never Land," 1 (second quotation); Foster, "White Gold Makes a Gleaming City" (third quotation); Pat Hanna, "Super Supper Club Set for Vail," *Rocky Mountain News*, December 18, 1964, 114; "Plush, New Night Club Opens in Vail Village," *Denver Post*, December 20, 1964, 67; "Vail," in Colorado Ski Country USA, *Manual of Colorado Skiing and Winter Sports, 1964–1965* (Denver: Colorado Ski Country USA, 1964), 37–39; Valhalla at Vail, ad in *Vail Trail*, February 18, 1966 (fourth quotation); Pasquale Marranzino, "Booming Vail Village," *Rocky Mountain News*, September 15, 1965, 41 (fifth quotation); numerous ads in *Vail Trail*, 1965–69.

121. J. A. Turner, "One Vail of No Tears"; Marieluise Murphy, "Vail," *Holiday Inn Magazine*, January 1968, 20; Horace Sutton, "Vail, Colorado—An Airless Aerie for Hardy Snow Birds and Ski Bunnies," *Houston Chronicle*, November 14, 1965, 17; Don Dooley, "Village That Skis Built," Men's and Recreation Section, *Milwaukee Journal*, March 28, 1965, 1; Vail Associates Ltd., ad in *Skiing*, October 1968.

122. Casewit, *United Air Lines Guide to Western Skiing*, 30; "Town Council Passes Next Year's Budget," *Vail Trail*, October 11, 1968, 8; D. Sage, interview.

123. "The Vail Project: Real Estate Development" (1960), 6, 11.

124. Bob Parker, Parker Pens column, *Vail Trail*, February 17, 1967, 10 (emphasis in original); Ted Kindel, "A Christmas Message from Our Mayor, Ted Kindel," *Vail Trail*, December 23, 1966, 1.

125. "The Vail Project: Real Estate Development" (1960), 6; Vail Corporation, Executive Committee, minutes, October 14, 1964, Box 1, VA Papers; Vail Associates Ltd., ad in *Skiing*, November 1963, 61. An addendum to the minutes cited here listed the (all male) employees of the Vail Ski School by nationality: two were Austrian, two German, one French, one Swiss, and one Italian. When Frenchman Roger Staub, an internationally known racer and freestyle skier, arrived to head the ski school in 1965, a *Vail Trail* profile made prominent mention of his being a bachelor. "New Director of Vail Ski School, Olympic Gold Medalist in Giant Slalom," *Vail Trail*, October 1965, 1.

126. On the matter of whiteness, see A. G. Coleman, "Unbearable Whiteness of Skiing." As Coleman shows, marketing skiing as a sport for whites was long-standing, industry-wide practice.

127. Parker, telephone interview, January 26, 1994; Vail Associates Inc., brochure, 1966–67 ski season, Hauk private papers; Vail Associates Ltd., ad in *Skiing*, October 1965; George Knox, "A Message from—Vail's Ugly People," *Vail Trail*, February 24, 1967, 2.

128. Bob Parker, "Looking Back on Vail," *Skiing*, December 1982, 46 (first and second quotations); Parker, telephone interview, January 12, 1994; Slifer, interview; Hauserman, *Inventors of Vail*, 75; Vail Associates Ltd., ad in *Skiing*, October 1963, 53 (third quotation).

129. Bob Parker, Parker Pens columns, *Vail Trail*, December 23, 1966, 9, and February 17, 1967, 10; "Of Interest to Women," *Vail Trail*, February 22, 1970, 14. Parker's mention of television referred to the fact that Vail received no television signal in its early years, due to its location in a steep, narrow valley surrounded by high mountains. In spring 1967, the question of whether to bring cable television to Vail sparked debate among locals. Among those opposed was Parker, who argued in his February 17 column that visitors "might want to get away from the omnipresent voice of television" and therefore that "it would be a selling point for Vail that we do not have TV." His side lost.

130. George Knox, "A Sense of Morality," *Vail Trail*, August 2, 1968, 2 (first quotation); Knox, "It Always Helps to Know," *Vail Trail*, July 28, 1967, 2 (second quotation); "The Vail Project: Real Estate Development" (1960), 5, 9.

131. Vail Associates Inc., Executive Committee, minutes, August 10, 1967, Box 1, VA Papers (first three quotations); Florence Steinberg, "Conventioneers Cognizant of the Complete Resort," *Eagle Valley Enterprise*, September 5, 1968, 5 (last two quotations). The places where the Vail Resort Association, the local chamber of commerce, ran its summer ads—in publications like *Venture*, *Status*, *National Geographic*, *Diplomat*, and the *New Yorker*—further suggested the affluent, educated clientele they were trying to reach. See "It's a Small World—We Made It That Way!" *Vail Trail*, October 4, 1968, 2.

132. Patricia Moore, "Vail Is Clean-Shaven Resort," *Denver Post*, April 11, 1969, 33; Curtis Casewit, "Super Salesman for Super Ski Resort," *Colorado Magazine*, September–October 1972, 10R; George Knox, "A New Era in Vail," *Vail Trail*, November 18, 1966, 2; Al Hills, "The Whiteford-Hills Resort Comprehension Test," *News Note*, October 23, 1970, 2 ("Subversive Employees" quotation); Peter Seibert, quoted in Canniff and Lapin, *This Is Vail*, 14.

133. Seibert, interview; Sharon Brown, "Profile: Image Maker, Bob Parker," *Vail Trail*, April 16, 1971, 7.

134. Casewit, *United Air Lines Guide to Western Skiing*, 36–37; "The Most Nearly Perfect Resort," *Ski*, August 1971, 70. Besides the CEOs listed, Vail by the late 1960s was also second home to astronaut Scott Carpenter, actor Henry Fonda, journalist and broadcaster Lowell Thomas, conductor Leonard Bernstein, oilman John Murchison, and members of the Uihlein family that owned the Schlitz brewing empire. By the early 1970s, the resort had also added U.S. Rep. Gerald Ford (soon to be vice president and then president) and his family to its roster of mostly conservative, corporate celebrities.

135. Skier-visit statistics are taken from Vail Corporation, memorandum, November 1960, Caulkins private papers; Vail Associates, annual report, 1968, 11; and Vail Associates, annual report, 1972, 2. Coverage of new construction included Marranzino, "Vail Ski Pass Starts Fast," 29; Willard Haselbush, "Spectacular Vail Village Rises in Colorado Sheep Pasture," *Denver Post*, December 29, 1963, 1D; Willard Haselbush, "Vail Village Resort Expansion Boosted," *Denver Post*, October 4, 1964, 87; "Vail Moves On—Not Resting on Laurels," *Rocky Mountain News*, October 31, 1965, 6B; "New Construction Tops 4 Million in Vail Village," *Vail Trail*, October 1965; Michael Howard, "Vail: Top Ski Resort Firmly Established," *Rocky Mountain News*, March 13, 1966, 8; William Logan, "Vail: Sky Is the Limit for Highland Jewel," *Rocky Mountain News*, October 3, 1966, 18; "Over $2.5 Million Construction Now in Progress—Building Business Booms with New Projects Underway," *Vail Trail*, June 23, 1967, 6; "Vail Area Building Booms; 500-Acre Suburb Added," *Denver Post*, June 25, 1967, 1H; "Vail Opens Two More Mountains," *Eagle Valley Enterprise*, October 19, 1967, 1; "The Vail Skyline Is an Ever-Changing Thing!," *Vail Trail*, November 10, 1967, 6; Willard Haselbush, "Expansion Announced for Vail," *Denver Post*, March 30, 1969, 1H; Vail Associates Inc., "The Vail Story," public-relations release, 1969, "Vail-1969" folder, historical clippings file, Vail Public Library; Willard Haselbush, "Vail Manor Luxury Complex Under Way," *Denver Post*, August 22, 1965, 1E; Willard Haselbush, "Resort Construction Booms in Vail," *Denver Post*, July 31, 1966, 4I; Harman, O'Donnell & Henninger Associates Inc., *Planning Study of the Gore Valley Area and the Town of Vail*, 8; and Linda Schoenwetter, "Land Values Will Soar," *Ski*, September 1969.

136. *Eagle Valley Enterprise*, December 26, 1963, 1; Haselbush, "Spectacular Vail Village Rises in Colorado Sheep Pasture," 1D; "Alpine-Type Village Going Up in Gore Creek Valley Area," *Rocky Mountain News*, December 29, 1963, 45; "Contemporary High Rises Will Go Up at Lion's Ridge," *Vail Trail*, October 5, 1969, 10; Olga Curtis, "Vail: There Is Also a Summertime," *Denver Post Mountain Living*, May 24, 1970, 30; "Vail Building Boom Moving Westward," *Vail Trail*, July 30, 1971, 19. The Condominium Ownership Act, originally Colo. Rev. Stat. 1963 § 118-15-1, is now Colo. Rev. Stat. § 38-33-101 et seq. As of May 1975, *Colorado Magazine* listed more condominium complexes in Vail than in any other resort. The resort towns of Summit County, especially Breckenridge, were also well represented. "Colorado Magazine's Condominium Directory," *Colorado Magazine*, May–June 1975, 55–61. See also Nance, *Recreational Condominiums in Summit County, Colorado*.

137. Slifer, interview; Vail Associates Inc., annual report, 1974, 4; Parker, telephone interview, January 12, 1994.

138. Sharon Brown, "Profile: Ted Kindel, Town Pioneer," *Vail Trail*, November 2, 1971, 8; George Knox, "Smile—You're On PR," *Vail Trail*, December 16, 1968, 2; "VRA Sponsors Employer-Employee Refresher Session," *Vail Trail*, December 9, 1966, 1. Even Vail's police could do their part for PR, Knox suggested, by learning customer-relations techniques and making sure not to intimidate visitors. "Our policemen should not look like cops; with a little imagination we're sure someone can come up with a uniform that would make them look far more distinctive," Knox mused in a 1969 piece. "Our Police Chief (and maybe we can even come up with a better title than that) should be a Public Relations man who also knows police work." Knox, "A Police Ambassador," *Vail Trail*, August 10, 1969, 2. VA's Bob Parker, too, believed that "our Officers should be trained in the handling of our guests." Town of Vail, Board of Trustees, meeting minutes, February 6, 1967.

139. The "unofficial town government" tag was Bob Parker's; see Parker, Parker Pens column, *Vail Trail*, April 15, 1966, 1. On the early evolution of Vail town government, including the resort association, see Philpott, "Visions of a Changing Vail," 133–42.

140. Sheika Gramshammer, "The Vail I Have Known," in official program of *Seventh Annual Jerry Ford Invitational Golf Tournament* (Barrett and Associates, 1983), 66, in "Vail" envelope, Pamphlet File, Colorado Historical Society; Parker, telephone interview, January 19, 1994; Lillian Miller, Lift Lines column, *Vail Trail*, December 16, 1966, 4 (quotation).

141. Gramshammer, "The Vail I Have Known"; Sharon Brown, "Profile: Vail Elementary School and Staff," *Vail Trail*, April 23, 1971, 10 (first quotation); L. Miller, Lift Lines column, *Vail Trail*, December 16, 1966, 4 (second quotation). On the idea that building a community from scratch was one of the joys of suburban living, see Henderson, "Rugged American Collectivism."

142. Slifer, interview; Marcia Sage, interview, Vail, July 22, 1993 (first quotation); L. Miller, Lift Lines column, *Vail Trail*, December 16, 1966, 4 (second quotation), and February 10, 1967, 4 (third quotation).

143. Sunday color sections like the *Denver Post Empire Magazine*, and lifestyle magazines like *Colorado Wonderland* in the 1950s and *Colorado Magazine* in the 1960s and 1970s, often did photo features on showpiece houses in Aspen, Vail, and other resort towns. In particular, *Colorado Magazine*'s Alpinehaus feature returned to Vail with some frequency. See, for example, "Alpinehaus: Happiness Is a Home in the High Country," Fall 1967, 32–34; Lorraine Burgess and Guy Burgess, "Alpinehaus : Victorian Retreat in the Mountains," Winter 1967, 34–36; Lorraine Burgess and Guy Burgess, "Alpinehaus," Summer 1968, 32–33, 48; "Alpinehaus: A Family Retreat at World-Famous Vail," September–October 1969, 32–34; Davis Dutton, "A Home for All Seasons," September–October 1975, 70–71. These photo features echoed the ones California-based *Sunset* magazine had been doing for years on innovative oceanfront houses, ski cabins, hunting lodges, and other vacation and "outdoor living" homes in the far western states.

144. Al Hills, letter to the editor, *Vail Trail*, April 16, 1971, 18.

145. Josef Staufer, letter to the editor, *Vail Trail*, September 7, 1969, 10; "Employee Housing Comes to Vail," *Vail Trail*, May 31, 1970, 1. The pernicious "downvalley effect"—in which resort workers are forced to live farther and farther from the resort, often in

squalid conditions, because they cannot afford the resort's skyrocketing real estate and housing costs—finally began to raise concerns in the 1990s and 2000s. See H. Clifford, *Downhill Slide*, esp. chap. 9; and Rademan, "Change Comes to the Mountains." The 1990s in particular saw a good deal of insightful journalism on this issue: see, for example, Ringholz, *Little Town Blues*, 117–19; Robert Weller, "Cost of Living Strips Ski Resorts, Cities of Needed Help," *Los Angeles Times*, March 19, 1995, B4; Ray Ring, "The New West's Service Economy," *High Country News*, April 17, 1995, 1, 8–14; Ringholz, *Paradise Paved*, 93–112; Michael Booth, "Where's a Worker to Live?," *Denver Post*, October 27, 1997, 1A, 11A; Judith Kohler, "'Greening' of the Back-to-Nature Movement Walls Off Shangri-La," *Los Angeles Times*, January 11, 1998, A1; and James Brooke, "Cry of Wealthy in Vail: Not in Our Playground!," *New York Times*, November 5, 1998, A18. Scholarly treatments include Travis, *New Geographies of the American West*, 143–49; Rothman, *Devil's Bargains*, 357–60; and A. G. Coleman, *Ski Style*, 201–2, 209–10.

146. Peter Seibert, quoted in Don Dooley, "Village That Skis Built," Men's and Recreation Section, *Milwaukee Journal*, March 28, 1965, 1; Vail Corporation, Executive Committee, minutes, December 15, 1964, Box 1, VA Papers.

147. Ruth, *Colorado Vacations*, 8; Hoyt, "Forecast for the Future," 307; Lamm and McCarthy, *Angry West*, 2–3.

148. In the Gallup Poll, Colorado regularly ranked as one of the top five states Americans would like to move to, usually trailing California, Florida, sometimes Arizona, and sometimes New York. Colorado's standing improved over time, from eighth in the 1940s, to fifth in 1950, to fourth in 1956, 1960, and 1966. During this same span of time, Colorado also consistently ranked among the top five most desirable states for a vacation (see note 4 in the introduction). In the 1956 poll, when asked what would be their reasons for moving to another state, respondents listed climate first, by a large margin, followed by job opportunities, nearness to family or friends, "regional preference" or "wanderlust," and scenery. Gallup polls no. 337 (December 12, 1944), question 7c; no. 414T (March 5–10, 1948), question 4a; no. 454 (March 26–31, 1950), question 1; no. 575 (November 11, 1956), questions 54a and 54b; no. 626 (March 28, 1960), question 2a; no. 723 (January 21–26, 1966), question 1b.

149. The raw numbers: Colorado's total population shot from 1,325,089 in 1950 to 1,753,947 in 1960 and 2,207,259 in 1970. In 1950, 92,519 Coloradans, or 7 percent, lived in the urban fringe; by 1960 the number was 351,918, or 20.1 percent, and by 1970 it was 609,950, or 27.6 percent. From 1950 to 1960, Colorado gained 428,858 new residents, with the six Denver metro counties (Denver, Adams, Arapahoe, Boulder, Douglas, Jefferson) accounting for 318,564, or 74.3 percent, of the gain. From 1960 to 1970, the statewide increase was 453,312, with the six metro counties contributing 301,737, or 66.6 percent, of the gain. In the 1960s, aside from the Front Range metropolitan corridor (the six Denver metro counties plus El Paso, Larimer, and Weld), ten other Colorado counties scored population gains of more than 20 percent, including all six of the tourist-oriented counties on the I-70 corridor: Gilpin (gained 587 people, or 85.7 percent); Clear Creek (2,026, or 72.5 percent); Summit (592, or 28.6 percent); Eagle (2,821, or 60.3 percent); Garfield (2,804, or 23.3 percent); and Pitkin (3,804, or 159.8 percent). U.S. Department of Commerce, Bureau of the Census, *Census of Population: 1960*, vol. 1, part 7, tables 2 and 6, and *1970 Census of Population*, vol.

1, part 7, tables 2 and 9; SPD, *Colorado Year Book, 1962–1964*, 376–77; "Final 1970 Census Figures for Colorado," *Colorado Business Review*, January 1971, 5–6.

CHAPTER 4. BLUEPRINTS FOR ACTION

1. Kirk, *Collecting Nature*, chap. 2, and Wolf, *Arthur Carhart*, provide overviews of Carhart's multifaceted career.

2. Carhart, *Water or Your Life*, 106; Carhart to Ross Sheffler, May 22, 1958, FF "Correspondence: May–July 1958," Box 3, Arthur Hawthorne Carhart Papers (hereafter Carhart Papers).

3. Carhart to Sheffler, May 22, 1958, FF "Correspondence: May–July 1958," Box 3, Carhart Papers (first quotation); Carhart, *Water or Your Life*, 107–9 (second quotation p. 107); Carhart, "Pattern for Murder" (third quotation p. 77, fourth quotation p. 26).

4. The classic treatment of the subject remains Hays, *Conservation and the Gospel of Efficiency*. See also Koppes, "Efficiency/Equity/Esthetics."

5. Good overviews of postwar environmental politics include Hays, *Beauty, Health, and Permanence*; Hays, *History of Environmental Politics Since 1945*; Rothman, *Greening of a Nation?*; Rothman, *Saving the Planet*, chaps. 4–6; Wellock, *Preserving the Nation*, chaps. 3–4; and Shabecoff, *Fierce Green Fire*. See also R. N. L. Andrews, *Managing the Environment, Managing Ourselves*, chap. 11; and two fine case studies, Huffman, *Protectors of the Land and Water*; and Judd and Beach, *Natural States*. Gottlieb, *Forcing the Spring*, and Montrie, *People's History of Environmentalism in the United States*, show that environmentalism by other names thrived long before the 1960s, including outside the middle class that is usually assumed to have invented it. At the same time, Rome, " 'Give Earth a Chance,' " explains why the movement did not materialize as a mass phenomenon until the 1960s.

6. There is a rich literature on sportsmen's relationship to conservation. On the question of how much credit sportsmen deserve for *originating* conservation, see Reiger, *American Sportsmen and the Origins of Conservation*; and T. R. Dunlap, "Sport Hunting and Conservation." More recent scholarship has weighed the social implications of sportsmen-supported conservation measures: see Warren, *Hunter's Game*; and Jacoby, *Crimes against Nature*.

7. Mark Harvey is one of the few historians to recognize the IWLA's pivotal postwar role, noting the part it (and especially its "western representative" Joe Penfold) played in the watershed Echo Park controversy. See M. W. T. Harvey, *Symbol of Wilderness*, 171–73.

8. Izaak Walton League of America, Summit County [CO] Chapter, *Come Up to the High Country*, brochure [1940s], in Colorado Room, Tutt Library Special Collections.

9. On the origins, expansion, and ethos of the Izaak Walton League, see Fox, *John Muir and His Legacy*, 159–72; and Voigt, *Born with Fists Doubled*. The quotation is from Fox, p. 162.

10. Barrows and Holmes, *Colorado's Wildlife Story*, 25, 56–57; Edna H. Hill, "Colorado and the League," *Outdoor America*, October 1948, 6.

11. *Outdoor America* devoted regular, admiring coverage to the activities of Colorado Ikes, particularly in 1950–51, an especially energetic time for them. See, for example,

"Chapter, Division Briefs: Colorado," June–July 1950, 14; "Mile High Chapter Plans $150,000 Lodge," June–July 1950, 15; "Chapter, Division Briefs: Colorado," March–April 1951, 15; "Johnny Grass Seed Forges Ahead," May–June 1951, 2; and "Colorado Captures Bulk of Membership Awards," May–June 1951, 25.

12. Carhart to J. N. Darling, May 15, 1943, FF "Correspondence: 1940–1943," Box 2, Carhart Papers. On the land grab, see Merrill, *Public Lands and Political Meaning*, 171, 192–94; and Steen, *U.S. Forest Service: A History*, 272–77. William Voigt looked back on the land grab and its historical context in *Public Grazing Lands* (which Voigt dedicated to, among others, Art Carhart). The controversy was also what turned Bernard DeVoto into a leading polemicist for conservation; on his involvement, see J. L. Thomas, *Country in the Mind*, 131–45; and Fox, *John Muir and His Legacy*, 224–27.

13. Kingery, *Colorado Mountain Club*, 76. Hal Rothman describes the state of the Sierra Club and other established conservation groups in the wake of World War II, and assesses the reasons for their political weakness at that time, in *Greening of a Nation?*, 15–20.

14. Arthur H. Carhart, "Raiders on the Range," *Trail and Timberline*, no. 339 (March 1947): 39–43.

15. "The Point of View of the Conservation Committee," *Trail and Timberline*, no. 339 (March 1947): 44.

16. Marjorie Peregrine, "Our Mountain Club Must Protect the Public Lands," *Trail and Timberline*, no. 340 (April 1947): 64.

17. Carhart may have personally influenced the Dude Ranchers' Association (DRA) to inveigh against the land grab. Charles C. Moore, then DRA president, was Carhart's longtime personal friend, and the two men likely exchanged information about the controversy and discussed how to respond. That said, the DRA might well have opposed the land grab even without Carhart's involvement. Moore was, in Carhart's words, a "militant conservationist," and one of the DRA's founding principles was the protection of fish and game. See Borne, *Dude Ranching*, 50, 146–48.

18. Arthur H. Carhart, "The Haul of the Wild," *Nation's Business*, March 1945, 25–26, 63; Arthur H. Carhart, "Hunting and Fishing Is Big Business," *Sports Afield*, August 1947, 19–21, 138–40; Arthur H. Carhart, "Hunting and Fishing Is Bigger Business," *Sports Afield*, June 1951, 30–31, 65–70; Arthur H. Carhart, "Hunting and Fishing—Bigger Business Than Ever," *Sports Afield*, July 1960, 22–23, 93–94.

19. Carhart, *All Outdoors*, KFEL-Denver, January 24, 1945, transcript in FF "Radio Scripts: KFEL, *All Outdoors*: Jan–Feb 1945," Box 21, Carhart Papers. *All Outdoors* was a semiweekly, quarter-hour radio show that Carhart began doing for KFEL in August 1944, not long after leaving the state's Game and Fish Department. He offered folksy tips on hunting, fishing, campfire cooking, and the like or explained the latest research concerning game management. But he devoted many shows to open lobbying for conservation causes.

20. Carhart, *Crisis Spots in Conservation*, 7, 8, 9.

21. Carhart, *Water or Your Life*, 108; Carhart, "Pattern for Murder"; Carhart to Richard M. Leonard, February 6, 1953, FF "Correspondence: 1953," Box 2, Carhart Papers; Carhart, *Crisis Spots in Conservation*, 11.

22. For antidiversion editorials and ads in the *Aspen Times*, see "Water Resources

Must Be Protected Now!," December 2, 1948, 1; "Little Water Planning for Western Slope," December 30, 1948, 1, 8; "WATER: Western Colorado's and Pitkin County's Most Vital Resource," April 21, 1949, 7; "NOW Is the Time!," April 28, 1949, 7; and "We Gave the Party," May 5, 1949, 8. On the founding of the Western Colorado Water Planning Association, see these *Aspen Times* articles: "Federation Formed to Fight For Water," March 24, 1949, 1; "Woodall Temporary Head Water Planners," May 19, 1949, 1; and "Woodall Elected Pres. W. Colo. Water Planners," June 23, 1949, 1. Aspen's tourist businesses went all out to show their support for the water-planning association: local hostelries (including the Hotel Jerome, owned by Walter Paepcke's Aspen Company) offered half-off rates to visiting delegates, while Paepcke's Aspen Skiing Corporation offered free chairlift rides. See "Large Crowd Expected For W.S.W.P.A. Meeting," *Aspen Times*, June 16, 1949, 1.

23. "Water Resources Must Be Protected Now!"

24. Wilkinson, *Crossing the Next Meridian*, chap. 6, remains an excellent introduction to western water law and its long-standing bias against nonconsumptive, nonextractive uses of water.

25. "Woodall Tells Directors No Diversion Agreement," *Aspen Times*, February 2, 1950, 1.

26. Tyler, *Last Water Hole in the West*, 292–93; "Water Association Sends Delegates to Denver," *Aspen Times*, August 9, 1951, 1.

27. Pitkin County Water Protection Association, *1953 Version: Rape of the Roaring Fork*, brochure (Aspen, 1953), in FF "Correspondence: 1953," Box 2, Carhart Papers.

28. On interaction between the IWLA and the water-protection association, see "Group to Fight Further Diversion of Water," *Aspen Times*, July 26, 1951, 1, 8; and "Water Association Sends Delegates to Denver," *Aspen Times*, August 9, 1951, 1. On the founding and early activities of the local chapter of Ikes, see "Izaak Walton League Elects New Officers," *Aspen Times*, December 24, 1953, 1; and "Izaak Walton League to Hear Kimball Talk," *Aspen Times*, January 7, 1954, 1.

29. See, for example, Carhart to John B. Oakes, January 17, 1956, FF "Correspondence: 1956," Box 2, Carhart Papers; and Carhart to Joe W. Anderson, February 14, 1959, FF "Correspondence: Jan–May 1959," Box 3, Carhart Papers. Oakes was the *New York Times*'s editorial writer and author of an occasional column on conservation; he took a keen interest in environmental issues and in the 1960s would serve on the Sierra Club Board of Directors and play a founding role in the Natural Resources Defense Council. Anderson was an assistant to House Democratic whip Carl Albert of Oklahoma.

30. For the complete text of the 1956 brochure, see "1956 Version—Rape of the Roaring Fork," *Aspen Times*, February 23, 1956, supplementary insert.

31. "Little Water Planning for Western Slope," *Aspen Times*, December 30, 1948, 1, 8.

32. John P. Burns, manager of the Glenwood Springs Chamber of Commerce, quoted in "Glenwood C.C. Manager In Favor of Diversion," *Aspen Times*, March 11, 1954, 1.

33. Carhart to Richard Leonard, August 25, 1953, and Leonard to John N. Spencer, August 20, 1953, both in FF "Correspondence: 1953," Box 2, Carhart Papers.

34. "Aspen Protests to Frying Pan-Arkansas Diversion Aired," *Pueblo Star-Journal and Sunday Chieftain*, August 31, 1952, 2.

35. M. W. T. Harvey, *Symbol of Wilderness*. That the Echo Park battle was primarily a battle for wilderness is not just a historians' fiction; it was also the sense of many conservationists at the time. No less than Sierra Club executive director David Brower, recognized by his contemporaries and by later historians as the leader of the Echo Park fight, acknowledged that the battle involved conservation groups of many different stripes, but he asserted that the "one thing they had in common was a devotion to the abstract concept that wilderness has values which our culture cannot afford to lose, and that this is an important part of living for something besides making a living." David R. Brower, "The Sierra Club on the National Scene," *Sierra Club Bulletin*, January 1956, 4.

36. *Sierra Club Bulletin*, February 1954, 5, 12. Though the *Bulletin* was a publication for Sierra Club members, this special issue, devoted entirely to the "Trouble in Dinosaur," was mass-mailed to a much wider readership by the Wilderness Society.

37. Carhart to Fred M. Packard, September 23, 1954, FF "Correspondence: Colorado River: 1954," Box 5, Carhart Papers. Packard was executive secretary of the National Parks Association.

38. Arthur H. Carhart, "The Statement in Behalf of the Outdoor Writers of America Association, Before the Task Force on Water Resources and Power, Commission on Reorganization, of the Executive Branch of the Government," May 17, 1954, typescript in FF "Correspondence: Jan–May 1954," Box 2, Carhart Papers; J. W. Penfold, "A Statement to the Secretary of the Interior in Connection with Split Mountain and Echo Park Dams," typescript in FF "Correspondence: Colorado River: 1950–1951," Box 5, Carhart Papers. Penfold's statement was delivered by proxy at an April 1950 hearing held by Interior Secretary Oscar Chapman, during which he heard from proponents and opponents of the plans for Echo Park, which had been made public only a few weeks earlier.

39. Carhart to Ira N. Gabrielson, March 20, 1954, FF "Correspondence: Colorado River: 1954," Box 5, Carhart Papers. Carhart and Penfold called the group the Colorado Citizens Committee for the same reason: "to avoid a specific name that would invite 'nature lover' ridicule" and also "to get in the positive implication of 'development.' " Carhart to Gabrielson, March 23, 1954, ibid. Gabrielson was president of the Washington, DC–based Wildlife Management Institute.

40. Carhart to Bus Hatch, April 28, 1954, and Carhart to Fred M. Packard, September 23, 1954, both in FF "Correspondence: Colorado River: 1954," Box 5, Carhart Papers. We do not know if Bohn actually joined Carhart and Penfold's citizens' group; Carhart's letters say only that Bohn expressed strong interest and that the group was trying to bring him on board. Other group members with interests in tourism included at least one dude ranch owner, a ski-area manager, and an official in the Denver Convention and Visitors Bureau. See Carhart to Ira N. Gabrielson, March 20, 1954, ibid., for attendance at the group's organizational meeting in March 1954.

41. Carhart, "Ride the Lazy Dinosaur." *Westways*, in which this article appeared, was (and is) the magazine of the Automobile Club of Southern California, the regional affiliate of the American Automobile Association. That Carhart offered his views in an auto club magazine suggests the type of leisure-seeker he was trying to reach.

42. Nello Cassai, "Echo Dam Would Open Superb Recreation Area," *Denver Post*, August 1, 1954, 3A.

43. Carhart, memo to William Voigt, Joseph Penfold, David Brower, Ira Gabrielson, and C. R. Gutermuth, April 28, 1955, FF "Correspondence: Colorado River: 1955," Box 5, Carhart Papers. Carhart's safety argument was repeated almost exactly in *This Is Dinosaur*, a book of photographs and essays that Wallace Stegner edited and Alfred Knopf published to publicize Echo Park and build nationwide sympathy for saving it. In the book, white-water rafting legend Dock Marston wrote that "the canyons of Dinosaur have had a reputation far worse than they deserved. . . . With good boats and good boatmen, these canyons are considerably less dangerous than the traffic of any American highway." The canyon was, in fact, a "playground," Marston reassured readers. Otis "Dock" Marston, "Fast Water," in Stegner, *This Is Dinosaur*, 58.

44. Penfold sketched out a road system in a 1951 memo, which he issued in his capacity as western representative of the IWLA, just after having run the river with Carhart and other dam opponents. See Penfold, "Memo: To Cooperators," July 31, 1951, FF "Correspondence: Colorado River: 1950–1951," Box 5, Carhart Papers. Carhart laid out his landscape plans most fully in a letter to Benton Stong, January 23, 1954, FF "Correspondence: Colorado River: 1954," Box 5, Carhart Papers. See also Arthur H. Carhart, "The Menaced Dinosaur Monument," *National Parks Magazine*, January–March 1952, 24–29. Some might see little sunlight between the Carhart-Penfold vision for auto tourism in Dinosaur and the recreational improvements dam proponents were promising. But Carhart, consistent with conservationist principles, saw a key difference: expertise. His plan sprang from his own professional expertise in landscape and recreation management, whereas dam proponents, he charged, knew nothing about such matters. "Nobody with training and background in . . . land-use planning," Carhart wrote in *National Parks Magazine*, would argue that replacing rivers with a reservoir was the way to improve recreation. The people pushing the idea were "engineers trained and interested in construction activities" or "water lawyers with a limited, somewhat soggy and backward-looking legal outlook." Letting such hacks manage Dinosaur's recreational resources would be like "accepting the diagnosis of a carpenter in a heart ailment, and then allowing him to operate on that organ with a brace and bit." Carhart, "Menaced Dinosaur Monument," 21.

45. Wagar corresponded frequently with Carhart and wrote prolifically on the need for recreation planning, lending academic legitimacy to the cause. For an early example, see Wagar, "Recreation in Relation to Multiple Use in the West." Colorado A&M is now Colorado State University.

46. Wagar, "Some Major Principles in Recreation Land Use Planning," 434.

47. On Mission 66, see Sellars, *Preserving Nature in the National Parks*, 180–95; and Barringer, "Mission Impossible: National Park Development in the 1950s." On Operation Outdoors, see Hirt, *Conspiracy of Optimism*, 157–60. On the state parks movement, see Landrum, *State Park Movement in America*; and Tilden, *State Parks*.

48. Joseph Penfold to Arthur Carhart, February 16, 1962, FF "Correspondence: 1962," Box 3, Carhart Papers. Historian Robin Winks, who has written the most detailed account of ORRRC to date, describes Penfold's thinking much as I have here; see Winks, *Laurance S. Rockefeller*, 121–22.

49. Penfold acknowledged as much in his letter to Carhart of February 16, 1962, FF "Correspondence: 1962," Box 3, Carhart Papers.

50. On Penfold's work in drafting the ORRRC bill and finding friends for it in Congress, see Winks, *Laurance S. Rockefeller*, 121–22; "Outdoor Resources Review," *Living Wilderness*, Fall–Winter 1956–57, 38–39; and Penfold's own recollections in a letter to Carhart, February 16, 1962, FF "Correspondence: 1962," Box 3, Carhart Papers. The Game and Fish Department publicist who helped Penfold draft the bill was Frank Gregg, editor of the agency's monthly magazine, who in 1957 would become executive director of the Izaak Walton League. (Years later, during the Carter administration, he would head the Bureau of Land Management.) Penfold himself humbly refused to take full credit for the idea that led to ORRRC. "No one can claim it as a wholly original idea," he wrote to Carhart in his letter of February 16, 1962, adding that the idea was not even all that new: back in the 1920s President Coolidge had appointed a Recreation Commission, "which in general had similar purposes" to what Penfold had in mind.

51. Outdoor Recreation Resources Review Commission (hereafter ORRRC), *Outdoor Recreation for America*. For a summary of the commission's recommendations, see pp. 5–10; for the declaration that outdoor recreation was vital to the national interest, see esp. 23–24. A summary of ORRRC's recommendations appeared in "Outdoor Recreation Review," *Living Wilderness*, Winter–Spring 1962, 3–11. Winks, *Laurance S. Rockefeller*, 129, lists some of the ORRRC proposals that actually came to pass; see also pp. 133–34 for Winks's summary of the commission's "major accomplishments."

52. ORRRC, *Outdoor Recreation for America*, 4.

53. See, for example, Hays, *Beauty, Health, and Permanence*, 54, 57, 117; and Winks, *Laurance S. Rockefeller*, 134.

54. Allott and other opponents kept saying it would be premature to pass a wilderness bill before ORRRC could finish its work, because only then could the commission decide whether the legislation was really needed. For a detailed account of Aspinall's maneuvers on the bill, see Schulte, *Wayne Aspinall and the Shaping of the American West*, 115–62. Some conservationists suspected Penfold and the IWLA of also dragging their feet. See, for example, M. W. T. Harvey, *Wilderness Forever*, 206. But in testimony before Congress in 1958, Penfold made clear that he and the IWLA backed the bill's immediate passage. In fact, he turned Allott's argument on its head, suggesting that enactment of wilderness legislation would speed the completion of ORRRC's work. "Wilderness Bill Hearings," *Living Wilderness*, Summer–Fall 1958, 38.

55. David E. Pesonen, "An Analysis of the ORRRC Report: 'Outdoor Recreation for America,'" *Sierra Club Bulletin*, May 1962, 13. Pesonen, the Sierra Club's conservation editor, had a first-hand reason for feeling bitter toward ORRRC: he had worked on the ORRRC study report on wilderness, and he felt the commission had disregarded it entirely. See M. P. Cohen, *History of the Sierra Club*, 280. The study report in question was ORRRC, *Wilderness and Recreation*.

56. M. W. T. Harvey, *Wilderness Forever*, 198. While some conservationists felt ORRRC had held up the wilderness bill, others credited ORRRC's eventual endorsement for getting the bill moving forward again. In fact, some conservationists of the 1960s considered the Wilderness Act to be a product of ORRRC and one of its crowning accomplishments.

57. The term "primitive area" dated from 1929, when the Forest Service started using

it to designate certain protected tracts in the national forests. Under new rules enacted in 1939, the agency began phasing out the term, reclassifying primitive areas as either "wilderness" or "wild areas." But when ORRRC released its report, in 1962, the reclassification process was still ongoing, and there remained a number of tracts called "primitive areas."

58. ORRRC, *Outdoor Recreation for America*, 113. ORRRC's six zones or "classes" of recreational land are explained on pp. 96–120.

59. The guidelines for recreation zoning may have rankled the Sierra Club more than anything else about ORRRC. The *Sierra Club Bulletin* assailed them as "vague and arbitrary," unrealistic and wishy-washy, effectively worthless. "Recreation resources are like people," the *Bulletin* objected. "They defy rigid classification." Consistent with the noncommittal nature of the whole ORRRC report (at least in the *Bulletin*'s critical view), the zoning proposal offered few guidelines to help planners choose between one zone and another; even more maddeningly, it generally failed to factor in existing land uses that were incompatible with recreation, thus ignoring the bitter political conflicts any effort at recreation zoning was sure to touch off. See Pesonen, "Analysis of the ORRRC Report," 9.

60. On Brower's disgust with Penfold and ORRRC, see M. P. Cohen, *History of the Sierra Club*, 280; and Winks, *Laurance S. Rockefeller*, 135–36. We do not know how much influence Penfold actually exercised within ORRRC. The consensus-minded tone of the commission's final report likely owed more to the leadership style of ORRRC chair Laurance Rockefeller, and the need to balance divergent interests, than to Penfold's singular role. In his biography of Rockefeller, Robin Winks credits the chairman with pushing the commission toward a more "people-oriented approach to resource management," noting that Rockefeller "persistently argued that conservation meant relating parks and outdoor recreational resources more directly to the needs of the people." If Winks is correct, this, more than Penfold's influence, might explain why the final report seemed to downplay the importance of wilderness in favor of higher-use recreation areas. On the other hand, Francis Sargent, executive director of ORRRC, later recalled that Penfold was one of the commission's hardest-working members, commanded a good deal of respect from his fellow commissioners, and often saw his viewpoint prevail. Winks, *Laurance S. Rockefeller*, 135–36; Voigt, *Born with Fists Doubled*, 145.

61. More broadly, this reflected Penfold's personal conviction that conservationists should care as much about the places people lived, worked, and played every day as they did about wilderness and wildlife habitat. See Voigt, *Born with Fists Doubled*, esp. 157–58, 163–64.

62. Howard Zahniser to Ira N. Gabrielson, October 22, 1959, FF "Correspondence: June-Dec 1959," Box 3, Carhart Papers.

63. On Carhart's planning around Trappers Lake, see Wolf, *Arthur Carhart*, chap. 4; Baldwin, *Quiet Revolution*, 29–42; Sutter, *Driven Wild*, 63–65; and Kirk, *Collecting Nature*, 28–29.

64. Carhart, *Planning for America's Wildlands*. On what Carhart hoped to accomplish by writing the book, see his letters to Charles H. Callison, July 27, 1958, FF "Correspondence: May–July 1958," Box 3; Robert W. Eisenmenger, October 22, 1960, FF

"Correspondence: Aug–Dec 1960," Box 3; Horace M. Albright, May 21, 1961, FF "Correspondence: Planning for America's Wildlands: 1961," Box 8; and Stanton W. Mead, May 31, 1961, FF "Correspondence: Jan-July 1961," Box 3, all in Carhart Papers.

65. On Carhart's belief in the need for comprehensive wildland planning, encompassing more than just "true wilderness," see especially his letters to Charlotte E. Mauk, March 24, 1949, FF "Correspondence: 1949," Box 2; John B. Oakes, January 31, 1957, FF "Correspondence: Jan–April 1957," Box 2; and James C. McClellan, March 16, 1959, FF "Correspondence: Jan-May 1959," Box 3, all in Carhart Papers. See also Carhart, *Planning for America's Wildlands*, 23.

66. Howard Zahniser to Ira N. Gabrielson, October 22, 1959, FF "Correspondence: June–Dec 1959," Box 3, Carhart Papers. On Zahniser's passion for pure, "primeval" wilderness, see M. W. T. Harvey, *Wilderness Forever*, 78–79, 110.

67. On Carhart's reasons for supporting Zahniser's wilderness bill, even as he continued to favor a more comprehensive approach to wildland planning, see his letter to John B. Oakes, January 31, 1957, FF "Correspondence: Jan–April 1957," Box 2, Carhart Papers. For the final compromise on what to call the zones in question, see Carhart, *Planning for America's Wildlands*, 69–82. Zahniser had leverage over the terminology Carhart used, not just because he was an acknowledged authority on wilderness, but also because the Wilderness Society was cosponsoring publication of Carhart's book and Zahniser had been tapped to referee the manuscript and write the introduction.

68. Carhart, *Planning for America's Wildlands*, 6–20, 34–35, 40–42, 69, 70, 75–79. On this last point—that land need not lack any trace of human history to be wilderness; that land once damaged by human activity could revert to wilderness condition—Zahniser had come to agree. See M. W. T. Harvey, *Wilderness Forever*, 110, 117, 119.

69. The "tops in the nation" pun had been a staple of Colorado tourist literature since Victorian times. The quotation here is from Governor Ed Johnson's greeting that appeared on the back of the official state highway map-brochure, *Colorful Colorado* (Denver: Colorado Department of Highways), in 1955 and 1956.

70. Colorado State Park and Recreation Board, *State Park System for Colorado*; Harold Lathrop, "State-Wide Park Development Involves Many Agencies," *Colorado Municipalities*, May 1961, 116–18, 138–19; Colorado State Planning Division, *Colorado, 1956–1958*, 145–46.

71. For a concise history of early American zoning that, like my account here, emphasizes property-value protection as the original intent, see P. Hall, *Cities of Tomorrow*, 58–62. Other useful treatments include M. Scott, *American City Planning Since 1890*, esp. chaps. 3 and 4 and pp. 483–92; and Toll, *Zoned America*. Fischel, "An Economic History of Zoning," offers an alternate explanation of zoning's emergence in the 1910s and 1920s but still stresses the desire to protect property values. On the evolution of zoning to serve ends not originally intended, like protecting aesthetic values or promoting desirable development, see M. Scott, *American City Planning Since 1890*, 483–92, 509–13; and E. D. Kelly, *Managing Community Growth*, esp. 14–15.

72. "Cooperation Assures Aspen's Future," *Aspen Times*, August 30, 1945, 1 (quotation); "Citizens Meet to Discuss City Planning," *Aspen Times*, September 6, 1945, 1.

73. Aspen, City Council, minutes, September 4, 1945; "Citizens Meet to Discuss

City Planning"; "Citizens Committee Meets, Talks, Acts," *Aspen Times*, September 13, 1945, 1.

74. Locals were told that Gropius, for one, was a "noted city planner" ("Citizens Meet to Discuss City Planning"), but of course the Bauhaus founder was primarily an architect, and city or community planning accounted for only a small part of his practice. The most thorough catalog of Gropius's work lists 125 projects between 1905 (the year of his first commission) and 1945. Of these, just seven involved any sort of community planning, very liberally defined. See Nerdinger, *Walter Gropius*. Gropius's pre-1945 community-planning projects appear on 58–61, 116–23, 230, 240–41, 248, and 274–77.

75. Walter Paepcke to Charles Wiley, September 26, 1945, and to Eugene Lilly, June 13, 1945, both quoted in J. S. Allen, *Romance of Commerce and Culture*, 132, 136; and see p. 137 for the demise of the planning project.

76. Aspen, City Council, minutes, February 18, March 5, and September 3, 1946, and January 6, April 7, April 15, and May 12, 1947.

77. V. E. Ringle, Aspen Quakings column, *Aspen Times*, June 5, 1947 (second quotation), 8; "Zoning Experts Will Meet With Aspenites," *Aspen Times*, July 10, 1947, 1 (third quotation); V. E. Ringle, "Council Should Pass the Zoning Ordinance," Aspen Quakings column, *Aspen Times*, July 31, 1947, 4 (first and fourth quotations).

78. Ruth E. Pike, "New Era for Aspen," *Colorado Municipalities*, November 1947, 220; Aspen, City Council, minutes, June 2, July 29, August 4, and August 11, 1947. Paepcke and Aspen mayor A. E. Robison chose the two experts—Allen Pritchard, executive secretary of the Colorado Municipal League; and Elmore Peterson, a member of the State Planning Commission—on the personal recommendation of Colorado Governor Lee Knous.

79. Aspen, Ordinance no. B-48 (1947). Official notice of this ordinance appeared in the *Aspen Times*, August 21, 1947, 6. See also Pike, "New Era for Aspen," 220–22, for a detailed explanation of the measure.

80. "People's Party Platform," ad, *Aspen Times*, October 29, 1953, 8; "A. E. Robison Re-Elected City of Aspen Mayor," *Aspen Times*, November 5, 1953, 1. While zoning rural space was certainly not a common practice at the time, there was precedent for it in other parts of the country. Rural zoning originated in the Upper Midwest in the 1930s—and there, too, it was born of efforts to promote tourism by preserving valuable recreational amenities. See Shapiro, " 'One Crop Worth Cultivating,' " chap. 3, esp. 134–37.

81. Aspen, City Council, minutes, August 2, September 7, October 4, December 6, and December 20, 1954; Pitkin County, Board of Commissioners, minutes, June 18, July 6 (quotation), August 3, November 12, and December 6, 1954, and February 18 and June 6, 1955; Pitkin County, Planning Commission and Board of Commissioners, *Zoning District Map* (1955). As with Aspen's 1947 zoning ordinance, the main objections to the first draft of the county ordinance came from landowners who feared that zoning would keep them from developing their property or selling it profitably to developers. And the tension between tourist boosters and boosters of older extractive industries resurfaced in the debate over county zoning. At least one local, Midnight Mine owner Frank Willoughby, urged that proposed restrictions on the "Tourist" zone be eased to allow for future mining on Aspen Mountain. See Pitkin County, Board of Commissioners, minutes, April 18, 1955 (discussion summarized in minutes of May 2, 1955).

82. "City Council Appoints Planning Commission," *Aspen Times*, February 2, 1956, 1; "Planning Project Underway," *Aspen Times*, February 23, 1956, 1; "Meeting on Zoning Tuesday, March 27," *Aspen Times*, March 22, 1956, 1; "Board Discusses Various Phases of City Zoning," *Aspen Times*, March 29, 1956, 1; "Zoning Meeting Well Attended Mon. Nite," *Aspen Times*, May 10, 1956, 1; Aspen, Ordinance no. 6 (Series of 1956); "City Zoning Ordinance Now Applies to All Construction," *Aspen Times*, July 19, 1956, 7. Official notice of the updated and expanded Aspen zoning ordinance appeared in the *Aspen Times*, July 5, 1956, 10–11.

83. Dorothy Fifield, "City Planning Urged to Guide Aspen's Growth," *Aspen Times*, January 11, 1951, 8; Dorothy Fifield, "City Planning Urged to Guide Aspen's Growth," *Aspen Times*, January 18, 1951, 6 (quotation).

84. Aspen, Ordinance no. 2 (Series of 1954) and Ordinance no. 6 (Series of 1956); "Public Meeting Agrees Water Comes First," *Aspen Times*, February 16, 1956, 1; "Hotel Owners Complain to City about Water Supply," *Aspen Times*, June 14, 1956, 9; "Sewer Bonds Voted," *Aspen Times*, June 21, 1956, 1; Ruth, *Colorado Vacations*, 128–29. On the broader effort to clean up roadside visual pollution, especially billboards, see Gudis, *Buyways*, part 3.

85. "The World Watches," editorial, *Aspen Times*, June 14, 1956, 4; "Sewer Bonds Voted." As a marker of how much Aspenites' attitudes had changed, consider that just seven years earlier, Aspen had rejected a proposed sewer and sanitation district, even though it too had been pitched as a way to attract new businesses and visitors. "Will Ask Approval of Complete Sewer System," *Aspen Times*, January 13, 1949, 1; "Sanitation Dist. Is Voted Down," *Aspen Times*, May 26, 1949, 1.

86. Created under the auspices of the State Planning Commission, the Coordinating Committee counted 39 sponsoring organizations, including several state and federal agencies and a wide variety of interest groups. Of these, 8 were business- or travel-booster groups, and 8 were "environmental" groups in the sense that their chief concern was resource conservation, outdoor recreation, beautification, landscape planning, or historic preservation (4 sponsoring agencies also fit into this environmental category: the State Planning Commission, State Game and Fish Department, State Historical Society, and National Park Service). Other sponsoring organizations included farm, labor, and professional interest groups. See Colorado Coordinating Committee for Planning and Zoning, *Let's Plan Colorado's Future*.

87. "Planning Meeting Set for Seven Western Slope Counties," *Colorado Information*, April 19, 1951, 3; untitled items in *Colorado Information Newsletter*, September 13, 1951, 3, and October 18, 1951, 3; Pitkin County, Board of Commissioners, minutes, July 2, 1951; Summit County, Board of Commissioners, minutes, July 2, 1951. Walter Paepcke's Aspen Company was among the businesses invited to send a representative to this Seven-County Area Planning and Zoning Committee; it is not clear if the company actually did. The planning principles adopted by the seven-county committee are listed in the Pitkin County commissioners' minutes of July 2, 1951.

88. In November 1955, Summit County commissioners authorized themselves to act as a planning commission, and they appointed an advisory panel with representatives from the incorporated towns of Breckenridge, Dillon, and Frisco. Then in June 1956, the

county commissioners joined with officials from the same three towns to create a joint town-county Regional Planning Commission. See Summit County, Resolution 55–18 (1955); and Summit County, Board of Commissioners, minutes, November 7, 1955, and June 4, 1956. For the angry reaction from local landowners, see the *Summit County Journal* (hereafter *SCJ*): "Secret Societies," May 25, 1956, 4; "Summit County Subjected to Planning Commission," June 15, 1956, 1; and "Property Owners Ask Meeting with Planning Commission," August 3, 1956, 1.

89. On Silverthorne (named for an old Blue River placer mining claim at the site), see items in the *SCJ*: "A New Town in the Making North of Dillon," July 6, 1956, 1; ad for Silverthorne Subdivision, July 23, 1960, 7; Mrs. Robert Offerson, Dillon Doings column, September 9, 1960, 3; "Silverthorne Lists Building Restrictions," October 14, 1960, 1; "Dillon Market Moved," January 13, 1961, 8; Clora Denning, Dillon Doings column, August 4, 1961, 3; and Denning, Silverthorne Doings column, September 1, 1961, 3. See also Virgil M. Cox, "'Newest Town in State' Slighted?," letter to the editor, *Denver Post*, February 8, 1962, 27.

90. "Straight Creek Tunnel, US 6 Route Urged for $78 Million Interstate Highway," *SCJ*, April 22, 1960, 1; "Dam Construction to Get Underway," *SCJ*, April 21, 1961, 1; "Family Ski Area Planned for Peak 8," *SCJ*, March 10, 1961, 1; "Forest Service Grants OK for Breckenridge Ski Resort," *SCJ*, July 7, 1961, 1; "Skiing Facilities to Be Ready for Use Dec. 15," *SCJ*, September 8, 1961, 1; "Ski Area Construction on Peak 8 Well Under Way," *SCJ*, October 13, 1961, 1; "Breckenridge Builds," *SCJ*, January 20, 1961, 6 (quotation).

91. Between April 1960, when the E. Lionel Pavlo Engineering Co. report came out, and April 1962, when Summit County commissioned its master plan, the *Summit County Journal* reported nearly every week on some big new development in the local real estate market, business scene, or physical landscape. See, for example, "Loveland Pass Village Plans Under Way," May 20, 1960, 1; "Loveland Pass Village Ready for Occupants," August 19, 1960, 8; Mrs. Walter Byron, "Business Enterprises Give Promise—New Breckenridge," January 20, 1961, 1; "Breckenridge Builds"; Mrs. Walter Byron, "Pros and Cons on the Development of Summit Co.," February 17, 1961, 1; "Breckenridge Bits," March 10, 1961, 2; "Blue River Estates to Open Breckenridge Office," May 19, 1961, 1; "Breckenridge Bits," May 19, 1961, 2; "Rounds Active in Area Development," September 1, 1961, 8; "Two New Businesses to Open in Breckenridge Soon" and "Breckenridge Bits," October 20, 1961, 2; "6000-Ft. Landing Strip Being Built North of Breckenridge," October 27, 1961, 1; "Ski Shop for Breckenridge," November 3, 1961, 1; "Breckenridge Town Council Held Lively Meeting," November 17, 1961, 1; "The Alpine Apothecary," November 24, 1961, 1; "Tax Sale Sells Out," December 22, 1961, 1; "Summit Co. Chamber of Commerce to Be Organized," December 22, 1961, 8; "Group Recommends C of C Unit for Each Area," January 12, 1962, 1; "Breckenridge Bits," January 19, 1962, 2; "Potpourri," February 9, 1962, 9; and "Frisco C. of C. Now Activated," February 18, 1962, 1. For a sense of the community anxieties unleashed by such rapid development, see Gilliland, *Frisco!*, 124, 127–30.

92. Summit County, Board of Commissioners, minutes, April 18, 1962, and June 21 and August 2, 1963. See also coverage in the *SCJ*: "Summit Co. to Participate in Urban Planning Project," April 27, 1962, 9 (first quotation); "County Comprehensive Plan Unveiling Wednesday Night," March 29, 1963, 1; "Eight-Point Program for Future Co.

Growth Given," April 12, 1963, 1; "Majority Favors County and Regional Planning," July 26, 1963, 1 (second quotation); "Town Board News," November 8, 1963, 4 (third quotation).

93. Mrs. Walter Byron, "Pros and Cons on the Development of Summit Co."; "Breckenridge Bits," *SCJ*, March 10, 1961, 2.

94. For this analysis of the open-space issue and its influence on American environmental thinking, I am indebted to Adam Rome's *Bulldozer in the Countryside*, esp. chap. 4. Rome credits Sam Hays, the dean of historians of the postwar environmental movement, for paying heed to the crucial but generally overlooked open-space issue, though Hays traces the issue only back to the 1970s, casting it as a product, not a progenitor, of popular environmentalism. See Hays, *Beauty, Health, and Permanence*, 92–95.

95. Huddleston, *Summit County, Colorado*, 56, 59–62 (quotations p. 60).

96. Ibid., esp. "Plan for Future Land Use," 54–65 (all quotations p. 60, emphasis in last quotation in original).

97. *Colorado Information*, September 27, 1962, 1.

98. [Feltner], *A Look Back*, 38–39; Barrows and Holmes, *Colorado's Wildlife Story*, 124–26; Colorado State Planning Division, *Colorado Year Book, 1962–1964*, 609–16. The legislature also enlarged the new Game, Fish and Parks Commission to ten seats, adding two at-large members representing parks and recreation interests. The merger did not work well; state parks remained underfunded, and hunting and fishing interests remained angry that funds once devoted to wildlife management were diverted to mass-recreation facilities, especially in or near cities. In 1972, Colorado went back to having separate agencies and separate funding for parks and for game and fish. But in 2011, over the objections of many who cited the failed merger of the 1960s, the state reversed course again, re-merging the agencies to create Colorado Parks and Wildlife. Barrows and Holmes, *Colorado's Wildlife Story*, 127–28; Jim Moss, "Colorado Division of Wildlife and Colorado State Parks to Combine July 1, 2011," *Recreation Law* blog, March 11, 2011, http://recreation-law.com/2011/03/11/colorado-division-of-wildlife-and-colorado-state-parks-to-combine-july-1-2011/ (accessed December 14, 2011); Joanne Ditmer, "State Parks and Wildlife Merger Is a Bad Idea," *Denver Post*, March 25, 2011; John W. Mumma, "A Shotgun Wedding for DOW and State Parks?," *Denver Post*, April 18, 2011; "Governor Signs Bill to Merge Wildlife, Parks Agencies," *Denver Post*, June 7, 2011.

99. [Feltner], *A Look Back*, 39; "Colorado Division Endorses User Fees," *Izaak Walton Magazine*, January 1964, 18; "Colorado Conference APPROVES Them [user fees]," *Izaak Walton Magazine*, June 1964, 14; "State Recreation Area Use Fee," *Jeepers in the News*, June 1965, 7. The legislature initially resisted user fees, but a compromise was struck under which only actual users of facilities (boaters, hikers, campground guests, etc.) would pay the fee; people simply driving through and sightseeing could still do so for free. See "Colorado Solons Oppose Commissioners on Park Fees," *Izaak Walton Magazine*, July 1964, 18–19; and "New and Better Facilities for Parks as a Result of Low Fees Based on Use," *Colorado Business*, June 1965, 6.

100. Colorado Department of Game, Fish and Parks, *Outdoor Recreation in Colorado* (first two quotations from p. 2, third from p. 18); [Feltner], *A Look Back*, 40.

101. For an especially explicit example of this thinking, see *The Use of Mountain Recreational Resources*, a report published in 1971 by the University of Colorado business

school, which called for "piecemeal" recreational development to give way to "an overall, long-range plan for the use of all [Colorado's] recreational lands. . . . In effect, it would amount to a kind of zoning as Arthur Carhart recommended some years ago." If Colorado adopted such an "organized system" of recreation planning and promotion, the report promised, "the rewards . . . are considerable. Tourism is a large factor in the Colorado economy. It could easily be the first." P. T. Thompson, *Use of Mountain Recreational Resources*, chap. 6 (quotations pp. 153, 161, 179).

102. For too long, Progressive conservation and popular environmentalism were studied in isolation from each other, but more recent scholarship, especially on the interwar and midcentury periods, has begun to reveal how the first shaded into, and helped shape, the second. Especially insightful examples include Sutter, *Driven Wild*; Phillips, *This Land, This Nation*; Beeman and Pritchard, *A Green and Permanent Land*; Maher, *Nature's New Deal*; Brooks, *Before Earth Day*; and Kirk, *Collecting Nature*.

103. The CMC journal, *Trail and Timberline*, always included club members' essays describing outings in the mountains of Colorado and other places. The accounts could be lyrical, whimsical, or even technical, but they were almost always personal. The quotations are from Hugh Kingery, "Statement of the Denver Group of the Colorado Mountain Club at the Hearings on the Wilderness Bill, Denver, Colorado, January 10–11, 1964," and "Statement: The Denver Group of the Colorado Mountain Club," typescripts in FF "Wilderness Comm," Colorado Open Space Collection (hereafter COS Collection).

104. See the following *Trail and Timberline* articles: E. H. Brunquist, "Wilderness Areas—Pros and Cons," no. 480 (December 1958): 169–175; F. A. Cajori, "Conservation and the Future," no. 489 (September 1959): 120, 127; Jack Reed, "The American People and the Wilderness," no. 500 (August 1960): 113–14; "Conservation," no. 514 (October 1961): 181; Roger Fuehrer, "Conservation News," no. 526 (October 1962): 171; "Denver Wilderness Bill Hearings Favor Saylor Bill 3 to 1," no. 542 (February 1964): 22; Estelle Brown, "Conservation News: Giant Steps," no. 548 (August 1964): 132.

105. For biographical information on Ed Hilliard, see Kirk, *Collecting Nature*, 89–93; and the obituary "Edward H. Hilliard, Jr.," *Living Wilderness*, Autumn 1970, 4.

106. "By-Laws of Conservation Council of Colorado, Inc.," undated typescript in FF "Cons. Council of Colo," COS Collection; Conservation Council of Colorado Inc., "Preliminary Statement of Objectives," February 20, 1961, typescript in COS Collection.

107. E. H. Hilliard Jr. and Dick Guadagno to twenty "recreational conservation groups," May 8, 1962, FF "Howdy the Raccoon Stash the Trash," COS Collection. Hilliard signed this letter on behalf of the Conservation Council of Colorado, Guadagno on behalf of the CMC's Conservation Committee; the letterhead was the Conservation Council's.

108. Hugh E. Kingery, "The Third Giant Step," *Trail and Timberline*, no. 549 (September 1964): 145; Brown, "Giant Steps," 132; "Conservation Conference at Breckenridge, Colorado—Summary," typescript in FF "Board of Directors: Minutes, 1965," Box 1: 1, Colorado Environmental Coalition Records (hereafter CEC Records); Roger P. Hansen, "A Blueprint for Action—Now or Never," speech at the CMC Breckenridge conference, September 27, 1964, typescript in FF "Organizational File: Recollections by Members for Organizational History," Box 2: 1, CEC Records; "Conference at Breckenridge—or Mission Accomplished," *Trail and Timberline*, no. 550 (October 1964): 164.

109. The COSCC recruiting letter sent to prospective member organizations declared that the time for "continuing in our traditional roles of representing rather particularized interests" was past and that recreational groups needed to "[broaden] our horizons to find common ground for cooperative action." But the council took pains to promise that "this can be done without sacrificing present organization autonomy." For an excerpt of the recruiting letter, as received by the Colorado White Water Association, see "Colorado Open Space Council," *The Spray*, February 1965, 2–3. As it so happened, the white-water group was very receptive to COSCC's message; not only did it become an active member but also its president, Clyde Jones, was named to COSCC's Steering Committee.

110. For the initial list of priorities, see "Conservation Conference at Breckenridge, Colorado—Summary," CEC Records; and "Conference at Breckenridge—or Mission Accomplished," *Trail and Timberline*, no. 550 (October 1964): 164.

111. For COSCC's 1965 statement of purpose, see "Colorado Open Space Coordinating Council, Inc.," typescript in FF "Organizational File: Recollections by Members for Organizational History," Box 2: 1, CEC Records.

112. Hansen, "Blueprint for Action—Now or Never," esp. 3–7, CEC Records; Kingery, "Third Giant Step," 144; "Conservation Conference at Breckenridge, Colorado—Summary," CEC Records; [Roger P. Hansen], "A Proposal for Support of the Colorado Open Space Foundation," May 1, 1966, typescript, and Roger P. Hansen, "Word and Phrase Study Outline of Key Conservation Issues," July 20, 1966, typescript, both in FF "Organizational File: Recollections by Members for Organizational History," Box 2: 1, CEC Records; Colorado Open Space Coordinating Council, Board of Directors, minutes, January 10, 1966, and "Resolution for a Quality Colorado Environment," July 18, 1966, typescript, both in FF "Board of Directors: Minutes 1966," Box 1: 1, CEC Records; "Colorado Open Space Coordinating Council Statement on State Parks," undated typescript in FF "Board of Directors: Policy Files—Parks and Recreation/Pesticides 1970s," Box 1: 2, CEC Records.

113. Hansen, "Blueprint for Action—Now or Never," emphasis in original, CEC Records.

114. George F. Jackson, "Statement on Behalf of S-174—The Wilderness Bill, for the Izaak Walton League of America and the Colorado Division of the League," typescript in FF "Wilderness 10/61—4/62," COS Collection; Bruce N. Berger to the Hon. Wayne N. Aspinall, May 28, 1964, FF "6/1—Wild Bill Ltrs," COS Collection; Ed Hilliard, "Statement on S-174 Wilderness Bill by E. H. Hilliard, Jr.," typescript in FF "Wilderness 10/61—4/62," COS Collection. Aspinall, powerful chair of the House Interior Committee, held up the wilderness bill for many years, but in 1964, after attaching key provisions to weaken it, he finally did vote for it.

115. "Colorado Open Space Coordinating Council, Inc.," emphasis added, CEC Records. This statement closely resembled a passage in Hansen's Breckenridge speech. See Hansen, "Blueprint for Action—Now or Never," 7, CEC Records.

116. "Resolution for a Quality Colorado Environment," 1, CEC Records; "Proposal for Support of the Colorado Open Space Foundation," 1 (emphasis in original), CEC Records. Geographer John Wright, after years of working for land trusts in the

Mountain West, came to a similar conclusion as I do here: Coloradans, he argues, tend to go about their environmentalism in a "businesslike" way, seeing it as essentially "a new, more responsible way of conducting commerce." The same market forces that brought prosperity to Colorado, Wright believes, came to drive its "expanding conservation sector" too. Wright, *Rocky Mountain Divide*, 255.

117. Roger P. Hansen, "Citizen Participation in Decision-Making," speech at the League of Women Voters Education Fund Conference, Salt Lake City, February 11–13, 1969, typescript in FF "Reports/Statements re: SW land," Box 1, Rocky Mountain Center on Environment Papers (hereafter ROMCOE Papers); article in the Public Service Company of Colorado magazine *Home and Community Service*, April 1967, quoted in Roger Hansen, "Colorado's New Conservation," *Trail and Timberline*, no. 584 (August 1967): 156.

118. Roger P. Hansen to Bob Parker, October 14, 1965, in FF "Publicity: Correspondence, 1965–1970," Box 5: 2, CEC Records.

119. On COSF, see "Proposal for Support of the Colorado Open Space Foundation," esp. 3, CEC Records; and the documents concerning COSF in FF "Board of Directors: Advisory Committee 1967–1968," Box 1: 2, CEC Records. On ROMCOE's business-friendly mission, see esp. Roger P. Hansen to Richard Olson, April 5, 1968, and Colorado Open Space Foundation Advisory Committee, minutes, February 15, 1968, both in ibid.; and the September 1968 brochure *ROMCOE: Rocky Mountain Center on Environment*, in envelope labeled "Rocky Mountain Center on Environment. Materials," Box 1, ROMCOE Papers.

120. "Executive Director's Report (Period 12/1/68 to 2/19/69)," in envelope labeled "Rocky Mountain Center on Environment. Executive Director's Report 1968–69," Box 1, ROMCOE Papers.

121. Bob Parker, quoted in Sharon Brown, "Profile: Image Maker, Bob Parker," *Vail Trail*, April 16, 1971, 7.

122. Roger P. Hansen, "Commerce and Conservation Meet," *Trail and Timberline*, no. 576 (December 1966): 206; Curtis Casewit, "Super Salesman for Super Ski Resort," *Colorado Magazine* (September–October 1972), 12R; Robert Parker, telephone interview, January 26, 1994.

123. The primitive area, part of the White River National Forest, had been designated in 1933. Under rules the Forest Service adopted in 1939 (see note 57 in this chapter), it was eligible for reclassification as a "wild area," which would have put it off-limits to other uses. But much to wilderness advocates' frustration, the Forest Service took decades to reclassify all the old primitive areas—and just as it was getting around to Gore Range–Eagles Nest, Colorado highway officials announced plans for the I-70 tunnel, putting the reclassification on hold. Michael Nadel, "The Pace of Wilderness Classification," *Living Wilderness*, Spring 1965, 20.

124. E. Lionel Pavlo Engineering Co., *Interstate Highway Location Study*, 10.

125. Gordon G. Gauss, "Bill Nearly Stymied Tunnel at Vail Pass," *Denver Post*, September 6, 1964, 61; Greg Pinney, "Forest Service Denies Buffalo Route Land Trade," *Denver Post*, September 3, 1967, 3. The relevant clause is at the very end of Section 3(b) of the Wilderness Act, 16 U.S.C. § 1132(b) (1964).

126. "Primitive Area Road Opposed," *Living Wilderness*, Autumn 1966, 44; "Gore Range–Eagle Nest Highway Intrusion," *Living Wilderness*, Spring and Summer 1967, 62; "News Items of Interest," *Living Wilderness*, Autumn 1967, 59; "Highway Route Threatens De Facto Wilderness in Colorado Rockies," *Sierra Club Bulletin*, November 1967, 3; William M. Blair, "Plan for Road in a Primitive Area Stirs a Dispute," *New York Times*, January 5, 1968, 43; "Secretary Rejects Interstate 70 Route," *Living Wilderness*, Spring 1968, 46–47; "No Trucks on Buffalo Pass," editorial, *New York Times*, May 20, 1968, 46.

127. "Colorado Open Space Coordinating Council, Inc., Roads Committee: Annual Report—10/1/66–9/3067," FF "Board of Directors: Roads Committee 1967," Box 1: 2, CEC Records; James [Richard] Guadagno, "Red Buffalo Route—Some Engineering and Cost Considerations," undated typescript in FF "R. Weiner," COS Collection; J. R. Guadagno, "The Red Buffalo Route," *Trail and Timberline*, no. 563 (November 1965): 232–34; Neuzil, *Interstate 70: Dillon to Dowd, Colorado*; Dennis R. Neuzil, "Uses and Abuses of Highway Cost-Benefit Analysis with Particular Reference to the Red Buffalo Route," *Sierra Club Bulletin*, January 1968, 16–21; Laycock, *Diligent Destroyers*, 138–41. Guadagno's findings in particular found their way into journalistic coverage of the controversy; see, for example, Monk Tyson, "Tunnel Foes to Be Heard," *Denver Post*, October 19, 1966, 27.

128. Kingery, "Statement of the Denver Group of the Colorado Mountain Club," 2; C. A. Kutzleb, "Gore Range-Eagles Nest Wild Area," *The Living Wilderness*, Summer 1956, 16; U.S. Department of the Interior, Bureau of Outdoor Recreation, Mid-Continent Region (Denver, Colorado), *Selection of a Highway Route*, 5; "Highway Route Threatens De Facto Wilderness in Colorado Rockies." Hansen argued that, in fact, highway officials were legally obligated to weigh environmental concerns. Under the Transportation Act of 1966, he pointed out, no highway project could take "land from a public park, recreational area, wildlife and waterfowl refuge or historical site . . . unless . . . there is no feasible and prudent alternative to the use of such land." "Frankly," Hansen told one reporter, "some would like to make a test case of Red Buffalo in the context of . . . the Transportation Act of 1966." See "Battle of Red Buffalo Pass," *Colorado Magazine*, Winter 1967, 21.

129. U.S. Department of the Interior, Bureau of Outdoor Recreation, *Selection of a Highway Route*, 16–17; "Statement of Harry R. Woodward, Director, Colorado Game, Fish and Parks Department, before the Special Legislative Study Committee on October 16, 1967: A Comparison of the Impact of Two Proposed Routes of I-70 upon Fish and Wildlife Resources," typescript in "Roads. Colorado. U.S. Highways. #70," Clippings Files, Denver Public Library, Western History/Genealogy Department.

130. "Colorado Open Space Coordinating Council, Inc. (COSCC) Activity Highlights, October 1, 1967 to September 30, 1968," typescript in FF "Newsletter: COSC Activity Highlights 1966–1971," Box 5: 1, CEC Records; resolution of the Board of Trustees, Town of Vail, quoted in "Battle of Red Buffalo Pass," 24.

131. "Interstate 70 Routing Stirs Vail-Area Anger," *Denver Post*, October 16, 1966, 6E; Monk Tyson, "Red Buffalo Pass: Tunnel Foes to Be Heard," *Denver Post*, October 19, 1966, 27; "Route Opponents Make Charge," *Denver Post*, October 21, 1966, 43; "Primitive Area Road Opposed," *Living Wilderness*, Autumn 1966, 44; "Battle of Red Buffalo Pass," 20; Lake County, Board of Commissioners, and Jess A. Larch, Leadville–Lake

County Regional Planning Commission, *Lake County I-70 Brief*, esp. 2–7, 16–18. Sam Huddleston's Summit County master plan, three years earlier, had advised county leaders to oppose the Red Buffalo route should the Highway Department pursue it; see Huddleston, *Summit County, Colorado*, 68–70.

132. "Ed Johnson Plea: Buffalo Pass Route Backed," *Denver Post*, October 8, 1967, 25; Ed C. Johnson, "Straight Creek Tunnels Offer State Great Economic Benefits," letter to the editor, *Denver Post*, October 27, 1967, 25.

133. Robert Parker, telephone interview, January 12, 1994; "Battle of Red Buffalo Pass," esp. 24; Merrill G. Hastings Jr., "Message from the Publisher," *Colorado Magazine*, Summer 1968, 5. Not all players in the Colorado tourist industry opposed Red Buffalo. In the same interview, for example, Parker noted that some members of the Vail Associates executive board questioned his opposition to the tunnel. And Rocky Mountain Motorists, the Colorado affiliate of the American Automobile Association, was one of the major voices to come out in favor of the tunnel; the organization's long-standing closeness with state highway officials seems to have influenced this decision. See Peter G. Ratcliffe, open letter to Rocky Mountain Motorists, *Trail and Timberline*, no. 586 (October 1967): 189.

134. The typical letter is Thomas M. Clougherty, "Wilderness Road Route Opposed," letter to the editor, *Denver Post Perspective*, August 20, 1967, 5; Shumate quoted in "Battle of Red Buffalo Pass," 24. Letters to the Highway Department reportedly ran 10 to 1 against the tunnel plan.

135. Joseph B. Schieffelin, "State Senator Questions Economy of Gore Range Route," *Denver Post Perspective*, October 22, 1967, 4; "Battle of Red Buffalo Pass," esp. 19, 22, 24; "Statement of Harry R. Woodward." On Dominick's pack trip, see William Logan, "I-70 Wilderness Route Tour Convinces Dominick," *Rocky Mountain News*, September 3, 1967, 5, 8; "Dominick: Vail Support Reaffirmed," *Denver Post*, September 3, 1967, 4; Logan, "Riding the Gore Range," *Rocky Mountain News Festival Magazine*, September 10, 1967, 1, 4; Logan, "Wildlife, Even Bears, Plentiful in Gore Range," *Rocky Mountain News*, September 11, 1967, 8. COSCC sponsored a separate horseback trip in to the primitive area, in July 1967, for state and federal agency officials and the press.

136. U.S. Department of the Interior, Bureau of Outdoor Recreation, *Selection of a Highway Route*, esp. v, 21–23. On the reactions of Transportation Secretary Alan Boyd, Commerce Secretary Alexander Trowbridge, and Interior Secretary Udall, see John Morehead, "Boyd Questions I-70 Route Choice," *Denver Post*, September 8, 1967, 65; "Battle of Red Buffalo Pass," 24; and Logan, "Udall: Prove Need for Route," *Rocky Mountain News*, September 6, 1967, 5. For the Oregon case, see Judd and Beach, *Natural States*, 116–23; and Mowbray, *Road to Ruin*, 118–24.

137. James Foster, "Freeman to Rule I-70 Will Bypass Wilderness Area," *Rocky Mountain News*, May 17, 1968, 1; Secretary of Agriculture Orville L. Freeman, "Decision on the Request by the Colorado Department of Highways to Route Interstate Highway 70 through Gore Range-Eagle Nest Primitive Area, Arapaho and White River National Forests," read into the record by Sen. Peter H. Dominick, May 17, 1968, 90th Cong., 2nd sess., *Congressional Record* 114, S5805 (emphasis in original).

138. Barney Brewer, quoted in David Sumner, "Colorado: The Last Decade,"

Colorado Magazine, July–August 1975, 16; [Roger Hansen], "Conservationists Win Red Buffalo (An Editorial)," *COSF Open Space Report,* May 31, 1968, 1–2.

139. Hastings, "Message from the Publisher," 5.

140. Bob Parker, Parker Pens column, *Vail Trail,* January 13, 1967, 1, 7. Parker expressed the same sentiments in a letter to the *Denver Post,* which was reprinted in the *Eagle Valley Enterprise,* October 14, 1965, 8; and quoted in *Vail Trail,* December 31, 1965, 4. Parker's well-received speech to the Third Colorado Open Space Conference in Vail in 1966 was devoted to a similar topic: the links between environmental protection and economic prosperity. See Hansen, "Commerce and Conservation Meet," 206.

CHAPTER 5. THE JOHN DENVER TENOR

1. Though in 1975, Denver did admit to marijuana and hashish use, belying his squeaky-clean image. "John Denver Puffs . . . ," *Chicago Tribune,* October 8, 1975, 2.

2. Concert description derived from "The Tom Sawyer of Rock," *Time,* September 17, 1973, 50; Starkey Flythe Jr., "John Denver: Mr. Clean with Hair and Guitar," *Saturday Evening Post,* January–February 1974, 58 (first quotation); Edwin Miller, "Sunshine Singer," *Seventeen,* March 1974, 112 (second quotation); Lynn Van Matre, "Denver's High Floats Past Critic," *Chicago Tribune,* October 6, 1974, 44; and Frank Starr, "John Denver: Nice, High—Not Deep," *Chicago Tribune,* April 16, 1975, A2. On John Denver as an emblem—including in the eyes of many Coloradans—of what made living in Colorado special, see T. Conover, *Lost in Aspen,* 81–82.

3. Van Matre, "Denver's High Floats Past Critic"; Starr, "John Denver: Nice, High—Not Deep"; Robert Hilburn, "Denver Strikes Emotional Chord," *Los Angeles Times,* May 13, 1975, F10; Grace Lichtenstein, "John Denver—Pop Music's Wholesome Guru," *New York Times,* March 28, 1976, 1, 18; Lynn Van Matre, "Denver Smile Puts a Happy Face on Others," *Chicago Tribune,* April 29, 1976, B6. The quoted review is Hilburn's; readers' letters quoted in Robert Hilburn, "High Dudgeon over John Denver," *Los Angeles Times,* September 14, 1974, A7.

4. Robert Hilburn, "John Denver's Sociological Bond," *Los Angeles Times,* September 3, 1977, B11.

5. Hilburn, "John Denver's Sociological Bond."

6. John Denver, "Rocky Mountain High," *Rocky Mountain High,* RCA Victor LSP-4731, 1972, LP. For a thoughtful historical analysis of Denver's nature songs and their implications for environmental thinking in the 1970s, see Filipiak, "'I've Seen It Rain Fire in the Sky.'" On Denver's life, see his autobiography, *Take Me Home;* J. M. Martin, *Rocky Mountain Wonder Boy;* and Flippo, "His Rocky Mountain Highness."

7. Colin Escott, liner notes to John Denver, *The Rocky Mountain Collection,* RCA 07863-66837-2, 1986, 2-CD set; John Denver, "Rocky Mountain High," *Rocky Mountain High,* RCA Victor, LSP-4731, 1972, LP. On another celebrity—Robert Redford—who became an icon of both environmentalism and the western outdoor lifestyle, see Nicholas, Bapis, and Harvey, *Imagining the Big Open,* part 5.

8. "Improve Highway 40 Now," editorial, *Steamboat Pilot,* April 28, 1960, 2.

9. See coverage in the *Clear Creek Mining Journal* (hereafter *CCMJ*): "6–40 Bottleneck

Easing Seen," October 7, 1954, 1; "Proposed Survey Route Presented to City Council as First Step in Seeking 4-Lane Highway Approval," April 22, 1955, 1; "Four-Lane Hiway Seems Assured," May 6, 1955, 1, 5; "Highway Right of Way May Take Bridal Veil Park; Route Plan Appears Uncertain," October 21, 1955, 1; "Citizens Aroused Over Highway Delays," March 30, 1956, 3; "Freeway Agreement Signed for Idaho Springs," April 13, 1956, 1, 4; "C of C Concerned with Town View from New Highway," February 7, 1958, 1; "C of C Members View City from New Highway," February 21, 1958, 1 (both quotations); "West End Business People Assured Highway Will Not By-Pass Them," April 18, 1958, 1; "Official Ceremony Opening $3,000,000 4-Lane Super Highway Set Tomorrow Morning," November 14, 1958, 1; and "Four-Lane Highway Opened Here Saturday; First of Three 'Bottleneck Buster' Highway Projects," November 21, 1958, 1, 3. See also "By-Pass Routes Proving Value," *Middle Park Times*, July 25, 1957, 10.

10. Anonymous highway engineer, quoted in Jean Wren, What's New in Georgetown column, *CCMJ*, March 19, 1964, 1.

11. On Lady Bird's highway beautification campaign, see Gould, "First Lady as Catalyst." A trip through the Rocky Mountain states in summer 1964 may have encouraged Lady Bird to choose this particular cause, notes Gould (p. 80). Melosi, "Lyndon Johnson and Environmental Policy," places the beautification initiatives in the wider context of the Johnson administration's "New Conservation" and dreams of the Great Society. Several treatises and polemics published in the early 1960s alleged that the interstate system, and the wider "car culture" that spawned it, were aesthetically devastating the American countryside. See, for example, Wood and Heller, *California Going, Going . . .*; Tunnard and Pushkarev, *Man-Made America*; and Blake, *God's Own Junkyard*. On antibillboard efforts and the broader struggle for control of roadside spaces, see Gudis, *Buyways*, part 3.

12. Odette Baehler, What's New in Georgetown column, *CCMJ*, November 4, 1965, 3; citizens' petition quoted in Odette Baehler, What's New in Georgetown column, *CCMJ*, February 16, 1967, 1. The purpose of this petition was to urge the town to install old-fashioned gaslights, instead of modern mercury-vapor lights, in the downtown district, for the sake of preserving the "charming atmosphere for which Georgetown is famous."

13. Odette Baehler, What's New in Georgetown columns, *CCMJ*, June 3, 1965, 1; March 19, 1964, 1; and October 15, 1964, 3.

14. "'Mothers March' to Protest Ski Rates at Aspen," *Denver Post*, October 2, 1960, 29C; "Residents of Aspen Stage Revolt over Ski Fees Hike," *Denver Post*, October 5, 1960, 23 (sign slogans); and *Aspen Times* coverage: "Our Sympathy to the Ski Corp.," editorial, September 23, 1960, 4; "Mothers to Picket," September 30, 1960, 1; F. George Robinson, "A Director Answers," letter to the editor, September 30, 1960, 10; "Protest March Held after Negotiations Fail," October 7, 1960, 1; Harald Pabst, "Directors Reply," letter to the editor, October 7, 1960, 2 (Ski Corp. executive quotation); untitled photograph, October 7, 1960, 10; Friedl Pfeifer, "Stockholders Reply," letter to the editor, October 14, 1960, 14; "The Economics of Lift tickets," editorial, December 2, 1960, 4; Peggy Clifford, Talk of the Times column, December 16, 1960, 12 (Clifford quotation).

15. On the Highway 82 setback, see "The Price of Compromise," editorial, and "Opposition to County Zoning Heard on Tuesday," *Aspen Times*, February 5, 1960, 1, 15; "Board Favors Setback," and "Zoning Is for Protection," editorial, *Aspen Times*, February

19, 1960, 1, 4; and "Commissioners Maintain 200-ft. Set-back," *Aspen Times*, March 11, 1960, 11. On the hotel, see "Council Causes Concern," "The Council Disappoints," editorial, Herbert Bayer, letter to the editor, and Robin Molny et al., "Aspen Architects Oppose Council Decision," *Aspen Times*, March 25, 1960, 1, 4, 5; Peggy Clifford, "All About Height," Talk of the Times column, *Aspen Times*, April 1, 1960, 6; and "Building Heights, Dogs Again Occupy Council," and Michael S. Annan, Everett L. Millard, Waddy Catchings, and Ivan B. Abrams, letters to the editor, *Aspen Times*, April 8, 1960, 2, 9, 11, 15.

16. Leo A. Daly Company, *Aspen Area General Plan: Final Report*, 1966, quotations from preface (unpaginated) and introduction (p. 1). Real estate agents and landowners grumbled about the proposed density controls in downtown Aspen, and the plan underwent adjustments based on public input, but according to the *Times*, "all concerned seem to agree with the plan in general." "Master Plan Gets P&Z Review Mon.," *Aspen Times*, March 31, 1966, 1; "The Plan and Density," *Aspen Times*, April 7, 1966, 2. See also P. Clifford, *To Aspen and Back*, 116–18.

17. On the crackdown on hippies and the alleged moral corruption of Aspen's youth, see P. Clifford, *To Aspen and Back*, 118–22; and Barlow-Perez, *History of Aspen*, 78. For some divergent viewpoints on the issue, see "Aspen's Vagrancy Law," editorial, *Aspen Times*, June 30, 1966, 2A; "New Laws Would Help," editorial, *Aspen Times*, July 14, 1966, 2A; and "Council Retains Old Vagrancy Law," *Aspen Times*, July 21, 1966, 7B.

18. P. Clifford, *To Aspen and Back*, 142–43. Holland Hills is in Basalt, eighteen miles down the Roaring Fork River from Aspen.

19. P. Clifford, *To Aspen and Back*, 89–91; H. S. Thompson, "Battle of Aspen" (all quotations).

20. H. S. Thompson, "Battle of Aspen."

21. H. S. Thompson, "Battle of Aspen" (all quotations); P. Clifford, *To Aspen and Back*, 135–41, 144–55. For coverage beyond Colorado of Thompson's campaign, see, for example, Anthony Ripley, "'Freak Power' Candidate May Be the Next Sheriff in Placid Aspen, Colo.," *New York Times*, October 19, 1970, 44; Bob Cromie, "A Loser If You Ever Saw One," *Chicago Tribune*, November 2, 1970, 26; and "The Law: Sheriffs 1970-Style," *Time*, November 16, 1970.

22. "Vail Having $15 Million Boom in Quiet Economy," *Denver Post*, August 2, 1970, 1G (first quotation); Al Hills, "Our Summer Place," *News Note*, June 24, 1970 (second quotation).

23. Pete Seibert, quoted in "State Hiw'y Dept Charged With 'Bad Faith,'" *Eagle Valley Enterprise*, July 28, 1966, 5; "It's the Time For—," editorial, *Vail Trail*, December 30, 1968, 2. In fairness, Seibert's negative view was undoubtedly influenced by the fact that Vail Associates was locked in a bitter legal dispute with the State Highway Department at the time, over the question of how much VA should be compensated for land lost to the interstate right-of-way. Predicting that the highway would damage Vail's attractiveness was one way VA could justify asking for more money.

24. Ted Kindel, "Kindel for Mayor," *Vail Trail*, October 14–21, 1966, 7; John McBride, letter to the editor, *Vail Trail*, November 4–11, 1966, 1 (emphasis added).

25. Ted Kindel, "Candidate for Mayor Makes Final Bid," and Ron Fricke, Christopher

B. Hall, and William H. Duddy, letter to the editor, *Vail Trail*, November 4–11, 1966, 1, 4, 7.

26. Vail Corporation, Board of Directors, minutes, February 26, 1966, Box 3, Vail Associates Papers; Town of Vail, Board of Trustees, minutes, September 23, 1968; John Kaemmer, letter to the editor, and George Knox, Tid-Bits column, *Vail Trail*, February 9, 1968, 3, 10; "Signs of the Times," *Vail Trail*, July 27, 1969, 6. Pete Seibert had originally pressed Holiday Inn to use a smaller sign, telling the chain that "the use of neon and animation would not be acceptable to Vail." But VA relented in the end. Later the garish lighted sign was replaced by a modest painted one, likely when the Town of Vail adopted a strict new sign ordinance in 1973. On Holiday Inn's immediately recognizable Great Sign and its eventual obsolescence, see Jakle, Sculle, and Rogers, *Motel in America*, 264–67, 278–79.

27. George Knox, "Let's Do Somethin'!," *Vail Trail*, June 21, 1968, 2. In this latter dispute, over the gingerbread Kuehn Tower, VA's Architectural Control Committee came to an agreement with the building owner and dismantled the tower about two months after it appeared. Said the committee in a statement: "The ability to maintain sound and continuing architectural control is necessary to preserve Vail's widely admired building standards. Without the ability to take a firm and positive stand in dealing with variances, Vail would very soon become just another one of the many blights among America's so-called 'Tourist Attractions.'" "Kuehn Tower Goes Kaput," *Vail Trail*, August 16, 1968, 1. See also "Is Kuehn Tower Keen . . . Or—? Let Us Know What You Think," *Vail Trail*, January 13, 1967, 5.

28. John P. McBride, letter to the editor, *Vail Trail*, February 11, 1966, 8; "New CROSS-ROADS of VAIL Project Inspired by Vail Growth Progress," *Vail Trail*, April 19, 1968, 4; "Denverites Buy Lodge at Vail," *Denver Post*, January 5, 1969, 3J; "Denver Men Buy the Lodge at Vail," *Eagle Valley Enterprise*, January 9, 1969, 1; "Broadmoor Hotel to Assist Lodge at Vail in Management," *Rocky Mountain News*, April 22, 1969, 48; "Restored and Enlarged Lodge (Broadmoor) at Vail to Be Greatest," *Vail Trail*, September 7, 1969, 5.

29. "Urban Renewal (Believe It or Not) Hits Vail," *Vail Trail*, November 30, 1969, 3; "Vail Complex to Replace Lodge," *Denver Post*, December 7, 1969, 4M; "Vail Construction to Total $12 Million," *Vail Trail*, June 1, 1969, 10; Connie Knight, "Vail's Summer Construction Underway," *Vail Trail*, May 31, 1970, 5; Peter J. Ognibene, "The Travail of Instant Tyrolia," *Denver Post Empire Magazine*, October 10, 1971, 11–15 (first quotation p. 13); Terry Minger, quoted in Town of Vail, Board of Trustees and Planning Commission, joint meeting minutes, August 5, 1970 (second quotation); Walter McC. Maitland, letter to the editor, *Vail Trail*, December 22, 1972, 54 (third quotation).

30. LionsHead Centre, ad, *Vail Trail*, September 14, 1969.

31. Joe Macy, interview, Vail, September 1, 1993; Morten Lund, "Their New Alps Versus Our New Alps," *Ski*, November 1971, 85–91ff; Peter Seibert, interview, Vail, January 6, 1994; "Vail's 1969 Expansion Plan Detailed," *Vail Trail*, February 24, 1969, 1.

32. Seibert, interview; David Sage, interview, Vail, July 22, 1993; Terrell J. Minger, interview, Denver, August 23, 1993. Seibert also claimed that VA was motivated by its ongoing dispute with the State Highway Department over the value of 110 acres of VA land that the department had condemned for construction of Interstate 70 (see also note 23 in this chapter). The Highway Department had offered an average of $2,400 an acre; VA appealed, contending the land was worth a minimum of $40,000 an acre. By selling Lions-Head land for high-density development, Seibert later explained, VA hoped to "justify

the value of the land they [state highway officials] were taking." In retrospect, he added, "what we should have done was settle that case and then back off and take another look at [the plans for LionsHead], but we went ahead." VA eventually did win its appeal. Seibert, interview; "State Hiw'y Dept Charged with 'Bad Faith'"; "Land Award Is Set for Vail Associates," *Denver Post*, November 15, 1967, 34; "Road Dept. Appeals Vail Award Ruling," *Denver Post*, November 3, 1968, 36.

33. "Vail Having $15 Million Boom in Quiet Economy"; "LionsHead at Vail: Focus of Vail's Building Boom Shifting to LionsHead Area," *Vail Trail*, March 25, 1971, 20–22; "Vail Building Boom Moving Westward," *Vail Trail*, July 30, 1971, 19; Mary Jo Allen, letter to the editor, *Vail Trail*, July 14, 1972, 25. Some LionsHead construction was done hastily and cheaply. David Sage, a real estate agent who sat on the town Planning Committee in the early 1970s, said that at LionsHead "a lot of times there was very cheap quality. Some of them [developers] got away with it. A lot of them came in from out of state for a project or two, hit and run." Sage cites the example of a Texas developer who neglected to make design accommodations for the cold winter climate. The building he slapped together constantly suffered from frozen bathrooms. D. Sage, interview.

34. Rod Slifer, interview, Vail, August 30, 1993; Carl R. Hansen, letter to the editor, *Vail Trail*, May 4, 1973, 24.

35. John Dobson, "Vail—How Big?," *Vail Trail*, April 9, 1971, 2 (quotation); John Dobson, "Our Mayor Speaks," *Vail Trail*, April 5, 1970, 3.

36. For a brief history of Boulder growth management, see League of Women Voters of Boulder Valley, "Did You Know? . . . The Story of Boulder, Colorado: Its Struggles to Reconcile Growth With Environmental Preservation," Boulder Community Network, http://bcn.boulder.co.us/lwv/lwvknow.html (accessed August 10, 2007). See also E. D. Kelly, *Managing Community Growth*, 53, 56–60, 96–97; and Wright, *Rocky Mountain Divide*, 77–87. A. L. Scott, "Remaking Urban in the American West," recounts Boulder's tumultuous growth and lifestyle politics in the 1960s and 1970s.

37. Vail actually annexed its first parcel, LionsHead, in 1969, before Minger took office. But after his 1970 appointment, and the election that same year of a strongly pro-annexation town council, Vail grabbed several more parcels, slapping zoning controls on all of them. By 1973, town limits reached all the way to East Vail, at the far eastern end of the valley. Efforts to annex East Vail itself began that year. Minger argued for annexation not just to control growth but also to expand the electorate to include the many resort workers who lived in Vail's "suburbs." Echoing the complaints of many Vail workers, he told the *Trail* that "a large percentage of the people who form the backbone of the community [and] make it work—waitresses, bartenders, etc. . . . live in the extremities of the valley and aren't able to voice their opinion by vote on the very things that their work makes possible." This democratic rationale made some Vailites nervous; Minger remembers that there was "a lot of concern about turning over land-use decisions and these other political decisions to . . . a lot of young people, a lot of ski instructors and bartenders and people like that who could vote." Terry Minger, quoted in Celia Roberts, "A Look at Annexation from Town and County," *Vail Trail*, August 31, 1973, 27; Pete Seibert, quoted in Don Dooley, "Village That Skis Built," Men's and Recreation Section, *Milwaukee Journal*, March 28, 1965, 1; Minger, interview.

38. In Colorado, home-rule communities enjoy more freedom and power over their own affairs than statutory municipalities, because the state constitution dictates that ordinances dealing with municipal matters and passed under a home-rule charter supersede state laws with which they might conflict. Prior to 1972, only towns with populations over two thousand could secure home rule; the 1971 Municipal Home Rule Act extended this option to smaller towns like Vail. Colo. Rev. Stat. § 31-2-201 et seq. On the legalities of home rule in Colorado, see Lorch, *Colorado's Government*, 55–56, 61–62.

39. Town of Vail, Board of Trustees, minutes, February 1, 1972; "Voters Okay Home Rule Commission," *Vail Trail*, April 21, 1972, 1; "Home Rule Charter Vote Draws Comments from Voters," *Vail Trail*, September 8, 1972, 25; "Home Rule Charter Passes," *Vail Trail*, September 15, 1972, 1. In April, voters embraced home rule and approved the creation of a charter commission by a lopsided 68 to 1 vote; in September, they voted for the finished charter 90 to 17. Minger favored home rule not just because, as he explained in a detailed *Trail* article, it would allow "flexibility and creativity in the exercise of local government functions," but also because he felt it would empower locals and invigorate local government. It would, he wrote, "place decision-making power in the hands of local citizens" and thus lead to "a potential increase in citizen interest and participation in local government." Terry Minger and Sharon Hobart, "The Home Rule Charter Plan," *Vail Trail*, April 7, 1972, 26. See also Town of Vail, Board of Trustees, minutes, February 1, 1972.

40. Stewart L. Udall, quoted in "Colorado: Growing, Growing, Gone?," *Colorado Investor Fact Sheet* 1, no. 9 (September 5, 1972): 1, 2, 3 (emphasis in original). See also Rigomar Thurmer, "The Second Vail Symposium . . . They Listened and Became Aware!," *Vail Trail*, August 11, 1972, 8–9. The 1972 bestseller that popularized the catch phrase "limits to growth" was Meadows et al., *Limits to Growth*. It was sponsored by the Club of Rome, an international group of concerned academics, diplomats, and businesspeople.

41. Robert W. Knecht, "Local, State and Federal Policies on Land Use," in *First Vail Symposium*, 15 (first and second quotations); Desmond Muirhead, quoted in "Colorado: Growing, Growing, Gone?," 5 (third quotation); Thomas A. Corcoran, "A Developer's View of Mountain Recreation Communities," in *First Vail Symposium*, 3 (fourth quotation); Udall, quoted in "Colorado: Growing, Growing, Gone?" (fifth quotation).

42. All quotations are from *First Vail Symposium*: John A. Dobson, "Welcome Speech"; Knecht, "Local, State and Federal Policies"; Corcoran, "A Developer's View"; Terry Minger, "Preface."

43. James M. Idema, quoted in Kenneth L. Peterson, "Colorado to Extend Quality Fishing," *Trout*, January–February 1963, 7; Van Gytenbeek, *Way of a Trout*, 107–9. On the origins of Trout Unlimited and its concern with mass-stocking, see Hazen L. Miller, "How Trout Unlimited Began," *Trout*, Summer 1969, 4–5; Jim Yuskavitch, "Taking Stock of Stocking," Robert Behnke, "The First Forty Years: From Rhetoric to Research," *Trout*, Winter 1999, 16–26, 52–54; and Halverson, *Entirely Synthetic Fish*, 114–18. On Trout Unlimited in Colorado, see "Pennsylvania, Colorado Get New TU Units," *Trout*, November–December 1963, 9; "Cutthroat Chapter Is Formed," *Trout*, September–October 1964, 9; "Now It's . . . Denver, National Headquarters," *Trout*, Winter 1969, 2; and Van Gytenbeek, *Way of a Trout*, 96, 99–100, 108, 113–14, 135–36, 137.

44. Quotations, respectively, from Paul R. Needham, "Counterfeit Catchables: The Wrong Kind of Trout Creel Insurance," *Outdoor America*, May 1959, 5–6; Robert E. Vincent, "Are We Taming Our Trout?" *Outdoor America*, June 1961, 7; and Idema, quoted in Peterson, "Colorado to Extend Quality Fishing." See also "Natural Foods Are Better for Trout," *Trout*, May–June 1963, 10–11.

45. Idema, quoted in Peterson, "Colorado to Extend Quality Fishing." See also Oren V. Shaw, "Disagrees on Dams," letter to the editor, *Trout*, January–February 1967, 4; and W. D. Klein, "Are We Polluting Our Streams with Trout?" *Trout*, Spring 1974, 22, 36, 38.

46. Van Gytenbeek, *Way of a Trout*, vii (first quotation); Fly Fisherman for Conservation Inc., quoted in "Quality Is the Word," *Trout*, March–April 1962, 2 (second quotation); Kenneth L. Peterson, "New Trout Philosophy Offers a Challenge," *Trout*, March–April 1965, 9 (third quotation). On the idea that fishery conservation was the keystone for a wider environmental agenda, and its proponents the leaders of a wider movement, see James R. Harlan, "Fish—Barometer of Pollution," *Outdoor America*, July 1960, 4–5; Conservation Council of Colorado Inc., "Preliminary Statement of Objectives," February 20, 1961, typescript in FF "Operation Rescue," Colorado Open Space Collection; Harold Hagen, "Aesthetics or Anaesthetics?" *Izaak Walton Magazine*, June 1962, 5–6; "Trout Can Play Role in Pure-Water Concept," *Trout*, May–June 1964, 3; Peterson, "New Trout Philosophy Offers a Challenge"; "Threats to West's Fishing," *Trout*, January–February 1965, 8–9; Keith Schuyler, "The Trout as a Symbol," *Trout*, May–June 1965, 6, 8–10, 13–14; "Impoundments Strip Streams of Souls," *Trout*, July–August 1965, 3; Martin K. Bovey, "Broad Effort of TU Told," *Trout*, March–April 1966, 8, 14; Bovey, "What TU Is, Does," *Trout*, May–June 1966, 5, 12; Roderick Haig-Brown, "Outdoor Ethics," *Trout*, May–June 1966, 8, 11, 14; and T. L. Marshall, "The Fish Stocking Program: What Is Its Future?" *Trout*, Summer 1974, 21, 28, 30.

47. COSCC, Board of Directors, minutes, May 10, 1965, and March 14, 1966, FF "Board of Directors: Minutes 1965," and FF "Board of Directors: Minutes 1966," Box 1: 1, Colorado Environmental Coalition Records (hereafter CEC Records). See also Peterson, "Colorado to Extend Quality Fishing"; "Ripples," *Trout*, May–June 1963, 14; "Council and Chapter News," *Trout*, Summer 1971, 7; and [Feltner], *Look Back*, 37. To get a strong sense of Trout Unlimited's agenda, see "Proposed American Trout Policy," *Trout*, March–April 1964, 6–7, 10.

48. On debates over recreational development in Vermont, see B. Harrison, *View from Vermont*, chap. 6. On Mineral King, see Harper, *Mineral King*; Schrepfer, "Perspectives on Conservation"; T. Turner, "Who Speaks for the Future?"; M. P. Cohen, *History of the Sierra Club*, 340–45, 392–96, 450–51; and U.S. Department of Agriculture (hereafter USDA), Forest Service, *Public Lands and Private Recreation*, 21–22.

49. Spence Conley, "Vail Wilderness Becoming Ski Paradise," *Rocky Mountain News*, March 25, 1962, 23; Jack Foster, "White Gold Makes a Gleaming City," *Rocky Mountain News*, March 10, 1963, 53; "Fabulous Resort Area Taking Shape at Vail," *Denver Post*, November 7, 1963, 32; William Logan, "Vail: Sky Is the Limit for Highland Jewel," *Rocky Mountain News*, October 3, 1966, 18; Richard J. Schneider, "Vail 'Master Plan' Seeks Wise Growth," *Rocky Mountain News*, August 13, 1973, 5; Jane Cracraft, "Overcrowding Resort Hit at Vail Symposium," *Denver Post*, August 8, 1971, 44; Ognibene, "Travail of Instant

Tyrolia"; Richard J. Schneider, "Plastic Bavaria II on Tap, Thanks to Forest Service," *Rocky Mountain News*, September 8, 1974; Steve Wynkoop, "Vail Area Facing Urbanized Future," *Denver Post*, July 15, 1973, 1; John G. White, "Eagle Fears Vail Syndrome," *Denver Post*, August 5, 1973, 49.

50. See Paul Hauk, "Breckenridge," in *Ski Area Chronologies, White River National Forest*, Ring Binder 2, Box 1, Paul I. Hauk Papers, Denver Public Library (hereafter Hauk Papers-DPL). Also see coverage in the *Summit County Journal* (hereafter *SCJ*): Mrs. Walter Byron, "Business Enterprises Give Promise—New Breckenridge," January 20, 1961, 1; "Forest Service Grants OK for Breckenridge Ski Resort," July 7, 1961, 1; "Breckenridge Bits," August 25, 1961, 2; "Rounds Active in Area Development," September 1, 1961, 8; and "Skiing Facilities to Be Ready for Use Dec. 15," September 8, 1961, 1. Ironically, the loudest objections to the Peak 8 permit came from Vail's Pete Seibert, who saw the upstart as a worrisome rival, given its being closer to Denver than Vail. Just two years after claiming that Vail would not undercut existing resorts, Seibert protested to the Forest Service that Peak 8 *would* undercut Vail. Vail Associates asked that Peak 8 be postponed until Vail could build up its business first. But the Forest Service, pointing out VA's earlier plea for *more* competition, granted Peak 8 its permit in July 1961. The mountain opened in December, a year before Vail. Hauk, "Breckenridge," Ring Binder 2, Box 1, Hauk Papers-DPL; Seibert, *Vail: Triumph of a Dream*, 89–91.

51. See the *SCJ*: "Breckenridge Bits," March 10, 1961, 2; Helen Rich, letter to the editor, September 15, 1961, 7; "Breckenridge Bits," September 15, 1961, 6; "Town Board News," May 22, 1964, 3; "Breckenridge Bits," January 1, 1965, 4.

52. Hauk, "Breckenridge," Ring Binder 2, Box 1, Hauk Papers-DPL; Willard Haselbush, "$3 Million Breckenridge Spa Taking Shape," *Denver Post*, January 6, 1963, 3D; "Million Dollars Raised for Breck Ski Expansion," *SCJ*, February 19, 1965, 6; "There's Still Gold in Them Thar Hills: 52 Million Dollars Earmarked for Breckenridge," *SCJ*, January 8, 1970, 1; "Breckenridge Contract Is Signed," *SCJ*, January 29, 1970, 1.

53. Paul Kaplan and Cindy Kaplan, letter to the editor, *SCJ*, January 22, 1970, 2. In 1997, Breckenridge in a sense became part of Vail when Vail Associates bought the resort, touching off a new era of expansion. VA bought Summit County's Keystone at the same time, and the entire company was renamed Vail Resorts.

54. Morten Lund, "Their New Alps Versus Our New Alps," *Ski*, November 1971, 85–91, 157–64; Morten Lund, "Their New Alps, Our New Alps: The Coming Despoliation of Colorado," *Ski*, December 1971, 80–82, 122–26; Morten Lund, "Smokey the Bear: Skiers' Friend or Foe?" *Ski*, October 1972, 62, 145–51.

55. Copper Mountain, ad, publication unknown [1971?], clipping in author's collection. On the development of Keystone and Copper Mountain, former White River National Forest ranger Paul Hauk's "chronologies" are indispensable; Hauk wrote detailed histories of these and all the other ski areas in the forest and compiled copies of original correspondence surrounding the planning and permitting process for each resort. See Hauk's *Ski Area Chronologies, White River National Forest*, Ring Binders 1–4, Box 1, Hauk Papers-DPL; Keystone and Copper Mountain appear in Ring Binder 3. Copper's distinctive design is described and pictured in USDA, Forest Service, *Planning Considerations for Winter Sports Resort Development*, 30–32.

56. USDA, Forest Service, *Planning Considerations for Winter Sports Resort Development*; Lund, "Smokey the Bear: Skiers' Friend or Foe?" 151 (emphasis in original).

57. No one has yet written a history of the Marble controversy, but Paul Hauk assembled a wealth of primary documents that will someday enable someone to do so; see Hauk Papers-DPL, Box 2. On Beaver Creek, see esp. Hauk, "Beaver Creek," in *Ski Area Chronologies, White River National Forest*, Ring Binder 2, Box 1, Hauk Papers-DPL. Seth Marx's corporate history, *Mountain Vision*, and Pete Seibert's personal account, *Vail: Triumph of a Dream*, are understandably slanted in favor of Beaver Creek's development, but both are useful for tracing the controversy. See also Simonton, *Vail: Story of a Colorado Mountain Valley*, 115–27; Fay, *History of Skiing in Colorado*, 113, 117–19; and A. G. Coleman, *Ski Style*, 195–96.

58. On the brewing national backlash against the mind-set of endless economic growth, see Collins, *More*, 132–52.

59. Richard D. Lamm, "The Ultimate Problem," *Trail and Timberline*, no. 534 (June 1963): 111–12. Lamm gleaned the idea of population growth being "the ultimate problem" from a 1962 speech to the CMC membership given by Sigurd Olson of the Wilderness Society.

60. Cal Queal, "Colorado's Big Land Squeeze," *Denver Post Empire Magazine*, May 4, 1969, 5.

61. Colorado Open Space Council, Board of Directors, minutes, April 8, 1971, FF "Board of Directors: Minutes 1971," Box 1: 1, CEC Records; Jim Monaghan, memo to Board of Directors, Colorado Open Space Council, March 1, 1973, FF "Board of Directors: Minutes 1973," Box 1: 1, CEC Records; Jim Kirksey, "Hogan Laments State Environmental Exploitation," *Denver Post*, September 16, 1970, 53; "Colorado's Population Puzzle Perplexes Many," *Colorado Investor Fact Sheet*, October 16, 1972, 3; Walker, *John A. Love*, 31, 41–42.

62. Marc Hodler, World Ski Federation president, quoted in "Denver '76: Olympic Challenge," *Colorado Magazine*, Midwinter 1969, 33. For examples of how the DOC used scenic clichés, Old West imagery, and other staples of Colorado tourist advertising, see the coffee-table-style "bid book," *Denver/The City* (Denver: Denver Organizing Committee for the 1976 Winter Olympics Inc., 1970). Also see the glossy *International Bulletins* that the DOC issued to the international press, beginning in fall 1968; a few issues are in Box 1, Protect Our Mountain Environment (Anti-Olympics Collection) (hereafter POME Collection). See also Pasquale Marranzino, "Our Great Bid for a Knockout," *Rocky Mountain News*, April 8, 1970, 45; and Bernard Kelly, "Denver's Winter Olympics Hopes—The Hour of Decision," *Denver Post Empire Magazine*, May 10, 1970, 14. On the evolution of the Olympics bid from the 1940s to 1970, see "Colorado Bids for 1956 Winter Olympic Games," *Rocky Mountain News*, April 23, 1949, 30; "Colorado Olympic Unit Set," *Denver Post*, December 27, 1964, 76; Lee Meade, "Colorado 'Breaks Ground' for '76 Winter Games," *Denver Post*, May 8, 1966, 62; "Denver to Bid for Winter Olympics," *Denver Post*, June 23, 1966, 1; "Ski Promoters Support Colorado Olympic Aims," *Denver Post*, November 13, 1966, 52; Richard O'Reilly, "'76 Winter Games Eyed by Colorado," *Rocky Mountain News*, January 4, 1967, 5; Bob Wirz, "Coordinating Group Formed for Olympics," *Denver Post*, March 31, 1967, 58; Ralph Moore, "Solons Support Olympic

Bid," *Denver Post*, April 21, 1967, 59; "Denverites Get Olympic Posts," *Denver Post*, May 11, 1967, 87; Charlie Meyers, "Good News Today: Denver Wins Olympic Step," *Denver Post*, December 18, 1967, 1; "Denver's Winter Olympics Bid," *Denver Post Empire Magazine* "Ski Country" supplement, November 10, 1968, 58; and Charlie Meyers, "Denver's Olympic Bid Paying Off, DOC Says," *Denver Post*, December 13, 1969, 10.

63. "Winter Olympics 'to Put Denver on Map,'" *Denver Post*, May 13, 1970, 21; see also Bernard Beckwith, "Denver Voted Olympicville, Winter of '76," "We Now Face Olympian Tasks," editorial, and "Solons Hail Denver's Choice," all *Denver Post*, May 13, 1970, 1, 30, 32; Bob Collins, "Jubilant Denver is Winner in 1976 Bid for Winter Olympics," *Rocky Mountain News*, May 13, 1970, 1; "Thanks, Olympians," editorial, *Denver Post*, May 15, 1970, 22; "Olympic 'Victors' Welcomed Home," *Denver Post*, May 16, 1970, 28; Ruth Sumners, "Denver Society Hails Olympians," *Rocky Mountain News*, May 18, 1970, 50. From the start, the drive to bring the Olympics to Colorado got positive press in both Denver dailies; *Rocky Mountain News* editor Jack Foster and *Denver Post* editor Palmer Hoyt even served on the Denver Organizing Committee that put together the winning bid. As the anti-Olympics backlash took shape in 1970–71, *News* reporting became somewhat more balanced, but the *Post*'s coverage still tilted strongly in favor of Olympics officials. The *Post* tended to either ignore critics of the games, portray them in a negative light, or bury stories about them deep in the paper; meanwhile, *Post* editorials scored the critics and staunchly insisted the Games would benefit Colorado. There were allegations that *Post* columnists were ordered not to write anything that might cast the Denver Olympics in a bad light, and that at least one column was spiked for taking too negative a tone. See Hornby, *Voice of Empire*, 53; "The Word from Olympus," *The Unsatisfied Man*, April 1971, 3; Richard O'Reilly, "Olympic Column Wipeout," *The Unsatisfied Man*, April 1972, 1.

64. See, for example, these letters to the *Denver Post*: Bernard E. Jones, "Ski Benefits," January 16, 1969, 19; Stan Perkins, "Delay Hosting Olympics," April 21, 1969, 19; Alice F. Ellis, "Objects to Spending for Olympics," June 22, 1969, 2G; Janeann Rogers, "Keep Colorado a Secret?," March 25, 1970, 4 (in the *Post*'s Zone 3 *Newsweekly*); Everett Pierce, "Olympic Killjoy," May 17, 1970, 2G; E. R. Murray, "Olympic Jam," May 29, 1970, 15; and Ron Kelemen, "Did You Ask Us about Olympics?," May 31, 1970, 2G. See also the column by Tom Gavin, "Winter Olympics—Big Snow Job," *Denver Post*, May 15, 1970, 21; and comments by Alan Merson, quoted in "Olympics Exploitation Hit," *Denver Post*, July 23, 1970, 12. The predictions about the future of I-70 are from, respectively, Joanne Ditmer, "Eyesore, U.S.A. In The Rockies?," *Denver Post*, May 17, 1970, 43; and the aforementioned letter by E. R. Murray.

65. Vance R. Dittman Jr. et al. to the Honorable John A. Love et al., June 1, 1968, FF 22, Box 1, POME Collection; "Olympics 1969," n.d., typescript in FF 19, Box 1, POME Collection; "Evergreen Share Sought in Olympics," *Denver Post*, May 2, 1969, 28; "Group Opposes Ski-Jump Plan," *Denver Post Zone 3 Newsweekly*, August 27, 1969, 5; "Olympic Plan Response Chilly," *Denver Post Zone 3 Newsweekly*, September 17, 1969, 3; Todd Phipers, "Evergreen Icy to Ski Jump Plan," *Denver Post*, June 7, 1970, 23; Gary Gerhardt, "Olympic Objections Cited in Evergreen," *Rocky Mountain News*, June 12, 1970, 8; Chuck Green, "Evergreen Expresses Olympiphobia," *Denver Post*, June 12, 1970, 76; Robert O. Redish Jr., "Successful Olympics Need Solid Backing," letter to the editor, *Denver*

Post, June 25, 1970, 25; "Olympics Exploitation Hit," *Denver Post*, July 23, 1970, 12; Joanne Ditmer, "Evergreen Due Consideration," *Denver Post*, August 16, 1970, 36; "Removal of Olympic Site Asked," *Denver Post*, August 18, 1970, 4; Mrs. Dale R. Patterson, "Reply to DOC," letter to the editor, *Denver Post*, October 13, 1970, 19; John Toohey, "Olympic Plans Draw Fire," *Denver Post*, October 25, 1970, 25; Pat McGraw, "POME: Cease Olympic Plans," *Denver Post*, October 30, 1970, 2; McGraw, "Evergreen Nordic Site Re-Evaluation Pledged," *Denver Post*, November 11, 1970, 76; McGraw, "Citizens Unit Asks DOC Funds Cutoff," *Denver Post*, January 10, 1971, 29; David H. Brown, "Call for Quiet from Evergreen," letter to the editor, *Denver Post*, January 19, 1971, 23; Cheryl Haynes, "Colorado asks: What's up, D.O.C.?" *dear earth* (April 1971, 7–11; Catherine Dittman, "Is All of This Expendable?" *Denver Audubon Society Newsletter*, April 1971, 2–4.

66. The suspect images appeared in the DOC's bid book, *Denver/The City*, 18, 84; the truth stretching about the Nordic, Alpine, and other event venues appeared in this and a companion volume, *Denver/Technical Information*. For excellent overviews of the DOC's serial blundering, see Whiteside, *Colorado: A Sports History*, chap. 5; M. S. Foster, "Colorado's Defeat of the 1976 Winter Olympics"; and Ted Farwell, as told to David Sumner, "The Olympic Bubble," *Colorado Magazine*, January–February 1973, 19–20, 26–40, 90. The most thorough (and devastating) exposé of the DOC's struggles with cost estimation and site selection was a six-part investigative series by Richard O'Reilly that ran in the *Rocky Mountain News* in April 1971: "Olympics—Good or Bad in Colorado?," April 4, 1971, 1, 5; "'60 Winter Olympics Cost Skyrocketed," April 5, 1971, 8, 16; "Snags Arise in Olympic Site Selection," April 6, 1971, 8, 22; "Olympic Alpine Site Conflict Brewing," April 7, 1971, 6, 8, 18; "Olympic Cost Estimates Vary Widely," April 8, 1971, 8, 18; "Benefits of Olympics Are Disputed," April 9, 1971, 8. See also Fred Brown, "Colorado Olympic Plan Termed Too General," *Denver Post*, January 4, 1970, 14; Ben Eastman Jr., "Adequate by Olympic Standards?," letter to the editor, *Denver Post Empire Magazine*, May 31, 1970, 4; Moras L. Shubert to "1976 Olympic Committee," June 9, 1970, FF 14, Box 1, POME Collection; Shubert, "Studies on Olympic Site," letter to the editor, *Denver Post*, January 25, 1971, 15; "DOC 'Can't Estimate' Olympics Costs," *Rocky Mountain News*, February 10, 1971, 10; Roger Rapoport, "Olympian Snafu at Sniktau," *Sports Illustrated*, February 15, 1971, 60–61; "Olympic Alpine Site Unsuitable," *Denver Post*, September 11, 1971, 32; "CU Students Evaluate Games Sites," *Rocky Mountain News*, September 11, 1971, 5; "Olympics Handling Rapped," *Denver Post*, February 10, 1972, 36; O'Reilly, "Olympic Committee Difficulties Evaluated, Criticized," *Rocky Mountain News*, February 20, 1972, 19–20; Fred Brown, "Solons Want More Specifics," *Denver Post*, March 3, 1972, 4; Bick Lucas, "Cost of Olympics Finally Revealed," *Denver Post*, March 26, 1972, 66; "DOC Expenses Something to Conceal," *Cervi's Rocky Mountain Journal*, March 30, 1972; John Jerome, "Goodbye, Denver Olympics," *Skiing*, February 1973, 68–70, 92–93.

67. State representative Richard D. Lamm, quoted in "How Many Care? The U.S. May Lose Out on the Winter Olympics," *Current Events*, January 31, 1973, 1–2; Richard Lamm, "Citizens Can Move Their Government," *Colorado Destiny*, September 2, 1972, Citizens for Colorado's Future Papers (hereafter CCF Papers); Bill Bruns, "Will Colorado Scrap Its Own 1976 Olympics?" *Life*, November 3, 1972, 81. Lamm was only one of many expressing such concerns; see, for example, Bob Saile, "Anti-Olympic Breeze

Blows," *Denver Post*, June 18, 1970, 89. Lamm's chief ally in the legislature, Rep. Bob Jackson of Pueblo, used similar rhetoric: "Why sell Colorado?" he asked in 1971. "Our state is attractive to us just because we have some uncluttered vistas and some pretty streams. . . . We should stop and think whether we want to change the open aspect of our environment here. I don't think we want to." Rep. Bob Jackson, quoted in Richard O'Reilly, "Benefits of Olympics Are Disputed," *Rocky Mountain News*, April 9, 1971, 8.

68. "Bill Seeks to Forbid State Olympic Cash," *Denver Post*, February 3, 1971, 2; "11 Dem Lawmakers Demand Details on Olympics Impact, Cost," *Denver Post*, February 3, 1971, 36; Cal Queal, "Yes, They Want No Olympics," *Denver Post*, February 7, 1971, 23; "Denver's Olympic Host Role Opposed," *Denver Post*, March 31, 1971, 81; "Colorado Open Space Council Position Concerning the 1976 Denver Winter Olympics," March 5, 1971, typescript in FF "Board of Directors: Policy Files—Miscellaneous 1960s–1970s," Box 1: 2, CEC Records; Bruce Robinson, "Sierra Club Reply on Olympic Planning," letter to the editor, *Denver Post*, September 22, 1971, 23; "Colorado Olympics Opposed," *Denver Post*, January 17, 1972, 23; "ROMCOE Declines Stand on Olympics," *Denver Post*, March 3, 1972, 21; "Olympics Planning Criteria Pushed," *Rocky Mountain News*, March 4, 1972; Lois Barr, "Olympics Plans Draw Fire," *Denver Post*, June 22, 1972, 17; "Anti-Olympic Vote Urged," *Denver Post*, November 3, 1972, 30. ROMCOE executive director Roger Hansen excoriated a federal impact statement for understating the damage the games would likely wreak. "Olympics Statement 'Vague, Inadequate,'" *Denver Post*, September 29, 1972, 14; Richard O'Reilly, "Olympics Impact Statement Ripped," *Rocky Mountain News*, September 30, 1972, 15.

69. "Georgetown Eyes Building Ordinance," *Denver Post*, May 19, 1970, 2; "Town to Preserve History," *Denver Post*, May 20, 1970, 44; Chuck Green, "Past Spared in Georgetown," *Denver Post*, June 14, 1970, 61; Jim Abbott, quoted in Joan White, "Georgetown Rumblings Portend Growth," *Denver Post*, July 18, 1971, 31; "Aspen Firms Claim Olympics Backing," *Denver Post*, January 5, 1972, 53; Guido Meyer, "Aspen as Games Site," letter to the editor, *Denver Post*, January 9, 1972, 26; "Chamber, Citizens at Odds," *Denver Post*, January 19, 1972, 24; "Aspen OKs Olympics with 'Ifs,'" *Denver Post*, January 21, 1972, 35; Joan Nice, "Views of Aspen's Sierra Club," letter to the editor, *Denver Post*, January 21, 1972, 23.

70. "Steamboat Springs Readies Nordic Events Bid," *Rocky Mountain News*, February 26, 1971, 5; "3 Alternate Areas Eyed for Olympics," *Rocky Mountain News*, March 6, 1971, 8; B. B. Brown et al., *Economic and Environmental Impact of the 1976 Winter Olympics— Alpine Events*; "Moving Olympics Alpine Sites Urged by U. Colo. Study," *Cervi's Rocky Mountain Journal*, December 16, 1971, 1, 3; "Steamboat Bids to Host Olympic Events," *Denver Post*, December 17, 1971, 25; Charlie Meyers, "5 Ski Areas Vie for DOC Site," *Denver Post*, January 5, 1972, 23; Richard O'Reilly, "Selection of New Olympic Alpine Events Site Near," *Rocky Mountain News*, January 5, 1972, 8; Charlie Meyers, "Avon Appears Favorite as Alpine Olympic Site," *Denver Post*, January 26, 1972, 60; "Colo. Reaction Varied in Choice of '76 Sites," *Denver Post*, February 1, 1972, 2; Bob Saile, "Alpine Site Snag Possible," *Denver Post*, February 8, 1972; Al Knight, "Avon Site on Forest Service Check List," *Rocky Mountain News*, February 9, 1972, 11; Richard O'Reilly, "Olympic Site Mulled as Potential Wilderness," *Rocky Mountain News*, February 10, 1972, 46; "No

Conflict Expected in Wilds, Alpine Plans," *Denver Post*, March 10, 1972, 2; "Charlie Meyers, "Steamboat Asks All Nordic Ski Events," *Denver Post*, April 4, 1972, 3; "The Olympic Torch?" undated clipping from *Steamboat Pilot* (quotation), Box 4, Rocky Mountain Center on Environment Papers (hereafter ROMCOE Papers); Towler, *History of Skiing at Steamboat Springs*, 97–98.

71. Jack Foster, "Tutt Tells What 1976 Games Will Mean to Colorado," *Rocky Mountain News*, March 6, 1971, 45; Charlie Meyers, "Olympic Referendum Move Kept Secret, but Vote Likely," *Denver Post*, November 25, 1971, 38; "Citizens' Unit Seeks to Move Olympics," *Denver Post*, January 5, 1972, 50; Keith A. Chamberlain, "Questions Olympic Benefits," and Glenn E. Hunter, "Rejects Honor," letters to the editor, *Denver Post*, January 18, 1972, 17; "Richard Lamm Hits Olympics as Land Promotion," *Denver Post*, January 19, 1972, 24; Tom Gavin, "'Glor-y Glor-y Col-O-Ra-Do!" *Denver Post*, February 18, 1972, 25 ("trouble with tourists" quotation); "CCF Still Hoping to Defeat Olympics," *Denver Post*, February 29, 1972, 21; Charles Carter, "Olympics Vote Proposed," *Denver Post*, March 14, 1972, 3; John Ashton, "Drive Launched for Referendum," *Denver Post*, March 16, 1972; "C of C Reaffirms Backing for Winter Olympics," *Rocky Mountain News*, March 25, 1972, 11; "'Laughing Stock of World': Harm Seen in Games Rejection," *Denver Post*, March 30, 1972; "Anti-Olympics Petitions Are Delivered," *Rocky Mountain News*, July 7, 1972, 7; "EPA: Olympics Spur to Growth," *Denver Post*, June 27, 1972, 15; Charlie Meyers, "Petitions on Balloting Delivered," *Denver Post*, July 7, 1972, 25; Frank M. Ashley, "Olympics and the State's Economy," letter to the editor, *Denver Post*, September 3, 1972, 38; W. R. Goodwin, "Games Once-in-Lifetime Opportunity, Says DOOC Chief," *Denver Post Bonus*, September 25, 1972, 3, 8; Bick Lucas, "Big 'Negative' Vote May Save Olympics," *Denver Post*, November 5, 1972, 46; "Questions and Answers . . . about the 1976 Olympic Winter Games," and "Colorado's 1976 Winter Olympics: A Statement from Governor John Love," leaflets distributed by Coloradans for the 1976 Winter Games, [1972], CCF Papers.

72. "Sabotaging the Olympics," editorial, *Rocky Mountain News*, January 27, 1971, 33; "Olympic Fears Unjustified," editorial, *Denver Post*, January 28, 1971, 22; C. Holmes Pierson, "Patriotism, Courtesy and the Olympics," letter to the editor, *Denver Post*, October 5, 1972, 31. On the loss of faith in experts and administrative elites by the late 1960s, and the growing cynicism that they were captive to narrow, self-serving interest groups, see R. N. L. Andrews, *Managing the Environment, Managing Ourselves*, 218–21. To counter such concerns, the DOC opened most of its meetings to the public in spring 1972 and reincorporated itself as the ostensibly more approachable Denver Olympic Organizing Committee (DOOC) in July 1972. But according to one insider, it was all window dressing: "actually no major change was made." Farwell, "Olympic Bubble," 90.

73. On efforts to discredit Olympics opponents, see "Sniping Clouds the Olympics without Solving Any Problems," *Denver Post*, January 12, 1971, 18; Pasquale Marranzino, "Let's Not Sabotage the Olympics," *Rocky Mountain News*, January 14, 1971, 45; "Sabotaging the Olympics," *Rocky Mountain News*, January 27, 1971, 38; "Olympic Fears Unjustified," *Denver Post*, January 28, 1971, 22; Jim Graham, "DOC Must Lead the Way," *Denver Post*, February 16, 1972; Bick Lucas, "DOC Has Obligation to Do Better Job," *Denver Post*, February 20, 1972, 76; Ken Pearce, "Currigan Urges Unity on '76 Olympic Games," *Denver*

Post, March 10, 1972, 2; Colorado Committee of 76, "This We Believe," ad in *Cervi's Rocky Mountain Journal*, March 30, 1972, 9; Norman Udevitz, "Small but Artful Activist Group Wielding Rare Power," *Denver Post*, October 11, 1972, 32; "Look at Olympics as Challenge: Vote No on Both Propositions," *Denver Post*, October 22, 1972, 29; C. Madeleine Gibson, "Why a 'No' Vote on Olympic Ban," letter to the editor, *Denver Post*, October 27, 1972 ("agitators" quotation); Save Our State Committee, ad in *Denver Post*, November 6, 1972, 31 ("hitch-hikers" quotation); and Jim Graham, "Olympics Are Needed, and Need a No Vote," *Denver Post*, November 5, 1972, 47. On the western tradition of invoking longevity in place to gain political advantage, see Wrobel, *Promised Lands*, chaps. 4–6.

74. On Olympics proponents as profiteers, see Robert A. Burns, "Businessmen Eye Olympic 'Gold Rush,'" *Rocky Mountain News*, February 28, 1971, 53; "Avon Selection to Benefit Vail Associates," *Denver Post*, February 2, 1972, 73; Sherry Keene, "Olympics Prime Bull Market in Vail Land, Stock," *Cervi's Rocky Mountain Journal*, February 7, 1972, 1; "Colorado's Financial Elite Plan 1976 Snow Job for Public," *Straight Creek Journal*, August 24, 1972, 3, 8–9; and "We Are Being Told We Must Pay Unknown Millions for a Ten-Day Event Which Will Profit Its Promoters and Encourage Unneeded Growth," *Colorado Destiny*, September 2, 1972, CCF Papers. On the deteriorating position of the DOC, see George Kane, "Shotgun Marriage of Colorado and Olympics," *Cervi's Rocky Mountain Journal*, January 6, 1972, 19; Charlie Meyers, "Key Problems Facing DOC," *Denver Post*, February 27, 1972, 26; Michael Balfe Howard, "News Survey Indicates Heavy Support for Olympic Referendum," *Rocky Mountain News*, March 13, 1972, 1; "Needed: New Direction for DOC," *Rocky Mountain News*, April 12, 1972; "What's Up DOOC?" *Colorado Investor Fact Sheet*, August 21, 1972, 1–4; Ron Wolf, "Legislators in Survey Oppose Games Funding," *Denver Post*, September 5, 1972, 3; "Olympics Amendment Confuses Colorado's Voters," *Denver Post*, October 1, 1972, 14; Charlie Meyers, "Voters to Determine Denver Olympics' Fate," *Denver Post*, October 29, 1972, 53; and Bruns, "Will Colorado Scrap Its Own 1976 Olympics?" *Life*, November 3, 1972, 81.

75. Richard O'Reilly, "Colorado Voters Reject 1976 Winter Olympics," *Rocky Mountain News*, November 8, 1972, 5, 6; Norm Udevitz, "Olympic Torch Put Out: Voters Reject Funding for '76 Olympics," *Denver Post*, November 8, 1972, 1, 3.

76. Richard D. Lamm, "Promotional Pollution: The Case for Not Holding the 1976 Winter Olympics in Colorado," speech to the Colorado Press Association, February 12, 1972, CCF Papers.

77. For postmortems of Colorado's 1972 elections, see Robert Threlkeld, "Haskell Victory a 'Major Political Upset,'" *Rocky Mountain News*, November 8, 1972, 5; Fred Brown, "Senate Veteran Allott Upset by Haskell," *Denver Post*, November 8, 1972, 1F; Jim Graham, "Olympic Vote Labels City, State Welshers," *Denver Post*, November 10, 1972; Lee Olson, "Colorado Voters Exerted Their Independence," *Denver Post*, November 19, 1972, 30; Steve Wynkoop, "Olympics Revisited: Wounds Unhealed," *Denver Post*, January 25, 1976, 1, 2; and Richard J. Schneider, "Opinions Still Divided on Idea of Winter Olympics in Colorado," *Rocky Mountain News*, February 6, 1976, 5, 12.

78. Schulte, *Wayne Aspinall and the Shaping of the American West*, 268–78.

79. Wiley and Gottlieb, *Empires in the Sun*, 131–32, 134. Vanderhoof, formerly speaker of the state house, and then lieutenant governor to John Love, had become governor in

July 1973 when Love resigned to become President Nixon's "energy czar." Another 1974 victory with roots in the Olympics battle was the election of Gary Hart to the U.S. Senate; Hart, a Denver lawyer, had been an outspoken opponent of the Olympics (as well as George McGovern's national campaign manager) in 1972.

80. Leonard Larsen, "Environment Key Word: 'Short' Legislature Far from 'Routine,'" *Denver Post Bonus*, January 20, 1970, 2; "Environmental Quality: A Business, Industry and Public Concern Confronted the 1970 General Assembly," *Coloscope*, April 1970, 2–3; Rocky Mountain Center on Environment, "Preliminary Study Outline for an Environmental Resources Inventory," January 1970, typescript in Box 1, ROMCOE Papers.

81. On the popularization and politicization of ecological principles in the 1960s and early 1970s, see Worster, *Nature's Economy*, chaps. 16–17; and Kingsland, *Evolution of American Ecology*, chaps. 7–8.

82. Useful discussions of environmental issues facing the 1971 legislature include Dick Prouty, "Cleaner Environment Legislative Aim," *Denver Post Bonus*, January 5, 1971, 8; Charles Roos, "Here Are Accomplishments of General Assembly," *Denver Post*, April 29, 1971, 38; "Environment: Public Concern Forced Legislative Focus but, the Results Are Not in Yet," *Coloscope*, May 1971, 2–3; Fred Brown, "Land-Use Legislation Cited," *Denver Post*, May 9, 1971, 36, 38; "Environmental Law: Did Anything Go Right?" *dear earth*, June 1971, 11–13. On the 1972 legislative session, see Fred Brown, "Land, Water Basic Issues for State," and Charles Roos, "Short Session Expected to Be Decisive," *Denver Post Bonus*, January 27, 1972, 2, 3, 5, 7; and "CML Legislative Report: 'Short' Session of the 48th General Assembly," *Colorado Municipalities*, July 1972, 151–55.

83. The quotation, reflecting the official stance of the Colorado Association of Commerce and Industry, is from "Viewpoint: We Must Not Spread Chaos," *Coloscope*, February 1971, 2.

84. Love, quoted in Prouty, "Cleaner Environment Legislative Aim"; "ROMCOE Position on Recommendations of Colorado Land Use Commission," March 3, 1971, typescript in FF "1970–1972 Colo. Organizations. Colorado Land Use Commission," Box 8, CEC Records. For overviews of the land-use reform movement nationwide, see Popper, *Politics of Land-Use Reform*; and Rome, *Bulldozer in the Countryside*, chap. 7.

85. On statewide zoning and other land-use reform proposals, and their unhappy fate in the 1970 legislative session, see "Parks, Recreation, and Environment Committee Recommendations," *Colorado Information*, January 1970, 12; untitled item in *Colorado Information Weekly Newsletter*, March 5, 1970; untitled item in *Colorado Information Weekly Newsletter*, April 23, 1970; "CML Legislative Report: Forty-Seventh Sine Die," *Colorado Municipalities*, June 1970, 157–58; Fred Brown, "Love Pleads Again for State Zoning," *Denver Post*, July 11, 1970.

86. For an overview of land-use legislation during these years, see James Monaghan, "A Short History of Land Use in Colorado," *Straight Creek Journal*, special section on "Land Use Colorado," March 5–12, 1974, 12. Monaghan was lobbyist for COSC.

87. Probably the most important land-use law passed in Colorado during these years, the 1974 Areas and Activities of State Interest Act (originally Colo. Rev. Stat. § 106-7-101, now Colo. Rev. Stat. § 24-65.1-101 et seq.), recognized the need to define areas

with significance beyond the local level ("areas of critical state concern"), but paradoxically it gave *local*, not state, government the powers to designate and regulate such areas. (These are still known in Colorado as "1041 powers," after the bill's original number, H.B. 1041.) The state Land Use Commission could approve or comment on such regulations but could not disapprove or overrule them.

88. Fred Brown, "Peoples' Lobbyists Growing in Number," *Denver Post Bonus*, January 27, 1972, 8.

89. The planning-region concept emphasized historical, topographical, economic, demographic, cultural, and transportation ties that transcended traditional county lines and rivalries. Some proposed that county lines be ignored altogether in defining such regions, since the political boundaries did not always take into account topographical barriers, demographic disparities, and the like. In 1968 the State Planning Office suggested joining Summit, Grand, and parts of Eagle, Pitkin, and Garfield Counties in a single planning region, because they had all become "primarily oriented towards recreation and tourism" and also shared a strong transportation link in Interstate 70. But in the end, state planners shied away from this innovative approach; the twelve planning regions they unveiled in late 1970 adhered to county lines. See Colorado State Planning Office, *Proposed Regional Delineation for the State of Colorado*, esp. 13–14. See also "The State of Planning," *Colorado Municipalities*, October 1970, 249–58.

90. Roger P. Hansen, "A National Land Use Policy," emphasis in original, paper prepared for the Council on Environmental Quality [1971], typescript in envelope "Rocky Mountain Center on Environment. A National Land Use Policy, et al.," Box 1, ROMCOE Papers.

91. Colorado Municipal League, resolutions for 1971–72, *Colorado Municipalities*, July 1971, 166–67; Frank Morison, "The Colorado Environment, 1971," *Coloscope*, December 1971, 3 (quotation).

92. On the inherent individualism and nonradicalism of political consumerism, see L. Cohen, *Consumers' Republic*, chap. 8; and Cross, *All-Consuming Century*, chap. 5, esp. 167–69. On the idea, new to the 1970s, of "lifestyle," and its limits, see Erwin, "Lifestyle."

93. Albert G. Melcher, "Colorado—and Its Future," *dear earth*, April 1971, 2. Melcher was field services director for ROMCOE when he wrote these words.

94. George F. Jackson, "President's Report," *Outdoor America*, August 1960, 14; "Are We Letting Izaak Down?" *Outdoor America*, June 1960, 2.

95. Joe Bach, letter to the editor, *Trail and Timberline*, no. 636 (December 1971): 236, 254; Kingery, *Colorado Mountain Club*, 81.

96. Roger P. Hansen to Laurence E. Riordan, October 27, 1965, FF "Publicity: Correspondence, 1965–1970," Box 5: 2, CEC Records.

97. Quotation from Hubert Stock, "The 4-Wheel Drive as a Trail User," *Jeepers in the News*, January 1974, 12. On the Jeep Club's early years, see Mary Green, "Jeep Club History," *Jeepers in the News*, October 1962, 1–2. From the early 1960s, *Jeepers in the News* (the club's newsletter) began to run more conservation news, advice on how to jeep in an environmentally responsible way, and notices of upcoming cleanup activities. See, for example, George H. Armishaw, "The Eleventh Commandment," April 1961, 2; Doris Derrough, "Colorado High Country U.S.A.: GeePee . . . PG . . . Jeep," July 1966, 28–29;

Jerry Covault, "Motorized Mountaineers," September 1966, 14; and Art Hassan, letter to president of the International Harvester Corp., April 5, 1971, reprinted in the May 1971 issue, p. 16. On the Jeep Club joining the Outdoor Roundtable, see John Lind, "Commander's Corner," *Jeepers in the News*, May 1964, 12.

98. See *Jeepers in the News*: "4-Wheel Drive Areas in Danger of Elimination," October 1969, 1–2 (quotation); John Gaylord, "Commander's Reports . . . Conservation," January 1969, 2; "Local Newspaper Pans Jeep Club in Efforts to End All 4-Wheeling in State," September 1969, 2; Gene Bates, editorial, December 1969, 2; "Year—2000," January 1971, 1–2; and George Thomas, "Wanted: Progress Dead or Alive," November 1971, 13.

99. Gene Morris, "President's Report," *Jeepers in the News*, July 1972, 18 (first, second, sixth, seventh, eighth, and ninth quoted phrases); Eric Julber, "Let's Open Up Our Wilderness Areas," *Jeepers in the News*, June 1972, 19 (third, fourth, and fifth quoted phrases). *Jeepers in the News* listed the home addresses of the club's leaders in the late 1960s and early 1970s.

100. Bill Sanford, "Commander's Corner," *Jeepers in the News*, March 1974, 2. The Jeep Club did join COSC in summer 1974—not because club leaders found new rapport with the coalition, but because they wanted leverage to tug it toward a more jeep-friendly position. For their part, COSC officials allowed the Jeep Club to join only on the condition that it purge language from its constitution that seemed to condone off-trail driving. See Bill Sanford, "Commander's Corner," *Jeepers in the News*, June 1974, 2; COSC, Board of Directors, minutes, May 2, 1974, FF "Board of Directors: Minutes 1974," Box 1: 1, CEC Records; "The Constitution of the Mile Hi Jeep Club of Colorado," n.d., typescript in FF "Mile High Jeep Club of Colo.," Box 3: 3, CEC Records.

101. James Kemp, vice chairman of the Eagles Nest Wilderness Committee, quoted in "Wilderness . . . or Lumber?" *Colorado Magazine*, July–August 1969, 13.

102. Brief for the Federal Appellants, US Court of Appeals, 10th Circuit, Nos. 404–70, 405–70, 406–70, Robert W. Parker, et al., Appellees, v. USA, Clifford Hardin, Edward P. Cliff, David S. Nordwall, James O. Folkestad, Kaibab Industries, Appellants, p. 5. It should be noted, though, that the Vail Associates executive board formally censured Parker for his very public stance, apparently worried that his antagonizing the Forest Service might jeopardize VA's permit to operate a ski area on national forest land. Curtis Casewit, "Super Salesman for Super Ski Resort," *Colorado Magazine*, September–October 1972, 12R–14R.

103. This point corroborates James Morton Turner's insight that, by this time, wilderness advocates found themselves embracing a more openly recreational rationale for wilderness protection, largely to win more popular support. J. M. Turner, "From Woodcraft to 'Leave No Trace,'" 463, 468–69, 472–73, 476, 479. On wilderness as a landscape packaged for consumption, see Talbot, "Wilderness Narrative and the Cultural Logic of Capitalism."

104. Amy Scott, in "Remaking Urban in the American West," makes a similar argument, using Boulder's case to show how "lifestyle liberals" and radicals, instead of quitting political action after the 1960s, instead "channeled their energies into local politics . . . to remake urban cultures and landscapes" (254).

105. The fees were based on the floor area of new buildings, so the developers of

larger projects ended up paying more into the town's recreation fund. Town of Vail, annual report, 1973, pp. 9, 10; Town of Vail, Ordinance no. 5 (Series of 1973); "Recreational Fund Ordinance Approved by Town Council," *Vail Trail*, March 23, 1973, 24. As early as 1969, when he was still assistant town coordinator, Terry Minger proposed "impact fees" on new developments, citing towns in other states that had implemented such fees and noting that courts had upheld municipalities' authority to do so. Terry Minger, memorandum to the Town of Vail Planning Commission, April 8, 1969, attachment to Town of Vail, Board of Trustees, minutes, April 16, 1969.

106. Town of Vail, Board of Trustees, minutes, March 20, 1973; anonymous letter, quoted in George Knox, "Structured Parking—Antholz Acquisition Draws Replies," *Vail Trail*, July 7, 1972, 4; Knox, "Our Last Chance!," *Vail Trail*, June 30, 1972, 2; Town of Vail, Board of Trustees, minutes, March 20, 1973; Town of Vail, Ordinance no. 6 (Series of 1973). The land, called the "Antholz property" after the ranch family that once owned it, is now home to a public park, outdoor amphitheater, and botanical garden.

107. Town of Vail, Ordinance no. 8 (Series of 1973), Article 16. This requirement was patterned on the National Environmental Policy Act.

108. Royston, Hanamoto, Beck & Abey and Livingston & Blayney, *Vail Plan*, 1–6, 6A; Livingston & Blayney, "Vail Planning Study: Parking: Preliminary Concepts," memorandum, [1973], Vail Public Library Historical Files; Bob Ewegen, "Automobile Target of Vail Bond Issue," *Denver Post*, August 14, 1973, 18; Minger, interview.

109. The plan did not go to a popular vote, but in a bond election Vailites voted overwhelmingly for two of the projects that anchored it: 229–8 in favor of the town buying the thirty-eight-acre meadow, 210–28 in favor of building the underground parking garage, and 222–16 in favor of a one-cent sales-tax hike to help pay for these two projects. "Bond Issues Pass Easily," *Vail Trail*, September 28, 1973, 1; Terry Minger, "The City Manager's Budget Message," in Town of Vail, budget, 1974, p. 5. For an example of business owners objecting to the plan-in-progress, see Town of Vail, Board of Trustees, minutes, June 5, 1973. For an example of a more enthusiastic reaction, see "Royston Presented Preliminary Plan at Trustee Meeting," *Vail Trail*, February 9, 1973, 7.

110. Royston, Hanamoto, Beck & Abey and Livingston & Blayney, *Vail Plan*, 3, 5.

111. Hauk, "Beaver Creek," Ring Binder 2, Box 1, Hauk Papers-DPL; Marx, *Mountain Vision*, 36–50 (quotation p. 48).

112. Hauk, "Beaver Creek," Ring Binder 2, Box 1, Hauk Papers-DPL; Marx, *Mountain Vision*, 49–50.

113. For a glimpse into the minds of those who designed this stretch of I-70, see Thurlow C. Reseigh, "Design Problems on Interstate Route 70, Denver to Utah Line," paper presented at the annual convention of the American Association of State Highway Officials, Denver, October 11, 1961. Reseigh was roadway plans engineer for the Colorado Highway Department at the time.

114. On the professional viewpoint of midcentury highway engineers, see L. W. Kemp, "Aesthetes and Engineers," esp. 763–77; Rose and Seely, "Getting the Interstate System Built," esp. 27–33; and T. Lewis, *Divided Highways*, 133–36, 169–71, 240. Beginning in the 1940s some engineers did embrace the "complete highway" concept, with its concern for roadside appearance and for fitting the highway to landscape contours. But,

Louis Kemp notes, many highway administrators were highly skeptical of the concept and insisted that any aesthetic design elements be justified on cost, safety, or other functional grounds (e.g., sinuous curves might reduce dangerous "highway hypnotism" and save the cost of slicing directly through hills).

115. A fascinating artifact is the guide to I-70 that the Highway Department published around 1970 to try to convince a by-then-skeptical public that the interstate had, in fact, been designed in harmony with nature all along. Colorado Division of Highways, *Interstate 70: Through the Colorado Rockies*.

116. Besides the moss rock, scenic mitigation around Georgetown also included planting the torn-up mountainside with wildflower seeds, some of which locals collected themselves. Also, in the valley just above town, Highway Department planners, consulting with town officials and the State Historical Society, shifted the roadway slightly to spare a buttress of the old Georgetown Loop narrow-gauge railroad bridge, which locals and the State Historical Society wanted to restore as a working historical exhibit. See Colorado Division of Highways, *Interstate 70: Through the Colorado Rockies*, 13; and coverage in the *CCMJ*: Odette Baehler, What's New in Georgetown columns, November 4, 1965, 3, and May 18, 1967, 1; and Wally Baehler, What's New in Georgetown column, July 27, 1967, 1. On the bridge at Genesee, see E. Christensen, "Lifelines," 3, 10. The bridge, designed by Frank Lundberg, was named a Prize Bridge by the American Institute of Steel Construction in 1971. For the view the bridge frames, see p. 125.

117. Barton, Stoddard, Milhollin and Higgins, and Taliesin Associated Architects of the Frank Lloyd Wright Foundation, *Vail Pass: Alignment Studies and Design Concepts*; C. L. Benson, "Highway in Harmony with Its Environment"; U.S. Department of Transportation, Federal Highway Administration, *I-70 in a Mountain Environment*; "Vail Pass Highway: Respecter of Mountain Ecology"; Montooth, "Landscape as an Extension of Architecture," 263–66.

118. Haley, *Wooing a Harsh Mistress*. On highway engineers' exasperation with having laypeople and politicians second-guess them on Glenwood Canyon, see Rose and Seely, "Getting the Interstate System Built," 35–36.

119. Haley, *Wooing a Harsh Mistress*.

120. Rocky Mountain Center on Environment, *Interstate 70 and the Glenwood Canyon Region*, p. VII-1.

121. John Gagnon, "Singing Star Discovers Canyon Wider Than It Looks," *Glenwood Post* (Glenwood Springs, CO), October 23, 1974, 1, 9; "Balladeer John Denver Gives Testimony a Tune," *Los Angeles Times*, February 28, 1977, A1.

122. Edwin Miller, "Sunshine Singer," *Seventeen*, March 1974, 112–13, 149; Colin Dangaard, "Denver Is on a Rocky Mountain High of Hits," *Chicago Tribune*, November 20, 1977, E2; Christopher Wren, "He Sings the Joy He Has in Living," *New York Times*, July 15, 1973, 111.

CONCLUSION: HOW TOURISM TOOK PLACE

1. ELF communiqué, October 21, 1998, quoted in Glick, *Powder Burn*, 3. Glick's riveting book is to date the definitive treatment of the case, though he wrote it before the

perpetrators were known. One participant turned state's witness in 2005, leading to the arrests of four others on charges related to the arson. One of the four committed suicide in jail; the other three were convicted in 2007. Two others involved in the early stages of the plot are believed as of this writing to have fled the country.

2. Deborah Frazier, "Vail Gets National Attention, Sympathy," *Rocky Mountain News*, October 25, 1998, 8A; John Cloud, "Fire on the Mountain," *Time*, November 2, 1998, 77. See also J. K. Perry, "Two Elk Fires Harmed Anti-Expansion Efforts," *Vail Daily*, December 14, 2005.

3. Riebsame, Gosnell, and Theobald, "Land Use and Landscape Change in the Colorado Mountains I"; Theobald, Gosnell, and Riebsame, "Land Use and Landscape Change in the Colorado Mountains II"; Travis, *New Geographies of the American West*, esp. introduction and chap. 1.

4. Christina Nelson, "Invading the West," *Denver Post Empire Magazine*, September 1, 1996, 11; "The West at War," *Newsweek*, July 17, 1995, 24–28; Jerome Cramer, "Cattlemen vs. 'Granola Bars,'" *Time*, September 30, 1991, 75; Kathy Khoury, "In Cactus Country, It's Corrals vs. Country Clubs," *Christian Science Monitor*, April 8, 1998, 3; Todd Wilkinson, "Rural Montana Rewrites Myth of Yuppie Sprawl," *Christian Science Monitor*, October 10, 1996, 1, 4; Ringholz, *Paradise Paved*; Todd Wilkinson, "Paradise Lost?," *Denver Post Magazine*, August 20, 1995, 10–13, 15.

5. See, for example, Judith Kohler, "Popular Western Resorts Become Trophy-Home Ghost Towns," *Los Angeles Times*, January 18, 1998, B1. For a serious effort to assess the impact of seasonal homes on communities and local economies, see Venturoni, *Social and Economic Effects of Second Homes*.

6. Good books named after, and focused on, the idea of a "New West" include Wiley and Gottlieb, *Empires in the Sun*; Riebsame, *Atlas of the New West*; Wilkinson, *Eagle Bird*; Limerick, *Something in the Soil*; Limerick, Cowell, and Collinge, *Remedies for a New West*; Ringholz, *Paradise Paved*; Nicholas, Bapis, and Harvey, *Imagining the Big Open*; Travis, *New Geographies of the American West*; Roche, *Political Culture of the New West*; Jackson and Kuhlken, *Rediscovered Frontier*; and Connors, *New West Reader*. An early use of the same term to mean the same thing was Adams, *New West: Landscapes along the Colorado Front Range*.

7. For two incisive cases against the concept of the "New West," raising some of the same objections I do here, see J. E. Taylor III, "Many Lives of the New West"; and Hyde, "Nothing New Under the Sun." Historian Patricia Limerick, probably the scholar most popularly associated with "New West" issues—and probably also the most thoughtful—herself points out that the term is not exactly new; see Limerick, *Something in the Soil*, 274–76.

8. Writers' Program of the Work Projects Administration in the State of Wyoming, *Wyoming*; Howe, *Rocky Mountain Empire*; Pomeroy, *In Search of the Golden West*, quotation is the title of chap. 6. The image of a cowboy on the ground and an airplane overhead seems to have been a recurring symbol of the Old-to-New West transition: not only did the Wyoming WPA guide use it, but so did the dust jacket of *Rocky Mountain Empire*. For other uses of the New West trope at midcentury, see J. E. Taylor, "Many Lives of the New West," 149–51.

9. "South Carolina: The New Plantations," *Economist*, October 16, 1993, 33; Elizabeth Levitan Spaid, "South Carolina's Island of Last Resort," *Christian Science Monitor*, March 8, 1995, 4; Sam Cook, "Trails, Trees, Traffic: State's Gorgeous Getaway Deals with Signs of the Times," *Duluth News-Tribune*, June 11, 1995, 1A, 14–16A; Keith Henderson, "'Sprawl-Mart' Endangers Vermont," *Christian Science Monitor*, December 6, 1993, 11–13; B. Harrison, *View from Vermont*, 241–44; David Holmstrom, "Key West: In a Community of Sun-Seekers and Tourists, One Man Goes to Extremes to Stand Up for His Island Home," *Christian Science Monitor*, March 9, 1994, 12–13. It is worth noting that conflicts over rural land and culture were no newer to the Midwest, South, or East than they were to the West. For especially perceptive studies of earlier conflicts, see B. Harrison, *View from Vermont*; Sherman, *Fast Lane on a Dirt Road*; Heasley, *A Thousand Pieces of Paradise*; Summers, *Consuming Nature*, esp. chaps. 5, 6; and Gibbons, *Wye Island*.

10. An unsettling introduction to this issue is D. Baron, *Beast in the Garden*.

11. Pergams and Zaradic, "Is Love of Nature in the US Becoming Love of Electronic Media?"; Pergams and Zaradic, "Evidence for a Fundamental and Pervasive Shift Away from Nature-Based Recreation"; Levi and Kocher, "Virtual Nature"; Louv, *Last Child in the Woods*.

12. On the challenges posed by global warming in the Rocky Mountain West, see B. Conover, *How the West Was Warmed*. On a climate-related crisis that is already well under way in the region, see [Nordhaus], *Bark Beetle Outbreaks in Western North America*; and Nikiforuk, *Empire of the Beetle*.

BIBLIOGRAPHY

MANUSCRIPT AND ARCHIVAL COLLECTIONS

Aspen Historical Society Written Material Files. Aspen.

Aspen Skiing Corporation/William V. Hodges Jr. Papers. Aspen Historical Society, Aspen.

Batten, Charles R. Papers. Collection no. CONS 8, Conservation Collection. Denver Public Library, Denver.

Bragdon, John Stewart. Records, 1949–61. Dwight D. Eisenhower Presidential Library and Museum, Abilene, KS.

Carhart, Arthur Hawthorne. Papers. Collection no. CONS 88, Conservation Collection. Denver Public Library, Denver.

Caulkins, George P., Jr. Papers, 1959–present. Private collection, Denver.

Citizens for Colorado's Future. Papers, 1971–72. Collection no. M78–1666, Western History Collection. Denver Public Library, Denver.

Cliff, Edward Parley. Papers. Collection no. CONS 14, Conservation Collection. Denver Public Library, Denver.

Club 20. Scrapbooks, loose-leaf notebooks, and files, 1954–present. Club 20 offices, Grand Junction, CO.

Cogburn, Elmer. Papers. Collection no. CONS 15, Conservation Collection. Denver Public Library, Denver.

Colorado Department of Local Affairs. Records. Colorado State Archives, Denver.

Colorado Department of Transportation. Records. Colorado State Archives, Denver.

Colorado Environmental Coalition. Records. Collection no. CONS 137, Conservation Collection. Denver Public Library, Denver.

Colorado Open Space. Collection no. CONS 104, Conservation Collection. Denver Public Library, Denver.

Colorado Ski and Snowboard Museum Photograph Collection. Colorado Ski and Snowboard Museum and Hall of Fame, Vail.

Colorado Ski Country USA. Records, 1965–89. Collection no. WH 1045, Western History Collection. Denver Public Library, Denver.

Denver Public Library Clippings Files, Western History and Genealogy Department. Denver.

Denver Public Library Government Documents Collection. Denver.

Draper, Benjamin Poff. Papers. Collection no. WH 1064, Western History Collection. Denver Public Library, Denver.

Eagle County Historical Society. Historical Files. Eagle Valley Library District, Eagle Branch, Eagle, CO.

Eisenhower, Dwight D. Papers as President of the United States, 1953–61 (Ann Whitman File). Administration Series, DDE Diary Series, Name Series, and Speech Series. Dwight D. Eisenhower Presidential Library and Museum, Abilene, KS.

Eisenhower, Dwight D. Records as President of the United States, 1953–61: White House Central Files. Alpha File and President's Personal File. Dwight D. Eisenhower Presidential Library and Museum, Abilene, KS.

Haney, Hal. Papers, 1950–2000. Collection no. WH 1484, Western History Collection. Denver Public Library, Denver.

Hauk, Paul I. Papers. Collection no. WH 1304, Western History Collection. Denver Public Library, Denver.

Hauk, Paul I. Papers, 1957–79. Private collection, Glenwood Springs, CO.

Norgren, Carl A. Papers. Dwight D. Eisenhower Presidential Library and Museum, Abilene, KS.

Norlin Library Pamphlet Collection. Archives. University of Colorado at Boulder Libraries, Boulder.

Protect Our Mountain Environment (Anti-Olympics Collection). Collection no. 735. Stephen H. Hart Library and Research Center, History Colorado Center, Denver.

Rocky Mountain Center on Environment. Papers. Collection no. CONS 65, Conservation Collection. Denver Public Library, Denver.

Shaw, Judge William R. Papers. Aspen Historical Society, Aspen.

Ski Industry Collection. University of Colorado at Boulder, Norlin Library, Western History Collection, Boulder.

Tutt Library Special Collections. Colorado College, Tutt Library, Colorado Springs.

Vail Associates. Papers, 1961–89. Collection no. WH 606, Western History Collection. Denver Public Library, Denver.

Vail Public Library Historical Files. Vail.

Vail Resorts. Photographs, 1960s–present. Vail Resorts Inc. offices, Vail.

PERIODICALS

Aspen Times. 1926–73.

Cervi's Rocky Mountain Journal, aka *Rocky Mountain Journal* (Denver). 1959–73.

Clear Creek Mining Journal (Idaho Springs, CO). 1955–68.

Colorado Business (Denver: Colorado State Chamber of Commerce). 1946–66.

Colorado Business Review (Boulder: Bureau of Business Research, University of Colorado). 1951–77.

Colorado Development Digest (Denver: Colorado Division of Commerce and Development). 1964–73.

Colorado Host (Denver: Colorado Visitors Bureau). 1958–64.

Colorado Information (Denver: Colorado State Association of County Commissioners, etc.). 1946–79.

Colorado Investor, aka *Colorado Investor Fact Sheet* (Denver). 1972–77.

Colorado Magazine, aka *Colorful Colorado/Rocky Mountain West* and later *Colorado and the West* and *Colorado/Rocky Mountain West* (Denver). 1965–80.

Colorado Motor Carrier, aka *Colorado Motor Carrier and Rocky Mountain Motor Carrier* and *Highland Highways* (Denver: Colorado Motor Carriers' Association). 1953–75.

Colorado Municipalities (Denver: Colorado Municipal League). 1945–75.

Colorado Outdoors (Denver: Colorado Department/Division of Game, Fish and Parks). 1952–72.

Colorado Resources Development Council Newsletter, aka *Colorado Development Council Newsletter* (Denver: Colorado Resources Development Council, Inc.). 1949–51.

Colorado Taxpayer Report (Denver: Colorado Public Expenditure Council). 1955–60.

Colorado Wonderland (Colorado Springs, later Boulder). 1949–56, 1959.

Coloscope (Denver: Colorado Association of Commerce and Industry). 1967–77.

COSCC Open Space Report, aka *COSF Open Space Report, COSC Newsletter,* and *The Conservator* (Denver: Colorado Open Space Coordinating Council, Inc.). 1966–73.

CRDC Progress (Denver: Colorado Resources Development Council, Inc.). 1948–49.

Daily Sentinel (Grand Junction, CO). 1954–75.

Denver Audubon Society Newsletter (Denver: Denver Branch, National Audubon Society). 1969–77.

Denver Post. 1924–80.

Denvertising (Denver: Advertising Club of Denver). 1954–62.

Eagle Valley Enterprise (Eagle, CO). 1945–73.

Ecologram: Environmental News for Business and Industry (Denver: Colorado Association of Commerce and Industry, Environmental Affairs Department). 1972–78.

Facts from the State Planning Division (Denver: Colorado State Planning Division). 1956–58.

Front Range Journal (Idaho Springs and Central City, CO). 1968–69.

Georgetown Courier (Georgetown, CO). 1945–57.

Glenwood Springs Sage (Glenwood Springs, CO). 1961–63.

Herald Democrat (Leadville, CO). 1932–72.

High Country News (Lander, WY; later Paonia, CO). 1970–present.

Holiday (Indianapolis, later Philadelphia). 1945–77.

Jeepers in the News (Denver: Mile-Hi Jeep Club of Colorado). 1958–75.

The Living Wilderness (Washington, DC: Wilderness Society). 1949–75.

Middle Park Times (Kremmling, CO). 1953–60.

Moly Mountain News, aka *Moly News* (Climax, CO: Climax Molybdenum Co.). 1949–61.

News from the Colorado Visitors Bureau (Denver: Colorado Visitors Bureau). 1965–68.

News Note (Vail). 1970.

Outdoor America, aka *The Izaak Walton Magazine: Outdoor America* (Chicago and Glenview, IL: Izaak Walton League of America). 1946–78.

Outdoor News (Denver: Colorado Department/Division of Game, Fish and Parks). 1968–72.

Over the Highways (Denver: Colorado Department of Highways). 1952–69.

Peak and Prairie (Denver: Rocky Mountain Chapter, Sierra Club). 1975–77.
Rocky Mountain Life (Denver). 1946–49.
Rocky Mountain News, aka *Denver Rocky Mountain News* (Denver). 1892–1980.
Rocky Mountain Sportsman and Western Wild Life (Denver). 1938–39.
ROMCOE Forum (Denver: Rocky Mountain Center on Environment). 1974–80.
Sierra Club Bulletin (San Francisco: Sierra Club). 1945–80.
Ski, aka *Ski Magazine* (Los Angeles). 1948–80.
Ski Illustrated (Concord, NH). 1936–38.
Skiing, aka *Rocky Mountain Skiing* (Denver, later New York). 1948–73.
The Spray (Denver: Colorado White Water Association). 1955–73.
Steamboat Pilot (Steamboat Springs, CO). 1953–60.
Summit County Journal (Breckenridge, CO). 1955–73.
Trail and Timberline (Denver: Colorado Mountain Club). 1918–80.
Trailways Magazine (Chicago: National Trailways System). 1937–50.
Trout (Saginaw, MI, later Denver: Trout Unlimited). 1962–75.
United Motor Courts Review (Denver: United Motor Court Association). 1954.
Vail Trail. 1965–2008.
Western Skiing, aka *Western Summer* (Los Angeles). 1945–48.

PROMOTIONAL MATERIALS

Aspen Chamber of Commerce. Pamphlets and print advertisements. 1952–60.
Aspen Company. Brochures and print advertisements. 1950–60.
Aspen Skiing Corporation. Pamphlets, brochures, and print advertisements. 1947–2002.
Best Western Motels. Pamphlets and brochures. 1948–67.
Burlington Route, aka Chicago, Burlington & Quincy Railroad. Pamphlets and print advertisements. 1922–63.
Carter Oil Company. Print advertisements and maps. 1957–59.
Clear Creek County Chamber of Commerce. Brochures and print advertisements. 1947–64.
Club 20. Brochures. 1955–92.
Colorado Advertising and Publicity Committee, dba Department of Development, Department of Public Relations, Sportsmen's Hospitality Committee, and Winter Sports Committee. Pamphlets, brochures, and print advertisements. 1941–63.
Colorado Association. Pamphlets and print advertisements. 1930–32.
Colorado Division of Commerce and Development, Advertising and Publicity Section. Pamphlets and brochures. 1964–68.
Colorado Dude and Guest Ranch Association. Pamphlets. 1935–2002.
Colorado Highway 6 Association. Pamphlets and print advertisements. 1956–57.
Colorado Motel Association. Brochure. 1963.
Colorado Ski Country USA. Annual guidebook (*Colorado Ski Country USA*, aka *Guide to Colorado Ski Country USA*). 1968–80.
Colorado State Chamber of Commerce. Pamphlets and brochures. 1956–64.

Colorado State Highway Department, later Colorado Department of Highways. Annual official state highway maps (*Travel Colorado Highways* and later *Colorful Colorado*). 1939–80.

Colorado Visitors Bureau. Pamphlets and annual *Manual of Colorado Skiing*. 1958–65.

Congress Motor Hotels, aka Congress of Motor Hotels. Pamphlets and print advertisements. 1957–60.

Continental Air Lines. Brochures and print advertisements. 1948–75.

Continental Oil Company, dba Conoco Travel Bureau. Pamphlets and maps. 1933–67.

Denver & Rio Grande Western Railroad. Pamphlets and print advertisements. 1892–1955.

Denver Convention and Visitors Bureau. Pamphlets, brochures, and print advertisements. 1925–72.

Frontier Airlines. Print advertisements. 1952–56.

Georgetown Civic Association. Brochure. [ca. 1953].

Grand County Lions Club. Brochure. 1936.

Idaho Springs Chamber of Commerce. Pamphlets, brochures, and print advertisements. 1898–1963.

Leadville Lions Club. Pamphlet. 1943.

National U.S. Highway 40 Association. Brochures and print advertisements. 1953–57.

Northern Colorado Highway Association. Brochure. [ca. 1940].

Rainbow Cottage Camp System, Inc. Brochure. [ca. 1935].

Union Pacific Railroad. Pamphlets and print advertisements. 1920–65.

United Air Lines. Print advertisements. 1946–75.

Vail Associates Inc., later Vail Resorts Inc. Pamphlets, brochures, and print advertisements. 1963–2002.

Western Air Lines. Print advertisements. 1946.

Western Colorado Chamber of Commerce. Pamphlet. 1922.

GOVERNMENT DOCUMENTS

Aspen, City of. Ordinances, 1945–75. Office of the City Clerk, Aspen.

Aspen, City of. City Council. Minutes, 1935–72. Office of the City Clerk, Aspen.

Aspen Regional Planning Commission. Records, 1954–55. Office of Community Development, City of Aspen.

Breckenridge, Town of. Ordinances, 1960–72. Office of the Town Clerk, Breckenridge.

Breckenridge, Town of. Board of Trustees. Minutes, 1945–72. Office of the Town Clerk, Breckenridge.

Breckenridge, Town of. Planning and Zoning Commission. Minutes, 1972. Office of the Town Clerk, Breckenridge.

Colorado. Department of Highways. Annual reports, 1953–69. Colorado State Archives, Denver.

———. Budgets. 1953–73. Colorado State Archives, Denver.

———. *Paths of Progress*. [1954?].

———. *A Major Link in America's Interstate System*. March 1956.

Colorado. Division of Highways. *Interstate 70: Through the Colorado Rockies.* Produced in cooperation with the Federal Highway Administration. [1970?].

Colorado. Department of Local Affairs. Division of Commerce and Development. Advisory Committee. Records, 1968–72. Colorado State Archives, Denver.

Colorado. Department of Local Affairs. Division of Local Government. *Problems of Local Government.* 1973.

Colorado. Department of Local Affairs. Division of Planning. *The Division of Planning: A Profile.* Information Services Report no. 1. Prepared by Gary Malmberg. April 1976.

———. *Colorado's Regions.* Information Services Report no. 2. Prepared by Gary Malmberg. April 1976.

———. *Colorado Winter Resource Management Plan.* August 1976.

———. *From Bonanza to Last Chance: Changing Economic Expectations in Colorado.* Prepared with the aid of the Thirteen Planning and Management Regions. March 1978.

———. *Growth and Human Settlement in Colorado: Working Draft for Discussion Purposes.* September 1977.

Colorado. Department of Natural Resources. *Colorado's Natural Resources: Opportunity and Challenge.* Prepared by Morris E. Garnsey and Roma K. McNickle, University of Colorado. [1957].

———. *A Critical Survey of Several Forecasts of the Population of Colorado.* Prepared by William Petersen, University of Colorado. July 1957.

———. *Mineral Resources.* Prepared by F. M. Van Tuyl and E. H. Crabtree, Colorado School of Mines. July 1957.

———. *Climate as a Natural Resource.* Prepared by Loren Crow, Denver, and Robert Low, High Altitude Observatory, Boulder. November 1957.

———. *Fish and Wildlife Resources.* Prepared by Ira N. Gabrielson, Wildlife Management Institute, Washington, DC. November 1957.

———. *Recreation Resources and Facilities.* Prepared by L. J. Crampon and Ronald D. Lemon, University of Colorado, Bureau of Business Research. November 1957.

———. *Water Resources of Colorado.* Prepared by Stefan H. Robock, Midwest Research Institute, Kansas City, MO, based on statements by the Colorado Water Conservation Board, Colorado State Department of Public Health, Office of the State Engineer, U.S. Bureau of Reclamation, U.S. Soil Conservation Service, and U.S. Geological Survey. November 1957.

Colorado. Department of Natural Resources. Division of Game, Fish and Parks. *1970 Colorado Comprehensive Outdoor Recreation Plan.* [1970].

Colorado. Department of Natural Resources. Division of Parks and Outdoor Recreation. *The Colorado Division of Parks and Outdoor Recreation Historical Summary.* [1990].

Colorado. Department of Natural Resources. Geological Survey. *The Governor's Conference on Environmental Geology.* Special Publication no. 1. [1969].

Colorado. Division of Natural Resources. Department of Game, Fish and Parks. *Outdoor Recreation in Colorado: A Digest of the State of Colorado's Comprehensive Plan for Providing Outdoor Recreation.* 1965.

Colorado Environmental Commission. *Colorado: Options for the Future; Final Report of the Colorado Environmental Commission.* 1972.

Colorado. Highway Planning Committee. *The Committee Reports to John Q. Public on the Long Range Highway Plan.* [1949?].

Colorado. Land Use Commission. *Progress Report: Colorado State Land Use Plan and Management System.* February 1972.

Colorado. Mineral Resources Board. *Mineral Resources of Colorado.* Prepared under the supervision of John W. Vanderwilt. 1947.

Colorado. State Advertising and Publicity Committee. Annual reports, 1941–63.

―――. *Telling the World About Colorado: General Report 1941–1942, State of Colorado Advertising and Publicity Committee.* 1942.

―――. *Making the World Colorado Conscious: General Report 1941–1946.* 1946.

Colorado. State Advertising and Publicity Department [sic]. *Annual Report, Fiscal Year 1950–51.* 1951.

Colorado. State Board of Immigration. *Colorado: The Western Slope.* 1930.

―――. *The Northwest Plateau, Including the Moffat Tunnel District.* 1930.

Colorado. State Highway Commission/State Highway Advisory Board. Minutes, 1913–72. Central Files, Colorado Department of Transportation, Denver.

Colorado. State Park and Recreation Board. *A State Park System for Colorado: Digest of a Study Including Recommendations for a Long-Range Program.* February 1959.

Colorado. State Planning Commission. *The Present Status of the Highways of the State, and a Preliminary Plan for the Future System, [with] A Condensed Summary of the History of Highway Financing and Construction.* April 1937.

―――. *Year Book of the State of Colorado, 1937–1938.* [1938].

―――. *Suggested Outline for Economic Development in Colorado.* 2 vols. January 1945.

―――. *Ten Years of State Planning in Colorado.* Prepared by Elmore Petersen. November 1945.

―――. *Year Book of the State of Colorado, 1945–1947.* [1947].

―――. *State of Colorado Year Book, 1951 to 1955.* [1955].

―――. *Report for 1955 of the Colorado State Planning Commission to the Governor of Colorado and the Colorado General Assembly.* January 1956.

Colorado. State Planning Commission and Colorado Water Conservation Board. *Public Land Ownership in Colorado: Tabulation and Maps.* April 1944.

Colorado. State Planning Division. *Colorado, 1956–1958: Year Book of the State of Colorado.* [1958].

―――. *Colorado Year Book, 1962–1964.* [1964].

Colorado. State Planning Office. *A Proposed Regional Delineation for the State of Colorado.* Prepared by Richard E. Hart. July 1968.

―――. *Annexation: Colorado Legislative Notebook for Local Officials and Planning Commissions, Revised thru 1970/2nd Regular Session, 47th General Assembly.* [1970?].

―――. *County Zoning: Colorado Legislative Notebook for Local Officials and Planning Commissions, Revised thru 1970/2nd Regular Session, 47th General Assembly.* [1970?].

―――. *Improvement Districts in Cities and Towns: Revised thru 1970, 2nd Regular Session, 47th General Assembly.* [1970?].

―――. *Municipal Zoning: Colorado Legislative Notebook for Local Officials and Planning Commissioners, Revised thru 1970/2nd Regular Session 47th General Assembly.* [1970?].

Dillon, Town of. Ordinances, 1942–68. Office of the Town Clerk, Dillon, CO.

Dillon, Town of. Board of Trustees. Minutes, 1940–66. Office of the Town Clerk, Dillon, CO.

Eagle County. Board of Commissioners. Proceedings, 1960–73. Office of the County Clerk, Eagle, CO.

Federal Reserve Bank of San Francisco. *Western Power and Fuel Outlook.* Supplement to Monthly Review. November 1950.

Georgetown, Town of. Board of Selectmen. Minutes, 1938–71. Office of the Town Clerk, Georgetown, CO.

Granby, Town of. Board of Trustees. Minutes, 1949–60. Office of the Town Clerk, Granby, CO.

Grand County. Board of Commissioners. Minutes, 1945–64. Office of the County Clerk, Hot Sulphur Springs, CO.

Kremmling, Town of. Board of Trustees. Minutes, 1945–64. Office of the Town Clerk, Kremmling, CO.

Lake County. Board of Commissioners. Minutes, 1945–72. Office of the County Clerk, Leadville, CO.

Lake County. Board of Commissioners, and Jess A. Larch, Leadville–Lake County Regional Planning Commission. *Lake County I-70 Brief: Vail Pass or Red Buffalo Route.* [1966].

Northwest Colorado Council of Governments. *Work Program and Policies.* [1974?].

Outdoor Recreation Resources Review Commission. *Outdoor Recreation in America: A Report to the President and to the Congress by the Outdoor Recreation Resources Review Commission.* Washington, DC: GPO, 1962.

———. *Wilderness and Recreation: A Report on Resources, Values, and Problems.* ORRRC Study Report no. 3. Prepared by the Wildland Research Center, University of California. 1962.

Pitkin County. Board of Commissioners. Minutes, 1945–72. Office of the County Clerk, Aspen.

Pitkin County. Planning and Zoning Commission. Minutes, 1958–72. Office of the County Clerk, Aspen.

Pitkin County. Planning Commission and Board of Commissioners. *Zoning District Map.* 1955.

President's Council on Recreation and Natural Beauty. *From Sea to Shining Sea: A Report on the American Environment. Our Natural Heritage.* 1968.

Public Land Law Review Commission. *One Third of the Nation's Land: A Report to the President and to the Congress by the Public Land Law Review Commission.* 1970.

Summit County. Board of Commissioners. Minutes, 1945–72. Office of the County Clerk, Breckenridge.

Summit County. Planning Office. *The Visual Environment of Summit County Colorado: Examination—Analysis—Recommendations.* Prepared by David Vince. September 1974.

U.S. Congress. Senate. Committee on Public Works. *National Highway Program: Hearings Before a Subcommittee of the Committee on Public Works . . . on S. 1048, S. 1072, S. 1160,* and S. 1573, Bills Relating to the National Highway Program. 84th Cong., February 21, 23, 25, 28, March 2, 4, 10, 11, 14, 16, 18, 22, 23, 24, 28, 29, 31, April 1, 13, 14, and 15, 1955.

U.S. Department of Agriculture. Forest Service. *Outdoor Recreation in the National Forests.* Agriculture Information Bulletin no. 301. September 1965.

———. *Planning Considerations for Winter Sports Resort Development.* Prepared in cooperation with the National Ski Areas Association. 1973.

U.S. Department of Agriculture. Forest Service. Intermountain Forest and Range Experiment Station (Ogden, UT). *Skiing Trends and Opportunities in the Western States.* USFS Research Paper INT-34. Prepared by Roscoe B. Harrington. 1967.

U.S. Department of Agriculture. Forest Service. Pacific Northwest Research Station (Portland, OR). *Public Lands and Private Recreation Enterprise: Policy Issues from a Historical Perspective.* General Technical Report PNW-GTR-556. Prepared by Tom Quinn. 2002.

U.S. Department of Agriculture. Forest Service. Rocky Mountain Forest and Range Experiment Station (Fort Collins, CO) and Intermountain Forest and Range Experiment Station (Ogden, UT). *The Forest Resource of Colorado.* U.S. Forest Service Resource Bulletin INT-3. Prepared by Robert L. Miller and Grover A. Choate. 1964.

U.S. Department of Agriculture. Forest Service. Rocky Mountain Region. *Final Environmental Impact Statement for the White River National Forest Land and Resource Management Plan, 2002 Revision.* [2002].

U.S. Department of Agriculture. Forest Service. White River National Forest, Holy Cross Ranger Station. Records, 1957–present. Minturn, CO.

U.S. Department of Agriculture. Soil Conservation Service. *An Appraisal of Outdoor Recreation Potentials in Eagle County, Colorado.* Produced in cooperation with the Eagle County Technical Action Panel. April 1968.

———. *An Appraisal of Outdoor Recreation Potentials in Garfield and Pitkin Counties, Colorado.* Produced in cooperation with the Garfield and Pitkin Counties Technical Action Panel. June 1968.

———. *An Appraisal of Outdoor Recreation Potentials in Grand and Summit Counties, Colorado.* Produced in cooperation with the Middle Park Technical Action Panel. June 1968.

———. *Outdoor Recreation Potential: Colorado.* June 1973.

U.S. Department of Commerce. Bureau of the Census. *Census of Population: 1960; Volume 1: Characteristics of the Population; Part 7: Colorado.* 1963.

———. *1970 Census of Population; Volume 1: Characteristics of the Population; Part 7: Colorado.* January 1973.

U.S. Department of the Interior. Bureau of Land Management. *Room to Roam: A Recreation Guide to the Public Lands.* January 1968.

U.S. Department of the Interior. Bureau of Outdoor Recreation. Mid-Continent Region (Denver). *The Selection of a Highway Route: Choices and Values; A Report on the "Red Buffalo" Section of Interstate Highway 70 in Colorado.* January 1968.

U.S. Department of the Interior. Geological Survey. *Mineral Resources of the Gore Range–Eagles Nest Primitive Area and Vicinity, Summit and Eagle Counties, Colorado.* 1970.

U.S. Department of the Interior. National Park Service. *Study of Alternatives: Georgetown–Silver Plume Historic District, Colorado.* September 1989.

U.S. Department of the Interior. Office of the Secretary. Division of Information. *The Natural Resources of Colorado.* 1963.

U.S. Department of Transportation. Federal Highway Administration. Office of Development. In cooperation with the Department of Agriculture, Forest Service. *I-70 in a Mountain Environment: Vail Pass, Colorado.* Prepared by the Colorado Department of Highways. 1978.

Vail, Town of. Articles of incorporation, 1966. Records of the Colorado Department of State, Colorado State Archives, Denver.

———. Ordinances, Series of 1966–74. Office of the Town Clerk, Vail.

———. Budgets, 1969–74. Historical Files. Vail Public Library, Vail.

———. Annual reports, 1971–73. Historical files, Vail Public Library, Vail.

———. Home rule charter, 1972. Records of the Colorado Department of State, Colorado State Archives, Denver.

Vail, Town of. Board of Trustees. Minutes, 1966–73. Office of the Town Clerk, Vail.

Vail, Town of. Home Rule Charter Commission. Minutes, 1972. Office of the Town Clerk, Vail.

OTHER REPORTS AND PLANS

Allen, Gerald L. *Colorado Ski and Winter Recreation Statistics, 1969.* Boulder: University of Colorado, Graduate School of Business Administration, Business Research Division, 1970.

American Society of Planning Officials, with contributions from the Conservation Foundation, Urban Land Institute, and Richard L. Ragatz Associates Inc. *Subdividing Rural America: Impacts of Recreational Lot and Second Home Development.* Prepared for the Council on Environmental Quality; Office of Policy Development and Research, Department of Housing and Urban Development; and Appalachian Regional Commission. Washington, DC: GPO, 1976.

Barton, Stoddard, Milhollin & Higgins, and Taliesin Associated Architects of the Frank Lloyd Wright Foundation. *Vail Pass: Alignment Studies and Design Concepts.* Prepared for the Colorado Division of Highways. Denver, May 1972.

Bickert, Carl von E., Judith L. Oldham, and John J. Ryan. *A Profile of the Tourist Market in Colorado, 1968.* Prepared for the Colorado Division of Commerce and Development. Denver: University of Denver, Denver Research Institute, Industrial Economics Division, 1969.

Brown, Gerald E. *Master Plan for Future Land Use and Development of Eagle County, Colorado.* Prepared for the Eagle County Planning Commission. September 1973.

Burghardt, Galen, Jr., Joseph Winston, Jack Harbeston, and Consulting Services Corporation. *Study of Impact of Public Lands on Selected Regional Economies: A Study Prepared for the Public Land Law Review Commission.* Rev. ed. February 1970.

Colorado Coordinating Committee for Planning and Zoning. *Let's Plan Colorado's Future: A Guide to the Orderly Development of Rural and Urban Communities.* Denver: Colorado State Planning Commission, January 1953.

Colorado Ski Country USA. *An Impact Study [of] the Colorado Ski Industry: Its Impact on Mountain Counties and Communities*. [Denver, 1976?].

Crampon, L. J. *Business in the Small Cities of Colorado*. Prepared for the Board of Industrial Development Research. Boulder: University of Colorado, Bureau of Business Research, March 1949.

———. *Glenwood Springs Business Report*. Prepared for the Glenwood Springs Chamber of Commerce and the Board of Industrial Development Research. Boulder: University of Colorado, Bureau of Business Research, March 1949.

———. *Promoting Colorado's Industrial Potential*. Boulder: University of Colorado, Bureau of Business Research, July 1952.

———. *The Tourist and Colorado*. Boulder: University of Colorado, Bureau of Business Research, February 1956.

———. *The Tourist and Colorado, 1957: A Supplement to the 1955 Study*. Prepared with the assistance of the Colorado State Chamber of Commerce. Boulder: University of Colorado, Bureau of Business Research, October 1957.

———. *1960 Colorado Travel Review*. Boulder: University of Colorado, Bureau of Business Research, September 1960.

———. *The Development of Tourism*. Boulder: University of Colorado, Bureau of Business Research, [ca. 1963].

———. *Tourist Development Notes*. 3 vols. Boulder: University of Colorado, Graduate School of Business Administration, Business Research Division, [ca. 1964].

Crampon, L. J., and F. W. Ellinghaus. *1953 Colorado Statewide Summer Tourist Survey*. Published under a grant from the Colorado Advertising and Publicity Committee. Boulder: University of Colorado, Bureau of Business Research, December 1953.

Crampon, L. J., and Donald F. Lawson. *1953 Colorado Summer Tourist Traffic Flow Study*. Boulder: University of Colorado, Bureau of Business Research, August 1954.

Crampon, L. J., Donald F. Lawson, and F. W. Ellinghaus. *Report on the Economic Potential of Western Colorado*. Prepared for the Colorado Water Conservation Board. Boulder: University of Colorado, Bureau of Business Research, 1953.

Crampon, L. J., and Ronald D. Lemon. *Skiing in the Southern Rocky Mountain Region*. Prepared for the Ski Area Operators Committee of the Southern Rocky Mountain Ski Association. Boulder: University of Colorado, Bureau of Business Research, [1957].

E. Lionel Pavlo Engineering Co. *Interstate Highway Location Study, Dotsero to Empire Junction: State Project No. HPS-1-(20)*. Prepared for the Colorado Department of Highways. New York, 1960.

The First Vail Symposium: "The Role of the Mountain Recreation Community." Proceedings of the First Vail Symposium, July 30–31, 1971. Vail: Town of Vail and Vail Resort Association, 1971.

Foss, Phillip O., ed. *Outdoor Recreation and Environmental Quality: Proceedings of the Western Resources Conference, Fort Collins, Colorado, 1972*. Fort Collins: Colorado State University, Environmental Resources Center, 1973.

Gage Davis Associates Inc. *The Vail Mountain / Gore Valley Capacity Study*. Prepared for the U.S. Forest Service, Vail Associates Inc., Vail Resort Association, Town of Vail, and Eagle County. Boulder, June 1980.

Gilmore, John S., and Mary K. Duff. *The Evolving Political Economy of Pitkin County: Growth Management by Consensus in a Boom Community.* Denver: University of Denver, Denver Research Institute, March 1974.

Goeldner, C. R. *The Aspen Skier, Volume 1: Lift Survey.* Boulder: University of Colorado, Graduate School of Business Administration, Business Research Division, 1974.

———. *The Aspen Skier, Volume 2: Lodging Survey.* Boulder: University of Colorado, Graduate School of Business Administration, Business Research Division, 1974.

Goeldner, C. R., and Gerald Allen. *Colorado Ski and Winter Recreation Statistics, 1973.* Boulder: University of Colorado, Graduate School of Business Administration, Business Research Division, 1974.

Goeldner, C. R., and Yvonne Sletta. *The Breckenridge Skier.* Boulder: University of Colorado, Graduate School of Business Administration, Business Research Division, 1975.

Harman, O'Donnell & Henninger Associates Inc. *Planning Study of the Gore Valley Area and the Town of Vail.* Prepared for the Town of Vail. Denver, October 1969.

Howard, Needles, Tammen & Bergendorff and Singstad & Baillie. *Continental Divide Tunnels: Consolidated Report on Engineering Studies, Estimates of Construction and Other Costs, Estimates of Traffic and Revenue, and Methods of Financing as a Toll Project.* Prepared for the Colorado Department of Highways. Kansas City, MO, and New York, January 1954.

Huddleston, Sam L. *Leadville and Lake County, Colorado: The Master Plan.* Produced in cooperation with the Leadville–Lake County Regional Planning Commission. Denver, August 1963.

———. *Summit County, Colorado: The Master Plan.* Produced in cooperation with the Summit County Planning Commission. Denver: August 1963.

Leo A. Daly Company. *Aspen Area General Plan: Inventory Report, 1965.* Prepared for the City of Aspen, Planning and Zoning Commission, and Pitkin County, Planning and Zoning Commission. San Francisco, 1965.

———. *Aspen Area General Plan: Final Report, 1966.* Prepared for the City of Aspen, Planning and Zoning Commission, and Pitkin County, Planning and Zoning Commission. San Francisco, 1966.

Local Area Statistics on Eagle County, Colorado. Prepared for the Colorado Department of Employment, Resources and Community Development Division. Boulder: University of Colorado, Bureau of Business Research, March 1961.

Monarchi, David E. *Colorado State and Regional Population Projections. 1970 to 2000.* Prepared for the Colorado Department of Local Affairs, Division of Planning. Boulder: University of Colorado, Graduate School of Business Management, Business Research Division, July 1975.

Nance, James Vernon, Jr. *Recreational Condominiums in Summit County, Colorado: Locational Factors and Policy Implications.* Boulder: University of Colorado, Graduate School of Business Administration, Business Research Division, 1976.

National Research Council. Highway Research Board. Committee on Highway Organization and Administration. *Report of a Study of the Highway Laws, Organization, and Procedures of Colorado.* Part I: *Improving the Colorado State Highway Department through Administrative and Executive Action.* Washington, DC, July 1948.

———. *Report of a Study of the Highway Laws, Organization, and Procedures of Colorado*. Part II: *Legislative Requirements for Improved Highway Administration in Colorado*. Washington, DC, January 1949.

Neuzil, Dennis R. *Interstate 70: Dillon to Dowd, Colorado; A Case Study in Highway Economy*. Newark: University of Delaware, Department of Civil Engineering, 1967.

Pilot Study of the Colorado Tourist Industry. Denver: Colorado Resources Development Council, [ca. 1949].

Rocky Mountain Center on Environment. *Interstate 70 and the Glenwood Canyon: Choices for Posterity*. Denver, October 15, 1971.

Royston, Hanamoto, Beck & Abey, and Livingston & Blayney. *The Vail Plan*. Prepared for the Town of Vail. San Francisco, August 1973.

Standley, Stacy, III. *The Impact of the Vail Ski Resort: An Input-Output Analysis*. Boulder: University of Colorado, Graduate School of Business Administration, Business Research Division, 1971.

Summary of 1953 Colorado Statewide Tourist Survey. Prepared for the 1954 Governor's Travel and Hospitality Conference. Boulder: University of Colorado, Bureau of Business Research, May 1954.

Thompson, Phyllis T. *The Use of Mountain Recreational Resources: A Comparison of Recreation and Tourism in the Colorado Rockies and the Swiss Alps*. Boulder: University of Colorado, Graduate School of Business Administration, Business Research Division, 1971.

Wilcox, A. T., and G. B. Wetterberg. *Outdoor Recreation Resources . . . Eagle County, Colorado 1967*. Fort Collins: Colorado State University, College of Forestry and Natural Resources, Department of Recreation Resources, 1971.

BOOKS, ARTICLES, PAPERS, THESES

Abbott, Carl. "The Metropolitan Region: Western Cities in the New Urban Era." In *The Twentieth-Century West: Historical Interpretations*, edited by Gerald D. Nash and Richard W. Etulain, 71–98. Albuquerque: University of New Mexico Press, 1989.

———. *The Metropolitan Frontier: Cities in the Modern American West*. Tucson: University of Arizona Press, 1993.

———. *How Cities Won the West: Four Centuries of Urban Change in Western North America*. Albuquerque: University of New Mexico Press, 2008.

Abbott, Carl, Stephen J. Leonard, and David McComb. *Colorado: A History of the Centennial State*. 3d ed. Niwot: University Press of Colorado, 1994.

Ackermann, Marsha E. *Cool Comfort: America's Romance with Air-Conditioning*. Washington, DC: Smithsonian Institution Press, 2002.

Adams, Robert. *The New West: Landscapes along the Colorado Front Range*. Boulder: Colorado Associated University Press, 1974.

Akerman, James R. "Selling Maps, Selling Highways: Rand McNally's 'Blazed Trails' Program." *Imago Mundi* 45 (1993): 77–89.

Albanese, Catherine L. *Nature Religion in America: From the Algonkian Indians to the New Age*. Chicago: University of Chicago Press, 1990.

Allen, E. John B. *From Skisport to Skiing: One Hundred Years of an American Sport, 1840–1940*. Amherst: University of Massachusetts Press, 1993.

———. *The Culture and Sport of Skiing: From Antiquity to World War II*. Amherst: University of Massachusetts Press, 2007.

Allen, James Sloan. *The Romance of Commerce and Culture: Capitalism, Modernism, and the Chicago-Aspen Crusade for Cultural Reform*. Chicago: University of Chicago Press, 1983.

[Allen, Wayne L., Odette Baehler, George Simonds et al.]. *Historic Georgetown: Centennial Gazette, 1868–1968*. [Georgetown, CO: Georgetown Chamber of Commerce, 1968].

American Automobile Association. *Western Tour Book*, aka *Western Official AAA Tour Book*, *AAA Official Western Tour Book*, and *AAA Western Tour Book*. Annual editions. Washington, DC: American Automobile Association, 1926–58.

———. *Directory of Motor Courts and Cottages*. Washington, DC: American Automobile Association, 1939–40.

———. *Western Accommodations Directory*. Washington, DC: American Automobile Association, 1954–55 and 1958–59.

Andrews, Richard N. L. *Managing the Environment, Managing Ourselves: A History of American Environmental Policy*. 2d ed. New Haven, CT: Yale University Press, 2006.

Andrews, Thomas G. "'Made by Toile?' Tourism, Labor, and the Construction of the Colorado Landscape, 1858–1917." *Journal of American History* 92, no. 3 (December 2005): 837–63.

Aquila, Richard, ed. *Wanted Dead or Alive: The American West in Popular Culture*. Urbana: University of Illinois Press, 1996.

Aron, Cindy S. *Working at Play: A History of Vacations in the United States*. New York: Oxford University Press, 1999.

Athearn, Frederic J. *An Isolated Empire: A History of Northwestern Colorado*. 3d ed. Cultural Resources Series no. 2. Denver: Bureau of Land Management, Colorado State Office, 1982.

Athearn, Robert G. *Rebel of the Rockies: A History of the Denver and Rio Grande Western Railroad*. New Haven, CT: Yale University Press, 1962.

———. "The Tin Can Tourist's West." In *Montana and the West: Essays in Honor of K. Ross Toole*, edited by Rex C. Myers and Harry W. Fritz, 105–21. Boulder: Pruett, 1984.

———. *The Mythic West in Twentieth-Century America*. Lawrence: University Press of Kansas, 1986.

Athearn, Robert G., and Carl Ubbelohde. *Centennial Colorado: Its Exciting Story*. Denver: E. L. Chambers, 1959.

Atwood, Wallace W. *The Rocky Mountains*. American Mountain Series, vol. 3. New York: Vanguard Press, 1945.

Avila, Eric. *Popular Culture in the Age of White Flight: Fear and Fantasy in Suburban Los Angeles*. Berkeley: University of California Press, 2006.

Bailey, Alfred M. "High Country of Colorado." *National Geographic*, July 1946, 43–72.

Baker, Alan R. H. *Geography and History: Bridging the Divide*. Cambridge: Cambridge University Press, 2003.

Baldwin, Donald N. *The Quiet Revolution: The Grass Roots of Today's Wilderness Preservation Movement*. Boulder: Pruett, 1972.

Bancroft, Caroline. *Historic Central City: Its Complete Story as Guide and Souvenir.* Denver: Bancroft Booklets, 1951.

———. *Gulch of Gold: A History of Central City, Colorado.* Denver: Sage Books, 1958.

———. *Colorful Colorado: Its Dramatic History.* 2d ed. Boulder: Johnson Publishing, 1963.

———. *Famous Aspen: Its Fabulous Past—Its Lively Present.* Rev. ed. Boulder: Johnson Publishing, 1967. Update of *Famous Aspen: Its Complete Story as Guide and Souvenir.* Aspen: Aspen Times, 1951.

Baranowski, Shelley, and Ellen Furlough, eds. *Being Elsewhere: Tourism, Consumer Culture, and Identity in Modern Europe and North America.* Ann Arbor: University of Michigan Press, 2001.

Barlow-Perez, Sally. *A History of Aspen.* 2d ed. Basalt, CO: WHO Press, 2000.

Barnett, Gabrielle. "Drive-By Viewing: Visual Consciousness and Forest Preservation in the Automobile Age." *Technology and Culture* 45, no. 1 (January 2004): 30–54.

Baron, David. *The Beast in the Garden: A Modern Parable of Man and Nature.* New York: Norton, 2004.

Baron, Jill S., ed. *Rocky Mountain Futures: An Ecological Perspective.* Washington, DC: Island Press, 2002.

Baron, Robert C., Stephen J. Leonard, and Thomas J. Noel, eds. *Thomas Hornsby Ferril and the American West.* Golden, CO: Fulcrum, 1996.

Barringer, Mark. "Mission Impossible: National Park Development in the 1950s." *Journal of the West* 38 (January 1999): 22–26.

Barrows, Pete, and Judith Holmes. *Colorado's Wildlife Story.* Denver: Colorado Department of Natural Resources, Division of Wildlife, 1990.

Beeman, Randal S., and James A. Pritchard. *A Green and Permanent Land: Ecology and Agriculture in the Twentieth Century.* Lawrence: University Press of Kansas, 2001.

Belasco, Warren James. *Americans on the Road: From Autocamp to Motel, 1910–1945.* Cambridge, MA: MIT Press, 1979.

Belk, Russell W., Melanie Wallendorf, and John F. Sherry Jr. "The Sacred and the Profane in Consumer Behavior: Theodicy on the Odyssey." *Journal of Consumer Research* 16, no. 1 (June 1989): 1–38.

Benson, Cade L. "Highway in Harmony with Its Environment." *Civil Engineering* 46, no. 9 (September 1976): 56–59.

Benson, Jack A. "Skiing at Camp Hale: Mountain Troops during World War II." *Western Historical Quarterly* 15, no. 2 (April 1984): 163–74.

Benson, Maxine. "Dwight D. Eisenhower and the West." *Journal of the West* 34, no. 2 (April 1995): 58–65.

Berube, Alan, Audrey Singer, Jill H. Wilson, and William H. Frey. *Finding Exurbia: America's Fast-Growing Communities at the Metropolitan Fringe.* Washington, DC: Brookings Institution Press, 2006.

"Better Homes and Gardens" Family Camping. [Des Moines, IA]: Meredith Publishing Co., 1961.

Beyers, William B., and Peter B. Nelson. "Contemporary Development Forces in the Nonmetropolitan West: New Insights from Rapidly Growing Communities." *Journal of Rural Studies* 16, no. 4 (October 2000): 459–74.

Black, Robert C., III. *Island in the Rockies: The History of Grand County, Colorado, to 1930.* Boulder: Pruett, for the Grand County Pioneer Society, 1969.

Blackford, Mansel. *Fragile Paradise: The Impact of Tourism on Maui, 1959–2000.* Lawrence: University Press of Kansas, 2001.

Blain, Carmen, Stuart E. Levy, and J. R. Brent Ritchie. "Destination Branding: Insights and Practices from Destination Management Organizations." *Journal of Travel Research* 43 (May 2005): 328–38.

Blair, Edward. *Leadville: Colorado's Magic City.* Boulder: Pruett, 1980.

Blake, Peter. *God's Own Junkyard: The Planned Deterioration of America's Landscape.* New York: Holt, Rinehart and Winston, 1964.

Booth, Douglas E. *Searching for Paradise: Economic Development and Environmental Change in the Mountain West.* Lanham, MD: Rowman and Littlefield, 2002.

Borne, Lawrence R. *Dude Ranching: A Complete History.* Albuquerque: University of New Mexico Press, 1983.

Bowen, Ezra. *The Book of American Skiing.* Philadelphia: Lippincott, 1963.

Bowles, Samuel. *The Switzerland of America: A Summer Vacation in the Parks and Mountains of Colorado.* Springfield, MA: Samuel Bowles and Co., 1869. Repr., Denver: Clearing House Publications, 1977.

Boyer Lewis, Charlene M. *Ladies and Gentlemen on Display: Planter Society at the Virginia Springs, 1790–1860.* Charlottesville: University Press of Virginia, 2001.

Bradley, Seth B. "The Origin of the Denver Mountain Parks System." *The Colorado Magazine* 9, no. 1 (January 1932): 26–29.

Bramwell, Lincoln. "Wilderburbs: Nature, Culture, and the Rise of Rural Development in the Rocky Mountain West, 1960–2000." PhD diss., University of New Mexico, 2007.

Brooks, Karl Boyd. *Before Earth Day: The Origins of American Environmental Law, 1945–1970.* Lawrence: University Press of Kansas, 2009.

Brosnan, Kathleen A. *Uniting Mountain and Plain: Cities, Law, and Environmental Change along the Front Range.* Albuquerque: University of New Mexico Press, 2002.

Brosnan, Kathleen A., and Amy L. Scott, eds. *City Dreams, Country Schemes: Community and Identity in the American West.* Reno: University of Nevada Press, 2011.

Brown, Baird B., Gustav A. Byrom III, David R. Erickson, J. Leland Lindauer, Mark Ruttum, Steven P. Walker, and Charles W. Howe. *Economic and Environmental Impact of the 1976 Winter Olympics Alpine Events.* Boulder: University of Colorado, [1971].

Brown, David G., Kenneth M. Johnson, Thomas R. Loveland, and David M. Theobald. "Rural Land-Use Trends in the Coterminous United States, 1950–2000." *Ecological Applications* 15, no. 6 (December 2005): 1851–63.

Brown, Dona. *Inventing New England: Regional Tourism in the Nineteenth Century.* Washington, DC: Smithsonian Institution Press, 1995.

Brown, Jeffrey. "A Tale of Two Visions: Harland Bartholomew, Robert Moses, and the Development of the American Freeway." *Journal of Planning History* 4, no. 1 (February 2005): 3–32.

Brown, Robert L. *Holy Cross: The Mountain and the City.* Caldwell, ID: Caxton, 1970.

Brush, Helen N., and Catherine P. Dittman. *Indian Hills: The Place, the Times, the People.* 2d ed. Evergreen, CO: Jefferson County Historical Society, 1993.

Buchholtz, C. W. *Rocky Mountain National Park: A History.* Boulder: Colorado Associated University Press, 1983.

Buell, Lawrence. *The Environmental Imagination: Thoreau, Nature Writing, and the Formation of American Culture.* Cambridge, MA: Belknap Press of Harvard University Press, 1995.

Burns, James MacGregor, J. W. Peltason, and Thomas E. Cronin. *State and Local Politics: Government by the People.* 6th ed. Englewood Cliffs, NJ: Prentice-Hall, 1990.

Butsch, Richard, ed. *For Fun and Profit: The Transformation of Leisure into Consumption.* Philadelphia: Temple University Press, 1990.

Byers, William Newton. "Bierstadt's Visit to Colorado: Sketching for the Famous Painting, *Storm in the Rocky Mountains.*" *Magazine of Western History* 11, no. 3 (January 1890): 237–39.

Cai, Liping A. "Cooperative Branding for Rural Destinations." *Annals of Tourism Research* 29, no. 3 (2002): 720–42.

Cairns, Mary Lyons. *Grand Lake in the Olden Days: A Compilation of "Grand Lake," "The Pioneers" and "The Olden Days."* Denver: World Press, 1971. Repr., Frederick, CO: Renaissance House Publishers, 1991.

Campbell, Colin. "Consuming Goods and the Good of Consuming." *Critical Review* 8 (Fall 1994): 503–20.

Canniff, Mary Ellen, and Mervyn L. Lapin, eds. *This Is Vail.* Vail: King Kong Resources, 1970.

Carhart, Arthur H. *Colorado.* New York: Coward-McCann, for the Colorado Association, 1932.

———. "The Haul of the Wild." *Nation's Business,* March 1945, 25–26, 63.

———. "Hunting and Fishing Is Big Business." *Sports Afield,* August 1947, 19–21, 138–40.

———. *Crisis Spots in Conservation.* [Chicago]: Izaak Walton League of America, 1949.

———. *Hi, Stranger! The Complete Guide to Dude Ranches.* Chicago: Ziff-Davis, 1949.

———, ed. *Conservation, Please! Questions and Answers on Conservation Topics.* New York: Garden Club of America, with the American Museum of Natural History, 1950.

———. "Hunting and Fishing Is Bigger Business." *Sports Afield,* June 1951, 30–31, 65–70.

———. "Pattern for Murder." *Sports Afield,* March 1952, 40–41, 75–77, 81–83.

———. "Ride the Lazy Dinosaur." *Westways,* February 1953, 18–19.

———. *The National Forests.* New York: Knopf, 1959.

———. *Water or Your Life.* 1951. Rev. ed., Philadelphia: Lippincott, 1959.

———. "Hunting and Fishing—Bigger Business Than Ever." *Sports Afield,* July 1960, 22–23, 93–94.

———. *Planning for America's Wildlands: A Handbook for Land-Use Planners, Managers and Executives, Committee and Commission Members, Conservation Leaders, and All Who Face Problems of Wildland Management.* Harrisburg, PA: Telegraph Press, for National Audubon Society, National Parks Association, Wilderness Society, and Wildlife Management Institute, 1961.

Carr, Neil. "The Tourism-Leisure Behavioural Continuum." *Annals of Tourism Research* 29, no. 4 (2002): 972–86.

Casewit, Curtis W. *United Air Lines Guide to Western Skiing.* Garden City, NY: Doubleday, 1967.

————. "Victory at Vail." *Success! Unlimited*, January 1967, 4–7, 43.

————. "Miracle out of a Meadow." *Ford Times*, December 1967, 7–11.

Cassidy, Maribee. *Off Limits: Leadville in the Early 1940's*. Leadville, CO: Leadville Herald-Democrat, 1983.

Castle, Emery N., ed. *The Changing American Countryside: Rural People and Places*. Lawrence: University Press of Kansas, 1995.

Cherry, Conrad. *Nature and Religious Imagination: From Edwards to Bushnell*. Philadelphia: Fortress Press, 1980.

Chiang, Connie Y. *Shaping the Shoreline: Fisheries and Tourism on the Monterey Coast*. Seattle: University of Washington Press, 2008.

Childers, Michael W. *Colorado Powder Keg: Ski Resorts and the Environmental Movement*. Lawrence: University Press of Kansas, 2012.

Christensen, Bonnie. *Red Lodge and the Mythic West: Coal Miners to Cowboys*. Lawrence: University Press of Kansas, 2002.

Christensen, Erin. "Lifelines: The Story of Colorado's Public Road System." *Colorado Heritage*, Issue 3, 1987, 2–12.

Chronic, Halka, and Felicie Williams. *Roadside Geology of Colorado*. 2d ed. Missoula, MT: Mountain Press, 2002.

Clay, Grady. *Close-Up: How to Read the American City*. Chicago: University of Chicago Press, 1973.

Clayton, Susan, and Susan Opotow, eds. *Identity and the Natural Environment: The Psychological Significance of Nature*. Cambridge, MA: MIT Press, 2003.

Clements, Eric L. "Selling the Switzerland of America: Colorado's Railroads Promote Pleasure and Health Seeking, 1870–1930." *Colorado Heritage*, March/April 2009, 14–23.

Clifford, Hal. *Downhill Slide: Why the Corporate Ski Industry Is Bad for Skiing, Ski Towns, and the Environment*. San Francisco: Sierra Club Books, 2002.

Clifford, Peggy. *To Aspen and Back: An American Journey*. New York: St. Martin's, 1980.

Cocks, Catherine. *Doing the Town: The Rise of Urban Tourism in the United States, 1850–1915*. Berkeley: University of California Press, 2001.

Cohen, Lizabeth. *A Consumers' Republic: The Politics of Mass Consumption in Postwar America*. New York: Knopf, 2003.

Cohen, Michael P. *The History of the Sierra Club, 1892–1970*. San Francisco: Sierra Club Books, 1988.

Coleman, Annie Gilbert. "The Unbearable Whiteness of Skiing." *Pacific Historical Review* 65, no. 4 (November 1996): 583–614.

————. "Call of the Mild: Colorado Ski Resorts and the Politics of Rural Tourism." In *The Countryside in the Age of the Modern State: Political Histories of Rural America*, edited by Catherine McNicol Stock and Robert D. Johnston, 281–303. Ithaca, NY: Cornell University Press, 2001.

————. *Ski Style: Sport and Culture in the Rockies*. Lawrence: University Press of Kansas, 2004.

Coleman, Jon T. "The Prim Reaper: Muriel Sibell Wolle and the Making of Western Ghost Towns." *Mining History Journal* 8 (2000): 10–17.

Collins, Robert M. *More: The Politics of Economic Growth in Postwar America.* New York: Oxford University Press, 2000.

Colorado: The Colorful Centennial State. Denver: Golden West Publications, 1959.

Colorado Writers' Program, Work Projects Administration. *Colorado: A Guide to the Highest State.* American Guide Series. New York: Hastings House, 1941.

———. *Ghost Towns of Colorado.* American Guide Series. New York: Hastings House, 1947.

Connors, Philip, ed. *New West Reader: Essays on an Ever-Evolving Frontier.* New York: Nation Books, 2005.

Conover, Beth, ed. *How the West Was Warmed: Responding to Climate Change in the Rockies.* Golden, CO: Fulcrum, 2009.

Conover, Ted. *Whiteout: Lost in Aspen.* New York: Random House, 1991.

Conron, John. *American Picturesque.* University Park: Pennsylvania State University Press, 2000.

Convery, William J. "Ski Heil! The Highland Bavarian Corporation and the Origins of Commercial Skiing in Aspen." Paper presented in the Winter Speakers Series, Aspen Historical Society, Aspen, February 18, 1997.

Conzen, Michael P., ed. *The Making of the American Landscape.* 2d ed. New York: Routledge, 2010.

Coquoz, Rene L. *The Leadville Story: Brief Story 1860–1960.* Leadville, CO: By the author, [ca. 1963].

———. *The Invisible Men on Skis: The Story of the Construction of Camp Hale and the Occupation by the 10th Mountain Division, 1942–1945.* Leadville, CO: By the author, 1970.

Corbett, Theodore. *The Making of American Resorts: Saratoga Springs, Ballston Spa, Lake George.* New Brunswick, NJ: Rutgers University Press, 2001.

Cornell, Virginia Miller. *Ski Lodge: Millers Idlewild Inn; Adventures in Snow Business.* Carpinteria, CA: Manifest Publications, 1993.

Cox, William T. *Fearsome Creatures of the Lumberwoods.* Washington, DC: Judd and Detweiler, 1910.

Cresswell, Tim. *Place: A Short Introduction.* Malden, MA: Blackwell, 2004.

Cronin, Thomas E., and Robert D. Loevy. *Colorado Politics and Government: Governing the Centennial State.* Lincoln: University of Nebraska Press, 1993.

Cronon, William. *Nature's Metropolis: Chicago and the Great West.* New York: Norton, 1991.

———, ed. *Uncommon Ground: Toward Reinventing Nature.* New York: Norton, 1995.

Cronon, William, George Miles, and Jay Gitlin. "Becoming West: Toward a New Meaning for Western History." In *Under an Open Sky: Rethinking America's Western Past,* edited by William Cronon, George Miles, and Jay Gitlin, 3–27. New York: Norton, 1992.

Cross, Gary. *An All-Consuming Century: Why Commercialism Won in Modern America.* New York: Columbia University Press, 2000.

Cullen, Jim. *The American Dream: A Short History of an Idea That Shaped a Nation.* New York: Oxford University Press, 2003.

Culver, Lawrence. *The Frontier of Leisure: Southern California and the Shaping of Modern America.* New York: Oxford University Press, 2010.

Cunningham, Sharon A. *Manitou, Saratoga of the West.* [Colorado Springs]: El Paso County Medical Society Auxiliary, 1980.

Cutsinger, Jackie, and George Galster. "There Is No Sprawl Syndrome: A New Typology of Metropolitan Land Use Patterns." *Urban Geography* 27, no. 3 (April 1–May 15, 2006): 228–52.

Dallas, Sandra. *Vail*. Boulder: Pruett, 1969.

Davies, Pete. *American Road: The Story of an Epic Transcontinental Journey at the Dawn of the Motor Age*. New York: Henry Holt, 2002.

Davis, Clark. "From Oasis to Metropolis: Southern California and the Changing Context of American Leisure." *Pacific Historical Review* 61, no. 3 (August 1992): 357–86.

Davis, Kenneth S., and Frieda Kay Fall. *The Eisenhower College Collection: The Paintings of Dwight D. Eisenhower*. Los Angeles: Nash Publishing, 1972.

Davis, Susan G. *Spectacular Nature: Corporate Culture and the Sea World Experience*. Berkeley: University of California Press, 1997.

Dawson, Michael. *Selling British Columbia: Tourism and Consumer Culture, 1890–1970*. Vancouver: UBC Press, 2004.

DeLyser, Dydia. "'Good, by God, We're Going to Bodie!': Ghost Towns and the American West." In *Western Places, American Myths: How We Think About the West*, edited by Gary J. Hausladen, 273–95. Reno: University of Nevada Press, 2003.

Dempsey, Stanley, and James E. Fell Jr. *Mining the Summit: Colorado's Ten Mile District, 1860–1960*. Norman: University of Oklahoma Press, 1986.

Dennis, Richard. "History, Geography, and Historical Geography." *Social Science History* 15, no. 2 (Summer 1991): 265–88.

Denver, John. *Take Me Home: An Autobiography*. With Arthur Tobier. New York: Harmony Books, 1994.

Dercum, Edna Strand. *"It's Easy, Edna, It's Downhill All the Way."* Dillon, CO: SIRPOS Press, 1981.

Dorward, Sherry. *Design for Mountain Communities: A Landscape and Architectural Guide*. New York: Van Nostrand Reinhold, 1990.

Draper, Benjamin Poff. "Cultural Life in Georgetown, Colorado, 1859–1900." Master's thesis, University of Denver, 1936.

———. *Georgetown: High Points in the Story of the Famous Colorado Silver Camp*. [Denver?]: By the author, 1940.

———. *Georgetown Pictorial: An Illustrated Story of a Colorado Mining Town*. Denver: Old West Publishing Co., 1964.

Dugan, Ben M. *Berthoud Pass*. Charleston, SC: Arcadia, 2011.

Dunaway, Finis. *Natural Visions: The Power of Images in American Environmental Reform*. Chicago: University of Chicago Press, 2005.

Dunlap, Riley E., and Robert Bruce Heffernan. "Outdoor Recreation and Environmental Concern: An Empirical Examination." *Rural Sociology* 40, no. 1 (Spring 1975): 18–30.

Dunlap, Thomas R. "Sport Hunting and Conservation, 1880–1920." *Environmental Review* 12, no. 1 (Spring 1988): 51–60.

Dunlop, M. H. *Sixty Miles from Contentment: Traveling the Nineteenth-Century American Interior*. New York: Basic Books, 1995.

Dusenbery, Harris. *Ski the High Trail: World War II Ski Troopers in the High Colorado Rockies*. Portland, OR: Binford and Mort, 1991.

Eagle Chamber of Commerce. *Western Colorado: The Playground of America; Mt. of the Holy Cross and the Eagle River Valley, Eagle County*. Glenwood Springs, CO: Western Guide Publishing Co., 1929.

Eberhart, Perry. *Guide to the Colorado Ghost Towns and Mining Camps*. Denver: Sage Books, 1959.

Eckel, Edwin B. *Minerals of Colorado: A 100-Year Record*. Geological Survey Bulletin 1114. Washington, DC: U.S. Geological Survey, 1961.

Eisinger, Peter K. *The Rise of the Entrepreneurial State: State and Local Economic Development Policy in the United States*. Madison: University of Wisconsin Press, 1989.

Emore, Anna. *Dillon: The Blue River Wonderland*. [Dillon, CO]: Summit Historical Society, 1976.

Erwin, Robert. "Lifestyle." *Wilson Quarterly* 18, no. 1 (Winter 1994): 108–15.

Faragher, John Mack. "Bungalow and Ranch House: The Architectural Backwash of California." *Western Historical Quarterly* 32, no. 2 (Summer 2001): 149–73.

Fay, Abbott. *A History of Skiing in Colorado*. Ouray, CO: Western Reflections, 2000. Rev. ed. of *Ski Tracks in the Rockies: A Century of Colorado Skiing* [Evergreen, CO: Cordillera Press, 1984].

Feldman, James W. *A Storied Wilderness: Rewilding the Apostle Islands*. Seattle: University of Washington Press, 2011.

[Feltner, George]. *A Look Back: A 75 Year History of the Colorado Game, Fish and Parks Division*. Denver: Colorado Department of Natural Resources, Game, Fish and Parks Division, 1972.

Ferguson, Gary. *The Great Divide: The Rocky Mountains in the American Mind*. New York: Norton, 2004.

Fernlund, Kevin J., ed. *The Cold War American West, 1945–1989*. Albuquerque: University of New Mexico Press, in cooperation with the University of New Mexico Center for the American West, 1998.

Ferril, Thomas Hornsby. "Tourists, Stay Away from My Door." *Harper's Magazine*, May 1954, 77–81.

Fiege, Mark. *Republic of Nature: An Environmental History of the United States*. Seattle: University of Washington Press, 2012.

Filipiak, Jeffrey. "'I've Seen It Rain Fire in the Sky': John Denver's Popular Songs and Environmental Memory." In *Resounding Pasts: Essays in Literature, Popular Music and Cultural Memory*, edited by Drago Momcilovic, 86–111. Newcastle upon Tyne, England: Cambridge Scholars Publishing, 2011.

Findlay, John M. *Magic Lands: Western Cityscapes and American Culture after 1940*. Berkeley: University of California Press, 1992.

Fischel, William A. "An Economic History of Zoning and a Cure for Its Exclusionary Effects." *Urban Studies* 41, no. 2 (February 2004): 317–40.

Fischer, Frank. *Technocracy and the Politics of Expertise*. Newbury Park, CA: Sage, 1990.

Fischer, Frank, and Maarten A. Hajer, eds. *Living with Nature: Environmental Politics as Cultural Discourse*. New York: Oxford University Press, 1999.

Fleischmann, Arnold, and Joe R. Feagin. "The Politics of Growth-Oriented Urban Alliances: Comparing Old Industrial and New Sunbelt Cities." *Urban Affairs Quarterly* 23, no. 2 (December 1987): 207–32.

Flint, Anthony. *This Land: The Battle Over Sprawl and the Future of America.* Baltimore: Johns Hopkins University Press, 2006.

Flippo, Chet. "His Rocky Mountain Highness: The R.S. Interview with John Denver." *Rolling Stone,* May 8, 1975, 44–50, 72, 80.

Flores, Dan. *The Natural West: Environmental History in the Great Plains and Rocky Mountains.* Norman: University of Oklahoma Press, 2001.

Ford Motor Co. Publications Department. *Ford Treasury of the Outdoors.* New York: Simon and Schuster, 1952.

Forman, Richard T. T., Daniel Sperling, John A. Bissonette et al. *Road Ecology: Science and Solutions.* Washington, DC: Island Press, 2003.

Foster, Jack. *Adventures at Timberline.* Denver: Monitor Publications, 1963.

Foster, Mark S. "Colorado's Defeat of the 1976 Winter Olympics." *The Colorado Magazine* 53, no. 2 (Spring 1976): 163–86.

Fox, Stephen. *John Muir and His Legacy: The American Conservation Movement.* Boston: Little, Brown, 1981.

Francaviglia, Richard V. *Hard Places: Reading the Landscape of America's Historic Mining Districts.* Iowa City: University of Iowa Press, 1991.

Frush, Charles O. "A Century of Mining in Colorado." *Western Business Review* 3, no. 1 (February 1959): 3–10.

Fry, John. *The Story of Modern Skiing.* Hanover, NH: University Press of New England, 2006.

Furlough, Ellen. "Making Mass Vacations: Tourism and Consumer Culture in France, 1930s to 1970s." *Comparative Studies in Society and History* 40, no. 2 (April 1998): 247–86.

Gallegos, Robert, Tina Atencio, Celine Martinez, Debbie Lovato, and Josie Jaramillo. *From the County Seat to "Charlie" Vail: A Short History of the Growth and Development of Red Cliff, Gilman, Minturn and Vail.* [Minturn, CO: Foundation for Urban and Neighborhood Development, n.d.].

Garnsey, Morris E. *America's New Frontier: The Mountain West.* New York: Knopf, 1950.

Gatta, John. *Making Nature Sacred: Literature, Religion, and Environment in America from the Puritans to the Present.* New York: Oxford University Press, 2004.

Geisler, Charles C., Oscar B. Martinson, and Eugene A. Wilkening. "Outdoor Recreation and Environmental Concern: A Restudy." *Rural Sociology* 42, no. 2 (Summer 1977): 241–49.

Gibbons, Boyd. *Wye Island.* Baltimore: Johns Hopkins University Press, 1977.

Gillette, Ethel Morrow. *Idaho Springs, Saratoga of the Rockies: A History of Idaho Springs, Colorado.* New York: Vantage Press, 1978.

Gilliland, Mary Ellen. *Frisco! A Colorful Colorado Community.* Silverthorne, CO: Alpenrose Press and the Frisco Historical Society, 1984.

Glick, Daniel. *Powder Burn: Arson, Money, and Mystery on Vail Mountain.* New York: PublicAffairs, 2001.

Glickman, Lawrence B., ed. *Consumer Society in American History: A Reader.* Ithaca, NY: Cornell University Press, 1999.

Glotfelty, Cheryll. "The Riddle of Ghost Towns in the Environmental Imagination." *Western American Literature* 41, no. 3 (Fall 2006): 244–65.

Gober, Patricia, Kevin E. McHugh, and Denis Leclerc. "Job-Rich but Housing-Poor: The Dilemma of a Western Amenity Town." *Professional Geographer* 45, no. 1 (February 1993): 12–20.

Gómez, Arthur R. *Quest for the Golden Circle: The Four Corners and the Metropolitan West, 1945–1970.* Albuquerque: University of New Mexico Press, 1994.

Gottlieb, Robert. *Forcing the Spring: The Transformation of the American Environmental Movement.* Washington, DC: Island Press, 1993.

Gould, Lewis L. "First Lady as Catalyst: Lady Bird Johnson and Highway Beautification in the 1960s." *Environmental Review* 10, no. 2 (Summer 1986): 76–92.

Graf, Nelly. *No Vacancy.* Denver: University of Denver Press, 1951.

Graves, William. "California, the Golden Magnet." *National Geographic,* May 1966, 595–679.

Greider, Thomas, and Lorraine Garkovich. "Landscapes: The Social Construction of Nature and the Environment." *Rural Sociology* 59, no. 1 (Spring 1994): 1–24.

Gudis, Catherine. *Buyways: Billboards, Automobiles, and the American Landscape.* New York: Routledge, 2004.

Gulliford, Andrew. *Boomtown Blues: Colorado Oil Shale, 1885–1985.* Niwot: University Press of Colorado, 1989.

Gulliford, Andrew, and the Grand River Museum Alliance. *Garfield County, Colorado: The First Hundred Years 1883–1983.* [Glenwood Springs, CO]: Grand River Museum Alliance, 1983.

Gunn, Clare A. *Vacationscape: Designing Tourist Regions.* Austin: University of Texas, Bureau of Business Research, 1972.

Gunther, John. *Inside U.S.A.* New York: Harper and Brothers, 1947.

Gutfreund, Owen D. *20th-Century Sprawl: Highways and the Reshaping of the American Landscape.* New York: Oxford University Press, 2004.

Hafen, LeRoy R. "The Coming of the Automobile and Improved Roads to Colorado." *The Colorado Magazine* 8, no. 1 (January 1931): 1–16.

Hafen, LeRoy R., and Ann Hafen. *Our State: Colorado; A History of Progress.* Denver: Old West Publishing Co., 1966.

[Halaas, David Fridtjof, and Walter R. Borneman]. *The Story of a Valley: Georgetown Loop Historic Mining and Railroad Park.* Denver: State Historical Society of Colorado, 1984.

Haley, John L. *Wooing a Harsh Mistress: Glenwood Canyon's Highway Odyssey.* Greeley, CO: Canyon Communications, 1994.

Hall, Colin Michael. *Tourism and Politics: Policy, Power and Place.* Chichester, U.K.: Wiley, 1994.

Hall, Colin Michael, and Stephen J. Page. *The Geography of Tourism and Recreation: Environment, Place and Space.* London and New York: Routledge, 1999.

Hall, Peter. *Cities of Tomorrow: An Intellectual History of Urban Planning and Design in the Twentieth Century.* 3d ed. Malden, MA: Blackwell, 2002.

Halseth, Greg. *Cottage Country in Transition: A Social Geography of Change and Contention in the Rural-Recreational Countryside.* Montreal: McGill-Queen's University Press, 1998.

Halverson, Anders. *An Entirely Synthetic Fish: How Rainbow Trout Beguiled America and Overran the World.* New Haven, CT: Yale University Press, 2010.

Handler, Richard, and Eric Gable. *The New History in an Old Museum: Creating the Past at Colonial Williamsburg*. Durham, NC: Duke University Press, 1997.

Hankinson, Graham. "Relational Network Brands: Towards a Conceptual Model of Place Brands." *Journal of Vacation Marketing* 10, no. 2 (2004): 109–21.

Harper, John L. *Mineral King: Public Concern with Government Policy*. Arcata, CA: Pacifica Publishing Co., 1982.

Harrison, Blake. *The View from Vermont: Tourism and the Making of an American Rural Landscape*. Burlington: University of Vermont Press; Hanover, NH: University Press of New England, 2006.

Harrison, Julia. *Being a Tourist: Finding Meaning in Pleasure Travel*. Vancouver: UBC Press, 2003.

Harrison, Louise C. *Empire and the Berthoud Pass*. Denver: Big Mountain Press, 1964.

Harvey, David. *Justice, Nature and the Geography of Difference*. Malden, MA: Blackwell, 1996.

Harvey, Mark W. T. *A Symbol of Wilderness: Echo Park and the American Conservation Movement*. Albuquerque: University of New Mexico Press, 1994.

———. *Wilderness Forever: Howard Zahniser and the Path to the Wilderness Act*. Seattle: University of Washington Press, 2005.

Hauserman, Dick. *The Inventors of Vail*. Edwards, CO: Golden Peak Publishing Co., 2000.

Hausladen, Gary J., ed. *Western Places, American Myths: How We Think about the West*. Reno: University of Nevada Press, 2003.

Hays, Samuel P. *Conservation and the Gospel of Efficiency: The Progressive Conservation Movement, 1890–1920*. Cambridge, MA: Harvard University Press, 1959.

———. *Beauty, Health, and Permanence: Environmental Politics in the United States, 1955–1985*. Assisted by Barbara D. Hays. New York: Cambridge University Press, 1987.

———. *A History of Environmental Politics Since 1945*. Pittsburgh: University of Pittsburgh Press, 2000.

Heasley, Lynne. *A Thousand Pieces of Paradise: Landscape and Property in the Kickapoo Valley*. Madison: University of Wisconsin Press, with the Center for American Places, Santa Fe, NM, 2006.

Helphand, Kenneth I. *Colorado: Visions of an American Landscape*. Niwot, CO: Roberts Rinehart, 1991.

Henderson, Harry. "Rugged American Collectivism." *Harper's Magazine*, December 1953, 80–86.

Hendricks, Gordon. *Albert Bierstadt: Painter of the American West*. New York: Abrams; Fort Worth, TX: Amon Carter Museum of Western Art, 1974.

Heppenheimer, T. A. *Turbulent Skies: The History of Commercial Aviation*. New York: Wiley, 1995.

Herbers, John. *The New Heartland: America's Flight beyond the Suburbs and How It Is Changing Our Future*. New York: Times Books, 1986.

Higham, John. "The Reorientation of American Culture in the 1890s." In *The Origins of Modern Consciousness*, edited by John Weiss, 25–48. Detroit: Wayne State University Press, 1965.

Hinrichs, C. Clare. "Consuming Images: Making and Marketing Vermont as Distinctive Rural Place." In *Creating the Countryside: The Politics of Rural and Environmental*

Discourse, edited by E. Melanie DuPuis and Peter Vandergeest, 259–78. Philadelphia: Temple University Press, 1996.

Hirsch, Jerrold. *Portrait of America: A Cultural History of the Federal Writers' Project*. Chapel Hill: University of North Carolina Press, 2003.

Hirt, Paul W. *A Conspiracy of Optimism: Management of the National Forests Since World War Two*. Lincoln: University of Nebraska Press, 1994.

Hoelscher, Steven. "The Photographic Construction of Tourist Space in Victorian America." *Geographical Review* 88, no. 4 (October 1998): 548–70.

Hokanson, Drake. *The Lincoln Highway: Main Street across America*. Iowa City: University of Iowa Press, 1999.

Holbrook, Morris B., and Elizabeth C. Hirschman. "The Experiential Aspects of Consumption: Consumer Fantasies, Feelings, and Fun." *Journal of Consumer Research* 9, no. 2 (September 1982): 132–40.

Hooper, S. K. *"Around the Circle": One Thousand Miles through the Rocky Mountains*. Denver: Denver and Rio Grande Railroad, Passenger Department, 1892. Repr., Golden, CO: Outbooks, 1986.

Hornby, William H. *Voice of Empire: A Centennial Sketch of "The Denver Post."* Denver: Colorado Historical Society, 1992.

Howe, Elvon L., ed. *Rocky Mountain Empire: Revealing Glimpses of the West in Transition from Old to New, from the Pages of the Rocky Mountain Empire Magazine of "The Denver Post."* Garden City, NY: Doubleday and Co., 1950.

Huber, Thomas P. *Colorado: The Place of Nature, the Nature of Place*. Niwot: University Press of Colorado, 1993.

Huffman, Thomas R. *Protectors of the Land and Water: Environmentalism in Wisconsin, 1961– 1968*. Chapel Hill: University of North Carolina Press, 1994.

Huth, Hans. *Nature and the American: Three Centuries of Changing Attitudes*. Berkeley: University of California Press, 1957.

Hyde, Anne Farrar. *An American Vision: Far Western Landscape and National Culture, 1820– 1920*. New York: New York University Press, 1990.

———. "Cultural Filters: The Significance of Perception in the History of the American West." *Western Historical Quarterly* 24, no. 3 (August 1993): 351–74.

———. "Nothing New Under the Sun: Continuities in the West." *Pacific Historical Review* 67, no. 3 (August 1998): 393–99.

Jackson, J. B. *A Sense of Place, a Sense of Time*. New Haven, CT: Yale University Press, 1994.

Jackson, Kenneth T. *Crabgrass Frontier: The Suburbanization of the United States*. New York: Oxford University Press, 1985.

Jackson, Philip L., and Robert Kuhlken. *A Rediscovered Frontier: Land Use and Resource Issues in the New West*. Lanham, MD: Rowman and Littlefield, 2006.

Jacoby, Karl. *Crimes against Nature: Squatters, Poachers, Thieves, and the Hidden History of American Conservation*. Berkeley: University of California Press, 2001.

Jakle, John A. *The Tourist: Travel in Twentieth-Century North America*. Lincoln: University of Nebraska Press, 1985.

———. "Pioneer Roads: America's Early Twentieth-Century Named Highways." *Material Culture* 32, no. 2 (Summer 2000): 1–22.

Jakle, John A., and Keith A. Sculle. *Signs in America's Auto Age: Signatures of Landscape and Place*. Iowa City: University of Iowa Press, 2004.

———. *Motoring: The Highway Experience in America*. Athens: University of Georgia Press, 2008.

Jakle, John A., Keith A. Sculle, and Jefferson S. Rogers. *The Motel in America*. Baltimore: Johns Hopkins University Press, 1996.

Jansen-Verbeke, Myriam, and Adri Dietvorst. "Leisure, Recreation, Tourism: A Geographic View on Integration." *Annals of Tourism Research* 14, no. 3 (1987): 361–75.

Jasper, James M. *Restless Nation: Starting Over in America*. Chicago: University of Chicago Press, 2000.

Jay, John. *Skiing the Americas*. New York: Macmillan, 1947.

Jay, John, John O'Rear, Frankie O'Rear, and the editors of *Ski* magazine. *Ski Down the Years*. New York: Universal Publishing and Distributing Co., 1966.

Jobes, Patrick C. *Moving Nearer to Heaven: The Illusions and Disillusions of Migrants to Scenic Rural Places*. Westport, CT: Praeger, 2000.

Johnson, Michael L. *New Westers: The West in Contemporary American Culture*. Lawrence: University Press of Kansas, 1996.

Jordan, Robert Paul. "Our Growing Interstate Highway System." *National Geographic*, February 1968, 194–219.

Judd, Richard W., and Christopher S. Beach. *Natural States: The Environmental Imagination in Maine, Oregon, and the Nation*. Washington, DC: Resources for the Future, 2003.

Kammen, Michael. *Mystic Chords of Memory: The Transformation of Tradition in American Culture*. New York: Knopf, 1991.

Kelley, Ben. *The Pavers and the Paved*. New York: Donald W. Brown, 1971.

Kelley, Tim K. *Living in Colorado*. Boulder: Pruett, 1964.

Kelly, Eric Damian. *Managing Community Growth: Policies, Techniques, and Impacts*. 2d ed. Westport, CT: Praeger, 2004.

Kelly, George V. *The Old Gray Mayors of Denver*. Boulder: Pruett, 1974.

Kemp, Louis Ward. "Aesthetes and Engineers: The Occupational Ideology of Highway Design." *Technology and Culture* 27, no. 4 (October 1986): 759–97.

Kerbey, McFall. "Colorado, a Barrier That Became a Goal." *National Geographic*, July 1932, 1–63.

Kingery, Hugh E. *The Colorado Mountain Club: The First Seventy-Five Years of a Highly Individual Corporation, 1912–1987*. Assisted by Elinor Eppich Kingery. Evergreen: Cordillera Press, with the Colorado Mountain Club Foundation, 1988.

Kingsland, Sharon E. *The Evolution of American Ecology, 1890–2000*. Baltimore: Johns Hopkins University Press, 2005.

Kirk, Andrew Glenn. *Collecting Nature: The American Environmental Movement and the Conservation Library*. Lawrence: University Press of Kansas, 2001.

Kitsos, Thomas R., ed. *Land Use in Colorado: The Planning Thicket*. Boulder: University of Colorado, Bureau of Governmental Research and Service, 1974.

Klingle, Matthew W. "Spaces of Consumption in Environmental History." *History and Theory* 42, no. 4 (December 2003): 94–110.

Klucas, Gillian. *Leadville: The Struggle to Revive an American Town*. Washington, DC: Island Press, 2004.

Knight, MacDonald, and Leonard Hammock. *Early Days on the Eagle*. Eagle, CO: By the authors, 1965.

Knobloch, Frieda. "Creating the Cowboy State: Culture and Underdevelopment in Wyoming Since 1867." *Western Historical Quarterly* 32, no. 2 (Summer 2001): 201–21.

Knox, Paul L. *Metroburbia, USA*. New Brunswick, NJ: Rutgers University Press, 2008.

Kolb, David. *Sprawling Places*. Athens: University of Georgia Press, 2008.

Koppes, Clayton. "Efficiency/Equity/Esthetics: Towards a Reinterpretation of American Conservation." *Environmental Review* 11 (Summer 1987): 127–46.

Koshar, Rudy. *German Travel Cultures*. Oxford: Berg, 2000.

Krueckeberg, Donald A., ed. *Introduction to Planning History in the United States*. New Brunswick, NJ: Center for Urban Policy Research, Rutgers University, 1983.

LaBaw, Wallace L. *See and Ski in Colorado*. Broomfield, CO: Ingersoll Publications, 1966.

Lackey, Earl E. "Mountain Passes in the Colorado Rockies." *Economic Geography* 25, no. 3 (July 1949): 211–15.

Lamm, Richard D., and Michael McCarthy. *The Angry West: A Vulnerable Land and Its Future*. Boston: Houghton Mifflin, 1982.

Lamm, Richard D., and Duane A. Smith. *Pioneers and Politicians: Ten Colorado Governors in Profile*. Boulder: Pruett, 1984.

Landrum, Ney C. *The State Park Movement in America: A Critical Review*. Columbia: University of Missouri Press, 2004.

Lang, Robert, and Paul L. Knox. "The New Metropolis: Rethinking Megalopolis." *Regional Studies* 43, no. 6 (2009): 789–802.

Lavender, David. *The Rockies*. New York: Harper and Row, 1968.

Laycock, George. *The Diligent Destroyers: A Critical Look at the Industries and Agencies That Are Permanently Defacing the American Landscape*. Garden City, NY: Doubleday, 1970. Repr., New York: Ballantine/National Audubon Society, 1970.

Leach, William. *Land of Desire: Merchants, Power, and the Rise of a New American Culture*. New York: Pantheon, 1993.

Lears, T. J. Jackson. *No Place of Grace: Antimodernism and the Transformation of American Culture, 1880–1920*. New York: Pantheon, 1981.

———. "From Salvation to Self-Realization: Advertising and the Therapeutic Roots of the Consumer Culture, 1880–1930." In *The Culture of Consumption: Critical Essays in American History, 1880–1980*, edited by Richard Wightman Fox and T. J. Jackson Lears, 1–38. New York: Pantheon, 1983.

———. *Fables of Abundance: A Cultural History of Advertising in America*. New York: Basic Books, 1994.

Lefebvre, Henri. *The Production of Space*. Translated by Donald Nicholson-Smith. Oxford: Basil Blackwell, 1991.

Leich, Jeffrey R. *Tales of the 10th: The Mountain Troops and American Skiing*. Franconia, NH: New England Ski Museum, 2003.

Leonard, Stephen J., and Thomas J. Noel. *Denver: Mining Camp to Metropolis*. Niwot: University Press of Colorado, 1990.

Levi, Daniel, and Sara Kocher. "Virtual Nature: The Future Effects of Information Technology on Our Relationship to Nature." *Environment and Behavior* 31, no. 2 (March 1999): 203–26.

Lewis, James G. *The Forest Service and the Greatest Good: A Centennial History.* Durham, NC: Forest History Society, 2005.

Lewis, Michael, ed. *American Wilderness: A New History.* New York: Oxford University Press, 2007.

Lewis, Peirce. "The Galactic Metropolis." In *Beyond the Urban Fringe: Land-Use Issues of Nonmetropolitan America,* edited by Rutherford H. Platt and George Macinko, 23–49. Minneapolis: University of Minnesota Press, 1983.

———. "The Urban Invasion of Rural America: The Emergence of the Galactic City." In *The Changing American Countryside: Rural People and Places,* edited by Emery N. Castle, 39–62. Lawrence: University Press of Kansas, 1995.

Lewis, Tom. *Divided Highways: Building the Interstate Highways, Transforming American Life.* New York: Viking Penguin, 1997.

Liebs, Chester H. *Main Street to Miracle Mile: American Roadside Architecture.* Boston: Little, Brown, for the New York Graphic Society, 1985.

Limerick, Patricia Nelson. *The Legacy of Conquest: The Unbroken Past of the American West.* New York: Norton, 1987.

———. *Something in the Soil: Legacies and Reckonings in the New West.* New York: Norton, 2000.

Limerick, Patricia Nelson, Andrew Cowell, and Sharon K. Collinge, eds. *Remedies for a New West: Healing Landscapes, Histories, and Cultures.* Tucson: University of Arizona Press, 2009.

Löfgren, Orvar. *On Holiday: A History of Vacationing.* Berkeley: University of California Press, 1999.

Long, George W. "New Rush to Golden California." *National Geographic,* June 1954, 723–802.

Lorch, Robert S. *Colorado's Government: Structure, Politics, Administration, and Policy.* 5th ed. Niwot: University Press of Colorado, 1991.

Lotchin, Roger W. *Fortress California, 1910–1961: From Warfare to Welfare.* New York: Oxford University Press, 1992.

Louter, David. *Windshield Wilderness: Cars, Roads, and Nature in Washington's National Parks.* Seattle: University of Washington Press, 2006.

Louv, Richard. *Last Child in the Woods: Saving Our Children from Nature-Deficit Disorder.* Chapel Hill, NC: Algonquin Books of Chapel Hill, 2005.

Lyson, Thomas A., and William W. Falk, eds. *Forgotten Places: Uneven Development in Rural America.* Lawrence: University Press of Kansas, 1993.

MacCannell, Dean. *The Tourist: A New Theory of the Leisure Class.* New York: Schocken, 1976.

Maher, Neil M. *Nature's New Deal: The Civilian Conservation Corps and the Roots of the American Environmental Movement.* New York: Oxford University Press, 2008.

Malone, Michael P., and Richard W. Etulain. *The American West: A Twentieth-Century History.* Lincoln: University of Nebraska Press, 1989.

Marchand, Roland. *Advertising the American Dream: Making Way for Modernity, 1920–1940*. Berkeley: University of California Press, 1985.

Margolies, John, and Eric Baker. *See the USA: The Art of the American Travel Brochure*. San Francisco: Chronicle Books, 2000.

Mark, Joan. *The Silver Gringo: William Spratling and Taxco*. Albuquerque: University of New Mexico Press, 2000.

Marston, Ed, ed. *Reopening the Western Frontier*. Washington, DC: Island Press, 1989.

Martin, Curtis. "Political Behavior in Colorado." *Colorado Quarterly* 6, no. 1 (Summer 1957): 63–78.

Martin, James M. *John Denver: Rocky Mountain Wonder Boy*. New York: Pinnacle, 1977.

Martin, Russell. "Johnny Van and Club 20," *Straight Creek Journal*, November 20, 1975, 6–7.

Martinez, Patrick J., Patricia E. Bigelow, Mark A. Deleray, Wade A. Fredenberg, Barry S. Hansen, Ned J. Horner, Stafford K. Lehr, Roger W. Schneidervin, Scott A. Tolentino, and Art E. Viola. "Western Lake Trout Woes." *Fisheries* 34, no. 9 (September 2009): 424–42.

Marx, Seth H. *Mountain Vision: The Making of Beaver Creek*. [Beaver Creek, CO]: Beaver Creek Resort Company, [ca. 1996].

May, Kirse Granat. *Golden State, Golden Youth: The California Image in Popular Culture, 1955–1966*. Chapel Hill: University of North Carolina Press, 2002.

McCarthy, Tom. *Auto Mania: Cars, Consumers, and the Environment*. New Haven, CT: Yale University Press, 2007.

McCarty, Patrick Fargo. "Big Ed Johnson of Colorado: A Political Portrait." Master's thesis, University of Colorado, 1958.

McCloskey, Michael. "Wilderness Movement at the Crossroads, 1945–1970." *Pacific Historical Review* 41, no. 3 (August 1972): 346–61.

McEvoy, J. P. "'Silver Bill,' Practical Good Neighbor." *Reader's Digest*, September 1945, 19–22.

McKinsey, Elizabeth. *Niagara Falls: Icon of the American Sublime*. New York: Cambridge University Press, 1985.

McKinstry, Hugh. *The Future of Mining in Colorado . . . Some Geological and Economic Aspects*. Denver: Colorado State Chamber of Commerce, Mining and Petroleum Committee, [1959].

Meadows, Donella H., Dennis L. Meadows, Jørgen Randers, and William W. Behrens III. *The Limits to Growth: A Report for the Club of Rome's Project on the Predicament of Mankind*. New York: Universe, 1972.

Mehls, Steven F. *The Valley of Opportunity: A History of West-Central Colorado*. Cultural Resources Series no. 12. Denver: Bureau of Land Management, Colorado State Office, 1982.

———. *The New Empire of the Rockies: A History of Northeast Colorado*. Cultural Resources Series no. 16. Denver: Bureau of Land Management, Colorado State Office, 1984.

Melosi, Martin V. "Lyndon Johnson and Environmental Policy." In *The Johnson Years*, vol. 2, *Vietnam, the Environment, and Science*, edited by Robert A. Divine, 113–49. Lawrence: University Press of Kansas, 1987.

Merrill, Karen R. *Public Lands and Political Meaning: Ranchers, the Government, and the Property Between Them.* Berkeley: University of California Press, 2002.

Meyer, William B. *Americans and Their Weather.* New York: Oxford University Press, 2000.

Miller, Char, ed. *Cities and Nature in the American West.* Reno: University of Nevada Press, 2010.

[Miller, Jean, Carol Hoy, and Jim Wier]. *Winter Park: Colorado's Favorite for Fifty Years, 1940–1990.* [Denver]: Winter Park Recreational Association, 1989.

Miller, Jean, and Jim Wier, eds. "1859–1950 Skiing in Middle Park." Special issue, *Grand County Historical Association Journal* 4, no. 1 (January 1984).

———, eds. "A Dude Ranch Is . . . , 1874–1986." Special issue, *Grand County Historical Association Journal* 6, no. 1 (June 1986).

———, eds. "A Mountain, a Dream, a Train—Winter Park." Special issue, *Grand County Historical Association Journal* 9, no. 1 (December 1989).

Miller, Lyle. "The Hi-Ho, Lucky U, Bugs Bunny, and Sleepy Hollow: A History of Colorado Motels." *Colorado Heritage,* Autumn 1997, 2–21.

Mitman, Gregg. *Reel Nature: America's Romance with Wildlife on Film.* Cambridge, MA: Harvard University Press, 1999.

Mobil Travel Guide 1963/1964: Southwest and South Central Area. New York: Simon and Schuster, 1963.

Mohl, Raymond A., ed. *Searching for the Sunbelt: Historical Perspectives on a Region.* Knoxville: University of Tennessee Press, 1990.

Montooth, Charles. "Landscape as an Extension of Architecture." In *Landscape in America,* edited by George F. Thompson, 261–74. Austin: University of Texas Press, 1995.

Montrie, Chad. *A People's History of Environmentalism in the United States.* London: Continuum, 2011.

Moore, Deborah Dash. *To the Golden Cities: Pursuing the American Jewish Dream in Miami and L.A.* New York: Free Press, 1994.

Morgan, Gary. *Rails around the Loop: The Story of the Georgetown Loop.* Fort Collins, CO: Centennial Publications, 1976.

Morgan, Neil. *Westward Tilt: The American West Today.* New York: Random House, 1963.

Mormino, Gary R. *Land of Sunshine, State of Dreams: A Social History of Modern Florida.* Gainesville: University Press of Florida, 2005.

Morris, Leavitt F. "So You Want to Go Skiing!" *Christian Science Monitor Weekend Magazine,* January 3, 1948, 7.

Morrissey, Katherine G. *Mental Territories: Mapping the Inland Empire.* Ithaca, NY: Cornell University Press, 1997.

Mowbray, A. Q. *Road to Ruin.* New York: Lippincott, 1969.

Mutel, Cornelia Fleischer, and John C. Emerick. *From Grassland to Glacier: The Natural History of Colorado and the Surrounding Region.* 2d ed. Boulder: Johnson Books, 1992.

Myers, Debs. "Colorado." In *American Panorama West of the Mississippi: A "Holiday" Magazine Book,* 183–99. Garden City, NY: Doubleday, 1960.

Nash, Dennison. "Tourism as an Anthropological Subject." *Current Anthropology* 22, no. 5 (October 1981): 461–81.

Nash, Gerald D. *The American West in the Twentieth Century: A Short History of an Urban Oasis.* Englewood Cliffs, NJ: Prentice-Hall, 1973.

———. *The American West Transformed: The Impact of the Second World War.* Bloomington: Indiana University Press, 1985.

———. *The Federal Landscape: An Economic History of the Twentieth-Century West.* Tucson: University of Arizona Press, 1999.

Nash, Roderick Frazier. *Wilderness and the American Mind.* 4th ed. New Haven, CT: Yale University Press, 2001.

Needham, Richard. *Ski: Fifty Years in North America.* New York: Abrams, 1987.

[Neely, Cynthia C., Walter R. Borneman, and Christine Bradley]. *Guide to the Georgetown–Silver Plume Historic District.* Evergreen, CO: Cordillera Press, 1990.

Nelson, Jim. *Glenwood Springs: The History of a Rocky Mountain Resort.* Ouray, CO: Western Reflections, 1999.

Nelson, Mike, and the 9News Weather Team. *The Colorado Weather Book.* Englewood, CO: Westcliffe Publishers, 1999.

Nelson, Peter B., and William B. Beyers. "Using Economic Base Models to Explain New Trends in Rural Income." *Growth and Change* 29, no.3 (Summer 1998): 295–318.

Nerdinger, Winfried. *Walter Gropius: Der Architekt Walter Gropius, Zeichnungen, Pläne und Fotos . . . = Architect Walter Gropius, Drawings, Prints and Photographs . . .* Berlin: Bauhaus-Archiv; Cambridge, MA: Busch-Reisinger Museum; Berlin: Gebr. Mann Verlag, 1985.

Nicholas, Liza, Elaine M. Bapis, and Thomas J. Harvey, eds. *Imagining the Big Open: Nature, Identity, and Play in the New West.* Salt Lake City: University of Utah Press, 2003.

Nickerson, Norma Polovitz. *Foundations of Tourism.* Upper Saddle River, NJ: Prentice-Hall, 1996.

Nicolson, Marjorie Hope. *Mountain Gloom and Mountain Glory: The Development of the Aesthetics of the Infinite.* New York: Norton, 1959. Repr., Seattle: University of Washington Press, 1997.

Nikiforuk, Andrew. *Empire of the Beetle: How Human Folly and a Tiny Bug Are Killing North America's Great Forests.* Vancouver, BC: David Suzuki Foundation and Greystone Books, 2011.

Noel, Thomas J. "Paving the Way to Colorado: The Evolution of Auto Tourism in Denver." *Journal of the West* 26, no. 3 (July 1987): 42–49.

———. *Buildings of Colorado.* New York: Oxford University Press, for the Society of Architectural Historians, 1997.

Nord, Mark, A. E. Luloff, and Jeffrey C. Bridger. "The Association of Forest Recreation with Environmentalism." *Environment and Behavior* 30, no. 2 (March 1998): 235–46.

[Nordhaus, Hannah]. *Bark Beetle Outbreaks in Western North America: Causes and Consequences; Bark Beetle Symposium, Snowbird, Utah.* Edited by Barbara Bentz. Salt Lake City: University of Utah Press, [2009].

Norris, Scott, ed. *Discovered Country: Tourism and Survival in the American West.* Albuquerque, NM: Stone Ladder Press, 1994.

Notarianni, Gregory J. "Colorado Real Estate Practice in the Twentieth Century." *Colorado Lawyer* 26, no. 6 (June 1997): 169–72.

Novak, Barbara. *Nature and Culture: American Landscape and Painting, 1825–1875.* 1980. 3d ed. New York: Oxford University Press, 2007.

Nugent, Walter. *Into the West: The Story of Its People.* New York: Knopf, 1999.

O'Brien, Jack. "Skiing: Aspen Holiday." *Newsweek,* January 20, 1947, 81–82.

Ogden, John T. "From Spatial to Aesthetic Distance in the Eighteenth Century." *Journal of the History of Ideas* 35, no. 1 (January–March 1974): 63–78.

Olins, Wally. *On Brand.* London: Thames and Hudson, 2003.

Oppenheimer, Doug, and Jim Poore. *Sun Valley: A Biography.* Boise, ID: Beatty Books, 1976.

O'Rear, John, and Frankie O'Rear. *The Aspen Story, Including Skiing the Aspen Way.* New York: A. S. Barnes, 1966.

Ormes, Robert M. "Colorado's Friendly Topland." *National Geographic,* August 1951, 187–214.

———, ed. *Guide to the Colorado Mountains.* Denver: Sage Books, 1952.

Paasi, Anssi. "Place and Region: Regional Worlds and Words." *Progress in Human Geography* 26, no. 6 (2002): 802–11.

Patterson, James T. *Grand Expectations: The United States, 1945–1974.* New York: Oxford University Press, 1996.

Patterson, Steve, and Kenton Forrest. *The Ski Train.* Rev. ed. Golden, CO: Colorado Railroad Museum, 1995.

Pearce, Sarah J., and Roxanne Eflin. *Guide to Historic Aspen and the Roaring Fork Valley.* Evergreen, CO: Cordillera Press, 1990.

Peirce, Neal R. *The Mountain States of America: People, Politics, and Power in the Eight Rocky Mountain States.* New York: Norton, 1972.

Pergams, Oliver R. W., and Patricia A. Zaradic. "Is Love of Nature in the US Becoming Love of Electronic Media? 16-Year Downtrend in National Park Visits Explained by Watching Movies, Playing Video Games, Internet Use, and Oil Prices." *Journal of Environmental Management* 80, no. 4 (September 2006): 387–93.

———. "Evidence for a Fundamental and Pervasive Shift Away from Nature-Based Recreation." *PNAS* 105, no. 7 (February 19, 2008): 2295–2300.

Pfeifer, Friedl. *Nice Goin': My Life on Skis.* With Morten Lund. Missoula, MT: Pictorial Histories Publishing Co., 1993.

Phillips, Sarah T. *This Land, This Nation: Conservation, Rural America, and the New Deal.* Cambridge: Cambridge University Press, 2007.

Philpott, William. "Visions of a Changing Vail: Fast-Growth Fallout in a Colorado Resort Town." Master's thesis, University of Wisconsin at Madison, 1994.

———. "Consuming Colorado: Landscapes, Leisure, and the Tourist Way of Life." PhD diss., University of Wisconsin at Madison, 2002.

Pine, B. Joseph, II, and James H. Gilmore. *The Experience Economy: Work Is Theatre and Every Business a Stage.* Boston: Harvard Business School Press, 1999.

Poff, Chrys M. "The Western Ghost Town in American Culture, 1869–1950." PhD diss., University of Iowa, 2004.

Pollard, Tim. "The Birth and Early Years of Club 20." *Journal of the Western Slope* 11, no. 2 (Spring 1996): 25–36.

Pomeroy, Earl. *In Search of the Golden West: The Tourist in Western America*. New York: Knopf, 1957.

———. *The Pacific Slope: A History of California, Oregon, Washington, Idaho, Utah, and Nevada*. New York: Knopf, 1965.

———. "Computers in the Desert: Transforming the Simple Life." *Western Historical Quarterly* 25, no. 1 (Spring 1994): 6–19.

———. *The American Far West in the Twentieth Century*. New Haven, CT: Yale University Press, 2008.

Popper, Frank J. *The Politics of Land-Use Reform*. Madison: University of Wisconsin Press, 1981.

Potter, David M. *People of Plenty: Economic Abundance and the American Character*. Chicago: University of Chicago Press, 1954.

Power, Dominic, and Atle Hauge. "No Man's Brand—Brands, Institutions, and Fashion." *Growth and Change* 39, no. 1 (March 2008): 123–43.

Power, Thomas Michael. *Lost Landscapes and Failed Economies: The Search for a Value of Place*. Washington, DC: Island Press, 1996.

Power, Thomas Michael, and Richard Barrett. *Post-Cowboy Economics: Pay and Prosperity in the New American West*. Washington, DC: Island Press, 2001.

Pratt, Mary Louise. *Imperial Eyes: Travel Writing and Transculturation*. 2d ed. New York: Routledge, 2008.

Pred, Allan. "Place as Historically Contingent Process: Structuration and the Time-Geography of Becoming Places." *Annals of the Association of American Geographers* 74, no. 2 (1984): 279–97.

Price, Jennifer. *Flight Maps: Adventures with Nature in Modern America*. New York: Basic Books, 1999.

Pritchard, Sandra F. *Southern Summit: A Geographer's Perspective*. [Dillon, CO]: Summit Historical Society, 1984.

———. *Roadside Summit, Part II: The Human Landscape*. Dillon, CO: Summit Historical Society, 1992.

———. *Dillon, Denver and the Dam*. Dillon, CO: Summit Historical Society, 1994.

Purchase, Eric. *Out of Nowhere: Disaster and Tourism in the White Mountains*. Baltimore: Johns Hopkins University Press, 1999.

Rademan, Myles C. "Change Comes to the Mountains: Tourist Towns Face an Uncertain Future." *Planning* 69, no. 1 (January 2003): 16–19.

Rainey, Sue. *Creating "Picturesque America": Monument to the Natural and Cultural Landscape*. Nashville, TN: Vanderbilt University Press, 1994.

Rasker, Ray. "Your Next Job Will Be in Services. Should You Be Worried?" In *Across the Great Divide: Explorations in Collaborative Conservation and the American West*, edited by Philip Brick, Donald Snow, and Sarah Van de Wetering, 51–57. Washington, DC: Island Press, 2001.

Reiger, John F. *American Sportsmen and the Origins of Conservation*. 3d ed. Corvallis: Oregon State University Press, 2000.

Revis, Kathleen. "Colorado by Car and Campfire." *National Geographic*, August 1954, 206–48.

————. "Skiing in the United States." *National Geographic*, February 1959, 216–54.

Rhode, Paul. "The Nash Thesis Revisited: An Economic Historian's View." *Pacific Historical Review* 63, no. 3 (August 1994): 363–92.

Ribal, John Lee. "Changes in Tax Incidence in Eagle County, Colorado Before and After the Development of the Vail Ski Industry." PhD diss., University of Notre Dame, 1986.

Richey, Edward Duke. "Living It Up in Aspen: Post-War America, Ski Town Culture, and the New Western Dream, 1945–1975." PhD diss., University of Colorado, 2006.

Riddle, Ellen Ray. *Louis Dupuy and His Souvenir of France.* Mission Viejo, CA: John Ray Riddle, 1985.

Riebsame, William E., ed. *Atlas of the New West: Portrait of a Changing Region.* New York: Norton, for the Center of the American West, University of Colorado at Boulder, 1997.

Riebsame, W. E., H. Gosnell, and D. M. Theobald. "Land Use and Landscape Change in the Colorado Mountains I: Theory, Scale, and Pattern." *Mountain Research and Development* 16, no. 4 (1996): 395–405.

Rieser, Andrew C. *The Chautauqua Moment: Protestants, Progressives, and the Culture of Modern Liberalism.* New York: Columbia University Press, 2003.

Riley, Marilyn Griggs. "Sin, Gin, and Jasmine: The Controversial Career of Caroline Bancroft." *Colorado Heritage*, Spring 2002, 30–46.

Riley, Robert B. "Thoughts on the New Rural Landscape." *Places* 8, no. 4 (Summer 1993): 84–89.

Ringholz, Raye C. *Uranium Frenzy: Boom and Bust on the Colorado Plateau.* New York: Norton, 1989.

————. *Little Town Blues: Voices from the Changing West.* Layton, UT: Gibbs Smith, 1992.

————. *Paradise Paved: The Challenge of Growth in the New West.* Salt Lake City: University of Utah Press, 1996.

Ristow, Walter W. "American Road Maps and Guides." *Scientific Monthly* 62, no. 5 (May 1946): 397–406.

Robbins, William G. *Landscapes of Conflict: The Oregon Story, 1940–2000.* Seattle: University of Washington Press, 2004.

Roche, Jeff, ed. *The Political Culture of the New West.* Lawrence: University Press of Kansas, 2008.

Rocky Mountain Motorists. *Where to Vacation in Colorado*, aka *Official Travel Directory of Colorado, Official Rocky Mountain Travel Directory*, and *Rocky Mountain Travel Directory.* Annual editions. Denver: Rocky Mountain Motorists, American Automobile Association, 1928–73.

Rogers, James Grafton. *My Rocky Mountain Valley.* Boulder: Pruett, 1968.

Rojek, Chris. *Decentering Leisure: Rethinking Leisure Theory.* London: Sage, 1995.

Rojek, Chris, and John Urry, eds. *Touring Cultures: Transformations of Travel and Theory.* London and New York: Routledge, 1997.

Rollins, William. "Reflections on a Spare Tire: SUVs and Postmodern Environmental Consciousness." *Environmental History* 11, no. 4 (October 2006): 684–723.

Rome, Adam. *The Bulldozer in the Countryside: Suburban Sprawl and the Rise of American Environmentalism.* New York: Cambridge University Press, 2001.

———. "'Give Earth a Chance': The Environmental Movement and the Sixties." *Journal of American History* 90, no. 2 (September 2003): 525–54.

Roosevelt, Theodore. *Ranch Life and the Hunting-Trail*. New York: Century, 1888. Repr., Alexandria, VA: Time-Life Books, 1980.

———. *Outdoor Pastimes of an American Hunter*. New York: Scribner's, 1905. Repr., New York: Arno Press and the New York Times, 1970.

Rose, Mark H. *Interstate: Express Highway Politics, 1939–1989*. Knoxville: University of Tennessee Press, 1990. Rev. ed. of *Interstate: Express Highway Politics, 1941–1956* (Lawrence: University Press of Kansas, 1979).

Rose, Mark H., and Bruce E. Seely. "Getting the Interstate System Built: Road Engineers and the Implementation of Public Policy, 1955–1985." *Journal of Policy History* 2, no. 1 (1990): 23–55.

Rose, Mark H., Bruce E. Seely, and Paul F. Barrett. *The Best Transportation System in the World: Railroads, Trucks, Airlines, and American Public Policy in the Twentieth Century*. Columbus: Ohio State University Press, 2006.

Rothman, Hal K. *Devil's Bargains: Tourism in the Twentieth-Century American West*. Lawrence: University Press of Kansas, 1998.

———. *The Greening of a Nation? Environmentalism in the United States since 1945*. Fort Worth, TX: Harcourt Brace College, 1998.

———, ed. *Reopening the American West*. Tucson: University of Arizona Press, 1998.

———. *Saving the Planet: The American Response to the Environment in the Twentieth Century*. Chicago: Ivan R. Dee, 2000.

Rudzitis, Gundars. "Amenities Increasingly Draw People to the American West." *Rural Development Perspectives* 14, no. 2 (September 1999): 9–13.

Rugh, Susan Sessions. "Branding Utah: Industrial Tourism in the Postwar American West." *Western Historical Quarterly* 37, no. 4 (Winter 2006): 445–72.

———. *Are We There Yet? The Golden Age of American Family Vacations*. Lawrence: University Press of Kansas, 2008.

Rust, Daniel L. *Flying Across America: The Airline Passenger Experience*. Norman: University of Oklahoma Press, 2009.

Ruth, Kent. *Colorado Vacations: An Intimate Guide*. New York: Knopf, 1959.

Sabin, Edwin L. *"Around the Circle": A Thousand Miles through the Rockies on the Rio Grande*. Denver: Denver & Rio Grande Railroad, Passenger Department, 1907.

Sandweiss, Martha A. *Print the Legend: Photography and the American West*. New Haven, CT: Yale University Press, 2002.

Saxon, O. Glenn. *Colorado and Its Mining Industry (1859–1959)*. Denver: Colorado State Chamber of Commerce, Mining and Petroleum Committee, 1959.

Scamehorn, Lee. *High Altitude Energy: A History of Fossil Fuels in Colorado*. Boulder: University Press of Colorado, 2002.

Schafer, Mike, and Joe Welsh. *Classic American Streamliners*. Osceola, WI: Motorbooks International, 1997.

Scharff, Robert. *The Magic of Frontierland: Romantic and Ingenious Vacation Ideas in America's Colorful Western Wonderland*. New York: Grosset and Dunlap, with Frontier Airlines, 1968.

Scharff, Virginia. *Twenty Thousand Roads: Women, Movement, and the West*. Berkeley: University of California Press, 2003.

Schivelbusch, Wolfgang. *The Railway Journey: The Industrialization of Time and Space in the Nineteenth Century*. Berkeley: University of California Press, 1986.

Schmitt, Peter J. *Back to Nature: The Arcadian Myth in Urban America*. New York: Oxford University Press, 1969.

Schrepfer, Susan R. "Perspectives on Conservation: Sierra Club Strategies in Mineral King." *Journal of Forest History* 20, no. 4 (October 1976): 176–90.

Schullery, Paul. *American Fly Fishing: A History*. New York: Nick Lyons Books, 1987.

Schulman, Bruce J. *From Cotton Belt to Sunbelt: Federal Policy, Economic Development, and the Transformation of the South, 1938–1980*. New York: Oxford University Press, 1991.

Schulte, Steven C. *Wayne Aspinall and the Shaping of the American West*. Boulder: University Press of Colorado, 2002.

Schulten, Susan. "How to See Colorado: The Federal Writers' Project, American Regionalism, and the 'Old New Western History.'" *Western Historical Quarterly* 36, no. 1 (Spring 2005): 49–70.

Schwantes, Carlos Arnaldo. *Going Places: Transportation Redefines the Twentieth-Century West*. Bloomington: Indiana University Press, 2003.

Schwartz, Rosalie. *Pleasure Island: Tourism and Temptation in Cuba*. Lincoln: University of Nebraska Press, 1997.

Scott, Amy L. "Remaking Urban in the American West: Urban Environmentalism, Lifestyle Politics, and Hip Capitalism in Boulder, Colorado." In *The Political Culture of the New West*, edited by Jeff Roche, 251–80. Lawrence: University Press of Kansas, 2008.

Scott, Mel. *American City Planning Since 1890: A History Commemorating the Fiftieth Anniversary of the American Institute of Planners*. Berkeley: University of California Press, 1969.

Seaman, Wayne R. *The Fishes of Colorado*. Rev. ed. Denver: Colorado Department of Game and Fish, Education Department, 1959.

Searle, Captain Tex. *The Golden Years of Flying: As We Remember*. Orem, UT: Mountain Empire Publishing, 1998.

Sears, John F. *Sacred Places: American Tourist Attractions in the Nineteenth Century*. New York: Oxford University Press, 1989.

Secrest, Clark. "The Picture That Reassured the World." *Colorado Heritage*, Winter 1996, 31–35.

Seely, Bruce E. "The Scientific Mystique in Engineering: Highway Research at the Bureau of Public Roads, 1918–1940." *Technology and Culture* 25, no. 4 (October 1984): 798–831.

———. *Building the American Highway System: Engineers as Policy Makers*. Philadelphia: Temple University Press, 1987.

———. "The Saga of American Infrastructure: A Republic Bound Together." *Wilson Quarterly* 17, no. 1 (Winter 1993): 19–39.

Seibert, Peter W. *Vail: Triumph of a Dream*. With William Oscar Johnson. Boulder: Mountain Sports Press, with Vail Resorts Management Company, 2000.

Sellars, Richard West. *Preserving Nature in the National Parks: A History*. New Haven, CT: Yale University Press, 1997.

Sellers, Christopher. "Body, Place and the State: The Makings of an 'Environmentalist'

Imaginary in the Post-World War II U.S." *Radical History Review* 74 (Spring 1999): 31–64.

Shabecoff, Philip. *A Fierce Green Fire: The American Environmental Movement*. New York: Hill and Wang, 1994.

Shaffer, Marguerite S. *See America First: Tourism and National Identity, 1880–1940*. Washington, DC: Smithsonian Institution Press, 2001.

Shapiro, Aaron Alex. "'One Crop Worth Cultivating': Tourism in the Upper Great Lakes, 1910–1965." PhD diss., University of Chicago, 2005.

Shelton, Peter. *Climb to Conquer: The Untold Story of World War II's 10th Mountain Division Ski Troops*. New York: Scribner, 2003.

Sherman, Joe. *Fast Lane on a Dirt Road: Vermont Transformed, 1945–1990*. Woodstock, VT: Countryman Press, 1991.

Shumway, J. Matthew, and James A. Davis. "Nonmetropolitan Population Change in the Mountain West, 1970–1995." *Rural Sociology* 61, no. 3 (Fall 1996): 513–29.

Simonton, June. *Vail: Story of a Colorado Mountain Valley*. Dallas: Taylor Publishing Co., 1987.

Sirgy, M. Joseph, and Chenting Su. "Destination Image, Self-Congruity, and Travel Behavior: Toward an Integrative Model." *Journal of Travel Research* 38, no. 4 (May 2000): 340–52.

"Skiing: The New Lure of a Supersport." *Time*, December 25, 1972, 54–63.

Slotkin, Richard. *Gunfighter Nation: The Myth of the Frontier in Twentieth-Century America*. New York: Atheneum, 1992.

Smith, Duane A. *Mining America: The Industry and the Environment, 1800–1980*. Lawrence: University Press of Kansas, 1985.

———. "'The Bulliest Time': Theodore Roosevelt and Colorado." *Journal of the West* 34, no. 2 (April 1995): 8–15.

Smith, Steven L. J. "The Tourism Product." *Annals of Tourism Research* 21, no. 3 (1994): 582–95.

Smith, Thompson R. "Destruction and Appropriation: Local Culture and the Corporation in Steamboat Springs." Seminar paper, Yale University, 1982.

Smith, Valene L., ed. *Hosts and Guests: The Anthropology of Tourism*. Philadelphia: University of Pennsylvania Press, 1977.

Snepenger, David J., Jerry D. Johnson, and Raymond Rasker. "Travel-Stimulated Entrepreneurial Migration." *Journal of Travel Research* 34, no. 1 (Summer 1995): 40–44.

Souther, J. Mark. *New Orleans on Parade: Tourism and the Transformation of the Crescent City*. Baton Rouge: Louisiana State University Press, 2006.

Sprague, Marshall. *The Great Gates: The Story of the Rocky Mountain Passes*. Boston: Little, Brown, 1964.

———. *Newport in the Rockies: The Life and Good Times of Colorado Springs*. 4th rev. ed. Athens, OH: Swallow Press, 1987.

Sprague, Marshall, Libby Block, John Chapman, William E. Barrett, William Cox-Ife, Mary Chase, and Caroline Bancroft. *Enchanted Central City*. Central City, CO: Central City Opera House Association, [ca. 1956].

Starr, Kevin. *Americans and the California Dream, 1850–1915*. New York: Oxford University Press, 1973.

————. *Inventing the Dream: California through the Progressive Era.* New York: Oxford University Press, 1985.

————. *Material Dreams: Southern California through the 1920s.* New York: Oxford University Press, 1991.

————. *Embattled Dreams: California in War and Peace, 1940–1950.* New York: Oxford University Press, 2002.

————. *Golden Dreams: California in an Age of Abundance, 1950–1963.* New York: Oxford University Press, 2009.

Steen, Harold K. *The U.S. Forest Service: A History.* Centennial ed. Seattle: University of Washington Press; Durham, NC: Forest History Society, 2004.

Stegner, Wallace, ed. *This Is Dinosaur: Echo Park Country and Its Magic Rivers.* New York: Knopf, 1955.

Steinberg, Ted. *Down to Earth: Nature's Role in American History.* New York: Oxford University Press, 2002.

Sternberg, Barbara, and Gene Sternberg. *Evergreen: Our Mountain Community.* Evergreen, CO: Sternberg and Sternberg, 1987.

Sternberg, Dick. *Trout: The Complete Guide to Catching Trout with Flies, Artificial Lures and Live Bait.* Chanhassen, MN: Creative Publishing, 1988.

Sterngass, Jon. *First Resorts: Pursuing Pleasure at Saratoga Springs, Newport, and Coney Island.* Baltimore: Johns Hopkins University Press, 2001.

Stewart, George R. *U.S. 40: Cross Section of the United States of America.* Boston: Houghton Mifflin, 1953.

Stover, John F. *American Railroads.* 2d ed. Chicago: University of Chicago Press, 1997.

Strasser, Susan. *Satisfaction Guaranteed: The Making of the American Mass Market.* New York: Pantheon, 1989.

————, ed. *Commodifying Everything: Relations of the Market.* New York: Routledge, 2003.

Stroud, Hubert B. *The Promise of Paradise: Recreational and Retirement Communities in the United States since 1950.* Baltimore: Johns Hopkins University Press, 1995.

Summers, Gregory. *Consuming Nature: Environmentalism in the Fox River Valley, 1850–1950.* Lawrence: University Press of Kansas, 2006.

Sundbo, Jon, and Per Darmer, eds. *Creating Experiences in the Experience Economy.* Northampton, MA: Edward Elgar Publishing, 2008.

Sunset Books and Sunset Magazine editors. *New Homes for Western Living.* Menlo Park, CA: Lane Book Co., 1956.

"Sunset" Ideas for Family Camping. Menlo Park, CA: Lane Book Co., 1957.

"Sunset" Ideas for Outdoor Family Fun in the West. Menlo Park, CA: Lane Book Co., 1958.

"Sunset" Magazine: A Century of Western Living, 1898–1998; Historical Portraits and a Chronological Bibliography of Selected Topics. Stanford, CA: Stanford University Libraries, 1998.

Sunset Magazine and Books editors. *Western Ranch Houses by Cliff May.* Menlo Park, CA: Lane Book Co., 1958. Repr., Santa Monica, CA: Hennessey + Ingalls, 1997.

Sunset Magazine editors, in collaboration with Cliff May. *"Sunset" Western Ranch Houses.* San Francisco: Lane Publishing Co., 1946. Repr., Santa Monica, CA: Hennessey + Ingalls, 1999.

Sutter, Paul S. *Driven Wild: How the Fight against Automobiles Launched the Modern Wilderness Movement*. Seattle: University of Washington Press, 2002.

Szasz, Ferenc M. "Wheeler and Holy Cross: Colorado's 'Lost' National Monuments." *Journal of Forest History* 21, no. 3 (July 1977): 133–44.

Talbot, Carl. "The Wilderness Narrative and the Cultural Logic of Capitalism." In *The Great New Wilderness Debate*, edited by J. Baird Callicott and Michael P. Nelson, 325–33. Athens: University of Georgia Press, 1998.

Talmadge, Marian, and Iris Gilmore. *Colorado Hi-Ways and By-Ways: Picturesque Trails and Tours*. Vol. 1, *Denver and Northeastern Colorado*. Denver: Monitor Publications, 1959.

Taylor, Bayard. *Colorado: A Summer Trip*. New York: Putnam, 1867. Repr., Niwot: University Press of Colorado, 1989.

Taylor, Bob Pepperman. *Our Limits Transgressed: Environmental Political Thought in America*. Lawrence: University Press of Kansas, 1992.

Taylor, Frank J. "Colorado's Fabulous Mountains of Oil." *Reader's Digest*, June 1957, 132–38.

Taylor, Joseph E., III. "The Many Lives of the New West." *Western Historical Quarterly* 35, no. 2 (Summer 1994): 141–65.

———. *Pilgrims of the Vertical: Yosemite Rock Climbers and Nature at Risk*. Cambridge, MA: Harvard University Press, 2010.

Teale, Edwin Way. *Journey into Summer*. New York: Dodd, Mead, 1960.

Teisl, Mario F., and Kelly O'Brien. "Who Cares and Who Acts? Outdoor Recreationists Exhibit Different Levels of Environmental Concern and Behavior." *Environment and Behavior* 35, no. 4 (July 2003): 506–22.

Theobald, D. M., H. Gosnell, and W. E. Riebsame. "Land Use and Landscape Change in the Colorado Mountains II: A Case Study of the East River Valley." *Mountain Research and Development* 16, no. 4 (1996): 407–18.

Theodori, Gene L., A. E. Luloff, and Fern K. Willits. "The Association of Outdoor Recreation and Environmental Concern: Reexamining the Dunlap-Heffernan Thesis." *Rural Sociology* 63, no. 1 (March 1998): 94–108.

Thomas, Clive S., ed. *Politics and Public Policy in the Contemporary American West*. Albuquerque: University of New Mexico Press, 1991.

Thomas, John L. *A Country in the Mind: Wallace Stegner, Bernard DeVoto, History, and the American Land*. New York and London: Routledge, 2002.

Thomas, Thomas A. "Roads to a Troubled Future: Transportation and Transformation in Colorado's Interstate Highway Corridors in the Nineteenth and Twentieth Centuries." PhD diss., University of Colorado, 1996.

Thompson, Dr. Hunter S. "The Battle of Aspen." *Rolling Stone*, October 1, 1970, 30–37. Reprinted as "Freak Power in the Rockies" in Thompson, *The Great Shark Hunt: Strange Tales from a Strange Time*, 151–74. New York: Summit Books and Rolling Stone Press, 1979.

Tilden, Freeman. *The State Parks: Their Meaning in American Life*. New York: Knopf, 1962.

Toll, Seymour I. *Zoned America*. New York: Grossman, 1969.

Tompkins, Jane. *West of Everything: The Inner Life of Westerns*. New York: Oxford University Press, 1992.

Towler, Sureva. *The History of Skiing at Steamboat Springs.* [Steamboat Springs, CO: By the author?], 1987.

Travis, William R. *New Geographies of the American West: Land Use and the Changing Patterns of Place.* Washington, DC: Island Press, 2007.

Trenton, Patricia, and Peter H. Hassrick. *The Rocky Mountains: A Vision for Artists in the Nineteenth Century.* Norman: University of Oklahoma Press, in association with the Buffalo Bill Historical Center, Cody, WY, 1983.

Tuan, Yi-Fu. "Space and Place: Humanistic Perspective." In *Progress in Geography,* vol. 6, edited by Christopher Board et al., 211–52. London: Edward Arnold, 1974.

———. *Topophilia: A Study of Environmental Perception, Attitudes, and Values.* Englewood Cliffs, NJ: Prentice-Hall, 1974.

———. *Space and Place: The Perspective of Experience.* Minneapolis: University of Minnesota Press, 1977.

Tunnard, Christopher, and Boris Pushkarev. *Man-Made America: Chaos or Control?* New Haven, CT: Yale University Press, 1963.

Turner, Frederick Jackson. "The Significance of the Frontier in American History." In *The Frontier in American History,* 1–38. New York: Henry Holt, 1920. Repr., Tucson: University of Arizona Press, 1986.

Turner, James Morton. "From Woodcraft to 'Leave No Trace': Wilderness, Consumerism, and Environmentalism in Twentieth-Century America." *Environmental History* 7, no. 3 (July 2002): 462–84.

Turner, Tom. "Who Speaks for the Future?" *Sierra,* July–August 1990, 30–38, 67–72.

Tweto, Ogden. "Tectonic History of West-Central Colorado." In *Exploration Frontiers of the Central and Southern Rockies,* edited by Harry K. Veal, 11–22. Denver: Rocky Mountain Association of Geologists, 1977.

Twitchell, James B. *Adcult USA: The Triumph of Advertising in American Culture.* New York: Columbia University Press, 1996.

———. *Lead Us into Temptation: The Triumph of American Materialism.* New York: Columbia University Press, 1999.

Tyler, Daniel. *The Last Water Hole in the West: The Colorado–Big Thompson Project and the Northern Colorado Water Conservancy District.* Niwot: University Press of Colorado, 1992.

Ubbelohde, Carl, Maxine Benson, and Duane A. Smith. *A Colorado History.* 8th ed. Boulder: Pruett, 2001.

Urquhart, Lena M. *Glenwood Springs: Spa in the Mountains.* Boulder: Pruett, 1970. Updated ed. [Dallas, TX]: Taylor Publishing Co., 1985.

Urry, John. *Consuming Places.* London: Routledge, 1995.

"Vail Pass Highway: Respecter of Mountain Ecology." *Civil Engineering* 50, no. 6 (June 1980): 70–72.

Vale, Thomas R., and Geraldine R. Vale. *U.S. 40 Today: Thirty Years of Landscape Change in America.* Madison: University of Wisconsin Press, 1983.

———. *Western Images, Western Landscapes: Travels along U.S. 89.* Tucson: University of Arizona Press, 1989.

Vandenbusche, Duane, and Duane A. Smith. *A Land Alone: Colorado's Western Slope.* Boulder: Pruett, 1981.

Van Gytenbeek, R. P. *The Way of a Trout*. Philadelphia: Lippincott, with Trout Unlimited, 1972.

Van Liere, Kent D., and Francis P. Noe. "Outdoor Recreation and Environmental Attitudes: Further Examination of the Dunlap-Heffernan Thesis." *Rural Sociology* 46, no. 3 (Fall 1981): 505–13.

Venturoni, Linda. *The Social and Economic Effects of Second Homes*. Silverthorne: Northwest Colorado Council of Governments, 2004.

Vias, Alexander C. "Jobs Follow People in the Rural Rocky Mountain West." *Rural Development Perspectives* 14, no. 2 (September 1999): 14–23.

Vincent, D. E. *Climax Kids, 1956*. Bloomington, IN: AuthorHouse, 2004.

Voigt, William, Jr. *Public Grazing Lands: Use and Misuse by Industry and Government*. New Brunswick, NJ: Rutgers University Press, 1976.

———. *Born with Fists Doubled: Defending Outdoor America*. Iowa City, IA: Izaak Walton League of America Endowment, 1992.

Vorkinn, Marit, and Hanne Riese. "Environmental Concern in a Local Context: The Significance of Place Attachment." *Environment and Behavior* 33, no. 2 (March 2001): 249–63.

Voynick, Stephen M. *Leadville: A Miner's Epic*. Missoula, MT: Mountain Press, 1984.

———. *Climax: The History of Colorado's Climax Molybdenum Mine*. Missoula, MT: Mountain Press, 1996.

Wagar, J. V. K. "Recreation in Relation to Multiple Land Use in the West." *Journal of Forestry* 41, no. 11 (November 1943): 798–802.

———. "Some Major Principles in Recreation Land Use Planning." *Journal of Forestry* 49, no. 6 (June 1951): 431–35.

Walker, Donald L., Jr. *John A. Love: The Story of Colorado's Thirty-Sixth Governor*. Denver: University of Colorado at Denver, 2000.

Warren, Louis S. *The Hunter's Game: Poachers and Conservationists in Twentieth-Century America*. New Haven, CT: Yale University Press, 1997.

Washabaugh, William. *Deep Trout: Angling in Popular Culture*. With Catherine Washabaugh. Oxford: Berg, 2000.

Waterman, Charles F. *Fishing in America*. New York: Holt, Rinehart and Winston, 1975.

Wellock, Thomas R. *Preserving the Nation: The Conservation and Environmental Movements, 1870–2000*. Wheeling, IL: Harlan Davidson, 2007.

Wells, Christopher W. *Car Country: An Environmental History*. Seattle: University of Washington Press, 2012.

White, Richard. *"It's Your Misfortune and None of My Own": A History of the American West*. Norman: University of Oklahoma Press, 1991.

Whiteside, James. *Colorado: A Sports History*. Niwot: University Press of Colorado, 1999.

Wiebe, Robert H. *The Search for Order, 1877–1920*. New York: Hill and Wang, 1967.

Wiley, Marion C. *The High Road*. Denver: Colorado Department of Highways, Division of Highways, [1976].

Wiley, Peter, and Robert Gottlieb. *Empires in the Sun: The Rise of the New American West*. New York: Putnam, 1982.

Wilkinson, Charles F. *Crossing the Next Meridian: Land, Water, and the Future of the West*. Washington, DC: Island Press, 1992.

————. *The Eagle Bird: Mapping a New West*. New York: Pantheon, 1992.

Williams, Michael. *Americans and Their Forests: A Historical Geography*. Cambridge: Cambridge University Press, 1989.

Wilson, Alexander. *The Culture of Nature: North American Landscapes from Disney to the Exxon Valdez*. Toronto: Between the Lines, 1991.

Wilson, William H. *The City Beautiful Movement*. Baltimore: Johns Hopkins University Press, 1989.

————. "New Wine in Old Bottles: The Denver Mountain Parks Movement." *Colorado Heritage*, Issue 2, 1989, 10–33.

Winiwarter, Verena. "Nationalized Nature on Picture Postcards: Subtexts of Tourism from an Environmental Perspective." *Global Environment* 1 (2008): 192–215.

Winks, Robin W. *Laurance S. Rockefeller: Catalyst for Conservation*. Washington, DC: Island Press, 1997.

Withey, Lynne. *Grand Tours and Cook's Tours: A History of Leisure Travel, 1750 to 1915*. New York: Morrow, 1997.

Wolf, Tom. *Arthur Carhart: Wilderness Prophet*. Boulder: University Press of Colorado, 2008.

Wolfe, Mark. "How the Lincoln Highway Snubbed Colorado." *Colorado Heritage*, Autumn 1999, 3–21.

Wolle, Muriel Sibell. *Ghost Cities of Colorado: A Pictorial Record of Central City, Black Hawk and Nevadaville*. Boulder: By the author, 1933.

————. *Cloud Cities of Colorado: A Pictorial Record of Leadville, Robinson, Kokomo, Climax, Fairplay, Breckenridge*. Denver: Smith-Brooks Printing Co., 1934.

————. *Stampede to Timberline: The Ghost Towns and Mining Camps of Colorado*. Boulder: By the author, 1949.

————. *Timberline Tailings: Tales of Colorado's Ghost Towns and Mining Camps*. Chicago: Swallow Press, 1977.

Wood, Samuel E., and Alfred E. Heller. *California Going, Going . . .* Sacramento: California Tomorrow, 1962.

Woods, Kenneth B., Donald S. Berry, and William H. Goetz, eds. *Highway Engineering Handbook*. New York: McGraw-Hill, 1960.

World Tourism Organization. *Resolutions of International Conference on Travel and Tourism, Ottawa, Canada*. Madrid: World Tourism Organization, 1991.

Worster, Donald. *Nature's Economy: A History of Ecological Ideas*. 2d ed. Cambridge: Cambridge University Press, 1994.

Wright, John B. *Rocky Mountain Divide: Selling and Saving the West*. Austin: University of Texas Press, 1993.

Writers' Program of the Work Projects Administration in the State of Wyoming. *Wyoming: A Guide to Its History, Highways, and People*. New York: Oxford University Press, 1941.

Wrobel, David M. *Promised Lands: Promotion, Memory, and the Creation of the American West*. Lawrence: University Press of Kansas, 2002.

Wrobel, David M., and Patrick T. Long, eds. *Seeing and Being Seen: Tourism in the American West*. Lawrence: University Press of Kansas, for the Center of the American West, University of Colorado at Boulder, 2001.

Wyckoff, William. "Denver's Aging Commercial Strip." *Geographical Review* 82, no. 3 (July 1992): 282–94.

———. *Creating Colorado: The Making of a Western American Landscape, 1860–1940.* New Haven, CT: Yale University Press, 1999.

Wylie, Evan M. "Ghost Town on Skis." *Collier's*, February 7, 1948, 24–26, 52–53.

Wyman, Walker D. *Mythical Creatures of the U.S.A. and Canada.* River Falls: University of Wisconsin-River Falls Press, 1978.

Yetter, George Humphrey. *Williamsburg Before and After: The Rebirth of Virginia's Colonial Capital.* Williamsburg, VA: Colonial Williamsburg Foundation, 1988.

Yorke, Douglas A., Jr., John Margolies, and Eric Baker. *Hitting the Road: The Art of the American Road Map.* San Francisco: Chronicle Books, 1996.

Young, Allen. *Opera in Central City.* Denver: Spectrographics, 1993.

Zeman, Scott C. "High Roads and Highways to Romance: New Mexico Highway Journal and Arizona Highways (Re)Present the Southwest." *New Mexico Historical Review* 78, no. 4 (Fall 2003): 419–38.

Zim, Herbert S., in consultation with the University of Colorado Museum staff. *The Rocky Mountains.* New York: Golden Press; Racine, WI: Western Publishing Co., 1964.

ACKNOWLEDGMENTS

IN THE YEARS I'VE SPENT ON THIS PROJECT, COLORADO HAS BEEN THROUGH four governors and gained about 1.6 million in population, and I swear Denver's average daily high has risen a few degrees. Which is one way of saying that *Vacationland* has taken more time and trouble than I ever thought possible. But it always was, and has remained throughout, a true labor of love. One of its most essential groundings is my lifelong love of the Colorado landscape, a love rooted in childhood family car and camping trips, visiting small mountain towns, or playing in streams, woods, and meadows with my sister, making wildflower bouquets in Coors beer cans (not yet realizing there was anything wrong with picking wildflowers—or with Coors beer). In all the years since, that inspiration has never lessened. But many people have also inspired me, and have helped in every possible way to make this labor of love a reality. It's a great honor to acknowledge them here.

Telling someone you're a historian usually gets one of two reactions: "I always loved history" or "I always hated history." The difference is usually who taught the history. I've been blessed with teachers who brought history alive for me as a craft and a means of understanding; they inspired this book and my wider career. Richard Lopes was not a history teacher, but no teacher did more to make me love learning. I often "blame" my becoming a historian on Fred Engel, because he first showed me the discipline's rigors and rewards, kindling a passion for not just studying history but *doing* it. At Williams College, discussions spilled out of seminar rooms into hallways, faculty offices, dining halls, and even professors' homes; I thrived on the intellectual energy and teacherly dedication of Chris Waters, Joel Wolfe, Charles Dew, Regina Kunzel, Bill Darrow, Kathy Morrissey, and Scott Wong, and I hope this book reflects some of what they taught me. I owe a great debt to mentors at the University of Wisconsin–Madison, especially Linda Gordon and Charles Cohen, who were so generous of their time and set such a high scholarly standard from the start of my graduate studies; John Cooper, a model of meticulous scholarship and good citizenship and an unfailing source of collegial conversation; Tom Vale, who always had time to talk about the West we both love; and Arne Alanen, who gave me great insight and encouragement later in my time at Madison.

But the teacher to whom I owe the most is Bill Cronon. At every stage, from its initial conception to its final publication, he made this book possible. Beyond that, over the years, Bill introduced me to wondrous new ways of seeing, opened countless doors for me, took extra time for me, and urged me to research what (and where) I deeply cared about, persuading me that there really was room for that in the academy. Bill sets a famously high—if hopelessly unreachable—standard with his own storytelling and scholarship, but I've been equally inspired by his youthful curiosity and joy of discovery, respect for traditions and elders, passion for the details and meanings of place, devotion to the ethics of ecology and community, and unfailing decency and humanity. I just can't imagine a better mentor, and I will forever be grateful for his friendship. Thank you, Bill.

The research for *Vacationland* took me into the basements and back rooms of town halls and county courthouses, in search of obsolete community plans and musty volumes of meeting minutes. Everywhere I went, staffers with much more important work to do met my requests for these obscure old records with patience and professionalism. Thanks to the clerks and staff at the cities of Aspen, Idaho Springs, and Leadville; the towns of Breckenridge, Dillon, Eagle, Fraser, Frisco, Georgetown, Granby, Kremmling, Minturn, and Vail; and the counties of Clear Creek, Eagle, Garfield, Grand, Lake, Pitkin, and Summit. Special thanks to Julie Boyd, then the Dillon town clerk, who took time to educate me on municipal administration in small mountain towns.

Like all historians, I'm also indebted to archivists and librarians who made my research possible. Michael Edmonds of the Wisconsin Historical Society is justly beloved by Madison grad students; I benefited from his trademark kindness and good counsel at a critical early stage. At the Colorado State Archives, the staff when I did my research there, especially Jim Chipman, Erin McDanal, Jim Parker, George Orlowski, and Vera Welham, helped locate key state agency records. At Auraria Library, Michael Gryglewicz and Frank Tapp found the Pavlo report. At Vail Associates/Resorts, Jack Affleck let me look through files of historic images, while at Club 20, Greg Walcher opened old records, reflected on the organization's history, and treated me to lunch. Lisa Hancock and Sarah Oates made my time at the Aspen Historical Society very productive. Jim Leyerzapf made visits to the Eisenhower Library a great joy; the detective work he and I did together to track down a critical, long-lost book at the library is one of my favorite research moments ever. And I'm grateful to librarians and other helpers at the Colorado Department of Transportation; Colorado State Library; Vail Public Library; John Tomay Memorial Library in Georgetown; Pitkin County Library; Eagle Public Library; Auraria Library; the University of Colorado's Norlin Library; the University of Denver's Penrose Library; Colorado College's Tutt Library; the U.S. Geological Survey Library in Denver; the Colorado Ski and Snowboard Museum in Vail; and the Holy Cross Ranger Station, White River National Forest, in Minturn.

People at two other repositories deserve special thanks. I can't overstate how good the staff at the Denver Public Library's Western History Department have been to me. Thanks above all to Jim Kroll, Joan Harms, Phil Panum, John Irwin, Colleen Nunn, and Bruce Hanson for their interest in my work, endless supply of source ideas, knowledge of Colorado history, and warmth and good humor. I got invaluable help at earlier stages from DPL's Barbara Walton and the late Augie Mastrogiuseppe and Eleanor Gehres, and at a later stage from James Rogers and Wendel Cox. Then there's the Colorado Historical Society (now History Colorado), where I've spent more research time than anywhere else. Society librarians, especially Rebecca Lintz and Barbara Dey, were always generous with their time and extraordinarily patient as I wandered around their workspace and spent hours upon hours reeling through unindexed small-town newspapers on microfilm. Keith Schrum and Patrick Fraker aided and encouraged me greatly, and talks with Eric Paddock always yielded insights and inspiration. Over the years, my friends David Wetzel and Steve Grinstead helped me personally and professionally in too many ways to count. But most of all, I remember Stan Oliner, who took me under his wing years ago and proved an endless font of enthusiasm and energy, door-openings and dogged pursuit of rare sources, and fascinating and funny anecdotes about everything Colorado. Stan, you are another big reason I went through with this crazy business, and I will never forget all you did for me. I dearly miss our *Denver Post* runs and Duffy's lunches, and I dearly wish you could see this book.

Image research and permissions for this book proved difficult, but many kind people lent a hand, like Shelly Bellm; Robert C., Laura, and Norma Bishop; Amy Brooks; Rick Carroll; Gay Curlin; Valerie Doyle; Rosemary

Evetts; John Garnsey; Debra Gust; Chris Jarnot; Patricia Labounty; Laura
Libby; Matt Lutts; Joan Pinamont; Chris Romer; Peter Runyon; George
Ruther; Suzanne Silverthorn; Kathy Struss; Jay Walla; J. Kent Wimmer;
and Krista York-Woolley. Thanks especially to Jack Affleck, Coi Drum-
mond-Gehrig, Dick Lamm, Mirte Mallory, George Orlowski, Anna Scott,
and Derick Wangaard, who went extra miles to locate, reproduce, or otherwise help with the images I hoped for. I always knew maps would be essential to this book, and the staff at the University of Wisconsin Cartography
Lab crafted wonderful maps.

One delight of studying such recent history is having the chance to talk
with some of the people who made it. Sadly, several of them have since
passed. Even so, I'd like to thank George Caulkins Jr., Ernie Chavez, Ben
Duke Jr., Earl Eaton, Pepi Gramshammer, Joe Macy, Marcia and David Sage,
Fitzhugh Scott Jr., Pete Seibert, and Rôd Slifer for taking time to talk to me
and in many cases offering additional help. The remarkable Paul Hauk took
interest in this work and left a treasure trove of documents to mine. He,
along with Dick Lamm, Terry Minger, and Bob Parker, showed a rare ability and willingness to candidly assess their own work in historical context.
I doubt all these people will or would agree with all the conclusions I draw
in this book, but I hope they know how much I appreciate their kindness.

Some of the most valuable help came from people I *haven't* met: western historians and writers of an earlier generation, like Earl Pomeroy and
Wallace Stegner; local historians, who rarely get enough credit from academic historians, but without whom I could not have done such a place-cen-
tered project as this; and journalists like Allen Best, Joanne Ditmer, Philip
Fradkin, Brad Knickerbocker, Ed Quillen, and basically everyone at *High
Country News*, who've shed great insight on the political and social conflicts
and environmental dilemmas of today's West.

I'm a little biased, but I'm not sure any other historical subfield can boast
so many ridiculously brilliant scholars, who manage also to be so generous,
down-to-earth, and fun, as environmental and western history. For years
I've been sponging ideas off them, and I thank those who shared panels,
roundtables, reading groups, and workshops; commented on papers; and
took interest in my work. An incomplete list would include Mike Amund-
son, Kathy Brosnan, Connie Chiang, Mike Childers, Cam Cocks, Lawrence Culver, Kip Curtis, Mark Fiege, Jeff Filipiak, John Findlay, Anne
Hyde, Karl Jacoby, Kathy Jellison, Ari Kelman, Todd Kerstetter, Andy Kirk,
Matt Klingle, Howard Lamar, Patty Limerick, Char Miller, Kathy Morse,

Mary Murphy, Tom Noel, Brad Raley, Ray Rast, Duke Richey, Monica Rico, Peggy Shaffer, Aaron Shapiro, Paul Sutter, Jay Taylor, Sam Truett, Louis Warren, and David Wrobel. All of them, in one way or another, enlightened and encouraged me at key moments. Audiences at conferences of the Western History Association, American Society for Environmental History, Agricultural History Society, and Social Science History Association, and at the University of Wisconsin, Illinois State University, and the University of Denver, asked challenging questions and offered valuable criticism and praise alike. Susan Rugh and Annie Gilbert Coleman read the manuscript and pointed out ways to make it better; beyond that, both have been ongoing sources of good cheer and good ideas, and they set the bar for tourist and recreational history. And Hal Rothman took an early interest in this project and became another mentor, collaborating with me and boosting me at a time when I wasn't sure I had much to contribute. I'll never forget that, or him.

I'm humbled to be a part of the Weyerhaeuser Environmental Books series, and I thank the good people at the University of Washington Press for keeping faith in this project through the unexpectedly long process. Julidta Tarver took early interest and encouraged me in the revisions; Nicole Mitchell pushed the project forward at a critical moment; Julie Van Pelt greatly improved the manuscript with her eagle-eye editing and good humor; designer Dustin Kilgore and managing editor Marilyn Trueblood kept things organized and on track in the late stages. UWP's crack production and marketing staff made the book look good. As for Marianne Keddington-Lang, I cannot thank her enough for her patience, sage advice, gentle prodding, and moral support. It's largely because of her and Bill Cronon that this project survived the many delays and doubts I had about it.

Much-needed funding for my research, writing, presentations, and illustrations, came from the University of Wisconsin–Madison, the UW History Department, Illinois State University, the University of Denver (where I'm especially grateful to Anne McCall for her assistance), the Charles Redd Center for Western Studies at Brigham Young University, and the Denver Public Library. I thank Joy Hilliard for her generous support of environmental history scholarship; being chosen as a Hilliard Fellow at DPL was a great honor and a terrific boost to this project.

Many, many friends helped with this project over the years. Various of them read drafts, helped brainstorm ideas, asked piercing questions, shared research tips, inspired me with their own scholarship, and took my mind off my topic when that was exactly what I needed. From the phenomenal Madison grad student community, thanks especially to Sean Adams, Thomas Andrews, Will Barnett, Katie Benton-Cohen, Thea Browder, David Chang, Tracey Deutsch, Angela Ellis, Jim Feldman, Pam Foster Felt, Ted Frantz, Durba Ghosh, David Grace, Joe Hall, Maggie Hogan, Adam Land, Natasha Larimer, Katy Magee, Monica Najar, Mike Rawson, Jon Rees, Alexander Shashko, Kendra Smith-Howard, Jenka Sokol, Jamie Spiller, Dave Stradling, Chris Wells, and Brian Williams: all of you, whether you knew it or not, helped me greatly to get through it all. Lynne Heasley, Jared Orsi, Louise Pubols, Greg Summers, and Marsha Weisiger were an outstanding dissertator group; I'm thrilled my book can finally join all of theirs. Finally, to Eric Morser, Louise and Marsha (again), Sarah Fatherly, Sarah Marcus, and Andy Rieser: without your wise counsel; better judgment; shared pitchers, road trips, and restaurant and retail therapy runs; sense of humor; countless thought-provoking conversations; intellectual inspiration; and compassion, patience, and faith; there is no way this gets done or I get through.

At Illinois State University, another exceptional group of colleagues helped me through a whole new round of research and writing. For advice, insights, comfort food, and moral support, I thank the entire ISU history department, most of all Ray Clemens, Tony Crubaugh, Andrew Hartman, Richard Hughes, Larry McBride, Kate McCarthy, Lucinda McCray, Katrin Paehler, and the "breakfast club" of Clifton Jones, David MacDonald, and Lou Perez. Roger Biles and Diane Zosky provided timely help with the process. Mark Wyman set an example with his scholarship, warmth, decency, and love of the land. Talks with John Freed always made me think, and I am grateful for all his help. No one heartened me more, or made me feel more at home, than Richard Soderlund. Alan Lessoff took real interest in this work, read drafts, recommended readings, and brightened more days than he knows. And Amy Wood made me laugh and kept me sane (though she might beg to differ), and like Alan, she inspired me with her brilliance and forced me to sharpen my thinking. They are model colleagues and dear friends. At the University of Denver, I've again found terrific colleagues who've energized me through this project's last gasps. Sincere thanks to Yasmaine Ford Faggan, Mike Gibbs, Joyce Goodfriend, Carol Helstosky, Don Hughes, Rafael Ioris, Beth Karlsgodt, Jodie Kreider, Rahul Nair, Nick Rockwell, and Jonathan Sciarcon. I especially thank Liz Escobedo, Susan Schulten, and Ingrid Tague for doing so much to help me settle in at DU;

Susan in particular has taken interest in this project and been a great source of ideas and inspiration.

I owe yet another great debt to yet another group of colleagues: my students. At ISU, DU, and UW-Madison, whether in surveys or specialized classes, first-year courses or capstones, I've always found that I learn as much or more from my students than they likely do from me. They bring fresh new ways of seeing, challenge my views and/or push me to explain them better, and keep me from cocooning inside my own focus, reminding me to see my issues, people, and places in wider context. I can't possibly list all the students who've taught and inspired me over the years; I hope they don't mind a sincere blanket thanks.

And a raised glass of gratitude to loyal, longtime friends outside the history world, like Dylan Bloy, Matt Dunn, Holly Hacker, and especially Craig Kronhart, who have bolstered me in this work and everything else over these many years.

It's fitting that the last two paragraphs I'll write for this book get back to where it all began: my family. My very interest in history started with stories about my grandpa growing up in post-gold rush Cripple Creek. Over the years other family stories fascinated me—of migration and immigration, hand-built houses and curved-dash automobiles, farms, family trips, war, love, loss, and patterns of everyday life—and I began to wonder how such stories fit with the wider currents of the past. In ways unexpected, stories of my dad growing up in Colorado and my mom moving here as a young adult became grounding points for the issues I explore in this book. Yet there is a more basic reason for thanking family last and most emphatically: because they deserve ultimate credit for anything I've accomplished. There are my grandparents, who taught me lessons I'm still realizing; I often imagine talking to them about this book and so much else that has unfolded since they've gone. There is my extended family in Colorado, Michigan, and elsewhere. There is my (relatively) new California family, especially Barbara, Allen, Randy, and Noelle Balik, who are so unfailingly positive and have been so understanding when the crush of work kept me from being the same. There are my nephews and niece, Nicholas, Paulo, and Isabel Costa, who make me so proud and happy, and also make me laugh—and Amauri Costa: *estou muito feliz que você é meu irmão.* And there are my parents, Peter and Ruth Philpott, and sister, Kathy Philpott Costa. This is not the place to go into yet more detail, so I'll just say that they've helped me in infinite ways: setting me up for a lifetime of learning with dinner-table conversations, family trips, and walls of books; helping me hash out ideas over the phone; being practical when I wasn't; picking me up when I crashed; and showing faith when I had none. They are finally why my research, my career, and really every path in my life keeps taking me back to my roots, back to home.

Alongside these three closest friends I can now acknowledge three more, which makes me luckier than I ever could have hoped. Carly and Peter have done much more than distract me from work. Far more importantly, they've filled our home with writings and drawings, pets in jars and parking lots, stories and songs—and me with happiness and love. They've gotten me back in touch with the joy of discovery, of seeing the simplest things with wide, wondering eyes. They've renewed my yen for both teaching and learning, and my awe at the way one always becomes the other. They're not yet at the stage where they can read a draft or critique my analysis—and arguably I should never ask that of them anyway—but they have already taught and bettered me more than they can know. And then, Shelby Balik. She *has* read drafts. She *has* critiqued my analysis, edited my writing. When you're a historian, it's enormously helpful to have a much better historian in the same house; my work is immeasurably better because of her. But much more than that, she is all we promised each other, and so much more: an unwavering ally, a fair critic, an open mind, an obstacle-smasher, a kind and loyal soul, a pragmatic thinker, a sounding board, a travel partner, a historian of our lives together, a protector from demons, a muse, a speaker and a listener, a fellow lover of all the little things—my best friend.

INDEX

Page numbers in italics refer to illustrations, maps, or captions.

"1041 powers," 402n87

A

AAA. *See* American Automobile Association
Abbott, Jim, 271
active recreation, shift toward, 15–16, 132–33, 140, 311n32
adventures and thrills, as tourist marketing theme, 131, 132–33, 134–35, 140–41, 143, 357n42
advertising and marketing, basic techniques of, 20–21, 131. *See also* brands and branding; place packaging, tourist advertising and marketing; tourist advertising imagery; tourist advertising themes
Advertising and Publicity Committee (APC), aka Department of Development, Sportsmen's Hospitality Committee, and Winter Sports Committee: budget battle, 49–50, 323n62–324n65; climate, advertises, 64, 65, 67–68; Colorado entry for *Encyclopædia Britannica*, produces, 307n3; "Cool, Colorful Colorado" slogan, 61, 65,

328n99; corporate relocation and, 167; fishing and hunting and, 65, 132–33; at Governor's Travel and Hospitality Conference, 53; lure book, 51, 61, 69, 328n99; Old West imagery and, 69; predecessors, 323n59; "Prospector's Trail" and, 330n114; scenic descriptions by, 58; seasonal tourism and, 65–66; skiing and, 65, 66, 137, 142, 150; spearheads state promotion of tourism, 49, 50–51; statistical studies of tourism, funds, 54; tourist lifestyle and, 165–66; tries to sell Coloradans on tourism, 2, 2–4; "Victory Vacations" campaign, 44, 49. *See also* Colorado Division of Commerce and Development
affordable housing concerns, 171, 186–87, 216, 286, 298, 368n145. *See also* resort workers
airlines and air travel: airports in high country, 81, 317n26, 332n9–10; Denver as repair stop, 331n7; excitement over potential of, 80–81; at Governor's Travel and Hospitality Conference, 53; hindered by high country topography, 81–82, 332n12; service to Denver and the high country, 52, 81, 332n12; tourist boosting by, 52–53, 325n74
Ajax. *See* Aspen Mountain
Allen, E. John B., 311n32

Allen, James Sloan, 316n18, 320n42

Allott, Gordon, 138, 207, 274, 375n54

American Airlines, 331n7

American Automobile Association (AAA): accused of bias toward Highway 40, 337n43; Echo Park and, 373n41; guidebooks, 51, 324n69; Idaho Springs and, 338n48; membership of, 324n69; mountain driving, advice on, 83; promotes high country, 51; TripTiks, 51, 94. *See also* Rocky Mountain Motorists (AAA)

American Forestry Association, 135–36

American Hotel and Motel Association, 229

American national identity, nineteenth-century tourism and, 9–10, 311n28

ambiance. *See* atmosphere and ambiance

Anoe, Pearl, 307n3

Antholz property (Vail), acquired for open space, 404n106, 404n109

anti-urban escapism: camping and, 135; Colorado vacations marketed to, 6; John Denver and, 239–40; "magic lands" and, 172, 178; replaced by fears of nuclear war, 353n12; suburbia/suburban nature and, 151, 162, 178; tourist lifestyle and, 164, 187; Vail and, 177–78, 185, 187, 250, 252, 257, 259, 288; wilderness and, 210–11

après-ski scene, 149, 150, 358n54; in Aspen, 150, 319n37; at Georgetown's Red Ram, 153; in Vail, 178–79

Arapahoe Basin: chairlifts at, 143–44; founding of, 139–40; Interstate 70 route and, 110; skier-visit trends, 349n120, 355n30; wide trails at, 147

Arapaho National Forest, 133, 137–38, 139, 145, 358n52. *See also* Arapahoe Basin; Berthoud Pass; Breckenridge ski resort (Peak 8); Copper Mountain; Keystone; Loveland; Winter Park

architectural controls, 35, 170, 175–76, 178, 215, 287–88, 317n22, 365n119, 390n27

Areas and Activities of State Interest Act (CO, 1974), 401n87

Arizona Highways magazine, 51, 52

Arlberg Club, 16, 17, 137, 138, 143

Arlberg technique, 29, 141, 145, 356n40

Armstrong, Bill, 277

Aspen: airport, 81, 317n26, 332n9–10; arsons and bombings, 248; cleanup efforts, 36–37, 40–41, 213, 320n40; conversion of local landscape to tourism, 26, 27, 29, 30–32, 37, 40, 40–41, 42, 74–75, 246, 319n35, 319n39; discovered by Paepckes, 34; downtown, 250, 286, 389n16; fears of mass tourism in, 37–38, 39, 244–50, 247; fishing pressures around, 133; Four Seasons Club, 36, 40, 319n39; ghost town, depicted as, 72; glamour and celebrity mystique, 35, 36, 149; Goethe Convocation (1949), 39–42, 61, 319n38; hippies in, 248; Hotel Jerome, 25, 30, 37; "human scenery" in, 35–36; Hunter S. Thompson and, 245, 249–50; John Denver and, 240, 272; locals' enthusiasm for skiing, 19, 30, 138, 245–46; locals fight Fry-Ark, 197–200, 215, 372n22; locals push for Interstate 70, 110, 344n88; locals' role in fostering tourism, 3–4, 25, 30–31, 32, 35, 36–37, 40–41, 317n26, 320n40; master plans, 36–37, 212–15, 247–48, 389n16; mining and, 28, 30, 40, 44, 48, 321n53, 378n81; as model for rest of state, 26, 34, 42–43, 46; Mothers March (1960), 245–46; Olympics and, 267, 271–72; Paepcke's plans for, 27, 33–41; Pfeifer's plans for, 26, 28–32, 314n10, 315n12, 316n16; physical setting, 28, 40, 41–42; planning and zoning in, 212–15, 216, 221, 244–45, 246–48, 259, 286, 378n81; political battles over growth, 244–50; population growth, 31, 245; postwar newcomers to, 31–32, 35–36, 315n14; "quiet years," 28, 29; railroad and, 14, 80, 317n26; ranching and ranchland around, 31–32, 40, 332n9; real estate activity, 31, 34, 37, 245, 246, 248; Red Mountain subdivision, 31–32; sewer and sanitation district, proposed, 379n85; silver crash, 28; ski development before 1945, 19, 28, 30–32, 138, 314n6; ski development after the war, 37–39, 40; skiing, growing renown for, 28, 32, 39, 143, 316n16; social scene, 150, 179, 319n37; summer design conference and music festival, 41; Tenth Mountain Division and, 25, 30, 31–32, 139, 315n14; tourist lifestyle in, 26, 32, 213–14, 245, 249, 286; unaffordable housing in, 286; vacation ambiance, 35–37, 41–42, 152; West End, 34, 214. *See also* Aspen Mountain; Paepcke, Walter; Pfeifer, Friedl

Aspen Airways, 332n10

Aspen Area General Plan (1966), 247–48

Aspen Chamber of Commerce: county zoning, urges, 214; founded, 344n88; Fry-Ark and, 197–98

Aspen Company, 38, 332n10, 372n22, 379n87. *See also* Paepcke, Walter

Aspen Highlands, 138, 141, 149–50, 172, 356n40

Aspen Institute for Humanistic Studies, 41, 332n10

Aspen Lions Club, 320n40, 344n88

Aspen Mountain (Ajax): chairlift, 39, 143, 144, 319n35; Grand Opening (1947), 39, 43, 319n36; mining claims and leases on, 30–31; Pfeifer's plans for, 28, 30, 31, 32; Roch Run, 28, 29, 38, 145, 147; Ski Club and, 19, 28, 30, 32; ski development on, before war, 19, 28; summer chairlift rides, 144; too steep for novices and families, 148, 179; view from atop, 142, 144

Aspen Ski Club, 19, 28, 30, 32

Aspen Skiing Corporation: Breckenridge/ Peak 8 and, 263; Buttermilk Mountain and, 148–49; formation of, 38–39, 318n32; Mothers March and, 245–46; Olympics and, 272; water protection

efforts and, 372n22

Aspen Ski School, 32, 38, 141, 148, 314n10

Aspen Times, 3–4, 37, 48, 197–98, 245–46, 247, 249, 321n53. *See also* Ringle, Verlin

Aspinall, Wayne, 138, 207, 228, 230, 274–75, 383n114

atmosphere and ambiance: in Aspen, 27, 35–37, 41–42, 152, 213, 248; efforts to protect, 212, 213, 248, 288, 301; "experience economy" and, 56–57; in Georgetown, 153–56, 155, 244, 388n12; importance of, for tourism, 35, 42, 152, 297, 301; Old West, 53, 68–69, 156; in ski resorts, 150, 179; in Vail, 175–77, 178–79, 182, 288; zoning and, 212

Atomic Energy Commission (AEC), 46–47, 340n63

automobile, as transportation of choice, 82

automobile accessibility, as selling point for tourism, 79, 82–86, 93, 95, 128–30, 129, 136, 137, 156–57, 162, 164, 175, 185, 203, 204, 212, 234, 251, 352n6, 356n36

automobile clubs, and recreational promotion, 16. *See also* American Automobile Association; Rocky Mountain Motorists

Avila, Eric, 361n89

Avon, 338n46

B

"ballroom skiing," 148–49

Bancroft, Caroline, 314n10

Barnett, Gabrielle, 337n42

Basalt, 389n18

Bauhaus and New Bauhaus, 33, 35, 37, 316nn18–19

Bayer, Herbert, 35, 36, 214–15

Bean, Trafton, 170, 214, 215

Beardsley, George, 254

Beaver Creek, 265, 272, 290

Benedict, Fritz: in Aspen, 31–32, 263; in Vail, 175, 178, 180, 364n115, 365n119

Berge, Trygve, 150

Berthoud Pass: Highway 40 over, 17, 84, 86, 111, 335n26, 336n34; Interstate 70 route and, 111–12, 114; Midland Trail over, 335n28; traffic over, 336n34, 342n71, 346n99; tunnel sites proposed near, 114–15, 118, 119

Berthoud Pass ski area: chairlift at, 139, 143–44; development of, 17, 137, 139; skier-visit trends, 349n120, 355n30

Bierstadt, Albert, 13, 16, 57, 95, 142, 310n21

Bierstadt, Mount, 310n21

Bighorn subdivision (East Vail), 183, 263

Big Sky resort (Montana), 262

billboards, efforts to restrict, 215, 225, 276, 285

Black Gore Creek, 136. See also Gore Creek

Black Hawk, 71, 72

Blue River, 218

Board of Immigration, State, 323n59

Bohn, Eddie, 202, 345n90, 373n40

boosters, local. See chambers of commerce, local; highway associations

boosters and boosterism. See Sell Colorado campaign; tourist advertising and marketing; tourist advertising imagery; tourist advertising themes; tourist boosters and business interests; names of booster agencies and groups

Boulder, 114, 214, 256, 391n36, 403n104

Bowles, Samuel, 13, 57

Bow-Mar, 162, 163, 361n87

Bradley, Steve, 147–48

Bradley Packer, 148

Brandborg, Stewart, 224

brands and branding, 20–21; "Colorful Colorado," 4, 58, 61, 65, 327n86; "Cool, Colorful Colorado," 61, 65, 328n99; of highways, 76, 77–79, 92–93; "Ike's Vacation Land," 55; of natural landscape, 57–62, 61; of places, as ubiquitous contemporary phenomenon, 301–2; regions defined by, 302; "Rocky Mountain Empire," 50, 167, 300; Sidney Six, 76, 77–79; "Ski Country USA," 150–51,

359n66; "Switzerland of America," 13, 57, 58; Thompson's efforts to foil, 250; of towns, 244, 250; of Vail, 128, 351n4. See also tourist advertising and marketing

Breckenridge: condominiums at, 120, 367n136; COSCC founding conference at, 224–27; county planning and, 379n88; ghost town, depicted as, 72; growth in wake of Pavlo report, 122–23, 216–17, 350n124; growth due to Interstate 70, 120; inaccessibility of, 80, 87; Interstate 70 route location battle and, 113, 115; mining at, 87; Red Buffalo and, 234; ski development at, 122–23, 138, 216, 262–63, 350n124; zoning open space around, 218. See also Breckenridge ski resort

Breckenridge ski resort (Peak 8): Aspen Ski Corp. absorbs and expands, 263; European glamour at, 150; founding and early growth of, 122–23, 138, 216, 262–63, 350n124; Seibert's efforts to delay, 394n50; Vail Associates absorbs, 394n53

Bridge Street (Vail), 175, 176, 177, 364n117

Brower, David, 208, 224, 373n35

Brown, D. R. C. "Darcy," Jr., 31, 318n30

Brown, Estelle, 223

Brown, Harry, 318n30

Brown Palace Hotel (Denver), 55

Buckley, Ron, 345n91

Bureau of Outdoor Recreation, U.S., 206, 220; Red Buffalo and, 231, 233, 236

Bureau of Public Roads, U.S. (BPR), 100–101, 108–9, 117, 231, 334n25, 344n83

Bureau of Reclamation, U.S., 189–90, 196–97, 200–1, 352n9

Burlington Route, 80, 333n17, 352n7

business interests and business lobby: Colorado Association of Commerce and Industry (CACI), 280, 289; favor land-use reform, 277; fund Crampon tourism studies, 54; kill land-use reform, 279–80. See also tourist boosters

Clear Creek, 291
Clear Creek Canyon: Highway 6 built through, 95, 153; rail line abandoned, 80
Clear Creek County: Holy Cross Trail and, 89; local pride in, 244; Loveland tunnel and, 347n103; population growth in, 369n149; uranium rumors in, 47. *See also* Georgetown; Idaho Springs
Clear Creek valley: construction of Interstate 70 through, 242–43, 291; local attachment to landscape of, 244; Victorian tourists in, 14. *See also* Georgetown; Idaho Springs
Cliff, Edward, 354n25, 355n27
Clifford, Peggy, 246, 249
climate: emotional benefits of, 67; as selling point for tourism, 62–68, 66, 92; as selling point for tourist lifestyle, 162, 165, 167, 369n148
climate change, and future of vacationlands, 305–6
Climax (company town), 45–46, 46, 143
Climax molybdenum mine, 45–46, 46, 71, 112, 346n97, 349n120
Climax ski area, 19, 143
climbing, 16, 195. *See also* Colorado Mountain Club
Club 20: corridor-vs.-corridor rifts and, 94; Glenwood Canyon and, 295; highway lobbying and, 85, 94, 295, 334n24, 337n44; name of, 334n22; Olympics and, 271; pro-growth politicians and, 274, 275; tourist promotion by, 85, 94; tunnel debate and, 116
Cobb, Lew, 50, 323n62–324n64
Cocks, Catherine, 309n12
Cold War: Aspen as antidote to, 33–34; environmentalism and, 192; modern highways, rationale for, 86, 103; vacationland as refuge from, 353n12. *See also* uranium
Coleman, Annie Gilbert, 366n126
Colfax Avenue (Denver), 157–58, 159, 160
Collegiate Peaks Wilderness, 290

Colorado, popular image of: as refuge from cities, 187; scenic clichés, defined by, 60–62, 307n4; as ski destination/"Ski Country USA," 32, 136–37, 150–51; tourist lifestyle and, 165–68, 187, 369n148; as vacationland, 4–5, 44, 60–62, 64, 67–68, 187, 212, 239–40, 307n4, 369n148. *See also* tourist advertising and marketing; tourist advertising imagery; tourist advertising themes
Colorado Advertising and Publicity Committee. *See* Advertising and Publicity Committee (APC)
Colorado & Southern Railway (C&S), 80, 153. *See also* Georgetown Loop
Colorado Association, 323n59, 327n86
Colorado Association of Commerce and Industry (CACI), 280, 289
Colorado Automobile Club, 16
Colorado-Big Thompson Project (C-BT), 196, 352n9
Colorado Coordinating Committee for Planning and Zoning, 215–16, 379nn86–87
Colorado Department of Development. *See* Advertising and Publicity Committee (APC)
Colorado Department of Highways (Highway Department): environmentally sensitive highway design and, 291–96, 405nn115–16; Georgetown bypass and, 243; Glenwood Canyon and, 292–96; at Governor's Travel and Hospitality Conference, 53; Holy Cross Trail and, 88, 89–90; Interstate 70, lobbies for, 103; Interstate 70 route decision and, 111–18; Idaho Springs bypass and, 242–43; local resentment against, 106–7, 115, 337n43; mountain driving, advice on, 83; publicity photos supplied by, 83, 333n19; Red Buffalo and, 229–37, 232; snowplowing by, 83, 137, 333n19; state highway map-brochure, annual, 51, 61, 69, 83,

170, 214, 216; open landscape around, 218; as rest stop, 95, 338n46; suburban nature and, 170; tourist businesses in, 157

Dillon Reservoir, 170, 173, 216; view from highway, as "billboard," 234

Dinosaur National Monument, 201–3, 374nn43–44

Dobson, John, 255–56, 257–58

DOC. *See* Denver Organizing Committee (DOC)

domestic comforts, as tourist marketing theme, 135, 136, 158, 159, 159–60

Dominick, Peter, 235–36, 237

Dotsero, 345n94, 346n97

downvalley effect, 368n145; in Aspen/Roaring Fork Valley, 286; in Vail Valley, 186–87

Draper, Benjamin, 154–56, 329n108, 359n71

drug traffic, avoids Interstate 70, 124

Dude Ranchers' Association (Wyoming and Montana), 195, 371n17

dude ranching, as basis for conservation ethic, 190, 195, 211, 300, 373n40

Dunaway, Bil, 245–46

Durrance, Dick, 141, 356n41

E

Eagle, 78, 81, 89, 93, 262, 263, 338n46

Eagle County: density controls, 290; Interstate 70 route location battle and, 118, 120, 122–23, 346n97; mining in, 321n53; planning and zoning and, 216, 402n89; population growth in, 369n149; remoteness of, 87, 89, 96, 336n33; uranium and, 47, 127. *See also* Beaver Creek; Minturn; Red Cliff; Vail

Eagle County Development Corporation (ECDC), 183, 263

Eagle River valley, 335n28, 336n33. *See also* Eagle County; Vail

Eagles Nest Wilderness, 290. *See also* Gore Range-Eagles Nest Primitive Area

Earth Liberation Front (ELF), 298–99, 405n1

easiness, as selling point for outdoor sports, 133–34, 135–36, 140, 141, 143–44, 147–49, 179, 352n8, 357n42, 357n46

East Vail, 263, 391n37

Eaton, Earl, 127–28, 172, 351n1

Echo Park dam battle, 200–204, 370n7, 373n35, 373n38, 374nn43–44

ecological thinking: land-use reform and, 277–78; Lindsay urges, 257; sweeping environmental reform proposals and, 276–78, 402n89; thwarted by place packaging and consumerism, 280–81, 297, 303

Edwards, Joe, 249

Eisenhower, Dwight: as avatar of leisure culture, 55; fish stocking for, 134; heart attack, 73; lobbied by Johnson for interstate, 100, 103, 104–5, 339n59, 341n69–342n72, 344n83, 347n99; ORRRC and, 206; paints scenic clichés, 62, 63; vacations in Colorado, as publicity gold mine, 54–55, 59, 63, 65, 73, 132, 134

Eisenhower, Mamie, 55

Eisenhower Tunnel (formerly Straight Creek Tunnel), 114–16, 118–20, 122, 123

Eldora ski area, 263

Elisha, Laurence, 25, 30, 37, 315n12

emotions and emotional fulfillment. *See* personal and emotional meaning

Empire Magazine (Denver Post), 300, 368n143

Encyclopædia Britannica Book of the Year, Colorado entry in, 307n3

Environmental Defense Fund, 294

environmental identity, 313n48. *See also* personal and emotional meaning; place, personal attachment to; recreational consumerism; tourist way of life

environmental impact statements, 264–65, 279, 287, 292, 398n68, 404n107

environmentalism and environmental movement: advertised qualities of place as basis for, 199, 225, 250–59, 280, 288;

environmentalism and environmental movement: (*continued*)

in Aspen, 244–50, 286; Beaver Creek fight, 265; "big recreation," concerns about, 259–60; coalition-building efforts, 194–95, 223–25, 282–84; Colorado influence on, 194, 201–2, 204; critics and foes of, 264, 276, 294–95; early forms of, 191, 192, 196–97, 200, 204, 217, 222, 307n5; Echo Park fight, 200–204; ecological thinking and, 257, 276–78, 280–81, 297, 303, 402n89; emotional rhetoric of, 197, 199–200; in Evergreen, 269; experts, faith in, 222, 226–27, 266; falters in 1970s, 275–76; fishing and, 260–61; Fry-Ark project, fight against, 197–200; future prospects for, 305–6; Granby Dam fight, 189–90, 196–97; grassroots environmental groups, 269, 270, 272; grazing "land grab," fight against, 194–95; "hard facts," use of, 200, 202, 231; history of, 192, 307n5; Interstate 70, environmental concerns about, 229–37, 290–96; John Denver and, 240–41, 265, 294–97; land-use reform efforts, 277–81, 401n87; local environmental reforms, 286–90; Marble ski resort fight, 265; on national level, 257; "nature lover" stereotype and, 199–200, 201–2, 227–28, 373n39; Olympics battle, 267–75; personal and emotional stakes in, 22–23, 190–91, 197, 199–200, 222–23, 225–26, 227, 229, 238, 241, 244, 257, 259, 280, 281, 286, 297, 303–5; place packaging as basis for, 22, 126, 201, 203, 250–59, 280, 281, 288, 297, 301, 302–5; and political upsets of 1972, 274–75; population growth, concern over, 265–67, 272, 395n59; Progressive-style conservation and, 192, 193, 196–97, 204–5, 222, 227, 382n102; recreational consumerism as basis for, 22–23, 190–91, 192, 194–95, 197, 198–200, 201–4, 222–26, 231–33, 238, 259, 265–66, 303–5, 374nn43–44; recreational consumerism, hindered by, 276, 280–84, 288–89, 295–97; recreation planning and, 222, 226–27, 266; Red Buffalo tunnel controversy, 229–37, 232, 385n128, 386n131, 386n133; ski resort sprawl, concerns about, 261–65; sportsmen and sportsmen-conservationists, tensions with, 282–83; tourist advertising imagery, influenced by, 57, 190, 198, 250–59, 280, 288; tourist business interests, shared interests with, 191, 197–99, 200, 201–4, 205, 222, 227–29, 230, 233–38, 279, 288, 373n40, 384n116; tourist business interests, split from, 279–80; tourist lifestyle as basis for, 22–23, 204, 259, 268–70, 275, 286, 288; in Vail, 250–59, 280, 287–89; working class and poor, blind spot toward, 286, 303. *See also* wilderness

Eriksen, Stein, 149–50, 356n40

escapism. *See* anti-urban escapism

Evans, Mount, 16, 95

Evergreen: Olympics and, 268–69; suburban-style development in, 169

"experience economy," 56–57, 326n82

experts and technocrats: critics of, 106–8, 107, 115, 272–73; deference to, 101, 117–18, 122, 334n25; environmentalists' faith in, 222, 226–27, 266; highway planners as, 100–101, 102, 111, 334n25, 340n62, 349n113; Interstate 70, decide route of, 117–22, 349n114; Johnson's attacks on, 106–7, 107; Olympics and, 272; ORRRC and, 205; planning and zoning and, 214; Progressive-style conservation and, 192, 193, 196–97, 204–5, 222, 227, 382n102; recreational amenities, management of, 196–97, 374n44; recreation planning and, 205, 221, 226–27; resource management and, 192, 193. *See also* highway engineers and officials; highway planning and design; planning and zoning, local; recreation planning and zoning extractive industries: as economic base, 26–27; Pavlo on, 121, 349n120; weighed against tourism, 44–45, 48–49, 68, 71–72, 74, 121, 323n59, 329n108, 349n120. *See also* mining

exurbs: and new landscape patterns of vacationland, 168–70, 362n100; and Olympics, 268–69; packaged places in, 301–2. *See also* suburbia, suburban landscapes, and suburban ideals; tourist way of life; *specific places*

F

families: marketing tourism and recreation to, 6, 56, 58, 69, 70, 130, 135, 148–49, 159, 179–80, 181, 182; vacationland as paradise for, 130, 168; vacations as effort to strengthen, 308n8. *See also* children

Federal Aid Highway Act of 1944, 343n80

Federal Aid Highway Act of 1956 (Interstate Highway Act), 97, 108, 117, 343n80

Federal Writers' Project (FWP), guides to Colorado and ghost towns, 312n41

Ferril, Thomas Hornsby, 49

Findlay, John, 172

fishing: advertising clichés, 132–33, 134–35; as basis for river protection, 198–99; culture of, 261; emotional appeal of, 132–33; environmental protection and, 261; hatcheries and fish stocking, 133–35, 260–61, 354n21; fishing rules, 133, 353n13; images of, as logos for Colorado, 132; "improvement" of fish habitats for, 133, 353n14; IWLA and, 193, 282; and masculinity, 132–33; mass market, transformed for, 133–34; in national forests, 135, 354n22; novices and non-experts, transformed for, 133–34; promotion of, 131–35, 352n9; Romanticism and, 132, 261; as Rooseveltian adventure, 132–33, 134–35; scenic clichés and, 132; small towns, importance to, 131, 352n9; Summit County promotes, 352n9; wildness,

experience of, 132, 134–35

fish stocking and fish hatcheries, 133–34, 260–61, 354n21

Fiske, Billy, 314n6

Flat Tops, 208–9, 285, 290

Florida, postwar allure of, 6, 67, 277

Flynn, T. J., 314n6

Ford, Gerald, 367n134

Forest Service, U.S.: Beaver Creek and, 265, 290; Berthoud Pass and, 143; Breckenridge/Peak 8 and, 394n50; camping and, 136, 354n25; Carhart and, 16–17, 189, 208–9; fishing and, 131, 133; Gore Range-Eagle Nest Primitive Area and, 285–86, 384n123; at Governor's Travel and Hospitality Conference, 53; "improves" fish habitats, 133, 353n14; logging, commitment to, 136, 192–93, 286, 354n25, 355n27; NEPA and, 264–65; Operation Outdoors, 136, 205, 353n14, 354n25; Park Service vs., 354n25; recreation and, 16–17, 136–37, 354n25, 355n27; road building by, 136, 355n27; ski area design manual, environmentally sensitive (Wingle), 264, 266; ski area permits, 127–28, 138, 261, 264, 290, 314n6, 394n50; ski development master plan (1959), 128, 137–38, 261, 351n2; skiing and, 127–28, 136–38, 142, 290; Vail and, 127–28, 138, 351n2, 394n50, 403n102; Vail Pass design and, 292; wilderness and, 285–86, 290, 375n57, 384n123. *See also* national forests; *specific forests*

Foster, Jack, 171, 396n63

Four Seasons Club (Aspen), 36, 40, 319n39

four-wheeling, 283–84. *See also* Mile-Hi Jeep Club

Fox, Stephen, 193

France, ski resorts in, 253–54, 264

Fraser, 55, 59, 65, 73

Frazier, Walter, 36–37, 212–13, 214

Freeman, Orville, 236

Fremont Pass, 45, 336n33

Frisco, 18, 44, 94–95, 120, 218, 233–34,

Gore Range-Eagles Nest Primitive Area, 230–37, 232, 285–86, 290, 384n123

Governor's Conference on Parks and Recreation, annual, 219–20

Governor's Travel and Hospitality Conference, annual, 53, 54, 68–69

Gramshammer, Pepi, 150

Granby, 96, 114, 157, 158, 350n127

Granby Dam, 189–90, 196–97

Grand Army of the Republic Highway, 92–93

Grand County: contemporary resort development in, 124; Interstate 70 route location battle and, 120; railroad inaccessibility of, in nineteenth century, 14; uranium and, 47. See also Berthoud Pass; Fraser; Granby; Grand Lake; Hot Sulphur Springs; Kremmling; Winter Park

Grand Junction, 89, 111, 112, 235, 332n12, 346n97

Grand Lake, 19, 96

Grand River. See Colorado River

Grand Valley and Hot Springs Scenic Route, 335n28

grazing "land grab" of 1946–47, 194–95, 371n12, 371n17

Green Mountain Reservoir, 352n9

Green River, 201

Gregg, Frank, 375n50

grooming, of ski slopes, 129, 147–48

Gropius, Walter, 37, 212–13, 214, 378n74

growth, popular backlash against, 241–42, 265, 274–75. See also growth management; population growth: concern about; tourist and recreational development: as environmental problem

growth management: in Aspen, 246, 286; in Boulder, 256; in Vail, 254, 256, 287–89. See also planning and zoning, local; land-use reform

growth networks, 50

Guadagno, Dick, 231, 233, 385n127

Gunther, John, 49–50

Gutfreund, Owen, 334n25

Gypsum, 89

H

Hall, Colin Michael, 308n7

Haney, Hal, 307n3

Hansen, Roger: Beaver Creek and, 290; business-friendly image for COSCC, cultivates, 228; environmental coalition, calls for, 224; "nature lover" stereotype and, 227, 228; Olympics and, 398n68; private property, questions sanctity of, 279; recreation planning, favors, 226; Red Buffalo and, 237, 385n128; ROMCOE and, 229; sportsmen and, 283; tourist-boosting, sees common cause with, 227–28

Harding, Ed, 345n90

Harrison, Julia, 313n47, 326n81, 337n42

Hart, Gary, 401n79

Harvey, Mark, 200–201, 370n7

Haselbush, Willard, 171, 173

Haskell, Floyd, 274

Hastings, Merrill, 235, 236, 237, 268

Hauk, Paul, 351n2, 394n55, 395n57

Hauserman, Dick, 187, 351n1, 364n113

Hawaii, statewide zoning in, 277, 278

Hayden, Mount, 314n6

Hays, Samuel, 381n94

health-seeking, 67, 339n57

Heeney, 352n9

high country, meaning of, 11–12, 310n20

Highland-Bavarian Corporation, 314n6

Highway 6. See U.S. Highway 6

Highway 6 Association. See Colorado Highway 6 Association

Highway 40. See U.S. Highway 40

Highway 40 Association. See National U.S. Highway 40 Association

Highway 82, State, 214, 215, 246, 344n88

Highway 82 Association, 344n88

highway associations: corridor-vs.-corridor rivalries and, 93–94; COSCC and,

national identity, nineteenth-century tourism and, 9–10, 311n28

national parks and monuments: Denver (proposed), 16; Dinosaur, 201–3; Holy Cross, 89, 335n30; ORRRC and, 206; Rocky Mountain, 16, 195. *See also* National Park Service

National Park Service: camping and, 136; Colorado Coordinating Committee for Planning and Zoning and, 379n86; Forest Service vs., 354n25; at Governor's Travel and Hospitality Conference, 53; Mission 66, 136, 205, 354n25. *See also* national parks and monuments

National U.S. Highway 40 Association: boosterism and branding by, 90–92; Coloradans dominate, 345n90; Echo Park and, 202; Eisenhower mystique, use of, 55; at Governor's Travel and Hospitality Conference, 53; Interstate 70 route, campaigns for, 110–11; traffic counts and, 112, 346n96

nature and landscape: advertising depictions of, 20, 58–62, 61; consumer culture, natural things refracted through, 310n17; future prospects for, 305–6; highway planners' brazenness toward, 101; Interstate 70 assaults, 21, 105, 123, 124, 126, 290–91, 293, 293–94, 350n130; Interstate 70 harmonizes with, 98–99, 123, 124–25, 125, 291–94, 295; natural harmony, ideal of, 178, 257–59, 287; niche recreational markets and, 281–82, 297, 303; parcelized by place packaging, 126, 303; Romantic experience of, 15, 57–58, 59, 60, 141–42, 168, 309n15, 326n85; Romantic paintings of, 13, 60, 142, 310n21, 326n84, 327n90; simplified by tourist advertising, 20, 58–59, 64, 72–73, 74, 269. *See also* climate; environmentalism and environmental movement; ecological thinking; place packaging; scenery and scenic spots; scenic clichés; suburban nature; topography of

the high country; wilderness

"nature lover" stereotype: Aspenites and, 199–200; Carhart and, 200, 201–2, 373n39; Colorado environmentalists and, 227–28

Needham, Richard, 356n40

Neuzil, Dennis, 231

New Deal programs, and Colorado recreation, 17, 28, 90, 312n41, 335n30

New Mexico, highways across, 92, 100, 340n66

Newton, Quigg, 50

"New West," 300–301, 308n10, 406n7

New York Times: Fry-Ark and, 198; John Oakes of, 372n29; Red Buffalo and, 231

niche markets, recreational: COSCC and, 225, 282–83; ecological thinking, hindrance to, 280–81; environmental coalition building, hindrance to, 225, 281–84, 297; environmental values born of, 280–81, 303; jeepers as, 283–84; local environmental reform, encourages, 286; parcelization of landscape and, 303; sportsmen as, 282–83; wide-ranging environmental agendas, discourages, 282; wilderness as, 284, 285

Nielsen, Aksel, 55, 339n59, 341nn69–70, 344n83

Nitze, Paul, 318n32

novices and non-experts, tourist and recreational development catering to, 133–34, 140, 141, 147–49, 147, 179–80, 357n46

O

Oakes, John B., 372n29

Office of Road Inquiry, 334n25

oil shale, 47–48, 197, 198

Old West atmosphere and imagery: as advertising theme, 68–72, 70, 90; Aspen and, 41; Bow-Mar and, 162, 163; DOC and, 268, 395n62; Georgetown and, 71, 154–56, 155; Highway 40 and,

90; historic mining towns and, 71; modern mining, tension with, 71–72; motels and, 158; New West imagery, juxtaposed with, 300, 406n8; as tourist draw, 4, 53, 68–69, 156; Vail rejects, 365n119. *See also* ghost towns

Olson, Sigurd, 395n59

Olympics (1976), debate over, 241, 267–75, 396n63, 397n66

open-space protection: in Aspen, 244–45, 246, 247, 248, 286; in Boulder, 256; COSCC and, 225, 226, 236; as major concern in Colorado, 265, 267; as national issue, 217, 381n94; Olympics and, 267, 270; ORRRC and, 206; in Summit County, 217–18; in Vail, 178, 256, 287, 404n106, 404n109

Operation Outdoors (U.S. Forest Service), 136, 205, 353n14, 354n25

outdoor recreation. *See* recreational consumerism; tourism, participation in; tourist and recreational development; tourist way of life; *specific activities*

Outdoor Recreation in America (ORRRC), 206–8

Outdoor Recreation Resources Review Commission (ORRRC): as boost for conservationists, 205–6; Carhart and, 205–6, 208–11; Colorado origins of, 205–6, 207; critics of, 207, 208, 211, 375n55, 376n59; environmental movement, helps set agenda for, 207; influence and legacy of, 206–7; mass-use recreational areas and, 207–8, 209, 211, 212; *Outdoor Recreation in America*, 206–7; Penfold and, 205–7, 208, 375n50, 376n60; recreation planning after, 212, 218–21, 226; recreation zoning, call for, 207–9, 209, 211, 376n59; tourist lifestyle, advocates, 207; wilderness and, 206, 207–9, 209, 211, 375nn54–57, 376n60

Overland Park auto camp (Denver), 157

P

Pabst, Fred, 357n47

Paepcke, Elizabeth, 34–35, 41

Paepcke, Walter, 36; Aspen airport and, 40, 81, 332nn9–10; Aspen Institute and, 41; background and business career, 33, 316n19; cultural-commercial idealism of, 33–34, 39–40, 316nn18–19; death of, 245; Goethe Convocation and, 39–41, 319n38, 320n42; local residents, tells what to do, 35, 36–37, 40–41, 320n40; local water protection efforts and, 372n22; mass tourism, fears of, 37–38, 245; Pfeifer and, 37–38, 318n30; predicts new boom, 43; real estate purchases, 34, 35, 37, 40, 319n39; recruits newcomers to Aspen, 35–36, 149; resort-building vision for Aspen, 27, 33–41; skiing, ambivalence about, 37–39, 150, 319n37; Taxco, inspired by, 317nn22–23; transforms local landscape, 27, 35–37, 40–41, 42; Williamsburg, inspired by, 35; zoning, pushes for, 212–14, 378n78

Page, Stephen J., 308n7

Palmer, William Jackson, 57

Parker, Robert (Bob): as ally of COSCC, 228, 229; Colorado Open Space Conference speech, 387n140; on economic value of environmental quality, 229, 387n140; on eliteness as selling point, 182; on family-friendliness and wholesomeness of Vail, 179, 180; on harmony with nature in Vail, 178; on hospitality training for Vail police, 368n138; on Red Buffalo, 235, 386n133; Ski Country USA and, 359n66; on television in Vail, 366n129; on "total resort concept," 173; on tourism as environmental boon, 237–38, 387n140; on Vail Village design, 365n119; as wilderness advocate, 286, 403n102

Park Service. *See* National Park Service paving/improvement of highways, 17,

preservation based on, 244; personal identity based on, 22, 240, 280; tourism and claims to place, 8–9, 278; tourist advertising encourages, 10, 20–21, 22, 56–57, 67, 188, 238, 281, 297, 303. *See also* personal and emotional meaning; place, sense of; place packaging; regional geography, sense of; tourist lifestyle

place, sense of, 21, 313n46; advertised qualities of place as basis for environmentalism, 199, 225, 250–59, 280, 288; consumer culture comes to dominate, 5, 10, 297, 301–6, 304; consumption of place as means to good life, 10–11; place packaging shapes, 301–2; places as products, 5, 55–57; tourist advertising tries to mold, 9, 57, 58, 78, 150. *See also* place, personal attachment to; place packaging; regional geography, sense of; vacationland

place packaging: concept of, 5, 21, 131, 304; convenience as core principle of, 21, 130, 143, 147, 161–62, 175, 357n46; Echo Park and, 201, 203; environmental attitudes and environmentalism, influence on, 22, 126, 201, 203, 250–59, 280, 281, 288, 297, 301, 302–5; highways and, 21–22, 79, 84–85, 86, 93–94, 99, 126, 203, 337n42, 374n44; Interstate 70 corridor as, 22, 126; parcelizes the landscape, 126, 303; personal attachments to packaged places, 22, 188, 250–52, 280, 281, 297, 301; sense of place, shapes, 301–2, 304; for skiing, 142–49, 147, 150–51; suburbs as, 172; and tourist way of life, 130–31; of towns, by accumulation of tourist businesses, 152–53, 157; ubiquity of, 301–2, 304; Vail as, 172–86, 187; wilderness as form of, 285–86

planning and zoning, local: in Aspen/Pitkin County, 212–15, 216, 221, 244–45, 246–48, 259, 286, 378n81, 379nn86–87;

history of, 212, 377n71; inadequacy of, 277; as local prerogative, 278, 279; opposition to, 213, 216, 378n81; Paepcke and, 212–13, 214; property values and, 212, 213–14, 218, 377n71; to protect recreational amenities, 212–15, 217–18, 219, 256, 278, 286–88, 378n80, 379n86; small towns and rural counties urged to embrace, 215–16; as Soviet-style totalitarianism, 216; in Summit County, 216–18, 219, 379n88, 386n131; tourist business interests and, 206, 211–12, 213–15, 218; in Vail, 256, 287–88, 289, 391n37, 404n109. *See also* land-use reform; recreation planning and zoning

Planning for America's Wildlands (Carhart), 209–11, 377n67

planning regions, proposed, 279, 402n89

Pomeroy, Earl, 143, 300, 308n11

population dispersion, proposals for, 267, 277, 285

population growth: birth-control measures and, 267; concern over, 265–67, 270, 272, 395n59; in Denver suburbs, 188; Olympics and, 270, 272; tourism and tourist lifestyle spurs, 7–8, 187–88, 272, 308n10, 369n149

Powderhorn ski area, 263

Price, Jennifer, 310n17

primitive areas, 207–8, 285, 375n57, 384n123. *See also* wilderness

Pritchard, Allen, 378n78

Progressive-style conservation, 192, 193, 196–97, 204–5, 222, 227, 382n102. *See also* experts and technocrats

Project Plowshare, 340n63

property values. *See* real estate values

Prospectors' Trails, 70, 84, 330n114

Protect Our Mountain Environment (POME), 269, 274

Public Roads Administration (PRA), 97–98, 101. *See also* Bureau of Public Roads

Public Works Administration (PWA): and

Public Works Administration (*continued*)
Vail Pass construction, 90; and Winter
Park development, 17. *See also* Works
Progress Administration

Purgatory ski area, 263

Q

Queal, Cal, 170–71, 266–67

R

Rabbit Ears Pass, 335n26

railroads: abandon trackage in high
country, 80, 317n26, 331n4; airlines vs.,
81; arrive in Colorado, 13; auto travel,
forced to accede to, 333n17; declin-
ing traffic, 80, 331n2; circle tours and,
333n20; Climax mine and, 346n97,
349n120; frame scenery, 15; highways
follow earlier paths of, 87, 98; limit
spread of tourism in nineteenth
century, 14; Moffat Tunnel, 17, 18, 114,
349n120; promote tourism after WWII,
52, 61, 69, 70, 80, 325n73; "ski train" to
Winter Park, 17, 18, 349n120; streamliners to Colorado, 80; transcontinentals
shun Colorado, 97–98; Victorian tourism and, 13–15. *See also* Denver & Rio
Grande Western Railroad (D&RGW);
Georgetown Loop

ranch houses, 163, 361n92; architectural
influence of, 185; as design for "outdoor
living," 165; motels designed like, 159, 159

ranching and ranchland: in Aspen area,
31–32, 40, 197, 248, 319n39, 332n9;
conversion to leisure use, 31–32, 40, 128,
319n39; as economic base, 26, 44, 49,
68, 73–74, 349n120; Old West allure of,
68; as open space, 218, 219, 404n106; in
Summit County, 218, 219; in Vail Valley, 128, 404n106

Rand McNally, and early highways, 335n27

real estate values: in Aspen, 213–14; in new

Dillon, 170; in "New West," 299; in
Summit County, 218; in Vail, 182–83,
186–87, 252–54, 389n23, 390n32; zoning
and, 212, 213–14, 218, 377n71

recreational boosters and business interests. *See* tourist boosters and business
interests

recreational consumerism: Carhart
appeals to, 190–91, 194–95, 197, 204, 226,
373n41; COSCC and, 225–27, 282; dam
proponents appeal to, 203; Echo Park
and, 201–4, 373n41, 374nn43–44; environmental concern based on, 22–23,
190–91, 192, 194–95, 197, 198–200, 201–4,
222–26, 231–33, 238, 259, 265–66, 303–5,
374nn43–44; environmental movement hindered by, 276, 280–84, 288–89,
295–97; IWLA and, 193, 197, 282; nonradical nature of, 280–81; recreation
planning and, 205, 222; Sierra Club
appeals to, 193, 197; tourist promotion,
recreational enthusiasts' role in, 16, 17,
20, 138–39, 154; wilderness and, 210–11,
222–23, 285, 403n103. *See also* personal
and emotional meaning; place, personal attachment to: tourist advertising
and marketing; tourist way of life

recreational development. *See* tourist and
recreational development

recreation planning and zoning: Carhart
champions, 204–5, 208–12; Colorado
enthusiasm for, 212, 218–20, 226–27,
261, 266, 382n101; Colorado influence
on, 208–12; COSCC, early priority
of, 226–27; early proponents of, 204–5,
374n45; environmentalists seek, 226–27,
266; environmental movement, helps
set stage for, 222; Forest Service master
plan for ski development (1959), 128,
137–38, 261, 351n2; ORRRC advocates,
205–8, 209, 211–12, 218–19; Penfold and,
205–8; as Progressive-style conservation technocracy, 205, 221, 226–27;
recreational consumerism and, 205, 222;

State Highway Department. *See* Colorado Department of Highways

State Historical Society of Colorado, 62, 154, 156, 379n86, 405n116

State Planning Commission/Division, 48, 104, 214, 215, 307n3, 323n59, 379n86

state-sponsored tourist promotion, 2, 3–4, 49–50, 51, 61, 65, 69, 137, 323n59, 323n63, 324nn64–65, 324n67. *See also* Advertising and Publicity Committee (APC)

Staub, Roger, 150, 366n125

Steamboat Ski Resort, 81, 124, 263

Steamboat Springs: early skiing at, 18–19; highway association and, 93; Interstate 70 route and, 115, 124; resort development at, 124; Olympics and, 272; second thoughts about interstate in, 242; ski lift construction at, 143; Victory Highway and, 335n28

Stegner, Wallace, 374n43

Stewart, George, 90, 98

Storm in the Rocky Mountains—Mount Rosalie (Bierstadt), 310n21

Storm Mountain (Steamboat Ski Resort), 124, 263

Straight Creek tunnel site (later Eisenhower Tunnel), 114–16, 118–20, 122, 123

"strenuous life," and shift toward active recreation, 15–16, 132–33, 140, 311n32

sublime: nineteenth-century notion of the, 15, 326n84; skiing and experience of the, 141–42; ski lifts and the, 144. *See also* scenery and scenic spots; scenic clichés

suburban nature: camping and, 135–36; concept of, 6, 130, 151–52, 161–62, 187; in Denver suburbs, 161, 162–69, 163; Echo Park and, 203; in Evergreen, 169; in Georgetown, 154, 169–70; motels and, 158–62, 159; in New Dillon, 170; new landscape patterns of vacationland and, 168–70, 362n100; open-space concerns and, 217; recreation planning, support for, 222; in Vail, 130, 178, 184–86; wildness and, 210, 211. *See also* suburbia, suburban landscapes, and suburban ideals; tourist way of life

suburbia, suburban landscapes, and suburban ideals: around Denver, 161, 162–69, 163, 188, 274; in Evergreen, 169; in Georgetown, 169–70; "magic lands" and (Findlay), 172; motels appeal to, 158–62, 159; in new Dillon, 170; new landscape patterns of vacationland and, 168–70, 362n100; open-space concerns and, 217; packaged places and, 301–2; postwar suburban boom, 5, 130, 151, 152, 166, 188; tourism and tourist marketing, influence on, 6, 187; tourist lifestyle and, 11, 187–88; vacationland influences on, 161, 162–68, 163; in Vail, 130, 172, 175, 177–82, 184–86; Vail "suburbs," 183, 256, 258, 391n37; white identity and, 361n89; wildness and, 210, 211; zoning's origins and, 212. *See also* sprawl; suburban nature; suburbs of Denver; tourist way of life

suburbs of Denver, 161, 162–69, 163, 188, 274; Aspinall redistricting and, 274–75; Bow-Mar, 162, 163, 361n87; Eisenhower's real estate investments in, 344n83; population explosion in, 188; proliferation of, after World War II, 164; working-class, 186

Summers, Gregory, 350n131

Summit County: condominiums catch on in, 183, 367n136; fishing, efforts to promote, 352n9; Holy Cross Trail and, 88–89; Interstate 70 route and, 110, 114, 118, 120, 122–23, 138, 346n97, 347n103; IWLA chapter in, promotes tourism, 193; mining in, 322n53; planning and zoning in, 216–18, 219, 379n88, 386n131; planning region, proposed, 402n89; population growth in, 369n149; railroad service, loses, 80; real estate frenzy in, 216–17, 380n91; Red Buffalo and, 233–34, 386n131; remoteness of, before modern highways, 87; as tourist

Colorado lags in, after war, 49–50; conservation groups help with, 20, 193; coordination of, statewide, 49, 53–54, 68–69, 139; Eisenhower press coverage as form of, 54–55, 59, 63, 65, 73, 132, 134; natural attributes cast as recreational amenities, 55–68; ORRRC, influence on, 211–12; personal bond to place, encourages, 10, 20–21, 22, 56–57, 67, 188, 238, 281, 297, 303; places as products, 55–57; region and place, helps define, 93–94; scenery and, 4, 13, 20, 58–62, 61; state funding for, budget battle over, 49–50, 323n62–324n65; state-sponsored, 2, 3–4, 49–50, 51, 61, 65, 69, 137, 323n59, 323n63, 324nn64–65, 324n67; suburban ideals, influenced by, 6; "Victory Vacations" campaign, 44, 49. *See also* Advertising and Publicity Committee (APC); brands and branding; place packaging; skiing and ski area development; tourist advertising imagery; tourist advertising themes; tourist and recreational development; tourist boosters and business interests; *specific places*

tourist advertising imagery: Carhart influenced by, 190, 211, 221; climate clichés, 62–68, 66; environmental attitudes and environmentalism, influences, 57, 190, 198, 250–59, 280, 288; everyday parlance parrots, 59; fishing imagery, 132–33, 134–35; ghost town imagery, 72–73; Interstate 70, used to lobby Eisenhower for, 104; IOC parrots, 268; John Denver and, 240; mining imagery, use of, 68–72; Old West imagery, 68–72, 71, 90; press coverage parrots, 59; recreation zoning, influences, 211, 221; scenic clichés, 4, 20, 58–62, 61; simplifies nature and the landscape, 20, 58–59, 64, 72–73, 74, 269; suburban imagery, blurs with, 161, 162–68, 163

tourist advertising themes: adventures/ thrills, 131, 132–33, 134–35, 140–41, 143,

357n42; automobile accessibility, 79, 82–86, 93, 95, 128–30, 129, 136, 137, 156–57, 162, 164, 175, 185, 203, 204, 212, 234, 251, 352n6, 356n36; convenience, 82, 95, 131, 135–36, 160–62; easiness (of outdoor sports), 133–34, 135–36, 140, 141, 143–44, 147–49, 179, 352n8, 357n42, 357n46; escape from the city, 6, 74, 135, 151, 162, 164, 172, 177–78, 185, 187, 210–11, 250, 252, 257, 259, 288; family-friendliness, 6, 56, 58, 69, 70, 130, 135, 148–49, 159, 179–80, 181, 182; glamour and celebrity appeal, 35, 36, 139, 143, 149–50, 178–79, 311n52, 356n40, 366n125; historic ambiance, 4, 17, 53, 68–72, 90, 153, 154–56, 155; home-style comforts, 135, 136, 158, 159, 159–60; luxury, 6, 14–15, 65, 80, 143, 173–74, 177, 182; personal and emotional appeals, 10, 20–21, 42, 52, 56–57, 58–59, 67, 70–71, 74, 132–33, 211, 238, 302, 313n45; Romantic nature tropes, updated for twentieth century, 57–60, 141–42, 168, 309n15, 327n90; safety, 130, 131, 143, 148, 151, 352n8, 357n42; sex appeal, 66, 149, 179; social exclusivity, 179, 180–82, 187

tourist and recreational development: all-encompassing nature of, 27, 35–36, 37, 42, 152; Aspen as model for, 26, 34, 42–43, 46; atmosphere/ambiance, importance of, 35, 42, 152, 297, 301; Central City as model for, 43, 156; as colonialism, 8, 308n11; conversion of land to, 26, 27, 29, 30–32, 37, 40, 40–41, 42, 74–75, 128, 155, 156, 171, 246, 299–300, 319n35, 319n39, 378n81; disdain for tourists and doubts about tourist development, 45, 48–49; as economic engine, 7–8, 26–27, 43–44, 50, 73, 155–56; economic measures of, 2, 3, 54, 195–96, 200, 202, 206, 222, 321n48; as environmental boon, 222, 237–38, 266, 272; as environmental problem, 216–17, 241–45, 246–47, 247, 249, 259–60, 261–65, 266–67, 268, 269, 272, 270, 277, 285, 296–97, 299,

tourist and recreational development
(*continued*)

301; extractive industries, weighed against, 44–46, 48–49, 68, 71–72, 74, 121, 323n59, 329n108, 349n120; Georgetown as model for, 43; Interstate 70 and other highways as means to, 78–79, 82–86, 88–89, 94, 99–100, 103–4, 108, 109–10, 116–17, 120–21, 125–26, 128, 341n70, 348n109, 351n6; locals' role in fostering, 2, 3–4, 25, 29, 30–31, 32, 35, 36–37, 40–41, 183–84, 251, 288, 317n26, 320n40; mass-market/mainstream tastes, catering to, 133–35, 136, 137–38, 141, 143–49, 147, 151, 201–4, 205, 207–8, 209–11, 209, 212, 220, 227, 357n47, 376n60; mass tourism, fears of, 37–38, 145–47, 180, 221, 244, 245, 247, 252, 261, 390n26; mining, incompatibility with, 71–72, 74; national interest, matter of, 104, 206–7, 341n70; and natural harmony, ideal of, 178, 257–59, 287; and new ways of valuing land, 26, 34–35, 37, 128; novices and non-experts, catering to, 133–34, 140, 141, 147–49, 147, 179–80, 357n46; Pavlo on, 120–21; population growth spurred by, 7–8, 308n10; recreational enthusiasts' role in, 16, 17, 20, 138–39, 154; social dimensions of, 8, 308n11; suburban ideals, influenced by, 6; as threat to community identity and local character, 243–44, 246, 263, 271, 299, 301; as threat to tourist lifestyle and quality of life, 245–46, 249, 250–51, 263; as unreliable economic base, 48; wilderness as boon to, 228. *See also* place packaging; skiing and ski area development; tourist advertising and marketing; tourist boosters and business interests

tourist boosters and business interests: AAA/Rocky Mountain Motorists, 51, 324n69; airlines, 52–53, 325n74; backlash against, 245–46, 247, 248–50, 253–54, 273–74, 298–99; conservation groups

promote tourism, 20, 193; Denver civic boosters, 16; Denver Convention and Visitors Bureau, 51, 65, 69, 96, 158, 325n70, 330n114; Echo Park and, 373n40; environmentalism and environmental movement, shared interests with, 191, 195, 197–99, 200, 201–4, 205, 222, 227–29, 230, 233–38, 279, 288, 373n40, 384n116; environmentalism and environmental movement, split from, 279–80; Glenwood Canyon and, 295; Governor's Travel and Hospitality Conference, gather at, 53, 54, 68–69; highway associations, 76, 77–79, 90–93; Hilliard as, 223; idealism of, 20, 33–34, 38, 39–40, 237–38; IWLA and, 193; land-use reform, challenged by, 279–80; magazines, 51–52, 325n72; Olympics as dream of, 267–68; ORRRC and, 211–12; Pavlo assures, 121; railroads, 52, 61, 69, 70, 80, 325n73; recreation planning and, 205, 211–12, 221, 382n101; small tourist businesses, 51, 53, 152–53, 157, 359n67; small-town boosters, 51; statewide coordination of, 49, 53–54, 68–69, 139; variety of, 19–20; wilderness and, 228, 233–35, 236, 285–86, 403n103; zoning and, 214, 215, 218. *See also* motels; place packaging; tourist advertising and marketing; tourist and recreational development

tourist industry: patchwork nature of, 7, 49, 54. *See also* tourist and recreational development; tourist boosters and business interests

tourist infrastructure. *See* place packaging

tourist seasons: autumn, 65, 67, 329n104; efforts to balance out, 43, 139; fishing season, adjustments to, 353n13; seasonal work patterns in Vail, 250–51; spring ("mud season"), 65, 67, 329n104; summer, 3, 65, 328n102; winter, 43, 65–67, 66, 328n102. *See also* year-round tourism

tourist way of life: anxiety about threats to, 241, 274, 245, 246, 250–52, 254, 255,

259, 270; in Aspen, 26, 32, 213–14, 245, 249, 286; California and, 10–11, 164–65, 361n89; class exclusivity of, 186–87; concept of, 6–7, 10–11, 22, 130–31, 162–64; *Colorado Magazine* promotes, 237; corporate relocation, lure for, 166–68; Denverites and, 208; in Denver suburbs, 161, 162–68, 163; environmental values and environmentalism based on, 22–23, 204, 259, 268–70, 275, 286, 288, 302–5; Hilliard and, 223; IWLA and, 193; jeeping and, 283; John Denver and, 239–40, 273; Lamm and, 187, 270, 273; landscapes of, 168–70; new Dillon planned for, 170; nonradical tendencies of, 280–81; Olympics and, 270, 274; ORRRC endorses, 207; place packaging and, 130–31; population growth spurred by, 7–8, 187–88, 308n10; promotion of, in Colorado, 165–68; ranch house as architecture of, 163, 165; ski-resort sprawl as threat to, 263; suburbia as landscape of, 11, 161, 162–68, 163; Thompson and, 249; tourist development as threat to, 245–46, 249, 250–51, 263; tourist infrastructure sets stage for, 152; travel-lifestyle magazines, 51–52, 237; working class and poor, inaccessible to, 186; in Vail, 130–31, 170, 172, 184–86, 250–52, 254, 255–56, 288. *See also* recreational consumerism
Tourtelotte Park (Aspen Mountain), 39
Trail and Timberline (Colorado Mountain Club), 382n103
Trail Riders of the Wilderness program, 135–36
transmountain diversions, 196. *See also* water projects
Transportation Act of 1966, 385n128
Trappers Lake, Carhart zones for wilderness, 208–9
Travis, William R., 308n10, 362n100
trout: hatchery-raised, 133–35, 354n21; wildness of, 132, 134–35, 353n11

Trout Unlimited, 225, 260, 261, 283, 353n14
Tuan, Yi-Fu, 337n42
tunnels. *See* Continental Divide tunnel; Red Buffalo tunnel controversy
Turner, Frederick Jackson, 98
Turner, James Morton, 403n103
Two Elk Lodge arson (Vail), 298–99

U

Udall, Stewart, 236, 257, 294
underclass. *See* downvalley effect; resort workers
Union Pacific Railroad: avoids Colorado, 98; Sun Valley and, 364n115; trains to Denver, 80
United Air Lines, 52, 81, 325n74, 332n12
uranium, 46–47, 103, 112, 127, 351n1
urban clusters, planning and zoning for, 247–48, 267
Urry, John, 364n116
Use of Mountain Recreation Resources, The (University of Colorado), 381n101
user fees, 220, 381n99
U.S. Highway 6: arguments for Interstate 70 route along, 110, 111, 112, 346n97; boosting and branding of, 76, 77–79, 92–93, 337n39; designated in Colorado, 90, 336n33; difficult conditions on, 96; Interstate 70, chosen as route for, 118–20; Interstate 70 route location battle, 109–18; origins of, 90, 336n33; path of, 90, 336n33; paving/improvement of, 90, 91, 95, 96, 337n43, 338n44; Pavlo report and, 118–22; Sidney Six branding effort, 76, 77–79; traffic on, vs. U.S. 40, 90, 336n34; and tunnel battle, 113–14, 115, 347n103. *See also* Loveland Pass; Vail Pass
U.S. Highway 40: arguments for Interstate 70 route along, 111–12, 345n93, 346nn96–97; boosting and branding of, 90–92; difficult conditions on, 84, 96; Echo Park and, 202; favored by Johnson,

U.S. Highway 40 (*continued*)
112–13, 347nn99–101; historic mystique of, 90, 92; Interstate 70 route location battle, 109–18; loses out on Interstate 70 route, 118–20; origins of, 86–87, 90, 335n28; path of, 86–87, 335n26, 335n28; paving/improvement of, 17, 87, 335n29; Pavlo report on, 118–22; Pavlo report, consequences for, 123–24, 350n127; Stewart and, 90; traffic on, vs. U.S. 6, 90, 336n34; and tunnel battle, 114, 115. *See also* Berthoud Pass

U.S. 6 Roosevelt Highway Association, 92. *See also* Colorado Highway 6 Association

V

vacationland: American dream and, 10; Colorado's image as, 4–5, 44, 60–62, 64, 67–68, 187, 239–40, 307n4, 369n148; Denver suburbs and ideal of, 161, 162–68, 163; children and families, wholesome place for, 130, 151, 165–66, 168; future of, 305–6; high country's image as, 5, 27, 52, 54–55, 56, 57–75, 61, 66, 70, 86, 126; as multivalent term, 22; new landscape patterns of, 22, 168–70, 362n100. *See also* place packaging; recreational consumerism; suburban nature; suburbia, suburban landscapes, and suburban ideals; tourist advertising and marketing; tourist and recreational development; tourist way of life

Vail: advertised qualities of place, desire to protect, 250–59, 280; affordable housing concerns, 186–87, 368n145; Alpine design theme, 175–77, 176, 365n119; annexation by, 256, 391n37; anti-urban escapism, 177–78, 185, 187, 250, 252, 257, 259, 288; après-ski scene, 178–79; architectural controls, 176, 178, 365n119, 390n27; auto accessibility of, 128–30, 129, 178, 185, 251, 352n6; Bridge Street, 175, 176, 177, 364n117; building heights and architecture, concerns about, 252–54, 255, 390n27; condominiums in, 120, 183, 252, 253, 254, 367n136; conservatism of, 179, 180–82, 367n134; consumption, designed to encourage, 175, 176, 288, 289; conversion of land to leisure use, 128, 171; corporate image of, 182, 367n134; critics of, 177, 262; density, concerns about, 252–53; entrepreneurial zeal in, 183; environmental impact statements in, 287, 404n107; environmental movement in, 250–59, 280, 287–89; family- and child-friendliness of, 179–80, 181, 184; Forest Service and, 127–28, 138, 351n2, 394n50, 403n102; founding myth, 127–28, 171, 287; glamour of, 150, 178–79, 366n125; golf in, 171, 173, 178, 364n113; gondola, 143; growth management, 254, 256, 287–89; highway tourists, shuns, 180; Holiday Inn sign flap, 252, 390n26; home rule in, 256, 287, 392nn38–39; house architecture in, 185, 368n143; impact fees, proposed, 403n105; initial reports of, 170–71, 363nn105–6; Interstate 70 and, 120, 128–30, 129, 178, 250, 352n6; LionsHead, 253–54, 255, 256, 258, 288, 391nn32–33, 391n37; locals' anger at Vail Associates, 253–54, 298–99; locals' role in promoting tourism, 183–84, 288; as "magic land," 172, 177–78; mass tourism, fears of, 180, 252, 390n26; master plan of 1973 (*Vail Plan*), 287–88, 289, 404n109; as model of environmentally-friendly development, 123, 237–38, 257, 267; Mountain Haus, 253, 254; municipal recreation facilities in, 287, 288, 364n113; naming/branding of, 128, 351n4; natural harmony, as place of, 178, 257–59, 287; novices and non-experts, caters to, 179–80; Olympics and, 272; opening of, 171; open-space protection in, 178, 256, 287, 404n106, 404n109; overdevelopment concerns,

Voigt, William, Jr., 194, 371n12

W

WEYERHAEUSER ENVIRONMENTAL BOOKS

The Natural History of Puget Sound Country by Arthur R. Kruckeberg

Forest Dreams, Forest Nightmares: The Paradox of Old Growth in the Inland West by Nancy Langston

Landscapes of Promise: The Oregon Story, 1800–1940 by William G. Robbins

The Dawn of Conservation Diplomacy: U.S.-Canadian Wildlife Protection Treaties in the Progressive Era by Kurkpatrick Dorsey

Irrigated Eden: The Making of an Agricultural Landscape in the American West by Mark Fiege

Making Salmon: An Environmental History of the Northwest Fisheries Crisis by Joseph E. Taylor III

George Perkins Marsh, Prophet of Conservation by David Lowenthal

Driven Wild: How the Fight against Automobiles Launched the Modern Wilderness Movement by Paul S. Sutter

The Rhine: An Eco-Biography, 1815–2000 by Mark Cioc

Where Land and Water Meet: A Western Landscape Transformed by Nancy Langston

The Nature of Gold: An Environmental History of the Alaska/Yukon Gold Rush by Kathryn Morse

Faith in Nature: Environmentalism as Religious Quest by Thomas R. Dunlap

Landscapes of Conflict: The Oregon Story, 1940–2000 by William G. Robbins

The Lost Wolves of Japan by Brett L. Walker

Wilderness Forever: Howard Zahniser and the Path to the Wilderness Act by Mark Harvey

On the Road Again: Montana's Changing Landscape by William Wyckoff

Public Power, Private Dams: The Hells Canyon High Dam Controversy by Karl Boyd Brooks

Windshield Wilderness: Cars, Roads, and Nature in Washington's National Parks by David Louter

Native Seattle: Histories from the Crossing-Over Place by Coll Thrush

The Country in the City: The Greening of the San Francisco Bay Area by Richard A. Walker

Drawing Lines in the Forest: Creating Wilderness Areas in the Pacific Northwest by Kevin R. Marsh

Plowed Under: Agriculture and Environment in the Palouse by Andrew P. Duffin

Making Mountains: New York City and the Catskills by David Stradling

The Fishermen's Frontier: People and Salmon in Southeast Alaska by David F. Arnold

Shaping the Shoreline: Fisheries and Tourism on the Monterey Coast by Connie Y. Chiang

Dreaming of Sheep in Navajo Country by Marsha Weisiger

The Toxic Archipelago: A History of Industrial Disease in Japan by Brett L. Walker

Seeking Refuge: Birds and Landscapes of the Pacific Flyway by Robert M. Wilson

Quagmire: Nation-Building and Nature in the Mekong Delta by David Biggs

Iceland Imagined: Nature, Culture, and Storytelling in the North Atlantic by Karen Oslund

A Storied Wilderness: Rewilding the Apostle Islands by James W. Feldman

The Republic of Nature: An Environmental History of the United States by Mark Fiege

The Promise of Wilderness: American Environmental Politics since 1964
by James Morton Turner

Pumpkin: The History of an American Icon by Cindy Ott

Nature Next Door: Cities and Their Forests in the Northeastern United States
by Ellen Stroud

Car Country: An Environmental History by Christopher W. Wells

Vacationland: Tourism and Environment in the Colorado High Country
by William Philpott

Loving Nature, Fearing the State: Environmentalism and Antigovernment Politics before Reagan by Brian Allen Drake

Whales and Nations: Environmental Diplomacy on the High Seas by Kurk Dorsey

Tangled Roots: The Appalachian Trail and American Environmental Politics
by Sarah L. Mittlefehldt

Flies, Bedbugs, Cockroaches, and Rats: A History of Pests in the City
by Dawn Day Biehler

WEYERHAEUSER ENVIRONMENTAL CLASSICS

The Great Columbia Plain: A Historical Geography, 1805–1910 by D. W. Meinig

Mountain Gloom and Mountain Glory: The Development of the Aesthetics of the Infinite
by Marjorie Hope Nicolson

Tutira: The Story of a New Zealand Sheep Station by Herbert Guthrie-Smith

A Symbol of Wilderness: Echo Park and the American Conservation Movement
by Mark Harvey

Man and Nature: Or, Physical Geography as Modified by Human Action by George Perkins Marsh; edited and annotated by David Lowenthal

Conservation in the Progressive Era: Classic Texts edited by David Stradling

DDT, Silent Spring, and the Rise of Environmentalism: Classic Texts
edited by Thomas R. Dunlap

The Environmental Moment, 1968–1972 by David Stradling

Cycle of Fire by Stephen J. Pyne

Fire: A Brief History

World Fire: The Culture of Fire on Earth

Vestal Fire: An Environmental History, Told through Fire, of Europe and Europe's Encounter with the World

Fire in America: A Cultural History of Wildland and Rural Fire

Burning Bush: A Fire History of Australia
The Ice: A Journey to Antarctica